WINN LIBRARY.
Gordon College
Wenham, Mass. 0198

Operating Systems

McGRAW-HILL COMPUTER SCIENCE SERIES

RICHARD W. HAMMING
Bell Telephone Laboratories

EDWARD A. FEIGENBAUM
Stanford University

Bell and Newell   *Computer Structures: Readings and Examples*
Cole   *Introduction to Computing*
Donovan   *Systems Programming*
Gear   *Computer Organization and Programming*
Givone   *Introduction to Switching Circuit Theory*
Hamming   *Computers and Society*
Hamming   *Introduction to Applied Numerical Analysis*
Hellerman   *Digital Computer System Principles*
Kain   *Automata Theory: Machines and Languages*
Kohavi   *Switching and Finite Automata Theory*
Liu   *Introduction to Combinatorial Mathematics*
Madnick and Donovan   *Operating Systems*
Manna   *Mathematical Theory of Computation*
Newman and Sproull   *Principles of Interactive Computer Graphics*
Nilsson   *Artificial Intelligence*
Ralston   *Introduction to Programming and Computer Science*
Rosen   *Programming Systems and Languages*
Salton   *Automatic Information Organization and Retrieval*
Stone   *Introduction to Computer Organization and Data Structures*
Watson   *Timesharing System Design Concepts*
Wegner   *Programming Languages, Information Structures, and
          Machine Organization*

Operating Systems

Stuart E. Madnick
MASSACHUSETTS INSTITUTE OF TECHNOLOGY
ALFRED P. SLOAN SCHOOL OF MANAGEMENT
and Project MAC

John J. Donovan
MASSACHUSETTS INSTITUTE OF TECHNOLOGY
ALFRED P. SLOAN SCHOOL OF MANAGEMENT*
and Project MAC

*Formerly with the Department of Electrical Engineering, M.I.T.

McGraw-Hill Book Company

NEW YORK/ST. LOUIS/SAN FRANCISCO
DÜSSELDORF/JOHANNESBURG/KUALA LUMPUR
LONDON/MEXICO/MONTREAL
NEW DELHI/PANAMA/PARIS
SÃO PAULO/SINGAPORE/SYDNEY
TOKYO/TORONTO

OPERATING SYSTEMS

Copyright © 1974 by McGraw-Hill, Inc. All rights reserved.
Printed in the United States of America. No part of this publication
may be reproduced, stored in a retrieval system, or transmitted, in any
form or by any means, electronic, mechanical, photocopying, recording, or
otherwise, without the prior written permission of the publisher.

15 DODO 8321

Library of Congress Cataloging in Publication Data

Madnick, Stuart E
    Operating systems.

    (McGraw-Hill computer science series)
    Bibliography: p.
    1. Electronic digital computers—Programming.
I. Donovan, John J., joint author. II. Title.
QA76.6.M33   001.6'42   74-2040
ISBN 0-07-039455-5

QA
76.6
.M33

This book was set in Press Roman by Allen Wayne Technical Corp. The
editor was Kenneth J. Bowman; the designer was Allen Wayne Technical
Corp.; the production supervisor was Bill Greenwood.

To all those who have supported me when I most needed encouragement or help, from my high school teacher, Mr. Thornton; my college advisors, Professors Shan Kuo and Conrad Wogrin; my wife, Marilyn; my co-author, friend, and colleague Stuart Madnick; Professor Licklider; my friend James Nichols; to my M.I.T. friend and critic, Professor Paul MacAvoy.

DONOVAN

To my wife, Ethel, and my children, Howard, Michael, and Lynne.

MADNICK

Contents

Preface

Purpose of Book

This book presents advanced software techniques, especially focusing on operating systems. It presents material that will enable the reader to design, use, and analyze not only current operating systems but future ones as well. The presentation covers a spectrum ranging from specific implementation details to relevant theoretical results. The book is written as a text, with relevant problems, examples, and exercises.

Approach of Book

Our approach is to develop a framework based upon the concept of resource management. Within this framework, specific case studies are introduced as examples and relevant theory is presented where appropriate.

The book is unique in that it presents a comprehensive framework for the design, study, and implementation of operating systems. Most other texts either present miscellaneous theoretical results or use a case study approach. In the first case, the student may not learn where or how to apply the theoretical results. In the second, he may find it difficult to differentiate between fundamental concepts and design issues and arbitrary decisions.

The features we attempt to provide in this book are the following:

1 It is a package course. This is not just a collection of articles but an integrated textbook.

2 It is a text for upper undergraduate or graduate courses in computer science or management.

3 Questions appear at the end of each chapter.

4 A teacher's manual is available with solutions to the questions and possible course syllabuses.

5 The book is based on a class-tested course given at M.I.T. for several years. It has been used at other universities, such as the University of Rhode Island and the University of Pittsburgh, and at several industrial companies, for example, The Foxboro Company, U.S. Naval Underwater Systems Center.

6 The text relates to existing operating systems. We draw examples particularly, though not exclusively, from IBM's System/370.

7   The book uses a framework approach that our students find conceptually enjoyable and understandable.

8   Emphasis is given to relevant material. We have found that most students cannot appreciate theoretical results without some practical motivation.

9   A complete sample operating system is presented. Studying an operating system is similar to riding a bicycle—you can write the equations to show the bicycle will balance but you can never ride the bicycle until you actually try.

10 A comprehensive and annotated bibliography is provided to enable the reader to delve further into the topics introduced in the text.

11 Teaching aids are available. In addition to this book, we have made the following available through the M.I.T. computation center:
    a   A 360 machine simulator written in PL/I.
    b   Grading programs for simple assembly language problems.
    c   Sample PL/I problems and a facility for running them.
    d   Sample I/O and interrupt problems.
    e   An environment simulator for testing and running different process schedulers (dispatchers).
    f   An I/O environment simulator for testing and evaluating different I/O scheduling algorithms.
    g   A fast PL/I compiler—this uses the same source as IBM's PL/I(F) and produces the same object code, but in less time.
    h   A submonitor system for running student jobs.

All the programs listed in 11 above are described in our book, *Software Projects: Pedagogical Aids for Software Education and Research* (see page 581), which describes all the programs listed in 11 above. Specifically, the description for each program consists of three sections:

1   A student guide—sample of student handouts for the package.

2   A teacher's guide—descriptions of how a teacher would operate the program.

3   A maintenance manual—a complete description of the implementation of the program.

Uses of Book

As noted above, this book is primarily a text on an upper undergraduate or graduate level. As a prerequisite to the material presented, the student should be familiar with the concepts of an assembler, loader, compiler, and should have programming experience in some high-level language. Assembly language programming is desirable. A good background can be found in the text *Systems Programming* by John J. Donovan.

We see four ways in which this book may be used as a text:

1   As an intensive one-semester course in operating systems.

2   As a two-term sequence:
    a   First term: course introducing the concepts and practice of I/O programming and interrupt processing. The course would provide the conceptual frame-

work necessary for further study in operating systems as well as the practical experience for programming real-time systems, minicomputers, and specialized applications (e.g., patient-monitoring computers).

    b Second term: high-level course focusing on the concepts, design, implementation, and relevant theory of operating systems.

3 To formulate courses using individual sections of the book, e.g.,

    a Chapter 2—a course devoted to applications of real-time programming, I/O programming, and interrupts.

    b Chapter 7—a workshop or lab course constructing sample operating systems.

    c An overview course on operating systems, skipping the details of Chapter 2 and focusing on the theory and concepts of Chapters 3, 4, 5, and 6.

4 As a course for professionals or for self-study using the problems and solutions manuals.

    The book is aimed at helping the student in the following areas:

    a Designing operating systems

    b Understanding relevant theory

    c Using techniques presented in operating systems in other applications

    d Using operating systems

    e Buying or evaluating operating systems

As a text, the book covers the topics mentioned in the recent study by the ACM COSINE Committee, "An undergraduate course in operating systems." The text further covers material contained in two courses of Curriculum 68 as described by the ACM Curriculum Committee in Computer Science[1] : (A2) Advanced Computer Organization and (A8) Large Scale Information Systems. The book covers material as reported by ACM Curriculum Committee on Computer Education for Management focusing on Curriculum for Graduate Professional Programs in Information Systems.[2] These are (C10) Introduction to Computer Systems and Programming; (C11) Information Structure and Files (Chapter 6 of this book); (C2) Computer Systems; (D2) System Design; and (D3) Systems Development Projects (Chapter 7).

In Chapter 2 we present the basic material of machine structures, machine language programming, I/O programming, and interrupt handling. We feel that a person knowledgeable in operating systems must not be intimidated by "pushing bits." This chapter uses the IBM System/370 for detailed examples (this is the only chapter that is heavily machine-dependent).

In Chapters 3, 4, 5, and 6 we develop the framework for the analysis and design of operating systems. In our view of an operating system, the system is a manager of resources. (We differentiate four resources: memory, processors, devices, information.) These chapters discuss the techniques and issues involved in managing these resources and develop the framework for managing them through examples, starting with the simplest and moving to the most complicated. The maximum function (taking the most complicated example of each resource) of these chapters

---

[1] **Communications of the Association of Computing Machinery (CACM), Vol. 11, No. 3, p. 151 (March, 1968).**

[2] **Communications of the Association of Computing Machinery (CACM), Vol. 15, No. 5, p. 363 (May, 1972).**

is a system like MULTICS, whereas the minimum function is a system such as IBM's OS/360 Primary Control Program (PCP).

In Chapter 7 we design an operating system using the framework developed in previous chapters. We start with the general strategy, develop descriptions of the databases and routines, and finally present the code for an operational implementation.

When the management of all these resources is put in one system, we note that they are not independent. For example, the processor management technique may depend upon whether or not the system uses a paged or swapping memory management technique. In Chapter 8 we explore the interrelationships among the managers of these resources and develop techniques for performance evaluation.

Chapter 9 analyzes various existing systems within the framework developed, and Chapter 10 contains an annotated bibliography of the field.

Stuart E. Madnick
John J. Donovan

Acknowledgments

We list here the people who assisted us in writing this book.

We thank Charles A. Ziering, our head teaching assistant, and particularly acknowledge his reliability. We especially note his contributions to Chapters 4 and 8, as he confirmed (and corrected) most of our figures, and his work on the solutions manual.

We thank our teaching assistants, Paul Gregory, Judy Piggins, Harry Forsdick, Jeff Bunza, Mike Knaur, and Suhundra Umarji, for contributing to the questions, David Schwartz for his work on the bibliography, Chad Carpenter and Jeff Buzen for proofreading, and Anne Beer for her assistance with the index.

Chapter 7 evolved from the thesis work of John DeTreville and was further refined by Richard Swift.

We give special note to those M.I.T. students who went through early versions of our course and survived—we thank them for their constructive criticisms.

We thank Ellen Nangle, who has once again edited, proofread, and typed a book singlehandedly.

We especially appreciate the fine editing of Irene Gunther, the perseverance of Nora Braverman, and the innovative styling of Irving Weinstock, all of Allen Wayne Technical Corp.

We thank Professors Michael Scott-Morton and John Little of the Sloan School for providing a healthy environment within the Management Science group for producing this book.

Stuart E. Madnick
John J. Donovan

Framework of Book 1

This book has two major objectives: to teach the fundamentals of advanced software engineering (including asynchronous operation, interrupt processing, operating system interfaces, and hardware-software tradeoffs), and to enable the reader to design and analyze operating systems.

Modern computer hardware is very powerful (see Figure 1-1a) and can be used for many purposes. But the hardware often provides an awkward or difficult-to-use interface to the world. In order to tame this "bare machine," we have developed operating systems that can manage the basic hardware resources and provide a more hospitable interface to users and their programs (see Figure 1-1b). Operating systems have become so essential to efficient computer operation that many people view them as inseparable from the hardware.

There are many important reasons for studying operating systems; the most notable are: (1) for special-purpose usage you may have to design your own operating system or modify an existing one; (2) the selection of the operating system and its options is a major decision for most computer installations; (3) the user must interact with the operating system in order to accomplish his task since it is his primary interface with the computer; and (4) many concepts and techniques found in operating systems have general applicability in other applications. The framework presented in this book is especially suited to addressing these issues.

The term *operating system* denotes those program modules within a computer system that govern the control of equipment resources such as processors, main storage, secondary storage, I/O devices, and files. These modules resolve conflicts, attempt to optimize performance, and simplify the effective use of the system. They act as an interface between the user's programs and the physical computer hardware.

These modules are sometimes collectively called the *Control*, the *Monitor*,[1] the *Executive*, the *Supervisor*, or the *Operating System*. Applications-oriented modules,

---

[1] Not to be confused with a *Monster*.

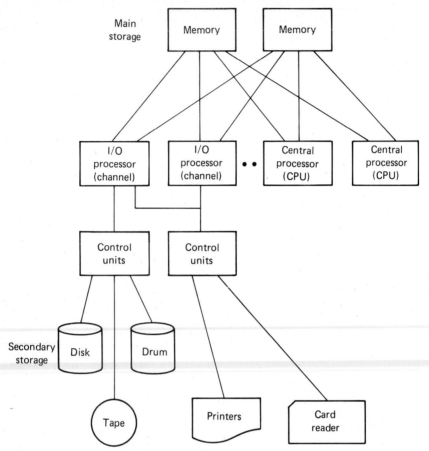

Figure 1-1a Basic computer hardware (bare machine)

language processors, library routines, and debugging aids are not included in our definition of an operating system. These are merely users of the operating system and are covered adequately elsewhere (Donovan, 1972; Knuth, 1968).

1-1 IMPORTANCE OF OPERATING SYSTEMS

Computers have become essential to society in such traditional applications as payroll and banking where the volume of operations performed makes them indispensable. For example, in the mid-1950s the Bank of America pioneered the use of computers in banking after realizing that, in the foreseeable future, it would require the entire adult population of California to handle checks manually (Fano, 1972). Computers are now being used in new fields, such as the design of automobiles, improved medical care, and space exploration; future applications are being envisaged in the areas of learning, acquiring knowledge, and artificial intelligence.

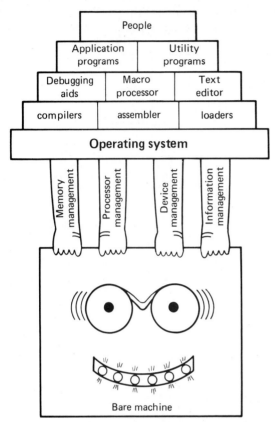

Figure 1-1b Relationship of operating system to basic
computer hardware

Over 20 billion dollars a year are spent on computer products and services. It is
estimated that 70 percent of that amount goes into software development, maintenance, data processing salaries, and other software-related activities. Every indication is that the applications and availability of computers will continue to expand.

What controls the computer and acts as intermediary between the user and the
computer? It is the operating system. The operating system is a program that, when
executed, controls the operation of the computer. For example, the operating
system performs the task of scheduling the use of the computer. Sophisticated
operating systems increase the efficiency and consequently decrease the cost of
using a computer. For example, the operating system may provide for simultaneous
operation by allowing one user's program to execute while the printout of an earlier
user is being completed.

This book develops a framework for the study, design, and implementation of
operating systems. The framework includes both small systems (e.g., our sample
operating system in Chapter 7) and large systems (e.g., OS/VS, as in the case
studies of Chapter 9).

1-2 BASIC CONCEPTS AND TERMINOLOGY

This section introduces the basic concepts of computer hardware structure, programming, and operating system terminology.

1-2.1 Computer Hardware Structure Terminology

Many different computer hardware configurations exist. Figure 1-1a depicts one possible configuration.

Instructions and data are stored in the *main storage*, historically called *core memory* (the terms *main storage, memory,* and *core* are often used interchangeably). Connected to the memory are various processors. A *processor* is a hardware device capable of interpreting instructions and performing the indicated operation (e.g., addition). Instructions as well as data are stored in the memory in coded form.

A computer system has one or more *Central Processing Units* (CPU). A *CPU* is a processor that manipulates and performs arithmetic operations upon data in the memory. It also executes instructions that control the other processors. For example, the CPU may execute a START I/O (SIO) instruction to initiate an I/O processor.

In many modern systems certain processors are specialized to perform specific tasks efficiently and/or inexpensively. For example, the *I/O* (Input and Output) *processors* are designed to control I/O devices and handle the movement of data between the memory and the I/O devices. These processors range from being specialized for a certain I/O device to being quite sophisticated, simultaneously executing several I/O instructions and controlling several I/O devices.

Almost any conceivable device from a laser to a milking machine can be (and has been) used as an I/O device. Many of the more common devices (card readers, printers, disks, drums, tapes, etc.) require control circuitry that is applicable to other devices. For reasons of economy, this common hardware is sometimes separated out into a device called a *control unit*.

There may be many user programs competing for the system resources, such as memory, CPUs, I/O processors, control units, devices, etc. What decides which users are to have access to the resources and how long a user may have a resource? What prevents the system from collapsing if a device becomes inoperable? What assigns the "path" to a device through the I/O processors and control units? What manages all of these resources? The answer to all of these questions is the operating system.

1-2.2 Programming Terminology

Figure 1-1a depicts the hardware of a computer system. In most installations there is an even larger dollar investment in software than in hardware. *Software* is the collection of programs or data that are used to perform certain tasks. A *program* is a sequence of instructions. (Programs are sometimes loosely called "code"). Programs are placed into memory and interpreted (executed) by a processor. While not in use, programs are often stored in some secondary storage device, such as a disk, drum, or tape.

A system may have "prepackaged" programs available to users (routines to perform: square roots, searching, sorting, compilers, assemblers, translators). How are these prepackaged routines managed and who keeps track of where they are? Once again it is the operating system.

A lone user facing a formidable system such as the one shown in Figure 1-1a might become discouraged. Suppose this lone user is a Harvard student who has just learned how to program the CPU. He wants to execute a program to add 49 to numbers read from punched cards. How does he read cards? Must he also learn how to program the I/O processor? This is obviously too much to expect from a novice. Fortunately, the operating system usually provides routines for the I/O processors; in general, the operating system assists in the construction and execution of user programs.

The operating system provides an environment in which particular software packages can execute. An example is a compiler, which is a program that translates a *source program* (e.g., a FORTRAN program) in a high-level language to a corresponding machine language program, or *object program*. Most modern compilers interact closely with the operating system both during the compilation of source programs and the execution of the object code. During compilation the compiler needs the operating system to read the source program, print its listing, and punch its output decks. At execution time the object code produced by compilers such as PL/I requires a sophisticated *run-time environment*. ALLOCATE and FREE statements require the assistance of the operating system's memory management facilities. PL/I ON CONDITIONS need interrupt handlers provided by the operating system.

1-2.3 Operating System Terminology

A user submits his job to the operating system. A *user* is anybody that desires work to be done by a computer system. A *job* is the collection of activities needed to do the work required. A job may be divided into several steps (job steps). *Job steps* are units of work that must be done sequentially, for example, the three steps, compile, load, execute. Once the operating system accepts a user's job, it may create several processes. A *process* (or *task*) is a computation that may be done concurrently with other computations. Figure 1-2 depicts the relationship between user, job, process, and address space.

Another view of a process is the locus of points of a processor executing a collection of programs. The collection of programs and data that are accessed in a process forms an *address space*. Figure 1-2 depicts two sample address spaces—one for an I/O process, the other for a CPU process.

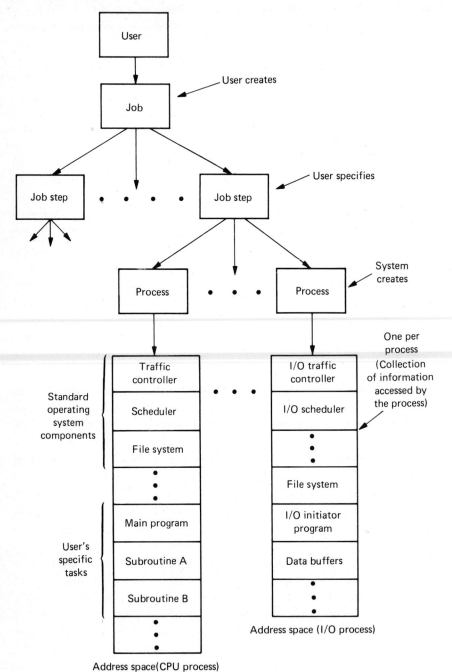

Figure 1-2 User, job, job step, process, and address space

Note that the actual code for the file system portion of the operating system may be the same for both address spaces. If code is to be shared in this manner, it must be pure, or locks must be set to prevent race conditions. *Pure code* (sometimes called *reentrant code*) is code that does-not modify itself.

The operating system must map the address spaces of processes into physical memory. This task may be assisted by special hardware (e.g., a paged system) or it may be performed primarily by software (e.g., a swapping system).

Multiprogramming is a term given to a system that may have several processes in "states of execution" at the same time. A process is in a state of execution if the computation has been started but has not been completed or terminated (error completion). (Note: a process may be in a state of execution and not be executing; that is, some intermediate results have been computed but the processor is not currently working on this process.)

Another feature found in most contemporary computer systems is special hardware and instructions used by the operating system. These instructions, which are usually not available to the ordinary user, are commonly called *privileged instructions*. Most contemporary computers have at least two states of execution—a *problem state (user state, slave state)* and a *supervisor state (executive state, master state)*. In the supervisor state the processor can correctly execute privileged instructions. Obviously, one privileged instruction is to change the state of the machine. Others may start the I/O processors, change the protection rights of parts of memory, or change the interrupt status of the machine.

Protection hardware is often used to control access to parts of memory. For example, the operating system may deem certain parts of memory to be not writable. That is, a user program may be prohibited from altering the operating system programs.

Interrupt hardware allows the operating system to coordinate operations going on simultaneously; it also allows the nonsequential flow of a program. An *interrupt* is a mechanism by which a processor is forced to take note of an event (in much the same manner as you may be interrupted from reading this book by a relative or friend). Hardware may exist to mask certain interrupts. We have all "masked" out our mothers at times.

We should note here that many computer configurations do not have all these special instructions or hardware. (The IBM 1130 has no general masking facilities.) What limitations does the lack of these facilities place on the user or purchaser of such a system? On the other hand, many large systems have even more elaborate hardware facilities than those referred to here to assist the operating system, especially in the I/O processors. What does a user gain from these special features? This book will attempt to answer both these questions.

1-3 AN OPERATING SYSTEM RESOURCE MANAGER

We will present a framework for the study of operating systems based on the view that the operating system is a manager of resources. In this section we discuss these resources and define what the modules of the operating system must do to manage them; in Section 1-4 we present a model to demonstrate the sequencing of the management of these resources (process view); and in Section 1-5 we present a model to demonstrate the interrelationship and primitive functions of these modules (hierarchical and extended machine view).

These three views are not in conflict with one another; they represent three dimensions of one object—an operating system. Each view aids in the understanding and study of an operating system, and together they form the framework for this book. The models used are extensions of the work of others, most notably, Dijkstra (1968), Donovan (1972), Hansen (1970, 1971), Saltzer (1966), and Madnick (1969).

The primary view we take in this book is that the operating system is a collection of programs (algorithms) designed to manage the system's resources, namely, memory, processors, devices, and information (programs and data). All these resources are valuable, and it is the function of the operating system to see that they are used efficiently and to resolve conflicts arising from competition among the various users.

The operating system must keep track of the status of each resource, decide which process is to get the resource (how much and when), allocate it, and eventually reclaim it.

We distinguish between the resources of memory, processors, I/O devices (disks, tapes, teletypes) and information because of the inherent differences in their characteristics. We recognize that in a broad sense they are all devices and have many similarities. However, such abstractions do not appear to be useful at present for the development of relevant theory or techniques for the managing of the resources.

Viewing the operating system as a resource manager, each manager must do the following:

1 Keep track of the resources.
2 Enforce policy that determines who gets what, when, and how much.
3 Allocate the resource.
4 Reclaim the resource.

We have grouped all the programs of the operating system into four resource categories. On the following pages we have listed these categories together with their major functions and the typical names given to some of the routines that perform these functions.

1-3.1 Memory Management Functions

1 Keep track of the resource (memory). What parts are in use and by whom? What parts are not in use (called *free*)?

2 If multiprogramming, decide which process gets memory, when it gets it, and how much.

3 Allocate the resource (memory) when the processes request it and the policy of 2 above allows it.

4 Reclaim the resource (memory) when the process no longer needs it or has been terminated.

1-3.2 Processor Management Functions

1 Keep track of the resource (processors and the status of processes). The program that does this has been called the *traffic controller* (Saltzer, 1969).

2 Decide who will have a chance to use the processor; the *job scheduler* chooses from all the jobs submitted to the system and decides which one will be allowed into the system, i.e., have any resources assigned to it. If multiprogramming, decide which process gets the processor, when, and how much; this is called the *processor scheduler*.

3 Allocate the resource (processor) to a process by setting up necessary hardware registers; this is often called the *dispatcher*.

4 Reclaim resource (processor) when process relinquishes processor usage, terminates, or exceeds allowed amount of usage.

It should be pointed out that in making the decision as to which job gets into the system many factors must be considered. For example, a job that is requesting more memory or tape drives than the system has should not be allowed into the system at all. That is, it should not have any resource assigned to it. Why isn't the job scheduler a part of memory management or device management? Because historically the major consideration used in admitting a job to the system was the amount of processor time allocated to it. Furthermore, the record-keeping operations for job scheduling and processor scheduling are very similar. Therefore, we have chosen to place these modules in processor management.

1-3.3 Device Management Functions

1 Keep track of the resource (devices, channels, control units); this is typically called the *I/O traffic controller*.

2 Decide what is an efficient way to allocate the resource (device). If it is to be

shared, then decide who gets it, and how much he is to get; this is called *I/O scheduling*.

3 Allocate the resource (device) and initiate the I/O operation.

4 Reclaim resource. In most cases the I/O terminates automatically.

The method of deciding how devices are allocated depends on the flexibility of the device. Some devices cannot be shared (e.g., card readers) and must therefore be *dedicated* to a process. Others may be *shared* (e.g., disks); hence, there is more flexibility, and there are complications in the allocation of these devices. Others may be made into *virtual devices*. For example, the operation of punching on a card punch could be transformed into a "write" onto a disk (a virtual card punch), and at some later time a routine would copy the information onto a card punch. Virtualizing card reader, card punch, and printer devices is performed by *SPOOLing routines*. The virtual devices approach allows (1) dedicated devices to be shared, hence, more flexibility in scheduling these devices; (2) more flexibility in job scheduling; and (3) better match of speed of device and speed of requests for that device.

1-3.4 Information Management Functions

1 Keep track of the resource (information), its location, use, status, etc. These collective facilities are often called the *file system*.

2 Decide who gets use of the resources, enforce protection requirements, and provide accessing routines.

3 Allocate the resource (information), e.g., *open* a file.

4 Deallocate the resource, e.g., *close* a file.

1-3.5 Resource Management Summary

It is our contention that all the resource management functions of an operating system fall into the above four categories. We can use this framework to analyze existing operating systems, design new operating systems, and study theoretical work in context.

In Chapters 3, 4, 5, and 6, we will explore the management of these four resources in depth, examining operating systems from the bits to the broad overview. In Chapter 2 we will deal specifically with the bits.

Since our view of an operating system is based on the management of four separate resources—memory, processors, devices, and information—it is important to define the way these resources interrelate. Although, for simplicity, management of these resources can be viewed initially as being independent, there are subtle interdependencies that must be understood. Chapter 8 presents some of these.

The resources and the operating system's management of them are much like the wood, bricks, nails, etc. that go into building a house. There are various ways of "putting it together," all of which conform to acceptable standards; however, some ways are awkward and others elegant. Section 1-5 suggests one way of putting it together. A complete sample operating system based upon this view is described in Chapter 7. Besides serving as an example, that chapter implicitly presents some useful approaches to putting an operating system together, and does so on a level of detail not generally reached in other chapters. Except for the examples of computer structures in Chapter 2, this book is relatively machine-independent. Particular machine examples are used only to demonstrate concepts.

1-4 AN OPERATING SYSTEM—PROCESS VIEWPOINT (WHERE THESE RESOURCE MANAGERS ARE ACTIVATED)

In the last section we stated that an operating system consisted of a collection of programs to manage resources. What is the relationship among these programs? When in the life of a process does each of these programs come into play? To explain these interrelationships, and the sequencing between the resource manager modules, we present a view of the life of a process.

We will use an example to develop this view. Figure 1-3 depicts three processes (users' jobs) coexisting in a multiprogrammed system.

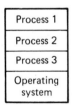

Figure 1-3 Multiple processes in a multiprogrammed system

The life cycle of a process can be represented by the transitions between the three states illustrated in Figure 1-4:

Run: The process has been assigned a processor and its programs are presently being executed.

Wait: The process is waiting for some event (e.g., an I/O operation to be completed).

Ready: The process is "ready to run," but there are more processes than processors and it must wait for its turn on a processor.

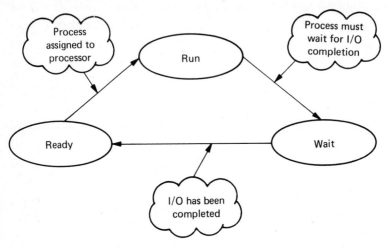

Figure 1-4 Simple states of a process

In Figure 1-4 sample reasons for the process state transitions are given; for example, if a "running" process must wait for I/O completion, it becomes a "waiting" process.

The process states of Figure 1-4 have been simplified. They assume that all the processes already existed in the system and that they will continue running forever. A more complete and realistic process life cycle is represented in Figure 1-5.

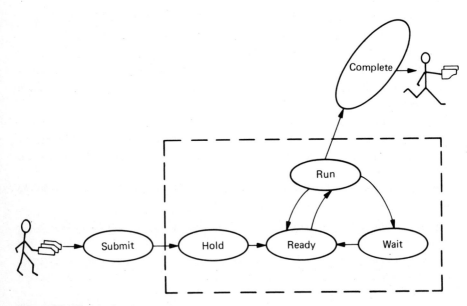

Figure 1-5 Model of process states

We have added three states:

Submit: A user submits a job to the system; the system must respond to the user's request.

Hold: The user's job has been converted into internal machine readable form, but no resources have been assigned to the process (the job has been SPOOLed onto disk). Resources must be allocated to move it to the ready state.

Complete: The process has completed its computation and all its assigned resources may be reclaimed.

In general, the operating system will take a process through all its states. These states and transitions are depicted in Figure 1-6, where the circles denote states and the clouds denote routines within the operating system that may be involved when a process switches from one state to another. There exists an identical diagram for each process in the system.

As Figure 1-6 shows, process management plays an important role in sequencing a process through its states. Let us go through an example using Figure 1-6. A user submits his job to the system, perhaps by placing his deck into a card reader (submit state). The job consists of several decks of programs preceded by job control cards. The job control cards pass information to the operating system as to what resources the job will need. The SPOOLing routine reads the job and places it onto a disk (*hold state*). To find storage space for the machine readable copy of the user's job, the SPOOLing routine must call information management, which keeps track of all information and available space in the system.

At some later time, the job-scheduling routine scans all the SPOOLed files on the disk and picks a job to be admitted into the system. In picking a job, the scheduler will call memory management to determine if sufficient main memory is available, and call device management to determine whether devices requested by the job are available. The job scheduler determines the device requirements from the user's job cards.

Once the job scheduler decides that the job is to be assigned resources, the traffic controller is called to create the associated process information, and memory management is called to allocate the necessary main storage. The job is then loaded into memory and the process is ready to run (*ready state*).

When a processor becomes free, the process scheduler scans the list of ready processes, chooses a process, and assigns a processor to it (*running state*).

If the running process requests access to information (e.g., read a file), information management would call device management to initiate the reading of the file. Device management would initiate the I/O operation and then call process management to indicate that the process requesting the file is awaiting the completion of the I/O operation (*wait state*).

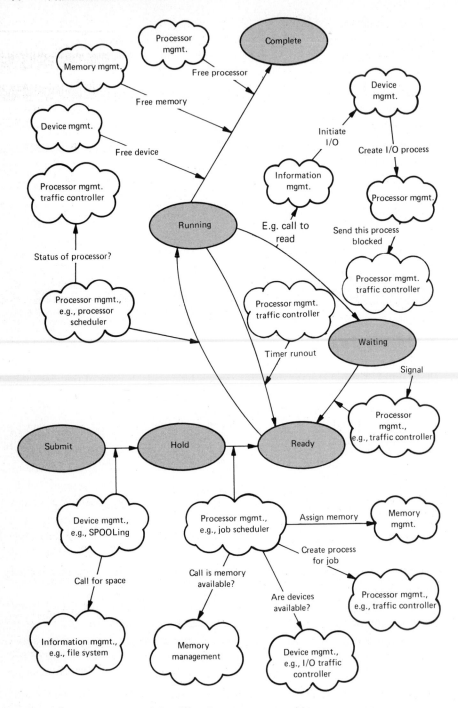

Figure 1-6 Operating system's handling of process state transitions

When the I/O is completed the I/O hardware sends a signal to the traffic controller in process management, which places the process back into the ready state.

If the process should complete its computation when it is run again, then it is placed into *completed state* and all allocated resources are freed.

The process states of Figure 1-6 represent one possible view of the life cycle of a process. In a more complex operating system it may be desirable to define even more states (see Chapter 4). On the other hand, if an operating system were designed without the process concept in mind, it might be difficult for an observer to determine clearly the state of a process at any given time.

1-5 OPERATING SYSTEMS—HIERARCHICAL
AND EXTENDED MACHINE VIEW

In the previous sections we noted the need to *identify* the system resources that must be managed by the operating system and, using the process view, we indicated *when* these resource managers come into play. We must now answer the question, *"How* are these resource managers called into play, and *where* do they logically reside in regard to each other?" Does the scheduler call upon the services of memory management? Does memory management ever call the scheduler? Is the process concept only for the user or is it employed by the operating system also? This section presents a hierarchical view of an operating system to show how the modules relate. We realize that there is no absolutely right or wrong way to organize these modules. We feel, however, that the hierarchical approach results in a simple, clean structure that is easy to analyze and implement.

1-5.1 Extended Machine Concept

In Section 1-2.1 we introduced the basic hardware features of contemporary computers. This was the view of a *bare machine*—a computer without its software clothing. A bare machine is not the environment desired by most programmers. You might wish to write a program, such as:

1	MOVE C,B	SET C = B
2	FIND-SPACE 80,X	FIND 80 BYTES OF "FREE" SPACE AND SET X = LOCATION
3	READ-CARD X	READ A CARD INTO AREA X
4	COMPARE X(2),'/*'	ARE THE FIRST TWO BYTES OF AREA X A "/*"?
5	TRANSFER-MATCH END	IF SO, TRANSFER TO END

Statements 1, 4, and 5 correspond closely to typical computer instructions, as on a System/370. Statements 2 and 3, on the other hand, may require tens, hundreds, or even thousands of instructions to be correctly and efficiently accomplished on a modern computer since they involve interaction with some of the key system resources, such as memory and I/O.

The instructions to perform these kinds of resource management functions are usually provided by the operating system. The user program can request these services by issuing special *supervisor call* instructions that act much like subroutine calls but transfer control to the operating system rather than to one of the user's subroutines. Thus as far as the user is concerned, statements 2 and 3 are legal instructions for the extended machine even though they do not correspond to instructions of the bare machine. The operating system provides many "instructions" in addition to the basic hardware instructions. The sum of these instructions is called the instruction set of the *extended machine*. This situation is graphically represented in Figure 1-7. The kernel of the operating system runs on the bare machine; user programs run on the extended machine.

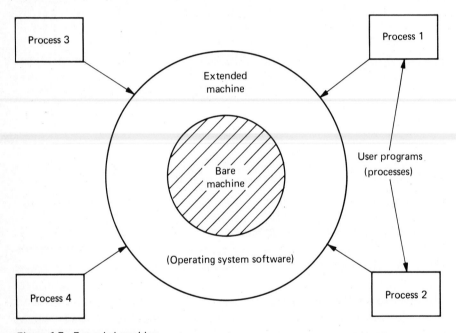

Figure 1-7   Extended machine

1-5.2 Hierarchical Machine Concept

We still have to explain how the operating system is put together. Most of the early operating systems consisted simply of one big program. As systems became larger and more comprehensive, this "brute force" approach became unmanageable. Eventually, it became clear that the extended machine approach could be applied to the operating system in two ways (see Figure 1-8): (1) key functions needed by many system modules could be separated into an "inner extended machine," and (2) certain modules could be separated out and run on the extended machine in essentially the same way as user processes.

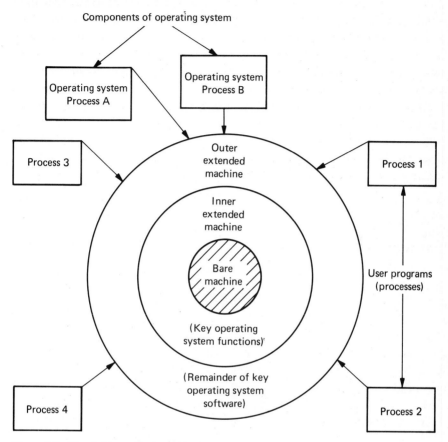

Figure 1-8 Simple hierarchical machine

In order to use the hierarchical approach, we must answer the original question: *Where* does each module of the operating system belong? In the inner extended machine, the outer extended machine, or as a process? Furthermore, the inner/outer extended machine concept can be generalized into *levels of extended machines* and the operating system processes can interrelate and be generalized into *layers of processes*. All those modules of the system that reside in the extended machine, as opposed to those that operate as process layers, are collectively called the *kernel* of the operating system. There is, at present, no firm rule to indicate how many levels should be used, what modules should go into which levels, what should be in the kernel, etc.

Two of the earliest designs using the hierarchical concepts were the T.H.E. operating system developed by Dijkstra (1968) and the modular file system design of

Madnick (1969). Similar strategies are now being employed in the design of complex application programs under such names as *modular programming* or *structured programming*. Both in this section and in our design of a complete sample operating system in Chapter 7, we have selected intrinsically clear and basic functions to be placed in the kernel and have separated as many tasks of the operating system as possible into separate system processes. Figure 1-9 illustrates the hierarchical structure that will be discussed in this book. All the processes (shown as boxes in Figure 1-9) use the kernel and share all the resources of the system. Some of the processes are the "parent" or "controller" of others. We have denoted this relationship by the wavy lines indicating separate process layers.

In a *strictly hierarchical* implementation, a given level is allowed to call upon services of lower levels, but not on those of higher levels. For example, if we designed an interprocess message management module that must call upon services of the memory management module, the memory module must be in a lower level than the message module and must not call upon process message management. In Figure 1-9, this requirement is shown by placing these modules in levels 2 and 3, respectively.

What function should be placed in the lowest level, level 1? The one that is used by all resource managers—keeping track of the allocation of resources. This requires the synchronization of the resource allocation. The corresponding primitive operations are frequently called the *P operator* (noting that a resource is seized or requested) and *V operator* (noting that a resource has been released). These synchronization primitives operate upon a software mechanism called a *semaphore* (from Webster's definition: "a telegraphic apparatus for signaling by means of arms, lanterns, flags, etc.").

The semaphore may be as simple as a switch (*binary semaphore*) or may have an integer value (*counting semaphore*). A semaphore is associated with each resource in the system. When a resource is requested, the P operator is used to test the corresponding semaphore; if it is off, P turns it on and returns. If the semaphore is already on, then P makes a note that the requesting process has been placed in WAIT state waiting for the resource associated with that semaphore. Later, a V operator issued by another process releases the resource, turns the semaphore off, and awakens any processes waiting for that resource.

In Chapter 4 the process synchronization operations will be more formally explained; a sample implementation is presented in Chapter 7. It is important to note that since most modules of the operating system need to use P's and V's, these functions are placed in the core of the kernel (level 1).

Examples of the primitive functions in the various levels of the kernel are:

Level 1: Processor Management Lower Level
The P synchronization primitive

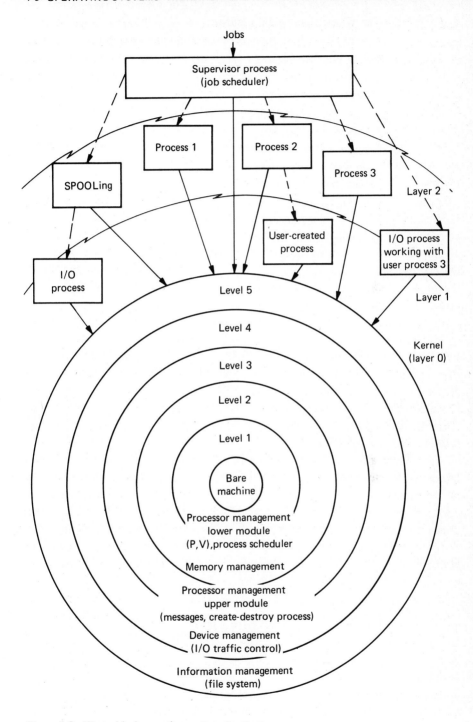

Figure 1-9 Hierarchical operating system structure

The V synchronization primitive

Process scheduling—the mechanism of multiprogramming

Level 2: Memory Management

Allocate memory

Release (free) memory

Level 3: Processor Management Upper Level

Create/destroy process

Send/receive messages between processes

Stop process

Start process

Level 4: Device Management

Keep track of status of all I/O devices

Schedule I/O

Initiate I/O process

Level 5: Information Management

Create/destroy file

Open/close file

Read/write file

The kernel comprises routines needed to support the operation of processes. What functions of the resource managers can be performed in a separate process? To make such a decision, one must ask which functions can be performed independently and concurrently, as opposed to those that must be performed serially. Nothing can be gained by placing serially executed functions in a separate process. The functions of the operating system that may be executed concurrently with the execution of a user's processes are those of the job scheduler, remote terminal handling, and the input/output SPOOLing routines; let us, then, make these separate processes.

Each user could have a separate I/O process for each device to oversee his specialized I/O. In flexible systems the system may also allow the user to create as many processes as he wishes. This is especially useful for certain parallel numerical computations and for handling real-time process control and timesharing functions.

1-6 AN EXAMPLE—OS/MVT USING OUR VIEW

Let us make a very cursory presentation of IBM's OS/MVT (Multiprogramming with a Variable Number of Tasks). (See also IBM, 1.) We will not elaborate on each resource, since that is the function of the rest of this book, nor will we present an in-depth treatment of OS/MVT (or any other 370 operating system) since we will treat this as one of our case study examples in Chapter 9. However, we hope to demonstrate here the application of our approach.

1-6.1 Memory Management—OS/MVT

Within an operating system the memory management modules are concerned with the assignment of primary memory to user jobs and with keeping track of memory use. Memory is allocated to each job as a contiguous block called a partition. In Figure 1-10, memory is divided into partitions with each job assigned to a partition. OS/MVT allows up to 15 partitions (jobs).

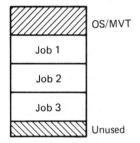

Figure 1-10 OS/MVT memory allocation

1-6.2 Processor Management—OS/MVT

The processor management modules are concerned with the assignment of a processor to a job. There are three major modules of processor management: the job scheduler, the processor scheduler, and the traffic controller.

The job scheduler is concerned with choosing which job will be started next and converted to processes. There are several schedulers available as part of OS/MVT. A simple version provides a FCFS (First Come First Served) sequencing. Other versions are described in Chapters 4 and 9.

Another important module within processor management is the processor scheduler. In a multiprogramming system that has several processes in a state of execution, the processor scheduler chooses which process is assigned to a processor and how long that process will have the processor. OS/MVT's processor scheduler chooses which process is to be assigned to the processor strictly on a priority basis. Once a process has a processor, it keeps it until (1) it does some I/O; (2) it makes an error; (3) it finishes; or (4) a higher priority process wants the processor. However, there is an option that allows "timeslicing," (a processor is assigned to a process for a fixed amount of time). When that fixed amount of time (slice) is up, the processor may be assigned to another process.

1-6.3 Device Management—OS/MVT

The device management modules are concerned with the assigning of devices to jobs and the efficient operation of these devices. Once the job scheduler selects a job, it may request any device.

OS/MVT provides for multiprogramming in which a user's job is executed intermittently with other jobs. One may ask how I/O is handled. For example, if two jobs are trying to print results on a single printer, must the operator cut up the final output paper containing the intermingled results of each job and paste the output together? The answer is no. In general, there are three ways in which device management may assign devices: dedicated, shared, and virtual. Printers cannot be shared without cutting and pasting output. We could dedicate a printer to a job, but this might interfere with efficient device operation. OS/MVT handles devices such as the printer by virtual assignment. In particular, it uses SPOOLing. The SPOOLing modules cause all printing to be done on a virtual (imaginary) printer, for example, the disk. At some later time the SPOOLing modules take all the information "printed" on the disk and actually print it on the printer at maximum speed.

SPOOLing is only one of the device management modules. Others include modules for assigning channels, control units, and other devices.

1-6.4   Information Management—OS/MVT

The information management modules are concerned with the organization, assignment, protection, and retrieval of data sets (files). The user specifies which files his job will need by means of Job Control Statements. The actual reading, writing, and storage of information is performed by OS/MVT's Data Management Services, which are invoked via Access Method modules. The user's program needs only to refer to files by symbolic names; the physical storage and mapping are performed automatically.

1-7   OTHER VIEWS OF AN OPERATING SYSTEM

There are many other ways to view an operating system, which we will not present in detail. However, a short discussion of these other views may help the reader by giving him a better perspective of an operating system.

1-7.1   Historical View

It is difficult to present an accurate account of operating system developments, since many important concepts were first introduced long before they became generally accepted. For example, the concepts of paging and virtual storage were first demonstrated on the Atlas System in 1959 (Fotheringham, 1961), then used in a few general systems during the mid-1960s, and finally announced as part of IBM's standard product line in 1972. Our brief historical view and the chart in Figure 1-11 are based upon the historical summaries of Saul Rosen (Rosen, 1969) and Robert F. Rosin (Rosin, 1969).

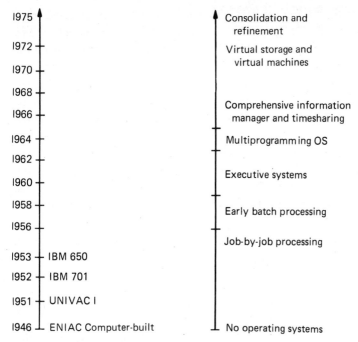

Figure 1-11   Historical development of operating system

1-7.1.1 JOB-BY-JOB PROCESSING

In the early systems, since run times were quite long and debugging was clumsy, each programmer operated the computer personally—loading decks, pushing buttons, examining storage locations, etc.

1-7.1.2 EARLY BATCH PROCESSING

As time went on and computers got to be faster and more expensive, it became too costly to allow a computer to sit idle while a user manually loaded his jobs. Thus monitor programs were developed that allowed users to "batch" their jobs together, which constituted an automatic job sequencing. The batch monitor was invoked only at the end of each job's processing to initiate the start of the next job.

1-7.1.3 EXECUTIVE SYSTEMS

As computers became more complex, especially with regard to I/O device management, executive systems were developed that permanently resided in memory and provided Input/Output Control Services (IOCS) for user jobs. Many other services, such as run-time limits, accounting, etc., were incorporated into these executive systems.

1-7.1.4 MULTIPROGRAMMING OPERATING SYSTEMS

The input/output bottleneck increased as systems became even larger and faster. Multiprogramming was used as a technique to enhance the throughput efficiency. As byproducts, extensive I/O standardization and numerous job control languages and executive systems were developed.

1-7.1.5 COMPREHENSIVE INFORMATION MANAGEMENT AND TIMESHARING

With the increased use of the computer for sophisticated data processing instead of just for numerical computation, it was necessary to standardize and simplify the storage and handling of data. Extensive information management facilities, often called data management or filing systems, were introduced. At the same time, the concept of direct user interaction via timesharing techniques was incorporated into several systems.

1-7.1.6 CONSOLIDATION AND REFINEMENT

In the rapid and somewhat chaotic growth of operating systems, many important concepts emerged, disappeared, and then reappeared again, often in different forms. The example of paging has already been noted earlier in the chapter. In recent years, there has been considerable effort to consolidate and refine all the advances of the past. The merging of the multiprogramming-batch philosophy with time-sharing technology to form operating systems capable of both batch and timesharing operations is an example of these trends.

1-7.2 Functional View

Most users wish to use the computer only to solve particular problems. They have no interest in paging, segmentation, SPOOLing, etc. Such users want only that the system provide them with a number of packages to assist them in defining and solving their problems. Although such packages are important, we do not consider them part of the operating system and will not, therefore, deal with them in this book.

Examples of these packages are:

1 Assembly language translators
2 Compilers, such as FORTRAN, COBOL, and PL/I
3 Subroutine libraries, such as SINE, COSINE, and SQUARE ROOT
4 Linkage editors and program loaders that bind subroutines together and prepare programs for execution
5 Utility routines, such as SORT/MERGE, tape copy, etc.
6 Application packages, such as circuit analysis or simulation
7 Debugging facilities, such as program tracing and terminal "core dumps"

1-7.3   Job Control Language and Supervisor Services Interface View

Many users view the operating system principally in terms of the way they must communicate with it. This communication is normally in two forms: (1) Job Control Language, which identifies a user's job and its requirements to the system and (2) supervisor services interface, i.e., the way a user's program, while running, calls upon the operating system for services.

The job control language for a complex, flexible, modern operating system is often very extensive (Brown, 1970; Cadow, 1970). The user may specify accounting and priority information, the programs to be run, and the resources needed (input and output). A typical job might look as follows:

```
                                                             Comments

//            JOB      NAME = DONOVAN, ACCOUNT = 6.251,
                       TIMELIMIT = 5, PRIORITY = 8

//STEP1       EXEC     PL1                               ⎫
//OUTPUT      DD       UNIT=TAPE9,VOLUME=SER=             ⎪
                       0123,DCB=(RECFM=FB,                ⎬  First job step,
                       LRECL=80,BLKSIZE=800)              ⎪  a PL/I compilation
//INPUT       DD       *                                  ⎪
           ≡  PL/I program                               ⎭
/*
//STEP2       EXEC     LINKER,COND=(4,LT,STEP1)          ⎫  Second job step,
//OUTPUT      DD       DSNAME=REAL.LIVE.FILE              ⎪  link PL/I output with
//INPUT       DD       DSNAME=&STEP1.OUTPUT               ⎬  library (only if no
//SYSLIB      DD       DSNAME=PLI.LIBRARY                 ⎪  compile errors of
/*                                                        ⎭  severity level over 4)
//STEP3       EXEC     REAL.LIVE.FILE,MEMORY=100K        ⎫  Third job step,
//OUTPUT      DD       UNIT=PRINTER                       ⎬  execution of user's
//INPUT       DD       *                                  ⎪  program
           ≡  input data                                 ⎭
/*
```

By using the full facilities of a Job Control Language, the user can specify detailed control over the operation and sequencing of the steps of his job. For example, the operation of certain later steps can be made conditional upon the results of earlier steps, for example, COND = (4,LT,STEP1) in our example. In fact, JCL, in such cases, becomes in effect a powerful macroscopic programming language.

The user supervisor services interface is often implicit, especially when programming is done in high-level languages. In assembly language it becomes necessary to explicitly invoke the supervisor services either by Supervisor Call Instructions or by system-provided macroinstructions. The simple program portion described in Section 1-5.1 might actually be programmed as:

1	MVC	C,B	SET C = B
2	SVC	13	FIND 80 BYTES OF "FREE" SPACE AND SET
	DC	A(80,X)	X = LOCATION
3	SVC	01	READ CARD INTO AREA SPECIFIED BY X
	DC	C'CARD'	
	DC	A(X)	
4	CLC	X(2),=C'/*'	ARE FIRST TWO BYTES OF AREA X AN
			"/*"?
5	BE	END	IF SO, TRANSFER TO END

The SVC is the Supervisor Call Instruction used on the IBM System/370 series of computers.

For many users, the JCL and SVC interfaces are their main view of an operating system.

1-8   GENERAL DESIGN CONSIDERATIONS

1-8.1   Software Design Procedure

A design procedure for software is based on the following steps:

1 Make a clear statement of the problem.
2 List the relevant databases.
3 Specify the format of those databases.
4 Devise an algorithm.
5 Look for modularity.
6 Repeat steps (1) through (5) on each module.

In designing an operating system, the first iteration of (1) through (5) would produce a statement of the facilities desired in the system. In step (5) it would be noted that an operating system could be functionally divided into four managers. The presentation in this book could then be used in the first three iterations of these steps. That is, all modules would be divided into four categories of resource managers. The second iteration would pinpoint the key functions within each manager (keep track, policy, allocate, and deallocate). The third iteration would require the development of algorithms to perform these functions. The fourth iteration would involve recognizing basic table maintenance functions, databases, and queue handling.

1-8.2   Implementation Tools

Just as a modern carpenter does not build a house with simply a hand saw, hammer, and nails, a modern programmer cannot work efficiently without the help of tools that offer him sufficient flexibility. Such tools permit him to perform alone work that previously required many programmers, and, in fact, if he uses the software tools effectively, he can do the work both faster and more elegantly.

We shall briefly mention a few tools that greatly improve the effectiveness of a system's designer and implementer: high-level languages, timesharing, and structured programming. Briefly, the use of high-level languages, as opposed to assembly languages, may increase programmer clarity and productivity considerably. The use of a timesharing system with powerful information management capabilities provides both rapid and easier debugging as well as simplified control and maintenance of the source code modules. The term *software factory* has been used by several groups to describe such a facility. Structured programming, as noted in the section on extended machines, is an approach to simplify the conceptual design of large systems and ease the implementation and debugging of the system.

We advocate using high-level languages even for implementing an operating system. Yet in Chapter 7 our sample operating system is actually written in assembly language! Hypocrites? No. If we analyze the MULTICS operating systems 95 percent of MULTICS is in a high-level language (PL/I); the 5 percent left in assembly language are the very basic and machine-dependent portions. The sample operating system of Chapter 7 is so small that it consists only of these very primitive functions.

1-8.3 Documentation

Good documentation is a must. Most operating systems use very simple algorithms but very complicated databases. One technique for documenting such systems is to give a framework of the interaction of all modules. Then for each module give the data structure (e.g., PL/I style) with a brief statement of what the module does to the structures. The sample operating system design description in Chapter 7, although not necessarily ideal, presents a good illustration of the level of documentation appropriate. If a timesharing system is used for system development support as a software factory, it is possible to use the information management and text-editing facilities to maintain up-to-date documentation online.

1-9 PRELUDE OF THINGS TO COME

Chapter 2 presents a background on the hardware environment of systems. Using the view of the operating system as a resource manager, Chapters 3, 4, 5, and 6 (memory, processor, device, and information management, respectively) present a discussion of each of these managers. In these chapters we present a spectrum of techniques for managing each resource. In some instances, we describe specific algorithms, giving the databases used and usually a flowchart as well. Chapter 8 explains and gives examples of interdependencies in the management of these resources. Chapters 7 and 9 describe our sample operating system and then give a summary of certain existing operating systems using the framework developed in Chapters 3, 4, 5, and 6.

Chapter 10 gives an annotated bibliography of many of the important works in this field. We have also cross-referenced the bibliography to allow the reader to select further readings in specified areas. Appendix A gives a specification of the IBM/370, which is used in some examples in the text, and appendix B gives an introduction to microprogramming.

1-10 SUMMARY

The operating system is a manager of resources. It manages these resources using certain mechanisms according to any number of policies and goals (e.g., high utilization of system devices, high throughput of jobs).

This book introduces a framework based on the operating system as a resource manager. We identify four resources: memory, processors, devices, and information. When are these functions executed? The process state model gave us a framework as to when each of these functions took place. Where are these functions executed? The hierarchical model gave us a structure of where each one of these functions took place.

QUESTIONS

1-1 What is the difference between the following?
  1 process and processor
  2 user, job, and process

1-2 List two advantages of multiprogramming.

1-3 One may make the following analogy:
  Boss is comparable to CPU
  Secretary is comparable to I/O channel
  Typewriter is comparable to I/O device
  1 State how a boss, secretary, and typewriter communicate with each other (e.g., boss with his secretary).
  2 How is each scheduled? Consider priorities, preemption, and interruption and which can be interrupted by whom (e.g., who can interrupt the boss?).
  3 Repeat 1 and 2 for the group: CPU, I/O channel, I/O device.

1-4 Divide all the following instructions into privileged and nonprivileged. For each instruction state your reasons.
  1 Set tape drive on fire.
  2 Raise π (pi) to the 'x' power.
  3 Stop CPU.
  4 Read the clock.
  5 Clear memory.
  6 Disable all interrupts (masking).
  7 Change value of instruction address register.

1-5 Assume that you are head of the check-sorting division of a bank, which processes 50,000 checks a day for its 99,999 customers. That is, 50,000 checks are distributed among 99,999 bins.
  Two sorting methods are proposed.
  1 Linear—the bins are lined up in a row. A person takes about 99,999/10 seconds (about 1,000 seconds) to find the right bin and deposit the check in it.

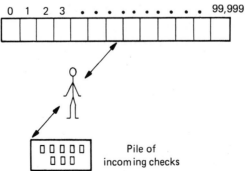

2 Bucket sort—11,110 intermediary bins are used. Based on first digit of check, he places it in one of ten bins. After all the checks have been so processed, he goes to one of these bins and processes each check into 10 other bins based upon the second digit, etc. Processing each such check action takes about 10/10 = 1 second.

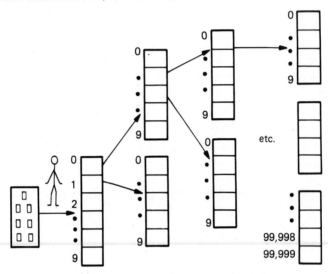

a How long would it take to process all the checks using methods 1 and 2?

b Using method 2, which steps could be done in parallel (as separate processes)? That is, how many people could be used?

c If parallel processing were used in method 2, how long would it take to sort all the checks?

1-6 We make an analogy between a warehouse with many shelves and a memory with many locations. Assume a large number of items have arrived and will continue to arrive. The task of the warehouse manager (memory manager) is to store these items on the shelves.

Give an example of how the four memory manager functions of Section 1-3 are performed; for example,

1 How does the manager keep track of space?

2 If the loading dock has many items on it, how does the manager decide which item to store first?

3 How are shelves allocated?

4 What does the manager do when one item is removed from the shelves?

1-7 We can make an analogy between managing a restaurant and managing processors when the following are analogous.

Cook—processor

Maitre d' (cook's boss)—processor manager

Customers' orders—processes—they are all demanding processing, e.g., they want their meal.

Customers—users

Give an example of how the four processor manager functions of Section 1-4 are performed, e.g., how does the boss keep track of resources—the processors and processes, etc.?

1-8 We can make an analogy between managing a post office and managing devices where the mail trucks are devices and the letters are the I/O request. (*Note:* the post office does not decide where your letters go or just how they get there.)

Give an example of how the four device management functions of Section 1-3.3 are performed for the post office. Be sure to consider the following in function 2. If one letter arrives, do you assign it a truck and send the truck away (fast delivery for that letter, but you could run out of trucks) or do you wait until the truck is full (efficient use of device but slow delivery, e.g., a truck to Lynn, Mass. may take a year to fill)? Thus, discuss the tradeoff between fast response (sending the letter on the first truck) and good utilization (wait until the truck is full).

1-9 We make an analogy between a librarian and an information manager. Give an example of how the four information management functions of Section 1-3 are performed for a library.

1-10 We can make a process state model of you.

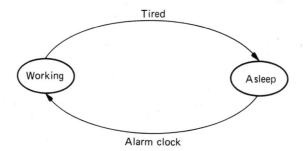

Where you have two states, asleep or working, you make the transition from the working state to the asleep state when you are tired.

1 Add three more states, e.g., eating.

2 Indicate all possible transitions between the five states.

1-11 One technique or view found useful is the structured programming or hierarchical view (our third view is in Section 1-5.2). Let us explore the advantages of this view for building an operating system by the analogy of a carpenter building a house. His basic parts involved are nails, glass, cement, putty, and wood.

1   What are the disadvantages for a carpenter who uses only very basic parts, e.g., nothing preassembled?

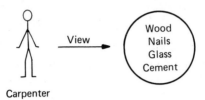

2   Alternately, a carpenter could use higher level primitives, e.g., window assemblies. List such primitives.

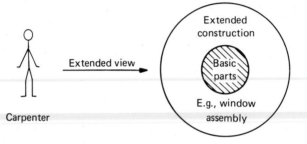

What are some advantages to this view?

3   Order the extended primitives of 2, e.g., if a large assembly uses a smaller one then the larger one is above the smaller (a door assembly may include a window assembly).

1-12   Define briefly an alternate Job Control Language from that of the figure on page 25. The alternate should cover the same kinds of meanings but have other advantages, e.g., possibly more English-like (e.g., file input is STEP1.OUTPUT).

1-13   Given a primitive batch system with no multiprogramming as discussed in Section 1-7.1.2 where jobs (e.g., source decks to be compiled, loaded, and executed) were submitted to an operator. The operator physically loaded the deck of cards associated with the job into a card reader. For each job the operator was given information as to some of the resources the job needed (e.g., tapes and printers) and the maximum length of time the job would take to execute.

1   List all steps (your list should be between 5 and 15 steps) that the operator must perform. Include decision operations (e.g., choosing which job runs first) as well as physical operations (e.g., mount tape).

2 The MIT Computation Center reports that the average job executes for 48 seconds. How much time would an operator spend performing the steps you have listed (e.g., how much total time to process a job)?

3 Which steps could be done in parallel? (More than one operator is available).

4 Using the same time per step that you used for part 2 and allowing for parallel processing, how much time would it take to process the job?

5 Which steps could be automated, that is, become part of the operating system?

1-14 Below is a flowchart of a simple operating system with no multiprogramming for processing jobs.

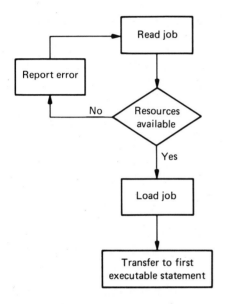

1 Devise a Job Control Language for such an operating system.

2 Extend this language to include the concept of a job step and conditional executing of a job step.

3 Modify the above flowchart to handle 2 above.

1-15[2] Question 1-14 asked you to design a simple operating system. In this question you are to design a replacement for IBM's OS/MVT.

1 Provide complete flowcharts.

2 Complete and debug an implementation.

---

[2] For the instructor who assigns all odd-numbered problems.

I/O Programming, Interrupt Programming, and Machine Structure

2

The purpose of this chapter is to:

1 Present the concepts of I/O programming, interrupts, and asychronous computation

2 Present the basic computer structures that must be understood to implement an operating system

3 Present the IBM System/370, which will be used in many examples in following chapters

4 Present machine language (assembly language) programming, I/O programming, and interrupt programming

5 Present an introduction to the important resources an operating system must manage (the processor, I/O channels, main storage, I/O devices)

The chapter is a self-contained introduction to contemporary computer system structure (computer hardware). The intention is not to be comprehensive but rather to familiarize the reader with the central concepts common to such systems. The reader may need to refer to other sources, such as programming manuals, in order to understand certain examples and questions.

In the ensuing pages we will deal with the general structure of a computer system, the operation and initiation of I/O processes, the handling and synchronization of parallel processing, and interrupt processing.

While we do not necessarily advocate programming the operating system in assembly language,[1] we feel this language is a useful vehicle for understanding

---

[1] The terms *machine language* and *assembly language* are used interchangeably in this chapter. We are primarily concerned with machine language (basic computer hardware) but use assembly notation to simplify the reading. The reader may wish to refer to other references, such as Donovan's *Systems Programming,* for a more detailed discussion.

the structure and capabilities of a computer system as well as the mechanics of implementing an operating system.

We think that knowledge of these details is essential for anyone actually implementing or studying an operating system. Therefore, before providing a broad, theoretical framework, we present the concepts of assembly language, I/O programming, and interrupt processing using examples from present-day computers. The examples are taken from both the IBM System/360 and the IBM System/370 (IBM, 2, 3, 4, 5).[2] We have chosen the System/370 for the following reasons:

1 It is the common language of the computer industry.
2 It is similar to many other contemporary computer languages.
3 It has a reasonable machine language, I/O language, and interrupt structure.
4 It provides a set of metaphors that make it possible to understand other machines.

In cases where other machines display important features that are significantly different, we introduce those machines.

This chapter is divided into four sections:

1 General computer system structure
2 CPU structure—assembly language programming
3 I/O structure—I/O programming
4 Interrupt structure—interrupt programming

The reader need only concern himself with the sections that are unfamiliar to him. For example, we anticipate that for many readers Sections 2-1 and 2-2 will serve as a review, whereas Sections 2-3 and 2-4 will provide new material.

2-1 MACHINE STRUCTURE

Figure 2-1 provides an example of a computer system.

Instructions and data are stored in main storage (traditionally called core or memory); the terms main storage, memory, and core are often used interchangeably. Several processors (hardware devices that interpret instructions) are connected to the memory. In most modern systems the processors may become specialized into I/O processors and central processors. The I/O processors, commonly called *channels,* are primarily concerned with input and output operations, while the Central Processing Units (CPUs), are primarily concerned with executing instruc-

---

[2] The IBM System/360 and System/370 are series of computer systems in common use. The System/370 is the newer series and will normally be used in examples. Most examples should apply to both series.

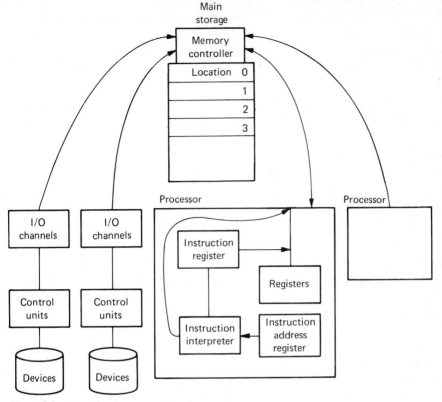

Figure 2-1 Example of a computer system

tions for arithmetic and logical operations. There may be several CPUs and I/O processors within the same system.

The I/O processors often have a set of instructions that differ from the CPUs, both in format and in meaning. Section 2-2 of this chapter is concerned with programming the CPU, while Section 2-3 deals with the programming of I/O processors.

Most CPUs consist of a set of working registers used as accumulators, index registers, and base registers. The CPU also consists of some internal registers, for example, instruction register and instruction address register. Instructions are fetched from memory, placed into the instruction register, and interpreted, The instruction address register contains the memory address of the next instruction to be executed.

2-2 ASSEMBLY LANGUAGE PROGRAMMING
The purpose of this section is to familiarize the reader with the 370 and the 370 assembly language. It is written primarily for the reader who is somewhat familiar

with the concept of assembly language and machine language and the reader who needs a review of the 370. There are many introductory books on assembly language programming (Altucher, 1966; Kapur, 1970; IBM, 6, 7), and the manuals of most manufacturers are helpful.

Our purpose, therefore, is not to describe the 370 in great detail, but only those features essential to the understanding of the functions and mechanisms of an operating system.

2-2.I General Approach to a New Computer

In this section we present an approach that might be adopted by a user wishing to become familiar with a new computer. Specifically, we list a series of questions concerning the central processor of the IBM/370, and then answer them. Since the I/O channel can be viewed as just another computer, we answer these same questions with regard to the I/O processors.

1 *Memory*

What is the memory's basic unit, size, and addressing scheme?

2 *Registers*

How many registers are there? What are their sizes, functions, and inter-relationships

3 *Data*

What type of data can be handled by the computer? Can it handle characters, numbers, logical data? How are these data stored?

4 *Instructions*

What are the classes of instructions on the machine? Are there arithmetic instructions, logical instructions, symbolic instructions? What are their formats? How are they stored in memory?

5 *Special Features* (pertinent to operating systems)

The answers to questions 1, 2, 3, and 4 supply sufficient familiarity with machine structure for most users. However, the user who must design or understand an operating system must be familiar with additional hardware features. These features are:

a *Status of a Program* How does the CPU keep track of which instruction to execute? Does the CPU differentiate between operating system state and user state?

b *Input/Output Processing* How is input and output handled? If separate I/O processors are used, how does the CPU communicate with them?

c *Interrupts* What kinds of interrupts exist? How are interrupts handled?

d *Masking* Can interrupts be ignored or suspended?

e *Protection* Is there hardware available that can prevent the reading, writing, or execution of parts of memory?

f *Timers* Is there a clock on the system that can be accessed or set?

g *States* Does the CPU have different states? Does the CPU have privileged instructions that may be executed only in certain states?

h *Microprogramming* Can the user change the instructions of the machine? Can anyone?

2-2.2 Machine Structure—360 and 370

In this section we will answer preceding questions in the context of the IBM/370. The material is generally applicable to the 360 also.

2-2.2.I MEMORY

The basic unit of memory in the 370 is a byte—8 bits of information. That is, each addressable position in memory can contain 8 bits of information. There are instructions to operate on contiguous bytes as follows:

UNIT OF MEMORY	BYTES	LENGTH IN BITS
Byte	1	8
Halfwood	2	16
Word	4	32
Doubleword	8	64

The size of the 370 memory is up to 2^{24} bytes (about 16 million).

The addressing on the 370 memory may consist of three components. Specifically, the value of an address equals the value of an offset plus the contents of a base register plus the contents of an index register. We will give examples of this addressing later.

In general, operations on units of memory are specified by the low-order byte address. For example, when addressing a word (4 bytes) the address is that of the low-order byte, for example, location 104 as illustrated below:

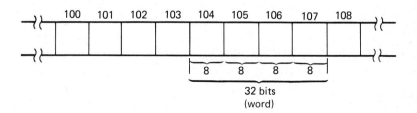

32 bits
(word)

2-2.2.2 REGISTERS

The 370 has 16 general purpose registers, each consisting of 32 bits. There are four floating-point registers consisting of 64 bits each. In addition, there are 16 special control registers, each 32 bits. The 370 has a 64-bit Program Status Word (PSW) that contains the value of the instruction address, protection information, and interrupt status.

The general purpose registers may be used for various arithmetic and logical operations and as base registers. When the programmer uses them in arithmetic or logical operations, he thinks of these registers as scratch pads to which numbers are added, subtracted, compared, and so forth. When used as base registers, they aid in the formation of the address. Take for example the instruction:

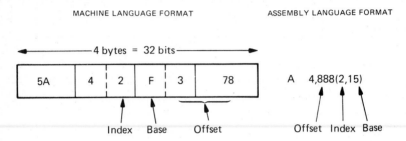

This is interpreted as an add instruction. A number is to be added to the contents of general register 4. The location of the number is 888 (offset) plus the contents of register 2 (index) plus the contents of register 15 (base). That is, the sum of those three numbers is the address the contents of which we wish to add to the contents of register 4.

The base/offset addressing has several advantages. It aids the process of relocation since relative addresses are used in the instructions rather than direct absolute addresses. In addition, it decreases the amount of space required for specifying an address. The 370 may have up to 2^{24} bytes of main storage. This would require 24 address bits if direct addressing were used. In comparison, the base and offset fields together use only 16 bits.

2-2.2.3 DATA

The 370 provides instructions for processing several different types of data, such as binary integers, binary floating point, decimal integers, and character strings. The principal data formats are shown in Figure 2-2.

All data and instructions are physically stored as a sequence of binary ones and zeros. Thus a 16-bit fixed-point halfword with decimal value +300 would be stored in binary as '0000 0001 0010 1100'. For the sake of convenience, binary numbers are usually written in the hexadecimal (base 16) number system rather than the binary (base 2) number system. The *hexadecimal digits* are given in Appendix A.

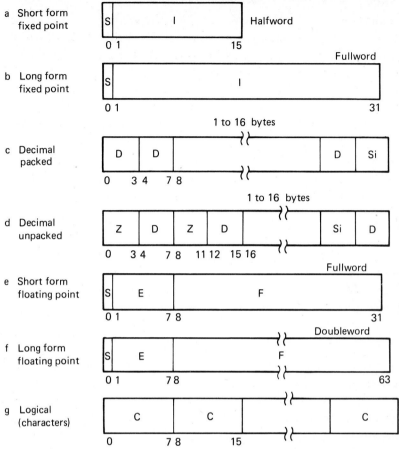

C = Character code (8 bits)
D = Binary coded decimal digit (4 bits)
E = Exponent
F = Fraction
I = Integer
S = Sign bit
Si = Sign code (4 bits)
Z = Zone code (4 bits)

Figure 2-2   Data formats for the System/370

Note that every hexadecimal digit can be replaced by exactly four binary digits and vice versa. Thus when we have the number +300 in decimal, which equals B'0000 0001 0010 1100' in binary, its hexadecimal equivalent is

X' 0   1   2   C '.

Fixed-point numbers may be stored in either a halfword or a fullword (Figures 2-2a and 2-2b).

The 370 allows the storage of numbers in decimal form (Figures 2-2c and d), that is, numbers may be stored not as binary numbers but in a format closely approximating the decimal representation. For example, the number 12 could appear in one byte where the first four bits contain a decimal 1 (0001) and the second four bits would contain a decimal 2 (0010). Decimal forms are useful in business data processing.

The 370 allows floating-point numbers (Figures 2-2e and f), logical data, and character strings (Figure 2-2g) to be represented in memory, as Figure 2-2 shows.

There are instructions to operate on all these types of data.

2-2.2.4 INSTRUCTIONS

The 370 has arithmetic, logical, transfer, and special I/O instructions. There are five basic formats of these instructions. An instruction may require either two bytes, four bytes, or six bytes. Appendix A lists all the available instructions and their formats. For example, the word

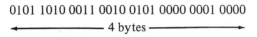

0101 1010 0011 0010 0101 0000 0001 0000

◄─────────── 4 bytes ───────────►

would be interpreted as an RX format add instruction, adding to register 3 the contents of the address (16 + contents of register 5 + contents of register 2).

2-2.2.5 SPECIAL FEATURES

Status of a Program   The Program Status Word is an internal register that specifies the status of the CPU. Its format in Basic Control Mode[3] is as follows.

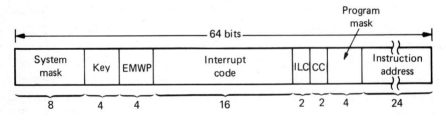

How does the 370's CPU know what instruction to take next? How does the CPU know what interrupted it? How does the CPU know if it has masked certain interrupts? How does it know if it is in the privileged state? The answer to all these questions is through the PSW.

We will briefly explain the relevant parts of each field of bits. In Section 2-4 we will give examples of how these fields are used in interrupt processing. (See Appendix A for the meaning of all bits in the PSW.)

The *instruction address* contains the address of the next instruction to be executed.

---

[3] On the 370 there are two different formats for the PSW. In Basic Control Mode (E = 0), the PSW is essentially compatible with the PSW of the earlier 360. Extended Control Mode (E = 1), in conjunction with the control registers, provides some special features that will not be discussed until Chapter 3.

The EMWP field (E = extended mode; M = machine check mode; W = wait state mode; P = problem state mode) has two bits that are relevant to our discussion, W and P. The P bit denotes the mode of the CPU (0 = supervisory or 1 = user problem). Certain "privileged" instructions may be executed only in supervisory mode. The W bit indicates that the processor either is running (W = 0) or is stopped, possibly waiting for an interrupt (W = 1).

The *interrupt code* contains coded information as to the type of interrupt last received. (See Appendix A for the exact codes.)

The *system mask* indicates whether the CPU wishes to accept interrupts from a specific channel. Bits 0 through 5 must be turned on if channels 0 through 5, respectively, are allowed to interrupt the CPU. If bit 6 is on, all channels 6 or above are allowed to interrupt. If bit 7 is on, external interrupts (clock timer, operator emergency button, etc.) are allowed. If the I/O interrupts are masked and an interrupt occurs, then the hardware automatically suspends (holds) that interrupt for later processing.

The *program mask* contains information to mask some other types of interrupts. If such an interrupt is masked and occurs, it is lost (ignored). Note that not all types of interrupts are maskable. (Similarly, you personally may find it impossible to mask certain interrupts, e.g., mothers' interrupts usually get processed.)

The *key* is for protection purposes, and is explained in the section on protection. The Instruction Length Code (ILC) contains the length of the *last* instruction executed, not the present one. This allows the programmer to trace back one instruction. The Condition Code (CC) contains the current value of the condition code. The CC is automatically set by certain instructions, such as arithmetic, comparison, etc.

Input/Output Processing The 370, in common with most contemporary large-scale systems, has separate processors that do most of the I/O. These I/O computers or processors are called channels. The CPU, however, is usually in charge and initiates the I/O by executing such instructions as START I/O. The START I/O is actually a communication to the channel to start executing its program.

The CPU of the 370 has several instructions relating to I/O. (Note that the channel that actually does the I/O has many more instructions, such as read, write, eject page, etc.) The three principal instructions are: START I/O, which initiates the I/O channel to start executing its program; HALT I/O, which stops the channel; and TEST I/O, which tests the status of a device, control unit, or channel. In Section 2-3 we will discuss these 370 instructions. These instructions do not themselves perform any I/O; they are merely a method by which the CPU communicates with the I/O processor.

Interrupts Can the CPU be interrupted? The answer is yes. In Section 2-4 we discuss and give examples of specific mechanisms used on the 370. Most other machines have similar hardware mechanisms for handling interrupts. An interrupt is an occurrence that causes the processor to take some immediate action. If while you are reading this page (you being the processor), a friend asks for your attention, you have been interrupted. Your procedure would be to write down the page number you were on (hardware), and then determine what he or she wants (software) and whether or not you wish to satisfy the request.

The 370 has a mechanism for being interrupted, saving its status, determining what general class of interrupt occurred, and executing an appropriate interrupt routine.

Masking   There are times when you may not want to be interrupted. In such circumstances, you would like to mask out the interruption. Similarly, the operating system may wish to mask out new interrupts while it is working on previous ones.

The CPU of the 370 can mask certain interrupts; specifically, when certain bits are set in the Program Status Word, an I/O interrupt remains pending; other interrupts, when masked, are ignored.

Protection   The main storage on the 370 is divided into blocks of 2,048 bytes. A lock (a four-bit number, 0 to 15) is associated with each memory block, as illustrated in Figure 2-3. These locks may be set and examined by appropriate privileged instructions. Before an access is allowed to storage, a comparison is made between the lock associated with the storage block and the protect key in the PSW. The access is allowed only if the lock and key match or if the PSW contains the "master key" (a key of 0).

There are actually two types of locks on the 370: read/write protect; or only write protect. If a lock is set for only write protect (i.e., the "fetch protect" not set), then read accesses are allowed even if the lock and key don't match. The examples in Figure 2-3 illustrate some valid and invalid accesses. If the access is not permitted, a protection interrupt occurs.

Timers   There are several clocks and timers available on the 370:

1   The Time-of-Day clock (TOD) is a special 64-bit binary register. This register is incremented every μs. By convention, the TOD is initialized so that zero corresponds to January 1, 1900 midnight Greenwich Mean Time. The TOD may be examined or reset by appropriate instructions.

2   The Clock Comparator is a companion 64-bit register to the TOD. Whenever the Clock Comparator is less than the value of the Time-of-Day clock, an external interrupt is generated. This can be used to establish an "alarm clock."

3   The CPU Timer is another special 64-bit register that is automatically decremented every μs. When the timer is negative, an external interrupt is generated. This can be used like an egg timer by placing the time limit in the CPU timer and then receiving the interrupt when the time has elapsed.

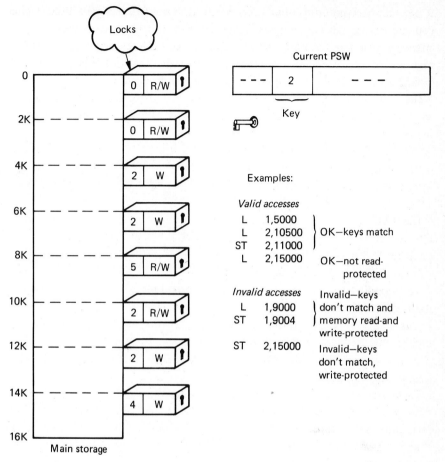

Figure 2-3 Example of 370 protection keys

4 The Interval Timer is largely for 360 compatibility. The interval timer is a 32-bit word at main storage location 80. This word is decremented every 1/300th of a second. Whenever the interval timer switches from positive to negative, an external interrupt occurs. For most purposes, the CPU Timer is more accurate and appropriate than the Interval Timer.

Each of the clock and timer facilities may be used separately or in combination with the others.

States The 370 CPU may be operating in either of two modes: *supervisor mode* (PSW bit 15 = 0) or *problem mode* (PSW bit 15 = 1). When in problem mode, also called *user mode* or *nonprivileged mode,* certain "privileged" instructions are not allowed. If the user attempts to use such an instruction, a privileged operation program interrupt occurs. Privileged instructions include those that (1) alter the PSW,

(2) alter the storage protection locks, and (3) interact with the I/O. The specific privileged instructions are indicated in Appendix A.

Microprogramming (Rosen, 1969; Wilkes, 1969) Most models of the 370 series use microprogramming, but no readily available facilities are provided to enable users to change the microprograms (see Appendix B).

2-2.3 Machine Language

In this section we will discuss machine language (the actual code executed by a computer). Again, our examples are taken from a 370-type computer, but are easily applicable to other machines. After reading this section, the reader should refer to one of the many books or manuals that discuss the machine language of the particular machine that he will be using.

We will not write machine language in ones and zeros, nor will we use hexadecimal numbers. Rather we will use a mnemonic form of machine language. Figure 2-4 depicts the add instruction discussed previously in Section 2-2.2.2.

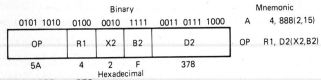

Note: $888_{10} = 378_{16}$

Figure 2-4 Mnemonic form of machine language

Let us now examine a simple machine language program to add three numbers (21, 41, 52) together. This program is shown in Figure 2-5. We assume that the instructions and data were loaded starting at location 1000_{16}.

Machine language		Mnemonic language		Comments
Loc Contents (hexadecimal)		Loc Contents (decimal)		
1000	05F0	4096	BALR 15,0	SET BASE REG 15 = 1002_{16} (4098_{10}).
1002	5810F012	4098	L 1,18(0,15)	LOAD '21'
1006	5A10F016	4102	A 1,22(0,15)	ADD '41'
100A	5A10F01A	4106	A 1,26(0,15)	ADD '52'
100E	5010F01E	4110	ST 1,30(0,15)	STORE ANSWER
1012	07FE	4114	BCR 15,14	RETURN TO CALLER (RETURN ADDRESS IN REG 14)
1014	00000015	4116	21	DATA
1018	00000029	4120	41	----
101C	00000034	4124	52	----
1020	----	4128	----	RESULT

Figure 2-5 A sample machine language program

The reader may wish to refer to the appropriate manuals for the meanings of the above instructions (IBM, 6, 7). We will briefly comment on the Branch and Link via Register (BALR) and the Branch Conditional via Register (BCR) instructions. The BALR instruction may be used in various forms; in this particular case (i.e., the second operand is 0) it places the address of the next instruction into the register designated by the first operand. Thus it places the number 1002_{16} (or 4098_{10}) in register 15. Since the BALR places a specific address into a register without requiring a reference to memory, it is a handy means of establishing the initial contents of a base register. Note that this program uses register 15 as the base register. Make sure you understand why and how this works.

What do we do when our little program has completed? There is no tidy way to stop a 370; furthermore, it is uneconomical to do so. Therefore, each program returns to its caller ("parent program"), which may be either another user subroutine or the operating system itself. By convention, the return address is left in register 14 by the caller. When the program has finished its job, it does an unconditional branch (branch code = 15) to the address specified in register 14—i.e., BCR 15,14.

2-2.4 Assembly Language

As the reader should quickly realize, writing programs in hexadecimal machine language or even in easier mnemonic machine language is highly burdensome and time-consuming. Assembly language provides an easier way to write programs while allowing the programmer to have just as much direct control over the specific instructions.

The key advantage of assembly language is that it allows the programmer to refer to storage locations by means of symbolic names, as shown in Figure 2-6. The tedious conversion to the 370 base/offset addressing is done automatically by the assembler. If the assembler is to compute the offset field of instructions automatically, it must know what register can be used as a base register and what that register will contain. The USING instruction answers both those questions and thus makes it possible for the assembler to produce correct code. The USING instruction is a *pseudo-op*. (A pseudo-op is an instruction to the assembler, as opposed to a machine-op, which is an instruction to the machine.) The Define Constant (DC) and Define Storage (DS) statements are pseudo-ops that instruct the assembler to place a 21, a 41, and a 52 in three consecutive fullwords in memory and leave one more for the answer.

START or CSECT is a pseudo-operation that tells the assembler where the beginning of the program is and allows the user to give a name to the program. In this case the name is EXAM.

END is a pseudo-operation that tells the assembler that the last card of the program has been reached.

EXTERNAL SYMBOL DICTIONARY

```
SYMBOL    TYPE ID  ADDR   LENGTH  LD ID
EXAM      SD   01  001C00 000024
```

```
LOC    OBJECT CODE  ADDR1 ADDR2  STMT  SOURCE STATEMENT
001000                            1 EXAM   START X'1000'     IDENTIFIES NAME OF PROGRAM.
001000 05F0                       2        BALR 15,0         SET REG 15 TO ADDRESS OF
                                  3 *                        NEXT INSTRUCTION.
001002                            4        USING *,15        PSEUDO-OP TELLING ASSEMBLER THAT
                                  5 *                        REG 15 IS BASE REGISTER AND CONTAINS
                                  6 *                        ADDRESS OF NEXT INSTRUCTION.
001002 5810 F012    01014         7        L    1,FIRST      GET '21'.
001006 5A10 F016    01018         8        A    1,SECOND     ADD '41'.
00100A 5A10 FC1A    0101C         9        A    1,THIRD      ADD '52'.
00100E 5010 F01E    01020        10        ST   1,ANSWER     STORE ANSWER.
001012 07FE                      11        BR   14           RETURN TO CALLER (REG 14
                                 12 *                        SHOULD CONTAIN RETURN ADDRESS
                                 13 *                        AS SET BY BALR 14,15 SUB CALL).
001014 00000015                  14 FIRST  DC   F'21'
001018 00000029                  15 SECOND DC   F'41'
00101C 00000034                  16 THIRD  DC   F'52'
001020                           17 ANSWER DS   F            RESERVE SPACE FOR ANSWER.
                                 18        END
```

CROSS-REFERENCE

```
SYMBOL  LEN   VALUE  DEFN   REFERENCES
ANSWER  00004 00102C 00017  001C
EXAM    00001 001000 00001  0007
FIRST   00004 001014 00014  0007
SECOND  00004 001018 00015  0008
THIRD   00004 00101C 00016  0009
```

Figure 2-6 A sample assembly language program

2-2.5   A Sample Assembly Language Program

Before completing the machine/assembly language section of this chapter, we will present a more comprehensive example. The reader is encouraged to study and understand this example since portions of it will be used again later.

Let us write a subroutine that will perform integer exponentiation. When this subroutine is called, register 1 points to (contains the address of) a halfword as shown below:

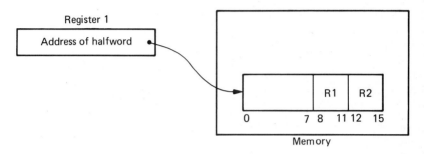

R1 and R2 denote registers such that the contents of the register denoted by R1 is raised to the power of the contents of R2. The exponentiated result is placed in the register denoted by R1.

For example, if the halfword contained

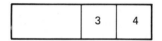

and register 3 contained a 10 and register 4 contained a 2, then the subroutine would place a 100 in register 3.

The algorithm must handle three cases:

   if exponent = 0, return 1

   if exponent < 0, return 0 (we assume integer arithmetic)

   if exponent > 0, loop to multiply and return answer

The overall algorithm is described in the flowchart of Figure 2-7.

Figure 2-8 contains the actual assembly listings of the EXPON subroutine. The first column on the left (LOC) gives the relative location (relative to beginning of program) of each statement of the program. The CSECT and USING pseudo-ops do not result in any assembly code; thus they do not take any memory space at execution time. The column OBJECT CODE contains the hexadecimal machine language equivalent to the statements. The column headed ADDR contains the offset value of the second operand of each instruction.

The assembler gives a cross-referenced listing indicating the symbol, its length, its address relative to the beginning of the program, the statement number in

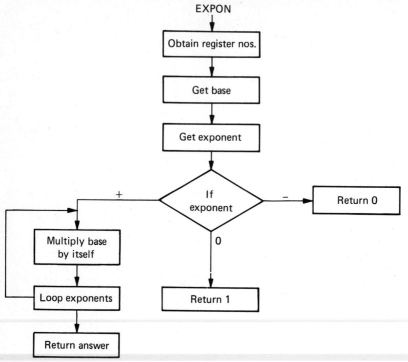

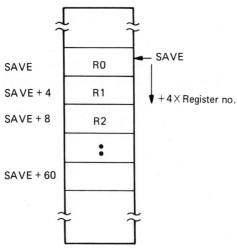

Figure 2-7 Flowchart for EXPON subroutines

which the symbol is defined, and, lastly, the statement numbers in which the symbol was referenced.

A few notes may be helpful in understanding the code in Figure 2-8, especially statements 15 and 16. We have stored all the registers in an area called SAVE, as illustrated below:

```
LOC    OBJECT CODE   ADDR1 ADDR2  STMT  SOURCE STATEMENT

                                    1 EXPON   CSECT              THIS SUBROUTINE IS CALLED BY THE
                                    2 *                          SEQUENCE:  L    15,=V(EXPON)
                                    3 *                                     BALR 14,15
CCC000              00050           4         USING EXPON,15     TELL ASSEMBLER REG 15 HAS
                                    5 *                          BASE ADDRESS OF EXPON.
CCC000  900F F050                   6         STM   0,15,SAVE    SAVE ALL THE REGISTERS.
CCC004  1822                        7         SR    2,2          ZERO OUT REGISTER 2.
CCC006  4320 1001                   8         IC    2,1(0,1)     LOAD BYTE 2 OF THE INSTRUCTION.
CCC00A  8C20 0004                   9         SRDL  2,4          SHIFT EXP REGISTER INTO REG 3.
CCC00E  8830 001C                  10         SRL   3,28         RIGHT SHIFT EXP REG IN REG 3.
CCC002                             11 RBASE   EQU   2            REG 2 CONTAINS BASE REG NO.
CCC003                             12 REXP    EQU   3            REG 3 CONTAINS THE EXP REG NO.
CCC004                             13 BASE    EQU   4            REG 4 CONTAINS THE BASE.
CCC005                             14 EXP     EQU   5            REG 5 CONTAINS THE EXPONENT.
CCC012  8920 0002                  15         SLL   RBASE,2      MULTIPLY BASE REG NO. BY 4.
CCC016  8930 0002                  16         SLL   REXP,2       MULTIPLY EXP REG NO. BY 4.
CCC01A  5842 F050                  17         L     BASE,SAVE(RBASE)  FETCH THE BASE.
CCC01E  5853 F050                  18         L     EXP,SAVE(REXP)    FETCH THE EXPONENT.
CCC022  1255                       19         LTR   EXP,EXP      TEST IF EXP NEG, ZERO, POS.
CCC024  4740 F03C                  20         BM    NEG          TRANSFER IF NEGATIVE EXPONENT.
CCC028  4780 F042                  21         BZ    ZERO         TRANSFER IF ZERO EXPONENT.
CCC02C  1874                       22         LR    7,BASE       INITIALIZE RESULT.
CCC02E  47F0 F034                  23         B     ENDLOOP      MULTIPLY EXP TIMES.
CCC032  1C64                       24 LOOP    MR    6,BASE       MULTIPLY.
CCC034  4650 F032                  25 ENDLOOP BCT   EXP,LOOP     LOOP EXP NO. OF TIMES.
CCC038  47F0 F046                  26         B     DONE
CCC03C  1877                       27 NEG     SR    7,7          IF NEG EXP, RESULT = 0.
CCC03E  47F0 F046                  28         B     DONE
CCC042  4170 0001                  29 ZERO    LA    7,1          IF ZERO EXP, RESULT = 1.
CCC046  5072 F050                  30 DONE    ST    7,SAVE(RBASE)  PUT ANSWER IN SAVE AREA REG.
CCC04A  98CF F050                  31         LM    0,15,SAVE    RESTORE THE REGISTERS.
CCC04E  07FE                       32         BR    14           RETURN TO CALLER.
CCC050                             33 SAVE    DS    16F          SPACE TO SAVE THE 16 REGISTERS.
                                   34         END
```

CROSS-REFERENCE

SYMBOL	LEN	VALUE	DEFN	REFERENCES
BASE	00001	000004	00013	0017 0022 0024
DONE	00004	000046	00030	0026 0028
ENDLOOP	00004	000034	00025	0023
EXP	00001	000005	00014	0018 0019 0025
EXPON	00001	000000	00001	0004
LOOP	00002	000032	00024	0025
NEG	00002	00003C	00027	0020
RBASE	00001	000002	00011	0015 0017 0030
REXP	00001	000003	00012	0016 0018
SAVE	00004	000050	00033	0006 0017 0018 0030 0031
ZERO	00004	000042	00029	0021

Figure 2-8 Code for EXPON

Since the contents of each register takes up four bytes in the SAVE area, to get the location of register RBASE, we must multiply the register number by 4 (which is the same as shifting it two binary places to the left).

2-3 I/O PROGRAMMING

The early computer systems (e.g., IBM 1401 and 1620) had three basic components: (1) the CPU, (2) the main storage unit (memory), and (3) I/O devices (peripheral equipment). These components were interconnected as illustrated in Figure 2-9.

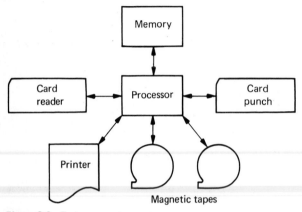

Figure 2-9 Early computer system

The Central Processor Unit and memory correspond essentially to the general machine structure presented in Figure 2-1, but the early systems also contained I/O instructions such as READ A CARD, PUNCH A CARD, and PRINT A LINE to operate the I/O devices one at a time. An ADD instruction may take one ms of CPU time and a READ CARD instruction 500 ms (at 100 cards per minute maximum speed) of CPU time on an early computer.

As computer systems evolved, performance was upgraded by increasing CPU speed and memory size. For example, memories with 1,000 bytes at one ms per access have been replaced by models with over a million bytes at less than one μs. per access—a thousandfold increase in speed and size. In similar fashion CPUs have improved so that the typical instruction time is less than one μs.

The disparity in speeds between the I/O devices and the CPU motivated the development of *I/O processors* (also called *I/O channels* since they provide a path, or channel, for the data to flow between I/O devices and the main memory). I/O processors are specialized processing units intended to operate the I/O devices. Since these units may be simple, specialized, and not too fast, they are generally much less expensive than a conventional CPU. Figure 2-10 depicts a computer system with a separate I/O channel for each device. If all input and output are executed via the channel, the CPU is free to perform its high-speed computations without wasting time on operations such as reading cards. Furthermore, since it is possible to be operating several channels simultaneously, many card readers, punches, and printers may function at the same time. However, to obtain these benefits, the operating system may have to supervise these operations.

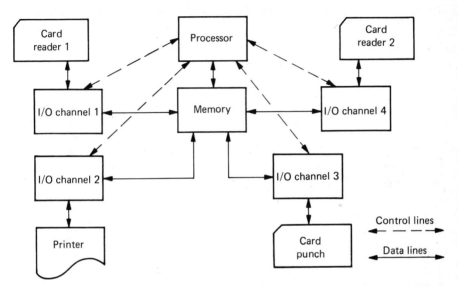

Figure 2-10   Computer system with I/O channels

2-3.1 Types of I/O Channels

Although the basic idea remains the same, I/O channels come in all shapes and sizes, ranging from very simple processors to highly complex CPUs. Though I/O processors are inexpensive, they are generally still too costly to make it feasible to use one channel per device; this had led to the development of selector and multiplexor channels.

In both cases multiple devices may be connected to each channel (up to 256 devices per channel on the 370). A *selector channel* can service only one of its devices at a time—i.e., one device is *selected* for service. These channels are normally used for very high-speed I/O devices, such as magnetic tapes, disks, and drums. Thus each I/O request is usually completed quickly and then another device selected for I/O.

A *multiplexor channel* is able to simultaneously service many devices (up to 256). It is able to accomplish this only for slow I/O devices, such as card readers, card punches, and printers.

A *block multiplexor channel* is a compromise solution that allows multiple-channel programs for high-speed devices to be active on the same I/O channel. The block multiplexor performs one channel instruction for one device and then, automatically, switches to perform an instruction for another device, and so on.

The block multiplexor channel resembles the selector in that, at any given time, it services only one device; however, it resembles the multiplexor in that it does not have to wait until the entire channel program is completed before it can service another device. A typical 370 configuration is illustrated in Figure 2-11.

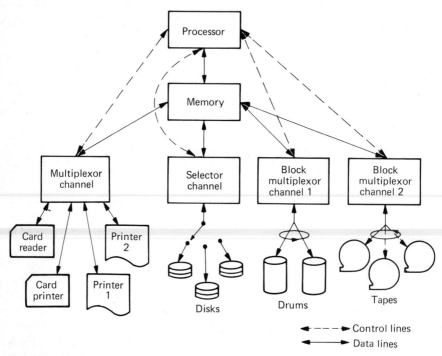

Figure 2-11   370-type system configuration

2-3.2 I/O Programming Concepts

Needless to say, the "three ring circus" of Figure 2-11 does not necessarily function efficiently without a considerable amount of effort. It is the function of the operating system to act as ring master and coordinate all the processors. In order to explain the problems that the operating system must handle, we will present some basic concepts relating to I/O programming.

The Central Processing Unit typically communicates with the I/O processor by means of specific instructions, such as START I/O and HALT I/O. The I/O processor may communicate with the CPU by means of interrupts (which are explained in Section 2-4).

The I/O processor interprets its own set of instructions. To make clear the distinction between CPU instructions and I/O channel instructions, we will call the latter *I/O commands*. The programs written in these sets of commands are known as *I/O programs* and their generation is loosely called *I/O programming*. Typically, programmers do not write their own I/O programs, but call a system-supplied function that provides the I/O programs for them. The monitor system tailors the I/O programs to the particular needs of the user and activates their execution.

2-3.3 I/O Processor Structure—360 and 370

In this section we analyze the I/O processor using the same approach used for the central processor in Section 2-2. We set forth and answer the five basic questions that should be posed when approaching a processor, and present some examples of I/O programs. I/O processors have not achieved the same standardization of instructions as have Central Processing Units. However, their functions can be generalized rapidly. We will take examples of I/O programming from the 370-type configuration.

2-3.3.1 MEMORY

What is the memory's basic unit, size, and addressing scheme? The memory is the same as that used by the 370's Central Processing Unit, the basic memory unit is a byte, and size is up to 2^{24} bytes. For addressing, the I/O channel uses a 24-bit absolute address.

2-3.3.2 REGISTERS

How many registers are there? What are their sizes, functions, and interrelationships? The I/O channel has no explicit registers, but does have an instruction address register and a data counter. Some I/O devices have internal registers similar to the internal CPU working registers used for instructions.

2-3.3.3 DATA

What types of data can be handled by the processor? Primarily, only logical character data can be handled (a string of consecutive bytes from 1 to $2^{16}-1$ in length). Some I/O devices may include some types of code conversions on the data (e.g., code conversions from EBCDIC to BCD). The I/O processor also uses sense data pertaining to the state of an I/O device and may read and act on this type of data.

2-3.3.4 INSTRUCTIONS

What classes of commands does the processor interpret? There are three basic groupings of I/O commands:

1 Data transfers: read; read backwards; write; sense (read device status)

2 Device control: control (page eject, tape rewind, etc.)

3 Branching: transfers of control within the channel program

The channel fetches the channel commands [Channel Command Words (CCW)] from memory and decodes them according to the following format.

Opcode	Data addresses	Flags	unused XXXXX	Count

```
0       7 8                      31 32  36 37        47 48          63
```

The *opcode* (bits 0-7) indicates the command to be performed; it actually consists of two parts: 2 to 4 operation bits and 4 to 6 modifier bits. The operation bits are standard while the modifier bits vary for each type of device.

The *data address* (bits 8-31) specifies the beginning location of the data field referenced by the command. The *count field* specifies the byte length of the data field. The data address and count are used primarily for the data transfer-type commands.

The *flag bits* further specialize the command. The principal flags are:

1 The *command chain* flag (bit 33) denotes that the next sequential CCW is to be executed on normal completion of the current command. (*Note:* under default conditions, i.e., all flags = 0, the channel stops at completion of current command.)

2 The *data chain* flag (bit 32) denotes that the storage area designated by the next CCW is to be used with the current command, once the current data area count is exhausted.

3 The *suppress length indication* flag (bit 34) suppresses the indication to the program of an incorrect length (see Figure 2-12).

4 The *skip* flag (bit 35) specifies suppression of transfer of information to storage.

5 The *programmed controlled interruption* flag (bit 36) causes the channel to generate an interruption condition when this CCW takes control of the channel.

A group of multiple CCWs linked together by command chains, data chains, or transfers is called a *channel program*. The CPU starts the channel executing a channel program.

2-3.3.5 SPECIAL FEATURES

Status The channel has an internal register that acts as the instruction address register. (A multiplexor or block multiplexor actually has several such registers, one per device.) In addition, three specific words of memory are used for status information. The Channel Address Word (CAW), which starts at location 72_{10} in core, contains the address of the first instruction to be executed by the channel. The channel refers to the CAW only during the execution of the Start I/O (SIO) instruction by the CPU. The Channel Status Word (CSW), actually a doubleword, contains coded information indicating the status of the channel. The format of the CSW, located at location 64, is as follows:

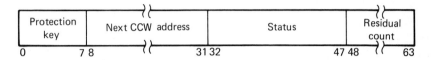

Key—protection key being used by channel

Address—address of next channel command

Status—e.g., building on fire, I/O completed, I/O error occurred, etc.

Count—how many bytes of the last CCW were not processed? (usually zero unless the channel abnormally terminated an I/O operation)

I/O Not applicable; the channel does all its own I/O.

Interrupt Not applicable, channel can generate interrupts to the CPU but is not itself interrupted.

Masking Not applicable, since no channel interrupts.

Protection The protection key (bits 0-4 of CAW) is copied by the channel at START I/O time and forms the protection key for all I/O data transfer commands.

Timer No facility for accessing.

States All commands may be used in an I/O program: there is no supervisor/problem state distinction within the channel program. (The START I/O CPU instruction is, of course, privileged.)

Microprogramming The user has no facility to change or add channel command opcodes.

2-3.4 Examples of I/O Programs

Let us write a program to skip to the top of a new page, print two lines, and eject to the next page. Figure 2-12 contains four I/O commands coded in hexadecimal to perform our task.

Appendix A presents the I/O command opcodes for various devices; the I/O program above is intended for a model 3211 printer device. The first command (opcode 8B) causes the printer to advance the paper to the top of the next page. In Appendix A this opcode can be found under the 3211 description Skip to Channel N Immediately (opcode 1NNNN001). Thus $8B_{16} = 10001011_2$ means Skip to Channel 1 Immediately.

LOCA-TION	OPCODE	DATA ADDRESS	FLAG	UNUSED	COUNT	
400	8B	XXXXXX	40	00	XXXX	SKIP TO NEW PAGE
408	01	010008	60	00	0008	PRINT LINE
410	0B	XXXXXX	40	00	XXXX	ADVANCE 1 LINE
418	89	010010	00	00	0014	PRINT 20-CHARAC-TER LINE; EJECT TO NEXT PAGE AND STOP

010008	'GOOD DAY'
010010	'YOU ARE NOW ON A 370'

Figure 2-12   Example of an I/O channel program

The channel referred to is not an I/O channel. There is a control tape or chain that is internal to the printer and has holes or marks in several columns (channels). By convention, channel 1 has a mark that corresponds to the top of the page. This is necessary since various sizes of paper may be used in the printer (regular size 11-inch long paper, 13-inch legal-length paper, etc.). The second command, opcode $= 01_{16}$, prints the eight characters stored at location 010008 (GOOD DAY). The next command, opcode $= 0B_{16}$, advances the paper by one line. This command is necessary because the 01 opcode above does not cause the paper to move, and without the command three 01's in a row would all print to be on the same line—this would save a lot of paper but would generally be a bit difficult to read. The second and third commands could have been combined into the single Write, Space 1 after Print command, opcode $= 09_{16}$. The final command, opcode $= 89_{16}$, prints the 20 characters that are stored at location 010010_{16} (YOU ARE NOW ON A 370) and then skips to the top of the next page.

In Figure 2-12 all of the I/O commands except the last have the command chain flag set (40_{16}). In addition, the Suppress Length Indication (SLI) flag (20_{16}) is required in the second CCW (flag $60 = 40 + 20$) since the data count of 8 bytes is different from the standard data count of 132 bytes used by a 3211 printer. If the SLI flag were not set, the I/O program would stop after executing the second command. The SLI should also be used in the last CCW, but since the I/O program is going to stop then anyway, it is not really needed. The data address field and count fields are not used in control commands such as Skip 1 Line and Eject to New Page.

Figure 2-12 depicts the hexadecimal representations of the channel commands. One may ask if there is a corresponding assembly language version. The answer is "sort of." The 370 assembly language provides a pseudo-op CCW, which facilitates I/O programming. The assembly language version of the program of Figure 2-12 is depicted in Figure 2-13.

$\vdots$

	CCW	X'8B',*,X'40',1	SKIP TO NEW PAGE
	CCW	X'01',DATA1,X'60',8	PRINT LINE
	CCW	X'0B',*,X'40',1	ADVANCE 1 LINE
	CCW	X'89',DATA2,0,20	PRINT 20 CHARACTER LINE; EJECT TO NEXT PAGE AND STOP

$\vdots$

DATA1	DC	C'GOOD DAY'
DATA2	DC	C'YOU ARE NOW ON A 370'

$\vdots$

Figure 2-13 Example of an assembly language I/O program

The CCWs have four fields: opcode, address, flags, and count, separated by commas. The assembler will automatically determine the correct address for data areas, such as DATA1, and place it in the CCW address field.

The I/O program of Figure 2-13, although clearer than the hexadecimal version of Figure 2-12, is still difficult to read. With a little cleverness, however, the programmer can develop a fairly good mnemonic assembly language, as shown in Figure 2-14.

$\vdots$

	CCW	EJECT,*,CONTINUE,1	EJECT TO NEW STUDY
	CCW	PRINT,DATA1,CONTINUE+SLI,8	PRINT LINE
	CCW	ADVANCE1,*,CONTINUE,1	ADVANCE 1 LINE
	CCW	PRINTEJT,DATA2,STOP,20	PRINT 20 CHARACTER LINE; EJECT TO NEW PAGE AND STOP

$\vdots$

DATA1	DC	C'GOOD DAY'
DATA2	DC	C'YOU ARE NOW ON A 370'

$\vdots$

EJECT	EQU	X'8B'	OPCODE TO SKIP TO NEW PAGE
PRINT	EQU	X'01'	OPCODE TO PRINT A LINE
ADVANCE1	EQU	X'0B'	OPCODE TO ADVANCE 1 LINE
PRINTEJT	EQU	X'89'	OPCODE TO PRINT 1 LINE AND EJECT TO NEW PAGE
CONTINUE	EQU	X'40'	FLAG FOR COMMAND CHAIN
SLI	EQU	X'20'	FLAG FOR SUPPRESS LENGTH INDICATION, SLI
STOP	EQU	X'00'	FLAG TO STOP CHANNEL PROGRAM

$\vdots$

Figure 2-14 Mnemonic assembly language I/O program

2-3.5   Communications between the CPU and the Channel

Now that we have seen how the channel itself works, we will examine how it communicates with the CPU. The purpose of having a channel is to free the CPU from having to control detailed I/O operations. The CPU and the channel are usually in a master/slave relationship. This means that the CPU tells the channel when to start and commands it to stop or change what it is doing. On the other hand, the channel cannot usually start any operation unless instructed by the CPU.

There are two types of communications between the CPU and the channel: (1) CPU to channel I/O instructions initiated by the CPU and (2) channel to CPU interrupt initiated by the channel.

This section will describe the first of these types, the relationship between I/O instructions and the channel. The second type of communication, description of the I/O interrupts, will be left for Section 2-4.

All CPU I/O instructions have the following format:

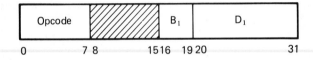

The channel and device number are specified by the sum of the contents of register B_1, and the contents of the D_1 field. Bits 16–23 of the sum contain the channel address, while bits 24–31 contain the device on the channel.

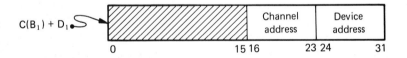

We are mainly concerned with three CPU I/O instructions:

1   START I/O (SIO): Two items are needed to start I/O: (1) the channel and device number and (2) the beginning address of the channel program. A START I/O instruction, such as SIO X'00E', specifies the channel number 0 and device number 0E. Locations 72–75 in memory contain the CAW, which specifies the start of the channel program.

2   TEST I/O (TIO): The CPU indicates the state of the addressed channel and device by setting the Condition Code (busy or not). The CC can then be tested by the standard branch conditional instruction.

3   HALT I/O (HIO): Execution of the current I/O operation at the addressed I/O device and channel is abruptly terminated.

After executing an SIO or a TIO, the CPU gets a Condition Code of either:

8 ~ OK (not busy)

2 ~ busy

1 ~ not operational

4 ~ indicates that there is a lot more to tell us in the CSW, which was just stored at location 64.

The Channel Status Word provides the detail status of an I/O device or the conditions under which an I/O operation has been terminated. The CSW may be set in the process of I/O interrupts and sometimes during execution of START I/O, HALT I/O, and TEST I/O. The format of the CSW is:

Protection key	0000	Command address	Status	Count
0 3	4 7	8 31	32 47	48 63

An SIO causes I/O to start only if the channel returns a Condition Code of 8. If any other CC is returned, the channel has rejected the I/O request. The reason for the rejection can be found in the CC or CSW.

Although the I/O interrupt mechanism has some powerful capabilities, as explained in Section 2-4, it is not needed to perform simple I/O processing. For example, assuming that I/O interrupts are disabled, the following sequence will start up an I/O program and check that it completes correctly:

```
              .
              .
           LA    1,CCWADDR      SET I/O PROGRAM
           ST    1,72           ADDRESS INTO CAW
           SIO   X'00E'         START I/O ON DEVICE X'00E'
           BC    4+2+1,ERROR    IF NOT CC=8, THEN ERROR
   TESTIO  TIO   X'00E'         TEST IF I/O COMPLETED YET
           BC    4+2,TESTIO     IF STILL BUSY, TEST AGAIN
              .
              .
```

If we monitored the Condition Code of each Test I/O, the sequence would be:

TIO CONDITION CODE

2 ~ busy
2 ~ busy
 .
 .   I/O in progress
2 ~ busy

4 ~ CSW stored   I/O completed

8 ~ OK (not busy)

loop completed, CC ≠ 4 or 2.

There could be thousands of TIO Condition Code = 2 results. For example, it takes about 60 ms to print a line (at 1,000 lines per minute). If each TIO and Branch Conditional (BC) instruction took one μs, there would be 30,000 iterations of the loop, each with CC = 2 (busy). This is one reason why the interrupt mechanism is preferred. When the I/O is finally completed, an *interrupt pending* condition occurs—the channel wants to tell the CPU that the I/O is complete but I/O interrupts are masked off. The next TIO does not get a CC = 2, since the device is no longer busy. Instead, it gets a Condition Code = 4, which means that the Channel Status Word information has been placed into locations 64–71.

At this point, the program could examine the CSW status field to check that indeed the I/O had completed correctly. Since the channel has given the CPU all the available information, it automatically clears the interrupt pending condition (i.e., deletes the interrupt). Thus the next TIO will find the device is not busy and there are no interrupts pending, and therefore return a Condition Code = 8 indicating that everything is finished.

2-3.6 I/O Example Using Single Buffering

For our example, we wish to read and print a series of cards. One simple strategy would be as depicted in Figure 2-15 and coded in Figure 2-16.

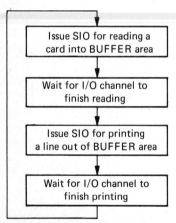

Figure 2-15 Single-buffering program for reading a card and printing

This sample program does not really take advantage of the I/O channels, since whenever the CPU is running, the channels are idle, and whenever a channel is running, the CPU is idle (issuing TIOs) and waiting for the channel to finish. Furthermore, if we assume that the rated speed of the card reader (device X′00C′) is 1,000 cards per minute and that of the printer (device X′00E′) 1,000 lines per minute, we see that the program has the additional drawback that we can only

EXTERNAL SYMBOL DICTIONARY

```
SYMBOL   TYPE ID  ADDR    LENGTH  LD ID
LIST     SD   01  001000  000099

  LOC    OBJECT CODE  ADDR1  ADDR2  STMT  SOURCE STATEMENT
                                          LIST
                                     1         START X'1000'      ESTABLISH BASE REGISTER.
001000  05F0                         2         BALR  15,0         TELL THE ASSEMBLER.
001002                               3         USING *,15
001002  8000 F096          01098     4         SSM   =X'00'       TURN ALL I/O INTERRUPTS OFF.
                                     5   *
001006  4110 F036          01038     6  LOOP   LA    1,READ       SET CAW TO CHANNEL
00100A  5010 0048          00048     7         ST    1,CAW          PROGRAM FOR READING.
00100E  9C00 000C          0000C     8         SIO   X'00C'       START READER.
001012  9D00 000C          0000C     9         TIO   X'00C'       WAIT UNTIL READER
001016  4770 F010          01012    10         BNZ   *-4            IS FINISHED.
                                    11   *
00101A  4110 F03E          01040    12         LA    1,PRINT      SET CAW TO CHANNEL
00101E  5010 0048          00048    13         ST    1,CAW          PROGRAM FOR PRINTING.
001022  9C00 000E          0000E    14         SIO   X'00E'       START PRINTER.
001026  9D00 000E          0000E    15         TIO   X'00E'       WAIT UNTIL PRINTER
00102A  4770 F024          01026    16         BNZ   *-4            IS FINISHED.
00102E  47F0 F004          01006    17         B     LOOP         PROCESS NEXT CARD.
                                    18   *
001032  000000000000                19  READ   CCW   X'02',BUFFER,X'00',80   READ A CARD.
001038  020001048000000050          20  PRINT  CCW   X'09',BUFFER,X'00',80   PRINT A CARD.
001040  090001048000000050          21  BUFFER DS    CL80         80-BYTE BUFFER AREA.
001048                              22   *
                                    23  CAW    EQU   72           CAW = LOCATION 72.
000048                              24         END
                                    25

001098  00                                           =X'00'
```

(executed by CPU — statements 1–18; executed by channel — CCW statements)

RELOCATION DICTIONARY

```
POS.ID  REL.ID  FLAGS  ADDRESS
  01      01      08    001039
  01      01      08    001041
```

CROSS-REFERENCE

```
SYMBOL   LEN    VALUE   DEFN   REFERENCES
BUFFER  00080  001048  00021  0019  0020
CAW     00001  000048  00023  0007  0013
LIST    00001  001000  00001
LOOP    00004  001006  00006  0017
PRINT   00008  001040  00020  0012
READ    00008  001038  00019  0006
```

Figure 2-16 Code for single-buffering program for reading and printing cards

63

process (read and print) cards at a rate of 500 cards per minute. This means, in effect, that whenever the reader is working, the printer is idle, and vice versa. Finally, this program does not worry about other practical issues, such as handling I/O errors or ever completing. (*Note:* it will try to run forever.) This scheme has the sole redeeming property of being very simple; all that can be said for it is that it does work.

2-3.7 I/O Example Using Double Buffering

Can we improve on the previous example so as to increase our rate from 500 cards processed per minute up to 1,000 cards per minute? Yes, by using a technique called *double buffering*. Our problem was that we could not read the next card into our single buffer until we finished printing out the present contents. With double buffering, we first read a card into buffer area 1; then, while printing out this area, we read the next card into buffer area 2; when we are finished printing buffer area 1, we then can start reading into buffer area 1 and repeat this process. Figure 2-17 depicts the general strategy and Figure 2-18 shows a program that accomplishes this double buffering.

GENERAL STRATEGY OF CPU PROGRAM USING DOUBLE BUFFERING

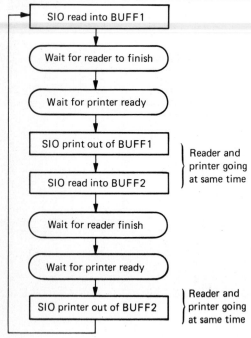

Figure 2-17 Double buffering for reading and printing cards

```
LOC     OBJECT CODE        ADDR1  ADDR2   STMT   SOURCE STATEMENT

001000                                      1   LIST    START X'1000'    ESTABLISH BASE REGISTER.
001000  05F0                                2           BALR  15,0       TELL THE ASSEMBLER.
001002                                      3           USING *,15
001002  8000 F11E                 01120     4           SSM   =X'00'     TURN ALL I/O INTERRUPTS OFF.
                                            5   *
001006  4110 F05E                 01060     6   LOOP LA  1,READ1         SET CAW TO READ1 CHANNEL
00100A  5010 0048                 00048     7        ST  1,CAW              PROGRAM (BUFFER1).
00100E  9C00 000C          0000C            8        SIO X'00C'           START READER.
001012  9D00 000C          0000C            9        TIO X'00C'           WAIT UNTIL READER
001016  4770 F010                 01012    10        BNZ *-4                IS FINISHED.
                                           11   *
00101A  4110 FC6E                 01070    12        LA  1,PRINT1         SET CAW TO PRINT1 CHANNEL
00101E  5010 0048                 00048    13        ST  1,CAW              PROGRAM (BUFFER1).
001022  9D00 000E          0000E           14        TIO X'00E'           MAKE SURE THAT THE PRINTER
001026  4770 F020                 01022    15        BNZ *-4                IS NOT BUSY.
00102A  9C00 000E          0000E           16        SIO X'00E'           START PRINTER.
                                           17   *
00102E  4110 F066                 01068    18        LA  1,READ2          SET CAW TO READ2 CHANNEL
001032  5010 0048                 00048    19        ST  1,CAW              PROGRAM (BUFFER2).
001036  9C00 000C          0000C           20        SIO X'00C'           START READER.
00103A  9D00 000C          0000C           21        TIO X'00C'           WAIT UNTIL READER
00103E  4770 F038                 0103A    22        BNZ *-4                IS FINISHED.
                                           23   *
001042  4110 FC76                 01078    24        LA  1,PRINT2         SET CAW TO PRINT2 CHANNEL
001046  5010 0048                 00048    25        ST  1,CAW              PROGRAM (BUFFER2).
00104A  9D00 000E          0000E           26        TIO X'00E'           MAKE SURE THAT THE PRINTER
00104E  4770 F048                 0104A    27        BNZ *-4                IS NOT BUSY.
001052  9C00 000E          0000E           28        SIO X'00E'           START PRINTER.
                                           29   *
001056  47F0 FC04                 01006    30        B   LOOP             PROCESS NEXT CARD.
                                           31   *
00105A  0C000C0000000000                   32   READ1   CCW X'02',BUFFER1,X'00',80   READ CARD INTO BUFFER1.
001060  0200108000000050                   33   READ2   CCW X'02',BUFFER2,X'00',80   READ CARD INTO BUFFER2.
001068  0200100000000050                   34   PRINT1  CCW X'09',BUFFER1,X'00',80   PRINT CARD FROM BUFFER1.
001070  0900108000000050                   35   PRINT2  CCW X'09',BUFFER2,X'00',80   PRINT CARD FROM BUFFER2.
001078  0900100000000050                   36   BUFFER1 DS  CL80                      80-BYTE BUFFER AREA.
001080                                     37   BUFFER2 DS  CL80                      80-BYTE BUFFER AREA.
0010D0                                     38   *
                                           39   CAW     EQU 72                        CAW = LOCATION 72
000048                                     40           END
001120  00                                 41           =X'00'
```

Figure 2-18 Code for double-buffering program for reading and printing cards

2-3.8   Multiple Card Buffering

In the two previous examples we used four simple one-command I/O programs and two single-card buffers. If we wished to print exactly 60 lines per page, the channel could be made to work a little harder without any changes to the CPU program:

1) Use two 60-card buffers:

BUFFER1	DS	60CL80	60-card buffer
BUFFER2	DS	60CL80	60-card buffer

2) Change the I/O programs as follows:

```
READ1        ⎧CCW      X'02',BUFFER1,X'40',80
             ⎢CCW      X'02',BUFFER1+80,X'40',80
60 CCWs      ⎨ .
             ⎢ :
             ⎩CCW      X'02',BUFFER1+59*80,X'00',80

PRINT1       ⎧CCW      X'8B',*,X'40',1
             ⎢CCW      X'09',BUFFER1,X'60',80
61 CCWs      ⎢CCW      X'09',BUFFER1+80,X'60',80
             ⎨
             ⎢ :
             ⎩CCW      X'09',BUFFER1+59*80,X'00',80
```

Likewise for READ2 and PRINT2.

With these changes, 60 cards at a time are read and printed, each batch on a new page. The changes do not appreciably increase efficiency or speed, but have other benefits that will be explained later in Section 2-4.5.

2-4   INTERRUPT STRUCTURE AND PROCESSING

We have mentioned interrupts briefly in the preceding sections. There are various ways to implement and define interrupt mechanisms; in this section we will use the operational definition:

An *interrupt* is (1) a response to an asynchronous or exceptional event that (2) automatically saves the current CPU status to allow later restart, and (3) causes an automatic transfer to a specified routine (called an interrupt handler).

For example, Figure 2-19 depicts the execution path of an interrupted processor. Up to point 1 the processor was executing a program; then the interrupt occurred and forced the processor to transfer to the interrupt routine 2. At the termination of the interrupt routine the processor resumed processing the original program at point 3.

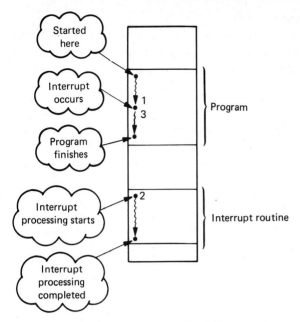

Figure 2-19 Locus of a process through an interrupt

2-4.1 Interrupt Types

Let us now work our way through the interrupt definition and relate it to the facilities provided by the 370. (The complete details of interrupt processing are beyond the scope of this book. What we are presenting here is a framework for the handling of interrupt conditions.)

The various types of interrupts are divided into five classes on the 370; some examples of each class are listed below:

1 Input/Output Interrupt
   a Invalid I/O command
   b I/O channel end (channel finished)
   c I/O device end (device finished)
2 Program Interrupt
   a Invalid CPU instruction
   b Fixed-point arithmetic overflow
   c Storage protection violation
3 Supervisor Call Interrupt (SVC instruction)
4 External Interrupt
   a Interval timer going off

    b Operator's interrupt button

    c CPU-to-CPU communication interrupt

5 Machine-check Interrupt (possible hardware failure was detected)

2-4.2 Interrupt Mechanism

Now we must consider how CPU status can be saved and control transferred to an interrupt handling routine. The "state" or current condition of the CPU is stored in a doubleword register called the Program Status Word. This corresponds to the CSW of the I/O processor. The PSW is used to control instruction sequencing and to hold and indicate the status of the system in relation to the program currently being executed. The active or controlling PSW is the "current" PSW. By storing the PSW during an interruption, the status of the CPU can be preserved for inspection or reloading. By loading a new PSW, or part of one, the state of the CPU can be changed.

The format of the PSW is as follows:

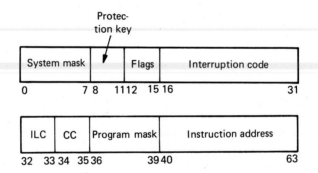

The individual fields were explained briefly in Section 2-2.2.5; for a more detailed explanation see the 370 Principles of Operation Manual (IBM, 2, 5) or Appendix A.

Bits in the PSW may be used to mask certain interruptions. When masked, I/O, external, and machine-check interruptions may be inhibited temporarily, but kept pending. The program mask may cause 4 of the 15 program interruptions to be ignored. The other program interruptions and the supervisor call interruption cannot be masked.

The programmer has at his disposal various status switching instructions. These include: Load PSW (LPSW), Set Program Mask (SPM), Set System Mask (SSM), Supervisor Call (SVC), and Set Storage Key (SSK). Most of these are privileged instructions and can be executed only in supervisor mode (i.e., if the P bit in the flags field of the current PSW is 0).

Each of the five classes of interrupts—I/O, program, supervisor call, external, and machine-check—has associated with it two doublewords, called "old" and "new"

PSWs, stored in the main memory at predetermined storage locations. When an interrupt occurs, the interrupt hardware mechanism (1) stores the current PSW in the old position and (2) loads the current PSW from the new position. Thus the instruction sequence transfers to the interrupt handler routine specified; at the same time many of the other PSW fields might also have been changed due to the new PSW. At the conclusion of the interrupt routine (3) there is usually an LPSW instruction to make the old PSW current again. The system is restored to the status ante quo and the interrupted program continues. These special interrupt locations and the three-step sequence are depicted in Figure 2-20.

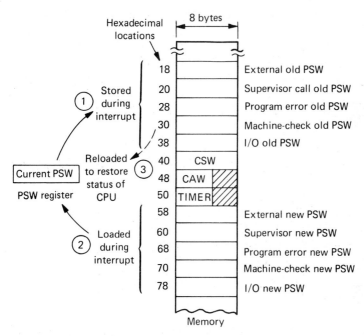

Figure 2-20 Special interrupt locations

2-4.3 Interrupt Handler Processing
The interrupt routine can access the appropriate old PSW to ascertain the condition that caused the interrupt. The old PSW contains an interrupt code and the location of the program being executed when the interrupt occurred.

Each of the program interrupt and external interrupt causes has a unique interrupt code: invalid operation = 01; privileged operation = 02; fixed point overflow = 08, etc., for program interrupts. When an I/O interrupt occurs, the PSW interrupt code indicates the channel and device causing the interrupt. The CSW status field, which is automatically set at the same time, contains information that indicates the cause of the interrupt; CSW bit 36 = 1 means channel end (channel finished work); CSW bit 37 = 1 means device end (device finished work), etc. The interrupt code set by an SVC interrupt corresponds to the one-byte immediate data field of the SVC instruction.

There are various circumstances in which it is necessary to prohibit interrupts. For example, when an I/O interrupt occurs for a device, such as the card reader, the current status is stored in the I/O old PSW location. If, while processing the interrupt, another I/O interrupt occurs for another device, such as the printer, the current status is again stored in the I/O old PSW location, destroying its previous contents. As a result, the original PSW stored is lost and it is impossible to restore original conidtions. This situation is normally handled by either: (1) completely masking (prohibiting) interrupts while processing an interrupt, or (2) temporarily masking interrupts until the old PSW is safely copied and stacked elsewhere. This is called *interrupt queuing*. Other situations requiring interrupt masking are illustrated by examples in Section 2-5.

2-4.4   Example of Exceptional Interrupt Processing

Hypothetically, let us assume that IBM is about to release a new computer system, the 371 (it's a "little bit better" than the 370). The new machine is exactly like a 370 except that the 371 has a new exponentiation opcode, EXP R1,R2, which takes $c(r1)^{c(r2)} \rightarrow c(r1)$. The machine opcode for EXP is 00. We would like to run object programs using this opcode on our old 370. However, when a 370 executes a 00 opcode, a program interrupt will occur. Our task is to write an interrupt handler that makes our 370 behave like a 371. Figure 2-21 contains a flowchart for our handler. We can use the EXPON routine from Section 2-2.5 to do the hard work, as shown in Figure 2-22.

In the main program, the programmer must provide the proper environment for the interrupt by setting the program interrupt new PSW with the address of his interrupt routine, as done in statement 6 of Figure 2-22.

Statements 30 through 79 give the code for the interrupt handler. Because program interrupts can be caused by many other conditions, three checks must be made to insure that a true EXP instruction caused the interrupt:

1   A program interruption code of $X'0001'$ must be in bits 16–31 of the program PSW starting at location 40.
2   An instruction length code of $B'01'$ must be in bits 32 and 33 of the program old PSW indicating a halfword instruction.
3   Finally, the operation code must be checked by subtracting 2 from the current instruction address in bits 40–63 of the program old PSW to get the location of the interrupted instruction.

Notice the use of the unused word at location $X'54'$ as a temporary save area in order to establish a base register. Control is eventually returned to the interrupted program by reloading the program old PSW at statement 74.

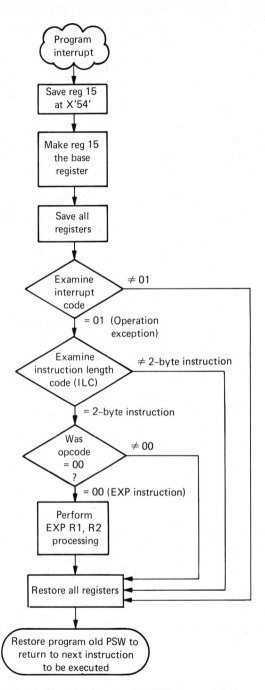

Figure 2-21 Flowchart for EXPON interrupt handler

```
LOC      OBJECT CODE            ADDR1  ADDR2   STMT  SOURCE STATEMENT

001000                                          1            EXPON    START X'1000'
001000   C5C0                                   2                     BALR  12,0            SET BASE.
001002                                          3                     USING *,12            TELL ASSEMBLER.
000068                                          4            PROGNPSW EQU   X'68'            LOCATION OF PROGRAM NEW PSW.
000028                                          5            PROGOPSW EQU   X'28'            LOCATION OF PROGRAM OLD PSW.
001002   D207 0068 C1C6        00068  01108     6                     MVC   PROGNPSW(8),=A(0,PROGINT)  SET PROGRAM NEW PSW.
                                                7            *
                                                8            *
                                                9            *     START MAIN PROGRAM.
001008   1811                                  10                     SR    1,1             SET REG.1 = 0.
00100A   0011                                  11                     DC    X'0011'         PERFORM 'EXP 1,1' (0**0=1).
00100C   5010 C02A             0102C           12                     ST    1,RESULT1       SAVE RESULT.
001010   4120 0002             00002           13                     LA    2,2             SET REG.2 = 2.
001014   4130 0004             00004           14                     LA    3,4             SET REG.3 = 4.
001018   0023                                  15                     DC    X'0023'         PERFORM 'EXP 2,3' (2**4=16).
00101A   5020 C02E             01030           16                     ST    2,RESULT2       SAVE RESULT.
00101E   5830 C10E             01110           17                     L     3,=F'-2'        SET REG.3 = -2.
001022   0023                                  18                     DC    X'0023'         PERFORM 'EXP 2,3' (16**-2=0).
001024   5020 C032             01034           19                     ST    2,RESULT3       SAVE RESULT.
001028   07FE                                  20                     BR    14              RETURN TO CALLER.
                                               21            *
                                               22            *     SAVE RESULTS HERE.
                                               23            *
00102C                                         24            RESULT1  DS    F               ** RESULT SHOULD BE 1.
001030                                         25            RESULT2  DS    F               ** RESULT SHOULD BE 16.
001034                                         26            RESULT3  DS    F               ** RESULT SHOULD BE 0.
                                               27            *
                                               28            *     EXP PROGRAM INTERRUPT HANDLER.
                                               29            *
001038   5CF0 C054             00054           30            PROGINT  ST    15,X'54'        SAVE REG.15 IN UNUSED LOCATION.
00103C   05F0                                  31                     BALR  15,0            SET UP BASE REGISTER.
00103E                                         32                     USING *,15            ...
00103E   900E F086             010C4           33                     STM   0,14,SAVEAREA   SAVE REGISTER 0-14.
001042   D203 FCC2 0054 01100  00054           34                     MVC   SAVEAREA+15*4(4),X'54'  MOVE REG.15 INTO SAVEAREA.
                                               35            *     ** TEST IF EXP PROGRAM INTERRUPT.
001048   9501 002B             0002B           36                     CLI   PROGOPSW+3,X'01'   IS IT OPERATION EXCEPTION?
00104C   4770 F07C             010BA           37                     BNE   RETURN          NO, IGNORE INTERRUPT.
```

Figure 2-22 EXPON program interrupt handler

```
001050  1B22          38          SR    2,2                 GET INSTRUCTION LENGTH FIELD
001052  4320 002C     39          IC    2,PROGOPSW+4        FROM OLD PSW.
001056  8820 0006     40          SRL   2,6                 ...
00105A  8920 0001     41          SLL   2,1                 ...
00105E  5920 F006     42          C     2,=F'2'             WAS IT A 2-BYTE INSTRUCTION?
001062  4770 F07C     43          BNE   RETURN              NO, IGNORE INTERRUPT.
001066  5810 002C     44          L     1,PROGOPSW+4        GET ADDRESS OF NEXT INSTRUCTION.
00106A  1B12          45          SR    1,2                 MOVE BACK 2 BYTES TO INTERRUPTED INST.
00106C  9500 1000     46          CLI   0(1),X'00'          IS IT EXP INSTRUCTION ('00' OP)?
001070  4770 F07C     47          BNE   RETURN              NO, IGNORE INTERRUPT.
                      48  *                                 ** PERFORM EXP SIMULATION NOW.
001074  1B22          49          SR    2,2                 ZERO OUT REGISTER 2.
001076  4320 1001     50          IC    2,1(0,1)            LOAD BYTE 2 OF INSTRUCTION.
00107A  8C20 0004     51          SRDL  2,4                 SHIFT EXP REGISTER INTO REG 3.
00107E  8830 001C     52          SRL   3,28                RIGHT SHIFT EXP REG IN REG 3.
000002                53  RBASE    EQU   2                   REG 2 CONTAINS BASE REG NO.
000003                54  REXP     EQU   3                   REG 3 CONTAINS THE EXP REG NO.
000004                55  BASE     EQU   4                   REG 4 CONTAINS THE BASE.
000005                56  EXP      EQU   5                   REG 5 CONTAINS THE EXPONENT.
001082  8920 0002     57          SLL   RBASE,2             MULTIPLY BASE REG NO. BY 4.
001086  8930 0002     58          SLL   REXP,2              MULTIPLY EXP REG NO. BY 4.
00108A  5842 F086     59          L     BASE,SAVEAREA(RBASE)  FETCH THE BASE.
00108E  5853 F086     60          L     EXP,SAVEAREA(REXP)    FETCH THE EXPONENT.
001092  1255          61          LTR   EXP,EXP             TEST IF EXP NEG, ZERO, POS.
001094  4740 F06E     62          BM    NEG                 TRANSFER IF NEGATIVE EXPONENT.
001098  4780 F074     63          BZ    ZERO                TRANSFER IF ZERO EXPONENT.
00109C  1874          64          LR    7,BASE              INITIALIZE RESULT.
00109E  47F0 F066     65          B     ENDLOOP             MULTIPLY EXP TIMES.
0010A2  1C64          66  LOOP     MR    6,BASE              MULTIPLY.
0010A4  4650 F064     67  ENDLCOP  BCT   EXP,LOOP            LOOP EXP NO. OF TIMES.
0010A8  47F0 F078     68          B     DONE
0010AC  1B77          69  NEG      SR    7,7                 IF NEG EXP, RESULT = 0.
0010AE  47F0 F078     70          B     DONE
0010B2  4170 0001     71  ZERO     LA    7,1                 IF ZERO EXP, RESULT = 1.
0010B6  5072 F086     72  DONE     ST    7,SAVEAREA(RBASE)   PUT ANSWER IN SAVE AREA REG.
0010BA  980F F086     73  RETURN   LM    0,15,SAVEAREA       RESTORE THE REGISTERS.
0010BE  8200 0028     74          LPSW  PROGOPSW            RETURN TO INSTRUCTION AFTER INTERRUPT.
0010C4                75  SAVEAREA DS    16F                 SPACE TO SAVE THE 16 REGISTERS.
                      76          END
001108  00000000000C1C38  77      =A(0,PROGINT)
001110  FFFFFFFE          78      =F'-2'
001114  00000002          79      =F'2'
```

Figure 2-22 EXPON program interrupt handler (continued)

73

2-4.5 Example of Asynchronous Interrupt Processing

Let us consider our read card/print card program from Sections 2-3.6 and 2-3.7 again. In both cases the central processor is kept busy 100 percent of the time; but doing what? It keeps testing the I/O status (TIO) waiting for the I/O to complete. Thus, more than 99 percent of the time is really wasted. In this example we want to put this CPU time to better use by using the interrupt facility. The CPU will then spend most of its time performing some computation. When an interrupt signals that it is necessary to start the next I/O, the processor will quickly start the I/O and then resume the computation. Figure 2-23 illustrates the overall strategy.

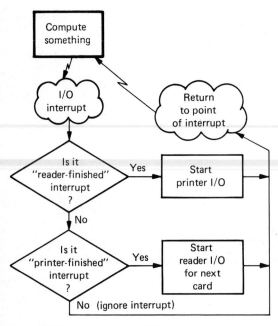

Figure 2-23 Interrupt-driven I/O processing

An actual program that incorporates this strategy is shown in Figure 2-24. In this case, the "useful computation" is to count from 1 to 1,000,000. In general, the user may have some more substantial computation in mind. As in the preceding example, the programmer must provide the proper initialization to the interrupt handler. This requires:

1 Setting I/O interrupt new PSW to the address of the I/O interrupt handler
2 Priming the "pump" by starting the first I/O to read a card
3 Setting the system mask to accept I/O interrupts

```
LOC     OBJECT CODE      ADDR1  ADDR2   STMT   SOURCE STATEMENT

001000                                    1   CCUNT   START  X'1000'             SET BASE.
001000  05F0                              2           BALR   15,0                TELL ASSEMBLER.
001002                                    3           USING  *,15
00C048                                    4   CAW     EQU    X'48'               LOCATION OF CHANNEL ADDRESS WORD.
0CC040                                    5   CSW     EQU    X'40'               LOCATION OF CHANNEL STATUS WORD.
000078                                    6   IONPSW  EQU    X'78'               LOCATION OF I/O NEW PSW.
00C038                                    7   IOOPSW  EQU    X'38'               LOCATION OF I/O OLD PSW.
001002  D207 0C78 FOCE  00078  010D0      8           MVC    IONPSW(8),=A(0,INT) SET I/O NEW PSW (INTERRUPT ADDR).
001008  D203 0048 FOD6  00048  01CD8      9           MVC    CAW(4),=A(READ)     SET CAW TO READ A CARD.
00100E  8000 FOEA       010EC            10           SSM    =X'FF'              ENABLE INTERRUPTS.
001012  9C00 000C       0000C            11           SIO    X'00C'              START READER FOR FIRST CARD.
                                         12   *
                                         13   *                                 START COMPUTATION.
                                         14   *
001016  5810 FODA       010DC            15           L      1,=F'1000000'       START COUNTING FROM 1 TO
00101A  1800                             16           SR     0,0                 1000000.
00101C  5A00 FODE       010E0            17   LOOP    A      0,=F'1'             (ADD 1).
001020  4610 FC1A       0101C            18           BCT    1,LOOP              (DECREMENT COUNTER UNTIL 1000000).
001024  07FE                             19           BR     14                  FINALLY FINISHED, RETURN TO CALLER.
```

Figure 2-24 Single I/O buffering while counting to 1,000,000

75

```
                                    20  *
                                    21  *   INTERRUPT HANDLER.
                                    22  *
001026 50F0 0054           00054    23  INT       ST    15,X'54'             SAVE REG 15 AT UNUSED LOCATION.
00102A 05F0                         24            BALR  15,0                 SET UP INTERRUPT HANDLER BASE REG.
00102C                              25            USING *,15                 ...
00102C 9104 0044           00044    26            TM    CSW+4,X'04'          WAS THIS A DEVICE END INTERRUPT?
001030 4780 F01C           01048    27            BZ    RETURN               NO, IGNORE THIS INTERRUPT.
001034 D501 003A F0BC 003A C003A    28            CLC   IOOPSW+2(2),=X'000C'   IS IT READER INTERRUPT?
00103A 4780 F024           01050    29            BE    READINT              YES, READER INTERRUPT.
00103E D501 003A F0BE 003A C003A    30            CLC   IOOPSW+2(2),=X'000E'   IS IT PRINTER INTERRUPT?
001044 4780 F032           0105E    31            BE    PRINTINT             YES, PRINTER INTERRUPT.
001048 58F0 0054           00054    32  RETURN    L     15,X'54'             RESTORE ORIGINAL CONTENTS OF REG 15
00104C 82C0 0038           C0038    33            LPSW  IOOPSW               AND I/O OLD PSW (RETURN TO MAIN PROG).
                                    34  *   ** READER INTERRUPT HANDLER.
001050 D203 0048 F0B8 00048 010E4   35  READINT   MVC   CAW(4),=A(PRINT1)    START PRINTER AND PRINT CARD
001056 9C00 000E           0000E    36            SIO   X'00E'               JUST READ.
00105A 47F0 F01C           C1048    37            B     RETURN               RETURN TO POINT OF INTERRUPTION.
                                    38  *   ** PRINTER INTERRUPT HANDLER.
00105E D203 0048 F0AC 00048 01CD8   39  PRINTINT  MVC   CAW(4),=A(READ1)     START READER TO GET
001064 9C00 000C           0000C    40            SIO   X'00C'               NEXT CARD.
001068 47F0 F01C           C1048    41            B     RETURN               RETURN TO POINT OF INTERRUPTION.
                                    42  *
                                    43  *
00106C 0CC00000                     44  READ1     CCW   X'02',BUFFER1,X'00',80   READ 80-BYTE CARD.
001070 0200108000000050             45  PRINT1    CCW   X'09',BUFFER1,X'00',80   PRINT 80-BYTE CARD.
001078 0900108000000050             46  BUFFER1   DS    CL80                 BUFFER FOR 80-BYTE CARD.
C01080                              47            END
0010D0 0CC000C000001026             48            =A(0,INT)
0010D8 00001070                     49            =A(READ1)
0010DC 00F4240                      50            =F'1000000'
0010E0 CCC0C0C1                     51            =F'1'
0010E4 00001078                     52            =A(PRINT1)
0010E8 000C                         53            =X'000C'
0010EA 000E                         54            =X'000E'
0010EC FF                           55            =X'FF'
```

Figure 2-24   Single I/O buffering while counting to 1,000,000 (continued)

Once these steps have been completed, the computation statements 15–19 can commence and the I/O will be handled entirely by the interrupt handler. This is often called *interrupt-driven processing*.

The interrupt handler consists of statements 20–55. In general, the interrupt handler is a physically separate user subroutine or a part of the operating system. Thus, it must set up its own base registers for correct addressing, as shown in the example of the preceding section.

There are various possible causes for an I/O interrupt. Even if no errors occur, normal functioning may cause multiple interrupts; three may be (1) channel-end interrupts, (2) control-unit-end interrupts, or (3) device-end interrupts. It is possible for the channel to finish its work before the device does. Consider the printer, for example. The channel must transfer the data bytes to be printed from memory to the printer's internal buffer. If this is the last CCW in the I/O program, the channel is no longer needed and a channel-end interrupt occurs. The printer device, by itself, can print this last line from its buffer and adjust the paper form appropriately. When the printer has finally finished these tasks, it causes a device-end interrupt. The existence and particular ordering of these interrupts is dependent upon the specific type of device, control unit, and channels being used—there are separate manuals that describe the particulars. In our printer example, we must wait for a device-end interrupt to tell us that the printer is no longer busy. This information is obtained from the CSW, as illustrated by statements 26 and 27.

After verifying the type of interrupt (device-end), it is necessary to determine which device caused the interrupt. This information is found in the Interrupt Code portion of the I/O old PSW. If the device end was from the reader (X'00C'), then start I/O for the printer. If from the printer (X'00E'), start I/O for the reader. Interrupts from other devices are ignored.

In this example, the interrupt handler only executes about 13 instructions to process each interrupt. If we assumed a processor speed of one million instructions per second, that is, 13 μs. The reader and printer, at a rate of 1,000 cards per minute, take 60 ms to complete each request. Thus, the I/O processing involves 13 μs of CPU every 60 ms; that consumes only .02 percent of the CPU time, leaving 99.98 percent for other computational purposes.

A more efficient I/O handler could be written by using double buffering, to increase card read/card print rate from 500 per minute to 1,000 per minute, and by using multi-CCW I/O programs to decrease the frequency of interrupts from every 60 ms to every 3.6 seconds. These techniques were outlined earlier in Section 2-3.7.

Actual I/O handlers must handle other concerns, such as error conditions and when to stop the I/O functioning. A more complete example is presented in the next section.

2-5 EXAMPLES OF I/O AND INTERRUPT PROCESSING PROGRAMS

To conclude this chapter, let us briefly discuss two useful examples as opposed to the somewhat contrived, simple ones.

2-5.1 IPL Program Example

In the examples of the preceding sections we assumed that the programs were already in memory. How did they get there? There are toggle switches and knobs on the processor's control panel that could be used, but that is an awkward and slow process. You may suggest the loader. But how did the loader get there? How about the operating system? But how did *it* get there? Sounds hopeless? The answer lies in the Initial Program Load (IPL) program (IBM, 3, 4). An actual IPL program is shown in the flowchart of Figure 2-25; the corresponding code is in Figure 2-26. This particular program fits on four 80-byte cards as indicated. But how does this program get into memory? Fortunately, the computer hardware provides us with a little help. When the computer operator pushes the IPL button, the following actions occur automatically:

1 24 bytes are read from the first record of the device selected on the IPL device address switches (i.e., the computer reads 24 bytes from the first card in the card reader). These bytes are placed in locations 0–23.

2 An SIO is performed using the IPL device address and CAW value of 8 (i.e., location 8 is used as the first CCW). This can be a multi-CCW I/O program.

3 When the I/O program completes, the 8 bytes at location 0–7 are used as they would be in the case of an old/new I/O PSW. That is, the interrupt code is stored in locations 2–3 and then the 8 bytes become the current PSW.

Although these particular steps are specific to the IBM 360/370, a similar method is used on most computer systems.

In the IPL program of Figure 2-26 the initial I/O program is five CCWs' long. Note that the last CCW is not even in memory when the I/O starts, but that is all right as long as it is loaded, by the first CCW, by the time it is needed. This process is often called bootstrap loading (one small portion loads a larger portion, which loads a larger portion, and so on).

The IPL program uses the interrupt mechanism to clear all of memory, that is, it keeps setting locations to zero until an addressing violation occurs.

The IPL program is intended to load an object program as produced by the standard IBM assembler. This might be the operating system itself or just a user's program, such as our earlier example programs, if an operating system were not needed.

After the user's program has been loaded, the IPL program stops and waits for an external interrupt. This gives the computer operator an opportunity to make any final changes by using the console toggle switches. When everything is ready, the operator presses the STOP button followed by the PSW restart button and the IPL program transfers control to the user's program.

This same process is used for loading any operating system. A disk- or tape-device unit is normally used as the IPL device instead of the card reader, but the overall algorithm is the same.

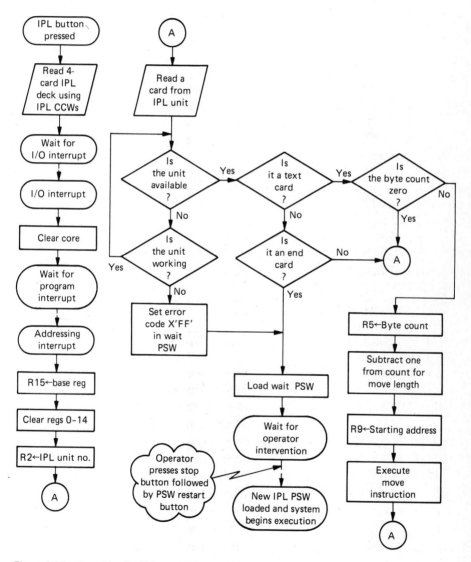

Figure 2-25 Flowchart for IPL program used with sample operating system

Figure 2-26 Sample IPL program

LOC	OBJECT CODE	ADDR1	ADDR2	STMT	SOURCE STATEMENT	
000000				1	IPLPROG	CSECT
000000				2		USING *,0 ESTABLISH ADDRESSIBILITY
				3	*	CARD 1 CONTAINS ONLY THE NEXT 24 BYTES
000000	0000000000000070			4	IPLPSW	DC X'00000000',A(START)
000008	0200001840000050			5	CCW1	CCW X'02',CCW3,X'40',80
000010	0200006040000050			6	CCW2	CCW X'02',NEWPROG-8,X'40',80
				7	*	CARD 2 STARTS HERE
000018	020000A800000050			8	CCW3	CCW X'02',NEWPROG+64,X'00',80
000020	0002000000000000			9	DEAD	DC X'0002000000000000' FINAL WAIT PSW
000040				10	CSW	EQU 64 CHANNEL STATUS WORD (CSW).
000048				11		ORG *+X'20'
000048	000000E0			12	CAW	DC A(READCCW) CHANNEL ADDRESS WORD (CAW).
00004C				13		DS F
000050	FFFFFFFF			14	TIMER	DC F'-1' TIMER (INITIALLY SET TO -1).
				15		ORG *+X'14'
				16	*	CARD 3 STARTS HERE
000068	0000000000000088			17	NEWPROG	DC F'0',A(L2) FOR ADDRESS INTERRUPT CAUSED
000070	05F0			18	START	BALR 15,0 BY ZEROING CORE.
				19		USING *,15 BASE REGISTER 15
000072	4110 F076		000E8	20		LA 1,BUFFER GET ADDRESS OF END OF
000076	9200 F076	000E8		21		MVI BUFFER,X'00' THIS PROGRAM.
00007A	D2FF 1001 1000	00001	00000	22	L1	MVC 1(256,1),0(1) ZERO CORE UNTIL YOU CAUSE
000080	4111 0100		00100	23		LA 1,256(1) AN ADDRESSING INTERRUPT.
000084	47F0 F008		0007A	24		B L1
000088	980E 0400		00400	25	L2	LM 0,14,X'400' CLEAR REGISTERS
00008C	4820 0002		00002	26		LH 2,2 GET IPL UNIT ADDRESS IN REG 2
000090	9C00 2000		00000	27	LL1	SIO 0(2) READ IN THE OBJECT DECK
000094	9D00 2000		00000	28	L3	TIO 0(2) IF AVAILABLE, SEE WHAT KIND
000098	4780 F03A		000AC	29		BE L4 OF CARD WAS READ.
00009C	9102 0044	00044		30		TM CSW+4,X'02' IF EXCEPTION, SET FLAG
0000A0	47E0 F022		00094	31		BNO L3 AND STOP.
0000A4	92FF 0027	00027		32		MVI DEAD+7,X'FF' SET ERROR CODE IN PSW

```
0000A8  8200 0020            00020   33  *              CARD 4 STARTS HERE
0000AC  95E7 F078            C000EA  34  L6     LPSW  DEAD             LOAD PSW TO WAIT FOR OPERATOR.
0000B0  4780 FC4E            000C0   35  L4     CLI   BUFFER+2,C'X'    IS IT A TXT CARD?
0000B4  95D5 F078            000EA   36         BE    L5
0000B8  4780 F036            0CCA8   37         CLI   BUFFER+2,C'N'    IS IT AN END CARD?
0000BC  47F0 F01E            00090   38         BE    L6
0000C0  9500 F081            000F3   39         B     LL1              IGNORE ALL OTHERS.
0000C4  4780 F01E            00090   40  L5     CLI   BUFFER+11,X'00'  IF ZERO COUNT, IGNORE
0000C8  4350 F081            000F3   41         BE    LL1                THIS CARD.
0000CC  C650                         42         IC    5,BUFFER+11      OTHERWISE, GET COUNT FOR
                                     43         BCTR  5,0              MOVING TEXT INTC CORE AT THE
0000CE  5890 F07A            000EC   44         L     9,BUFFER+4       CORRECT LOCATICN.
0000D2  4450 F068            000DA   45         EX    5,MOVE           MOVE TEXT.
0000D6  47F0 F01E            00090   46         B     LL1              GET ANOTHER CARD.
0000DA  D200 9000 F086 00000 000F8   47  MOVE   MVC   0(0,9),BUFFER+16
0000E0  0200 00E800000050            48  READCCW CCW  X'02',BUFFER,X'00',80
0000E8                               49  BUFFER DS    CL80             CARD BUFFER.
                                     50         END
```

Figure 2-26 Sample IPL program (continued)

2-5.2 I/O Buffering Example

The preceding interrupt handler examples were rather straightforward; the exceptional condition interrupts were synchronous and behaved like traditional subroutine calls, and the asynchronous I/O example operated completely independently of the computational program. When the computational program and the interrupt handler must communicate, there are some interesting problems to consider. The following example illustrates this point. Furthermore, the issues raised should provide a concrete basis for the process communication and synchronization and device-scheduling concepts presented in the chapters that follow.

2-5.2.1 PRINTER UTILITY ROUTINE

As noted in Chapter 1, a user program seldom directly issues I/O instructions such as SIO and TIO. I/O handling is provided by the operating system and appears to the user program in the form of special subroutines or SVCs. In this example, we present a simple printer utility routine. It may take only a few instructions to print a line, but as seen in the earlier examples, more complex routines are required to attain maximal processor utilization and I/O throughput (e.g., double buffering and interrupt-driven handling). Chapter 5 covers these issues in depth.

In this sample printer package, the user utilizes a simple subroutine with two entry points. The entry point PRINTSET is called only once to initialize the printer package; thereafter, the entry PRINT is called whenever the program wishes to have a line printed.

2-5.2.2 STRUCTURE OF THE EXAMPLE

This example consists of five subprograms. The MAIN subprogram represents a typical user program that utilizes the print package. In this case, the MAIN subprogram generates and then prints random numbers (see the sample output in Figure 2-28).

The print package consists of four subprograms:

1 PRINTSET   This subprogram is called only once by MAIN. It initializes a number of variables and sets the I/O new PSW.

2 PRINT   This subprogram is called by MAIN to print each output line. If the printer is "ready," it causes the I/O to start immediately. If the printer is "busy" working on an earlier request, the new request is queued ("remembered") so that the I/O can be started when the printer becomes ready later. In either case, it then returns to the caller.

3 PRINTINT   This subprogram handles the I/O interrupt. It checks to see if there were any errors; if there were, it attempts to recover by reissuing the I/O request. If there were none, and a line of output has been queued by PRINT, the I/O is started at this time.

4 SIOSTART   This is a common routine used by both PRINT and PRINTINT.

SIOSTART actually sets up the appropriate CCWs and then issues the SIO instruction to start the I/O.

The structure of this sample print package is depicted in Figure 2-27. A common set of data is shared by all four routines of the print package in order to keep track of requests as well as to provide a means for communication and synchronization among the routines. These data elements are included in Figure 2-27.

As noted earlier, this print package uses double-buffer techniques. Thus, there are two buffers used, BUFFER1 and BUFFER2, and four items of information associated with each buffer:

1 BUFFNXT: an address pointer to the other buffer.

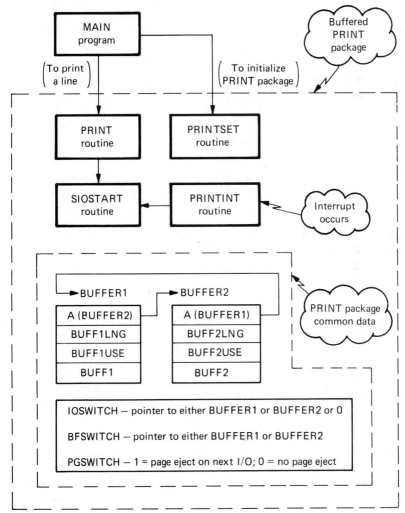

Figure 2-27   Structure of the print package

2 BUFFUSE: flag information (0 or 1).

1 = buffer contains information waiting to be or currently being printed (buffer "full").

0 = buffer contents have been printed so that buffer can be reused (buffer "empty").

3 BUFFLNG: if buffer is full, this item indicates the length of the print line (from 1 to 132 bytes).

4 BUFF: if buffer is full, this item is a copy of the actual line to be printed (up to 132 bytes long).

In addition to the buffer information, there are four other general data items:

1 IOSWITCH: if printer I/O is in progress, IOSWITCH is a pointer to either BUFFER1 or BUFFER2, whichever is being printed (thus, whenever IOSWITCH is nonzero, we say that I/O is "active"). If printer I/O is not in progress, IOSWITCH is zero (in this case, we say that I/O is "inactive").

2 BFSWITCH: BFSWITCH is a pointer that alternates between BUFFER1 and BUFFER2. At any given time, BFSWITCH indicates which buffer is to be used to hold the user's next print request.

3 PGSWITCH: flag information (0 or 1).

1 = cause a page eject for next print line.

0 = normal single space for next print line.

4 CCSWITCH: This is a pointer to the start of the CCW chain currently being executed (if any). This is used solely for I/O error handling and reentry.

Although this program is fairly simple in comparison to an entire operating system, it illustrates many basic points and should be studied carefully. Nevertheless, it should be noted that although this program was carefully written and debugged, we make no guarantee that it handles every case or even that it is particularly efficient.

2-5.2.3 MAIN PROGRAM

This MAIN program is primarily a "dummy" program to test the print package. In our example, it happens to be a program that generates and prints 200 random numbers, each random number being between 0 and 100. The basic algorithm is derived from the randomizing function

$$r_{i+1} = 23 \times r_i + 17 \ (\text{modulo } 2^{32} -1)$$

The actual random number, R, is computed from r by normalizing it to the desired range 0 to 100. To introduce an extra degree of randomness, the previous two random numbers, $R_{j-1} \times R_{j-2}$ values of r_i are skipped in the determination of R_j. The flowchart of MAIN and sample output is shown in Figure 2-28. As stated earlier, the particulars of the MAIN program are largely irrelevant since our primary concern is the print package.

Flowchart:

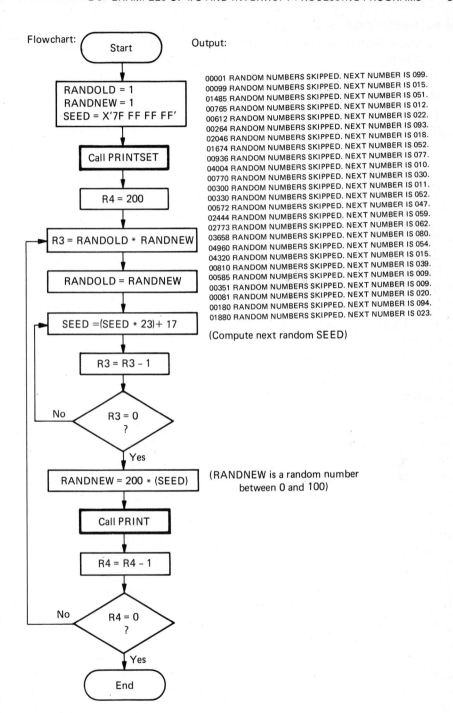

Output:

00001 RANDOM NUMBERS SKIPPED. NEXT NUMBER IS 099.
00099 RANDOM NUMBERS SKIPPED. NEXT NUMBER IS 015.
01485 RANDOM NUMBERS SKIPPED. NEXT NUMBER IS 051.
00765 RANDOM NUMBERS SKIPPED. NEXT NUMBER IS 012.
00612 RANDOM NUMBERS SKIPPED. NEXT NUMBER IS 022.
00264 RANDOM NUMBERS SKIPPED. NEXT NUMBER IS 093.
02046 RANDOM NUMBERS SKIPPED. NEXT NUMBER IS 018.
01674 RANDOM NUMBERS SKIPPED. NEXT NUMBER IS 052.
00936 RANDOM NUMBERS SKIPPED. NEXT NUMBER IS 077.
04004 RANDOM NUMBERS SKIPPED. NEXT NUMBER IS 010.
00770 RANDOM NUMBERS SKIPPED. NEXT NUMBER IS 030.
00300 RANDOM NUMBERS SKIPPED. NEXT NUMBER IS 011.
00330 RANDOM NUMBERS SKIPPED. NEXT NUMBER IS 052.
00572 RANDOM NUMBERS SKIPPED. NEXT NUMBER IS 047.
02444 RANDOM NUMBERS SKIPPED. NEXT NUMBER IS 059.
02773 RANDOM NUMBERS SKIPPED. NEXT NUMBER IS 062.
03658 RANDOM NUMBERS SKIPPED. NEXT NUMBER IS 080.
04960 RANDOM NUMBERS SKIPPED. NEXT NUMBER IS 054.
04320 RANDOM NUMBERS SKIPPED. NEXT NUMBER IS 015.
00810 RANDOM NUMBERS SKIPPED. NEXT NUMBER IS 039.
00585 RANDOM NUMBERS SKIPPED. NEXT NUMBER IS 009.
00351 RANDOM NUMBERS SKIPPED. NEXT NUMBER IS 009.
00081 RANDOM NUMBERS SKIPPED. NEXT NUMBER IS 020.
00180 RANDOM NUMBERS SKIPPED. NEXT NUMBER IS 094.
01880 RANDOM NUMBERS SKIPPED. NEXT NUMBER IS 023.

(Compute next random SEED)

(RANDNEW is a random number
between 0 and 100)

Figure 2-28 MAIN program (generates and prints random numbers)

2-5.2.4 PRINTSET ROUTINE

PRINTSET is both simple and self-explanatory, as Figure 2-29 shows. It initializes switches to indicate that both buffers are empty and that I/O is inactive. It sets the I/O new PSW (at location 78_{16}) so that I/O interrupts cause control to transfer to PRINTINT. Finally, it allows for interrupts once all conditions have been initialized.

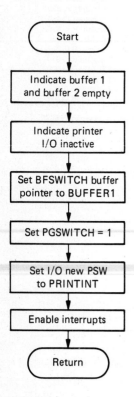

Figure 2-29 PRINTSET routine (initialization)

2-5.2.5 PRINT ROUTINE

When called with a request to print a line, PRINT examines the buffer that is to be used next (designated by the pointer BFSWITCH). If the buffer is already full (i.e., I/O is already queued due to a previous request), PRINT must "wait" via a LPSW until the I/O is completed. If the buffer is empty or becomes empty due to I/O completion, the print line and its length are moved into the selected buffer area. The buffer is then marked full. If I/O is already in progress due to the printing of the contents of the alternate buffer, PRINT immediately returns to its caller. On the other hand, if the printer is currently idle, PRINT calls the SIOSTART utility routine to set up the necessary CCWs and initiate the I/O. It then returns to its caller. Figure 2-30 is the flowchart for PRINT.

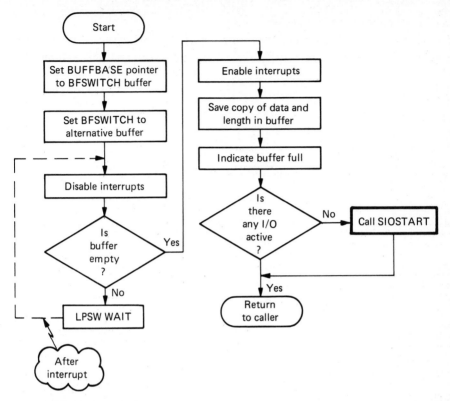

Figure 2-30   Print subroutine

2-5.2.6 SIOSTART ROUTINE

SIOSTART is a utility routine shown in Figure 2-31 that initiates I/O or restarts I/O after an error condition. It sets the IOSWITCH pointer to indicate that I/O is active and designates the buffer in use. It checks to see that the printer is ready, although this check is merely a precaution since SIOSTART should never be called when the printer is busy. SIOSTART modifies the PRINTCCW CCW to indicate the buffer to be printed and its length. The SLI bit is used in PRINTCCW since lengths other than 132 bytes may occur. If a page eject has been requested (i.e., PGSWITCH = 1), the CAW is set to the page eject CCW (EJECTCCW) that precedes PRINTCCW, and PGSWITCH is reset to 0. Otherwise, the CAW is set to PRINTCCW.

After all these steps have been completed, the SIO is issued. If it is accepted by the channel and device, SIOSTART returns to its caller. Otherwise, SIOSTART waits for the device to become ready again via a TIO loop and then retries the SIO.

2-5.2.7 PRINTINT ROUTINE

PRINTINT takes control whenever there is an I/O interrupt. It first saves all the registers and sets up a base register for its use. If the I/O interrupt is not from the

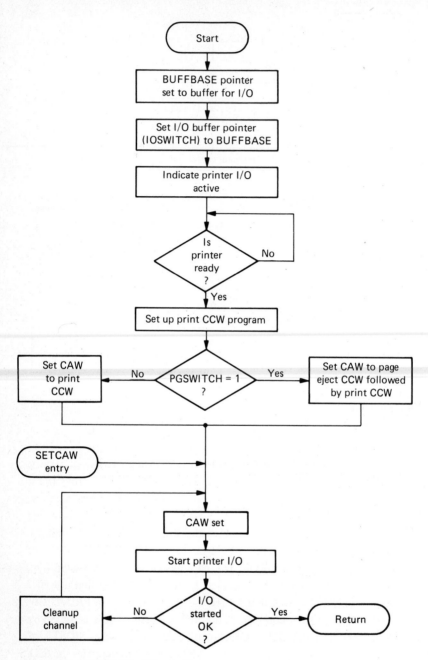

Figure 2-31 SIOSTART utility routine

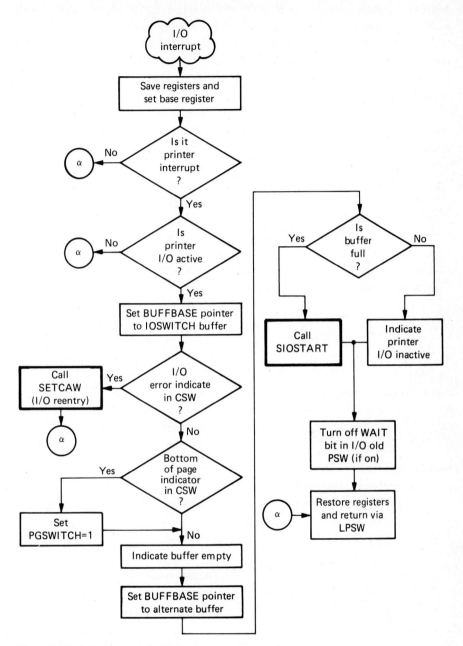

Figure 2-32   Print interrupt handler

printer or if there were no printer I/O active, the interrupt is ignored. If any errors were encountered, as indicated by CSW status bits (unit check, data check, etc.), the I/O is restarted via the SETCAW entry to the SIOSTART routine and control is returned to the interrupted routine until the next interrupt occurs. If the "bottom of page" indicator was set in the CSW, PGSWITCH is set to 1 so that a page eject will occur as part of the next I/O print sequence.

Assuming that the I/O interrupt indicated correct completion of the print request, the buffer is marked "empty." (This buffer is designated by the IOSWITCH pointer.) PRINTINT then checks the alternate buffer to see if it is full. If it is full, I/O is initiated via a call to SIOSTART and control is returned to the interrupted program. If it is empty, there is no more print work to do at this time, so the IOSWITCH is set to "inactive" and control is returned to the interrupted program.

At the time the I/O interrupt occurred, the CPU might have been in the wait state waiting for the interrupt (see the PRINT routine). If an LPSW X'38' were to be issued, the CPU would revert back to the wait state. Thus, the wait state bit is turned off in the I/O old PSW before the LPSW X'38' is issued. The PRINTINT flowchart is depicted in Figure 2-32.

2-5.2.8 DISCUSSION QUESTIONS

Although this program is just a simple example, it is important that the reader study it carefully in order to understand the subtle relationships between I/O and interrupts. In particular, the reader should be able to answer the following questions:

1 If the printer is an IBM 1403 that is rated at 1000 lines per minute, it can print a line in about 60 ms. How long does it take the MAIN program to produce a line of printed output? That is, how long is it between successive calls to PRINT? In particular, is it more or less than 60 ms?

Assume that each simple instruction (Load, Add, etc.) takes 1 μs and the Multiply instruction takes 10 μs.

2 a What advantages are there to this double-buffered printer technique? (Consider your answer to question 1 above.)

  b What advantages would there be for a single-buffered technique? How useful would it be?

3 a How could you change this program so as to make it triple-buffered? (It should be easy; if it isn't, you've done it wrong.)

  b What advantages are there for triple buffering?

4 In the PRINT subroutine we notice the following sequence of events (see Figure 2-30):

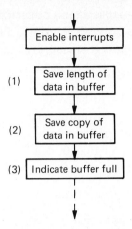

a Would there ever be any noticeable difference if we merely rearranged this sequence, such as (3), then (2), then (1)? (Remember that interrupts are possible during this sequence.)

b What would be the effect of the ordering (2), then (3), then (1), i.e., what problems could occur?

5 Why in PRINT was it necessary to disable interrupts before testing buffer empty?

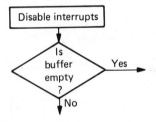

6 Why wasn't it necessary to disable interrupts before testing if I/O active?

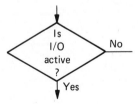

7 Why wasn't it necessary to disable interrupts in SIOSTART?

Questions 4-7 illustrate some of the important synchronization problems in operating systems. The reader should take the time to figure out the answers. These problems will be studied in the chapters on processor management and device management.

2-5.2.9   ANSWERS TO SELECTED DISCUSSION QUESTIONS (1 and 4)

Question 1   The time between successive calls to PRINT from MAIN varies depending upon the random numbers generated. This time is approximately

$$T_j = R_{j-1} \times R_{j-2} \times 14 \ \mu s + K$$

The inner loop takes about 14 μs based upon the stated timing assumptions. K represents the remainder of the instructions; it should be less than 100 μs. R_{j-1} and R_{j-2} are the last two random numbers generated. The product $R_{j-1} \times R_{j-2}$ can take on values from 1 to 10,000; thus T may range from as low as about 100 μs to as high as 140 ms. In particular, it could be either less than or greater than 60 ms!

This varying timing is typical of the behavior of actual programs (an assembler, compiler, etc.) where the processing time between I/O requests may vary depending upon the particular input being processed at that instant.

Question 4   Since interrupts can occur during the sequence in question, the PRINTINT subroutine could gain control at any point. If we reversed the sequence to (3), (2), (1), and an interrupt were to occur immediately after (3), we would experience the events shown in Figure 2-33.

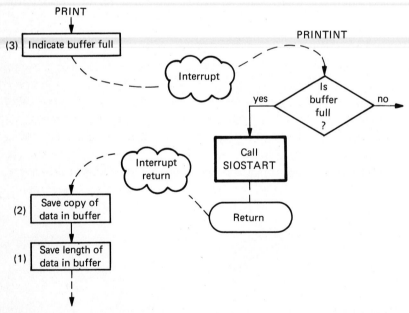

Figure 2-33   Interrupt sequence

Notice that under these circumstances PRINTINT would start the I/O for the new print line *before it is even in the buffer.* This would result in printing the previously printed line that had been in the buffer. In fact, since PRINT (when it regains control) will start to move data into the buffer, the actual line printed may be some strange merging of the old line and the new line, depending upon the relative timings of the printer I/O and the PRINT routine.

As an exercise, consider what would happen if the interrupt were to occur after (2) in the sequence (3), (2), (1). Would this still cause an error?

There are two common solutions to problems such as those we have described. One approach is to determine a "safe sequence" (by the way, convince yourself that the sequence (1), (2), (3) is safe, i.e., an interrupt could occur at any point and still not cause any errors). Another is to disable interrupts (e.g., SSM = X'00') during the sequence. This latter approach is generally discouraged since the system's ability to respond rapidly is seriously compromised if excessive and/or unnecessary use of the "disabled interrupt state" is used, especially if the sequence is long and time-consuming. As a general rule-of-thumb, interrupts should not be disabled unless absolutely necessary.

2-6 SUMMARY

Let us consider this chapter in the context of the design and analysis of operating systems. In all our examples, we issued our own I/O (device management) and handled all CPU interrupts (processor management). Techniques that increased efficiency and utilization were also presented. These tasks are actually the responsibility of the operating system, not the normal programmer. The operating system schedules the I/O and CPU in the manner it sees fit, based on some particular objective, such as maximum system throughput, highest user priority, etc.

This chapter presented concrete examples of contemporary computer structures, including machine language, I/O programming, and interrupt hardware, providing a basis for the understanding and appreciation of the resources that are to be managed by the operating system. The following chapters will present, in logical order, the techniques and concepts required to manage these resources efficiently.

QUESTIONS

2-1

    1 What is an I/O channel? What function does it serve in a computer system?

    2 How does the CPU communicate with the channel? How does the channel pass information back to the CPU?

    3 What are the functions of the Program Status Word (PSW) and the Channel Status Word (CSW)? What similarities exist between them?

    4 What purpose does the Channel Address Word (CAW) serve? Why don't we need a corresponding program address word for the CPU?

    5 What is the difference between an I/O operation (TIO, SIO, etc.) and a channel command word?

2-2 If the 370 encountered the following CCW, what would you expect to happen?

CCW X'09',LINE,X'20',120

2-3 What would happen if the 370 had the following PSW and location/register values?

```
PSW - X'00A00000000EA634'
Register 15 - X'000EA600'
Loc (Hex)      Value (Hex)

0EA634         D2030048F0409C00000E078E0A6F
0EA640         A00EA648
0EA648         8B00000060000001
0EA650         090EA6602000000D
0EA660         E8D6E440C1D9C540E6D9D6D5C7
```

2-4 Define and briefly explain the following terms:

    1 Channel

    2 SIO

    3 CSW

    4 CAW

    5 CCW

    6 Selector Channel

    7 Multiplexor Channel

    8 System Mask

2-5

    1 When the following CCW is executed by the channel, what will happen if an IBM 3211 printer is selected?

```
           CCW     X'09',DATA,0,3
DATA       DC      C'WIN'
```

    2 What would have happened if an IBM 3210 remote terminal was selected by the channel? What about an IBM 3505 card reader?

2-6   In Figure 2-34 are portions of a 370 assembly language routine which includes
       I/O operations and channel command words.
           Assume channel X'00E' is connected to a 3505 card reader and channel
       X'00B' to a 3211 printer. Channel command codes and flags for these devices
       may be found in Appendix A.
       1   Briefly, what does the program do?
       2   What is the function of the TIO and BC instructions on lines 5 and 6
           and 13 and 14? Why don't similar instructions occur before the other
           two SIO instructions?
       3   It would save space if we used just one buffer area rather than two, as are
           used in this program. What is the advantage of using two buffers? Would it
           be of further benefit to use more than two?
       4   During execution of WALDO, location 120 (decimal) contains the
           following hexadecimal value:

           000400000F0A8248

           a   When an I/O interrupt occurs during the execution of WALDO, signal-
               ing the termination of one of the I/O operations initiated by the pro-
               gram, to what location is control transferred to process the interrupt?
           b   What interrupts are masked off during the execution of the interrupt
               routine? Which ones are explicitly enabled?
           c   What protection keys are allowable for storage references during the
               execution of the interrupt routine?

2-7   Typically, the user has certain control over interrupts. On the 370, there are
       three general classes of control:

           Ignore—user can specify that interrupt be ignored (i.e., does not occur
           at all)
           Postpone—user can specify that interrupt be postponed (queued) but
           will occur when mask is removed
           Mandatory—interrupt can be neither ignored nor postponed

       For each of the following interrupts, state which class of control is appro-
       priate and briefly explain. (You don't have to remember 370 rules; use your
       common sense).
       1   Supervisor Call (SVC)
       2   Protection Violation (program interrupt)
       3   I/O Completion
       4   Fixed-point Overflow (program interrupt)

2-8   Interrupt Structure—Masking
       1   What are the purposes of masking interrupts?
       2   If you mask an interrupt what will happen to that interrupt?

STMT		SOURCE STATEMENT	
1	WALDO	START	0
2		BALR	15,0
3		USING	*,15
4	CAW	EQU	72
5	TEST1	TIO	X'00B'
6		BC	7,TEST1
7		MVC	CAW(4),=A(CHAN2)
8		SIO	X'00B'
9		MVC	CAW(4),=A(CHAN1)
10		SIO	X'00E'
11	TEST2	TIO	X'00E'
12		BC	7,TEST2
		.	
		.	process and modify data in
		.	BUFFER1
13	TEST3	TIO	X'00B'
14		BC	7,TEST3
15		MVC	CAW(4),=A(CHAN4)
16		SIO	X'00B'
17		MVC	CAW(4),=A(CHAN3)
18		SIO	X'00E'
19	TEST4	TIO	X'00E'
20		BC	7,TEST4
		.	
		.	process and modify data in
		.	BUFFER2
21		B	TEST1
22		BR	14
23	CHAN1	CCW	X'02', BUFFER1, X'00', 80
24	CHAN2	CCW	X'09', HEADER, X'AO', 15
25		CCW	X'00', BUFFER2, X'40', 80
26		CCW	X'11', TRAILER, X'20', 16
27	CHAN3	CCW	X'02', BUFFER2, X'00', 80
28	CHAN4	CCW	X'09', HEADER, X'AO', 15
29		CCW	X'00', BUFFER1, X'40', 80
30		CCW	X'11', TRAILER, X'20', 16
31	HEADER	DC	CL15 'START MESSAGE:'
32	TRAILER	DC	CL16 'MESSAGE FINISHED'
33	BUFFER1	DS	CL80
34	BUFFER2	DC	CL80 'INITIAL MESSAGE'
35		END	

Figure 2-34 Portions of a 370 assembly language routine

3   Some interrupts cannot be masked. For each of the following interrupts
     tell whether they can or cannot be masked and the reasons for their
     maskability.
     a   External
     b   I/O from device X'00E'
     c   Operation Exception
     d   Privileged Operation
     e   Protection (be careful)
     f   Addressing
     g   Fixed-point Overflow
4   If starting at location X'78' you found X'FF0C000F0E86A8' what
     problems would you expect?

2-9   Discuss briefly the differences and similarities between the Interruption Code
      field of the PSW (bits 16–31); the Condition Code field of the PSW (bits
      34–35); and the Status field of the CSW (bits 32–47).

2-10 What is the difference between system mask and program mask in the PSW?

2-11 In Figure 2-22, statement 30, why is register 15 stored in absolute location
      54? Why not save it by using statement 33 STM 0,15?

2-12 A typical I/O initiator program has code as follows:

```
        . . .
        SSM     OFF             TURN ALL INTERRUPTS OFF
        TIO     XXX             LOOP UNTIL DEVICE OK
        BNZ     *-4
        LA      1,CCWLIST       SET CAW
        ST      1,CAW
        SIO     XXX             INITIATE I/O
        BNZ     ERROR
        LPSW    WAIT            WAIT UNTIL I/O COMPLETE
        . . .
WAIT    DC      X'FF02 0000 0000 0000'
        . . .
```

1   Why is the SSM (Set System Mask) needed? That is, why should interrupts
     be disabled in the sequence above?
2   Under what circumstances might it be safe to eliminate the SSM instruc-
     tion? That is, when can the above sequence be safely followed while
     interrupts are enabled?
3   What would be wrong if WAIT was changed to

WAIT   DC   X'0002 0000 0000 0000'?

2-13

1 How many addressable I/O devices may be attached to the 7 channels?

2 You are a TWA system programmer developing an online airline reservation system. The system runs on an IBM S/360 and you wish to have 10,000 terminals that can access the system. How would you address all the terminals? You may consider developing any new device you want to attach to the basic S/360 system, but you may *not* alter the structure of the basic system.

2-14 Is the following statement true or false? "When a program interrupt occurs, the CPU automatically transfers to location 104 (decimal)." Why?

2-15 There are five classes of interrupts on the 370:

1 External
2 Supervisor call
3 Program
4 Machine check
5 Input/output

On certain computers, interrupts are divided into two kinds: synchronous and asynchronous.

1 Define a meaning. for synchronous and asynchronous interrupts.

2 How would you divide the 370 interrupts into these two kinds?

2-16

1 What does the priority of an interrupt mean? There are five classes of interrupts on the 370. List them in the order of priority and briefly describe what causes each to occur. In each class, explain why you think the designers gave it its relative priority. Would you suggest any re-ordering of these priorities?

2 What are the reasons for having five different types of interrupts? Can you see any reason for adding any new types? (If so, explain the type.) Can you see any reason to break down the classes any further? (If so, explain why for each.) Is the 370 interrupt class structure aesthetically pleasing to you?

2-17

1 What is the effect of masking off a certain type of interrupt? How is this masking accomplished?

2 Which of the five general types of interrupts (I/O, program, machine check, etc.) can be masked off?

3 Give an example of a situation in which you might want to mask off

each of the following types of interrupts. In each case, explain why you would want to prevent these interrupts from occurring.

   a fixed-point-overflow exception

   b all I/O interrupts

   c I/O interrupts from certain specified channels only

4 What happens to the PSW when an interrupt occurs? How do we return to where we left off after processing the interrupt?

5 What happens if a fixed-point-overflow exception occurs during the execution of the interrupt-handling routine for program interrupts? How can this situation be remedied once it has occurred? How could it have been prevented entirely?

2-18 When do the following interrupts occur?

   1 Channel end

   2 Program controlled interrupt

   3 Device end

2-19 Why do you get separate interrupts for channel end and device end on the 370? (Think in terms of what you gain.)

2-20 On the 370 the load instruction has a counterpart in the store instruction. However, there is no such counterpart to the LPSW (load PSW) instruction.

   1 Can you simulate a store PSW instruction? If so, how?

   2 Why might the operating system ever want to know the current PSW?

2-21 In Figure 2-18, statement 4, why was the system mask set?

2-22 You are an interrupt routine that prints a message when a program interrupt occurs. An interrupt has occurred and you have done what you are supposed to have done and want to ignore the erroneous instructions and return to the program that was interrupted. You look at location 56 and find the following hexadecimal contents:

FFA10004A000B204

   1 To which location in memory should you return?

   2 What is the starting address of the last instruction executed prior to the interrupt?

   3 What type of error caused this interrupt?

   4 The instruction that caused the interrupt was trying to access a certain location α (alpha) in the memory. What is one storage key value that was *not* assigned to the block in which α is contained?

2-23 Consider the programs HARRY, INT, and CCW in Figure 2-35.

   1 Assuming that the device at X'00E' is an IBM 3211 printer, what will happen if this set of programs is loaded and executed starting at HARRY?

Assume that the main routine HARRY is called by a BALR 14,15 instruction. (A short answer will do.)

2 Assume that HARRY is called twice by the following sequence of instructions:

```
L       15,=A (HARRY)
BALR    14,15

L       15,=A (HARRY)
BALR    14,15
```

Go through the three routines and simulate to your own satisfaction what happens and then answer the following question: Why isn't the code in lines 6 and 7 of HARRY a potential infinite loop?

3 What is the function being performed by lines 6–7 of HARRY and lines 7–9 of INT?

4 What hardware instruction could be used to do the same task as the lines mentioned in 3 above? Indicate what changes should be made.

2-24

1 Define a more mnemonic language for I/O programming than that of CCW.

2 IBM has chosen to use system macros to handle the I/O rather than have the user write "I/O language" programs. What are the merits of this approach over those of the assembler?

2-25 On the System/370 the operating system uses two hardware facilities to protect itself: (1) storage protection keys and (2) supervisor/problem state mode to restrict use of instructions, such as, SSM, SIO, etc.

1 Describe, in general, how storage protection keys work.

2 Describe, in general, how supervisor/problem state mode works.

3 Propose a modification to hardware that could allow the storage protection mechanism to handle all protection requirements (i.e., eliminate supervisor/problem state mechanism). (*Hint:* consider assigning the current PSW a location in memory.) Explain it.

4 Could the supervisor/problem state mechanism be extended to handle storage protection? Why or how?

2-26

1 What is the difference between a protection key and a protection lock?

2 If the protection key of the current PSW matches the lock associated with a block of core storage, can any type of access be made to that block?

3 If they do not match, under what circumstances can access be made?

4 The 370 has only two types of locks, a fetch or a fetch and write lock. Can the effect of an execute lock be simulated on a 370 (i.e., a block can be read but not executed)? How?

```
STMT        SOURCE    STATEMENT

    1  HARRY        START
    2               ENTRY FLAG
    3               EXTRN INT,CCW
    4               BALR    15,0
    5               USING *,15
    6  LOOP         CLC     FLAG,=F'0'
    7               BNZ     LOOP
    8               LA      1,1
    9               ST      1,FLAG
   10               MVC     NIOPSW (8),IOPSW
   11               MVC     CAW (4), =A (CCW)
   12               SIO     X'00E'
   13               BR      14
   14  NIOPSW       EQU     120
   15  CAW          EQU     72

   16  IOPSW        DC      A (0,INT)
   17  FLAG         DC      F'0'
   18               END
```

```
STMT          SOURCE    STATEMENT

    1  INT          START
    2               EXTRN FLAG
    3               ST      15,8
    4               BALR    15,0
    5               USING   *,15
    6               STM     1,2,SAVE
    7               SR      1,1
    8               L       2,=A (FLAG)
    9               ST      1,0 (2)
   10               LM      1,2,SAVE
   11               L       15,8
   12  DONE         LPSW    OIOPSW
   13  OIOPSW       EQU     56
   14  SAVE         DS      2F
   15               END
```

```
STMT          SOURCE    STATEMENT

    1  CCW          START
    2               CCW     X'09',FIRST,X'80',14
    3               CCW     X'00',ANS,X'80',4
    4               CCW     X'00',SECOND,X'00',6
    5  ANS          DC      C'6802  LOSES.'
    6  SECOND       DC      C' WINS.'
    7  FIRST        DC      C'THE ANSWER IS '
    8               END
```

Figure 2-35 Programs HARRY, INT, CCW

2-27   On the 370 there exist four bits for locks. Thus core may be partitioned among 16 possible users. Can these same four bits be used for partitions of more than 16 users? How?

2-28   Rewrite the program of Figure 2-24 to include the double-buffering facilities of Section 2-3.7.

2-29   Write the assembly language implementation of the routines presented in the I/O buffering example of Section 2-5.2.

Machine Problems and Design Questions[4]

2-30   The execution of an instruction such as "A 1, 889" will result (on the 360) in a program interrupt because it does not address a full word boundary. Write an interrupt routine for the 360 which would receive and perhaps correct such an addressing error, that is, make the 360 behave like the 370 which can operate on data that are not aligned.

2-31   The IBM 360 and IBM 370 are very similar computers, but the 370 has a few new additional features. You are given the binary deck of a 370 program and wish to run it on your old 360. After talking to the author of the program, you find that the program should run on your 360 except for the occurrence of 370 MVCL (Move Long) instructions.

When such an instruction is encountered by the 360, it is treated as a program interrupt. If you write a program interrupt handler that "simulates" the effect of the MVCL instruction and then resumes execution at the next instruction, you should be able to run this program. Write such an interrupt handler!

You should assume that this is the only program interrupt condition expected and the Program Interrupt New PSW has been set to A(0,MVCLSIM) where MVCLSIM is the name of your interrupt handler.

---

[4]NOTE: The questions in this section may be used as design questions and/or machine problems. As design questions, the answer would contain flowcharts and documentation. As machine problems, the answers must be implemented. On most machine configurations the student will have difficulty implementing these problems since these machines prevent the normal user from doing I/O programming or interrupt programming. However, the implementation may be accomplished in any one of the following ways:

1   If the student has access to a stand-alone 370 (e.g., 370/135 or a machine he can run in supervisor state), he may implement these machine problems directly.
2   If the student has access to a large 370 batch system where there is reluctance to turn over the bare machine to a student, he may use our simulator. The simulator simulates the 370 in such a way that the user has access to a "virtual 370." The simulator is written in PL/I and may be obtained through the authors.
3   If another machine is available (e.g., PDP 8), the instructor or the student may modify most questions to become applicable to an available machine.
4   If a terminal is available to the virtual machine/370 (VM/370) system, they may implement these problems directly on the virtual machine.

Move Long (MVCL) Description

OE	R1	R2

R1 and R2 each designate an even/odd pair of general registers. For example, OE28 instruction encountered and

reg2 = 00001800,   reg3 = 00001000
reg8 = 00043700,   reg9 = 00001000

then 4,096 bytes (1,000 hex) will be moved from location 43700_{16} to location 1800_{16}.

(*Note:* the actual 370 MVCL instruction is slightly more complex. We will only consider cases such as the above where lengths of both fields are the same.)

2-32 One class of interrupts on the IBM 370 computer is known as the *program* interruption. When this interrupt occurs, the hardware signals that the execution of a particular instruction called for something abnormal to be done. For example, in a fixed-point addition (A, AR), if the result of the operation requires more than 32 bits to be represented, a program interrupt would occur. The status field Interruption Code (IC) of the current Program Status Word (PSW) would be set to indicate that a fixed-point overflow occurred (0008) and the entire current PSW would be put into the program old PSW (loc 28_{16}). Finally, the contents of the program new PSW (loc 68_{16}) are put into the PSW and the next instruction (whose address is contained in the low-order 3 bytes of the program new PSW) is executed. This last sentence is equivalent to saying that control is transferred to the program interrupt handler.

In this machine problem we ask you to write that interrupt handler.

The problem is split up into three levels of difficulty. A solution to the problem will consist of the following two items:

- An assembly language program with one comment for each statement.
- A 1–2 (max) page description of what you have done and what tests you have performed in your solution to the problem; alternatively, you can submit for partial credit an explanation as to why your program failed.

1 Write an interrupt handler for program interrupts that performs the following tasks:

a Processes just program interrupts caused by fixed-point overflows; it should ignore all other types of program interrupts (by returning directly to the instruction following the one that caused the interrupt).

    b Analyzes the instruction that caused the interrupt and puts as the value in the register indicated by the R1 field the largest positive number representable in 32 bits. You need only process the A and AR instructions. (The largest positive number is a reasonable value to put there in some cases.)

    c Of course you should save and restore registers so that they reflect an unchanged condition to the interrupted program (with the exception of the register indicated by the R1 field).

    d Return to the instruction following the one that caused the interrupt.

    e Do not forget to produce evidence (e.g., TRACE output) that proves your features work.

2 Choose one of the following:

    a Alter the design of your program interrupt handler so that a Supervisor Call Interrupt can occur from within your program interrupt handler. The effect of this requirement is to say that while processing one interrupt, your program can be interrupted and another interrupt handler takes control. You will have to write an SVC interrupt handler. In order to make things interesting, your SVC handler should keep a count of how many SVCs have been executed since the IPL button was pushed. After rating the occurrence of an SVC, the handler should return to the next instruction (i.e., the SVC interrupt handler only counts the number of SVCs executed and returns control).

    b Alter the design of your program interrupt handler so that your main program runs in user mode and the interrupt handler runs in privileged mode. To test that your main program indeed is in user mode, attempt to execute a privileged instruction in your main program. This will cause a program interrupt to occur. The program interrupt handler should discover that the program interrupt was a "privileged operation" interruption and should keep a count of how many privileged operations have been attempted from user mode.

3 Upon the occurrence of a fixed-point overflow print out on the printer a messsge that says:

"FIXED POINT OVERFLOW AT XXXXXX"

where XXXXXX is the hexadecimal representation of the absolute address of the instruction that caused the fixed-point overflow. The code that causes this action should be contained within the program interruption handler.

Memory Management

The memory management modules of an operating system are concerned with the management of primary memory. By *primary memory* we mean the memory that the processors directly access for instructions and data (see Figure 1-1). Primary memory is frequently called *core* memory in historical reference to the magnetic ferrite core technology that was used for many years. Specifically, memory management is concerned with four functions:

1 Keeping track of the status of each location of primary memory, i.e., each location is either allocated or unallocated ("free").
2 Determining allocation policy for memory, i.e., deciding to whom it should go, how much, when, and where. If primary memory is to be shared by one or more processes concurrently, then memory management must determine which process' requests will be satisfied.
3 Allocation technique—once it is decided to allocate memory, the specific locations must be selected and allocation information updated.
4 Deallocation technique and policy—handling the deallocation (reclamation) of memory. A process may explicitly release previously allocated memory, or memory management may unilaterally reclaim the memory based on a deallocation policy. After deallocation, status information must be updated.

The policies chosen for memory management may be influenced by the desire to keep memory management modules small and simple, or by the need to increase user flexibility or system efficiency. In this chapter we present a spectrum of policies and techniques; some of these make possible a greater utilization of memory, while others provide the user with more flexibility—though sometimes at the cost of greater complexity, higher hardware costs, or increased overhead. The techniques we describe are:

1   Single contiguous memory management

2   Partitioned memory management

3   Relocation partitioned memory management

4   Paged memory management

5   Demand-paged memory management

6   Segmented memory management

7   Segmented and demand-paged memory management

8   Other memory management schemes

Recalling our hierarchical extended machine viewpoint (Figure 1-9), we note that the memory management modules are usually neither on the highest level of an operating system (i.e., they are usually called by other levels) nor on the lowest. However, we have chosen to discuss memory management first, as it is presently a key distinguishing characteristic of most operating systems. We see that a clearly distinguishing feature between the SDS940 and the OS360/MVT operating systems is memory management (paged versus partitioned).

In this chapter we emphasize the role of memory management in relation to job processing. However, within a computing system there may be a variety of different requirements that relate to memory management. In some cases, these may involve wholesaler versus retailer relationships; in others, different algorithms may be chosen merely because they are more efficient or more appropriate for certain situations.

The particular techniques presented in this chapter cover most memory management applications. For example, in a particular operating system/user environment, the job processing memory management may be based on a demand-paged allocation strategy. The user's processes then may suballocate assigned memory into individual data areas based on a partitioned allocation technique. At the same time, the operating system may use a relocatable partition approach in handling its own dynamic system tables. For these reasons, an operating system may provide a multiplicity of memory management facilities that can be used for different purposes.

To keep the analysis as simple as possible, we will direct our attention to the job processing memory management requirements. The other cases can be analyzed in a similar manner. The sample operating system in Chapter 7 illustrates some of these other cases.

In order to illustrate the impact of memory management on system efficiency, the concept of multiprogramming is introduced in this chapter. A more extensive treatment of multiprogramming is found in Chapter 4.

For each of the memory management policies and techniques to be studied, the analysis is divided into four sections:

1 An overview of the approach and concepts employed

2 A description of any special hardware facilities required or recommended

3 A description of the particular software algorithms and processing required

4 A discussion of the advantages and disadvantages of the particular strategy

3-1 SINGLE CONTIGUOUS ALLOCATION

Single contiguous allocation is a simple memory management scheme that requires no special hardware features. It is usually associated with small stand-alone computers (or minicomputers) with simple batch operating systems, e.g., IBM OS/360 Primary Control Program, IBM 1130 Disk Monitor System, IBM 7094 Fortran Monitor System. In such systems there is no multiprogramming, and a one-to-one correspondence exists between a user, a job, a job step, and a process. Thus the terms user, job, or process may be used interchangeably. In this chapter, for the sake of simplicity, we will always assume the one-to-one correspondence: only the term "job" will be used. Memory is allocated to the job, as depicted in Figure 3-1.

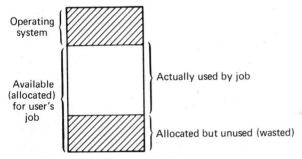

Figure 3-1 Single contiguous allocation

Memory is conceptually divided into three contiguous regions. A portion of memory is permanently allocated to the operating system. All of the remainder of memory is available (and allocated) to the single job being processed. The job actually uses only a portion of the allocated memory, leaving an allocated but unused region of memory. For example, if there are 256K bytes of memory, a simple operating system may require 32K bytes, leaving 224K bytes allocated for user jobs. If a typical job requires only 64K bytes, then 160K bytes of memory (over 50 percent of all memory) are unused. This unused memory cannot necessarily be returned to the manufacturer since there may be a few jobs that require having the entire 224K bytes available.

If we examine how the four functions of memory management are handled, we see the simplicity and hence the principal advantage of this scheme:

1 Keeping track of memory—it is allocated entirely to one job.

2 Determining factor on memory policy—the job gets all memory when scheduled.

3 Allocation of memory—all of it is allocated to the job.

4 Deallocation of memory—when the job is done, all memory is returned to free status.

3-1.1 Hardware Support

No special hardware is required for contiguous allocation. Sometimes a primitive hardware protection mechanism is desirable to ensure that the user's programs do not accidentally or maliciously tamper with the operating system. This mechanism may consist of a bounds register and a supervisor-user mode of the CPU. The bounds register contains the address of the protected area (which includes the operating system). If the CPU is in user mode, on each reference to memory the hardware checks to assure that it is not an access to the protected area. If an attempted access is made, an interrupt occurs and control is transferred to the operating system. In supervisor mode the operating system can access the protected area as well as execute privileged instructions that change the contents of the bounds register. Other techniques, such as the IBM 370's locks-and-keys protection mechanism, could be used to accomplish the same effect. The mode can be changed from user to supervisor only when control is transferred to the operating system (usually due to an interrupt).

3-1.2 Software Support

A flowchart of a single contiguous allocation is depicted in Figure 3-2. This algorithm is called when the job scheduler of processor management wishes to schedule a job to be run. The algorithm is called only when no other job is using memory.

3-1.3 Advantages

The major advantage of this scheme lies in its simplicity: an operating system using this scheme may require as little as 1K bytes in entirety in contrast to the 256K bytes or more needed by more sophisticated operating systems. Another advantage is that it does not require great expertise to understand or use such a system.

3-1.4 Disadvantages

A major disadvantage of this scheme lies in the fact that memory is not fully utilized. We note three inefficiencies. First, some memory is not being used at all (see the wasted area in Figure 3-1). Second, on most systems with channels, there are times when no portions of memory are actively being used by the CPU at all,

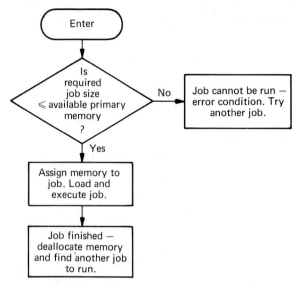

Figure 3-2 Single contiguous allocation

as when the job has initiated an I/O request and is waiting for the channel to complete its operations. The memory containing the user's CPU programs is not being utilized while CPU is waiting. What percent of the time is a CPU waiting for I/O? Every program is different, but a typical job on the IBM 360/65 may be waiting 65 or 70 percent of the time if single allocation is used. Therefore, both memory and processors are underutilized. Third, some portions of memory that contain the user's address space have information that is never accessed. For example, among the collection of programs and data that comprise the job, there exist routines, such as error routines, that will often not be executed. Why must these be loaded when they take up memory space?

Another disadvantage is the lack of flexibility that this scheme offers the user. For example, his address space (total program size) must be smaller than main memory, or else jobs cannot be run.

In summary, the disadvantages are: (1) Poor utilization of memory, (2) poor utilization of processors (waiting for I/O), and (3) user's job being limited to the size of available main memory (with the exception perhaps an overlay mechanism).

3-2 INTRODUCTION TO MULTIPROGRAMMING

Many of the inefficiencies associated with single contiguous memory allocation stem from the problem of matching a fixed set of available resources to a varying resource demand. The physical hardware resources of a computer system can be varied only over relatively long time periods—for example, by adding or removing an increment (say 64K) of memory. These physical changes usually are made only once or twice a year. At the same time, the resource requirements of the different jobs to be run may vary significantly. We could try to force programmers to develop all jobs with identical resource requirements. However, this would be extremely difficult, if not impossible. A more successful approach would be to operate on more than one job at a time and distribute the resources among these jobs. This technique, called *multiprogramming*, is the interleaved or concurrent execution of two or more processes. Multiprogramming is examined in detail in Chapter 4 (Processor Management). We will briefly introduce the concept in this section to clarify the memory management techniques to be discussed.

3-2.1 Example of Multiprogramming

Figure 3-3 depicts three jobs to be run. Each job requires some processor time for its computation, C_i, as well as some use of the I/O channels for its input/output, I_i. In addition, each job's address space requires some memory, M_i. For simplicity, we have modeled each job as if it performed its computation, then did its I/O; this cycle is repeated continuously. Let us assume that there are 100K bytes of available memory. If only Job 1 were run, 30K bytes would be used, and the remaining 70K would be wasted. Furthermore, $\dfrac{I_1}{C_1 + I_1}$ of the processor time would be spent waiting for input/output.

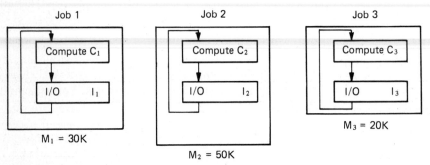

Figure 3-3 Models of three jobs to be multiprogrammed

Alternatively, we could place the address spaces for Jobs 1, 2, and 3 in main memory at the same time (30K + 50K + 20K = 100K bytes). This would fully utilize the 100K-byte main memory. Processor management would assign the processor to Job 1. After performing computation C_1, instead of stopping the processor while waiting for I_1 completion, processor management could assign the processor to Job 2. Likewise, when Job 2 reached I_2, the processor could be reassigned to Job 3. When Job 3 reaches I_3, we could immediately assign the processor again to Job 1 if I_1 had been completed (i.e., $I_1 \leqslant C_2 + C_3$). Thus, the processor would wait only $I_1 - (C_2 + C_3)$ time units instead of I_1. Through the use of multiprogramming, the processor utilization is much higher than when one job is run at a time. In many cases it is possible to complete two or three jobs in almost the same amount of time required to complete one uniprogrammed job.

3-2.2 Measures of System I/O Wait Percentage

Real processes are not as simple as the models in Figure 3-3. The computation and I/O are intermingled in complex ways. A useful aggregate parameter is the job's percent of I/O wait time, ω, which equals

$$\frac{\text{total I/O wait time}}{\text{total I/O plus total CPU time}}$$

This can easily be measured on most computers by running the process uniprogrammed and noting the percent of time that the processor is in the wait state. Several studies have shown that, on the average, typical jobs run on medium-to large-scale computers, such as the IBM 360/65 or 370/158, have an I/O wait time percentage of about 65 percent. Of course, individual jobs may deviate considerably from this average.

If we have two jobs, each with ω = 50 percent, and they are multiprogrammed, is the *effective system I/O wait percentage*, ω', reduced to 0? Well, if the model of Figure 3-3 held, we would have $C_1 = I_1 = C_2 = I_2$. Thus, C_2 could be executed concurrently with I_1 and likewise C_1 during I_2. However, as noted above, this model is oversimplified. Figure 3-4, for example, illustrates the processes as intermixed periods of computation and I/O. Each period, C_{11}, I_{12}, C_{13}, etc., is assumed to be of equal length in this example. Note that each job has an I/O wait percentage of 50 percent. If we tried to multiprogram them, we could match I_{12} with C_{21}, and I_{22} with C_{13}. However, when Job 1 wishes to perform input/output at I_{14}, we find that Job 2 also needs input/output at I_{23}. Thus the processor is idle while waiting for I_{14} or I_{23} to complete.

Generalizing the model of Figure 3-4, we can use probability theory to estimate

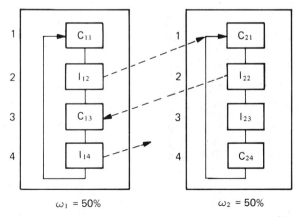

Figure 3-4 More detailed model of computation and I/O within a process

the effective system I/O wait percentage. That is, the system must wait only when all processes require I/O at exactly the same time. If we are multiprogramming n processes, each with the same I/O wait percentage, ω, the system I/O wait percentage, ω', is approximated by $\omega' = \omega^n$.

For example, if $\omega = 50$ percent, we have the estimates:

NUMBER OF PROCESSES, N	SYSTEM I/O WAIT PERCENTAGE, ω'
1	$(.50)^1 = 50\%$
2	$(.50)^2 = 25\%$
3	$(.50)^3 = 12.5\%$
4	$(.50)^4 = 6.3\%$
5	$(.50)^5 = 3.1\%$
6	$(.50)^6 = 1.6\%$

Unfortunately, the table above, although a useful approximation, is not quite correct. In order for the probability assumptions to hold, it is necessary for all processes to advance "one step" each time period. This would be true if we had n processors and n channels available, in which case ω' would indicate the probability of all n processors being idle at the same time (i.e., the same as tossing n coins and having all come up heads). It is reasonable to assume n concurrent I/O operations, especially with multiple multiplexor channels available; however, since we have only one processor, work builds up for this single processor. This situation can be mathematically solved using a probability theory technique called *birth-and-death Markov process*. This technique will be discussed in Chapter 4. In this approach, the system I/O wait percentage can be better approximated by the formula:

$$\omega' = \frac{\left(\dfrac{\omega}{1-\omega}\right)^n}{n! \displaystyle\sum_{i=0}^{n} \frac{\left(\dfrac{\omega}{1-\omega}\right)^i}{i!}}$$

Values of ω' are presented in Table 3-1. This formula results in lower values of ω' than the $\omega' = \omega^n$ estimate since one processor, rather than n processors, is kept busy trying to do all the work.

3-2.3 Relevance of Multiprogramming to Memory Management

The reader must realize that the formulas presented are only approximations. The important result to note is that, in general, system I/O wait time is reduced by increasing the *degree of multiprogramming*, i.e., the number of processes being multiprogrammed. The memory management algorithms that follow attempt to allocate the memory resource in order to maximize the degree of multiprogramming.

I/O Wait Percentage for Individual Job (ω)

Number of Jobs Being Multiprogrammed (n)	5.0	10.0	15.0	20.0	25.0	30.0	35.0	40.0	45.0	50.0	55.0	60.0	65.0	70.0	75.0	80.0	85.0	90.0	95.0
1	5.0	10.0	15.0	20.0	25.0	30.0	35.0	40.0	45.0	50.0	55.0	60.0	65.0	70.0	75.0	80.0	85.0	90.0	95.0
2	0.1	0.6	1.3	2.4	4.0	6.0	8.6	11.8	15.5	20.0	25.2	31.0	37.6	45.0	52.9	61.5	70.7	80.2	90.0
3	0.0	0.0	0.1	0.2	0.4	0.9	1.5	2.5	4.1	6.3	9.3	13.4	18.9	25.9	34.6	45.1	57.2	70.6	85.1
4	0.0	0.0	0.0	0.0	0.0	0.1	0.2	0.4	0.8	1.5	2.8	4.8	8.1	13.1	20.6	31.1	44.7	61.4	80.2
5	0.0	0.0	0.0	0.0	0.0	0.0	0.0	0.1	0.1	0.3	0.7	1.4	2.9	5.8	11.0	19.9	33.6	52.5	75.3
6	0.0	0.0	0.0	0.0	0.0	0.0	0.0	0.0	0.0	0.1	0.1	0.4	0.9	2.2	5.2	11.7	24.1	44.1	70.4
7	0.0	0.0	0.0	0.0	0.0	0.0	0.0	0.0	0.0	0.0	0.0	0.1	0.2	0.7	2.2	6.3	16.3	36.2	65.7
8	0.0	0.0	0.0	0.0	0.0	0.0	0.0	0.0	0.0	0.0	0.0	0.0	0.1	0.2	0.8	3.0	10.4	28.9	60.9
9	0.0	0.0	0.0	0.0	0.0	0.0	0.0	0.0	0.0	0.0	0.0	0.0	0.0	0.1	0.3	1.3	6.1	22.4	56.3
10	0.0	0.0	0.0	0.0	0.0	0.0	0.0	0.0	0.0	0.0	0.0	0.0	0.0	0.0	0.1	0.5	3.4	16.8	51.7
11	0.0	0.0	0.0	0.0	0.0	0.0	0.0	0.0	0.0	0.0	0.0	0.0	0.0	0.0	0.0	0.2	1.7	12.1	47.2
12	0.0	0.0	0.0	0.0	0.0	0.0	0.0	0.0	0.0	0.0	0.0	0.0	0.0	0.0	0.0	0.1	0.8	8.3	42.7
13	0.0	0.0	0.0	0.0	0.0	0.0	0.0	0.0	0.0	0.0	0.0	0.0	0.0	0.0	0.0	0.0	0.3	5.4	38.5
14	0.0	0.0	0.0	0.0	0.0	0.0	0.0	0.0	0.0	0.0	0.0	0.0	0.0	0.0	0.0	0.0	0.1	3.4	34.3
15	0.0	0.0	0.0	0.0	0.0	0.0	0.0	0.0	0.0	0.0	0.0	0.0	0.0	0.0	0.0	0.0	0.1	2.0	30.3
16	0.0	0.0	0.0	0.0	0.0	0.0	0.0	0.0	0.0	0.0	0.0	0.0	0.0	0.0	0.0	0.0	0.0	1.1	26.4
17	0.0	0.0	0.0	0.0	0.0	0.0	0.0	0.0	0.0	0.0	0.0	0.0	0.0	0.0	0.0	0.0	0.0	0.6	22.8
18	0.0	0.0	0.0	0.0	0.0	0.0	0.0	0.0	0.0	0.0	0.0	0.0	0.0	0.0	0.0	0.0	0.0	0.3	19.4
19	0.0	0.0	0.0	0.0	0.0	0.0	0.0	0.0	0.0	0.0	0.0	0.0	0.0	0.0	0.0	0.0	0.0	0.1	16.3
20	0.0	0.0	0.0	0.0	0.0	0.0	0.0	0.0	0.0	0.0	0.0	0.0	0.0	0.0	0.0	0.0	0.0	0.1	13.4

Table 3-1 System I/O wait percentage when multiprogrammed (ω')

3-3 PARTITIONED ALLOCATION

Partitioned allocation, in its various forms, is one of the simplest memory management techniques for supporting multiprogramming. Main memory is divided into separate *memory regions* or *memory partitions*. Each partition holds a separate job's address space, as illustrated in Figure 3-5.

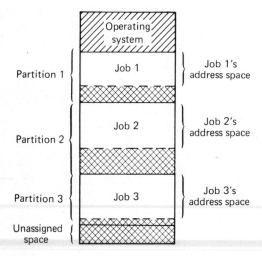

Figure 3-5 Partitioned allocation

The four functions of memory management are easily handled by this technique as follows:

1 Keeping track of the status of each partition (e.g., "in use" or "not in use," size).
2 Determining who gets memory—this is handled largely by the job scheduler.
3 Allocation—an available partition of sufficient size is assigned.
4 Deallocation—when the job terminates, the partition is indicated "not in use" and is available for future allocation.

Details of these functions are presented in the software support section.

3-3.1 Hardware Support

Very little special hardware is needed to support partitioned allocation. A memory protection mechanism is desirable to prevent one job from disrupting either the operating system or other jobs, whether accidently or maliciously. There are many ways to do this. We could use two bounds registers to bracket the partition being used. If the job tried to access memory outside the partition, a protection interrupt would occur. There are two disadvantages to this scheme:

1 The bounds registers must be changed every time that the processor is reassigned for multiprogramming.

2 It is difficult to extend this protection to the I/O channel. A job in partition 1 may try to instruct the channel to read data into an area in partition 3. We could provide bounds registers for every I/O channel, with multiple registers required for multiplexor channels. Alternatively, the operating system that initiates all I/O operations could try to check the channel program by software, although this would be a time-consuming burden.

The 370 protection mechanism handles these requirements fairly well. Each partition is assigned a separate protection key (1 through 15); key 0 is reserved for the operating system. Since the hardware actually associates the keys with each 2K-byte block of memory, partitions must be multiples of 2K, and all locks within a partition are set to the same value. Then, whenever the processor is reassigned, the "key" field within the new Program Status Word is set to the corresponding partition's key. Similarly, the I/O channels also use the protection key mechanism.

3-3.2 Software Algorithm

The partitioned allocation approach, like most of the memory management techniques to be presented, has numerous variations. Two common versions are *static partition specification* and *dynamic partition specification*.

3-3.2.1 STATIC PARTITION SPECIFICATION

By *static specification*, we mean that memory is divided into partitions prior to the processing of any jobs. This is similar to the technique used in IBM's OS/360 MFT (Multiprogramming with a Fixed number of Tasks). The partition specification may be designated by the computer operator or it may be built into the operating system. An example of a static partition specification table is given in Figure 3-6.

Partition Number (protection key)	Size	Location	Status
1	8K	312K	IN USE
2	32K	320K	IN USE
3	32K	352K	NOT IN USE
4	120K	384K	NOT IN USE
5	520K	504K	IN USE

Figure 3-6 Static partition specification table

Each job step supplied by a user must specify the maximum amount of memory needed. A partition of sufficient size is then found and assigned. The software algorithm to handle the allocation and deallocation is a simple one.

The technique of static specification is especially appropriate when the sizes and frequency of jobs are well known. In such a case, the partition sizes are chosen to correspond closely to the most common job sizes. However, there can be considerable memory wasted if the sizes and frequencies of jobs are not known, or if they are diverse. For example, if many jobs of sizes 1K, 9K, 33K, and 121K are to be run, we could assign these to partitions as follows:

PARTITION	PARTITION SIZE	JOB SIZE	WASTED SPACE
1	8K	1K	7K
2	32K	9K	23K
3	32K	9K	23K
4	120K	33K	87K
5	520K	121K	399K
	712K	173K	539K

In this case, all the partitions are assigned in the best possible way, yet only 173K of the available 712K is actually used. Thus, over 75 percent of the available memory is wasted. This is, of course, an extreme case, but similar situations can and do occur in actual systems.

3-3.2.2 DYNAMIC PARTITION SPECIFICATION

By dynamic specification, we mean that partitions are created during job processing so as to match partition sizes to job sizes. Dynamic partition allocation schemes are used in many instances that do not involve the operating system. The techniques have been called partitioned memory, dynamic storage allocation, controlled storage, and garbage collection. (For example, when the PL/I ALLOCATE statement is executed, a new storage area must be allocated; conversely, when the FREE statement is executed, the storage is released. This type of activity occurs within the partition and need not concern the operating system.)

Numerous schemes exist for accomplishing dynamic partition allocation. Tables must be made up with entries for each free area and each allocated partition, specifying the size, location, and access restrictions to each partition.

Figure 3-7 depicts a possible table organization for accomplishing these purposes. Two separate tables are used, one for the allocated areas and the other for maintaining the status of the unallocated, or free, areas. Since the tables are not necessarily completely filled, the status fields indicate whether the corresponding entry is currently in use (containing allocated or available area information) or not in use (an "empty entry").

Partition Number (protection key)	Size	Location	Status
1	8K	312K	ALLOCATED
2	32K	320K	ALLOCATED
3	–	–	EMPTY ENTRY
4	120K	384K	ALLOCATED
5	–	–	EMPTY ENTRY
- - -	- - -		

Allocated Partition Status Table

Free Area	Size	Location	Status
1	32K	352K	AVAILABLE
2	520K	504K	AVAILABLE
3	–	–	EMPTY ENTRY
4	–	–	EMPTY ENTRY
- - -	- - -	- - -	

Unallocated Area Status Table

Figure 3-7 Dynamic partition specification tables

An example of dynamic partition specification is presented in Figure 3-8. At some point three partitions are allocated, each containing a job of corresponding size (Figure 3-8a). Three additional jobs are then selected to be multiprogrammed, and new partitions of the appropriate sizes are created from the unallocated free areas (Figure 3-8b). Eventually, the partitions can be deallocated after the corresponding job is terminated. Figure 3-8c depicts the memory status after Jobs 2 and 3 terminate.

Various algorithms are available to accomplish the allocation and deallocation functions. Examples of algorithms, based on the tables of Figure 3-7, are shown in Figures 3-9 and 3-10. Certain obvious steps must be performed for allocation. First, a free area at least as large as the partition desired must be found. Second, if the area is larger than needed, it must be split into two pieces—one becomes the allocated partition, the other becomes a smaller free area. Conversely, when a partition is deallocated, we try to merge it with any adjacent free areas so as to make one contiguous free area rather than many small pieces. (See, for example, the handling of Job 3's partition in Figure 3-8b and c).

The tables illustrated in Figure 3-7 represent one way of keeping track of memory usage. In actual implementations a different approach is often used. The key problem is that the number of entries needed in the partition table and the free table actually depends upon the number of partitions and free areas that exist at any time—i.e., the number is not constant. The simple table approach is therefore somewhat inefficient since most of the entries are not used. A better scheme would be

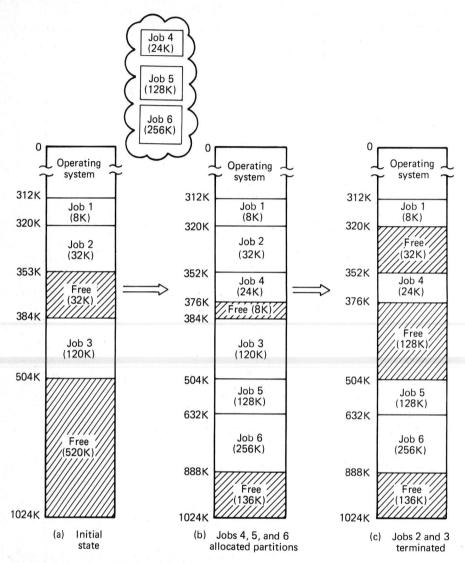

Figure 3-8 Partition allocation and deallocation

to append the table information to each partition or free area. The entries could then be chained together using address pointers. This approach is used in the sample operating system presented in Chapter 7. (The reader may wish to glance at Section 7-8 at this time.)

There are two common variations on the algorithms presented in Figures 3-9 and 3-10. These schemes are called *first fit* and *best fit* (Johnson, 1973; Knuth, 1968) and are outlined in the following sections.

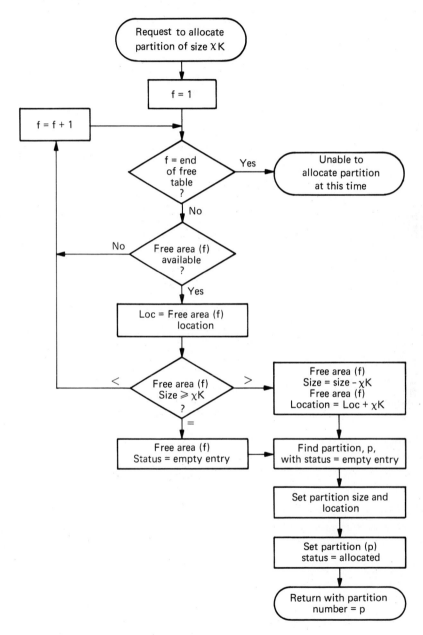

Figure 3-9 Partition allocation algorithm

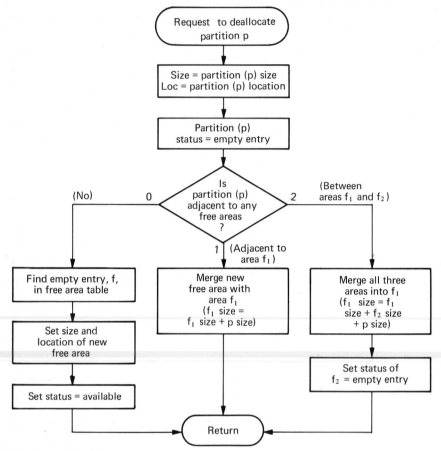

Figure 3-10 Partition deallocation algorithm

3-3.2.3 FIRST FIT PARTITION ALGORITHM

In the first fit algorithm the free table is kept sorted by location (i.e., each consecutive entry corresponds to a free area that starts at a higher memory address). This ordering can be maintained quite easily if the entries are chained together as suggested above. When it is necessary to allocate a partition, we start at the free area at the lowest memory address and keep looking until we find the *first* free area big enough for the partition to *fit*.

There are two major advantages to the first fit technique: (1) The question "Is partition adjacent to any free area?" in the deallocation algorithm (Figure 3-10) can usually be answered by searching only half the table. (Also, the adjacent free area at the lower memory address, if any, is always found first.) (2) The technique essentially favors using the free areas at low memory address whenever possible. This tends to allow a large free area to form at high memory addresses. Thus, when a very large partition size is needed, there is a good chance of finding a large enough free area.

3-3.2.4 BEST FIT PARTITION ALGORITHM

The only major difference between the best fit algorithm and the first fit algorithm is that the free table is kept sorted by size (i.e., the first entry corresponds to the free area with the smallest size). Thus the first free area we find that is large enough for the desired partition is the *best fit* (i.e., it is the free area closest in size but larger than or equal to the desired partition size). The technique described in Section 7-8 is a best fit algorithm.

There are three major advantages to the best fit technique: (1) On the average, the best fit free area can be found by searching only half the table. (2) If there is a free area of exactly the desired size, it will be selected—this is not necessarily true for first fit. (3) If there is no free area of exactly the desired size, the partition is carved out of the smallest possible free area and does not destroy a large free area that may be needed intact to satisfy a later request for a large partition.

Best fit has a major disadvantage in that the free area is usually not exactly the right size and must be split into two pieces. Due to the best fit criteria, the resulting free area is often quite small—so small that it may be almost worthless. In other words, the tendency is toward the development of a large number of very small free areas rather than of one large free area.

3-3.2.5 FRAGMENTATION PROBLEM

Several factors must be considered in selecting a partitioned memory algorithm. Speed and simplicity are among them; however, these are fairly easy to judge. A more important concern is the effect of fragmentation, the development of a large number of separate free areas (i.e., the total free memory is fragmented into small pieces). For example, referring to Figure 3-8c, if a request were made for a partition of size 138K, it would not be possible to allocate such a partition. Although a total of 296K bytes of free memory is available, there is no single free area larger than 136K.

Fragmentation can be overcome by using techniques other than partitioned allocation. We shall discuss two of these techniques, relocation and paging, in Sections 3-4 and 3-5.

The problem of fragmentation in partitioned allocation can be minimized by a careful selection of the specific algorithms to be used. For each of the algorithms discussed—static partition, dynamic first fit, and dynamic best fit—there are situations where it is most appropriate and others where it is least appropriate. By "situation," we usually mean the sequence of partition allocation and deallocation.

For example, a sequence might be:

Job 1 needs 140K

Job 2 needs 16K

Job 3 needs 80K

Job 1 terminates

Job 3 terminates

Job 4 needs 80K

Job 5 needs 128K

and so on

A particular situation is considered "bad" for an algorithm if it cannot satisfy a request immediately (i.e., a partition cannot be allocated until some allocated partitions are deallocated) while other algorithms could satisfy the request. The reader should work through the sequence above for first fit and best fit starting with 256K bytes of free area. Is the sequence a bad situation for either algorithm? Why? The reader is encouraged to develop sequences that are good or bad for each algorithm. Static allocation should be included by choosing static partition sizes.

The choice of a "best" particular algorithm depends upon the expected sequence characteristics (e.g., all jobs are the same size, or jobs are mostly 64K with a few 256K jobs). There are many more algorithms in addition to first fit and best fit; the reader may wish to examine the references (Knuth, 1968; Madnick, 1966; Ross, 1967).

3-3.2.6 MULTIPLE PARTITION ALGORITHM

The use of multiple partition allocation can sometimes decrease the fragmentation problem. A job usually consists of several separate memory segment portions, that is, separate subroutines and data arrays. Each individual portion must be logically contiguous (e.g., $A(i + 1)$ should follow $A(i)$) but the portions themselves need not be contiguous as long as adequate protection facilities are available. Thus a job requiring 100K of memory may actually consist of five 20K portions. This job can be allocated either one 100K partition, or five 20K partitions, or two 40K partitions and one 20K partition, and so on. This approach is called *multiple partition allocation* since more than one partition can be allocated to a job. Furthermore, with this kind of scheme it is possible for a job to request the allocation of additional memory during execution—for loading a special error-handling subroutine, for example—since this new portion does not have to be contiguous with any of the job's current portions. A memory allocation scheme similar to the above was used in the ill-fated IBM OS/360 VMS (Variable Memory System). (This system was never officially announced or delivered to customers; it was replaced by OS/MVT, which uses a dynamic partition scheme.)

Multiple partition allocation gives more flexibility to memory management (i.e., there is more than one way to satisfy the job's needs), but it doesn't eliminate fragmentation. Each free area fragment is, on the average, much smaller, but there are many more of them. In fact, the number of portions is actually a disadvantage.

In the case of a wide diversity in minimal portion sizes for jobs (e.g., an array of 50,000 elements, each of 4 bytes, would require a 200,000 byte contiguous area), it would be unlikely that a free area large enough for these large portions could be found. For example, it is possible for a single job requiring a mere 100K bytes allocated as fifty 2K portions to fragment a million-byte memory so that there would be no free area larger than 20K bytes; this might be smaller than the minimum portion size needed by most other jobs. This example is an extreme case, but such situations have been observed.

In cases where all portions were approximately the same size, multiple partition allocation would become much more attractive. Another variation on this approach, segmentation, is presented in Section 3-7.

3-3.3 Advantages

Partitioned allocation offers three major advantages:

1 It facilitates multiprogramming, hence, more efficient utilization of the processor and I/O devices.

2 It requires no special costly hardware.

3 The algorithms used are simple and easy to implement.

One question that may arise at this point is how much memory a system needs under a partitioned system. That is, how much memory should be bought? The answer depends on at least two factors: (1) average size of job and (2) percent of utilization of processor desired.

It has been observed on several 360/65 and 370/155 installations (Lehman, 1968) that a typical job requires about 128K bytes, and, if run alone, would spend 65 percent of its time in the I/O wait state. The performance model from Section 3-2.2 and Table 3-1 indicates that in order to keep average system I/O wait time below 10 percent, four jobs must be multiprogrammed to reduce the wait to 8 percent and five to decrease it to 3 percent. This suggests that about 640K bytes of memory would be adequate. There must, however, be a reserve to compensate for fragmentation. If we assume that one third of memory is wasted due to fragmentation, then our needs rise to 960K bytes. Thus, about one million bytes would be a good estimate of memory needs. Of course, memory must be even larger to hold the operating system itself. Typically, somewhere in the range of 256K to 512K would be needed for a sophisticated multiprogramming system, but a particular operating system may require less or more.

3-3.4 Disadvantages

There are several disadvantages to partitioned memory that reduce memory utilization:

1 Fragmentation can be a significant problem. It is possible to find job sequences that result in memory utilization well below 10 percent. The extent of this problem depends on the typical job sequences and algorithms used.

2 Even if memory is not fragmented, the single free area may not be large enough for a partition. For example, we have a 512K memory and a job sequence containing a few 300K jobs, but mostly 256K. If a 300K partition is allocated, the remaining 212K bytes are wasted since they are too small for any of the other jobs.

3 It does require more memory than a single contiguous allocation system (as well as a more complex operating system) in order to hold more than one job.

4 As with contiguous allocation, memory may contain information that is never used. Furthermore, a job's partition size is limited to the size of physical memory.

3-4 RELOCATABLE PARTITIONED MEMORY MANAGEMENT

An obvious solution to the fragmentation problem (as previously exemplified in Figure 3-8c) is to periodically combine all free areas into one contiguous area. This can be done by moving the contents of all allocated partitions so that they become contiguous, as illustrated in Figure 3-11. This process is called *compaction* (or *recompaction*, since it is done many times). The term "burping" the memory has also been used to describe this technique.

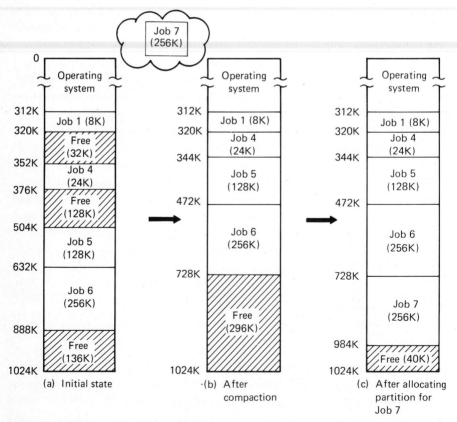

Figure 3-11 Relocatable partition compaction

Although it is conceptually simple, moving a job's partition doesn't guarantee that the job will still run correctly at its new location. This is because there are many location-sensitive items, such as: (1) base registers, (2) memory referencing instructions, (3) parameter lists, and (4) data structures (e.g., lists, chains, etc.) that use address pointers. To operate correctly, all location-sensitive items must be suitably modified. For example, in Figure 3-11, Job 4 is moved from location 352K to 320K. All addresses within Job 4's partition must then be decreased by 32K. This process of adjusting location-sensitive addresses is called *relocation* and is analogous to the operation of a relocating loader (Donovan, 1972; Presser, 1972).

Unfortunately, relocation of a job's partition can be quite difficult. In particular, how does the operating system identify the address pointers that must be altered? If the number 364000 appeared in Job 4's partition, is it an address pointer to be relocated or merely a variable representing the company's accounts payable? Some existing software techniques and conventions could be used (Reiter, 1967), but these are usually either inefficient or highly restrictive.

Another possible solution exists to the relocation problem: we could reload all jobs to be relocated and restart them from the beginning. The relocating loader is capable of handling the initial static relocation. However, besides being extremely crude (i.e., many hours of computation may have to be repeated), this restart may not be feasible if the program has already performed some irreversible actions (e.g., you may be issued two or more payroll checks, especially if your name is at the beginning of the alphabet).

Several hardware techniques have been developed to cope with this relocation problem. Most of them are based on the concept of a *mapped memory*, that is, the address space "seen" by a job is not necessarily the same as the physical memory address used. This concept is sometimes called virtual memory, but we shall reserve that term for a particular class of address mappings to be introduced in Section 3-6. Section 3-4.1 presents some techniques that can be used.

Except for the process of compaction and relocation, the relocatable partition allocation schemes are very similar to the previously discussed partitioned allocation techniques.

3-4.1 Hardware Support

There are two common approaches to the relocation problem, both of which require (or, at least, would benefit from) special hardware support. One approach, based upon the data typing concept, physically records the type of value stored in every memory location. For example, we could add 2 bits to every word to designate the value type (e.g., 00 = integer, 01 = floating point number, 10 = character, 11 = address pointer). These bits are never seen by the typical user program but are automatically set by the hardware. For example, the statement A = B not only sets A to the value of B but also copies the type information. Thus, address pointers may be manipulated and moved around within the program. When it is necessary to compact and relocate, the operating system, using privileged instructions, can exam-ine the type code information and thereby find each address pointer to be modi-fied. Hardware of this type is available on computers such as the Burroughs 5500 and 6700.

Address mapping by means of data typing is possible because the user program has a somewhat special view toward address pointers. These cannot be arbitrarily examined or manipulated; thus the user cannot become location-sensitive because there is no way the program can determine its location (e.g., the question "Am I loaded at location X?" cannot be asked!).

The data typing approach has several disadvantages. It requires extra bits on every word, compaction may be slow since the type bits on every word must be examined, and it is incompatible with the general structure of most contemporary computers (in particular, the System/370).

Another common hardware solution uses dynamic relocation by means of base-bounds relocation registers. This technique is used on several computers, such as the DEC PDP-10, the Univac 1108, and the Honeywell 6000 series. Two special privileged registers, the *base relocation register* and the *bounds register*, are accessi-ble only by the operating system. On every memory reference, the content of the base relocation register is automatically added to the effective address. (The effec-tive address is the final reference address computed by the processor; this includes any index or 370-type base register adjustments.)

At the left of Figure 3-12a is the address space of Job 4 (from Figure 3-11a), which is separated from the physical location of its partition on the right. Before relocation, it is obvious that the instruction LOAD 1,370248 (Load Register 1 from Location 370248) at 360800 will load the value 015571 into register 1. (For ease of reading, we will use direct effective addresses in instructions rather than the 370 base plus displacement notation.)

After relocation, the LOAD instruction of Figure 3-12b is at location 328032. Since none of the instructions or registers have been changed, the effective address for the data to be loaded is still 370248 even though the intended data value has been moved to 337480. To produce correct results, the operating system must set the relocation register to −32768 (320K − 352K = −32K). When the instruction LOAD 1,370248 is encountered, −32768 is automatically added to the effective address, 370248, to determine the actual physical memory location to be accessed −in this case, 370248 − 32768 = 337480. Thus the value 015571 is loaded into register 1 as intended. Note that nothing within the job's address space has been changed, nor is the program aware of its actual physical memory location. Every instruction, LOAD, ADD, BRANCH, and so on, will behave as if the partition were at 352K, even though it has been moved to 320K.

Since this relocation adjustment is done automatically as each instruction is executed, it is called *dynamic relocation*.

Protection could be implemented by using techniques such as the 370 locks and keys, but more commonly a bounds register is set to the maximum address in the

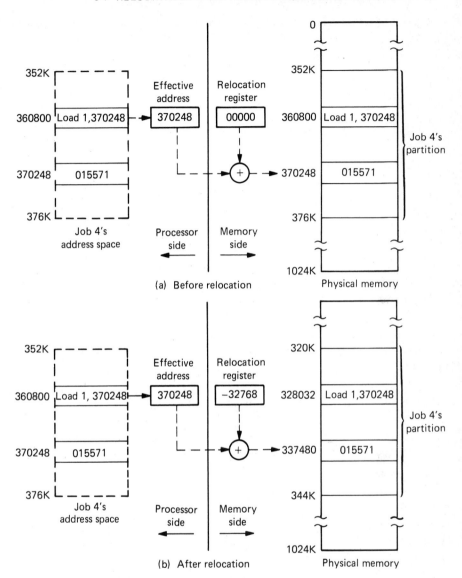

Figure 3-12 Use of relocation register

job's address space (376K in our example above). If the job attempts to access any location beyond the address specified in the bounds register, a protection interrupt will occur.

3-4.2 Software Algorithm

Since the starting point of a job's address space is unrelated to the physical location of the partition, it is useful to start the address space at location 0. This means that each job "thinks" that it is loaded at location 0 in memory. Thus the addresses within Job 4 would be initially set up as in Figure 3-13, no matter where its initial partition is located. If this software convention is used, all relocation register values will be positive. Furthermore, protection is accomplished, since the hardware will detect any effective address that is negative or exceeds the value of the bounds register.

Although, logically, there should be a separate pair of base and bounds registers for each partition, this is not a necessary or an economical approach. Prior to starting a job running, a single pair of registers are set to the base and bounds for that job's partition. When the job must wait during multiprogramming, the contents of these registers are saved (along with other status information, such as the PSW) so that they can be reloaded when the job is restarted.

The partition management algorithms raise basically the same concerns as those discussed in Section 3-3. One major additional concern is the question "When should compaction be done?" Two alternatives suggest themselves. The first is to compact immediately after a partition is deallocated so that there would always be only one contiguous free area—and no fragmentation. The free area table maintenance and partition allocation would then become very easy. However, compaction can be a time-consuming operation. For example, if we could move partitions only at a rate of 1,000,000 bytes per second (using a facility such as the 370 MVC or MVCL instructions), it would take about half a second to compact a small deallocated partition in the middle of a 1024K-byte memory.

The second alternative would be to operate exactly as with the nonrelocatable partition algorithms described in Section 3-3, but to compact memory whenever

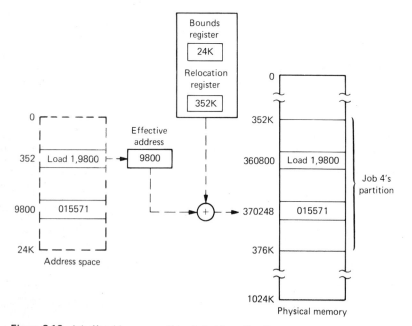

Figure 3-13 Job 4's address space if loaded at Location 0

a large enough free area was not available. Compaction would occur much less frequently than in the immediate compaction scheme above, but the table maintenance would be much more complex. Figure 3-14 depicts the overall flow of such an allocation algorithm.

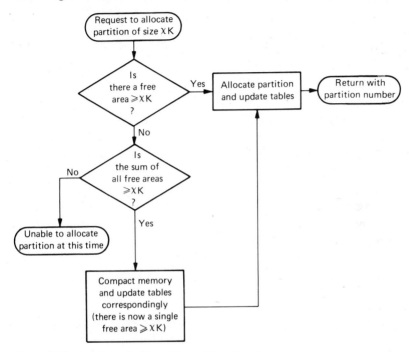

Figure 3-14   Overview of relocatable partition allocation

3-4.3 Advantages

The relocatable partition scheme eliminates fragmentation and thus makes it possible to allocate more partitions. This allows for a higher degree of multiprogramming, which results in increased memory and processor utilization.

3-4.4 Disadvantages

Several potential disadvantages must be considered:

1 Relocation hardware increases the cost of the computer and may slow down the speed (although usually only slightly).

2 Compaction time may be substantial.

3 Some memory will still be unused because even though it is compacted, the amount of free area may be less than the needed partition size. This wasted space is approximately equal to one-half the average job partition size.

4 As with partitioned allocation, memory may contain information that is never used. Furthermore, a job's partition size is limited to the size of physical memory.

3-5 PAGED MEMORY MANAGEMENT

The relocatable partitioned allocation approach represented one solution to the fragmentation problem through the use of address mapping to allow the individual free areas to be coalesced into one contiguous free area. This was necessary because we required that a partition be a contiguous area. We were able to relax the contiguity requirement in the multiple partition algorithm variation, but this did not always decrease fragmentation. Another way to avoid the contiguity requirement is through paged memory management.

For paged memory management each job's address space is divided into equal pieces, called *pages*, and, likewise, physical memory is divided into pieces of the same size, called *blocks*. Then, by providing a suitable hardware mapping facility, any page can be placed into any block. The pages remain logically contiguous (i.e., to the user program) but the corresponding blocks are not necessarily contiguous. As in the relocatable partitioned scheme, the user programs are unaffected by the mapping because it has no visible effect upon the address space.

For the hardware to perform the mapping from address space to physical memory, there must be a separate register for each page; these registers are often called *page maps* or Page Map Tables (PMTs). They may be either special hardware registers or a reserved section of memory.

Since each page can be separately relocated, there is no need for a job's partition to be completely contiguous in memory; only locations in a single page must be contiguous. Obviously, the choice of page size has a substantial effect on the usefulness of this scheme. If the page size is too large, it becomes comparable to the size of the job's partition, and the scheme is then essentially one of relocatable partition. If the page size is too small, it is necessary to have many page map registers, which greatly increases the cost of the computer system. As a result of these and other concerns, most paging systems use a page size of from 1K to 4K bytes.

A simple example, using a 1000-byte page size, is shown in Figure 3-15. Job 2, which has an address space of 3000 bytes, is divided into three pages. The page table associated with Job 2 indicates the location of its pages. In this case, page 0 is in block 2, page 1 is in block 4, and page 2 is in block 7. The LOAD 1,2108 instruction at location 0518 (page 0, byte 518) in Job 2's address space is actually stored at physical location 2518 (block 2, byte 518). Likewise, the data 015571 logically located at 2108 is stored at physical memory location 7108.

The paged memory management approach solves the fragmentation problem without physically moving partitions. For example, in Figure 3-15 there are 2000 bytes of available memory, but they are not contiguous. If there were a fourth job requiring 2000 bytes, we could compact memory, as is done with relocatable partitions, to produce a single 2000-byte free area. Alternatively, we can assign Job 4's two pages to the available blocks, such as page 0 = block 3 and page 1 = block 9. If the PMT is set correspondingly, the address space will still appear contiguous without making it necessary to physically move any partitions. A scheme of this type is

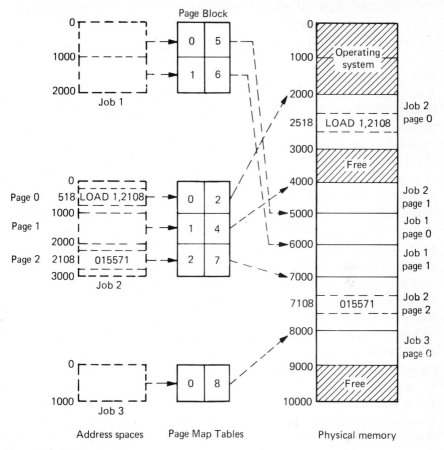

Figure 3-15 Page mapped memory

used in several contemporary computers, for example, the XDS 940, XDS Sigma 7, and CDC 3300.

The four functions of memory management are performed as follows:

1 Keeping track of status—accomplished through two sets of tables:

    a Page Map Tables—one per address space, each containing one entry for each page.

    b Memory Block Tables—one in system, containing one entry for each memory block with information on the use of that block (e.g., allocated or available).

2 Determining who gets memory—this is largely decided by the job scheduler. Memory may be assigned to the user simply by giving him the first set of free blocks found.

3 Allocation—all pages of the job must be loaded into assigned blocks and appropriate entries made in the Page Map Table and Memory Block Table.

4 Deallocation—when the job is done, blocks must be returned to free status by adjusting entries in block table.

3-5.1 Hardware Support

A hardware mechanism is needed to perform the mapping from each instruction's effective address to the appropriate physical memory location, functioning in a manner analogous to the relocation register hardware. There must be a separate "register" for each page. These may be actual high-speed registers or a special area of physical memory.

3-5.1.1 HIGH-SPEED PAGE MAP REGISTERS

If one million bytes of memory were available, and the block size were 4000 bytes, up to 250 pages would have to be mapped. But 250 high-speed registers would be quite expensive; because of the high cost, this technique is seldom used. Nevertheless, the high-speed registers scheme can be made more attractive in several ways. First, if each job's address space is limited to a relatively small size, such as 100K bytes, no more than 25 registers will ever be needed for each job's address space. Second, since only one job is running at a time, only one set of hardware page mapping registers will be needed. These registers must be saved and reset whenever the processor is switched to a new job because of multiprogramming. This technique is used on the XDS 940.

3-5.1.2 PAGE MAP TABLES

For large address spaces, and to eliminate the overhead of continually resetting the page mapping registers, the use of Page Map Tables in physical memory has become popular. The following hardware description is a slightly simplified version of the Dynamic Address Translation (DAT) facility—another name for page mapping—available on the IBM System/370.

To simplify address mapping, the page size is usually chosen to be a power of two, e.g., 1024 (1K) bytes, 2048 (2K) bytes, or 4096 (4K) bytes. In this way, if the page size is 4K bytes on the 370, the page number is precisely bits 8 through 19 of the effective address (see Figure 3-16). The effective address is 24 bits long, as generated by the processor. The DAT mechanism automatically separates the effective address into two parts: bits 8 through 19 become the 12-bit page number and bits 20 through 31 become the 12-bit byte offset within the page. Using the PMT, the page number is replaced by the block number to produce the resultant physical memory address to be used.

If the Page Map Table is to be stored in main memory, the hardware must know the location. We could assign a specific location, as done for the "old" and "new" PSWs, CAW, CSW, etc. This would, however, necessitate changing the entire table every time the processor switched jobs. Instead, the PMT is allowed to be stored

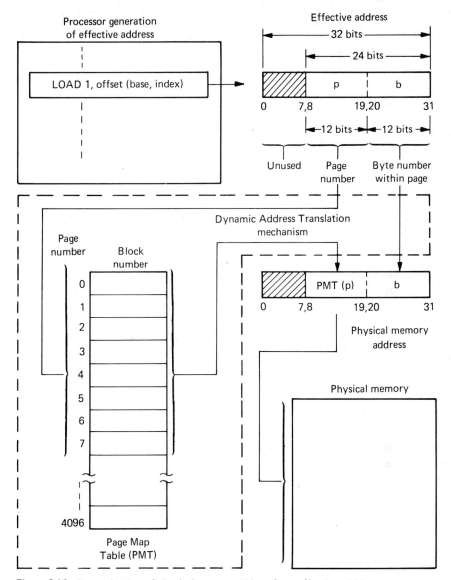

Figure 3-16 Determination of physical memory address from effective address

at any location in memory, the specific location used being indicated by the contents of a special Page Map Table Address Register (PMTAR). When the processor is switched to a new job, only the PMTAR has to be changed to indicate the location of the new job's PMT.

Portions of the simple example of Figure 3-15 are redrawn in Figure 3-17 to indicate the relationships between the pages, the blocks, the PMTAR, and the PMTs. The page size used in this diagram is 4096 (4K) bytes. There are various ways to encode the PMT entries. The block number stored in each entry must be 12 bits on the 370; this 12-bit number can be stored in a 16-bit halfword (2 bytes) as follows:

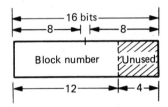

A job's address space can be up to 16 million bytes (4096 4K pages) on the 370. If each job's Page Map Table were 4096 entries long, each entry being 2 bytes, it would require 8192 bytes. Since most jobs use 256K bytes (64 pages) or less, we do not want to use a 8192-byte Page Map Table to store a mere 128 bytes (64 PMT entries).

This problem is remedied by making the tables only as long as needed, the length of the table being stored as part of the Page Map Table Address Register, as shown in Figure 3-17. This length acts like the bounds register discussed in Section 3-4.1 by indicating the maximum length of the job's address space.

3-5.1.3 HYBRID PAGE MAP TABLES

If the dynamic address translation hardware were implemented by using PMTs in memory exactly as described in the preceding section, the computer would run at about half its normal speed (i.e., incurring 100 percent overhead). Recall that every address reference to memory must be mapped. If the PMTs are stored in main memory, then every reference to memory will really require two accesses—one to map the page number to block number and another to actually access the desired data or instruction.

A hybrid scheme, combining aspects of the high-speed mapping registers and the PMTs, is often used to overcome this speed problem. A small number (e.g., 16) of special high-speed registers are used to hold portions of the PMTs. Whenever possible, these registers are used to dispense with accessing the PMT in memory. Entries from the PMT are loaded into these registers automatically by the hardware. These special registers and associated hardware to manage them are often called an *associative memory* or a *table look-aside buffer*. This mechanism can usually reduce the mapping overhead from 100 percent to less than 10 percent. Since the associative memory is handled automatically by the hardware, its existence is usually invisible

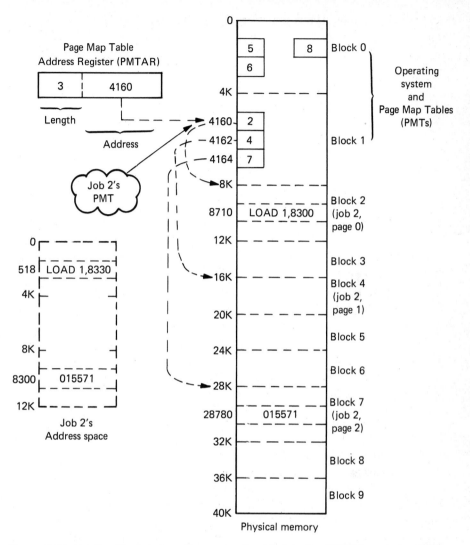

Figure 3-17 Relationship between the pages, the blocks, the PMTAR, and the PMTs

to the operating system as well as to the user jobs. The operating system is aware only of the PMTs. Some of the concepts underlying the use of such a two-level table will be discussed in Sections 3-6 and 3-10.3.

3-5.2 Software Algorithm

There are three basic table types that must be managed by the operating system software: the *Job Table* (JT), the *Memory Block Table* (MBT), and the PMTs. Each job has a separate entry in the Job Table indicating the location and length of its

PMT as well as other status information. The Memory Block Table indicates the status of each memory block—either allocated or available. Figure 3-18 illustrates the tables that may be used for the situation depicted in Figures 3-15 and 3-17.

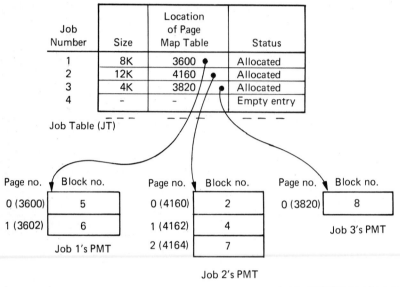

Job Number	Size	Location of Page Map Table	Status
1	8K	3600	Allocated
2	12K	4160	Allocated
3	4K	3820	Allocated
4	–	–	Empty entry

Job Table (JT)

Page no.	Block no.
0 (3600)	5
1 (3602)	6

Job 1's PMT

Page no.	Block no.
0 (4160)	2
1 (4162)	4
2 (4164)	7

Job 2's PMT

Page no.	Block no.
0 (3820)	8

Job 3's PMT

Page Map Tables (PMTs)

Block no.	Status
0	Operating system
1	Operating system
2	Job 2
3	Available
4	Job 2
5	Job 1
6	Job 1
7	Job 2
8	Job 3
9	Available

Memory Block Table (MBT)

Figure 3-18 Tables used by paged memory allocation software

3-5.2.1 ADDRESS SPACE ALLOCATION

A simple algorithm for address space allocation is presented in Figure 3-19. A similar algorithm, roughly the reverse, is used to deallocate an address space. The only nonobvious step is Allocate a Page Map Table with N Entries. Where do we get such a table? One solution is to reserve some space in the operating system area for PMTs. Individual PMTs can be allocated from this area by using techniques similar to partitioned memory management where each PMT is treated as a partition. When a job terminates, its PMT partition can be deallocated.

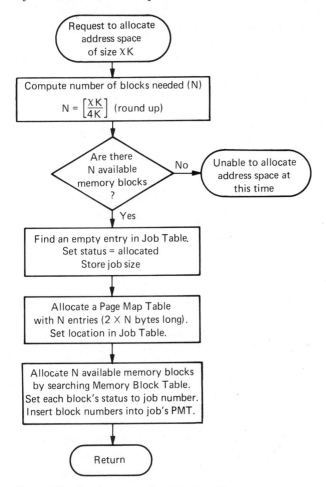

Figure 3-19 Paged memory allocation algorithm

3-5.2.2 OVERLAPPING ADDRESS SPACE

As in Relocatable Partitioned Memory Management, each job's address space is assumed to be independent of and separate from the other jobs. This provides an effective protection mechanism since it is impossible for one job to access the memory containing the address space of any other job on the operating system. (Simple lock and key protection may still be necessary since the I/O channels do not usually contain address mapping hardware.)

It is sometimes desirable to have the address spaces overlap partially in order to make some subroutines and/or data areas accessible to all jobs. For example, there may be an area in the operating system where the current date is stored for reference. This overlapping can be accomplished as shown in Figure 3-20. All jobs are loaded starting at 8K in their address spaces; locations 0 to 8K are part of the operating system's address space. If address spaces overlap, it is necessary to provide additional protection in addition to the address mapping. This can be accomplished by the lock and key mechanism. Alternatively, the mapping hardware could be extended so that some of the unused bits in each page table entry could be used to indicate whether reading and/or writing are permitted in that page.

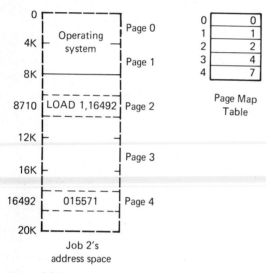

Figure 3-20 Overlapping address spaces (see Figure 3-17)

3-5.3 Advantages

The paged memory scheme eliminates fragmentation and thus makes it possible to accommodate the address spaces for more jobs simultaneously. This allows for a higher degree of multiprogramming, which results in increased memory and processor utilization. The compaction overhead required for the relocatable partition scheme is also eliminated.

3-5.4 Disadvantages

Several potential disadvantages must be considered:

1 The page address mapping hardware usually increases the cost of the computer and at the same time slows down the processor.

2 Memory must be used to store the various tables, principally the PMT. Processor

time (overhead) must be expended to maintain and update these tables.

3 Even though fragmentation is eliminated, a similar phenomenon, called *internal fragmentation* or *page breakage*, does occur. Jobs are assigned whole blocks of memory. If a job requires 5K bytes and the block size is 4K, two blocks must be allocated (i.e., 8K is allocated but only 5K was needed). On the average, half a page is wasted for each job. A tradeoff must be made between cutting wastage due to page breakage, which favors small pages, and reducing the number of entries in the Page Map Tables, which favor large pages. Knowledge of the average job's size is important in resolving this conflict.

4 Some memory will still be unused if the number of available blocks is not sufficient for the address spaces of the jobs to be run. For example, if two blocks totaling 8K bytes are available, they cannot be used if the minimum job size to be run is over 8K bytes. This wasted space, exclusive of page breakage, is approximately equal to one-half the average job's address space.

5 Finally, as in the previous memory management techniques, memory will often contain information that is seldom used. Furthermore, a job's address space is limited to the size of physical memory.

3-6 DEMAND-PAGED MEMORY MANAGEMENT

In all the previous schemes a job could not be run until there was sufficient available memory to load its entire address space. This restriction often resulted in unused free areas even though there were jobs waiting to be loaded and run. Furthermore, the pressure on programmers to keep their job's address space small was often counterproductive. Several studies have shown that if a job must be designed to operate in a constrained address space size, the cost of programming increases rapidly (Boehm, 1973).

These problems could be resolved by using extremely large main memories. At present this approach, although simple, is not usually economically feasible. Another approach is to use the operating system to produce the illusion of an extremely large memory. Since this large memory is merely an illusion, it is called *virtual memory* (Denning, 1970). These are two major virtual memory techniques: demand-paged memory management and segmented memory management. Segmented memory management will be discussed in Section 3-7.

Whereas the preceding memory management techniques attempted to approximate 100 percent memory utilization, demand-paged memory management can logically attain a utilization greater than 100 percent! That is, the sum of all the address spaces of the jobs being multiprogrammed may exceed the size of physical memory. This feat is accomplished by removing the requirement that a job's entire address space be in main memory at one time; instead only portions of it have to be loaded.

Consider Figure 3-15 where three jobs are loaded in memory with two 1000-byte blocks unused. How could we handle a fourth job that requires 4000 bytes (i.e., it needs four blocks but only two are available)? We could do as indicated in Figure 3-21, that is, load only two of Job 4's pages. Job 4 would then run correctly as long as it only references information in these two pages (e.g., the LOAD 1,1120 instruction at location 100 in Job 4's address space would work correctly).

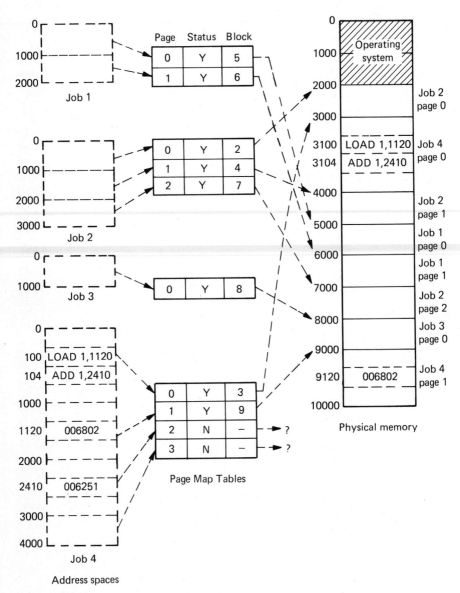

Figure 3-21 Demand-paged-mapped memory

Is it reasonable to try to run a job without loading its entire address space? Yes, because most programs use only a small amount of their entire address space during any particular run of the job. There are many reasons for this, such as:

1 User-written error-handling routines are used only when an error occurs in the data or computation (hopefully a rare event).

2 Certain options of the programs are mutually exclusive or not requested on every run (e.g., sort the payroll by name or by employee number).

3 Many tables are assigned a fixed amount of address space even though only a small amount of the table is actually used (e.g., if a symbol table for an assembler is set to handle 1,000 symbols and only 100 symbols are used in a particular run, 90 percent of the table is unused).

4 Many routines are commonly used at mutually exclusive times during a run (e.g., the input phase routines, the computation phase routines, and, finally, the output phase routines). Even if all these routines are used, they do not have to be in physical memory at the same time.

Two key questions remain to be answered: What do we do if a job references an area of address space not in physical memory? How do we decide which pages to keep in memory? Notice in Figure 3-21 that the ADD 1,2410 instruction at location 104 in Job 4 references a page that is not in memory. To handle this case, we extend the PMT hardware to include a status bit (i.e., Y = yes, reference is okay; N = no, reference is impossible).

If the address mapping hardware encounters a page table entry with status = N, it generates a *page interrupt*. Note that this is different from a protection interrupt, in that it is not a user program error. The operating system must process this interrupt by loading the required page and adjusting the page table entries correspondingly. The instruction can then be restarted. We say this page was "loaded on demand" (i.e., page 2 of Job 4's address was loaded because the page interrupt indicated that the job needed—demanded—the page). Thus, this scheme is called *demand-paged memory management*. In particular, when a job is initially scheduled for execution, usually only its first page is actually loaded. All other pages needed by the job are subsequently loaded on demand. This guarantees that an unnecessary page is not loaded.

Where are these pages loaded from when demanded? A copy of the job's entire address space is stored on a secondary storage device (e.g., magnetic disk or drum). When a page is needed in main memory, it is read from the secondary storage device.

The demand-paged memory management technique is very attractive because it does not constrain the address spaces to the size of physical memory. But there are some complications. In Figure 3-21 when we get to instruction ADD 1,2410 at location 104, page 2 must be loaded into physical memory for Job 4. Since all the memory blocks are now in use, where can page 2 be placed? This requires a technique called variously *page swapping, page removal, page replacement, page turning,* or *page cannibalizing.*

Once memory has become filled with pages it is possible to load another page only by first removing one of the pages presently in memory. The *replaced* page is copied back onto the secondary storage device before the new page is loaded (i.e., the two pages *swap* places between memory and secondary storage). How do we decide which page to *remove* from memory? Replacement algorithms have been the subject of considerable research (Belady, 1966; Coffman, 1968; Denning, 1970, 1972; Gustavson, 1968; and Randell, 1968). (See Section 3-6.2.)

Removing a page from memory and then immediately needing it again due to a page fault referencing that page would be very unfortunate. The phenomenon of excessively moving pages back and forth between memory and secondary storage has been called *thrashing* since it consumes a lot of the computer's energy but accomplishes very little useful results. Thrashing and its avoidance have received considerable research attention (Denning, 1968, 1970). In order to assist the operating system software in making these page replacement decisions, the hardware usually maintains some information on page usage. An example of such information is presented in Section 3-6.1, which deals with hardware support.

Demand paging is used in many contemporary operating systems, such as VS/1, VS/2, and VM/370 on the IBM System/370, MULTICS on the Honeywell 6180, and VMOS on the UNIVAC Series 70/46.

The four functions of memory management become both more complex and more flexible in a paged memory environment:

1 Keeping track of status—this is accomplished through three sets of tables:
   a Page Map Tables—one per address space
   b Memory Block Tables—one in system
   c File Map Tables—one per address space
2 The policy of who gets memory and when—partially determined by the job scheduler, but, on a dynamic basis, it is also determined by the demand page interrupts.
3 Allocation—when a block must be allocated, an available block must be found and the status of the block altered.
4 Deallocation—if it is not possible to find an available block for allocation, one of the allocated memory blocks must be deallocated and reassigned. When a job terminates, all the blocks it was using become available.

3-6.1 Hardware Support

The address mapping hardware via Page Map Tables, as described in Section 3-5, is needed for demand paging. Three key additions to the hardware are required.

1 A status bit in the Page Map Table to indicate whether the page is in main memory or secondary storage.

2 Interrupt action to transfer control to the operating system if the job attempts to access a page not in main memory

3 Record of individual page usage to assist the operating system in determining which page to remove, if necessary.

These requirements are met on the IBM System/370 (when operating in Extended Control Mode—i.e., when address translation is turned "on") as follows.[1] The PMT entry described earlier in Section 3-5.1.2 is altered so that one of the previously "unused" bits is used to indicate whether to generate an interrupt if that entry is accessed (I = 1 means generate interrupt).

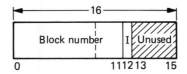

If a *page interrupt condition* (also called *page exception interrupt* or *page fault*) is encountered, a program interrupt with code = 17 occurs. Furthermore, the logical address that was referenced is stored in the word at location 144 in memory. The operating system can determine from this word which page needs to be loaded.

There are 2 additional bits associated with each block of memory. (These 2 bits are actually stored as part of the lock register on each 2K memory block.) The *reference bit* is automatically set to 1 whenever any location in that block is referenced (i.e., load, store, or execute). The *change bit* is set to 1 whenever any location in the block is changed (i.e., stored into). The operating system software can reset these bits using the Set Storage Key privileged instruction. On other hardware implementations, such as the Honeywell 6180, these bits are stored in the PMT entry.

Other facilities may be provided by the hardware to assist the operating system. For example, the operating system usually runs in *absolute mode* or *basic control mode* (i.e., like a 360 without dynamic address mapping). The address mapping can be selectively turned on by instructions such as Load Real Address (LRA), which translates a virtual address into its corresponding physical memory address.

---

[1] The Extended Control Mode is in effect when the "E" bit in the PSW (bit 12) is set to 1. The System/370 provides hardware support for either 2K or 4K pages. The mode of operation (2K or 4K) is determined by the setting of bits 8 and 9 of control register 0. In this chapter only the 4K mode is described.

If the page is not in memory, a specific condition code is set rather than an interrupt being generated. This facility is important for handling input/output requests, as explained in the next section.

3-6.2 Software Algorithm

Demand-paged memory management provides tremendous flexibility for the operating system and, consequently, has received considerable attention. In this section we can discuss some of the major algorithms only; the reader is directed to the references for more extensive coverage.

3-6.2.1 FILE MAP REQUIREMENT

Demand-paged memory management must interact with information management to access and store copies of the job's address spaces on secondary storage (information management is discussed in Chapter 6). We will assume that each page has a unique secondary storage address, called its *file address*. This address logically is part of each PMT entry, such as

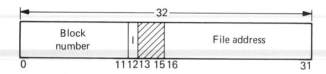

if the file address were 16 bits long. Although the Page Map Table is tied directly to the address mapping hardware, the format of the file address (and related status information) is handled solely by the software, and may be variable. Thus, the file information is usually stored in a separate table called the File Map Table, which is not used by the hardware.

The relationship of the File Map Table to the Page Map Table and the Memory Block Table is illustrated in Figure 3-22. Recall that these tables all reside as part of the operating system area in main memory and that there are separate Page Map and File Map Tables for each address space. In this diagram Job 2 has only two of its three pages in main memory. A copy of all three pages is available on a secondary storage device.

3-6.2.2 OVERVIEW OF PAGE INTERRUPT PROCESSING

In the previous memory management schemes, allocation of memory was completely static. That is, memory was allocated or rearranged only when a job started or terminated. In demand paging, it is necessary to allocate and deallocate memory during the job's execution. The memory management routines are invoked by means of the page interrupt.

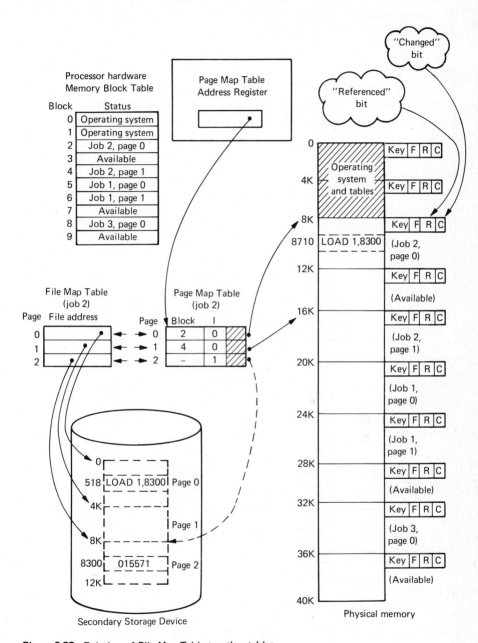

Figure 3-22 Relation of File Map Table to other tables

In demand paging there is very close interaction between the hardware and software, which is simply illustrated in Figure 3-23. The first part of this flowchart, the most frequently executed section, is implemented as part of the address mapping hardware. The second part is implemented as an interrupt handler routine within

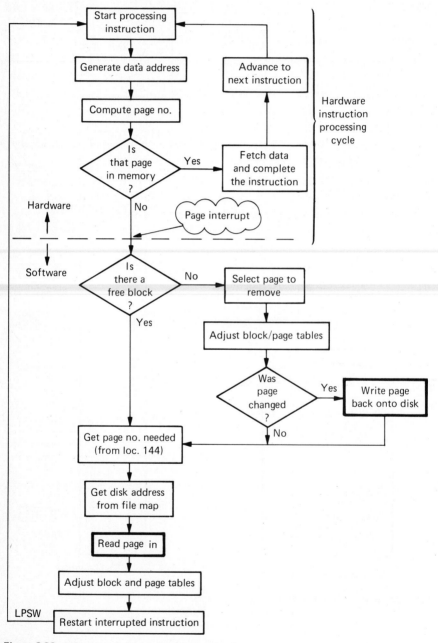

Figure 3-23 Interaction between hardware and software

the operating system. In some experimental research systems, much more of this flowchart has been incorporated into the hardware (Liskov, 1972). In future systems, the operating system will be tied even more closely to the hardware.

In the flowchart of Figure 3-23, the question "Is that page in memory?" is answered by the status of the page interrupt bit in the PMT entry (i.e., 0 means "yes," 1 means "no"). Recall that the same type of checking must be done for all data addresses in an instruction (e.g., the Move Characters instruction references two data areas) and for the instruction itself. In fact, on the System/370 it is possible to encounter up to eight page interrupts while processing one instruction!

Figure 3-24 illustrates this point. The Move Characters (MVC) instruction at location 12286 actually occupies 4 bytes (12286, 12287, 12288, and 12289). Half the instruction is in page 2, the other half in page 3. Both pages must be in memory at the same time. Furthermore, the data fields to be moved, A and B, likewise cross two pages each. Thus, all six pages must be in memory. If the MVC instruction is requested by means of an Execute (EX) instruction, as shown at location 4094, two more pages will be needed in memory. If none of these pages happened to be in memory, eight page interrupts would, in fact, be experienced. In other situations, such as the System/370 Move Characters Long (MVCL), and on other computers with multilevel indirect addressing an essentially unlimited number of page interrupts could occur.

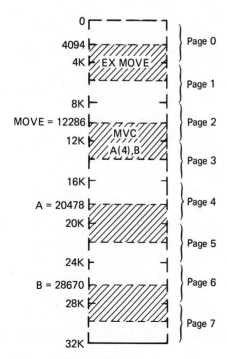

Figure 3-24 Situation that can result in eight page interrupts

Returning to the flowchart of Figure 3-23, the question "Is there a free page?" is answered by examining the Memory Block Table for an available block. If a block is available, the requested page number is extracted from the interrupt information word at 144. The secondary storage address for that page is obtained from the File Map Table. After the page has been copied into memory, the Page Map and Memory Block Tables must be adjusted. The instruction can then be restarted. If there is no available block, it is necessary to remove a page from memory. After selecting the page, its "changed" bit is examined. If it has not been changed, the copy of the page on secondary storage must still be identical—thus, there is no need to write the page back onto secondary storage. Otherwise, the page is written out and the memory block is available for use.

Processing a page interrupt as described above may require one or two input/output operations for reading or writing pages (called *page I/O's*). In order to minimize processor idle time waiting for page I/O completion, multiprogramming is frequently used just as for I/O operations generated explicitly from the user's job. The use of multiprogramming does, however, tend to complicate the record keeping.

As an example, there must be another memory block status in addition to allocated and available. This new status is called *in transit*. Consider the situation where a page is being loaded into memory for Job 1 and the processor is assigned to Job 2. Job 2 immediately experiences a page interrupt and needs a memory block. If Job 1's block is marked "allocated," the page interrupt handler may try to remove it—but it isn't even fully loaded yet! If it had been marked "available," it might be assigned to Job 2, in which case pages for Job 1 and Job 2 would be loaded into the same block! "In transit" means that the block should not be considered for assignment at this time. When the page I/O is completed, the status can be changed to allocated or available, as appropriate.

In many systems the frequency of page I/O can become very high. In these cases very high-speed secondary storage devices and sophisticated device management techniques are employed. These topics are discussed in Chapter 5.

3-6.2.3 PAGE REMOVAL ALGORITHMS

In the flowchart of Figure 3-23, the only nonobvious step is "select page to remove." How is this selection done? It could be done quite simply by always removing the page occupying memory block 3 (i.e., the first block after the operating system area). But this scheme, though simple, is also dangerous. In the situation of Figure 3-24, where eight page interrupts are encountered in one instruction, each page interrupt would remove the page just loaded and we would never get all eight pages loaded. Thus, the instruction would never get executed. This is an extreme case of the thrashing phenomenon mentioned earlier.

What is the best page to remove? Intuitively, it is the page that will never be needed again or, at least, not for a long time. Such algorithms, called MIN (Belady, 1969) or OPT (Mattson, 1970), have been studied. Unfortunately, they require advance knowledge of future page interrupts. (This is similar to the stock market algorithm for choosing which stock to buy—clearly, it is the one that is going to rise the highest). Thus, MIN and OPT are primarily of theoretical value. They can be used to serve as a measure of the effectiveness of realizable algorithms (i.e., algorithms that do not require future knowledge).

There are many schemes for replacement algorithms. The replacement aspect of paging is an area in which there exists relevant theoretical work. We will discuss the following topics:

1 FIFO (First in-First Out)
2 LRU (Least Recently Used)
3 Tuple-coupling

The basic idea behind replacement, and the problems involved, can be illustrated by an analogy. Let's say you are in charge of a supermarket. At present all your shelves are full. A new product is introduced, and you wish to sell it. Where do you put it? Obviously, you must replace a product already on your shelf. The question is: Which one? Can you devise an algorithm to give your shop clerk?

One algorithm would be to replace the product that has been on your shelves the longest (it has had its chance, and is now probably out of date). This algorithm would correspond to a FIFO algorithm. Is FIFO a good algorithm for your stock clerk? Probably not, as the products that are replaced would be those that you have been selling for 50 years, such as sugar or tea.

A better algorithm might be for your clerk to go around blowing the dust off the products—and then replace the product with the most dust on it, i.e., the product that is not selling, not being accessed. This corresponds to an LRU algorithm.

A measure of the effectiveness of your replacement algorithm is how often you had to go to your cellar to fetch a product you had replaced. If your replacement algorithm is a good one, you would not have to go very often.

What would happen to the effectiveness of your page algorithm (number of "fetches" to your cellar) if you were to replace only half of a product (reduce the page size by half)? That is, you don't replace all the JELL-O but only the raspberry, orange, and lemon flavors. This may result in a tremendous reduction of page fetches as compared to those that would be incurred by replacing all of a product. Such reductions would, however, occur only if you replaced that portion of the product that was accessed very infrequently. They would not take place if raspberry, orange, and lemon were the only flavors you sold. How many more fetches could result from replacing all the JELL-O as compared to replacing only half? Intuitively, you may think the number of fetches could at most double. It has, however, been proven that the number could be even more than double (Madnick, 1973).

Is there a way to limit the worst case? It can be done by adding a property to the paging algorithm used. This property is called *tuple coupling*, which assures that the fetches under the worst case never go up by more than a factor of two over the fetches that would have been incurred if page size had not been halved.

Good luck with your supermarket. Now let's get back to computers.

3-6.2.4 MODEL OF PAGE REMOVAL PERFORMANCE AND PROGRAM BEHAVIOR

In order to evaluate the effectiveness of alternate page removal algorithms, it is necessary to use a performance model. We will describe a simple but useful model. Since the effectiveness of a page removal algorithm depends on the particular program being run, we must also examine *program behavior*.

We abstract the program under consideration first into an execution trace and then into an address trace, and, finally, into a page trace (see Figure 3-25). An *execution trace* is a list of the exact instructions executed, in order, for the program. An *address trace* lists the addresses needed for each instruction's execution. A *page trace* lists the corresponding pages needed for the address trace. Note that the page trace is sufficient to characterize a program's execution. If the ADD 1,2410 instruction of Figure 3-25 were changed to a SUB 1,2464, pages 0 and 2 would still be needed—only page requests are important, not the specific instructions.

EXECUTION TRACE			ADDRESS TRACE	PAGE TRACE (page size = 1000 bytes)
100	LOAD	1,1120	100	0
			1120	1
104	ADD	1,2410	104	0
			2410	2
108	STORE	1,1124	108	0
			1124	1
112	MOVE	1140(4),	112	0
		3998	1140	1
			3998	3,4 $\begin{bmatrix} 3998, 3999, \\ 4000, 4001 \end{bmatrix}$
116	HALT		112	0

Figure 3-25 Execution, address, and page traces

Our simple performance model uses three parameters: (1) a page trace, P; (2) a specific memory size, M; and (3) a replacement algorithm, R. A sample analysis, using FIFO replacement, is shown in Figure 3-26. The page trace, P, is displayed

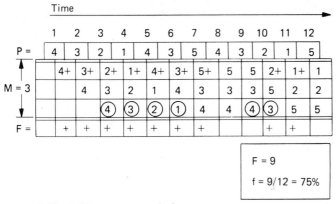

Figure 3-26 FIFO page trace analysis

along the top. In this example, the memory size is only three blocks, M = 3. Whenever a page is loaded into memory, the page number is added to the list of pages in memory and a mark is made in row F. The columns of M indicate the pages in memory at each instance of time.

Whenever there is a page reference for which the page needed is not in memory, that event is called a *page fetch*, or *page failure*, situation. For example, the third page reference is for page 2, but only pages 3 and 4 are in memory—thus, a page fetch is required. Whenever the page required is in memory, such as in the eighth page reference in Figure 3-26 (page 4 needed; pages 5, 3, and 4 are in memory), that event is called a page success and no page loading is necessary.

Performance is usually measured in terms of the *success function*, S, or the *failure function*, F, the number of successes or failures, respectively. If $|P|$ is the number of page references in the page trace, then $S + F = |P|$. Another useful measure of performance is the success frequency function, $s = \frac{S}{|P|}$ or failure frequency function, $f = \frac{F}{|P|}$. Note that $f = 1 - s$. In the example of Figure 3-26, there were nine failures out of twelve references, resulting in a failure frequency, f, of 75 percent. In practical systems with many more memory blocks and much longer page traces, f is usually below 1 percent.

Due to the address mapping hardware, the physical position of a page in memory is unimportant, thus we can use the ordering of the pages in the columns of the page trace analysis to assist us in simulating the replacement algorithm. For example, in FIFO removal, when it is necessary to remove a page, we wish to select the page that has been in memory the longest. In Figure 3-26 the columns are kept ordered so that the "oldest" page is always at the bottom and the "newest" page is at the top. The removal algorithm's choice for removal is always circled in Figure 3-26. In an actual implementation of FIFO removal, the clock value indicating when a page was loaded can be stored and, for removal, a search can be made for the "oldest" time. It is usually more efficient to maintain an ordered list, usually by means of pointers, similar to Figure 3-26 so that the page to be removed can be selected without a lengthy search.

Figure 3-27 illustrates an ordering mechanism by extending the use of the Memory Block Table (previously described in Figure 3-18). Each memory block entry indicates the "next oldest" entry. A separate variable is used to indicate the "oldest" entry and, thereby, starts the chain and also specifies the page to be removed next. Whenever a page is loaded into memory, it is placed at the end of the "oldest" chain and at the beginning of the "newest" chain. The example presented in Figure 3-27 represents the final ordering of Figure 3-26, that is, page 1, page 2, and page 5—going from "newest" to "oldest."

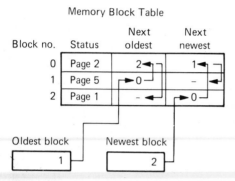

Figure 3-27 Page removal record keeping

3-6.2.5 FIFO REMOVAL

FIFO removal, as described in the preceding section, is a simple algorithm to implement, yet it eliminates the possibility of loading a page and immediately removing it.

FIFO has three key disadvantages: (1) if a page is frequently and continually used, it will eventually become the oldest and will be removed—even though it will be needed again immediately; (2) some strange side effects can occur; and (3) other algorithms have been found to be more effective.

The most noted side effect, called the *FIFO anomaly* (Belady, 1969), is that under certain circumstances adding more physical memory can result in poorer performance. Figure 3-28 presents the same page trace as Figure 3-26, but with a larger memory, M = 4 instead of M = 3.

In spite of this larger memory, the failure frequency function rises from 75 percent to 83 percent, even though, intuitively, one would expect a larger memory to result in better performance.

The actual occurrence of page traces that result in this anomaly are, of course, very rare. Nevertheless, this perverse phenomenon, coupled with the other objections noted, has caused FIFO to drop from favor.

	1	2	3	4	5	6	7	8	9	10	11	12
P =	4	3	2	1	4	3	5	4	3	2	1	5
M = 4 ↑	4+	3+	2+	1+	1	1	5+	4+	3+	2+	1+	5+
		4	3	2	2	2	1	5	4	3	2	1
			4	3	3	3	2	1	5	4	3	2
↓				4	4	④	③	②	①	⑤	④	3
F =	+	+	+	+			+	+	+	+	+	+

$$F = 10$$
$$f = \frac{10}{12} \approx 83\%$$

Figure 3-28 Example of FIFO anomaly

3-6.2.6 LRU REMOVAL

Many different page removal algorithms have been proposed and tested. One of the most popular techniques is called *Least Recently Used* (LRU). It selects for removal the page that has not been referenced for the longest time. FIFO, in contrast, removes the page that has been in memory for the longest time, regardless of how often and when it was referenced. LRU is based on the theory that if a page is referenced, it is likely to be referenced again soon. Conversely, if it hasn't been referenced for a long time, it is unlikely to be needed in the near future. This is also the basis for the *theory of locality*, which will be explained further in Section 3-6.3.

An LRU page trace analysis, as shown in Figure 3-29, puts the most recently referenced page on the top of the M list. The least recently used page thus falls to the bottom of the M list and is the candidate for removal. LRU has been found to possess many interesting theoretical properties; in particular, it is a member of a class of removal techniques called *stack algorithms* (Mattson, 1970). These algorithms function in such a way that increasing memory size can never cause the number of page interrupts to increase, in contrast to the FIFO anomaly. Figure 3-29 illustrates LRU removal for two memory sizes, M = 3 and M = 4. Notice that the top three elements of each column are always identical, e.g., after the seventh page reference, M = 3 contains 5,3,4 and M = 4 contains 5,3,4,1. This phenomenon does not occur with FIFO, as illustrated in Figures 3-26 and 3-28.

Let M(P,c,t) represent the list of pages that will be in memory for a page trace P, a memory size c, and reference time t. For the page trace P of Figure 3-29 and LRU removal, M(P,3,7) = 5,3,4 while M(P,4,7) = 5,3,4,1. It has been proven (Mattson, 1970) that for stack algorithms, such as LRU, $M(P,c,t) \supset M(P,c + 1,t)$ for all P,c and t. This has been called the *inclusion property* of stack algorithms.

	1	2	3	4	5	6	7	8	9	10	11	12
P =	4	3	2	1	4	3	5	4	3	2	1	5
	4+	3+	2+	1+	4+	3+	5+	4	3	2+	1+	5+
M = 3		4	3	2	1	4	3	5	4	3	2	1
			(4)	(3)	(2)	(1)	4	3	(5)	(4)	(3)	2
F =	+	+	+	+	+	+	+			+	+	+

(a) M = 3

F = 10

$f = \frac{10}{12} \approx 83\%$

	1	2	3	4	5	6	7	8	9	10	11	12
P =	4	3	2	1	4	3	5	4	3	2	1	5
	4+	3+	2+	1+	4	3	5+	4	3	2+	1+	5+
M = 4		4	3	2	1	4	3	5	4	3	2	1
			4	3	2	1	4	3	5	4	3	2
				4	3	(2)	1	1	(1)	(5)	(4)	3
F =	+	+	+	+			+			+	+	+

(b) M = 4

F = 8

$f = \frac{8}{12} \approx 67\%$

Figure 3-29 Example of LRU removal

The formal proof of the inclusion property is somewhat lengthy and will not be reproduced here. A simple motivation for it can be gained by considering how one might determine the value of M(P,c,t). For example, to determine M(P,3,7), start at the seventh page reference, which is page 5, then move backward in the page trace, and select the first three unique page numbers encountered; for M(P,3,7) this would be 5,3,4. For M(P,4,7) select the first four unique page numbers moving backward: 5,3,4,1. By "unique" we mean that the same page number should not be selected twice. An example of this requirement is seen for M(P,4,9) which is computed as follows:

t = 9 8 7 6 5 4

P(t) = 3 4 5 3̶ 4̶ 1

Thus, M(P,4,9) = 3,4,5,1. The page numbers 3 and 4 at times 6 and 7 are discarded since they have already been selected. Thus, for M(P,c,t) we start at the t-th page reference and move backward, selecting the first c unique page numbers. For M(P,c + 1,t) we select the first c + 1 unique page references. It should be fairly easy to see from this definition that M(P,c,t) ⊃ M(P,c + 1,t). That is, if a page number is selected for M(P,c,t), it must also be selected for M(P,c + 1,t). The inclusion property guarantees that increasing memory can not cause the number of page faults to increase.

3-6.2.7 LRU APPROXIMATION

An LRU removal algorithm should update the page removal status information *after every page reference.* (For FIFO removal this update was needed only when a page was loaded into memory.) This continual update would be prohibitively costly if done solely by software. But hardware LRU mechanisms tend to degrade execution performance while, at the same time, they substantially increase cost. As a result of these problems, true LRU removal is seldom used. Instead, simple and efficient algorithms that approximate LRU have been developed.

In Section 3-6.1, which describes hardware support, the *reference bit* was introduced. A reference bit is associated with each memory block, and this bit is automatically set to 1 by the hardware whenever that page is referenced. The single reference bit per block can be used to approximate LRU removal as suggested in Figures 3-30 and 3-31.

The page removal software periodically resets the reference bits to 0, while the execution of the user's job causes some reference bits to be set to 1. At any particular time, if the reference bit is 0, we know that page has not been referenced since the last time the reference bit was reset to 0. Thus, that page has "not been used recently" and is a candidate for removal; this is sometimes called the Not Used Recently (NUR) algorithm. The algorithm in Figure 3-30 cycles through the Memory Block Table looking for an unreferenced block. It resets the reference bit on all pages referenced while searching.

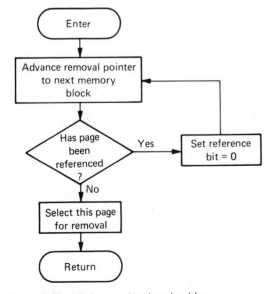

Figure 3-30 LRU approximation algorithm

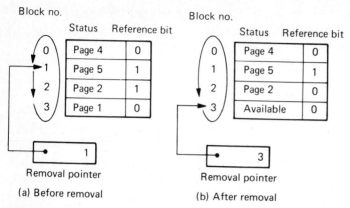

Figure 3-31 Example of LRU approximation

Figure 3-31 demonstrates the LRU approximation algorithm. In Figure 3-31a, block 1 (page 5) was the last page loaded. When a page is needed for removal, removal, the reference bits are examined starting at block 2. Block 3 (page 1) is selected for removal since its reference bit is still zero. All non-zero reference bits (e.g., block 2) are reset at the same time, as shown in Figure 3-31b. Block 0 (page 4) would be the next one selected for removal if a page interrupt occurred immediately.

Numerous LRU approximation variations are available. Algorithms, such as Figure 3-30, are easy to implement and provide a reasonable approximation to LRU. Corbato (1969) has reported on several other variations.

3-6.2.8 PAGE-SIZE ANOMALY

The page size is an important parameter of a demand-paged memory management system. The page size is usually determined by means of a compromise. On the one hand, we want to reduce PMT size and make page size large enough to compensate for the normally large access time required for secondary storage devices (1-byte page can be accessed and read in about 5 ms, whereas a 4096-byte page can be fetched in about 7 to 8 ms, only 56 percent more time)—these imply a large page size. On the other hand, we want to reduce page breakage—which implies a small page size. In most contemporary systems fairly large page sizes, between 1K and 4K bytes, are common. (For a significant exception, see the discussion of cache systems in Section 3-10.3.) Another important consideration is the effect upon the number of page interrupts.

Let us consider the effect of cutting the page size in half. If the original page trace references page p, the half-sized page trace would reference either page p′ or p″ depending on which half of the page was actually referenced—as determined by the actual address trace.

Let us call the large and small page sizes N and N/2 bytes, respectively. If the physical memory is 2N bytes, it can hold either two large pages or four small pages. Figure 3-32 illustrates the same page trace applied to both page sizes with LRU removal. In this example, only one part, p', of each large page, p, was really needed. Thus the small page size resulted in fewer page interrupts. The ratio, r = Fa/Fb = 0.5, indicates that the small page size resulted in half as many page interrupts. This phenomenon is called *compression* (Denning, 1970) since small page sizes can eliminate the need to load the unnecessary bytes of the larger page size.

Unfortunately, compression does not always occur. In Figure 3-33 both halves of each large page are actually needed. By dividing the page size in half, twice as many page interrupts are needed to load these pages. In this case, the ratio, r = Fa/Fb = 2, indicates that the small page size was not advantageous.

Actual programs with much longer page traces exhibit characteristics of both Figures 3-32 and 3-33. In selecting a page size for a system, the designer attempts to pick a favorable size as much as possible. It is useful to know the extreme cases or *performance bounds*. In the case of Figure 3-32, which is favorable to small pages, the ratio, r = Fa/Fb, could get very close to 0 by increasing the page trace by repeating the 1',2',3' sequence. For example, the page trace:

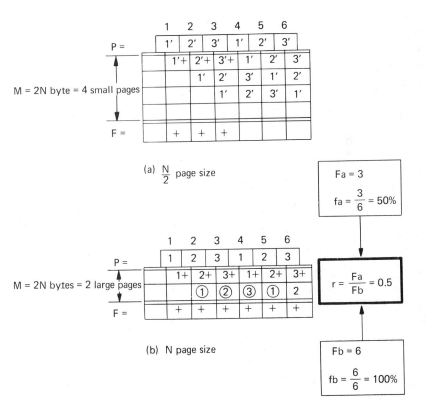

Figure 3-32 Small page size advantageous (Fa/Fb = 0.5)

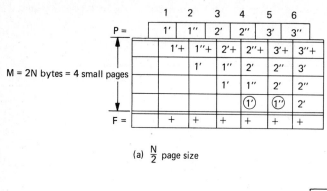

(a) $\frac{N}{2}$ page size

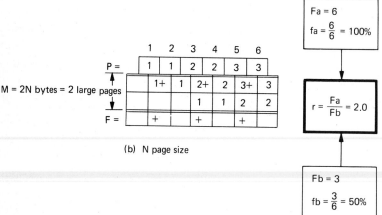

(b) N page size

Figure 3-33 Large page size advantageous (Fa/Fb = 2.0)

$$P = 1',2',3',1',2',3',1',2',3',1',2',3'$$

results in a ratio $r = \frac{3}{12} = 0.25$. In general, a page trace of this pattern with a length P_1 has a ratio $r = \frac{3}{P_1}$. For large P_1, $r \approx 0$.

Figure 3-33 may be considered the extreme unfavorable case for the smaller page size, since both halves of every large page are always needed. This case results in a ratio $r = 2$. An even more unfavorable situation is illustrated in Figure 3-34 where $r = 2.2$. If $r = 2$ is not the worst case, what is the worst case? It has been proven (Madnick, 1973) that, when using LRU removal, there exist page trace patterns such that the performance ratio $r = Fa/Fb$ asymptotically approaches the bound $\frac{M}{N} + 1$. Thus, for example, in a demand-paging system with a physical memory, M, of 1024K bytes and a page size, N, of 4K bytes, reducing the page size to 2K bytes can result in an increase of $\frac{1024K}{4K} + 1 = 257$-fold (i.e., a 25,600 percent increase in page interrupts).

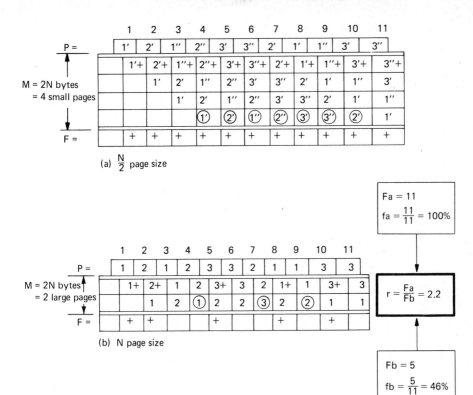

Figure 3-34 Small page size very unfavorable (Fa/Fb = 2.2)

3-6.2.9 TUPLE-COUPLING APPROACH TO PAGE REMOVAL

Due to the development of high-performance secondary storage devices with small access times, there is considerable interest in using small page sizes in the hope that typical page traces will be favorable for small page sizes. The use of such page sizes would be even more encouraging if a limit could be placed on the possibly unfavorable situations. A technique called *tuple-coupling* (Madnick, 1973) has been developed that guarantees that the ratio r will not exceed 2 (i.e., the worst case bound is reduced from $\frac{M}{N} + 1$ to 2). This technique imposes certain conditions that require minor modifications to conventional page removal algorithms such as LRU or FIFO.

The basic concept behind the tuple-coupling approach is simple. First, the two portions, p′ and p″, of each original larger page, p, must be identifiable (i.e., the set of pages is viewed as a collection of 2-tuples). Second, the removal ordering policies must be applied to both elements of a tuple (i.e., the tuples are coupled in regard to ordering decisions) so that a page p′ or p″ is never removed unless the corresponding large page p would also have been removed from M. The particular implementation of this approach may vary slightly, depending on the

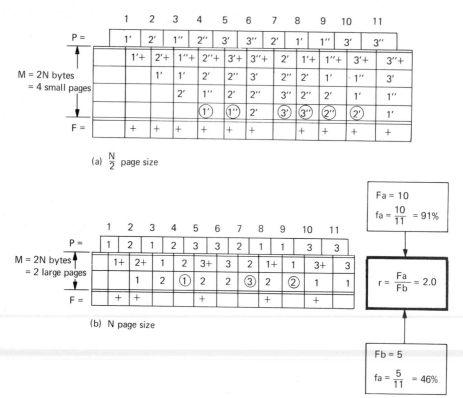

Figure 3-35 LRU removal with tuple-coupling

removal algorithm, e.g., LRU, FIFO, to be used. Any removal algorithm to which the tuple-coupling approach can be incorporated is said to be "tuple-couple-able."

Figure 3-35 illustrates the application of the tuple-coupling approach to the LRU removal example of Figure 3-33. It should be noted that, in this case, r has indeed been limited to 2 although it had a value of 2.2 when normal LRU removal was used. The method of tuple-coupling used in this LRU example is to move both p' and p'' to the top of the list if (1) either of them is referenced and (2) the other is already in M.

3-6.3 Performance and Program Behavior Considerations

Demand paging can provide good system performance by making it possible to multiprogram more jobs at the same time (i.e., remove the constraint imposed by the size of physical memory). Virtual memory, although "virtual," is not completely "free." The handling of page interrupts imposes a "cost" in terms of increased processor utilization due to operating system overhead and increased I/O loads due to page I/O's. In weighing these tradeoffs it is necessary to consider the characteristics of program reference behavior.

3-6.3.1 ADDRESS REFERENCE PATTERNS

Figure 3-36 (from Hatfield, 1972) illustrates the address reference pattern of an actual System/360 program. To understand this diagram, it is helpful to imagine a tiny light bulb connected to each byte of memory. This light bulb is turned on briefly whenever the corresponding byte is referenced either as data or as an instruction. Now imagine a camera aimed at the bulbs, which are lined up on a long column. The camera shutter is opened, and the program is allowed to run briefly turning lights on and off; the shutter is closed and the film advanced. This process is repeated until the program finally terminates. Thus, in Figure 3-36, each vertical column indicates the locations referenced during each brief time interval. The vertical axis is marked to indicate the beginning and end of each 4K page. Notice, for example, that pages 25 through 28 are not referenced until near the end of the program's execution. This diagram was actually produced by simulating the program's execution to determine the address trace as described in the preceding section.

It is important to note, as Figure 3-36 demonstrates, that the program's reference pattern is not random. Very definite patterns correspond to different phases of the

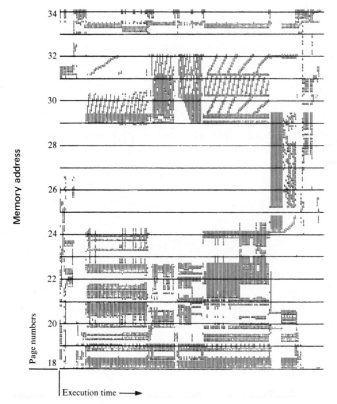

Figure 3-36 Sample memory reference pattern (from Hatfield; 1972)

execution time (e.g., input processing, table setup, computation, table searching, etc.). Particular program actions can be recognized–such as linear processing of a large table–which show up as "ramps" in the diagram.

In order to attain good program paging performance, it is important for the programmer to try to *cluster* or *localize* references as much as possible. For example, if a large matrix A(n,m) is stored in the order: A(1,1), A(1,2), . . ., A(1,m), A(2,1), A(2,2), . . . , A(2,m), etc., it is better, if possible, to sequence through the matrix in an order such as A(1,1), A(1,2), A(1,3), etc., rather than the order A(1,1), A(2,1), A(3,1), etc. There are many other suggestions for efficient programming in a demand-paging environment (Hatfield, 1971; Morrison, 1973).

3-6.3.2   PARACHOR CURVE

A parachor curve is a graph of the total number of page interrupts a program encounters as a function of the amount of physical memory available for holding pages. Figure 3-37 illustrates a parachor curve for an actual System/360 program (obtained from Madnick, 1973). Although each program has its own unique parachor curve, the shape of Figure 3-37 is quite typical.

Notice that when a program is constrained to a small amount of memory, it encounters a large number of page interrupts. When memory is increased by 8K bytes, from 32K to 40K, the number of page interrupts decreases by 1715. When memory is increased from 64K to 72K, also an 8K increase, the page interrupts decrease only by 309.

Most programs have a threshold beyond which incremental increases in memory have relatively little advantage, while a small decrease in memory results in a dramatic increase in page interrupts. This particular point varies considerably depending on the program; one study (Coffman, 1968) indicates that the physical memory size threshold is often around half the total address space (virtual memory) size. In Figure 3-37 the total address space size is 256K bytes. This threshold has often been called the program's *working set size,* referring to the fact that for each program a minimum number of pages is needed in memory in order for it to work efficiently. (This is not the formal definition of working set, which appears below.)

3-6.3.3   WORKING SET THEORY

The parachor curve provides an aggregate measure of a program's paging behavior (Bard, 1973). A program's behavior is not uniform throughout its execution, as Figure 3-36 illustrates. Furthermore, in a multiprogramming environment the number of memory blocks for a job is not necessarily constant since multiple jobs are competing for the physical memory.

A more local measure of performance is the *incremental working set size*, which is the number of pages referenced by a program over some interval of time (Denning, 1968). $W(t, \Delta t)$, which is the list of pages referenced between times $t - \Delta t$ and t, is

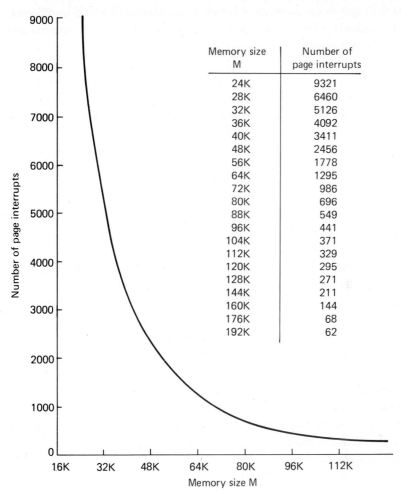

Memory size M	Number of page interrupts
24K	9321
28K	6460
32K	5126
36K	4092
40K	3411
48K	2456
56K	1778
64K	1295
72K	986
80K	696
88K	549
96K	441
104K	371
112K	329
120K	295
128K	271
144K	211
160K	144
176K	68
192K	62

Figure 3-37   Sample of a parachor curve

called the *working set*. The *working set size*, w(t, Δt), is the number of pages in W(t, Δt). The working set size is a monotonic function of Δt, that is, the longer the interval, the more pages that will be referenced up to a limit, L, which is the total number of pages actually needed. L must be less than or equal to the total address space size.

By choosing a Δt interval such as 10 ms or 10,000 instructions (in our example we often measure in terms of instructions executed rather than actual elapsed time), it is possible to estimate the program's current memory requirements—working set size—during execution. In this way the operating system can determine which jobs should be assigned more memory blocks and which jobs can yield memory blocks.

In order to adjust for the time variation in a program's working set size and to ensure that paging does not become excessive due to memory overcommitment, it is necessary to coordinate the actions of memory management and processor management. There is no sense in assigning a processor to a job if insufficient memory is available to hold that job's working set. Chapter 8 presents an analysis of this phenomenon.

3-6.3.4 LOCALITY

Efficient operation of a virtual memory system is dependent upon the degree of *locality of reference* in programs. Locality can be divided into two classes: temporal locality and spatial locality (Madnick, 1973).

Temporal locality refers to an observed property of most programs, i.e., once a location—data or instruction—is referenced, it is often referenced again very soon. This behavior can be rationalized by program constructs such as loops, frequently used variables, and subroutines.

Spatial locality refers to the probability that once a location is referenced, a nearby location will be referenced soon. This behavior can be rationalized by program constructs such as sequential instruction sequencing, linear data structures (e.g., arrays), and the tendency of programmers to put commonly used variables near one another.

The degree of locality varies from program to program. In general, it is desirable to develop programs with a high degree of locality. Appropriate programming techniques are discussed in Morrison, 1973 and Brawn, 1968.

3-6.4 Advantages

Demand-paged memory management has all the advantages discussed earlier with regard to paged memory management. In particular, fragmentation is eliminated and compaction is not necessary.

There are several additional advantages:

1 *Large virtual memory* A job's address space is no longer constrained by the size of physical memory. This provides better compatibility between large and small computers (e.g., a 512K-byte job that is normally run on a 1024K computer can be run on a 256K computer if necessary).

2 *More efficient use of memory* The portions of a job's address space that are not used—or seldom used—will not be kept in physical memory. Often 25 percent or more of a job's address space need never be loaded since these parts are used only under peculiar circumstances (e.g., error routines).

3 *Unconstrained multiprogramming* The degree of multiprogramming was usually limited by the size of physical memory in the previously discussed schemes. That is, the sum of the jobs' address space sizes must be less than or equal to physical memory size. In demand paging, there is no such limit. It is possible, though not necessarily desirable, to multiprogram 50 or 100 jobs on a computer with only 256K bytes of memory.

3-6.5 Disadvantages

In addition to the disadvantages mentioned for paged management in Section 3-5.4 (hardware costs, page breakage, processor overhead, and memory space for tables), new concerns arise in the case of demand-paged management:

1 The number of tables and amount of processor overhead for handling page interrupts are greater than in the case of the simple paged management technique.

2 Due to the lack of an explicit constraint on a job's address space size or amount of multiprogramming, it is necessary to develop approaches to prevent thrashing (i.e., an exorbitant amount of processor overhead is being consumed by the system to handle paging interrupts while very little progress is being made on user jobs). Under extreme thrashing situations, over 99 percent of processor time may be consumed by overhead activities and less than 1 percent by user jobs. (Some techniques for thrashing avoidance are presented in Chapter 8.)

3-7 SEGMENTED MEMORY MANAGEMENT

In the previous memory management approaches the physical memory was handled in various ways, e.g., partitioned, relocated, paged, etc.; yet these actions were invisible to the user's program. A linear and contiguous address space was always provided. Are there other ways of presenting the address space so as to facilitate efficient memory utilization and programmer convenience? Yes, segmentation is such a way.

A *segment* can be defined as a logical grouping of information, such as a subroutine, array, or data area. Thus, each job's address space actually consists of a collection of segments, as illustrated in Figure 3-38. *Segmentation* is the technique for managing these segments.

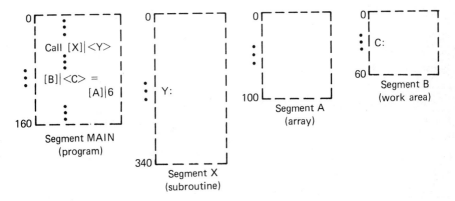

Figure 3-38 Segmented address space

In a segmented environment all address space references require two components: (1) a segment specifier and (2) the location within the segment. For example, references may be as follows:

CALL	[X]|⟨Y⟩	TRANSFER TO ENTRY POINT Y WITHIN SUBROUTINE X.
LOAD	1,[A]|6	LOAD THE 6TH LOCATION OF ARRAY A INTO REGISTER 1.
STORE	1,[B]|⟨C⟩	STORE REGISTER 1 INTO LOCATION C WITHIN SEGMENT B.

Although the segmented address space is explicit and "visible" to the programmer, the differences between this space and conventional address space need not affect his programming. In most programming languages there are statements, such as:

CALL Y;

C = A(6);

In a single linear address space the compiler and/or loader must convert these segmentlike references into a single address. For example, if Y is an entry point at location 120 within subroutine X and subroutine X is loaded at location 3460, then CALL Y becomes CALL 3580. Likewise, if A is an array of bytes at location 3800, A(6) refers to location 3806. Notice that the original structure is lost in this transformation. If an error occurred at location 3803, there is no explicit indication of the fact that 3803 is really A(3).

Typically, in a segmented address space, each segment is assigned a number, such as [X] = 3, [A] = 5. Then, CALL Y becomes CALL [3]|120 and A(6) becomes [5]|6, explicitly indicating the segment and location within the segment being referenced.

A segmented address space can be implemented by using address mapping hardware similar to that used for paged memory management. Figure 3-39 illustrates a Segment Map Table (SMT) that indicates the address of each segment in memory. The conversion of the two-part segmented address into a linear physical memory address is done automatically during execution rather than statically by the compiler or loader.

Due to the similarities between the page and segment address mapping hardware, the distinction between paging and segmentation is often confused. We will attempt to emphasize the conceptual differences in this section. The major difference is that a segment is a "logical" unit of information—visible to the user's program— and is of arbitrary size. A page is a "physical" unit of information—strictly used for memory management, invisible to the user's program—and is of a fixed size, e.g., 4K bytes. In retrospect, a segment is a more precise form of the job "portion" notion introduced in the multiple partition allocation discussion (Section 3-3.2.6).

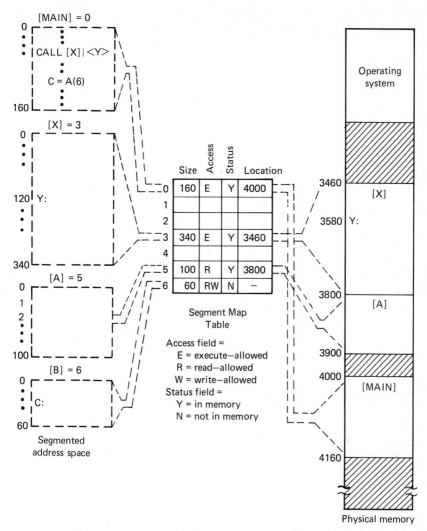

Figure 3-39 Segmented-mapped memory

Segmented memory management can offer several advantages (Dennis, 1965, 1966; Daley, 1969; Randell, 1967; Denning, 1970). It can:

1 *Eliminate fragmentation* By moving segments around, fragmented memory space can be combined into a single free area.

2 *Provide virtual memory* By keeping only the actively used segments in main memory, the job's total address space size may exceed the physical memory size.

3 *Allow dynamically growing segments or automatic bounds checking* If a segment's size must be increased during execution (e.g., table space full), the "out-of-range" reference can be detected by the size component of each

entry in the Segment Map Table. This detection can trigger either dynamic space allocation—increased segment size—or an error indication, depending on the operating system's handling of this condition.

4 *Dynamic linking and loading* In most systems, subroutines and data areas are located and added to the job's address space statically during the linking and loading process prior to the start of execution (Donovan, 1972; Presser, 1972). For a large program with many subroutines this linking process can be complex and time-consuming, sometimes requiring more time than the actual execution. It frequently happens that many of the subroutines linked are not actually called during any particular run. Thus, by deferring the linking until the segment is explicitly referenced, unnecessary linking is avoided.

5 *Facilitate shared segments (data areas and procedures)* If two jobs are using a square root routine, it is wasteful and possibly undesirable to have two separate copies exist in main memory.

6 *Enforced controlled access* Access to each segment should be controlled. A table of constants should be restricted to read accesses only, whereas a work-space segment may be written as well as read. A pure procedure segment should not be written because of the danger of accidental destruction, nor read because it allows "stealing" of procedures; access should be restricted to allow execution only. In a shared segment environment, these key privileges, Read, Write, and Execute, may be assigned on the basis of the segment involved and the user of the segment.

Segmented memory management has been used in certain commercial computers, primarily the Burroughs B5000 and its successors, since the early 1960s. More recently, the segmented approach has been adopted by the Honeywell 6180 MULTICS system, and, to a somewhat lesser extent, the IBM System/370 OS/VS2 system.

The four functions of memory management in a segmented environment combine some of the aspects of relocatable partitioned and demand-paged memory management:

1 Keeping track of status is done through four main sets of tables:

a Segment Map Tables—one per address space

b Unallocated Area Table—one in system

c Active Reference Table—one per address space

d Active Segment Table—one in system

2 The policy of who gets memory and when may be determined statically by the job scheduler if virtual memory use is limited (i.e., virtual memory size is comparable to physical memory size). In a general virtual memory environment, memory requirements are determined on a dynamic basis by segment "demand" interrupts.

3 Allocation—when a segment must be allocated, a large enough available area must be found. Compaction may be performed, if necessary.

4 Deallocation—if it is not possible to find a large enough available area for segment allocation, one or more of the currently allocated segments must be deallocated. The memory released becomes available space. When a job terminates, all the memory used by its segments becomes available.

3-7.1 Hardware Support

There are numerous variations on the hardware implementation of segmented memory management. We will present the key hardware support concepts in this section. The references provide more details and alternatives (Dennis, 1966, 1967; Daley, 1969; Denning, 1970).

3-7.1.1 FORMATION OF SEGMENTED ADDRESS

In a segmented environment it is necessary to generate a two-component, segment number and byte number address. One way to accomplish this is to have two separate address fields in each instruction, such as:

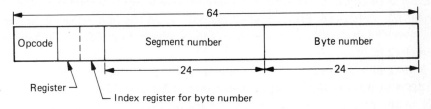

This allows easy formulation of instructions, such as:

LOAD 1,[5]|⟨8⟩

where 5 is the segment number and 8 is the byte number within the segment. In order to shorten the length of such an instruction as well as to provide more flexibility, segment base registers and byte base registers can be used, possibly with segment and/or byte offsets in the instruction. This addressing approach is used in the Burroughs 5500 and Honeywell 6180.

Another approach is to generate the effective address, using linear address formation techniques, and to interpret certain bits of the resulting effective address as a segment number and the remaining bits as the byte number. For example, the IBM System/370 can interpret the 24-bit effective address as an 8-bit segment number and a 16-bit byte number as follows:

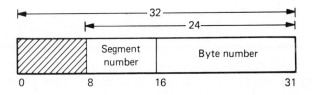

allowing up to 256 separate segments, each up to 64K bytes long. By using a 32-bit effective address, as provided on certain versions of the IBM System/360 Model 67 (a special model of the System/360 series designed for timesharing usages), it is possible to provide more and larger segments—up to 4096 segments, each up to one million bytes long. The Honeywell 6180, in comparison, allows up to 256K segments, each up to one million bytes.

The latter approach, using a single address field within the instruction, has the advantage (or disadvantage—depending on viewpoint) that the segmented address space can be made to be invisible to the user programs. Due to the single address formation, the last byte of one segment (if it is maximum size) is logically adjacent to the first byte of the next segment. This means that four adjacent 64K segments can be treated as a single 256K segment. This is not usually permitted when there are separate segment and byte address fields in the instruction.

3-7.1.2 ADDRESS MAPPING

The segment address mapping hardware required is similar to the page mapping hardware described in Section 3-6.1. However, several significant differences arise from the differences between segments and pages. Because segments are of arbitrary size, it is necessary to check that the reference byte address is within the segment's range.

Protection at the segment level is usually much more desirable than protecting pages or memory blocks, since segments represent logical entities that are meaningful to the programmer. Thus, the address mapping mechanism must check that access is permitted.

Since segments may be removed from main memory and placed on secondary storage, it is necessary to indicate whether the segment is currently in memory. If it is not, an interrupt to the operating system must occur. To help the operating system decide which segments to keep in memory and which to remove, "referenced" and "changed" bits may be used in each Segment Map Table Entry (SMTE).

Figure 3-39 depicts a general Segment Map Table format and Figure 3-40 indicates the sequence of operation that occurs in the process of address mapping. Specific implementations may omit certain features, such as the access protection or reference/change information, or may include additional features, such as the "ring protection" mechanism of the Honeywell 6180 (Graham, 1968).

3-7.2 Software Algorithm

Many of the operating system software algorithms needed to support segmentation are similar to the corresponding actions associated with demand paging. In this section we will explain how the six advantages of segmented memory management mentioned earlier are attained. It must be understood that many, if not all,

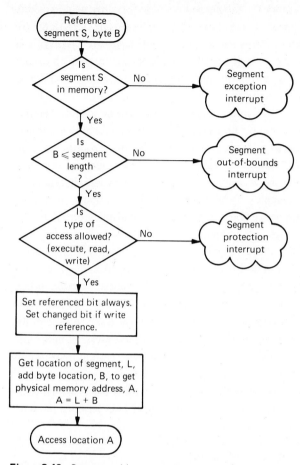

Figure 3-40 Segment address mapping

of these advantages can be gained by using other memory management techniques. However, segmentation, in general, makes the implementation much simpler.

3-7.2.1 ELIMINATION OF FRAGMENTATION

The Segment Map Tables act as multiple relocation/bound registers. By the readjustment of the location field in an entry, a segment may be moved around in memory without any apparent change to the job. In Figure 3-39, the three free areas can be combined into one large area by moving segments X, A, and MAIN.

3-7.2.2 PROVIDING VIRTUAL MEMORY

Virtual memory can be accomplished in a manner similar to demand paging. Copies of all segments are kept on secondary storage. Whenever a segment not in memory is referenced, a *segment exception interrupt* occurs. The operating system must find room in memory for the needed segment, possibly by compacting memory or removing a segment, and then load the segment into memory.

There has been considerable controversy over the advantages and disadvantages of providing virtual memory by segmentation or demand paging. A major advantage claimed for segmentation is that segments, meaningful units of information, are swapped. For example, if a reference is made to a location in a 400-byte segment, only those 400 bytes must be loaded into memory instead of a page of constant-size 4K bytes. Likewise, if an array of size 16K bytes is needed, the entire array segment is loaded at once rather than via four separate page interrupts. On the other hand, managing variable size segments may be a major problem for virtual memory. Storing segments of arbitrary size on secondary storage frequently leads to complex space assignment, wasted space, or serious restrictions on the size of segments (e.g., these must be multiples of 1K bytes). Likewise, manipulating these segments in memory may result in excessive overhead due to compaction. The fact that a segment must be completely loaded has several serious implications. Even if only 1 byte is needed from a 512K-byte segment, the entire segment must be loaded. A more severe restriction occurs if one wants to use a 200,000-word array, i.e., an 800K-byte segment, and main memory is only 512K bytes. No single segment may be larger than physical memory.

The technique of combining segmentation and paging, to be described in Section 3-8, eliminates most of these problems. If paging is not used, certain conventions can be established to keep these problems to a minimum. For example, segments must be kept relatively small, and stored as multiples of some basic size (such as 1K bytes), and virtual memory size must not be much larger than physical memory in order to minimize the amount of segment swapping.

3-7.2.3 ALLOWING DYNAMIC GROWING SEGMENTS

The length of certain data segments depends on the input data. An assembler's symbol table size, for example, depends on the number of symbols used in the input source program. In such a situation, it is desirable to provide dynamic growing segments. This means that the programmer may imagine that the segment is of arbitrary length and merely add new entries successively to the segment. In actuality, the segment's length starts out being very small. Whenever the programmer attempts to store a new entry into the segment, an "out-of-bounds" interrupt occurs. The operating system then gains control and must increase the length of the segment. This may require compaction or even removal of another segment from memory. After moving the segment to the larger area, the segment's location and length fields in the Segment Map Table are adjusted.

Many data segments are intended to be of fixed size. In these cases, the out-of-bounds interrupt is used to indicate an error condition. The handling of each particular segment is determined by the attributes of the segment. The *append attribute*, if present, signifies that automatic growth is intended.

3-7.2.4 DYNAMIC LINKING AND LOADING

Large, complex programs may consist of hundreds of separate subroutines. It is costly to link together all these subroutines and load them all into memory at one time, especially if many of them are not likely to be needed during any particular run. In a *dynamic linking and loading* environment, only the main program is initially loaded. If it references any other procedures, those segments are loaded and addressing links established at the time of reference. This is often called *deferred linking* or *deferred binding* since the linking of subroutines is postponed until a reference is explicitly made.

There are several ways to accomplish dynamic linking. Segmentation is not necessary for the implementation but it does help. The technique used by the MULTICS system requires two additional hardware facilities: indirect addressing and a linkage fault indicator.

If location 100 contains the number 320 and location 320 contains 400, for *direct addressing* LOAD 100 means load the contents of location 100 (i.e., 320).

Indirect addressing, designated by LOAD* 100, uses the contents of the data operand as a forwarding address for the direct address. In this case, LOAD* 100 is treated as LOAD 320 and the contents of location 320 (i.e., 400) are loaded. Figure 3-41 illustrates the differences between direct and indirect addressing.

The word that contains the direct address, when indirecting, is called the *indirect word*. In addition to the direct address, it may also contain additional status bits. For example, an indirect word may have the format shown in Figure 3-42.

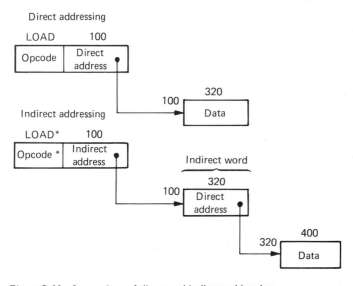

Figure 3-41 Comparison of direct and indirect addressing

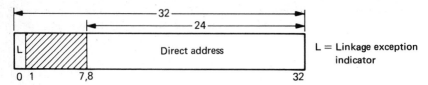

Figure 3-42 Format of indirect word

If the linkage exception indicator is set to 1, a *linkage exception interrupt* occurs whenever this word is used as an indirect word. If the indicator is 0, indirect addressing proceeds as described earlier.

These two mechanisms, indirect addressing and linkage exception, can be used to implement a dynamic linking facility, as illustrated in Figure 3-43. When a program has a symbolic reference to another segment, such as LOAD [X]|⟨Y⟩, the compiler or assembler generates an indirect addressing instruction instead (see location 60 on Figure 3-43a). The indirect word has the linkage exception indicator set and the direct address specifies the location of a character string representing the symbolic reference (e.g., 7" [X]|⟨Y⟩").

If the LOAD [X]|⟨Y⟩ instruction is executed, the linkage exception will occur. The operating system then gets control, determines that the cause was due to a linkage exception, and finds the symbolic name at location 3|108 from the interrupt information. The required segment [X] must be located with the assistance of information management (Chapter 6). It is assigned a segment number, in this case, segment number 4, and the indirect word is changed to reflect the correct segment and byte address for [X]|⟨Y⟩. The postlinkage situation is shown in Figure 3-43b. The interrupt instruction at 3|60 can be restarted by a Load PSW. This time the desired data, 015571, is correctly loaded. Henceforth, all future use of that instruction in segment [MAIN] will operate without linkage interrupt.

Several techniques can be used to decrease the overhead incurred by dynamic linking. For example, all references to the same symbolic address can employ the same indirect word. In Figure 3-43, if there were also a STORE 1,[X]|⟨Y⟩ instruction, it would be converted to STORE* 1,3|100 since 3|100 contains the indirect word used to link all references to [X]|⟨Y⟩. Thus the first use of such a reference in a procedure performs the link for all other uses of that symbolic reference.

Due to separate compilation of procedures, these linkage indirect words are local to each procedure. To save much of the work and to ensure the consistency of the conversion, once a symbolic reference is made, a copy of the reference and its assigned address is saved in an Active Reference Table (ART), also called Active Name Table or Known Segment Table in the literature. Thus, when a linkage exception occurs, the Active Reference Table is consulted (in the hope that another procedure has already caused that symbolic segment reference to be assigned a segment number) before resorting to information management and an

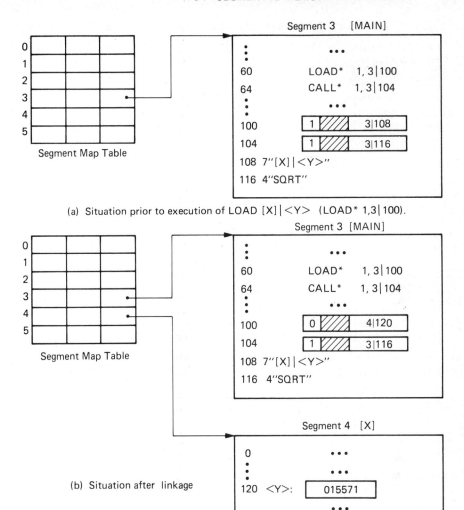

(a) Situation prior to execution of LOAD [X]|<Y> (LOAD* 1,3|100).

(b) Situation after linkage

Figure 3-43 Dynamic linkage

elaborate linkage process. If it is already in the Active Reference Table, the linkage indirect word is merely copied from the ART.

Several additional considerations arise concerning dynamic linking. One such consideration is that the linking process alters the linkage indirect word; thus the physical alteration of the segment during execution is in direct conflict with the concept of *pure procedures* where the procedure is not allowed to be changed during execution. One way to retain the purity of the procedure segment in a dynamic linking environment is to place all alterable information, including linkage indirect words as well as certain temporary variables, internal variables, etc., in a separate segment called the *linkage segment* or *impure segment*. Thus, for each source program, the compiler must generate at least two separate object segments—one pure and one impure. This requirement is satisfied by both the IBM System/360 PL/I compiler and the Honeywell MULTICS PL/I compiler.

There are many implementation alternatives with regard to the use of and interaction between these two segments. Figure 3-44 depicts a simplified view of the MULTICS mechanism (Dennis, 1965; Daley, 1968). Separate base registers are used during execution to address the current procedure segment (procedure register) and current linkage segment (linkage register). Both the indirect instruction and linkage indirect word use these base registers. Figure 3-44 illustrates the form of the procedure and linkage segments as produced by the compiler and prior to dynamic linkage. K1 and K2 constants are established by the compiler. The linkage process may proceed exactly as described earlier and still maintain the purity of the procedure segment.

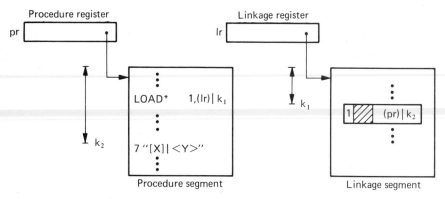

Figure 3-44 Separation of procedure and linkage segments

The intersegment transfer (i.e., subroutine call) introduces several additional complications. The register values, parameters, and return address are normally saved in a subroutine linkage stack segment. A stack register indicates the current stack area. In order to transfer control from one procedure segment to another, the procedure base register, linkage base register, and stack base register must be correctly changed. The approach used in the MULTICS system is described in Daley (1968) and Organick (1972).

3-7.2.5 SHARED SEGMENTS

As noted in most of the previously described memory management schemes, if two jobs used the same procedure, such as the square root subroutine, a separate copy of the subroutine was placed in each job's address space. This occurs frequently with many common procedures, such as subroutine libraries, system utilities (e.g., compilers, assemblers, etc.), and standard application programs. Under these circumstances, most of memory may be filled with duplicate copies of procedures. Segmentation, in conjunction with the dynamic linking facility, provides ways to eliminate this duplication.

Figure 3-45 presents the address space for two jobs with the common procedure COS duplicated for each job. Segment numbers are assigned dynamically as a result of the dynamic linking process. Since it is not possible to predict which procedures

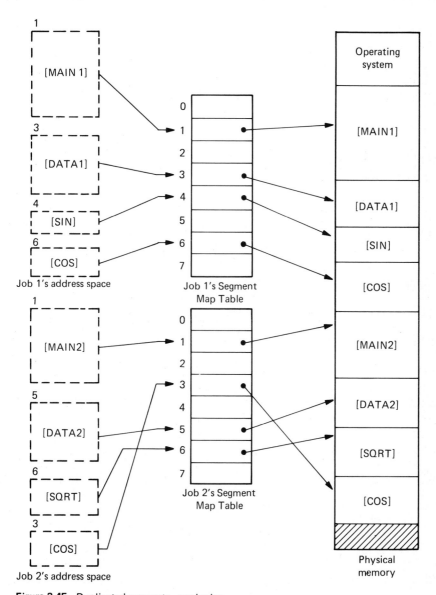

Figure 3-45 Duplicated segments—no sharing

will be used by each job in advance, the common procedures do not necessarily have the same segment numbers. COS, for example, is segment number 6 in Job 1's address space but is segment number 3 for Job 2. Use of shared segments is illustrated in Figure 3-46 where the Segment Map Table Entries for COS for both jobs point to the same physical copy of the COS subroutine. (Linkage segments and stack segments are not explicitly shown in these figures, although their presence is assumed.)

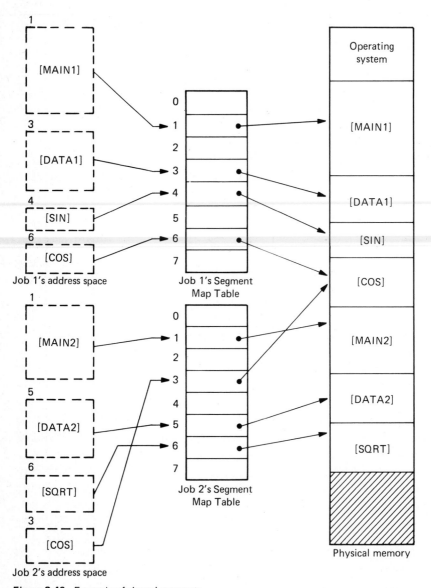

Figure 3-46 Example of shared segments

To be effectively shared in a multiprogramming environment, procedures must be *concurrently reusable* (also called *reentrant* or *pure procedures*). A pure procedure operates only on variables in registers or in separate data segments associated with the job; it never stores into, nor does it alter itself. Thus, the procedure segments, which are pure, may be safely shared while the linkage segments must be unique to each job. The fact that the linkage segments are not shared makes it possible to assign different segment numbers to the same procedure since segment numbers occur explicitly only in linkage segments, which may be different for each job.

A systemwide Active Segment Table (AST) is used to coordinate segment sharing. When a sharable segment is first referenced by any job in the system, an entry is made in the AST. This entry indicates the current status of the segment (i.e., in memory or not), the name of the job using that segment, and the segment number used by that job. Subsequently, when any other job symbolically references a segment, the AST is checked by the dynamic linker for possible duplication. If the segment is already in the AST, this job's name is added to the list of current users of that segment and the Segment Map Table is set to share the same physical copy of the segment.

The AST has to be examined only the first time a job references such a segment; subsequent references are made either automatically via the linked linkage indirect words or by use of the Active Reference Table. It is important to distinguish between the uses and purposes of the AST and ART. There is only one AST in the entire system; it is used to set Segment Map Table Entries to share the same physical segment. There is a separate ART for each job; it is used to set linkage indirect words so that the same segment number is used for a segment throughout the job.

When a segment is removed from memory, the segment exception indicator must be set in each SMTE sharing that segment. The AST provides the necessary information to find all these entries.

Conversely, when a segment is reloaded into memory due to a reference by one job, that copy is made available to all other jobs sharing that segment. This process of adjusting entries can be simplified by use of *indirect word* hardware. A bit in each SMTE indicates whether the address portion points directly to the actual segment (this is *segment direct word* mode) or to a word that points to the segment (this is *segment indirect word* mode). In this latter case, the address can be kept in the AST and all SMTEs will permanently point to the appropriate AST entry. When a segment is removed or reloaded, only the AST entry has to be modified.

The detailed implementation of segment sharing can be complex but it offers significant savings in main memory usage. For example, if 10 jobs were concurrently using the PL/I compiler, each would ordinarily require a separate copy. A typical PL/I compiler may require 256K bytes of procedure segments plus about 32K bytes of data segments for tables and variables. Ten copies would require 10 X (256K + 32K) = 2880 K bytes, almost 3 million bytes! If the procedure segments are shared, the memory requirement drops to 256K + 10 X 32K = 576K— an 80 percent reduction.

3-7.2.6 ENFORCED CONTROLLED ACCESS

If each job had a separate and disjoint address space, then protection of segments would serve primarily to detect programming errors, such as an attempt to alter a procedure segment. Extensive use of sharing, as described above, increases the importance of controlled access. If a pure procedure segment is being shared, we must prohibit any job from modifying this segment—either accidentally or maliciously. In addition, we usually prohibit any job from "reading" a procedure segment. There are two primary reasons for this restriction: (1) an attempt to read a procedure segment usually indicates a programming error and (2) the procedure may be *proprietary* (i.e., it is "owned" by someone who charges for use of that program), in which case we wish to prevent a user of this program from "stealing a copy." If a segment has only *execute access* status, it may be called as a procedure to be executed, but reading and writing (i.e., LOADs and STOREs) are prohibited.

Not only procedures, but also data segments may be shared. For example, a segment containing a table of major cities and their population may be used by several jobs simultaneously. To prevent unintentional alteration or programming error, this segment should have only *read access* status—attempted writing or execution of this segment would be prohibited.

Since the access control information is contained in each Segment Map Table (see Figure 3-39), it is not necessary for each job to have the same access restrictions. If we have a data segment that contains the current stock market prices, we can allow one job *write access* to periodically update the prices while restricting all other jobs to *read access*. Methods of determining the appropriate access permitted to each user are described in more detail in Chapter 6. A conceptually simple scheme shown in Figure 3-47 employs a matrix where one side lists all jobs (or, more typically, users) and the other side lists all segments. The intersection indicates the access privileges of a user to a particular segment. Access control has been the subject of considerable research; an extensive summary can be found in Graham (1972) and Hoffman (1969).

3-7.3 Advantages

The advantages of segmentation have been described in detail earlier in this section. In summary, segmentation (1) eliminates fragmentation, (2) provides virtual memory, (3) allows dynamic segment growth, (4) assists dynamic linking, (5) facilitates shared segments, and (6) enforces controlled access. Most of these features contribute directly to efficient utilization of memory.

Users

Segments	Donovan	Madnick	Ziering	Bad guy	• • •
SQRT	E	RWE	E	E	
PL/I	RWE	E	E	None	
Stock price	RW	R	R	R	
Payroll	R	RW	R	None	
• • •					

Figure 3-47 Access control matrix

3-7.4 Disadvantages

Segmentation has many of the same disadvantages as the other advanced memory management schemes: increased hardware cost, processor overhead for address mapping, the need for additional memory space for tables, and increased complexity in the operating system. Additional problems are caused by the following:

1 Considerable compaction overhead is incurred in order to support dynamic segment growth and eliminate fragmentation.

2 There is difficulty in managing variable size segments on secondary storage.

3 The maximum size of a segment is limited by the size of main memory.

4 It is necessary to develop techniques or constraints to prevent segment thrashing (the counterpart of page thrashing).

3-8 SEGMENTED AND DEMAND-PAGED MEMORY MANAGEMENT

One way to gain the logical benefits of segmentation and remove many of the disadvantages is to combine the segmentation and paging mechanisms. Instead of treating each segment as a single contiguous entity, each one can be subdivided into pages. By physically manipulating these pages, rather than the entire segment, problems of compaction, secondary storage handling, and limitation on segment size are removed. This approach has been employed in the IBM System/370 and the Honeywell 6180.

3-8.1 Hardware Support

There are, as usual, numerous variations possible for the hardware implementation. We will briefly describe the System/370 hardware; the Honeywell 6180 is quite similar and is described in Bensoussan (1969), Daley (1968), and Organick (1972).

The IBM System/370 Dynamic Address Translation (DAT) feature supports either 2K- or 4K-byte pages and segments of maximum size of either 64K or 1024K bytes. The choice of page and segment sizes is determined by control register settings made by the operating system. The following description applies to the 4K-byte page and 64K-byte segment settings.

The 24-bit 370 effective address is split into three parts: (1) segment number, (2) page number, and (3) byte number, as follows:

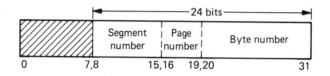

The hardware thus supports an address of up to 256 segments where each segment may consist of up to 16 pages (64K bytes).

The mapping from virtual address to physical address is accomplished by a series of tables, as depicted in Figure 3-48. The Segment Table Register (control register 1) indicates the location and length of the current Segment Map Table. Each Segment Map Table Entry indicates the location and length of a Page Map Table— unless the segment exception interrupt indicator is set. Each Page Map Table Entry (PMTE) indicates the corresponding block number for each page of that segment—unless the page exception interrupt indicator is set.

To decrease hardware costs as well as save bits in the various table entries, certain restrictions are imposed, as noted in Figure 3-48. For example, the Page Map Table address field in each SMTE should require a full 24-bit address. However, by requiring PMTs to start at an address that is a multiple of 8, only 21 bits are needed in the SMTE (i.e., the last 3 bits of the address are always zeros). The unused bits of each entry provide a convenient means for future changes to the hardware—such as protection bits in SMTEs, reference/change bits in PMTEs, and an increased number of segments by extending the length field in the Segment Table Register.

In order to prevent serious performance degradation due to accesses to the SMT and PMT, a *Translation Lookaside Buffer* (TLB)—an associative scratch pad memory—is automatically used by the hardware to eliminate most SMT and PMT accesses. The use of the TLB can generally keep address translation overhead below 10 percent. (See Section 3-10.3 for a related discussion.)

3-8.2 Software Algorithms

The algorithms presented in both the demand-paged and segmented memory management sections are directly applicable. Only minor modifications are

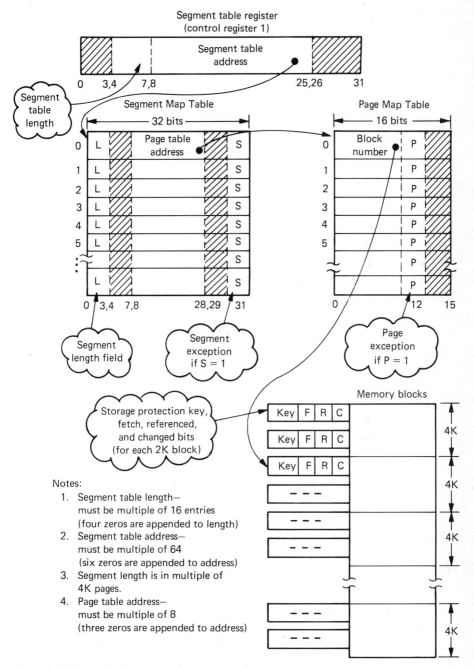

Figure 3-48 System/370 segmentation-page mapping hardware

necessary to eliminate duplication of effort. Figure 3-49 illustrates the interaction between the address translation hardware and the software algorithms.

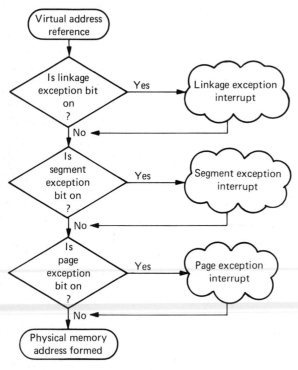

Figure 3-49   Hardware-software interaction

For most address references the translation is performed automatically without any software intervention. The handling of each of the interrupts is summarized below.

1 *Linkage Exception Interrupt* Assign segment number to symbolic segment name, set segment exception bit in SMTE, make entry in Active Reference Table, and convert linkage indirect word to use segment number.

2 *Segment Exception Interrupt* Create entry in Active Segment Table (unless entry already exists), set up Page Map Table (with page exception bits on) and File Map Table in the ASTE, set SMTE to point to PMT.

3 *Page Exception Interrupt* Find available block (removing a page from memory if necessary), load needed page, set PMTE appropriately.

Many of the operations of a segmented demand-paged memory management system closely approximate the operations of information management described in Chapter 6.

3-8.3   Advantages

The combination of segmentation and demand paging provides all the advantages previously listed in Sections 3-6.4 and 3-7.3

3-8.4   Disadvantages

The disadvantages of increased hardware cost, processor overhead, and complexity can be quite significant in a segmented and demand-paged memory management scheme.

In addition, the problems of page breakage and memory needed for SMTs and PMTs persist, as do the dangers of thrashing prevalent in both demand paging and segmentation.

The successful operation of systems such as IBM's OS/VS-2 and Honeywell's MULTICS indicate that these disadvantages can be kept to a minimum. Segmented demand-paged memory management is currently the most general and flexible approach to large-scale general purpose memory management.

3-9   OTHER MEMORY MANAGEMENT SCHEMES

There are many variations to the basic memory management schemes that have been presented. Several key variations will be discussed in this section.

3-9.1   Swapping

In demand paging and segmentation, pages and segments, respectively, were swapped between main memory and secondary storage. This approach can be employed in conjunction with the other memory management techniques.

The early M.I.T. Compatible Time-Sharing System, CTSS, used a basic single contiguous allocation memory management scheme—only one job was in memory at a time. After running for a short period, the current job's entire address space was swapped onto secondary storage to allow another job to run in main memory. (A more detailed discussion of the CTSS memory management algorithm is presented in Chapter 9.) Many contemporary small-scale timesharing systems use this *swapping technique.*

In a similar manner the partitions of a partitioned or relocatable partitioned memory management system can be swapped. In OS/360, if a high priority job arrives for processing and insufficient main memory is available, one or more jobs may be removed from main memory and swapped onto secondary storage. (This process is called *roll-out.*) At a later time, when the high-priority job has completed, the low-priority jobs may be reloaded into main memory. (This is *roll-in.*) The Time-Sharing Option (TSO) of OS/360 uses extensive swapping of user partitions to provide a CTSS-like facility. Roll-out/roll-in can be awkward in a partitioned environment since the partition must be reloaded into exactly the same location from which it was removed. In a relocatable partitioned environment, as provided by the DEC PDP-10 and Honeywell 6000 computer series, the partition may be reloaded into any available space that is sufficiently large, as long as the relocation base register is correctly set.

Swapping as described in this section is quite crude since the job's entire address space must be swapped back and forth. If job sizes are kept very small, as is often true of timesharing application programs (such as the editor), the swapping overhead may be minimal. For large jobs, the overhead incurred in swapping may be significant.

3-9.2 Overlays

A more refined form of the above swapping technique, which swaps only portions of the job's address space, is called *overlay management*. Overlays, normally used in conjunction with single contiguous, partitioned, or relocatable partitioned memory management, provide essentially an approximation to segmentation—but without the segment address mapping hardware.

Figure 3-50a illustrates the relationship between the procedures in a job's address space. This diagram indicates that procedure A calls only procedures B and C, procedure B calls only procedure F, whereas procedure C calls only D and E. As a result of this relationship, we notice that B never calls C and C never calls B. Thus, procedures B and C do not have to be in memory at the same time. By assigning procedure addresses as shown in Figure 3-50b, instead of using 190K bytes to hold the job's address space in memory, a maximum of only 100K bytes are needed. Whenever an interprocedure reference is made, control is transferred to a special *overlay supervisor* that loads the destination procedure, if necessary.

In most automatic overlay systems, as used in the IBM 1130 Disk Monitor System and OS/360, the user must explicitly state the overlay structure in advance. The swapping of overlays can become excessive if there are many alternating calls to mutually exclusive procedures. For example, a loop such as:

```
DO I = 1 TO 1000;
    CALL B(I);
    CALL C(I);
END;
```

in procedure A would cause procedures B and C to be swapped 1,000 times each.

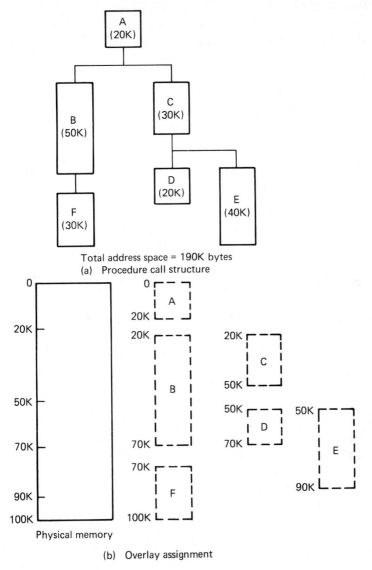

Total address space = 190K bytes
(a) Procedure call structure

Physical memory

(b) Overlay assignment

Figure 3-50 Overlay memory management

3-10 FUTURE TRENDS IN MEMORY MANAGEMENT

Computer system technology is a rapidly changing and evolving field. The memory management techniques presented in this chapter will undoubtedly undergo change in the future. In this section some identifiable trends are discussed. The three key topics discussed are: (1) larger main memories, (2) storage hierarchies, and (3) more operating system functions in hardware.

3-10.1   Large Main Memories

Main memory technology has been the subject of considerable research for many years and as a result costs have been decreasing. From the mid 1960s to the early 1970s the price for comparable memory has dropped, often to 1/8th its original price (e.g., memory on the 360/65 was about $1.60 per byte, the memory for the newer 370/168 is about $0.20 per byte). Tenfold price reductions have been predicted for this decade, and even hundredfold reductions have been foreseen through exploitation of existing experimental technologies.

These dramatic price reductions will make very large main memories economically feasible in the future. Systems with 10M or even 100M bytes of main memory may become commonplace. These developments may be interpreted as decreasing the importance of memory management since there will be so much main memory available. However, the authors doubt that memory will get large enough and cheap enough to satisfy the demands of all users. In the past, as memories became larger and processors faster, programmers merely wrote larger and more complex programs that were not previously possible. Many of the new applications in knowledge-based systems and artificial intelligence demand even larger memories. For example, how much memory will be needed for a computer to communicate in English, or to "see" objects through a televisionlike camera and manipulate them?

Nevertheless, we do believe that many of the constraints of the past will diminish, and a better understanding of the necessary hardware structure will result in more effective and more efficient memory management techniques.

3-10.2   Storage Hierarchies

The various page swapping and segment swapping techniques presented are examples of the use of storage hierarchies. In simple terms, a *storage hierarchy* is an ordering of storage devices on the basis of speed and cost so that only the most important information is kept on the expensive fast devices and the least important information is kept on the inexpensive slow devices (Madnick, 1973). As the definition of "importance" changes, the information is moved appropriately in the hierarchy. Human information processing is a clear example of the storage hierarchy process. In general, we keep our most important information "in our heads." Slightly less important information is kept in notebooks, filing cabinets, etc. Libraries and other comprehensive information storage repositories act as the slowest yet least expensive storage for all presently unimportant information. When some information suddenly becomes important, we sign the book out of the library for home use. If the information is sufficiently important, we can buy the book or even memorize the information.

Automatic two-level hierarchies, usually main memory and high-speed direct access secondary storage, have been used extensively in page swapping and segment swapping systems. Figure 3-51 illustrates the range of prices and performances

DEVICE	RANDOM ACCESS TIME (seconds)	MAXIMUM TRANSFER RATE (byte/sec)	PRICE ($/byte)	TYPICAL CAPACITY (bytes)
1. Cache Store (IBM 3165)	1.6×10^{-7} (160 ns)	1×10^8 (100M b/s)	8.8×10^0 ($8.80)	1.6×10^4 (16K)
2. Main Store (IBM 3360)	1.44×10^{-6} (1.44 μs)	1.6×10^7 (16M b/s)	5×10^{-1} (50¢)	5.12×10^5 (512K)
3. Bulk Store (AMS SSU)	1.3×10^{-4} (130 μs)	8×10^6 (8M b/s)	8.8×10^{-2} (8.8¢)	2×10^6 (2M)
4. Large Store (IBM 2305-2)	5×10^{-3} (5 ms)	1.5×10^6 (1.5M b/s)	2.2×10^{-2} (2.2¢)	1.1×10^7 (11M)
5. Mass Store (IBM 3330)	3.8×10^{-2} (38 ms)	8×10^5 (800K b/s)	4.5×10^{-4} (.045¢)	2×10^8 (200M)
6. Archival Store (Grumman MASSTAPE)	6×10^0 (6 sec)	6×10^5 (600K b/s)	2.2×10^{-5} (.0022¢)	1.6×10^{10} (16B)

Figure 3-51   Spectrum of available storage device technologies (Madnick, 1973)

available with existing storage device technologies. (Since these figures change quite rapidly, they should be used for comparative purposes only.) It should also be noted that there is a difference of about seven orders of magnitude in performance and five orders of magnitude in price between the fastest and slowest devices listed. (Recall that seven orders of magnitude is a 10,000,000-fold difference.) Ideally, an automatic storage hierarchy encompassing all these technologies would provide the user with an enormous virtual memory with an average cost comparable to the cheapest (slowest) device and an average speed comparable to the fastest (expensive) device. Section 3-10.3 illustrates some approaches to developing aggregate performance estimates.

Considerable experimentation and theoretical research are still needed to solve many of the problems associated with the implementation of automatic multilevel storage hierarchies. Their solution will depend on cooperation among operating system designers, hardware technology specialists, and theoreticians. We should see considerable activity in these areas in the future.

3-10.3   Hardware Support of Memory Management

As the cost of computer electronics decreases, more operating system functions can be economically placed in the control of hardware or firmware (see Appendix B for an explanation of firmware). In the VENUS experimental computer system (Liskov, 1972) most of the segmentation and demand paging algorithms were placed under hardware/firmware control.

The *buffer memory* or *cache memory* mechanism used on computers such as the IBM System/360 Model 85 and System/370 Models 155, 158, 165, and 168 is the hardware counterpart of the demand paging mechanism presented in Section 3-6. There is a definite tradeoff in main memory technologies between speed and cost. High-speed main memory (i.e., memory operating at access speeds of less than 200 nanoseconds) is much more expensive than slower-speed main memory (i.e., memory operating at access speeds greater than 500 nanoseconds), as shown in Figure 3-51.

Thus, we are faced with a choice between high-speed, but costly, main memory or slower, but much less expensive, main memory. By combining a small amount of high-speed memory, called the *cache* or *buffer* memory, with a large amount of lower-speed memory, called the *main memory,* a hardware virtual memory system can be constructed with an approximate speed of the high-speed memory but with an average cost of the inexpensive memory. The specific technique used on the IBM System/370 models is presented in the sections that follow (IBM, 9; IBM, 10; IBM, 11; IBM, 12; Liptay, 1968; Mattson, 1970).

3-10.3.1 BUFFER BLOCK ADDRESS FORMATION

In our previous discussions of memory management, we noted that the final result of all address mappings was a *physical memory address.* This address was then used by the memory hardware to retrieve or store the specified information. What does the hardware actually do with this address? The typical actions of the memory unit are discussed in Section 5-2.2. In the systems to be discussed here, all information is physically packaged in blocks of 32 bytes (called a *memory block*). Whenever the hardware must alter a byte, the 32-byte block containing the specified byte is fetched, the byte is changed, and the block is returned to storage (often called the *read/write cycle*). Furthermore, these blocks are organized in terms of *rows* of 4096 bytes (128 blocks) each. A block within a row is designated by its *column number.* Figure 3-52a illustrates the row, column, byte organization.

Thus, each physical memory address, as shown in Figure 3-52b, is actually split up by the memory unit hardware into a row number, column number, and byte number in order to actually reference the physical information. All this transformation is done automatically by the memory unit hardware and is completely transparent to the operating system as well as to the user programs. (A note for the benefit of "hardware experts": these rows and columns do not necessarily relate to physical *memory banks*—nor *interleaved memory*—which are handled at an even more basic level in the memory unit hardware. These topics will not be discussed here.) The number of rows is determined by the size of main memory.

3-10.3.2 BUFFER STORAGE UNIT

In a *buffer storage system,* also called a *cache storage system,* a special *buffer storage control* unit is placed between the processor and the actual main storage

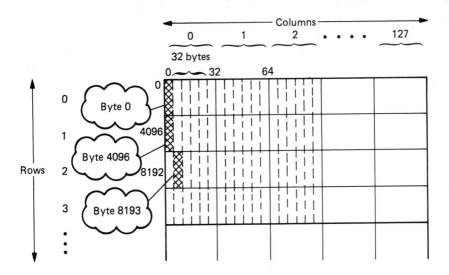

(a) Physical memory addressing in terms of rows, columns, and bytes

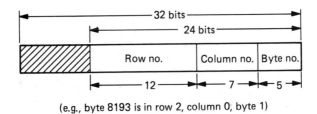

(e.g., byte 8193 is in row 2, column 0, byte 1)

(b) Interpretation of physical memory address in terms of row, column, and byte numbers

Figure 3-52   Row, column, and byte addressing

unit. The buffer control unit consists of two key parts: a small *buffer memory* and a *buffer contents index array*, as shown in Figure 3-53a.

A simple buffer memory, as in Figure 3-53b, is divided into 32-byte blocks in the same way as main memory. There are as many blocks in the buffer memory as there are columns in the main memory; in this example, there are 128 blocks. Thus, the buffer memory consists of 128 × 32 bytes = 4096 bytes. The buffer memory blocks are used to hold copies of main memory. The index array indicates which main memory row the buffer block copy came from. In Figure 3-53b there are three blocks from main memory, M_2, contained in the buffer memory, M_1.

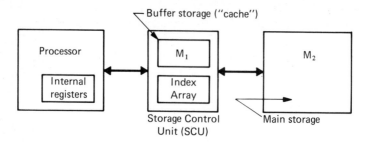

(a) Organization of buffer memory hardware

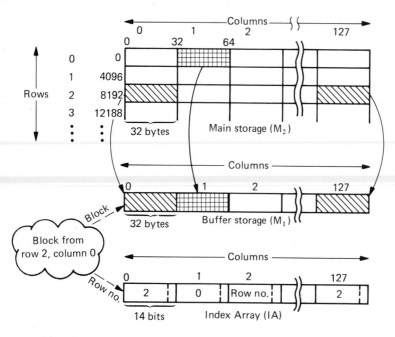

(b)   Relationship of buffer memory blocks to main memory blocks

Figure 3-53 Buffer memory system

These three blocks are:

1 locations 32–63 (row 0, column 1)
2 locations 8192–8229 (row 2, column 0)
3 locations 12156–12137 (row 2, column 127)

If a copy is made of a block from M_2, it is always and *only* stored in the corresponding column of M_1. The index array indicates the corresponding row number.

3-10.3.3 BUFFER MANAGEMENT ALGORITHM

An algorithm for the management of the buffer memory is presented in Figure 3-54. Whenever a fetch request is generated, a check is made to determine if the requested byte is contained in an M_1 buffer memory block. If it is, there is no need to access the M_2 main memory. If it is not in M_1, the block is fetched from M_2 and stored into the appropriate block of M_1. This algorithm is simple enough to be economically incorporated entirely into the hardware.

Whenever a buffer block is changed due to a store request, the corresponding M_2 memory block is updated; this is called *store through*. Thus, any buffer block may be replaced at any time since the main memory copy is always identical.

To illustrate the operation of the buffer memory algorithm, consider the following brief program segment:

	LOCATION	MEMORY CONTENTS	
		$\vdots$	
	64	00000017	DATA WORD 4 BYTES LONG
	68	$\vdots$	
START HERE →	4096	ADD 1, 64	INSTRUCTIONS 4 BYTES LONG
	4100	GOTO 4096	
	4104	$\vdots$	

This program will execute a small loop that continually adds the contents of location 64 (the number 17) to processor register 1. This particular program is not especially outstanding but will illustrate many important points. In fact, this program is functionally quite similar to an array processing program, such as:

SUM = 0; DO I = 1 TO 100; SUM = SUM + A(I); END;

but with some of the indexing and looping conditions eliminated.

The above program results in the following processor reference requests:

1 Fetch instruction from location 4096 (ADD 1,64).
2 Fetch data from location 64.
3 Fetch instruction from location 4100 (GOTO 4096).
4 Fetch instruction from location 4096.
5 Fetch data from location 64, etc.

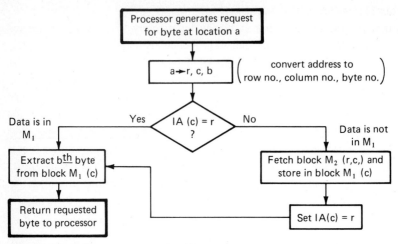

Figure 3-54 Buffer management algorithm

If we assume that M_1 is initially empty and use the buffer management memory algorithm of Figure 3-54, the following events occur:

1 Fetch instruction from location 4096.

    a $4096 \rightarrow r = 1, c = 0, b = 0$.

    b $IA(0) \neq 1$ (initially M_1 empty).

    c Block M_2 (1,0), locations 4096–4127, is fetched from M_2 and stored in $M_1(0)$.

    d Set $IA(0) = 1$.

    e Fetch request completed.

2 Fetch data from location 64.

    a $64 \rightarrow r = 0, c = 2, b = 0$.

    b $IA(2) \neq 0$ (initial conditions).

    c Block $M_2(0,2)$, locations 64–95, is fetched from M_2 and stored in $M_1(2)$.

    d Set $IA(2) = 0$.

    e Fetch request completed.

3 Fetch instruction from location 4100.

    a $4100 \rightarrow r = 1, c = 0, b = 4$.

    b $IA(0) = 1$ (from event 1d).

    c Instruction is extracted from $M_1(0)$ bytes 4–7.

    d Fetch request completed.

4 Fetch instruction from location 4096.

    a $4096 \rightarrow r = 1, c = 0, b = 0$.

    b $IA(0) = 1$ (from event 1d).

c Instruction is extracted from $M_1(0)$ bytes 0–3.

d Fetch request completed.

5 Fetch data from location 64.

a $64 \rightarrow r = 0, c = 2, b = 0$.

b $IA(2) = 0$ (from event 2d).

c Data are extracted from $M_1(2)$ bytes 0–3.

d Fetch request is completed.

Notice that references 1 and 2 required access to M_2, but references 3, 4, 5, etc., had to access M_1 only. This sample program works out especially well, and is typical of most conventional programs.

3-10.3.4 PERFORMANCE ANALYSIS

How does the use of a buffer memory help performance? Due to locality of reference, as described in Section 3-6 (demand-paged memory management), the required data will frequently be contained in M_1, thereby eliminating many references to M_2 (i.e., most references take the "Data is in M_1" path of Figure 3-54). Empirical evidence as well as simulation studies have shown that 90 percent or more of the references can be satisfied by referencing only M_1 buffer memory. This percentage is called the *success frequency function*, which was defined in Section 3-6. The actual value of the success frequency function depends on the program being executed and the particulars of the buffer management algorithm.

The combined buffer memory–main memory hierarchy can be viewed as a virtual memory with statistically defined characteristics. The key characteristics of interest are: (1) S, the effective size, (2) C, the effective cost per byte, and (3) T, the effective access time per byte. These virtual memory characteristics may be computed as follows:

$$S' = S_2$$

$$C' = \frac{S_1 \times C_1 + S_2 \times C_2}{S_2}$$

$$T' = f_1 \times T_1 + f_2 \times T_2$$

where:

S_1 is the total size of M_1

S_2 is the total size of M_2

C_1 is the cost per byte of M_1

C_2 is the cost per byte of M_2

T_1 is the average access time for M_1

T_2 is the average access time for M_2

f_1 is the success frequency function for M_1

f_2 is $1 - f_1$

The IBM System/370 Model 158 has reportedly attained a buffer success frequency of about 90 percent on the average. The correspondingly effective performance can be computed as follows:

	M_1	M_2	M'
Size (S)	8K	1M	1M
Cost (C) per byte	$4.00	50¢	53¢
Access (T)	230ηs	1μs	307ηs

Thus, we can see that the effective performance of the overall virtual memory, M', has a size and cost comparable to M_2 and an access time comparable to M_1. The comparison of these performances is illustrated dramatically in Figure 3-55.

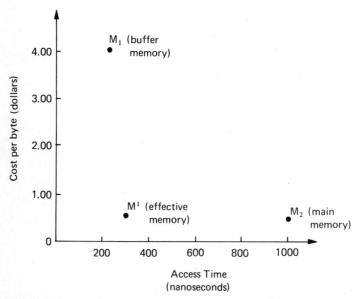

Figure 3-55 Comparison of memory performances

3-10.3.5 OTHER CONSIDERATIONS

For the sake of brevity, this presentation of the buffer memory system has simplified many important considerations. The appropriate references should be studied for more details (Liptay, 1968; Mattson, 1970; Wilkes, 1965; Madnick, 1973).

The algorithm used for assigning buffer memory blocks to main memory blocks always assigns a particular memory block to the same buffer memory block (i.e., to the one with the same column number). This is called a *completely constrained set associative mapping.* The technique is simple and compact, and requires no lengthy searching, but it does have drawbacks. Notice, for example, that only a single block from a column may be in M_1 at one time regardless of the number of rows. If the sample program on page 193 were changed to:

```
       . . .
4096   ADD       1,0
4100   GOTO      4096
       . . .
```

since both the instructions ($r = 1$, $c = 0$) and the data ($r = 0$, $c = 0$) come from the same column, they would have to be stored in $M_1(0)$. Every time the data reference were made, the copy of the instructions in $M_1(0)$ would be replaced by a copy of the data, and vice versa. Thus, there would be two references to M_2 for every iteration of the loop and M_1 would be almost completely useless. This problem is called a *buffer conflict.*

One solution to the buffer conflict problem is to have several "separate" M_1's, each with its own index array. If this is done, it is possible to have several blocks from the same column in the buffer storage unit at the same time. Since the probability of a buffer conflict is only about 1 in 128 (number of columns) it is probably necessary (except under very unusual circumstances) to have only either 2 or 4 M_1 blocks per column to minimize the problem. This is illustrated in Figure 3-56.

The IBM System/370 model 158 has two buffer blocks per column, whereas the more powerful Model 168 has four. The use of multiple blocks per column, identified as a and b in Figure 3-56, results in a new problem, *buffer replacement strategy.* For example, if a reference were made to location 4096 ($r = 1$, $c = 0$) and it were not in M_{1a}, or M_{1b}, a decision would have to be made as to which block (a or b) should be replaced by the block from 4096 to be fetched from M_2. A Least Recently Used strategy is normally used to resolve this problem.

3-11 SUMMARY

In this chapter we have presented a spectrum of memory management schemes, each of which generally had all the advantages of its predecessor and solved some

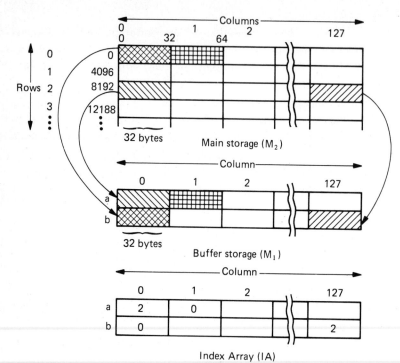

Figure 3-56 Multiple buffer blocks per column

of the disadvantages of its predecessor, although at a cost of increased complexity and overhead.

We have spent a considerable amount of time on memory management because it is usually the most significant distinguishing characteristic between contemporary operating systems and because it has been the object of considerable research.

QUESTIONS

3-1 Develop a sequence of jobs, similar to that shown in Section 3-3.2.5, with memory requirements and termination times that perform well for each of the following partitioned algorithms in turn, but not for the other two.
1 Static partitions
2 Best fit
3 First fit

3-2 We have presented two partitioned memory management algorithms, best fit and first fit. Yet another algorithm has been proposed: "worst fit." Worst fit always tries to assign the job to the largest partition found.
1 Comment on implementation.
2 Comment on expected performance.
3 Show a sequence of jobs where worst fit is better than best fit or first fit.
4 Show a sequence of jobs where worst fit is bad.

3-3 Assume the following:
- Average job size is 256K bytes.
- There are 1024K bytes of memory.
- If partitioned memory is used, then one-third of memory is wasted due to fragmentation.
- Alternatively, if recompactable partitions are used, then half of a partition size is wasted.
- I/O wait time is 70 percent.
- Average job run time is 10 seconds.
- Recompacting can be done at a rate of 1,000,000 bytes/second.
- Recompacting overhead time is 1 millisecond.

1 Does it pay to recompact? Show why, e.g., memory wasted, system I/O wait time.
2 For what memory size, if any, would your answer to (1) change?
3 For what job run time does your answer to (1) change?
4 If a relocation partition scheme were used, then all jobs would run 5 percent slower because of address computations of the relocation hardware. How do your answers to (1), (2), and (3) change?

3-4 Yet another algorithm for partitioned memory allocation has been proposed. In this algorithm all free areas are sorted in ascending addresses (similar to first fit). If a small amount of memory, e.g., less than 32K is requested, the proposed algorithm searches the free storage area list starting from the bottom. If a large memory partition is requested, the algorithm starts at the top of the list and works down.

1 Find some job sequence where this technique is demonstrably better than first fit and best fit.

2 Discuss the advantages of this technique, i.e., when it is good and when it is bad.

3-5 We defined the relocatable partitions memory management technique in terms of a single relocation register per job.

1 What benefits can be obtained by having two relocation registers? (List one benefit and explain.)

2 Would we have to change the processor address generation process to use two relocation registers? Why or why not? (If yes, how?)

3-6

1 Establish a set of software conventions or restrictions for all programs so that they could be relocated (as in a relocation partition scheme) on a 360.

2 Can you relocate on this machine without such conventions? If so, give an example.

3-7

1 What is multiprogramming? Why is it used?

2 What is fragmentation? How can it be overcome?

3 What is the difference between a page and a segment?

4 What is a pure procedure? What is the advantage of using pure code?

3-8

1 For each of the memory management schemes, describe briefly the major drawbacks.

2 While schemes such as segmented-paged allocation may be considered as the "best" for memory management, often such schemes are not feasible (i.e., you would not use the same scheme for MULTICS as for a 4K minicomputer). For any four of the memory management schemes, describe an environment in which it might be preferable to other schemes.

3-9 When you begin to talk about large multiprogrammed systems, you find that one important function of memory management is related to the idea of program sharing. Specifically, suppose four different processes wish to perform PL/1 compilations at the same time. The physical code of the PL/1 compiler is obviously the same for each process, with each process requiring a different set of "work areas." A program as complex as a PL/1 compiler is likely to be very large in terms of its core requirement. It would be nice, then, to allow the four processes to share the same physical area of core associated with the instructions for the compiler. In each of the following cases describe how a compiler that allowed this kind of sharing to take place could be written.

    1 A partitioned memory system like that IBM 360/370 family

    2 A two relocation register machine like the PDP-10

    3 A paged system like the IBM 370

    4 A segmented system like the HIS 6180 (MULTICS)

3-10 We have discussed seven methods of memory management in detail. These methods present a broad spectrum of flexibility in handling the problems of memory management, and an equally broad range of complexity in their approach to the problem. They are listed in the table below in order of increasing complexity. For each one indicate what problem or problems are solved by going to it from the method above it in the list, and what new hardware features (if any) and software features (if any) are needed to accomplish the transition.

MEMORY MANAGEMENT SCHEME	PROBLEM SOLVED	NEW HARDWARE NEEDED	NEW SOFTWARE NEEDED
Single contiguous allocation	——	——	——
Partitioned allocation			
Relocatable partitioned allocation			
Paging			
Demand paging			
Segmentation			
Segmentation with paging			

3-11

1 Define the user's address space.

2 What is its mapping into core for:

  a Single contiguous allocation?

  b Relocatable partitioned allocation?

  c Segmentation with demand paging?

3-12

1 Given a machine with multiple relocation and bounds registers, how would you implement a paging scheme with multiprogramming?

2 How would you implement multiprogramming with an arbitrarily large number of users given only a 1-bit protect key? (You must still protect users from one another.)

3-13 What purpose does the "changed bit" per page serve in a demand-paged system?

3-14 Consider a paged memory management environment (i.e., without demand paging).

1 If memory size is M bytes, average partition size is P bytes and page size is N bytes (Page Map Table Entry size n is ideally $\log_2 \frac{M}{N}$ bits), what is optimal page size N so as to minimize wasted memory in paged memory management (i.e., sum of page breakage plus PMTs)? Express your answer in terms of M and P.

2 Solve for the case of M = 512K and P = 128K bytes.

3 Does your answer to (2) change much if the PMTE size is constrained to be in multiples of bytes (i.e., $n = \dfrac{\log_2 \left(\frac{M}{N} \right)}{8}$ roundup)? When is this constraint significant?

3-15 Channels, as we have discussed them, require real physical addresses in their CCWs. If we were to use a paged memory without making hardware modifications to the I/O channel, a problem would arise had we attempted a read or write operation and, in the midst of its processing, the relevant page were chosen for removal. Two possible solutions exist:

- Temporarily wire down the buffer into real memory and change the CCWs to real addresses. That is, somehow keep the paging software from selecting the buffer page(s) for removal.

- Set aside a buffer within the (nonpaged) temporary storage area of the operating system and when I/O is complete (for a read) move the data into the page(s) in the virtual memory.

1 How would you implement scheme 1, i.e., what databases and/or routines would have to change? How would you determine which pages must be wired down?

QUESTIONS   **203**

2 If a user's buffer crossed a page boundary and his two pages were not contiguous in real core, how would you accomplish a read operation under scheme 1?

3 Under scheme 2 we are assuming that real memory is divided into a paged section and an operating system area. If a user requests I/O and there is no room left in the operating system area for his buffer, would he have to wait for space to be freed or could the operating system recover part of the paged area for use as a buffer? If the latter, how would this be done, and what problems would it create?

4 What will determine which is a better scheme? List one advantage and disadvantage for each scheme.

5 Would I/O handling be simplified if the channel could process CCWs with virtual addresses (rather than requiring real addresses)? If so, why would it be simplified and how would it be done?

3-16 In this problem we want to study the effect of changing page size in a demand-paged environment.

Consider the following sequence of memory references from a 460-word program:

10, 11, 104, 170, 73, 309, 185, 245, 246, 434, 458, 364

1 Show the page trace table for this sequence assuming a page size of 100 words, with 200 words of primary memory available to the program and a FIFO replacement algorithm. Find the success frequency for this page trace under these conditions.

2 Now reduce the page size to 50 words and produce the page trace table and success as above, indicating the pages here as 1', 1'', 2', 2'', etc.

3 Do the same for a page size of 200 words.

4 Discuss your results. Would you expect the behavior you found here to hold true when page sizes are halved or doubled?

5 What a priori advantages are gained by using smaller pages? What are the offsetting factors? Keep in mind that transferring 200 words of information to main memory takes *less* than twice as long as transferring 100 words, because of the way secondary storage operates.

6 Repeat (1) through (3) for a primary memory size of 400 words.

7 What is the effect of making more memory available to the program? Would you expect this effect to occur always? Why or why not? What changes might be expected if the page trace were much longer, as it would be in a real program?

8 It is unlikely that the page trace we have examined here would be found in the execution of an actual program. Why? Would you expect the

success frequency of an actual program under similar conditions to be higher or lower than those found here?

3-17 If we have the following hardware configuration,

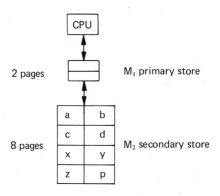

the paging scheme would be to pull pages from M_2 into M_1 when they are needed and to push pages from M_1 out to M_2 when space in M_1 is needed.

The following table produces a representation of what happens when the above page trace is inputted into a FIFO replacement algorithm where the number of pages in M_1 is 2.

Page trace P	a	a	b	b	c	c	a	b	
Page fetches F	*		*		*		*	*	F = 5
M_1 contents	a	a	b	b	c	c	a	b	
	–	–	a	a	b	b	c	a	

The most useful piece of information this table produces is the number of page fetches (faults) generated. It is this figure divided by the total number of references (length of page trace) and subtracted from 1 that is called the success frequency s.

$$f = \frac{F}{P} = \frac{5}{8} = .625$$

$$s = 1 - f = .375$$

For the rest of this problem let P be the page trace:

P = abacabdbacd

1 Produce a page trace table similar to the one above for page trace P using a FIFO removal algorithm and a primary memory whose size is two pages. What is the success frequency of this paging algorithm?

2 A Least Recently Used removal algorithm requires that when a page is to be removed, the page chosen should be the one that has been unused for the longest time. Repeat (1) using LRU.

3 Explain briefly why there was one extra page fault for the FIFO removal algorithm. In other words, what characteristics of page trace P lead LRU to perform better than FIFO?

4 Repeat (1) and this time let the memory size of M_1 be three pages.

5 Explain briefly what happened in (4). Specifically, what effect has the size of M_1 had on S? Is this result necessarily a general trend? What effect would changing the size of M_2 have on S?

6 The FIFO and LRU removal algorithms seem intuitively good methods. A Most Recently Used removal algorithm would seem intuitively bad. Try (1) again with an MRU removal algorithm. What does this indicate about our intuition and the generality of the characteristics of a single page trace such as P?

3-18

1 With a given multilevel memory system the success function seems to exhibit dependencies on the job mix currently in execution. Where do these dependencies come from and what can be done to minimize them?

2 What hardware and software tricks are used in multilevel memory systems to improve the success function as defined above, and what properties of programs do they exploit?

3 Given the individual specifications of access time, bandwidth, cost, size of components, and the success functions, how do you calculate the overall access time, bandwidth, cost, and size for the multilevel system configured as follows?

CPU - - - - - M1 - - - M2 - - - M3

f_{12} = success function for M1
f_{23} = success function for M2
B_1, B_2, B_3 = bandwidths for M_1, M_2, M_3
t_1, t_2, t_3 = access time for M_1, M_2, M_3
c_1, c_2, c_3 = cost/bit for M_1, M_2, M_3
s_1, s_2, s_3 = size in bits for M_1, M_2, M_3
B = overall bandwidth
t = overall access time
c = overall cost/bit
s = overall size

3-19 In discussing virtual memory, we have considered the user's view of his address space. Two possible views of a user's address space are shown below. In the first, the user's address space includes the operating system; in the second, it contains only the user's program area. Having an area in one's address space does not necessarily give the user access to it. Under OS/360, the user's address space includes the operating system as well as other users in the system, but this does not (theoretically) allow him to clobber these other areas because of the protect key system.

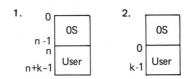

1 Under scheme 2, how would the user communicate with (e.g., call) the operating system?
2 Describe the differences between the two schemes in terms of a user's passing an argument by location to an operating system routine (e.g., reading a card into the user's specified buffer area).

3-20 The Interstellar Blundering Manufacturer Corporation has decided to develop and produce a computer. Two groups were assigned to develop the system; both came up with almost exactly the same system except for the memory system. Group A proposed an automatic two-level (buffer memory) memory system whereas group B proposed a conventional memory system.

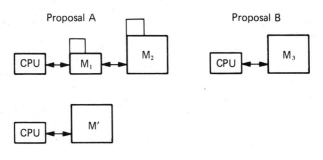

	Z (bytes)	τ (seconds)	C (cost/byte)
M_1	10^4	10^{-7}	10^2
M_2	10^6	10^{-6}	10^1
M'	10^6	τ'	C'
M_3	10^6	2×10^{-7}	2×10^1

A prototype model A was built and equipped with two counters, K_1 and K_2. K_1 is incremented every time a "fetch" is satisfied by M_1 and K_2 is incremented whenever a "fetch" must be made to M_2. After a year of actual use, it was found that $K_1/(K_1 + K_2) = 0.90$. As a result, group A suggested that their two-level memory may be viewed as equivalent to a conventional memory system with memory M'.

1 What is a reasonable estimate for τ'?

2 What is a reasonable estimate for C'?

3 What assumptions did you have to make to answer (1) and (2)?

4 If M' assumptions are considered, is there any user circumstance where A would be preferred to B? If so, what circumstance?

5 If M' assumptions are considered, is there any user circumstance where B would be preferred to A? If so, what circumstance?

3-21

1 MULTICS is a paged and segmented system. The Segment Map Table in MULTICS is itself a segment and is called the Descriptor Segment (DS). All segments, including the DS, are paged in MULTICS. A special register, called the Descriptor Base Register (DBR), points to the Page Map Table for the DS. What is involved in address calculation in a system such as MULTICS? Specifically, what steps must be taken in accessing a location addressed in the form segment/offset? The idea of this question is not to bring out detailed information about MULTICS, but rather to make you think about the hardware or software overhead for addressing in a paged and segmented system.

2 In the MULTICS system it is possible to contain the DSs for several users in core at the same time, loading the DBR with the appropriate DS base address when a particular user program is running. In one implementation the procedure that switches among users (SWAP_DBR) operates under address translation mode and has the same *segment number* in everybody's name space (i.e., the offset within the Descriptor Segment of the core address of the procedure is the same for everybody: $k_A = k_B$). It is then possible to switch users by executing a single instruction—the one that changes the contents of the DBR. Discuss the complications introduced if the switching procedure (SWAP_DBR) had a different segment number for each user.

3-22 Demand paging and demand segmentation are two memory management techniques that may give a user a larger virtual memory.

1 State when segment swapping is better.

2 Under what circumstances is one preferable to the other, and why?

3-23 You are given a machine with segmentation (but not paging) hardware, and you are asked to implement a demand paging system on this machine. To do this, you can use only software; no hardware additions may be made to the machine.

1 How would you do this? Be specific. Consider the hardware involved in segmentation, and what facilities are needed for paging.

2 Is it possible to do the same thing in reverse? In other words, if you were given a machine with paging hardware, could you use it to implement a segmented system? If so, indicate briefly how this could be done. If not, explain why not.

3-24 On most contemporary computers the I/O processors require "real" absolute addresses even if the CPU has virtual memory addressing. This means that the operating system must convert the channel programs in the user's address space to "real" channel programs that the I/O processors can handle.

1 If a demand-paged memory environment is assumed, what actions and tests must be made prior to conversion of the channel programs?

2 What additional memory block state is needed?

3 How can the data chaining CCW feature be used to handle I/O buffers that cross page boundaries?

4 Describe and flowchart the translation algorithm.

5 Is the translation algorithm simpler or more complex in a segmented memory environment? Why?

Processor Management

4

Processor management is concerned with the management of the physical processors, specifically, the assignment of processors to processes. Examining Figure 4-1, we can identify the following modules: the job scheduler, which creates the processes and, in a nonmultiprogrammed environment, would decide which process is to receive a processor; the processor scheduler, which, in a multiprogramming environment, decides which of the ready processes receives a processor, at what time, and for how long; and the traffic controller, which keeps track of the status of the process. There is a similar state diagram for every process in a system. In most systems it is necessary to synchronize processes and jobs, a task that is also performed by modules of processor management.

We discuss three topics in this chapter: job scheduling (Abell, 1970; Browne, 1972; Coffman, 1968), process scheduling—including traffic controller (Baskett, 1970; Hansen, 1971; Kleinrock, 1970; Lampson, 1968; Oppenheimer, 1967; Varney, 1971; Buzen, 1971), and synchronization of jobs and processes (Bernstein, 1969; Dijkstra, 1968; Haberman, 1971; Horning, 1973; Spier, 1969).

Figure 4-1 depicts the domains of job scheduling and process scheduling. The job scheduler can be viewed as a macroscheduler, choosing which jobs will run. The process scheduler can be viewed as a microscheduler, assigning processors to the processes associated with scheduled jobs.

The user views his job as a collection of tasks he wants the computer system to perform for him. The user may subdivide his job into job steps, which are sequentially processed subtasks (e.g., compile, load, execute). The system creates processes to do the computation of the job steps.

Job scheduling is concerned with the management of jobs, and processor scheduling is concerned with the management of processes. In either case, the processor is the key resource.

In a nonmultiprogramming system no distinction is made (and none need be) between process scheduling and job scheduling, as there is a one-to-one correspond-

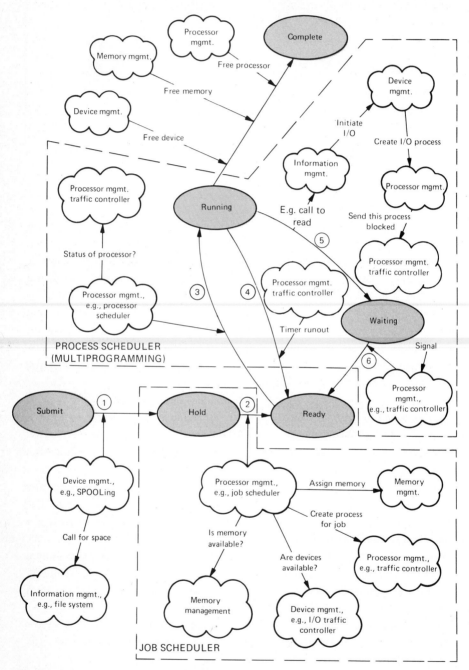

Figure 4-1 Process view of an operating system

ence between a job and its process and only one job is allowed in the system at a time. In such a simple system the job scheduler chooses one job to run. Once it is chosen, a process is created and assigned to the processor.

For more general multiprogramming systems, the *job scheduler* chooses a small subset of the jobs submitted and lets them "into" the system. That is, the job scheduler creates processes for these jobs and assigns the processes some resources. It must decide, for example, which two or three jobs of the 100 submitted will have any resources assigned to them. The *process scheduler* decides which of the processes within this subset will be assigned a processor, at what time, and for how long.

4-1 STATE MODEL

Let us pretend we are a job and follow our path through the states of Figure 4-1.

My friendly programmer wrote my program code several days ago. He submitted my code and appropriate control cards to the computing center (*submit state*). An operator took my code and caused it to be read into the computer and copied onto a disk where a job scheduler could examine it (*hold state*). Eventually, the job scheduler chose me to run and set up a process for me (*ready state*). To get my process into a ready state faster on a manually scheduled system, my friendly programmer might have inserted a green card (a five-dollar bill) in front of my deck. After being scheduled and set up by the job scheduler, my process was finally assigned a processor to execute my code (*running state*) by the process scheduler module. At that time I was given a "time quantum," i.e., a time limit for running. When that time quantum was up, I still was not completed. Therefore, my process was sent back into the ready state.

Sometime later the process scheduler gave my process another time quantum and assigned a processor (running state). During this time quantum my process almost finished but still had to print my answer. Therefore, my process initiated another process, an I/O process, and had to wait (*blocked state*) until my I/O was completed.

My I/O process has a similar state diagram—it became *ready* when my CPU process initiated I/O. When the I/O process finished, it signaled my blocked process that it was through.

When the operating system received the signal that my I/O process was finished, the traffic controller module changed my CPU process from the blocked state to the ready state again. This time when the process scheduler assigned a processor to my process (running state), I finished all my work (*completed state*).

We can identify the following modules of processor management.

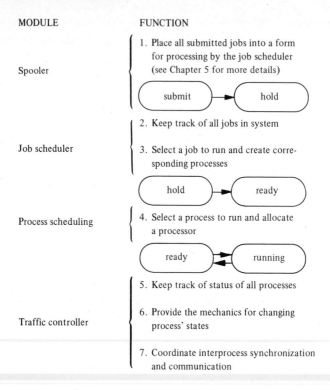

MODULE	FUNCTION
Spooler	1. Place all submitted jobs into a form for processing by the job scheduler (see Chapter 5 for more details) submit → hold
Job scheduler	2. Keep track of all jobs in system 3. Select a job to run and create corresponding processes hold → ready
Process scheduling	4. Select a process to run and allocate a processor ready ⇄ running
Traffic controller	5. Keep track of status of all processes 6. Provide the mechanics for changing process' states 7. Coordinate interprocess synchronization and communication

4-1.1 Job Scheduler

We have shown the process view of an operating system in Figure 4-1, n .ing the scope of job scheduling. The job scheduler is the "super" manager, which must:

1 Keep track of the status of all jobs. It must note which jobs are trying to get some service (hold state) and the status of all jobs being serviced (ready, running, or blocked state).

2 Choose the policy by which jobs will "enter the system" (i.e., go from hold state to ready state). This decision may be based on such characteristics as priority, resources requested, or system balance.

3 Allocate the necessary resources for the scheduled job by use of memory, device, and processor management.

4 Deallocate these resources when the job is done.

4-1.2 Process Scheduling

Once the job scheduler has moved a job from *hold* to *ready*, it creates one or more processes for this job. Who decides which processes in the system get a processor, when, and for how long? The process scheduling modules make these decisions.
Specifically, the following functions must be performed:

1 Keeping track of the status of the process (all processes are either running, ready, or blocked). The module that performs this function has been called the *traffic controller* (Saltzer, 1966).

2 Deciding which process gets a processor and for how long. This is performed by the *processor scheduler.*

3 Allocation of a processor to a process. This requires resetting of processor registers to correspond to the process' correct state. This task is performed by the traffic controller.

4 Deallocation of a processor, such as when the running process exceeds its current quantum or must wait for an I/O completion. This requires that all processor state registers be saved to allow future reallocation. This task is performed by the traffic controller.

4-1.3 Job and Process Synchronization

On the job level there are usually mechanisms for passing conditions between job steps. For example, we might want to prevent job step 4 from being performed if job step 1 had failed.

On the process level there must be mechanisms to prevent race conditions. A race condition exists when the result of a computation varies, depending on the timing of other processes. For example, one process requests a printer while another process is printing; if the printer were to be also assigned to the second process, the output would be intermixed between the two processes. We must have a mechanism to stop the second process from running until the first process releases the printer.

The P and V operators and semaphores are one set of mechanisms for coordinating the assignment of processors to processes (Dijkstra, 1968). In addition, we must be aware of possible deadlock situations in cases where there are two processes, each of which is waiting for resources that the other has and will not give up. In this situation, no processor can be assigned to either process.

4-1.4 Structure of Processor Management

The three main sections of this chapter, job scheduling, process scheduling, and synchronization, are all concerned with the assignment of processors to processes. Hence, they are all included in this chapter on processor management. In some cases, especially with job scheduling, interaction with the other resource managers takes place.

In summary, processor management operates on two levels—assigning processors to jobs and assigning processors to processes.

On the job level, processor management is concerned with such questions as which jobs will be run and which will run first. At this first level processor management is not concerned with multiprogramming. It assumes that once a job is scheduled, it will run. Job scheduling can run concurrently with other users' programs or other system functions. Thus job scheduling may itself be a separate process, as shown in Figure 4-2.

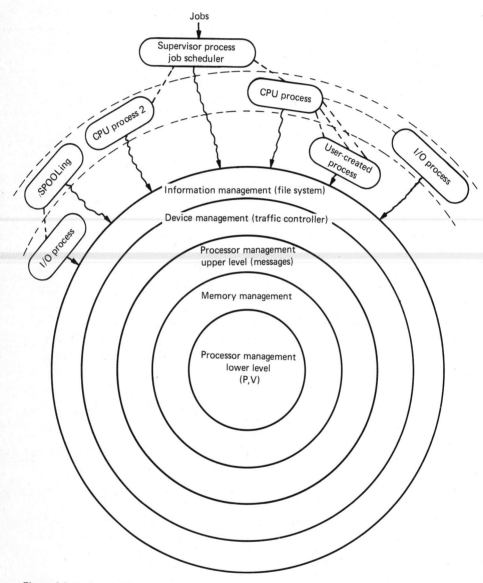

Figure 4-2 Hierarchical view of computer-based operating system levels for a real or extended machine

Once a job is scheduled, the system must perform the functions of creating processes, destroying processes, and sending messages between processes. In a general system these functions may be requested by users' processes, job scheduler, and other processes. Thus the functions may be common to all address spaces (see Figure 4-2–Processor Management Upper Level).

In a multiprogramming environment the process scheduler and the synchronization mechanisms may be called by all modules of the system. Thus they form the very center of the kernel of a system (Figure 4-2–Processor Management Lower Level). This model of system structure is the basis for the sample operating system presented in Chapter 7.

The job scheduler is like the coordinator of a contest; he decides who will enter the contest but not who will win it. The process scheduler decides which participant will win. In a nonmultiprogramming environment only one contestant is allowed to enter.

4-2 JOB SCHEDULING

The functions of the job scheduler may be done quite simply, quite elaborately, or dynamically.

In a timesharing system such as the Compatible Time Sharing System (CTSS) (Crisman, 1965), the job scheduling policy may consist of admitting the first 30 users that log in (i.e., arrive). A simple two-level priority algorithm allows a user with a higher priority to force the logout (i.e., termination) of a lower priority user. The user to be logged out is chosen on the basis of the processor time he has used: the one who has used the most processor time gets logged out.

The job scheduling algorithm of a batch system such as OS/VS-2 can be sophisticated. It takes into account not only the time a job arrives but also priority, memory needs, device needs, processor needs, and system balance.

In this section we discuss some simple job scheduling policies. (In Chapter 9 we discuss the sophisticated job schedulers of some other systems.) We focus on the policies of job scheduling and their implications, dealing first with systems without multiprogramming, then with more general multiprogramming systems.

4-2.1 Functions

The job scheduler can be viewed as an overall supervisor that assigns system resources to certain jobs. Therefore, it must keep track of the jobs, invoke policies for deciding which jobs get resources, and allocate and deallocate the resources.

We have chosen not to spend a great deal of time on extremely detailed mechanisms for performing the functions of job scheduling. The reader may refer to Chapters 7 and 9 for as much detail regarding a particular scheduler as he wishes (right down to the code). We are mainly concerned here with the factors that go into scheduling, and the consequences that result. For example, if job scheduling is done by reference to memory needs only, what is the effect on turnaround time as compared with other scheduling policies?

Before discussing different policies, let us briefly address ourselves to the function of keeping track of jobs in a system. One mechanism for keeping track of jobs is to have a separate Job Control Block (JCB) for each job in the system. When a process is placed in hold state (Figure 4-1), a JCB is created for it with entries regarding its status and position in a job queue.

Job identification
Current state
Priority
Time estimate
etc.

Figure 4-3 Job Control Block

Figure 4-3 illustrates the type of information that may be contained in a Job Control Block. Some information, such as priority and time estimate, is obtained from the job control cards submitted with the job. Other information, such as current state, is set by the operating system (see Section 5-6.3 for further discussion of the JCB).

4-2.2 Policies

The job scheduler must choose from among the "hold" jobs those that will be made "ready" to run. In a small computing center this function may be done by an operator. He may choose arbitrarily, choose his friends, or choose the shortest job. In larger systems, e.g., OS/360, all submitted jobs may be first stored on a secondary storage device whereupon the job scheduler can examine all such jobs. It can then choose which jobs will have system resources committed to them and hence will be run.

We should note the following:

The key concept is that there are more jobs that wish to run than can be efficiently satisfied by the resources of the system.

In particular:

a most resources are finite (e.g., tapes, memory)

b many resources cannot be shared or easily reassigned to another process.

Scheduling is considered a policy issue because its goals are usually subjective (and sometimes contradictory). For example, how would you rank the following goals?

1 Running as many jobs as possible per day (only run short jobs)

2 Keeping the processor "busy" (only run computation-intensive long jobs)

3 Fairness to all jobs (what does "fair" mean?)

Typical considerations one must deal with in determining a job scheduling policy are:

1 Availability of special limited resources (e.g., tapes)

   a If you give preference, someone can "cheat." For example, if you always first run the job that requests a plotter, then some users will always request a plotter.

   b If you don't give preference, some user suffers an extra delay (e.g., must wait for tape to be mounted or plotter adjusted after having waited to be scheduled).

2 Cost–higher rates for faster service.

3 System commitments–processor time and memory–the more you want, the longer you wait.

4 System balancing–mixing I/O-intensive and CPU-intensive (at M.I.T., for example, you specify A-, B-, or C-type job).

5 Guaranteed service–setting a specific waiting time limit (1 hour) or a general limit (within 24 hours). (At least don't lose the job!)

6 Completing the job by or at a specific time (e.g., 5 PM).

Once the job scheduler has selected a collection of jobs to run, the process scheduler attempts to handle the microscopic scheduling (dynamic assignment of processor to processes). Even ignoring time quanta limits, a process will typically run less than 100 ms before becoming blocked to await I/O completion or a similar event.

The job and process scheduler may interact. The process scheduler may choose to "postpone" ("roll out") a process and require that it go through the macro-level job scheduling again in order to complete. This is especially true in a timesharing system as discussed in Section 4-6. It is impossible to expose all the subtleties of the above considerations. In the following sections we present a few simple examples.

4-2.3 Job Scheduling in Nonmultiprogrammed Environment

In this section let us assume no multiprogramming; that is, once a process has been assigned a processor, it does not release the processor until it is finished. We will first examine a simple example of scheduling jobs using a policy of trying to reduce the *average turnaround time*. Since there is no multiprogramming, we assume one CPU process is created for each job. Thus the terms *job* and *process* may be used interchangeably.

4-2.3.1 JOB SCHEDULING USING FIFO

Assume jobs arrive as indicated in Figure 4-4.

JOB NO.	ARRIVAL TIME	RUN TIME
1	10.00	2.00 hrs
2	10.10	1.00 hrs
3	10.25	0.25 hrs

Figure 4-4 Sample job arrival time

Job 1 arrived at 10 AM, and the job control card estimated that it would run for two hours. We assume that the estimate is in fact how long the job runs.

If we use a First In First Out (FIFO) algorithm, the jobs will be run as depicted in Figure 4-5. Average turnaround is computed as follows.

$$T = (\sum_{i}^{n} T_i) \times \frac{1}{n} \quad \text{where} \quad \begin{aligned} T_i &= F_i - A_i \\ F_i &= \text{finish time} \\ A_i &= \text{arrival time} \end{aligned}$$

JOB NO.	ARRIVAL TIME	START TIME	FINISH TIME	TURNAROUND TIME
1	10.00	10.00	12.00	2.00 hrs
2	10.10	12.00	13.00	2.90 hrs
3	10.25	13.00	13.25	3.00 hrs
				7.90 hrs

Average turnaround = 2.63 hrs

Figure 4-5 Jobs scheduled using FIFO

4-2.3.2 JOB SCHEDULING USING SHORTEST JOB FIRST

Is there a way to reduce the average turnaround time using a different scheduling algorithm? Figure 4-6 uses a scheduling algorithm that runs the "hold" job with the shortest run time first. That is, when Job 1 arrives, it is run. While Job 1 is running, Jobs 2 and 3 arrive. We choose to run Job 3 next because it has a shorter estimated run time than Job 2.

JOB NO.	ARRIVAL TIME	START TIME	FINISH TIME	TURNAROUND TIME
1	10.00	10.00	12.00	2.00 hrs
2	10.10	12.25	13.25	3.15 hrs
3	10.25	12.00	12.25	2.00 hrs
				7.15 hrs
Average turnaround = 2.38 hrs				

Figure 4-6 Scheduling jobs using shortest job first

Note that this algorithm did reduce the average turnaround, but was it "fairer" than that of FIFO? Ask Job 2—he doesn't think so!

4-2.3.3 JOB SCHEDULING USING FUTURE KNOWLEDGE

Is there any way to further improve the average turnaround time? For example, would future knowledge be helpful? If at 10 AM we knew that two short jobs were going to arrive shortly, would we run Job 1? Figure 4-7 depicts the result of a scheduling algorithm that has "future knowledge."

JOB NO.	ARRIVAL TIME	START TIME	FINISH TIME	TURNAROUND TIME
1	10.00	11.50	13.50	3.50 hrs
2	10.10	10.50	11.50	1.40 hrs
3	10.25	10.25	10.50	0.25 hrs
				5.15 hrs
CPU idle = .25 hr				
Average turnaround = 1.72 hrs				

Figure 4-7 Scheduling jobs using future knowledge

Note that we did reduce average turnaround time, but we "wasted" .25 hours of CPU time and probably made Job 1 an unhappy customer. The fact that allowing the CPU to be idle can improve turnaround time helps to explain why many computation centers would prefer to leave the CPU idle during the normally busy afternoon rather than start up a 1-hour low-priority job.

These job scheduling algorithms have several problems:

1 When one system using an algorithm that did not run long jobs immediately closed down after five years of operation, it was rumored that jobs were found that had been lost for over three years!

2 Future knowledge is rare (if you have it, we would suggest you use it in the stock market, not in scheduling!).

3 Run times are usually estimated approximations.

4 Other resources must be considered, such as memory requirements, I/O devices, etc.

Nevertheless, the examples of Figures 4-5 through 4-7 do indicate the benefits a good job scheduler can offer (2.63 hours average turnaround were reduced to 1.72). In large installations that run thousands of jobs a day, there may be hundreds of jobs in "hold" state to choose from at any given time.

4-2.3.4 MEASURE OF SCHEDULING PERFORMANCE

In the above examples we have used turnaround time as a measure of scheduling performance. Many other measures exist, however. For example, if a 1-minute job is scheduled and run immediately, it has a turnaround time of 1 minute. On the other hand, if a 1-hour job is scheduled and run immediately, it has a 1-hour turnaround time. Does this mean that the 1-hour job was treated poorly? No, since it is impossible to have a turnaround time that is less than the run time. In order to normalize these differences, we can define another measure, called the weighted turnaround time (W), which is $W = \frac{T}{R}$. T is the turnaround time, as computed earlier, and R is the actual run time.

In the examples of Figure 4-5, 4-6, and 4-7, the average weighted turnaround times are 5.3, 4.05, and 1.37, respectively. In these cases scheduling policies that improved turnaround time also improved weighted turnaround time. Is this always true? Some counter examples in the following sections will show it is not. For these reasons it is important that we define the measure of performance before answering the question: "Is that a 'good' scheduling algorithm?"

4-2.4 Job Scheduling in Multiprogrammed Environment

In the previous sections we discussed some simple job scheduler policies and techniques. In particular, we noted that, if our policy was to minimize average turnaround time, T, we should always run the job with the shortest run time.

For simplicity, we assumed that jobs were run one at a time. However, most systems actually use some form of multiprogramming. The function of the job scheduler in a multiprogramming environment is to select the jobs to be run.

Let us assume a simple process scheduling algorithm so that we can focus on the job scheduler. In Section 4-3 we shall discuss other process scheduling algorithms, but for now let us assume a round robin where each process in the system is assigned a processor for some small time quantum. That is, if n jobs are running (multiprogramming) simultaneously, they each get an equal share of run time.

4-2.4.1 JOB SCHEDULING WITH MULTIPROGRAMMING BUT NO I/O OVERLAP
How does a multiprogramming environment affect the scheduling? Figure 4-8 gives an example of a job mix.

JOB NO.	ARRIVAL TIME	RUN TIME
1	10.0	0.3 hr
2	10.2	0.5 hr
3	10.4	0.1 hr
4	10.5	0.4 hr
5	10.8	0.1 hr

Figure 4-8   Job arrival and run times

Figures 4-9a and b show the results of an FIFO scheduling algorithm, assuming no multiprogramming. Figure 4-9a graphically depicts times when the jobs are in core.

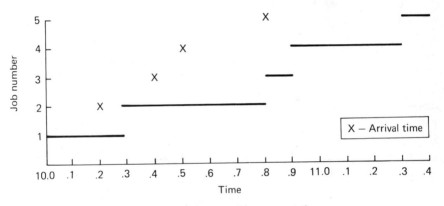

Figure 4-9a   FIFO — no multiprogramming: graphic representation

JOB NO.	ARRIVAL TIME	START TIME	FINISH TIME	TURNAROUND TIME	WEIGHTED TURNAROUND TIME
1	10.0	10.0	10.3	0.3	1.00
2	10.2	10.3	10.8	0.6	1.20
3	10.4	10.8	10.9	0.5	5.00
4	10.5	10.9	11.3	0.8	2.00
5	10.8	11.3	11.4	0.6	6.00
				2.8 hrs	15.20

Average turnaround, T = .56
Weighted average turnaround, W = 3.04

Figure 4.9b   FIFO—no multiprogramming: tabular representation

Figure 4-10 presents an analysis of the same job mix with multiprogramming but assuming no I/O (i.e., all jobs use only CPU). We assume a small timeslice; i.e., if two jobs are in memory, we assume they will be there twice as long, since the CPU alternately spends a short time with each.

At this point we can introduce the concept of *CPU headway* (Sekino, 1972). CPU headway is the amount of CPU time spent on a job. If two jobs are being multiprogrammed, each job's CPU headway will be equal to half of the clock time elapsed. We use this concept to help calculate when a job will finish in a multiprogramming environment.

In the example of Figure 4-10 we have assumed the availability of unlimited main memory and I/O devices; thus, a job may be started as soon as it arrives.

Note that Job 1 arrived at 10AM and was to run for .3 hours. However, after Job 1 had run for .2 hours, Job 2 arrived and was placed in memory. During the time segment 10.2 through 10.4, the processor was timesliced (switched back and forth) between Job 1 and Job 2. Thus even though Job 1 had only .1 hours of execution left, the processor was servicing two jobs, and it took .2 hours to complete Job 1. The reader should verify the other times in Figure 4-10.

What is the conclusion? Does multiprogramming improve or hurt performance?

From Figures 4-9 and 4-10 one would conclude that multiprogramming hurt performance based upon average turnaround time. Average turnaround time is .56 without multiprogramming and .6 with multiprogramming. (Note that average weighted turnaround time improves!)

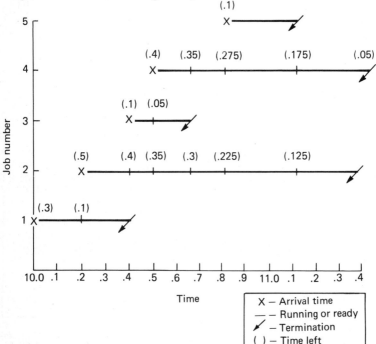

Figure 4-10a   Five jobs multiprogrammed — no I/O overlap

TIME	EVENT	NO. OF JOBS	% CPU PER JOB	ELAPSED TIME	HEAD-WAY PER JOB	JOB	TIME LEFT
10.0	Job 1 arrives					1	.3
10.2	Job 2 arrives	1	1	.2	.2	1 2	.1 .5
10.4	Job 3 arrives— Job 1 terminates	2	1/2	.2	.1	1 2 3	 .4 .1
10.5	Job 4 arrives	2	1/2	.1	.05	2 3 4	.35 .05 .4
10.65	Job 3 terminates	3	1/3	.15	.05	2 3 4	.3 .35
10.8	Job 5 arrives	2	1/2	.15	.075	2 4 5	.225 .275 .1
11.1	Job 5 terminates	3	1/3	.3	.1	2 4 5	.125 .175
11.35	Job 2 terminates	2	1/2	.25	.125	2 4	 .05
11.4	Job 4 terminates	1	1	.05	.05	4	

Figure 4-10b   Calculations for Figure 4-10a

JOB NO.	RUN TIME	START TIME	FINISH TIME	TURNAROUND TIME	WEIGHTED TURNAROUND TIME
1	0.3	10.0	10.4	0.4	1.33
2	0.5	10.2	11.35	1.15	2.3
3	0.1	10.4	10.65	0.25	2.5
4	0.4	10.5	11.4	0.9	2.25
5	0.1	10.8	11.1	0.3	3.0
				3.00	11.38

Average turnaround time, T = 0.6
Average weighted turnaround time, W = 2.276

Figure 4-10c   FIFO with multiprogramming

Even clearer examples can be found of multiprogramming hurting performance. Figure 4-11 shows four 1-hour jobs arriving simultaneously. In 4-11a all jobs are run in a multiprogrammed mode. Average turnaround time and weighted turnaround time equals 4 hours.

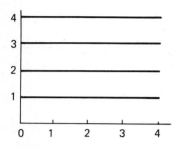

Average turnaround, T = 4
Average weighted turnaround, W = 4

(a) Jobs multiprogrammed

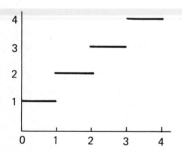

Average turnaround, T = 2.5
Average weighted turnaround, W = 2.5

(b) Jobs taken one at a time

Figure 4-11 Example of multi-programming hurting performance

In Figure 4-11b jobs are taken one at a time. That is, one job will finish in an hour; another will have to wait 2 hours; another, 3 hours; and the final one, 4 hours. Here average turnaround time and weighted turnaround time are 2.5 hours, clearly an improvement over multiprogramming.

Is multiprogramming always bad? No, not for certain job mixes. Study Figures 4-12 and 4-13.

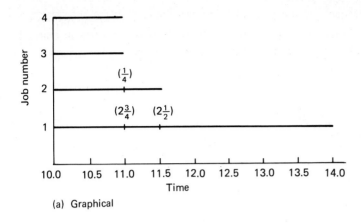

(a) Graphical

| | | | | | WEIGHTED |
JOB NO.	RUN TIME	START TIME	FINISH TIME	TURNAROUND TIME	TURNAROUND TIME
1	3.0	10.0	14.0	4.0	1.3
2	0.5	10.0	11.5	1.5	3.0
3	0.25	10.0	11.0	1.0	4.0
4	0.25	10.0	11.0	1.0	4.0
				7.5	12.3

Turnaround time, T = 1.88
Weighted turnaround time, W = 3.1

(b) Tabular

Figure 4-12   Example of scheduling with multiprogramming

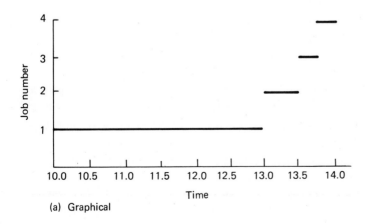

(a) Graphical

JOB NO.	RUN TIME	START TIME	FINISH TIME	TURNAROUND TIME	WEIGHTED TURNAROUND TIME
1	3.0	10.0	13.0	3.0	1.0
2	0.5	10.0	13.5	3.5	7.0
3	0.25	10.0	13.75	3.75	15.0
4	0.25	10.0	14.0	4.0	16.0
				14.25	39.0

Turnaround time, T = 3.56
Weighted turnaround time, W = 10.0

(b) Tabular

Figure 4-13 Example of scheduling without multiprogramming

If these jobs were run without multiprogramming (Figure 4-13) and the 3-hour job were run first, turnaround time, T, is 3.56 hours. Multiprogramming greatly improves the time, as shown in Figure 4-12, where T is only 1.88 hours.

4-2.4.2   JOB SCHEDULING WITH MULTIPROGRAMMING AND I/O OVERLAP

In actuality, part of a job's run time is I/O *wait* time that can be overlapped (i.e., the CPU can be used for other computations while the I/O is being handled by the I/O channel). How does this affect multiprogramming performance? Let us assume that 25 percent of a job's time is wait time. That is, for 25 percent of elapse time the CPU would be waiting for I/O *if* the job were run in a mono-programmed environment (all by itself).

However, in a multiprogrammed environment the processor could be assigned to another job during this wait time. It is possible, however, for all jobs to be waiting for I/O at the same time; thus the CPU may be still idle part of the time, as discussed in Section 3-2. The table of system wait percentages is reproduced again in Figure 4-14. The calculation of this table is described in Section 4-3.

In order to compute the average turnaround time, we need to determine when a job will complete. To do this, it is imperative to understand the concept of CPU headway, i.e., how much CPU "work" a job received in a given time interval.

Take two cases: first, if a job were run by itself and I/O wait were 25 percent, then in 1 hour of elapsed time only .75 hours of CPU headway would take place. Thus, if the CPU time needed were 1.5 hours, it would take 2 hours of elapsed time for that job to complete.

Now take the more complicated case of two jobs starting at the same time, both of which have I/O wait time of 25 percent and both of which need 1.5 hours of CPU time (i.e., 2 hours of elapsed time when monoprogrammed). When will they complete? Using the table of Figure 4-14 for two such jobs, the CPU will be idle 4

Percent wait time when monoprogrammed

Degree of multiprogramming	5.0	10.0	15.0	20.0	25.0	30.0	35.0	40.0	45.0	50.0	55.0	60.0	65.0	70.0	75.0	80.0	85.0	90.0	95.0
1	0.1	0.6	1.3	2.4	4.0	6.0	8.6	11.8	15.5	20.0	25.2	31.0	37.6	45.0	52.9	61.5	70.7	80.2	90.0
2	0.0	0.0	0.1	0.2	0.4	0.0	1.5	2.5	4.1	6.3	9.3	13.4	18.9	25.9	34.6	45.1	57.2	70.6	85.1
3	0.0	0.0	0.0	0.0	0.0	0.1	0.2	0.4	0.8	1.5	2.8	4.8	8.1	13.1	20.6	31.1	44.7	61.4	80.2
4	0.0	0.0	0.0	0.0	0.0	0.0	0.0	0.1	0.1	0.3	0.7	1.4	2.9	5.8	11.0	19.9	33.6	52.5	75.3
5	0.0	0.0	0.0	0.0	0.0	0.0	0.0	0.0	0.0	0.1	0.1	0.4	0.9	2.2	5.2	11.7	24.1	44.1	70.4
6	0.0	0.0	0.0	0.0	0.0	0.0	0.0	0.0	0.0	0.0	0.0	0.1	0.2	0.7	2.2	6.3	16.3	36.2	65.7
7	0.0	0.0	0.0	0.0	0.0	0.0	0.0	0.0	0.0	0.0	0.0	0.0	0.1	0.2	0.8	3.0	10.4	28.9	60.9
8	0.0	0.0	0.0	0.0	0.0	0.0	0.0	0.0	0.0	0.0	0.0	0.0	0.0	0.1	0.3	1.3	6.1	22.4	56.3
9	0.0	0.0	0.0	0.0	0.0	0.0	0.0	0.0	0.0	0.0	0.0	0.0	0.0	0.0	0.1	0.5	3.4	16.8	51.7
10	0.0	0.0	0.0	0.0	0.0	0.0	0.0	0.0	0.0	0.0	0.0	0.0	0.0	0.0	0.0	0.2	1.7	12.1	47.2
11	0.0	0.0	0.0	0.0	0.0	0.0	0.0	0.0	0.0	0.0	0.0	0.0	0.0	0.0	0.0	0.1	0.8	8.3	42.7
12	0.0	0.0	0.0	0.0	0.0	0.0	0.0	0.0	0.0	0.0	0.0	0.0	0.0	0.0	0.0	0.0	0.3	5.4	38.5
13	0.0	0.0	0.0	0.0	0.0	0.0	0.0	0.0	0.0	0.0	0.0	0.0	0.0	0.0	0.0	0.0	0.1	3.4	34.3
14	0.0	0.0	0.0	0.0	0.0	0.0	0.0	0.0	0.0	0.0	0.0	0.0	0.0	0.0	0.0	0.0	0.1	2.0	30.3
15	0.0	0.0	0.0	0.0	0.0	0.0	0.0	0.0	0.0	0.0	0.0	0.0	0.0	0.0	0.0	0.0	0.0	1.1	26.4
16	0.0	0.0	0.0	0.0	0.0	0.0	0.0	0.0	0.0	0.0	0.0	0.0	0.0	0.0	0.0	0.0	0.0	0.6	22.8
17	0.0	0.0	0.0	0.0	0.0	0.0	0.0	0.0	0.0	0.0	0.0	0.0	0.0	0.0	0.0	0.0	0.0	0.3	19.4
18	0.0	0.0	0.0	0.0	0.0	0.0	0.0	0.0	0.0	0.0	0.0	0.0	0.0	0.0	0.0	0.0	0.0	0.1	16.3
19	0.0	0.0	0.0	0.0	0.0	0.0	0.0	0.0	0.0	0.0	0.0	0.0	0.0	0.0	0.0	0.0	0.0	0.1	13.4
20	0.0	0.0	0.0	0.0	0.0	0.0	0.0	0.0	0.0	0.0	0.0	0.0	0.0	0.0	0.0	0.0	0.0	0.1	11.4

Figure 4-14   Table: percent wait time when multiprogrammed

percent of the time. What is the total CPU headway possible in 1 hour for both jobs? It is .96 CPU hours. If this is divided equally between the two jobs, each job gets only .48 hours of CPU headway per hour of elapsed time. Therefore, it will take 1.5 divided by .48 or 3.13 hours of total elapsed time to complete both of these jobs. This is a considerable improvement over the 4 hours that would have elapsed if these jobs were run monoprogrammed and processed serially.

Figure 4-15 presents the computation of the average turnaround time for the collection of jobs shown in Figure 4-10, but with 25 percent I/O wait time. The figure shows the major events (e.g., job arrival or finish), as was done in Figure 4-10. During these intervals between events a fixed number of jobs are running. The "Number of Jobs" column in Figure 4-15b is the number of jobs running in that period between the last event and the current event. Figure 4-14 determines the appropriate overall CPU wait time assuming that each job has a wait time of 25 percent. The column "% CPU per Job" is the percent of CPU time spent per job. Multiplying this times the elapsed time interval gives the CPU headway per job. Subtracting this headway from the previous CPU time left per job gives the new time left per job. We strongly urge the reader to verify the calculations of Figure 4-15.

Due to the effect of multiprogramming on turnaround time, the analysis frequently becomes quite complex. We assumed all of the jobs had a 25 percent I/O wait time. In real systems each job has a different I/O wait time percentage. Furthermore, typical I/O wait percentages reported on contemporary computers are usually in the range of 50 to 80 percent.

JOB	MONO-PROGRAM RUN TIME	START TIME	FINISH TIME	TURNAROUND TIME	WEIGHTED TURNAROUND TIME
1	0.3	10.0	10.356	0.356	1.187
2	0.5	10.2	11.05	0.850	1.700
3	0.1	10.4	10.581	0.181	1.810
4	0.4	10.5	11.158	0.658	1.645
5	0.1	10.8	11.025	0.225	2.250
				2.270	8.592

Turnaround time, T = .454
Weighted turnaround time, W = 1.718

Figure 4-15a   Job scheduling times for jobs with multiprogramming and I/O overlap: summary analysis

TIME	EVENT	NO. OF JOBS	CPU WAIT	% CPU PER JOB	ELAPSED TIME	JOB	HEAD-WAY PER JOB	CPU TIME NEEDED
10.0	Job 1 arrives					1		.225
10.2	Job 2 arrives	1	25	75	.2	1	.15	.075
						2		.375
10.356	Job 1 finishes	2	4	48	.156	1	.075	
						2	.075	.3
10.4	Job 3 arrives	1	25	75	.04375	2	.033	.267
						3		.075
10.5	Job 4 arrives	2	4	48	.1	2	.048	.219
						3	.048	.027
						4		.3
10.581	Job 3 finishes	3	0	33.3	.081	2	.027	.192
						3	.027	
						4	.027	.273
10.8	Job 5 arrives	2	4	48	.219	2	.105	.087
						4	.105	.168
						5		.075
11.025	Job 5 finishes	3	0	33.3	.225	2	.075	.012
						4	.075	.093
						5	.075	
11.05	Job 2 finishes	2	4	48	.025	2	.012	
						4	.012	.081
11.158	Job 4 finishes	1	25	75	.108	4	.081	

Figure 4-15b Job scheduling times for jobs with multiprogramming and I/O overlap: tabular analysis

The concepts of CPU headway and the turnaround time stretchout are important ones. Many advanced-usage charging policies adopted by computer centers attempt to determine the corresponding monoprogramming run times for jobs. This ensures that the charges for running a job will not vary because of other jobs that are being multiprogrammed at the same time (i.e., real elapsed time could be meaningless for charging purposes in a multiprogramming environment).

4-2.4.3 JOB SCHEDULING WITH MEMORY REQUIREMENTS AND NO I/O OVERLAP
In addition to CPU time, a job may need a certain amount of memory. Assuming finite memory and a relocatable partition scheme (one that eliminates fragmentation), what is the impact on turnaround time?

JOB NO.	TIME SUBMITTED	RUN TIME	MEMORY NEEDS
1	10.0	0.3 hr	10K
2	10.2	0.5 hr	60K
3	10.4	0.1 hr	50K
4	10.5	0.4 hr	10K
5	10.8	0.1 hr	30K

Figure 4-16 Sample job request for scheduling with memory needs

An analysis of the jobs using FIFO job scheduling, as shown in Figure 4-16, is depicted in Figure 4-17. We assume that available memory equals 100K and that there is multiprogramming with no I/O overlap. Note that although Job 3 arrived at 10.4, it could not start running until 11.2 since it needed 50K of core, and that was not available until 11.2.

The figures show that due to this memory constraint average wait time increased.

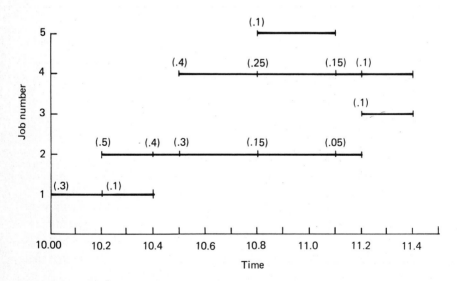

Figure 4-17a Multiprogramming core restrictions only: graphical

TIME	EVENT	NO. OF JOBS	% CPU PER JOB	ELAPSED TIME	HEAD-WAY PER JOB	CORE AVAIL-ABLE	JOB	TIME LEFT
10.0	Job 1 arrives Job 1 started					90	1	.3
10.2	Job 2 arrives Job 2 started	1	1	.2	.2	30	1	.1
							2	.5
10.4	Job 1 finishes Job 3 arrives	2	1/2	.2	.1	40	1	
							2	.4
10.5	Job 4 arrives Job 4 started	1	1	.1	.1	30	2	.3
							4	.4
10.8	Job 5 arrives Job 5 started	2	1/2	.3	.15	0	2	.15
							4	.25
							5	.1
11.1	Job 5 finishes	3	1/3	.3	.1	30	2	.05
							4	.15
							5	
11.2	Job 2 finishes Job 3 started	2	1/2	.1	.05	40	2	
							3	.1
							4	.1
11.4	Job 3 finishes Job 4 finishes	2	1/2	.2	.1	100	3	
							4	

Figure 4-17b Multiprogramming core restrictions only: tabular

JOB	RUN TIME	ARRIVAL	FINISH	TURNAROUND TIME	WEIGHTED TURNAROUND TIME
1	0.3	10.0	10.4	0.4	1.33
2	0.5	10.2	11.2	1.0	2.0
3	0.1	10.4	11.4	1.0	10.0
4	0.4	10.5	11.4	0.9	2.25
5	0.1	10.8	11.1	0.3	3.0
				3.6	18.58

Turnaround time, T = .72

Weighted turnaround time, W = 3.716

Figure 4-17c   Multiprogramming core restrictions only: summary results

4-2.4.4 JOB SCHEDULING WITH MEMORY AND TAPE CONSTRAINTS AND NO I/O OVERLAP

Let us now assume that the jobs also require a number of tape drives in addition to memory and CPU time. What is the impact on turnaround time now?

The job sample requests are indicated in Figure 4-18. We assume that the system has 100K memory and five tape drives.

JOB NO.	TIME SUBMITTED	RUN TIME	MEMORY NEEDS	TAPES NEEDED
1	10.0	0.3 hr	10K	2
2	10.2	0.5 hr	60K	1
3	10.4	0.1 hr	50K	4
4	10.5	0.4 hr	10K	2
5	10.8	0.1 hr	30K	3

Figure 4-18   Sample jobs with memory and tape needs

Figure 4-19 contains an analysis of this case. Note that we could not start Job 5 until enough tapes were freed. The added tape drive constraint caused the average weighted turnaround time to go up over the single memory constraint of Figure 4-17.

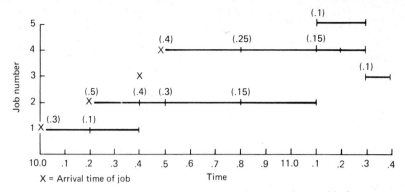

Figure 4-19a Multiprogramming with memory and tape needs: graphical

TIME	EVENT	NO. OF JOBS	% CPU PER JOB	ELAPSED TIME	HEAD-WAY PER JOB	CORE AVAIL-ABLE	TAPE AVAIL-ABLE	JOB	TIME LEFT
10.0	Job 1 arrives Job 1 started					90	3	1	.3
10.2	Job 2 arrives Job 2 started	1	1	.2	.2	30	2	1	.1
								2	.5
10.4	Job 1 finishes Job 3 arrives	2	1/2	.2	.1	40	4	1	
								2	.4
10.5	Job 4 arrives Job 4 started	1	1	.1	.1	30	2	2	.3
								4	.4
10.8	Job 5 arrives	2	1/2	.3	.15	30	2	2	.15
								4	.25
11.1	Job 2 finishes Job 5 started	2	1/2	.3	.15	60	0	2	
								4	.1
								5	.1
11.3	Job 4 finishes Job 5 finishes Job 3 started	2	1/2	.2	.1	50	1	3	.1
								4	
								5	
11.4	Job 3 finishes	1	1	.1	.1	100	5	3	

Figure 4-19b Multiprogramming with memory and tape needs: tabular

JOB	RUN TIME	ARRIVAL	FINISH	TURNAROUND TIME	WEIGHTED TURNAROUND TIME
1	0.3	10.0	10.4	0.4	1.33
2	0.5	10.2	11.1	0.9	1.80
3	0.1	10.4	11.4	1.0	10.00
4	0.4	10.5	11.3	0.8	2.00
5	0.1	10.8	11.3	0.5	5.00
				3.6	20.13

Turnaround time, T = .72
Weighted turnaround time, W = 4.026

Figure 4-19c   Multiprogramming with memory and tape needs: summary needs

4-2.5 Job Scheduling Summary

Minimal turnaround time is a rather common objective of a job scheduling algorithm. However, in actual systems we often find it necessary to modify this policy. Reasons might include the following:

1 Some "priority" concept can give certain jobs favored treatment—often for an extra charge.
2 Total throughput must be sufficient to get a day's work done in less than 24 hours. (Recall that some turnaround time techniques would actually let the CPU idle.)

In summary, we have tried to show that the designer must first determine his goals, e.g., low average turnaround, and then experiment with different scheduling algorithms for what he feels are representative job mixes.

Throughout Section 4-2 we tried different scheduling algorithms. The first three were tried with the same job mix. Some conclusions for this job mix would be:

1 First-In First-Out reduces the spread of wait times for each job.
2 Shortest Job First gives a low average turnaround time but clearly favors the short job.
3 Future Knowledge gives the best turnaround time but is difficult to implement.

We showed that in a multiprogramming environment certain job mixes had better turnaround times and other mixes did not. We included a more complicated analysis of scheduling in a multiprogramming environment with I/O overlap. Also taken into consideration were memory and device needs. Other job scheduling algorithms can be found in the case studies in Chapter 9.

4-3 PROCESS SCHEDULING

Section 4-2 discussed job scheduling, which is transition 2 of Figure 4-1. Process scheduling is concerned with transitions 3 and 4.

Once the job scheduler has selected a collection of jobs to run, the process scheduler attempts to handle the microscopic scheduling (i.e., the dynamic assignment of processor to process). The process scheduler is also called the *dispatcher* or *low-level scheduler* in the literature. In a multiprogrammed environment, a process typically uses the processor for only 100 ms or less before becoming blocked to wait for I/O completion or some other event.

In our multiprogramming examples of Section 4-2 we assumed a rather simple round-robin process scheduling algorithm where the processor is shared equally among jobs in memory. However, for reasons discussed in this section, we may wish to use more elaborate process scheduling algorithms.

The job and process scheduler may interact. The process scheduler may choose to postpone, or roll out, a process and require that it go through the macro-level job scheduling again in order to complete. This is especially true in a timesharing system.

In Figure 4-20 we see a single processor multiprogramming system. Processes A and D both request the use of a tape drive during execution. Let us assume there is only one tape drive available, and process A requests it first. The drive is assigned to process A. Later, when process D requests a tape drive, it must be blocked until process A releases the tape drive.

Being blocked is an attribute of the process, not the processor. It means that the processor will switch only among processes A, B, and C, and ignore process D. Usually process D will tie up a portion of memory, but in some systems it can be rolled out or paged out of memory onto secondary storage. In such a case, the blocking of process D has a logical effect that results in a redistribution of resources; the resources need not be wasted. This is an example of processor scheduling considerations that result from process synchronization requirements.

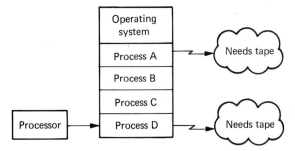

Figure 4-20 Single processor interlock

4-3.1 Functions

The process scheduler must perform the following functions:

1 Keep track of the state of processes.

2 Decide which process gets a processor, when, and for how long.

3 Allocate processors to processes.

4 Deallocate processors from processes.

As in the previous section, we are reluctant to get involved with the very detailed implementation techniques of processor scheduling, as they are highly machine-dependent and are not important to the concepts. The reader wishing to study the details should refer to the processor scheduling technique of the sample operating system contained in Chapter 7 or the case studies in Chapter 9. Here we will focus on policies.

Let us briefly discuss the function of keeping track of the status of the process. The module of the processor scheduler that performs these functions is called the traffic controller. One way of keeping track of the status of a process is to use a database associated with each process in the system called a Process Control Block (PCB). There is a separate PCB for each process; in fact, the PCB is the only really tangible part of a process (see Figure 4-21).

| Process identification |
| Current state |
| Priority |
| Copy of active registers |
| Pointer to list of other processes in same state |
| etc. |

Figure 4-21 Process Control Block

Frequently all PCBs in the same state (e.g., ready, blocked, etc.) are linked together; the resulting list is often given a special name such as *ready list*. The traffic controller is called whenever the status of a resource is changed. The block list may be further subdivided, one chain given for each reason that a process is blocked. Thus if a process requests a device and that device is already in use, the process is linked to the block chain associated with that device.

When the device is released, the traffic controller checks its block chain to see if any processes are waiting for that device. If so, these processes are placed back in ready state to rerequest the device. Alternatively, one of the processes may be assigned the device and placed in ready state, while all the other processes waiting for that device remain blocked.

4-3.2 Policies

The scheduling policy must decide which process is to be assigned a processor and for how long. The length of time a process is assigned a processor may depend on one, or some combination of, the following events:

The process is complete.

The process becomes blocked.

A higher priority process needs the processor.

A time quantum has elapsed.

An error occurs.

The decision as to which process is to run is made by scanning the PCB ready list and applying some policy.

The ready list can be organized in two ways:

1 Each time a process is put on the ready list (from hold, running, or blocked) it is put in its "correct" priority position in order. Then, when the processor becomes free, the top process on the list is run.

2 Processes are arbitrarily placed on the ready list. When it is necessary to find a process to run, the scheduler must scan the entire list of ready processes and pick one to run.

Typical process scheduling policies include the following:

1 *Round robin.* Each process in turn is run to a time quantum limit, such as 100 ms.

2 *Inverse of remainder of quantum.* If the process used its entire quantum last time, it goes to the end of the list. If it used only half (due to I/O wait), it goes to the middle. Besides being "fair," this works nicely for I/O-bound jobs.

3 *Multiple-level feedback variant on round robin.* When a new process is entered, it is run for as many time quantums as all other jobs in the system. Then regular round robin is run.

4 *Priority.* The highest priority ready job is selected. Priority may be purchased or assigned (e.g,. a nuclear reactor process may be run first).

5 *Limited round robin.* Jobs are run round robin until some fixed number of times. Then they are run only if there are no other jobs in the system.

6 *System balance.* In order to keep the I/O devices "busy," processes that do a lot of I/O are given preference.

7 *Preferred treatment to "interactive" jobs.* If a user is directly communicating with his process (i.e., an interactive process), the process is given the processor immediately after user input to provide rapid service.

8 *Merits of the job.* In some cases it is advantageous for the system itself to assign priorities. For instance, it may automatically assign high priorities to short jobs. Another example would be for the system to designate priorities so as to achieve a balanced load, such as to have one job with heavy input/output requirements (*I/O-bound*) and one job with very little input/output (*CPU-bound*) running concurrently. If all jobs are at one extreme, either the I/O channel will be overworked and the CPU idle, or vice versa. For maximal throughput it is thus advantageous for the system to assign priorities so as to maintain the proper mix and balanced load. Similarly, the system may desire to increase the priority of a job that is tying up resources (such as previously scheduled tape drives) in order to complete the job and release these resources for other use.

Other processor scheduling policies have been discussed in the literature (Buzen, 1973; Coffman, 1968).

As in almost any rationing situation, there is considerable controversy over what are equitable, efficient, or economical policies. The reader may wish to consult some of the references for additional details of scheduling policy; a considerable amount of computer folklore has developed in this area.

4-3.3 Process State Diagrams for Scheduling

It is often convenient and graphically clearer to use the process state diagram to help explain the process scheduling algorithm, as demonstrated in Figure 4-22. In this example, two ready states (low-priority ready and high-priority ready) are indicated. A process enters low-priority ready if it exceeds its time quantum while running, and high-priority ready when it moves from blocked to ready state.

A possible scheduler policy may be:

1 To select a process to run from the high-priority ready list

2 If there are no processes in high-priority ready, to select a process from the low-priority ready list.

The state transitions of Figure 4-22 have the effect of characterizing ready processes as either I/O-intensive (high-priority ready) or CPU-intensive (low-priority ready). The scheduler policy gives preference to I/O-intensive processes.

A more elaborate scheduling algorithm is indicated in Figure 4-23. This scheduling algorithm may be used in a timesharing operating system with a paging memory management. In particular, note that the blocked processes are divided into three groups (blocked for terminal I/O, blocked for disk or tape I/O, and blocked

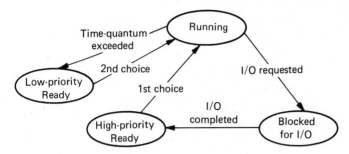

Figure 4-22 A set of scheduling state transitions

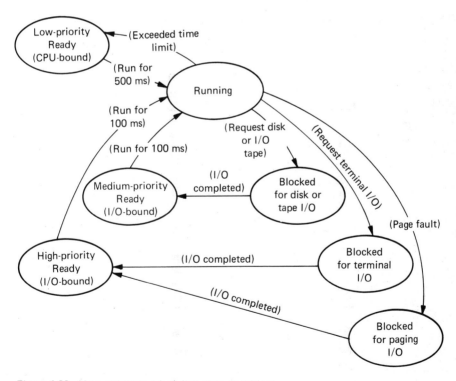

Figure 4-23 More elaborate scheduling state transitions

for paging I/O), and the ready processes are divided into three groups (CPU-bound, high-priority I/O-bound, and medium-priority I/O-bound.) The scheduling policy is to select a process from the high-priority ready list; if there is none, a process is selected from the medium-priority ready list. A low-priority process is run only if there are no higher priority processes.

There are many subjective policies implemented in this algorithm. For example, if a process runs for more than 100 ms (about 100,000 instructions) without requesting I/O, it is temporarily considered to be CPU-bound. In order to keep the I/O channels and devices busy, I/O-bound processes are always run before CPU-bound processes. If all I/O-bound processes are blocked, then a CPU-bound process is "given a crack" at the processor and furthermore is allowed to run five times as long (500 ms) before being stopped unless it becomes blocked by an I/O request. Note that terminal I/O completion puts the process into high-priority ready. This gives preferential treatment to "interactive" jobs immediately after an interaction.

Additional scheduler policies are presented as part of the case studies in Chapter 9.

4-3.4 Evaluation of Round-Robin Multiprogramming Performance

The state transition diagrams can also be used to model the status of the overall system, as shown in Figure 4-24a. If we assume that there are n processes in the system, state S_i corresponds to the situation where i processes are waiting for I/O completion (i.e., blocked for I/O). In state S_0, there are no processes in the blocked state; n-1 processes are ready and one is being run. On the other hand, in state S_n all n processes are waiting for I/O completion; no processes are runnable so the processor is idle.

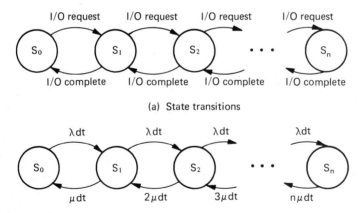

(a) State transitions

(b) Birth-and-death Markov process model

Figure 4-24   Model of system state

Can we determine the probability P_n of being in state S_n? Yes, the state transition diagram of Figure 4-24a can be converted to a *birth-and-death Markov process model* as shown in Figure 4-24b (Drake, 1967). We must label each transition arc with the probability of its occurrence in the next time instance. We define λdt as the probability that a running process will issue an I/O request in the next time instance ($1/\lambda$ can be interpreted as the average time between I/O requests). Likewise, we define μdt as the probability that an I/O request will be completed in the next time instance ($1/\mu$ may be interpreted as the average time for an I/O request to be completed).

Note that the arc from S_2 to S_1 is labeled $2\,\mu dt$, not μdt. This is because we are assuming that both I/O requests in progress have separate channels and each request has a completion probability of μdt. Thus, the probability of *either* request completing in the next instance is $\mu dt + \mu dt = 2\,\mu dt$. For similar reasons all arcs from state i to state i – 1 are labeled $i\,\mu dt$.

How do these λ's and μ's relate to our old friend the monoprogrammed I/O wait percentage, ω? It is easy to see that

$$\omega = \frac{\lambda}{\mu + \lambda}$$

If the I/O request rate, λ, is high, we have a large I/O wait percentage. If the I/O devices are very fast, high μ, the I/O wait percentage is small.

At the risk of grossly oversimplifying the mathematics, a birth-and-death Markov process can be solved for the probability of being in each state, P_i, by using the following two facts:

1 The number of $S_i \rightarrow S_{i+1}$ transitions must equal the number of $S_{i+1} \rightarrow S_i$ transitions (i.e., $p_{i,i+1}\,P_i = p_{i+1,i}\,P_{i+1}$). For Figure 4-24, this means that

$\lambda dt\, P_0 = \mu dt\, P_1$
$\lambda dt\, P_1 = 2\,\mu dt\, P_2$
$\lambda dt\, P_2 = 3\,\mu dt\, P_3$
etc.

2 The sum of all the state probabilities, P_i, must equal 1, that is,

$$\sum_{i=0}^{n} P_i = 1$$

These two facts are sufficient to solve for P_n, the probability that all n processes are waiting for I/O at the same time and the processor is idle. First, we note that

$$P_1 = \frac{\lambda dt}{\mu dt}\, P_0 = \left(\frac{\lambda}{\mu}\right) P_0$$

$$P_2 = \frac{\lambda dt}{2\mu dt} P_1 = \left(\frac{\lambda}{2\mu}\right) P_1 = \left(\frac{\lambda}{2\mu}\right) \left[\left(\frac{\lambda}{\mu}\right) P_0\right] = \frac{\left(\frac{\lambda}{\mu}\right)^2}{2} P_0$$

$$P_3 = \frac{\lambda dt}{3\mu dt} P_2 = \left(\frac{\lambda}{3\mu}\right) P_2 = \left(\frac{\lambda}{3\mu}\right) \left[\left(\frac{\lambda}{\mu}\right)^2 \frac{P_0}{2}\right] = \frac{\left(\frac{\lambda}{\mu}\right)^3}{3 \times 2} P_0$$

In general,

$$P_i = \left(\frac{\lambda}{\mu}\right)^i \frac{P_0}{i!} \qquad\qquad [4\text{-}1]$$

If

$$\sum_{i=0}^{n} P_i = 1$$

then

$$P_0 = 1 - \sum_{i=1}^{n} P_i$$

Using Eq. 4-1, we get

$$P_0 = 1 - \sum_{i=1}^{n} \left(\frac{\lambda}{\mu}\right)^i \frac{P_0}{i!}$$

With a bit of simple managing, we arrive at

$$P_0 = 1 - P_0 \left[\sum_{i=1}^{n} \left(\frac{\lambda}{\mu}\right)^i \frac{1}{i!}\right]$$

$$P_0 \left[1 + \sum_{i=1}^{n} \left(\frac{\lambda}{\mu}\right)^i \frac{1}{i!}\right] = 1$$

$$P_0 = \frac{1}{1 + \sum_{i=1}^{n} \left(\frac{\lambda}{\mu}\right)^i \frac{1}{i!}} \qquad\qquad [4\text{-}2]$$

By realizing that

$$\left(\frac{\lambda}{\mu}\right)^0 \frac{1}{0!} = 1$$

we can simplify

$$1 + \sum_{i=1}^{n} \left(\frac{\lambda}{\mu}\right)^i \frac{1}{i!}$$

to

$$\sum_{i=0}^{n} \left(\frac{\lambda}{\mu}\right)^i \frac{1}{i!}$$

Thus, Eq. 4-2 becomes:

$$P_0 = \frac{1}{\displaystyle\sum_{i=0}^{n} \left(\frac{\lambda}{\mu}\right)^i \frac{1}{i!}} \qquad [4\text{-}3]$$

Employing Eq. 4-1, we find that

$$P_n = \left(\frac{\lambda}{\mu}\right)^n \frac{P_0}{n!}$$

Using Eq. 4-3 for P_0, we obtain

$$P_n = \frac{\left(\frac{\lambda}{\mu}\right)^n}{n! \displaystyle\sum_{i=0}^{n} \left(\frac{\lambda}{\mu}\right)^i \frac{1}{i!}} \qquad [4\text{-}4]$$

Since

$$\omega = \frac{\lambda}{\mu + \lambda}$$

we can substitute

$$\left(\frac{\lambda}{\mu}\right) = \left(\frac{\omega}{1-\omega}\right)$$

to get:

$$P_n = \frac{\left(\frac{\omega}{1-\omega}\right)^n}{n! \sum_{i=0}^{n} \left(\frac{\omega}{1-\omega}\right)^i \frac{1}{i!}}$$

[4-5]

which is the result used originally in Section 3-2.2 and tabulated in Figure 4-14.

The reader must recall all the conditions on this formulation. We assumed that all processes had the same I/O wait percentage, ω, and that all processes were given equal treatment, as in round-robin scheduling. More complex situations can be modeled to determine performance, though the mathematics may become quite complex. (See Arden, 1969; Baskett, 1971; Buzen, 1973; Coffman, 1968; Hellerman, 1970; Kleinrock, 1970; McKinney, 1969).

4-4 MULTIPROCESSOR SYSTEMS

To enhance throughput, reliability, computing power, parallelism, and economies of scale, additional processors can be added to some systems. In early multiprocessor systems the additional processors had specialized functions, e.g., I/O channels. Later multiprocessing systems evolved to include the concept of one large CPU and several peripheral processors (CDC 6600). These processors may perform quite sophisticated tasks, such as running a display. A more common type of multiprocessing is a system having two or more processors, each of equal power, e.g., HIS 6180, IBM 158MP and 168MP, UNIVAC 1108, and Burroughs 6700. There is also the computer network, in which many different computers are connected, often at great distances from one another. Let us focus on the multiprocessor system with many CPUs, each of equal power.

There are various ways to connect and operate a multiprocessor system, such as (1) separate systems, (2) coordinated job scheduling, (3) master/slave scheduling, and (4) homogeneous scheduling. These techniques differ in degree of scheduling sophistication; each will be discussed in turn.

4-4.1 Separate Systems

Some systems, for example, the IBM System/360 Model 67, can be logically subdivided into two or more separate systems, each with one processor, some main memory, and peripheral devices. This is just like having two or more separate computing systems, all in the same room.

The advantage to this organization is that processors, memories, and I/O devices can be easily, though manually, switched. For example, the ensemble can be configured to be two systems, each with one processor, 512K bytes of memory, and 8 disk drives, or one system with one processor, 1024K bytes of memory, and 16 disk drives (second processor is unused); other such alternatives exist.

This configuration flexibility is useful if there are some jobs that require the full complement of memory and/or I/O device resources. Alternatively, if one processor is being repaired, all the other resources can be pooled into one large system rather than be allowed to sit idle.

In this separate system situation, there is no job or process scheduling between the processors except that which is accomplished manually.

4-4.2 Coordinated Job Scheduling

A variation on the separate system multiprocessor technique is the *coordinated job scheduling* approach (this is also called *loosely coupled multiprocessing*). Each processor is associated with a separate system. When a job arrives, it may be assigned to any system. The assignment of a job to a system may be based on a variety of requirements and policies, such as assigning the job to the system with the lightest load.

To accomplish this balancing, all job scheduling must be coordinated. This may be done manually, by a special-purpose computer (as done on the Octopus system at the Lawrence Radiation Laboratory), or by one of the actual processing systems (as done on IBM's OS/VS-2 Job Entry System).

4-4.3 Master/Slave Scheduling

The permanent assignment of a job to a system, as in the coordinated job scheduling technique, cannot handle the short-term balancing of resource demand. In a general multiprocessor system all memory and I/O devices are accessible to all processors. Memory and I/O devices are assigned to the processes, not to the processors. (This is also called *tightly coupled multiprocessing*). The processors are assigned to execute processes as determined by the process scheduler—except that there are now multiple processors available for assignment.

In a master/slave scheduling technique, one processor maintains the status of all processes in the system and schedules the work of all the slave processors.

This is analogous to the relationship between the CPU and I/O processors presented in Chapter 2. For example, the master processor selects a process to be run, finds an available processor, and issues a Start Processor instruction. The slave processor starts execution at the indicated memory location. When the slave encounters an exceptional event, such as an I/O request, it generates an interrupt to the master processor and stops to await further orders. Note that different slave processors may be assigned to a process at different times.

Figure 4-25 illustrates the manner in which multiple processors may be used for multiprogramming. Usually we visualize several separate processes as being in memory. In actuality, a process address space is often paged so that only part of it is in memory at one time; this allows a large number of processes to be active in the system.

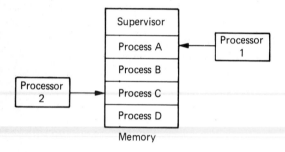

Processor 1 working on Process A

Processor 2 working on Process C

Figure 4-25   Multiprogramming with multiple processors

4-4.4   Homogeneous Processor Scheduling

The master slave scheduling approach, besides being conceptually undemocratic, has several performance and operational disadvantages. Under heavy scheduling loads, the master processor may become overloaded and cause a major bottleneck. A more democratic approach is to treat all processors equally, both as masters and slaves.

Under such conditions, the processor scheduling is logically decentralized. A list of processes and their status are stored so as to allow any processor to have access to the list—e.g., a common shared area of memory is used. Whenever a process is stopped due to I/O wait or timer limit, etc., its processor goes to the process state list, updates the process' status, and finds another process to run. Each processor uses the same scheduling algorithm to select the process to run next. If all processors are handled identically, no policy differences need exist with regard to a single processor or a multiple processor operating system.

It is necessary to establish good coordination and communication among processors in a decentralized operating system. The software lockout example presented in Section 4-5.4 illustrates this point.

4-5 PROCESS SYNCHRONIZATION

The problem of process synchronization arises from the need to share resources in a computing system. This sharing requires coordination and cooperation to ensure correct operation.

An example may illustrate some of these points. Figure 4-26 illustrates a typical rapid-service hamburger stand. You submit your order to the order clerk. He places your order on a turntable. The bagger takes orders off the turntable, one at a time, and puts the requested items into a bag. He then delivers the completed order to the cashier. The cashier processes these bags, one at a time, receiving money from you and giving you your order. Furthermore, there is a cook working in the back room, continually replenishing the supply of cooked hamburgers used by the bagger. In this example, each process (person) operates largely independently. The only communication is via certain shared areas: the *order list turntable,* the *cooked hamburger bin,* and the *checkout counter.*

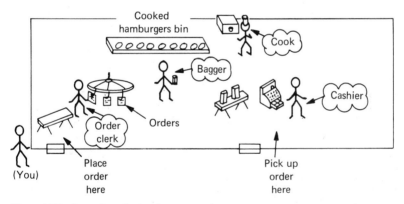

Figure 4-26 Operation of a hamburger stand

This simple example illustrates forms of communication and cooperation that we frequently take for granted. The bagger can fill orders only when there are orders to be processed. What does he do if there is a slack period and the order list is empty? He goes to sleep. How is he awakened when a customer arrives and places an order? The order clerk kicks him! It is a useful exercise to look for other necessary forms of communication and cooperation. For example, what prevents the cook from burying the stand under a pile of hamburgers 100 feet deep during a long slack period?

Analogous situations exist in a computing system among the processes. In some cases the coordination is forced upon them by the operating system because of the scarcity of resources, for example, the need to wait for access to an I/O channel. In other cases, a single job may consist of several processes that all work together. An information retrieval system, such as an airline reservation system, may have several processes performing separate tasks, as in our hamburger stand example. One task may accept requests, check for input correctness, and pass the request along to the "worker" process. The worker process accesses the data to find the necessary information and sends it to the "output" process. The output process routes the response back to the original requester.

Associated with processor allocation and interprocess communication are two synchronization problems, race condition and deadly embrace.

4-5.1 Race Condition

A *race condition* occurs when the scheduling of two processes is so critical that the various orders of scheduling them result in different computations. Race conditions result from the explicit or implicit sharing of data or resources among two or more processes. Figure 4-27 illustrates a simple form of race.

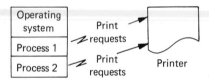

Figure 4-27 Simple race condition

In Figure 4-27 we assume that two processes are being run (multiprogrammed). Each process occasionally requests that a line be printed on the single printer. Depending on the scheduling of process 1 and 2, all the printout of process 1 may precede or follow the printout of process 2. But most likely the printout of each process will be interspersed on the printed paper.

One solution to this predicament is to require that a process explicitly *request* use of the shared resource (the printer in this case) prior to using it. When all use of the resource is completed (e.g., all printout completed), the resource may then be released by the process. The operations *request* and *release* are usually part of the operating system facilities handled by the traffic controller. If a process requests a resource that is already in use, the process automatically becomes blocked. When the resource becomes available as a result of a later release, the blocked process may be assigned the resource and made ready. Alternate solutions (e.g., SPOOLing) to the printer problem are discussed in Chapter 5.

In addition to physical devices, there are other shared resources, such as common tables (analogous to the order-list turntable of Figure 4-26), that require the same type of process synchronization.

For an example of such a race condition, consider Figure 4-28, which depicts a procedure for selecting a process from the ready list and placing it in the running state. This procedure is executed by the process scheduler. This algorithm works well for a single processor, but runs into trouble for multiple processors, as shown in Figure 4-29.

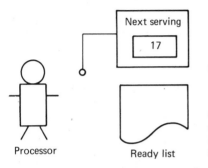

When current process is completed or postponed:

1 Find current process in ready list
2 Mark it "complete" or "postponed"
3 Note "next serving" number (17)
4 Find process 17 in ready list
5 Make note of process to be done
6 Adjust ready list for "next serving" number (18)

Figure 4-28 Scheduling (single processor)

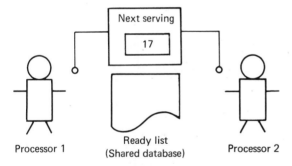

Processor 1   Ready list   Processor 2
                   (Shared database)

Assume both processors complete their current process at same time:

1 Processor 1 finds its current process in ready list
2 Processor 2 finds its current process in ready list
3 Processor 1 marks its current process
4 Processor 2 marks its current process
5 Processor 1 notes "next serving" (17)
6 Processor 2 notes "next serving" (17)
7 Processor 1 finds process 17 in ready list and notes it
8 Processor 2 finds process 17 in ready list and notes it
9 Processor 1 adjusts ready list "next serving" (18)
10 Processor 2 adjusts ready list "next serving" (19)

Now both processors are simultaneously working on the same process and process 18 has been skipped.

Figure 4-29 Scheduling (multiple processors)

Assume that two processes, each on a separate processor, go blocked at approximately the same time. After saving the status of the current processes, each processor determines the next process to be served. Since both processors use the same algorithm independently, they will choose the same process. Furthermore, in readjusting the selection criterion, it is possible to upset the ready list, for example, by bypassing a process as illustrated in Figure 4-29.

This problem is the direct result of multiple processors processing common databases asynchronously. There are usually many other such databases in an operating system, for example, the memory allocation map, the page allocation map, the I/O list, etc. An example of race conditions and their avoidance was presented in the I/O buffering problem in Section 2-5.2. Other examples can be found in the sample operating system presented in Chapter 7.

In order to resolve this problem, the processors that usually operate independently must be synchronized with regard to access to these common databases. Figure 4-30 illustrates the mechanism.

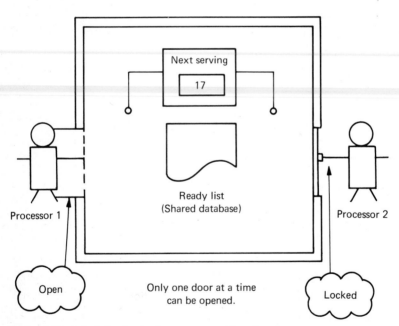

Figure 4-30 Scheduling (multiple processors with lockout)

Before accessing the ready list database, a processor checks a specific "lock bit." If it is not set, the database is not in use. In this case the processor may set the bit and commence operation on the database. When it has completed its function, the processor resets the bit. If a second processor requires access to the database in the interim, it will find the lock bit set and must wait until the lock is removed. Under this condition, the second processor is said to have undergone *software processor lockout* and is temporarily idled. This can happen to a second, third, or fourth processor, or to any number of processors at a time.

Note that cooperation is important. If a process "forgets" to release an allocated resource, that resource will never again be available for use by any other process. In practice, the operating system usually releases all resources allocated to a process when the process terminates.

4.5.2 Synchronization Mechanisms

Various synchronization mechanisms are available to provide interprocess co-ordination and communication. In this section several of the most common techniques will be briefly presented; the references provide more detail and additional alternatives (Dijkstra, 1965, 1968; Easton, 1971; Haberman, 1971; Hansen, 1970; Liskov, 1972; Saltzer, 1966).

4-5.2.1 TEST-AND-SET INSTRUCTION

In most synchronization schemes, a physical entity must be used to represent the resource. This entity is often called a *lock byte* or *semaphore*. Thus, for each shared database or device there should be a separate lock byte. We will use the convention that lock byte = 0 means the resource is available, whereas lock byte = 1 means the resource is already in use. Before operating on such a shared resource, a process must perform the following actions:

1   Examine the value of the lock byte (either it is 0 or 1).

2   Set the lock byte to 1.

3   If the original value was 1, go back to step 1.

After the process has completed its use of the resource, it sets the lock byte to zero.

If we call the lock byte X, the action prior to use of the shared resource is called LOCK (X) and the action after use is UNLOCK (X). These are also called REQUEST (X) and RELEASE (X), respectively. These actions can be accomplished on the IBM System/370 by using the following instructions:

```
LOCK (X)              UNLOCK (X)

TS    X               MVI   X, '00'
BNZ   *-4
```

Note that it is essential that the lock byte not be changed by another process between locking steps 1 and 2. This requirement is met by the System/370 Test-and-

Set (TS) instruction that performs both steps 1 and 2 as an indivisible operation. There are similar instructions available on most contemporary computers.

The reader should convince himself that the lock and unlock operations do, in fact, prevent race conditions. For example, consider the three processes:

```
PROCESS 1          PROCESS 2          PROCESS 3

    :                  :                  :
    :                  :                  :
LOCK (X)            LOCK (X)           LOCK (X)
    (critical
    : database      :  (...)           :  (...)
    : manipu-       :                  :
    lations)
UNLOCK (X)         UNLOCK (X)         UNLOCK (X)
    :                  :                  :
    :                  :                  :
```

The lock byte is initially 0. All possible timings of the processes should be considered.

4-5.2.2 WAIT AND SIGNAL MECHANISMS

The above mechanism is sufficient for synchronization but wasteful of processor resources. The blocked process doesn't really stop, instead it continually loops, testing the lock byte and waiting for it to change to zero. We don't want to waste such resources on a blocked process. Modified lock and unlock mechanisms can be defined as follows:

LOCK(X):

1   Examine the value of the lock byte (either it is 0 or 1).

2   Set the lock byte to 1.

3   If the original value was 1, call WAIT(X).

UNLOCK(X):

1   Set the lock byte to 0.

2   Call SIGNAL(X).

WAIT and *SIGNAL* are primitives of the traffic controller component of processor management. A WAIT (X) sets the process' PCB to the blocked state and links it to the lock byte X. Another process is then selected to run by the process scheduler. A SIGNAL(X) checks the blocked list associated with lock byte X; if there are any processes blocked waiting for X, one is selected and its PCB is set to the ready state. Eventually, the process scheduler will select this newly "awakened" process for execution.

The WAIT and SIGNAL mechanisms can be used for other purposes, such as waiting for I/O completion. After an I/O request (i.e., SIO instruction) has been issued, the process can be blocked by a WAIT(X) where X is a status byte associated with the I/O device (e.g., the lock byte can be stored in the device's Unit Control Block as shown in the sample operating system). When the I/O completion interrupt occurs, it is converted into a SIGNAL(X).

4-5.2.3 P AND V OPERATIONS ON COUNTING SEMAPHORES

A more general form of the LOCK/UNLOCK mechanism, called the P and V operations, has been defined by Dijkstra (1968). P and V operate on *counting semaphores,* which are variables that take on integer values—not just 0 and 1. The mechanisms can be defined as follows:

P(S):

1 Decrement value of S (i.e., $S = S - 1$).

2 If S is less than 0, WAIT(S).

V(S):

1 Increment value of S (i.e., $S = S + 1$).

2 If S is less than or equal to 0, SIGNAL(S).

Depending upon the initial value of the semaphores and the number of semaphores used, P and V can be used for many purposes. If one semaphore is used and its initial value is 1, P(S) and V(S) are identical to WAIT(S) and SIGNAL(S).

Of more interest is the use of these mechanisms in solving the "producer/consumer" problem (Dijkstra, 1968; Denning, 1971). The producer places items in a shared buffer that can hold n items for later use by the consumer—a good example is output buffer handling as employed in Section 2-5.2 or the "hamburger bin" in Figure 4-26. The producer must be prevented from placing an item in a full buffer and the consumer must be prevented from removing an item from an empty buffer. By using two semaphores, initially set as $S_1 = n$ and $S_2 = 0$, we can synchronize the processes as follows:

```
PRODUCER PROCESS, Pp          CONSUMER PROCESS, Pc

PRODUCE:                      CONSUME:
                              P  (S2)
    :  (produce item)         :  (remove item
    :                         ·   from buffer)
    P  (S1)                   V  (S1)
    :  (put item in buffer)   :  (consume item)
    :                         :
    V  (S2)
    GO TO PRODUCE             GO TO CONSUME
```

Once again, the reader should verify for himself that the correct synchronization does, in fact, occur. A simulated execution is a useful way to study semaphore coordination as shown in Figure 4-31 where n = 2. Notice that the producer is not allowed to add an item to a full buffer, nor is the consumer to remove an item from an empty buffer.

This same algorithm can be used by multiple producers and consumers. Other uses of the semaphore synchronization are illustrated in the sample operating system.

	ACTIONS		SEMAPHORE VALUES	
Event	P_p (Producer)	P_c (Consumer)	S_1	S_2
0	- - -	- - -	2	0
1	—	P(S_2) blocked	2	-1
2	P (S_1)	— (buffer	1	-1
3	V (S_2) unblocks P_c	— "empty")	1	0
4	P (S_1)	—	0	0
5	—	V (S_1)	1	0
6	V (S_2)	—	1	1
7	P (S_1)	—	0	1
8	V (S_2)	—	0	2
9	P (S_1) blocked	—	-1	2
10	— (buffer	P (S_2)	-1	1
11	— "full")	V (S_1) unblocks P_p	0	1
etc.				

Figure 4-31 Simulated execution of two synchronized processes

4-5.2.4 MESSAGE COMMUNICATION

The synchronization mechanisms we have discussed provide communication between processes indirectly by means of a shared buffer area and a shared lock byte or semaphore. Situations such as the producer/consumer problem can also be solved by providing direct process-to-process communication by means of the primitives SEND (P_r,M) and RECEIVE (P_s,M) where P_r and P_s are the names of processes and M is a message (i.e., a k-byte character string).

SEND (P_r,M) saves the message M for the receiver process P_r. RECEIVE (P_s,M) returns a message M, if there is one, to the requestor process; it also returns the name of the process P_s that sent the message. If there are no messages for the RECEIVE requestor, it becomes blocked until a message is sent to it. The buffering of messages and synchronization are handled automatically by the SEND and RECEIVE primitives.

Our sample operating system presents a detailed implementation of a message communication facility and numerous examples of its usage.

4-5.3 Deadly Embrace

A *deadly embrace* is a situation in which two processes are unknowingly waiting for resources that are held by each other and thus unavailable. Consider the two processes depicted in Figure 4-32.

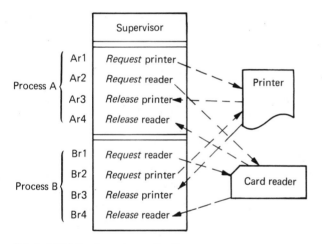

Figure 4-32   Deadly embrace situation

Processes A and B are sharing use of the printer and card reader by means of the request and release operations. Due to independent scheduling of the processes, the request and release operations may be interspersed in several different orders such as:

(1)   Ar1, Ar2, Ar3, Ar4, Br1, Br2, Br3, Br4

(2)   Br1, Br2, Br3, Br4, Ar1, Ar2, Ar3, Ar4

(3)   Ar1, Ar2, Br1, Ar3, Ar4, Br2, Br3, Br4

The reader should assure himself that these sequences are reasonable and perform correctly. Note that in number (3) process B is temporarily blocked by Br1 until process A issues Ar4.

Let us consider a sequence that starts with Ar1 (request printer for process A) and Br1 (request reader for process B). What happens next? If Ar2 (request reader for process A) occurs, process A must be blocked because the reader is already in use by process B. Then when Br2 (request for printer for process B) occurs, process B must also be blocked because the printer is in use by process A. We are confronted with a stalemate since each process is waiting for the other to release a needed resource—truly a deadly embrace.

The problem of deadly embrace can occur in many different ways in a multiprogramming system, especially in the use of multiple shared tables.

We will discuss the following techniques for handling deadly embraces:

1 Preallocate all shared resources.
2 Constrain allocation.
  a controlled allocation
  b standard allocation pattern
3 Detect and recover.

4-5.3.1 PREALLOCATE ALL SHARED RESOURCES

A safe and simple method of avoiding deadly embraces is to have the user declare *all* the devices and other resources he will use when submitting his job (Coffman, 1971; Fontao, 1971). The scheduler simply does not schedule any job until *all* the necessary resources are available. When they are assigned to the job, they are retained for the duration of the run. This technique is used on OS/360 for device allocation, but there are several disadvantages:

1 A user may not know before execution time all the devices his job will use.
2 It is necessary to wait until all resources are available even if some are not needed until the end of execution, which may be hours later.
3 It is wasteful for the system to commit a device to a job when there is only a small likelihood that the job will use that device. For example, a dump of a core image of a job on a printer may occur only if that user makes an error. Yet with this technique we must assign the printer to the job.
4 A particular job may not need all devices for the entire duration of the job; they could be released to some other job in a multiprogramming environment.

4-5.3.2 CONSTRAINED ALLOCATION TO AVOID DEADLY EMBRACE

Controlled Allocation (Haberman, 1969; Dijkstra, 1968)
As in Section 4-5.3.1 the user specifies all resources needed in advance except that the scheduler starts the job even when all of them are not immediately available. The concept here is to avoid allocating a resource to a job if there is any possibility of a deadly embrace. For example, consider a system with nine tape drives where

Job 1 needs up to six tape drives and Job 2 needs up to six tape drives. These jobs do not need all the tapes all the time; they will request the tapes when they are needed during execution. OS/360 would not let both of the jobs run. However, using controlled allocation, we could let both jobs run until we were faced with the situation depicted in Figure 4-33. If both jobs were to proceed past the double line, there would be a *possibility* of deadly embrace. This method allows only one job to proceed beyond that point until more tapes are released.

If we assigned four tapes to Job 1 and five tapes to Job 2, neither job could finish. We must avoid this situation. Note that if Job 1 completes before Job 2 requests its third tape, or if Job 2 gets to the point where it releases three tapes before Job 1 requests its first tape, and so on, neither job will have to wait at all.

Thus with this method, the job must:

1 Declare in advance the maximum resources needed.
2 Before a resource is assigned, go through the sequence to see if there is a possible deadly embrace; if there is not, assign the resource. Figure 4-34 presents an algorithm that accomplishes this step (Haberman, 1969).

The major problem with the constrained allocation method is that we must still know maximum needs in advance. Furthermore, the algorithm is too conservative. A job may not actually use its maximum needs after the point of detection; thus jobs may wait needlessly (i.e., the deadly embrace might not have occurred even if the jobs had been allowed to proceed).

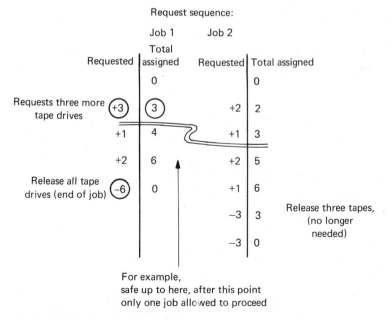

Figure 4-33 Sample of controlled allocation

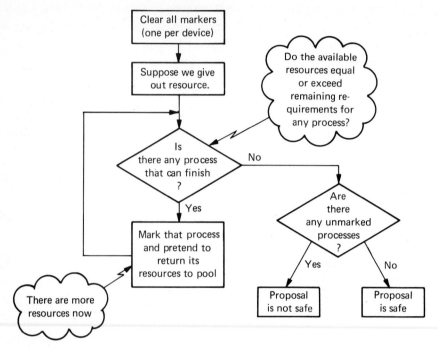

Figure 4-34 Algorithm for controlled allocation

Standard Allocation Pattern (Havender, 1968)

Another form of constrained allocation is the standard allocation pattern (Havender, 1968). In this scheme all resources are assigned a unique number (e.g., reader = 1, printer = 2, punch = 3, tape = 4, disk = 5, etc.). All allocation requests must be in *ascending* order. For example, reader(1), punch(3), tape(4) is a legal request sequence, while reader(1), tape(4), punch(3) is not. As long as the ascending order rule is followed, an allocation request is allowed if the resource is available—there are no other constraints. If not, the process must wait.

This scheme guarantees that there *cannot* be any deadly embraces. Note that we don't have to specify maximum needs in advance.

There are several problems with this approach. The standard sequence may not correspond to actual resource requirement ordering of the process. If the tape is needed immediately and the printer may be needed later, the printer must be requested prior to the tape request.

By assigning these unique numbers carefully, this standard order can be made a much less awkward constraint.

In general, this technique is used only inside very specialized systems. For example, OS/MVT uses it to allocate (lock) *internal* system tables; however, the facility is not available to users.

4-5.3.3 DETECT AND RECOVER

By being conservative all the techniques discussed above guarantee that deadly embrace cannot occur. The technique of detect and recover is more *daring,* since it will allow deadly embrace to occur as long as it can (1) detect it and (2) recover from the problem. Detection of deadly embraces is always possible, but it may be difficult. The following method may be used for detecting deadly embraces (Bensoussan, 1968; Murphey, 1968).

1 Arbitrarily assign each resource and process a unique number.

2 Allow processes to apply software locks when seizing resources.

3 Set up tables for keeping track of resources and processes as shown in Figure 4-35.

Resource Assignment Table (RATBL)

RATBL	No. of resource	Assigned to process no.
	1	
	2	
	3	
	•	
	•	

Process Wait Table (PWTBL)

PWTBL	Process	Resource being waited for
	1	
	2	
	3	
	•	
	•	

Figure 4-35 Resource and process status tables

4 Make appropriate RATBL and PWTBL entries as resources are seized and released.

5 When a locked resource is requested, use the deadly embrace detection algorithm illustrated in Figure 4-36.

Consider the following sequence that illustrates the detection process.

RATBL

Resource	Process
1	1
2	3
3	2
4	2
5	1

1 P_1 locks l_1

2 P_2 locks l_3

3 P_3 locks l_2

4 P_2 locks l_4

5 P_1 locks l_5

6 P_1 tries for l_3

   $J = 1$ $I = 3$

   $K = 2$

   K is not waiting for any resource $I' \rightarrow P_1$ waits

7 P_2 tries for l_2
   $J = 2$ $I = 2$
   $K = 3$
   no $I' \to P_2$ waits

8 P_3 tries for l_5
   $J = 3$ $I = 5$
   $K = 1$
   $I' = 3$
   $K' = 2$

PWTBL

Process	Resource
1	3
2	2
3	5

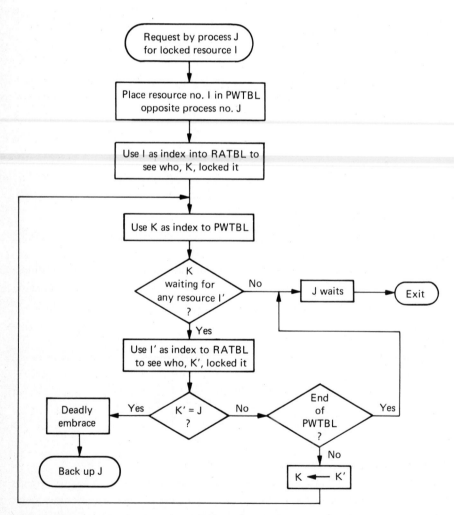

Figure 4-36 Algorithm for detecting a deadly embrace

$2 \neq J$ so set K = 2
$I' = 2$
$K' = 3$
$K' = J$! $\rightarrow$ DEADLY EMBRACE
          back up P_3

With this method no convention of ordering resource requests is needed. Release of resources may be monitored by the traffic controller, and devices reassigned as needed, with appropriate changes made to the RATBL and PWTBL.

To determine J properly, each request for a locked resource (causing entry to the detection algorithm) will require locking of RATBL and PWTBL until examination for deadly embrace is completed by the supervisor. Then the next request can be processed. Otherwise, a subsequent request, J', may change the tables, causing the supervisor (still on search J) to find a deadly embrace and back up processor J instead of J'. This queuing of requests will add more overhead to the time required for the supervisor to check things out.

When a deadly embrace is detected, it must be removed. Basically, this means that one of the jobs *must* release one or more resources to undo the deadly embrace. There is no general solution to the problem of recovery. In order to release a resource safely, the job must *backtrack* or *decompute* back to a point prior to allocation. Backtracking can be difficult; techniques used are:

1 Decompute algorithm (undo computation and state)—special for each routine.
2 Make a *snapshot* (or checkpoint) of the earlier state, which is then used to restore conditions to those prior to allocation.

This checkpoint technique is common for real-time computers and long-running data processing, since in any case it is needed for error restart.

There are several problems associated with the detect-and-recover strategy. Although detection is always possible, recovery (decompute) is not always possible or economically feasible. Even when recovery is possible, it is usually difficult.

4-5.3.4 RESEARCH ON DEADLY EMBRACE HANDLING

As the use of complex multiprogramming systems with shared resources has spread, the problems of deadly embrace have become a major concern for many systems. This has sparked much research (Coffman, 1971; Easton, 1971; Fontao, 1971; Haberman, 1969; Havender, 1968; Holt, 1972; Murphy, 1968; Needham, 1969).

4-5.4 Synchronization Performance Considerations

The use of synchronization mechanisms has an effect upon a process' and the overall system's performance. In this section a few key considerations are discussed and a sample analysis presented.

4-5.4.1 "SUSPEND" VERSUS "SPIN" LOCKS

In the operation of a multiple processor system, as described in Section 4-4, two different interlock situations must be considered. When a process becomes blocked due to a normal P operation, such as waiting for an I/O completion, the processor may be reassigned to some other process. This is called a *suspend lock* since the process is "suspended" and the processor is reassigned.

A similar locking mechanism is also used within the operating system itself, as illustrated by the ready list lock used to synchronize multiple processors in Figure 4-30. This case is somewhat different, however. What does the process do if it finds the ready list locked? Ordinarily it would suspend the current process and start running another ready process from the ready list. This can't be done in this case because it is the ready list itself that is locked! Thus, the process must keep the processor continually testing the lock (via Test-and-Set instruction, for example) until the lock is removed. Logically, the processor is kept "spinning its wheels," thus, this is called a *spin lock*. Many other such situations require spin locks in a multiple processor operating system.

4-5.4.2 ANALYSIS OF SOFTWARE PROCESSOR LOCKOUT

The spin lock situation described in Section 4-5.4.1 has been called a software processor lockout (Madnick, 1968). As the number of processes in the system increases, the frequency and duration of software lockouts also increase. In this section we analyze the effect of software lockout upon performance. For convenience and ease of understanding, a simple Markov model similar to the one discussed in Section 4-3.4 is used (Figure 4-37). Each processor is considered as independent. When a process is being executed, the interval of time before it becomes necessary to access a system database is described by a negative exponential distribution function with parameter $1/E$ (i.e., the expected execution interval between accesses is E time units). Similarly, the processor runs in the locked state for an expected interval of length L time units. The ratio $L/(E + L)$ may be loosely interpreted as the expected portion of total execution time that occurs in the locked state for a multiprogramming configuration with one processor (no processor lockout).

There are three possible states for an individual processor: (1) it is executing in the unlocked state on behalf of a process for an interval of time characterized by parameter $1/E$, after which it will attempt to access a system database; (2) it is executing in the locked state for an interval characterized by parameter $1/L$, after which it will remove the lock; or (3) it attempted to access the database but was idled by lockout.

In Figure 4-37, state S(i) represents the state with i processors attempting to access a system database (1 processor actually manipulating database, i − 1 processors awaiting access).

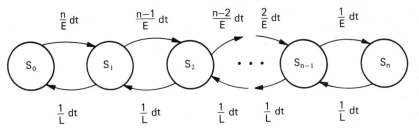

Figure 4-37 Markov model

The transitions from state i to state i - 1 have a probability of $(1/L)dt$, which means that the amount of time spent in the locked state by a processor is independent of the number of processors waiting to access a locked database. The transitions from state i to state i + 1 have probability $(n - i)(1/E)dt$, which means that each of the n - i processors in execution has probability $(1/E)dt$ of requesting access to the system databases. Solving for the steady state probabilities as we did in Section 4-3.4 (Drake, 1967), we find that

$$P_i = \frac{n!}{(n - i)!} \left(\frac{L}{E}\right)^i P_0 \qquad i = 1, \ldots, n$$

where

$$P_0 = \frac{1}{\sum\limits_{i=0}^{n} \frac{n!}{(n - i)!} \left(\frac{L}{E}\right)^i}$$

The performance criterion that interests us is the expected number of processors idled due to lockout:

$$E(idle) = \sum\limits_{i=2}^{n} (i - 1) P_i$$

The preceding formula becomes:

$$E(idle) = \frac{\sum\limits_{i=2}^{n} \dfrac{(i - 1)}{\left(\frac{E}{L}\right)^i (n - i)!}}{\sum\limits_{i=0}^{n} \dfrac{1}{\left(\frac{E}{L}\right)^i (n - i)!}}$$

This formula has been evaluated and graphed in Figures 4-38 and 4-39. Figure 4-39, for example, illustrates the effect of software lockout on a system characterized by a ratio of .05 for L/E. If there were 15 processors attached to such a system, we could expect that on the average 1 processor would always be idled by software lockout. Increasing the system to 40 processors results in an expected average of 19 idle processors, while a further increase to 41 processors would result in about 20 idle processors.

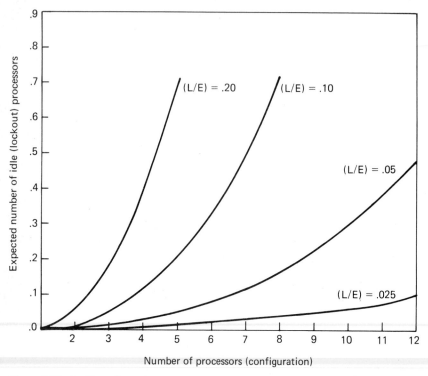

Figure 4-38 Small configurations

The notion of "idle" processors must be carefully understood. One way to look at the situation is to note that the 15-processor system has the effective power of 14 processors, whereas a 14-processor system has the effective power of 13.25 processors. Therefore, the fifteenth processor has a marginal effective power of 75 percent (¾ of a processor). Such a configuration is reasonable if either the marginal cost of the additional processor (and associated hardware) is less than 4 percent of the total system cost, assuming some economy of scale, or if the necessity for additional compute power outweighs the cost. On the other hand, under the same conditions, the marginal power of the forty-first processor is close to 0 percent.

What are likely values for L/E? Estimates such as 0.1 percent to 10 percent are likely for complex systems. Several operational single-processor operating systems spend up to 50 percent of execution time performing supervisory functions. If such systems were adapted for multiprocessing by indiscriminately locking whenever entering supervisor state, locked time (L) might easily exceed unlocked (E). A system must be designed with multiprocessor operation in mind to minimize lockout occurrences and curtail their duration.

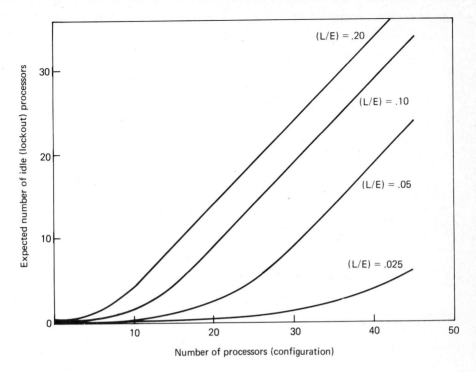

Figure 4-39 Large configurations

The ratio L/E may actually change when the number of processors is increased. Depending on the effectiveness of shared procedures and the amount of main storage added, the paging load could increase or decrease. Furthermore, if more processes are allowed on the system, the amount of time required by a locked priority scheduler would be expected to increase.

This simple model is not intended to produce a complete and precise mathematical solution to the entire problem of multiprocessor lockout. The quantitative results should, however, provide insight into its importance as a factor in the design of multiprocessor operating systems.

4-5.4.3 TECHNIQUES FOR REDUCING SYNCHRONIZATION OVERHEAD

The use of spin locks, as we have seen, has an adverse effect upon system performance; however, the more commonly used suspend locks increase overhead through the testing, setting, and resetting of locks. Several techniques are available for reducing synchronization overhead, and the relative merits of each must be weighed.

One approach is to use a single lock (or a very small number of locks) to cover all shared databases. The alternative is to identify all separate databases carefully and associate a separate lock with each. For example, we could divide the ready list into two or more separate ready lists (e.g., even-numbered processes and odd-numbered processes). Each ready list would then have a separate lock. Thus, in a two-processor system a processor could always find an unlocked ready list to use.

There are many factors to be considered in choosing between a *precise lock approach* (i.e., large number of separate locks) and an *overall lock approach* (i.e., one lock for all databases). In the precise approach considerable overhead is incurred in setting and resetting locks, even though the particular database is often not needed by any other process. This multitude of locks also greatly complicates debugging.

In the overall lock approach (also called brute force), the lock is *on* for long periods of time (up to 50 percent or more). This greatly increases the likelihood of software lockout and the resulting processor idle time.

4-6 COMBINED JOB AND PROCESS SCHEDULING

In many instances, the job scheduling and process scheduling algorithms must interact closely.

If we attempt multiprogramming too many processes at the same time, especially in a demand paging system, all the processes will suffer from poor performance due to an overloading of available system resources (this phenomenon, called *thrashing*, is analyzed in Chapter 8). On the other hand, in a conversational timesharing system, every user wants a "crack at the machine" as soon as possible—1-hour waits will not be tolerated.

As a compromise, we can adopt the philosophy that it is far better to give a few jobs at a time a chance than to starve them all! For example, we may allow two to five users to be ready at a time.

The basic concepts here are: (1) multiprogram "in the small" for two to five jobs, process-scheduling every few ms; and (2) timeshare "in the large," where every few 100 ms or seconds one ready job is placed in hold status and one of the hold status jobs is made ready. (See Figure 4-40.) Thus, over a period of a minute or so, every job has had its turn, and furthermore, the system runs fairly efficiently. Variations of

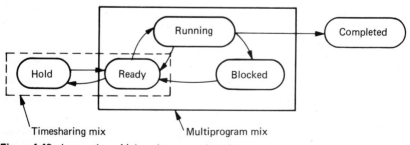

Figure 4-40 Interaction of job and process scheduling

this technique are used in many current operating systems, such as MULTICS (eligible processes) and CP/67 (Q1 and Q2 limits) which are discussed in Chapter 9.

4-7 SUMMARY

Processor management has major functions: (1) job scheduling, (2) process scheduling, and (3) traffic control (such as interprocess communication and synchronization).

Job schedulers range from very simple, even manually done, algorithms to complex automated schedulers that consider the mix of jobs waiting to be run (i.e., in the hold state) as well as the available resources of the system. A uniprogramming operating system or simple priority-based process scheduler does not provide the same degree of optimization available in an adaptive process-scheduling algorithm. In any type of system the interaction between job scheduling and process scheduling must always be carefully considered. If the job scheduler keeps dumping more and more jobs on an already overloaded process scheduler, system performance will suffer greatly.

Considerable research and study are still needed to resolve many of the problems connected with interprocess communication and synchronization. These features are very important to modern modular operating systems, as illustrated by their extensive usage in the sample operating system contained in Chapter 7.

QUESTIONS

4-1 Briefly define and differentiate the following terms:

1 processor

2 procedure

3 process

4-2 Is a process equivalent to a job? Can you think of a system design in which they are equivalent? In which they aren't? Explain.

4-3 The overhead involved in switching (by timeslicing or otherwise) from one job to another is in many instances not insignificant, even if all the jobs are core resident.

1 What pertinent information about a process needs to be changed, updated, or saved when switching processes?

2 Can you think of any additional hardware that would help perform these actions?

3 Switching from one process to another in a multiprogramming system commonly occurs when the process has exhausted its allotted quantum of time (e.g., 100 ms). What are some other reasons and/or criteria for switching processes?

4-4 Why can processors be assigned to any process in a multiprocessor system, rather than requiring a one-to-one correspondence between processor and process?

4-5 One machine design, the Honeywell H800, attempted to provide efficient multiprogramming by defining the state of each process as an entry in a special register table of known length that contains, among other things, the program counter and status information on the process. Switching is accomplished by means of a hardware feature that scans the table in round-robin fashion, executing a *single* instruction at a time per process. Using such a scheme (with or without hardware modification):

1 How could you implement a priority scheme for scheduling jobs or processes? Do you need one?

2 How do you handle the problem of saving or restoring registers, CAWs, CSWs, etc.?

3 How could you send a process blocked for I/O?

4 If the length of the process table is fixed to n entries, could you have more than n active processes? How would you implement this?

4-6 Let us consider the impact of changing from a partitioned allocation scheme to a relocatable partitioned scheme of memory management by studying the processing of six jobs. Each job has a specific priority, memory requirement, and CPU requirement. For simplicity, we will assume that all jobs are primarily computational with minimal I/O. Thus, if two such jobs are multi-programmed, each runs half as fast as if there were only one.

Each job is submitted at a particular time, which, of course, is not known to the system in advance. The system has 100K bytes of usable memory. The six jobs to be run are:

JOB NO.	ARRIVAL TIME	CPU TIME	MEMORY	PRIORITY
1	0.0	1.0	20K	1
2	0.5	1.0	60K	2
3	1.0	0.5	10K	3
4	1.5	2.0	30K	3
5	2.0	0.2	20K	1
6	2.5	0.1	20K	2

We can trace the systems processing as follows:

TIME	CPU USED PER JOB	JOBS			
.0		1(1.0)			
	.5				
.5		1(.5)	2(1.0)		
	.25				
1.0		1(.25)	2(.75)	3(.5)	
	.16				
1.5		1(.09)	2(.59)	3(.34)	
	.09				
1.77		1(0)	2(.5)	3(.25)	
	.12				
2.0		5(.2)	2(.38)	3(.13)	
	.13				
2.4		5(.07)	2(.25)	3(0)	6(.1)
	.07				
2.6		5(0)	2(.18)		6(.03)
	.03				
2.7			2(.15)		6(0)
	.15				
2.85			2(0)	4(2.0)	
	2.0				
4.85				4(0)	

We designate a job starting by an oval, e.g., (1), and terminating by a square, e.g., [1] . The number in parenthesis indicates amount of CPU processing time still required for that job, e.g., 1(1.0).

In the above example partitioned allocation was assumed. Thus, at time 1.0, memory looked as follows:

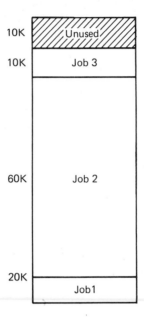

One way to measure the job scheduling effectiveness is to compute the job's turnaround time:

JOB NO.	FINISH TIME (F)	ARRIVAL TIME (A)	TURNAROUND TIME (F-A)
1	1.77	0.0	1.77
2	2.85	0.5	2.35
3	2.4	1.0	1.4
4	4.85	1.5	3.35
5	2.6	2.0	.6
6	2.7	2.5	.2

Average turnaround times:
Priority 1 (1 and 5) = 1.18 hr
Priority 2 (2 and 6) = 1.27 hr
Priority 3 (3 and 4) = 2.37 hr

1 State briefly how you would expect relocatable partitions to change the sequence of processing. How would you expect it to affect the average turnaround times?

2 Produce the actual processing trace and average turnaround times for a relocatable partitions scheme (assume recompact time to be negligible).

3 Did your answer to (2) meet your expectations stated in (1)? Would you expect these results in general? Why?

4 If the jobs performed a substantial amount of I/O, how would this affect the average turnaround times? Why would turnaround times be affected?

4-7 As an operating system designer, you have been commissioned to design the process and job schedulers of a new system. You have been told that high-priority jobs should be processed as quickly as possible, but that overall system throughput is also a major consideration. As a job scheduling scheme you have chosen to take all high-priority jobs before considering jobs of lower priority. In designing the process scheduler you are considering two schemes. The first is a priority scheme identical to the job scheduler. The second scheme first tries to run I/O-bound jobs, then "normal" jobs, then compute-bound jobs, regardless of user-specified priority. Discuss the two schemes with respect to overall system goals.

4-8

1 If recompaction could be performed by the I/O channels independent of the CPU (i.e., a CCW could move n bytes from location A to location B as the 370 MVCL instruction does), what problems would remain?

2 Assuming you wish to run the CPU (i.e., multiprogram) while the channel is recompacting, describe an algorithm to accomplish this safely. You may use flowchart, outlined description, etc.

4-9 We can describe much of processor management in terms of process state transition diagrams, such as:

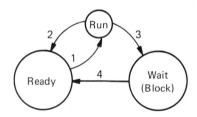

1 What "event" causes each of the marked transitions?

2 When we view all the processes in the system, we can see that a state transition by one process could cause another process to make a state transition also. Under what circumstances could transition 3 by one process immediately cause transition 1 by another process?

3 Under what circumstances, if any, could the following cause-and-effect transitions occur?

   a 2 → 1
   b 3 → 2
   c 4 → 1

4 Under what circumstances, if any, would the following transitions cause
   no other immediate transitions?
   a 1
   b 2
   c 3
   d 4

4-10 Consider the following diagram of state transitions for a process scheduler:

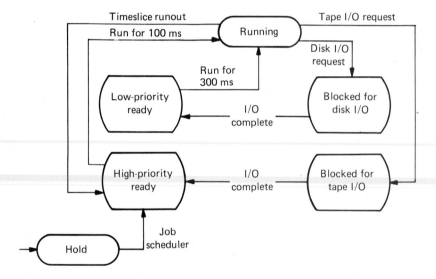

1 Describe the scheduling philosophy underlying this diagram.
2 Suggest a situation in which you might want to use such a scheduling
   scheme.

The job scheduler has chosen the following three jobs to be run by a system
under this scheduling scheme:

   Job 1 computes for 150ms, issues a tape request, computes for 150 ms,
   issues a tape request, computes for 150 ms, issues a tape request.
   Job 2 computes for 250 ms, issues a disk request, computes for 50 ms,
   issues a disk request.
   Job 3 computes for 250 ms, issues a tape request, computes for 250 ms,
   issues a tape request.

These three jobs are representative samples of the jobs submitted to this
system. Tape requests take 500 ms to complete; disk requests 100 ms.
Initially all jobs are ready, and whenever more than one job is in a ready
state, the scheduler chooses the job that has been in that state the longest

(round robin). You can assume that the job scheduler does not activate any more jobs until these three have finished.

3   Make a record of the execution of these three jobs by this system using the format shown below and recording the time and the status of each whenever any job makes a transition from one state to another.

TIME	RUNNING	HIGH-PRIORITY READY	LOW-PRIORITY READY	BLOCKED FOR TAPE I/O	BLOCKED FOR DISK I/O
t=0	1	2,3	—	—	—
.	.	.	.	.	.
.	.	.	.	.	.
.	.	.	.	.	.

4   Determine the turnaround time for each job and the fraction of time for which the CPU is idle.

5   Is the process scheduling scheme accomplishing its objectives as discussed in (1)? If not, why not?

6   What changes could be made in the scheduling scheme to make it perform better in general (i.e., reduce average job time as well as CPU idle time and turnaround time), given the types of jobs to be run on the system?

7   What policy should the job scheduler use in choosing jobs to be loaded in order to aid the process scheduler in accomplishing the aims of (6)?

4-11   Are the processor "race" and "interlock" problems the same between CPU and channel as between two CPUs? If not, how do they differ?

4-12   What is the difference between races and deadlocks? What can be done to prevent or alleviate them?

4-13   Consider a computer system with eight tape drives. All jobs to be run on this system use a maximum of three tape drives according to the pattern of usage shown on the graph below.

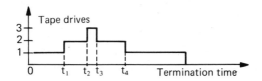

The t_is are different for different jobs, but in each case the interval $t_2 \rightarrow t_3$ is quite short. Various methods might be used for scheduling jobs on this system, such as:

1 Starting a job only if the maximum number of tape drives it will need are presently free; assigning these drives to the job for the entire duration of its processing
2 Using an embrace avoidance strategy, assuming that once a job requests a drive it will retain it for the remainder of its processing time
3 Using a less conservative embrace avoidance scheme based on the knowledge that once a job begins to release tape drives it never requests any more drives
   a Give a flowchart for each of the three strategies described above.
   b For each strategy determine the maximum number of jobs that could be multiprogrammed and the minimum and maximum number of tape drives in simultaneous use.

4-14 1 Primary memory in the S/360 is usually divided into units of 256K bytes called core boxes or memory modules. In the S/360-67, two CPUs can be configured with memory modules in essentially two ways. First, each CPU can be given access to one and only one memory module so that there are actually *two distinct systems* processing programs. Second, both memory modules can be accessible to the CPUs under the control of one operating system. When this was done once, total throughput was reduced by 25 percent over the first configuration of two separate systems. This decline has been attributed to interference between the CPUs. Give some sources of this interference.

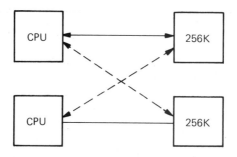

2 Considering the interference, why would anyone want to use the second configuration (other than Computing Center Machismo)?
3 It is necessary in the second configuration to prevent one processor from accessing a database while the other processor is making modifications to it; e.g., the job queue. One method of achieving processor lockout is to associate a byte with the database that indicates by its value whether a

processor is currently accessing it. If the byte is 0, the database is free for access; otherwise, the processor examining it is blocked from access. The following code purports to accomplish this. Will it work?

```
        SSM     INTOFF      DISABLE ALL I/O INTERRUPTS
        CLI     SWITCH,0    CHECK IF THE BYTE SWITCH
                            ASSOCIATED WITH THE DATA-
                            BASE IS 0
        BNE     ·BLOCKED    IF NON-0, THE PROCESSOR MAY
                            TRANSFER TO SOME ALTERNATE
                            CODE
        OI      SWITCH,1    NOTIFIES OTHER PROCESSORS
                            THAT DATABASE IS CLOSED TO
                            ACCESS
        SSM     INTON       REENABLE I/O INTERRUPTS
         .
         .
         .
        NI      SWITCH,0    WHEN FINISHED, SET THE SWITCH
                            TO 0
         .
         .
         .
INTOFF  DC      X'0'
INTON   DC      (APPROPRIATE MASK)
```

4 The test-and-set instruction was specifically designed to facilitate processor lockout. Explain why it works.

5 In the case of a program that is not parallel reentrant, only one processor at a time may execute it. To achieve processor lockout, it has been proposed that the program to be executed should have the following format.

```
                L       1,BRANCH
        LOOP    ST      1,LOOP

                        SERIALLY REENTRANT CODE

                L       1,STORE
                ST      1,LOOP
                 .
                 .
                 .
        STORE   ST      1,LOOP
        BRANCH  B       LOOP
```

How does this work? Compare this method with the use of the TS instruction.

6 What problems may arise if both the CPUs used the same low-core area in one of the memory modules (e.g., new PSWs, CAW)? Suggest a better scheme.

4-15

1 What is a deadly embrace?
2 Set the stage for a deadly embrace and explain how you would go about detecting it. (Examples need not be restricted to computer science.)
3 The general philosophies underlying both the scheduling of memory and I/O devices such as tape drives are not very different. Both deal with the problem of most efficiently assigning the available resource to as many users as possible (multiplexing) in order to achieve a more economical and effective use of the resource. This is because tapes, drums, etc., are serving the same purpose as core, i.e., information storage. The major difference is in the access times for retrieving any particular pieces of data.
   a We discussed the deadly embrace situation in relation to tape drives, etc., in the text (e.g., Figure 4-33). Is it possible to imagine a deadly embrace situation where the source under consideration is main memory under a demand paging allocation algorithm? Give reasons for your answer.
   b A deadly embrace avoidance technique, such as Haberman's (see Section 4-5.3.2), helps only in preventing a deadlock. Once a deadlock has occurred, there is often no way to get out of it. After studying (a) above give reasons why it might be impossible to break a deadlock once it has occurred.

4-16 In an effort to increase total computing power, a certain computer center has added a second CPU to its standard system, providing the ability to multiprocess with both CPUs. Since the second processor was very costly, no additional memory was added; both CPUs share the same physical core.
1 What problems would arise if both CPUs shared the same low core area (where the PSWs CSWs, etc., are kept)? Suggest a better scheme.
2 It is sometimes necessary to prevent one processor from accessing a database while the other is making modifications to it. This is called processor lockout. On what databases is processor lockout necessary? How could you lock out a processor?
3 After the addition of the second CPU, it was noted that total computing power was not doubled, but had increased only by a factor of 1.6. Give some possible explanation for this.

4-17 A computing system has 10 tape drives available. All jobs that run on the system require a maximum of four tape drives to complete, but we know that they start by running for a long period with only three; they request the one remaining drive for a short period when needed near the end of their operation. (There is an endless supply of these jobs.)

1 If the job scheduler operates with the policy that it will not start a job unless there are four unassigned drives, and it assigns those four drives to a job for its entire duration, what is the maximum number of jobs that can be in progress at once? What are the minimum and maximum number of drives that may actually be idle as a result of this policy?

2 Suppose a deadly embrace avoiding algorithm is in use instead of the overly restrictive policy outlined in (1). What is the maximum number of jobs that can be in progress at once? What are the minimum and maximum number of drives that may actually be idle as a result of this policy? Explain your answers.

3 Flowchart an algorithm that assigns tapes to multiple jobs but avoids deadly embraces (i.e., an algorithm for 2).

4-18 The following figure shows a canal with locks and two drawbridges on it. The drawbridges lie on a road which has been laid so as to avoid a marsh and which crosses the canal twice. Both the canal and the road carry traffic in one direction only. The principal traffic on the canal consists of barges. As a barge approaches bridge A, a warning is sounded when the barge is 100 meters from the bridge and, when the bridge is free of cars, it is drawn. The bridge stays drawn until the tail end of the barge has passed the bridge. A similar sequence is followed for bridge B. A typical barge is 200 meters long. Will a deadlock ever occur? If so, what would be the reasons? How could one detect a possible deadlock? Propose a solution to prevent a detected deadlock.

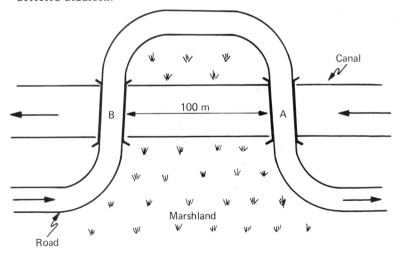

4-19 Give four examples of interprocess communication.

4-20 In actual operating systems (e.g., the sample operating system in Chapter 7) it is necessary to distinguish more than the three states (ready, running, and blocked) of a process. For example, what state is a process in if it has not been fully created? What state is a process in if it cannot be swapped until some event takes place?

1 Redraw the ready, running, blocked state diagram of a process, adding at least two additional "practical states."

2 Show all transitions.

3 What modules of the operating system would handle the new transitions?

4 Discuss the algorithms for (3).

4-21 What is the difference between a process being stopped for a software lockout in a multiprocessor system and a process being blocked in a multiprogramming system?

4-22 Work through the analysis of the sample job requests of Section 4-2.4.3 assuming a 25 percent I/O wait time. Compare these results with those of Section 4-2.4.2.

4-23 Define the operations of the order clerk, bagger, cook, and cashier of Figure 4-26 using the counting semaphores of Section 4.5.2.3. Present results in a form like P_p and P_c (Section 4-5.2.3).

4-24[1] A job scheduler has the task of deciding in what order jobs that have arrived in the system are to be run. At any given time, the job scheduler decides what job in the job queue, if any, will be initiated. The purpose of this assignment is to provide you with the opportunity of handling and making the policy decisions that fall to a job scheduler such as, for example, the job scheduler in the Attached Support Processor (ASP) system at the M.I.T. Information Processing Center. Your task, therefore, should you accept this assignment, is to write a job scheduler in PL/I.

In addition to deciding when each job will be run, the scheduler has these responsibilities:

---

[1] Essentially this question is to implement a job scheduler but it may be limited to a design question with no implementation by requiring flowcharts and design specifications. If the solution to this question is to be implemented, one of the following alternatives may be used:

1 Provide an environment for the student's solution by using our job scheduler environment simulator (Donovan, 1974).

2 Have the student write his own environment, which could be as simple as giving his scheduler sample job runs as data.

3 Write your own environment simulator.

For additional design problems that may be used for actual implementation on a computer system see *Pedagogical and Research Aids* (Donovan, 1974).

1 Organizing and maintaining a list of the jobs that have been submitted for running
2 Purging job entries from the list as they are terminated by the system
3 Maintaining and updating any other lists that may facilitate the scheduling process
4 Maintaining certain scheduling statistics and possibly using them to "tune" the scheduler dynamically for better performance

The system keeps its end of the bargain by supplying the scheduler with the following aids, in the form of utility programs:

1 Memory management
2 Device management
3 A system clock
4 Signaling when a job terminates
5 Transmission to the scheduler of JCL information for jobs that have arrived

For our scheduling purposes, you will not be concerned with printer, punch, disk, or any other device requirements of a job other than tape drive requirements. The imaginary system you will be working with will have 10 tape drives. The memory available will be 800K in nonrelocatable partitions; hence, fragmentation will be a factor. However, you, the job scheduler, do not have to keep track of memory or tape drives.

Your scheduler will actually be a collection of subroutines that are called by the system as scheduling decisions are needed. To be more specific, three of your routines will be called by the system:

1 J_ARRIV—job arrival routine
2 J_TERM—job terminate routine
3 J–SCHED—job start routine

The following pages provide description of the objectives of this machine problem, and enumerate the required and optional tasks to be performed. They also explain the general organization that your solution must have for interaction with the simulator, as well as the types and formats of data your solution must produce as results.

We begin with a functional description of the entry points in the student job scheduler.

1 J_ARRIV is the first routine the system will call. It will be called each time a job arrives at the system. The system will pass a pointer to a based structure containing all pertinent information about the job that has just arrived, including: job number, arrival time, maximum run time, core needed, tape drives needed, priority, and class (CPU-bound, balanced, I/O-bound). J_ARRIV's job is to put this information on the scheduler's list of jobs that have been submitted for running.

2 J_TERM will be called each time a job terminates. A pointer to a structure of data for the job to be terminated will be passed, and it is J_TERM's responsibility to purge that job from appropriate lists within the scheduler.

3 J_SCHED will be called all the rest of the time, i.e., whenever a job could possibly be scheduled. J_SCHED's task is to decide (1) whether or not to schedule a job at that time and (2) what job to schedule. If the scheduler chooses not to schedule another job at that time, it returns JOB NUMBER = 0. If it decides to schedule a job, it returns the NUMBER of the job it wants initiated. Note, for example, that after a big job terminates, a J_SCHED might be called three or four consecutive times before core is filled again; hence the fact that J_SCHED can pass only one JOB NUMBER at a time is not really a restriction.

To summarize, here is a list of the calls the system makes to the three major scheduler subroutines:

1 J_ARRIV—called when job arrives at system to inform scheduler to add job to job queue

2 J_TERM—called when job terminates

3 J_SCHED—called to schedule a job; answer: a job NUMBER or none

Hence a bird's-eye view of the system and interactions may look as follows:

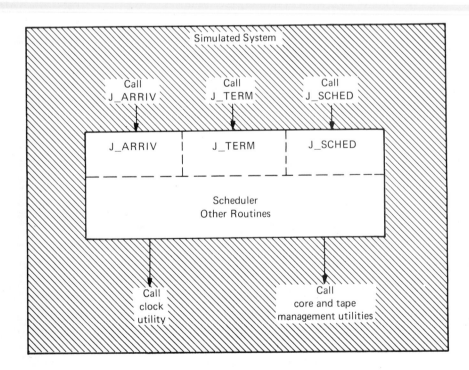

In other words, if you haven't gotten the idea by now, your assignment is to color in (via PL/I) the unshaded area in the diagram on page 280.

PART I   The first scheduler you are to write will consider only the following parameters for each job:

1   core needed
2   tape drives needed
3   priority of job
4   specified maximum run time
5   arrival time of job

In this part of the assignment, all jobs will be the same class (class B) so that job class will not be a scheduling consideration.

Useful statistics for the simulated system are listed below:

20 percent of all jobs run for 00.00 minutes (i.e., don't run—JCL errors, etc.)

50 percent of all 1-minute jobs run for less than ¼ minute

In general, the larger the specified maximum run time (MAXTIME) for a job, the more accurate that estimate is likely to be.

An average job has a MAXTIME of about 10 minutes; it uses approximately 150K of memory and about two tape drives.

PART II   The second scheduler assignment is to add job class (compute-bound, balanced, I/O-bound) to your scheduling considerations. The additional goal here is to maintain optimal job mixes in the system so as to maximize CPU efficiency and therefore minimize stretchout factors and turnaround times.

The following table summarizes the characteristics of various class jobs:

JOB TYPE	CPU TIME	OCCUPANCY TIME*
Compute-bound	1	1.5
Balanced	1	2.0
I/O-bound	1	4.0

*Occupancy time is the time a job would require if run alone in the system.

From the above numbers, it should be evident that, no matter what job mix you have, the total run time for jobs in a multiprogramming environment should be less than the sum of the occupancy times. It should also be evident that an *optimal* job mix would consist of some combination of compute-bound, balanced, and I/O-bound jobs. Just what the optimal job mix is for any given number of simultaneously active jobs is literally an open question—left open for your study and experimentation.

PART III   In addition to the tasks set in Parts I and II, several optional schedulers are in this part. In each of these additional optional assignments, the scheduler will be driven by a different administrative scheduling policy. You are to implement one of the following scheduling policy goals:

1 Maximum throughput—run all jobs in the shortest total time.

2 Turnaround limit—regardless of size, device requirements, or priority, turnaround time for any job must not exceed 60 minutes.

Keep in mind while trying to implement III-1 or III-2 that the goals of good overall turnaround time and excellent priority turnaround time should be sacrificed as little as possible.

3 Express service—in an effort to get users to switch their files from tape (your system is short on tape drives) to disk (you have disk drives that stand idle), you, the administrative policymaker, have decided to offer, for a limited time only, special express service, whereby lower-priority jobs that use no tape drives receive high-priority treatment for the same low-priority prices. However, so as not to upset high-priority users who are still paying high-priority prices, you have made users a threefold promise: (1) high-priority turnaround time will not be degraded as a result of the new express service; (2) high-priority users who use tape drives will still get at least as good a turnaround as express users; and (3) high-priority users who do not require tape drives will get the best turnaround times of anyone. Final note: you have made no promises to low-priority, non-express users.

4 Groups are encouraged to formulate and implement interesting and challenging scheduling policies (after discussing them with an instructor).

Device Management

5

In this chapter we group together the management of all devices other than the processor and memory for three reasons: (1) a separate chapter for each would not be warranted; (2) we can state some general concepts that are applicable to all; and (3) many contemporary systems consolidate all the modules that manage these devices.

This chapter focuses on the management of I/O devices. These include actual I/O devices, such as printers, card readers, tapes, disks, and drums, and supporting devices, such as control units or control channels. A brief discussion of I/O device characteristics is presented in Sections 5-2 and 5-3. Some readers may already be familiar with some of these devices; our purpose in these sections is to merely give a feel for the relative speeds and characteristics of the important devices. A large installation may devote over half the system cost to I/O devices. Therefore, it is desirable to use these devices in an efficient manner.

The basic functions of device management are:

1 Keeping track of the status of all devices, which requires special mechanisms. One commonly used mechanism is to have a database such as a Unit Control Block (UCB) associated with each device. (See Section 5-5.1 for a sample format of a UCB.)

2 Deciding on policy to determine who gets a device, for how long, and when. A wide range of techniques is available for implementing these policies. For example, a policy of high device utilization attempts to match the nonuniform requests by processes to the uniform speed of many I/O devices. There are three basic techniques for implementing the policies of device management:

    a Dedicated—a technique whereby a device is assigned to a single process.

    b Shared—a technique whereby a device is shared by many processes.

    c Virtual—a technique whereby one physical device is simulated on another physical device.

3 Allocation—physically assigning a device to process. Likewise the corresponding control units and channels must be assigned.

4 Deallocation policy and techniques. Deallocation may be done on either a process or a job level. On a job level, a device is assigned for as long as the job exists in the system. On a process level, a device may be assigned for as long as the process needs it.

This chapter will focus mainly on the policies of device management, since the techniques are heavily device-dependent and are changing rapidly with hardware advances. However, Chapter 7 gives an example of the implementation of a dedicated policy where each device is assigned solely to one job.

The module that keeps track of the status of devices is called the *I/O traffic controller*. We have called all modules associated with the operation of a single device the *I/O device handlers*. In our design of Figure 1-9, each I/O device has a device handler that resides in a separate process associated with that device. The I/O device handler's function is to create the channel program for performing the desired function, initiate I/O to that device, handle the interrupts from it, and optimize its performance. In short, the device handler performs the physical I/O. The *I/O scheduler* decides when an I/O processor is assigned to a request and sets up the path to the device.

5-1 TECHNIQUES FOR DEVICE MANAGEMENT

Three major techniques are used for managing and allocating devices: (1) dedicated, (2) shared, and (3) virtual.

5-1.1 Dedicated Devices

A *dedicated* device is allocated to a job for the job's entire duration. Some devices lend themselves to this form of allocation. It is difficult, for example, to share a card reader, tape, or printer. If several users were to use the printer at the same time, would they cut up their appropriate output and paste it together? Unfortunately, dedicated assignment may be inefficient if the job does not fully and continually utilize the device. The other techniques, shared and virtual, are usually preferred whenever they are applicable.

5-1.2 Shared Devices

Some devices such as disks, drums, and most other Direct Access Storage Devices (DASD) may be shared concurrently by several processes. Several processes can read from a single disk at essentially the same time. The management of a shared device can become quite complicated, particularly if utmost efficiency is desired. For example, if two processes simultaneously request a Read from Disk A, some mechanism must be employed to determine which request should be handled first. This may be done partially by software (the I/O scheduler and traffic controller) or entirely by hardware (as in some computers with very sophisticated channels and control units).

Policy for establishing which process' request is to be satisfied first might be based on (1) a priority list or (2) the objective of achieving improved system output (for example, by choosing whichever request is nearest to the current position of the read heads of the disk).

Shared devices are further discussed in Sections 5-2.2.3 and 5-5.

5-1.3 Virtual Devices

Some devices that would normally have to be dedicated (e.g., card readers) may be converted into shared devices through techniques such as SPOOLing. For example, a SPOOLing program can read and copy all card input onto a disk at high speed. Later, when a process tries to read a card, the SPOOLing program intercepts the request and converts it to a read from the disk. Since a disk may be easily shared by several users, we have converted a dedicated device to a shared device, changing one card reader into many "virtual" card readers. This technique is equally applicable to a large number of peripheral devices, such as teletypes, printers, and most dedicated slow input/output devices.

In Section 5-6 we discuss the techniques for virtualizing some devices and the problems associated with implementing these algorithms on particular systems that have memory limitations.

5-1.4 Generalized Strategies

Some professionals have attempted to generalize device management even more than is done here. For example, the call side of SPOOLing is similar to the file system and buffering bears striking similarity to SPOOLing. We could generalize even more and view memory, processors, and I/O devices as simple devices to which the same theory should apply. At present we realize that there are practical limitations to these generalizations, although at some time in the future more general theories may emerge that are applicable to all devices and that have direct practical applications. Therefore, while continuing our research to produce such general theories, we recognize that they will not emerge without thorough understanding of the issues presented in this book.

5-2 DEVICE CHARACTERISTICS—HARDWARE CONSIDERATIONS

Almost everything imaginable can be, and probably has been, used as a peripheral device to a computer, ranging from steel mills to laser beams, from radar to mechanical potato pickers, from thermometers to space ships. Fortunately, most computer installations utilize only a relatively small set of peripheral devices. Peripheral devices can be generally categorized into two major groups: (1) input or output devices and (2) storage devices.

5-2.1 Input or Output Devices

An *input device* is one by which the computer "senses" or "feels" the outside world. These devices may be mechanisms such as thermometers or radar devices, but, more conventionally, they are devices to read punched cards, punched paper tape, or messages typed on typewriterlike terminals. An *output device* is one by which the computer "affects" or "controls" the outside world. It may be a mechanism such as a temperature control knob or a radar direction control, but more commonly it is a device to punch holes in cards or paper tape, print letters and numbers on paper, or control the typing of typewriterlike terminals.

In previous chapters we have described some common I/O devices, such as printers and card readers (see the buffering examples of Chapter 2). In this chapter we will focus on the *storage devices*.

5-2.2 Storage Devices

A storage device is a mechanism by which the computer may store information (a procedure commonly called *writing*) in such a way that this information may be retrieved at a later time (*reading*). Conceptually, storage devices are analogous to human storage mechanisms that use pieces of paper, pencils, and erasers.

It is helpful to differentiate among three types of storage devices. Our differentiation is based on the variation of access times (T_{ij}) where:

T_{ij} = time to access item j, given last access was to item i (or current position is item i)

We differentiate the following types of storage devices:

1 *Serial Access* where T_{ij} has a large variance (e.g., tape)
2 *Completely Direct Access* where T_{ij} is constant (e.g., core)
3 *Direct Access* where T_{ij} has only a small variance (e.g., drum)

5-2.2.1 SERIAL ACCESS DEVICES

A *serial access* storage device can be characterized as one that relies on strictly physical sequential positioning and accessing of information. Access to an arbitrary, stored item requires a "linear search" so that an average access takes the time required to read half the information stored. A Magnetic Tape Unit (MTU) is the most common example of a serial access storage device. The MTU is based upon the same principles as the audio tape deck or tape cassette, but instead of music or voices, binary information is stored. A typical serial access device is depicted in Figure 5-1.

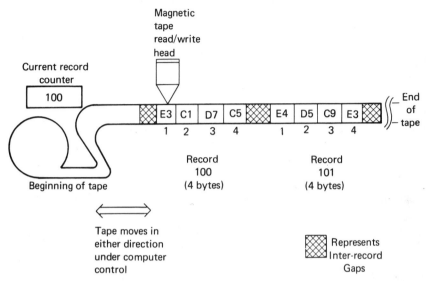

Figure 5-1   Magnetic tape unit

Information is usually stored as groups of bytes, called *records*, rather than single bytes. In general, a record can be of arbitrary length, e.g., from 1 to 32,768 bytes long. In Figure 5-1 all the records are four bytes long. Records may be viewed as being analogous to spoken words on a standard audio tape deck. Each record can be identified by its physical position on the tape; the first record is 1, the second, 2, and so on. The current record counter of Figure 5-1 serves the same function as the "time" or "number-of-feet" meter of audio tape decks. If the tape is positioned at its beginning (i.e., completely rewound), and we wish to read record number 101, it is necessary to skip over all intervening records (e.g., 1, 2, . . ., 99, 100) in order to reach record number 101.

In addition to obvious I/O commands, such as Read the Next Record or Write the Next Record, a tape unit usually has commands such as Read the Last Record (read backward), Rewind to Beginning of Tape at High Speed, Skip Forward (or Backward) One Record without Actually Reading or Writing Data. In order to help establish groupings of records on a tape, there is a special record type called a *tape mark*. This record type can be written only by using the Write Tape Mark command. If the tape unit encounters a tape mark while reading or skipping, a special interrupt is generated. Tape marks are somewhat analogous to putting bookmarks in a book to help find your place.

A 370 channel program using a magnetic tape unit might look like this:

```
CCW    X'07', - - -, X'40', - - -     REWIND TO BEGINNING OF TAPE
CCW    X'37', - - -, X'40', - - -     SKIP RECORD 1
CCW    X'37', - - -, X'40', - - -     SKIP RECORD 2
CCW    X'01', DATA1, X'40', 80        WRITE RECORD 3 FROM DATA1
CCW    X'01', DATA2, X'40', 80        WRITE RECORD 4 FROM DATA2
CCW    X'1F',- - -, X'40', - - -      WRITE TAPE MARK
CCW    X'07', - - -, X'00', - - -     REWIND TO BEGINNING AGAIN
```

A program can use a simple one-CCW channel program to read or write one record at a time.

Contemporary magnetic tape units, using half-inch-wide tape, usually store either 1600 or 6250 bytes in one linear inch of tape and can move the tape at speeds up to 200 inches per second. Even at this speed it would take about one minute to get to the middle record of a standard 2,400-foot tape starting from the beginning.

Typical characteristics of tape units are:

density—1600 bytes per inch (19,200 bytes per foot)

speed—200 inches per second (16 2/3 feet per second)

length—2400 feet long (i.e., capacity is about 46,000,000 bytes)

maximum access = 2 minutes

random (average) access = 1 minute

serial access (at one record read the next) $\approx$ 4 ms

$$\left.\begin{array}{l}\text{note}\\ T_{ij} \text{ wide}\\ \text{variance}\end{array}\right\}$$

Serial access storage devices are normally used for applications that require mainly sequential accessing, such as the copies of punched card decks, or the intermediate file copies produced by pass 1 of an assembler or loader. In current data processing, a large percentage of the applications are primarily sequential.

The Inter-record Gap (IRG) shown in Figure 5-1 is necessary due to the physical limitations of starting and stopping a tape. In order to read the next record in a stopped tape, the tape drive takes a finite amount of time to get up to speed. Similarly, after a record has been read, some tape goes by before it can be stopped.

The IRG is usually from 1/4 to 3/4 of an inch (approximately equivalent to 400 to 1200 bytes). The gap length for a specific device is a constant. Thus it is common to store records of greater than 1000 bytes; otherwise, 50 percent or more of the tape is wasted. For example, if we stored 80-byte records with a 3/4-inch IRG, only about 6.3 percent of the tape would be utilized (or 2.7 million out of a possible 47 million bytes).

To minimize gap waste, we frequently *block* records. *Blocking* is placing multiple logical records into one *physical record* (a block). Figure 5-2 depicts four 80-byte logical records (cards) in one 320-byte physical record (block).

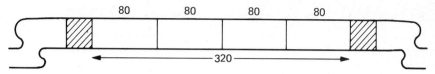

Figure 5-2 Blocked records

Blocks are typically 800 to 8000 bytes long. If they were any longer, there would be reliability problems and when read in, they would take up too much memory.

The mechanisms of blocking and deblocking will be elaborated further in Chapter 6. Basically, when the file system receives a request to read a logical record, this request is converted into a read of the appropriate blocked physical record that contains the logical record. The entire physical record is read into a buffer area in core, and the request is satisfied by extracting the logical record from the buffer area.

Substantial speed gains can be achieved if a table is kept aware of the contents of these buffer areas. For example, the next read request is usually for the next logical record, which probably is in the same physical record (now in the buffer area). There is thus no need to read the physical record again from the tape—the logical record may be extracted from the buffer area.

There are three major advantages to blocking:

1 Fewer I/O operations are needed since each I/O operation reads or writes multiple logical records at a time.

2 There is less wasted space since record length is larger than the Inter-record Gap length.

3 Smaller tape space is covered when reading many records (less distance to travel) since there is less wasted space.

There are also three major disadvantages:

1 Software overhead and routines are required to do the blocking, deblocking, and record keeping.

2 Buffer space is wasted (e.g., you might have wanted only 80 bytes but had to read 8000 bytes). On small machines this may be 10 percent or more of all memory.

3 There is more likelihood of tape errors since long records are being read.

5-2.2.2 COMPLETELY DIRECT ACCESS DEVICES

A completely direct access device is one in which the access time T_{ij} is a constant. Magnetic core memory, semiconductor memory, read-only wired memories, and diode matrix memories are all examples of completely direct access memories. Figure 5-3 depicts the workings of a core memory.

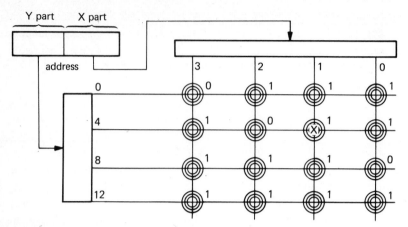

Figure 5-3   Core memory

In Figure 5-3 the 16 circles represent magnetic ferrite cores. All cores are connected by wires, each core having two selection wires through it. When the hardware receives a read request for some address, the address is decomposed into an x and y portion. The hardware then selects the appropriate core. This is done by passing current through the two selection wires. Only the core at the specified (x,y) coordinate receives a "double dose" of current; all other cores receive half the amount of current or no current at all. The double dose of current is sufficient to "flip" the magnetic field from 1 to 0.

One property of a magnetic core is that when it changes magnetic state it induces a current. A third sensing wire is passed through all the cores. If the appropriate core was 1 and it was switched to 0, a current would be induced in this wire. If it was already 0, there would be no induced current.

For example, in Figure 5-3, if a request to read bit 5 (binary 0101) were received, the hardware would decompose the address:

$$\underbrace{0\underbrace{1}_{y}\,0\underbrace{1}_{x}} \qquad \text{or} \qquad \begin{array}{l} y = 4 \\ \text{and} \\ x = 1 \end{array}$$

Thus, the sense output would be a 1 (the x core of Figure 5-3). Note that the process of reading a core destroys its information content (i.e., sets it to 0 always); thus an additional cycle is necessary to write the information back.

For core memory T_{ij} is constant for all i and j and is typically about 500 nanoseconds to 2 microseconds. Usually, this type of memory is used as *main memory*. Occasionally, if it is sufficiently inexpensive (and hence usually slower—greater than 2 microseconds), it is used as a storage device (e.g., IBM's Large Core Storage or CDC's Extended Core Storage). This use of completely direct access device is rare at present, but we may see more of it in the future (Risko, 1968).

Most contemporary computers use semiconductor (transistorlike) memories. The basic ideas are similar to the core memories described above, but semiconductor memories offer advantages in cost and speed. Typical semiconductor memories operate between 50 to 500 nanoseconds access time.

Although we say this type of storage device may be shared on the nanosecond level, it is limited in the sense that only one processor (CPU or I/O channel) can read a specific location (or block of locations) at a given time. Whenever more than one processor is accessing memory, especially if there is one CPU and several I/O channels, we frequently say that the channels are *memory cycle stealing*. Memory cycle stealing can degrade the performance of a system and is a factor with which the I/O traffic controller must contend.

5-2.2.3 DIRECT ACCESS STORAGE DEVICES (DASD)

A direct access device is one that is characterized by small variances in the access time T_{ij}. These have been called *Direct Access Storage Devices*. Although they do not offer completely direct access, the name persists in the field.

In this section we give two examples of DASD, fixed-head and moving-head devices.

5-2.2.3.1 *Fixed-Head Drums and Disks*
Figure 5-4 depicts a DASD storage device similar to a magnetic drum.

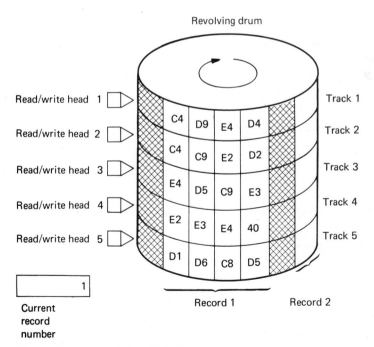

Figure 5-4 Fixed-head drum DASD

A magnetic drum can be simplistically viewed as several adjacent strips of magnetic tape wrapped around a drum so that the ends of each tape strip join. Each tape strip, called a *track*, has a separate read/write head. The drum continuously revolves at high speed so that the records repeatedly pass under the read/write heads (e.g., record 1, record 2, . . ., then record 1 again, record 2, . . ., etc.). Each individual record is identified by a track number and then a record number. For example, record (2,1) is X'C4C9E2D2', and record (5,1) is X'D1D6C8D5' in Figure 5-4. Typical magnetic drums spin very fast and have several hundred read/write heads; thus a random access to read or write can be accomplished in 5 or 10 ms in contrast to the minute required for random access to a record on a full magnetic tape.

Unlike the MTU, which could directly access only the preceding or following record, a DASD can access any record stored on the device. Thus it is necessary to specify the DASD address in the I/O channel commands. Logically, the I/O command would be:

READ (1) DASD record (2,1) into
        (2) memory address (14680)
        (3) length (80)

In most cases this request is actually broken into two parts: (1) DASD positioning and (2) data transfer operation. Thus, the above I/O command would become:

POSITION to DASD record (2,1)
READ into memory address (14680) length (80)

Once positioned, a DASD can be viewed as a serial device. If we wanted to read records (2,1), (2,2), and (2,3), the I/O commands could be simplified to:

POSITION to DASD record (2,1)
READ into memory address (14680) length (80)
READ into memory address (14760) length (80)
READ into memory address (14840) length (80)

For the 370, the DASD record address is usually 5 bytes, as follows:

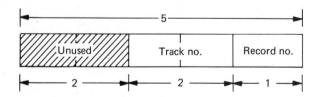

The purpose of the address section marked "unused" will be explained later. The positioning action on the 370 actually requires two channel commands, as follows:

```
GET     CCW X'31',ADDR,X'40',5      SEARCH ID: IS THIS THE RIGHT
                                              RECORD? IF YES, SKIP
                                              NEXT CCW

        CCW X'08',GET,X'40',- -     TRANSFER: IF NO, TRY AGAIN WITH
                                              NEXT RECORD

        CCW X'06',DATA,X'00',80     READ 80 BYTES OF DATA
ADDR    DC  X'0000000201'           TRACK 2, RECORD 1
DATA    DS  CL80                    80-BYTE DATA AREA
```

The Search ID Equal command compares the address of the record currently at the read/write head (or next record to arrive if in the midst of a record). If it is the desired record, the next CCW is skipped; otherwise the next CCW is executed. If the immediately following CCW is a Transfer back to the Search, a loop is formed that examines each record until the desired record arrives at the read/write heads.

Typical characteristics of a drum are:

rotation speed = 10 ms

maximum access = 10 ms

average (random) access = 5 ms

serial access (depending on length of record) $<$ 1 ms

T_{ij} — minor variance (1 order of magnitude)

capacity = 8 million bytes (256 heads * 32,000 bytes per track)

There are several key differences between a continuously spinning device, such as a drum, and a start/stop device, such as a tape. The drum does not stop rotating; therefore, we do not really need an Inter-record Gap on a drum (we used a gap on a tape to start and stop it). One use for a gap on a drum is to allow time for CPU computation when reading sequential records of a drum, for example, to let the IRG be roughly equivalent to the time needed both to process the last record and to start the I/O for the next record. Otherwise, we must wait for the device to rotate all the way around to get to the next record. This can make a significant difference in time for sequential processing (e.g., from 1 ms access to 10 ms access).

Another approach to handling this timing is to use a "hopscotch" pattern for storing records. For example, if there are 10 physical records (A, B, C, . . . J) to be stored on a drum that has 10 records per track, we could store them as follows:

Drum Record	Data Record
1	A
2	B
3	C
4	D
5	E
6	F
7	G
8	H
9	I
10	J

Let us assume that these records are frequently read sequentially (i.e., the job will need record A, then B, etc.). Assume the job takes 2 ms to process each record after reading it; after reading and processing record A (at drum record 1), the drum will have rotated to the beginning of drum record 4. (This is based on complete rotation in 10 ms or 1 ms for each of the 10 records.) In order then to read record B, the drum must rotate around to drum record 2 again, which will take 8 ms. Alternatively, the records could have been stored as follows:

Drum Record	Data Record
1	A
2	H
3	E
4	B
5	I
6	F
7	C
8	J
9	G
10	D

This time, after reading and processing record A, the drum will again have rotated to the beginning of drum record 4. We want data record B, which happens to be stored in drum record 4. Thus we do not have to wait for any additional rotation.

In comparing the two schemes for storing data records, notice that in the first scheme a program to process all 10 records would take approximately:

$$10 \times [1 \text{ ms (read record)} + 2 \text{ ms (process record)} + 8 \text{ ms (access next record)}]$$
$$= 10 \times 11 \text{ ms} = 110 \text{ ms}$$

The second scheme eliminates the "access next record" time and thereby reduces the time to:

$$10 \times [1 \text{ ms (read record)} + 2 \text{ ms (process record)}] = 10 \times 3 \text{ ms} = 30 \text{ ms}$$

In other words, the second scheme is almost four times faster. This difference becomes quite significant when there are 1,000 or 10,000 records to be processed.

Blocking is also helpful in improving the performance of sequential processing, since two or more consecutive data records are accessed in each drum record. If the drum uses Inter-record Gaps, blocking helps to minimize the amount of wasted space due to the IRGs.

5-2.2.3.2 *Moving-head Disks and Drums*

The magnetic disk is similar to the magnetic drum but is based upon the use of one or more flat disks, each with a series of concentric circles, one per read/write head. This is analogous to a phonograph disk. Since read/write heads are expensive, some devices do not have a unique head for each data track. Instead, the heads are physically moved from track to track; such units are called *moving-arm* or *moving-head* DASDs. Each arm position is called a *cylinder*.

In order to identify a particular record stored on the moving-head DASD shown in Figure 5-5, it is necessary to specify the arm position, track number, and record number. Notice that arm position is based upon radial movement whereas record number is based upon circumferential movement. Thus, to access a record, it is necessary to move to the correct radial position (if not already there) and then to wait for the correct record to rotate under the read/write head.

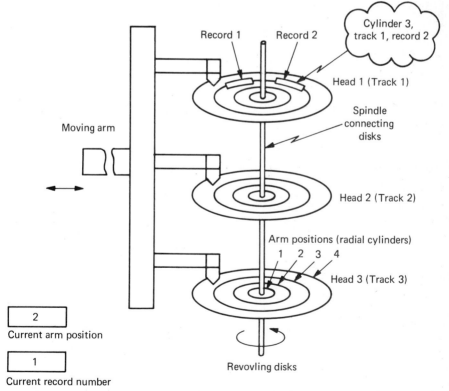

Figure 5-5 Moving-head disk DASD

On the 370 there is a separate I/O command, called a *Seek* operation, to position the arm. Once the arm is positioned, the device is created exactly like the magnetic drum described in Section 5-2.2.3.1. A Seek position is specified using six bytes, as follows:

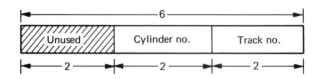

Unlike the record search done by the Search ID command, once the arm has been positioned at a cylinder, it stays at that position until another Seek command causes it to move. Thus, the seek command may be issued separately, which is called Preseeking, or it may be part of a long channel program.

Figure 5-6 shows the commands that can be used to read the record at Cylinder 3, Track 1, Record 2 assuming the area is not currently positioned at Cylinder 3.

```
          CCW  X'0B',ADDR,X'40',6              Seek cylinder.
SEARCH    CCW  X'31',ADDR+2,X'40',5            Search for desired record.
          CCW  X'08',SEARCH,X'40',- -          Keep trying to find.
          CCW  X'06',DATA,X'00',80             Read 80 bytes of data.
ADDR      DC   X'00 00 00 03 00 01 02'         Full address of
                                               Cylinder 3, Track 1,
                                               Record 2.
DATA      DS   CL80
```

Figure 5-6 CCW for reading record

Typical moving-arm disk DASDs have 10 to 50 tracks and 200 to 400 arm positions with characteristics such as:

$$
\left.
\begin{array}{l}
\text{maximum access} = 75 \text{ ms} \\
\text{(55 ms maximum arm movement,} \\
\text{20 ms maximum rotation)} \\
\text{average (random) access} = 30 \text{ ms} \\
\text{serial access} < 1 \text{ ms}
\end{array}
\right\}
\quad
\begin{array}{l}
T_{ij} - \text{minor variance} \\
\text{(less than two} \\
\text{orders of magnitude)}
\end{array}
$$

capacity = 100 million bytes (400 cylinders * 20 heads * 16,000 bytes per track)

5-2.2.3.3 *General Characteristics*

Some DASD devices allow keys to be associated with each record. The *keys* are assigned by the user and can denote the contents of a record. The controller for such devices allows commands to read or write a record addressed not by a track, arm, or cylinder, but rather by its key. For example,

Search key = HARRY instead of Search ID = 0201

There are often some constraints on DASDs that allow this form of addressing, e.g., the read head must already be positioned on the right cylinder.

Given the present trend toward reductions in the price of CPUs, it is probably better to keep a table in memory and not to use such searching on the disks, thus keeping the cost of the channels down.

The preceding examples are representative of storage devices, since in spite of numerous variations, all have similar characteristics.

5-3 CHANNELS AND CONTROL UNITS

Device management must also take responsibility for the channels and control units. The *channels*, as explained in Chapter 2, are the special processors that execute the channel programs (i.e., the CCWs). Due to the high cost of channels, there are usually fewer channels than devices. The channels must, therefore, be switched from one device to another. Further cost savings can be obtained by taking advantage of the fact that relatively few I/O devices are in use at one time. Thus, it is wise to separate the device's electronics from its mechanical components. The electronics for several devices can be replaced by a single control unit, which can be switched from one device to another. Figure 5-7 illustrates the relationship between channels, control units, and devices. Typically, there are up to eight control units per channel and up to eight devices of the same type per control unit.

In order to initiate an I/O operation, a path is required between memory and the device. For example, to access drum J requires the use of channel A and drum control unit D. If an I/O operation to drum G were in progress, it would not be possible to initiate I/O on drum J because channel A would not be available (the I/O on drum G requires use of channel A and control unit C).

The device management routines must keep track of the status of (1) channels, (2) control units, and (3) devices. Since the channels and control units are usually scarce, they frequently create a serious bottleneck. Several hardware techniques can be used to lessen this problem: independent device operation, device buffering, multiple paths, and block multiplexing.

5-3.1 Independent Device Operation

In many cases there is sufficient capability in the device to complete an I/O operation without further assistance from the channel or control unit. A disk seek operation, which might require 50 ms, only needs the channel long enough to transmit the seek address from memory to the disk—10 or 20 μs. The seek can be completed

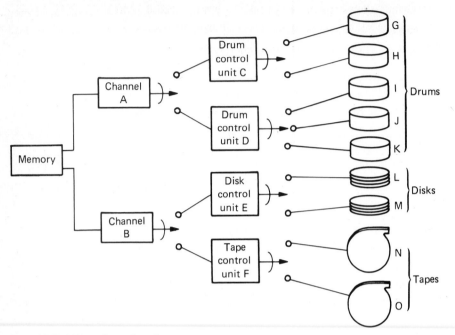

Figure 5-7 I/O configuration of a computer system

by the device alone. Likewise, there are operations that may require both the device and the control unit but not the channel for completion.

When an I/O operation is initiated, the entire path must be available. In order to indicate when parts of the path become available, there may be separate I/O completion interrupts: channel end, control unit end, and device end. The type of I/O completion interrupt is designated by the status bits in the Channel Status Word. If more than one part of the path becomes available at the same time, there will be only one interrupt but the status bits will indicate all available parts (e.g., both the channel end and control unit end bits will be on in the CSW).

If a *channel end* occurs, the channel is no longer busy, although the device may still be busy. An I/O operation can then be initiated on some other device using that channel.

5-3.2 Buffering

By providing a data buffer in the device or control unit, devices that would ordinarily require the channel for a long period can be made to perform independently of the channel. For example, a card reader may physically require about 60 ms to read a card and transfer the data to memory through the channel. However, a *buffered card reader* always reads one card before it is needed and saves the 80 bytes in a buffer in the card reader or control unit. When the channel requests that a card be read, the contents of the 80-byte buffer are transferred to memory at high speed (e.g., 100 μs) and the channel is released. The device then proceeds to read the next card and buffer it independently. Card readers, card punches, and printers are frequently buffered.

5-3.3 Multiple Paths

We could reduce the channel and control unit bottlenecks by buying more channels and control units. A more economical alternative, however, is to use the channels and control units in a more flexible manner and allow multiple paths to each device. Figure 5-8 illustrates such an I/O configuration. In this example there are four different paths to device E:

1 Channel A − Control Unit C − Device E
2 Channel A − Control Unit D − Device E
3 Channel B − Control Unit C − Device E
4 Channel B − Control Unit D − Device E

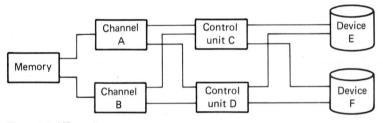

Figure 5-8 I/O configuration with multiple paths

If channel A and control unit C were both busy due to I/O for device F, a path could be found through channel B and control D to service device E. An actual I/O configuration may have eight control units per channel and eight devices per control unit rather than the sparse configuration of Figure 5-8. A completely flexible configuration would make all control units accessible to all channels and all devices accessible to all control units, thus providing possibly 256 alternate paths between memory and each device. For economic reasons, this extreme case, though feasible, is seldom found.

In addition to providing flexibility, a multiple path I/O configuration is desirable for reliability. For example, if channel A malfunctions and must be repaired, all the control units and devices can still be accessed through channel B. It is the responsibility of the device management routines to maintain status information on all paths in the I/O configuration and find an available route to access the desired device.

5-3.4 Block Multiplexing

On conventional 370 selector channels, the techniques of independent device operation and buffering are applicable only to the last CCW of a channel program. The channel and control unit remain connected to the device for the duration of the channel program. A 370 *block multiplexor channel* can be servicing multiple channel programs at the same time (e.g., eight channel programs). When the channel encounters an I/O operation such as a buffered or independent device operation that does not need the channel for awhile, it automatically switches to another channel program that needs immediate servicing. In essence, a block multiplexor channel represents a hardware implementation of multiprogramming for channel programs.

This type of channel multiprogramming could be simulated on a selector channel by making all channel programs only one command long. The device management software routines could then reassign the channel as necessary. However, this approach is not very attractive unless the central processor is extremely fast, since the channel switching must be done very frequently and very quickly.

5-4 DEVICE ALLOCATION CONSIDERATIONS

As noted at the beginning of this chapter, there are three major techniques of device allocation: dedicated, shared, or virtual. Virtual, which will be explained in Section 5-6, transforms a dedicated device into a shared device; thus, it is merely a special case of dedicated and shared allocation.

Certain devices require either manual actions or time-consuming I/O operations to be performed prior to use by a job, such as manually placing a deck of cards in a card reader's hopper or positioning a magnetic tape to the desired data record. To switch use of such a device among several jobs would require an excessive amount of work. Thus, these devices are dedicated to one job at a time and are not reassigned until that job releases the device—usually at the termination of the job. The assignment of a device to a job is usually performed in conjunction with the job-scheduling routines of processor management.

Due to the relative ease and speed with which a direct access device such as a magnetic drum or disk can be repositioned, it is possible to share it among several jobs running concurrently. A shared device is logically treated as if it were a group of dedicated devices. Each job using a shared device logically has a separate area to itself; the direct access property of the device makes it economical to switch back and forth among these areas. The device management routines may decide which shared device will be assigned to a job and what area of the device will be assigned. These decisions are also frequently made in conjunction with the job-scheduling routines.

For both dedicated and shared devices, static and dynamic allocation decisions must be made. The static decisions largely involve determining which dedicated and shared devices are to be assigned to the job. In general, device management tries to spread the allocation among devices so as to minimize channel and control unit bottlenecks. Often, the user can provide information on the job control cards indicating which of the devices will be used concurrently (these should be on separate channels) and which will be used at different times (these can be safely assigned to the same channel). The OS/360 Affinity (AFF) and Separation (SEP) job control language options serve this purpose (Brown, 1970; Cadow, 1970).

Since channels and control units are so scarce, they are seldom permanently assigned to a job. Instead, an assignment is made when a job makes an I/O request to device management. The assigned channel and control unit are deallocated and available for reassignment as soon as the I/O request is completed.

The static allocation decisions of device management are analogous to the static decisions of the job scheduler in processor management. The dynamic allocation is similar in purpose to the process scheduler of processor management. In the remainder of this chapter we will focus primarily on the dynamic allocation functions of device management.

5-5 I/O TRAFFIC CONTROLLER, I/O SCHEDULER, I/O DEVICE HANDLERS

The functions of device management can be conveniently divided into three parts:

1 *I/O traffic controller*—keeps track of the status of all devices, control units, and channels.

2 *I/O scheduler*—implements the policy algorithms used to allocate channel, control unit, and device access to I/O requests from jobs.

3 *I/O device handlers*—perform the actual dynamic allocations, once the I/O scheduler has made the decision, by constructing the channel program, issuing the start I/O instruction, and processing the device interrupts. There is usually a separate device handler for each type of device.

5-5.1 I/O Traffic Controller

Whereas the I/O scheduler is mainly concerned with *policies* (e.g., who gets the device and when), the I/O traffic controller is primarily concerned with *mechanics* (e.g., can the device be assigned?). The traffic controller maintains all status information.

The I/O traffic controller becomes complicated due to the interdependencies introduced by the scarcity of channels and control units, and the multiple paths illustrated earlier in Figures 5-7 and 5-8. The traffic controller attempts to answer at least three key questions:

1 Is there a path available to service an I/O request?

2 Is more than one path available?

3 If no path is currently available, when will one be free?

In order to answer these questions, the traffic controller maintains a database reflecting status and connections. This can be accomplished by means of Unit Control Blocks (UCB), Control Unit Control Blocks (CUCB), and Channel Control Blocks (CCB) as depicted in Figure 5-9. The first question can be answered by

Unit Control Block (UCB)

Device unit identification
Status of device
List of control units connected to this device
List of processes waiting for this device

Channel Control Block (CCB)

Channel identification
Status of channel
List of control units connected to this channel
List of processes waiting for this channel

Control Unit Control Block (CUCB)

Control unit identification
Status of control unit
List of devices connected to this control unit
List of channels connected to this control unit
List of processes waiting for this control unit

Figure 5-9 Control blocks

starting at the desired UCB and working back through the connected control units and channels trying to find a combination that is available. In a similar manner it is possible to determine all available paths. This second question may be important, especially when the I/O configuration is not symmetric, as shown in Figure 5-10. since choosing one path may block out other I/O requests. Thus, one path may conflict with fewer I/O requests than another path. In Figure 5-10, there may be up to five different paths to device H, yet only one possible path for either device G or I.

Under heavy I/O loads, it is quite likely that there will not be a path available at the time an I/O request is issued by a process. When an I/O completion interrupt occurs, one or more components (i.e., device, control units, and/or channel) become available again. We could try all I/O requests that are waiting to see if any can now be satisfied; if, however, hundreds of I/O requests were waiting, this could be a time-consuming approach. A more efficient approach would be to list all I/O requests that are "interested" in the component in the control block, as suggested in Figure 5-9. Only those particular I/O requests would then have to be examined.

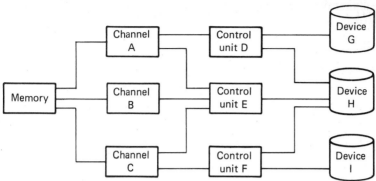

Figure 5-10 Assymetric I/O configuration

5-5.2 I/O Scheduler

If there are more I/O requests pending than available paths, it is necessary to choose which I/O requests to satisfy first. Many of the same concerns discussed in process scheduling are applicable here. One important difference is that I/O requests are not normally timesliced, that is, once a channel program has been started it is not usually interrupted until it has been completed. Most channel programs are quite short and terminate within 50–100 ms; it is, however, possible to encounter channel programs that take seconds or even minutes before termination.

Many different policies may be incorporated into the I/O scheduler. For example, if a process has a high priority assigned by the process scheduler, it is reasonable also to assign a high priority to its I/O requests. This would help complete that job as fast as possible.

Once the I/O scheduler has determined the relative orderings of the I/O requests, the I/O traffic controller must determine which, if any, of them can be satisfied. The I/O device handlers then provide another level of device-dependent I/O scheduling and optimization.

5-5.3 I/O Device Handlers

In addition to setting up the channel command words, handling error conditions, and processing I/O interrupts, the I/O device handlers provide detailed scheduling algorithms that are dependent upon the peculiarities of the device type. There is usually a different device handler algorithm for each type of I/O device.

5-5.3.1 ROTATIONAL ORDERING

Under heavy I/O loads, several I/O requests may be waiting for the same device. As noted earlier, there may be significant variations in the T_{ij} access time for a device. Certain orderings of I/O requests may reduce the total time required to service the I/O requests. Consider the drumlike device that has only four records stored in it (see Figure 5-11). The following four I/O requests have been received and a path to the device is now available:

1 Read record 4

2 Read record 3

3 Read record 2

4 Read record 1

There are several ways that these I/O requests can be ordered to accomplish the same result.

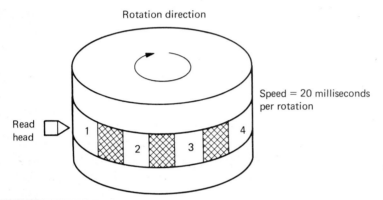

Figure 5-11 Simple drumlike device illustrating notational ordering

Ordering A

If the I/O scheduler satisfies the request by reading record 4, 3, 2, 1, then the total processing time equals $T_{?4} + T_{43} + T_{32} + T_{21} \approx 3$ revolutions (3/4 + 3 × 3/4 rotations), which equals approximately 60 ms. For the reading of record 4, since we do not know the current position of the drum, we assume 1/2 revolution (10 ms) to position it plus 1/4 revolution (5 ms) to read it.

Ordering B

If the I/O scheduler satisfies the request by reading record 1, 2, 3, 4, then the total processing time equals $T_{?1} + T_{12} + T_{23} + T_{34} \approx 1\text{-}1/2$ revolutions (3/4 + 3 × 1/4 rotations), which equals approximately 30 ms.

The results of ordering A and ordering B are the same, but there is a difference in speed of a factor of 2.

Ordering C

If we knew that "?" equaled record 3 (i.e., current read position is record 3), then the ordering 4, 1, 2, 3 ($T_{34} + T_{41} + T_{12} + T_{23}$) would be even better — exactly 1 revolution, which equals 20 ms.

In order to accomplish ordering C, it is necessary for the device handler to know the current position for the rotating drum. This hardware facility is called *rotational position sensing*.

Under heavy I/O loads, rotational ordering can increase throughput significantly (Abate, 1969; Coffman, 1969; Denning, 1969, 1970).

There are still some policy decisions that must be made in selecting a rotational ordering because some I/O requests are mutually exclusive. Drum requests, as described in Section 5-2.2.3.1, require a two-part address: track number and record number. If the requests are

track 1, record 1

track 1, record 3

track 2, record 2

track 2, record 3

track 3, record 1

then, requests 1 and 5 and requests 2 and 4 are mutually exclusive since they reference the same record number. Thus, either request 1 can be serviced on the first rotation and request 5 on the second rotation, or vice versa. Sorting the requests on the basis of record number is often called *slotting* since there is one I/O request "slot" per record number per revolution. All I/O requests for the same record number position must "fight" for the same slot. This congestion can be decreased if the hardware allows reading and writing from more than one track at a time, but this capability usually requires the use of an additional channel and control unit as well as more electronics in the device.

Some devices, such as the IBM 2305 Fixed Head Disk, can perform some of the rotational ordering and slotting automatically in the hardware. The control unit for the 2305 can accept up to 16 channel programs at the same time, via a block multiplexor-channel, and it attempts to process these I/O requests in an "optimal" order.

5-5.3.2 ALTERNATE ADDRESSES

The access time to read an arbitrary record on a drumlike device is largely determined by the rotational speed. For a given device this speed is constant.

The effective access time can be substantially reduced by recording each record at multiple locations on the device. Thus, there are several *alternate addresses* for reading the same data record. This technique has also been called *folding*.

Let us consider a device that has eight records per track and a rotation speed of 20 ms. If record A is stored on track 1, record 1, on the average it would take half a revolution—10 ms—to access record A. If a copy of record A is stored at both track 1, record 1 and track 1, record 5, then by always accessing the "closest" copy, using rotational position sensing, the effective access time can be reduced to 5 ms. Similarly, the effective access time can be reduced to 2.5 ms or even 1.25 ms by storing even more copies of the same data record.

Of course, by storing multiple copies of the same data record the effective capacity, in terms of unique data records, is reduced by the number of copies. If there are n copies per record, the device has been "folded" n times.

5-5.3.3 SEEK ORDERING

Moving-head storage devices, as described in Section 5-2.2.3.2, have the problem of seek position in addition to rotational position. I/O requests require a three-part address: cylinder number, track number, and record number. If the requests

cylinder 1, track 2, record 1

cylinder 40, track 3, record 3

cylinder 5, track 6, record 5

cylinder 1, track 5, record 7

were processed in the order shown, a considerable amount of time would be spent to move the seek arm back and forth. A more efficient ordering would be:

cylinder 1, track 2, record 1

cylinder 1, track 5, record 7

cylinder 5, track 6, record 5

cylinder 40, track 3, record 3

These requests are in *Minimum seek time order*, that is, the distances between seeks have been minimized.

There are many other possible seek orderings (Teorey, 1971, 1972). When rotational position is important, it is sometimes better to seek a further distance to get a record that will be at a closer rotational position. For an extreme example, if seek times were very small in comparison to the rotation time, the first ordering shown might be best since it accesses records in the order 1, 3, 5, 7. Determining this *minimum service time order* can be quite complex. It is further complicated by the fact that seek times, though monotonic, are not usually linear as a function of seek distance, i.e., the time to move the seek arm 20 cylinders is usually less than double the time to move it 10 cylinders.

In both the minimum seek time and minimum service time cases, the ordering was determined by the current I/O requests for that device. New I/O requests are likely to occur while the original ones are being satisfied. In retrospect, the ordering chosen on the basis of the original I/O requests may be poor when the new I/O requests are considered. Unless the system has a "crystal ball" feature, it is impossible to know what future requests will be. Several schemes have been used to minimize the negative effects of future I/O requests. Usually the ordering is reevaluated after each individual request has been processed so as to allow consideration of any new requests. *Unidirectional* or *linear sweep service time* ordering is a technique that moves the arm monotonically in one direction. When the last cylinder is reached or there are no further requests in that direction, the arm is reset back to the beginning and another sweep is started. This technique attempts to decrease the amount of back and forward arm thrashing caused by the continued arrival of new I/O requests.

5-5.4 Device Management Softward Overhead

Each of the device management algorithms discussed in the preceding sections provides additional device efficiency but at the cost of increased processor time (unless the algorithms are incorporated in the hardware, in which case there is increased hardware expense). The value of these algorithms depends upon the speed of the processor and the amount of I/O requests. If there are few I/O requests, multiprogramming of the processor alone may be sufficient to attain high throughput. If the processor is quite slow, the processor overhead may swamp the I/O advantages.

For example, a System/360 Model 30, with an average instruction time of 30 μs would take 30 ms to execute a 1,000-instruction reordering algorithm. If the I/O requests take less than 30 ms to service without reordering, there is no savings attained. However, reordering techniques do become very important on large-scale computers.

Virtual storage memory management increases the load on device management in two ways. First, the page swapping often introduces a large amount of I/O requests. Second, the device handler must handle translation from virtual memory addresses to physical memory addresses in the construction of CCWs, since most channels require physical memory addresses rather than virtual memory addresses.

Finally, device management must ensure the protection of each job's areas in main memory and secondary storage. In the extreme, this would require very careful analysis of all I/O requests and addresses referenced. This can be done because all I/O instructions are privileged and, thus, can be initiated only by the operating system. On the 360 it is possible to use the memory lock hardware to safeguard memory areas. Similar hardware features are often provided to protect secondary storage areas.

In total, a substantial amount of processor capacity is consumed by device management. This overhead is usually worthwhile since device management can significantly increase system throughput by decreasing system I/O wait time.

5-6 VIRTUAL DEVICES

5-6.1 Motivation

Devices such as card readers, punches, and printers present two serious problems that hamper effective device utilization.

First, each of these devices performs best when there is a steady, continuous stream of requests at a specified rate that matches its physical characteristics (e.g., 1,000 cards per minute read rate, 1,000 lines per minute print rate, etc.). If a job attempts to generate requests faster than the device's performance rate, the job must wait a significant amount of time. On the other hand, if a job generates requests at a much lower rate, the device is idle much of the time and is substantially underutilized.

Second, these devices must be dedicated to a single job at a time. Thus, since most jobs perform some input and output, we would require as many card readers and printers as we have jobs being multiprogrammed. This would normally be un-economical because most jobs use only a fraction of the device's capacity.

To summarize, these devices should have a steady request rate, whereas actual programs generate highly irregular requests. A small input/output-intensive program (e.g., a check-printing program) might generate thousands of print requests in a few seconds of CPU time. On the other hand, a compute-intensive program (e.g., de-termine the first 1,000 prime numbers) may print only a single line of output for every hour of CPU time. Buffering and multiprogramming, as illustrated in Chapter 2, help reduce these problems but are not capable of solving them completely. Furthermore, many other devices, such as plotters, graphic displays, and type-writer terminals, have similar problems.

5-6.2 Historical Solutions
These problems would disappear, or at least substantially decrease, if it were possible to use Direct Access Storage Devices for all input and output. A single DASD can be efficiently shared and simultaneously used for reading and/or writing data by many jobs, as shown in Figure 5-12. Furthermore, DASDs provide very high performance rates, especially if the data are blocked, thereby decreasing the amount of wait time for jobs that require substantial amounts of input/output.

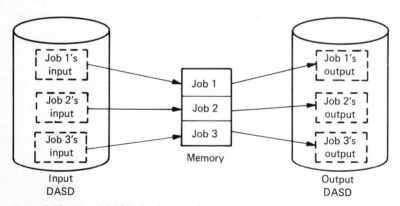

Figure 5-12 Use of DASDs for input and output

Although theoretically appealing, the use of DASDs for all input and output appears impractical. How do we get our input data onto the DASD in the first place? What do we do with the output data recorded on the output DASD? Consider for a moment walking into a drugstore with a disk pack and trying to convince the clerk that recorded on a specific part of the disk is your payroll check—and you wish to cash it!

5-6.2.1 OFFLINE PERIPHERAL OPERATIONS

Fortunately, a solution to this dilemma can be found in the three-step process illustrated in Figure 5-13. At step 1 we use a separate computer whose sole function is to read cards at maximum speed and record the corresponding information on a DASD. Two or more card readers may be used by computer 1, depending upon the amount of input that must be transcribed.

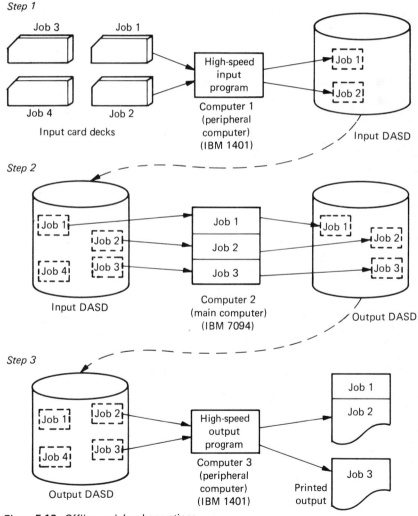

Figure 5-13 Offline peripheral operations

At step 2 the DASD containing the input recorded by computer 1 is moved over to the main processing computer (computer 2). This step corresponds to the one shown in Figure 5-12. Multiple jobs can be in execution, each reading its respective input from the input DASD and writing its output onto an output DASD. Note in this example that it is possible to multiprogram three jobs even though only two physical card readers are assumed to exist (on computer 1 at step 1).

Finally, at step 3, the output DASD is moved to a third computer that reads the recorded output at high speed and prints the information on the printers.

The three-step process described above was used quite extensively during the 1960s. The work performed by computers 1 and 3 was termed *offline peripheral processing* and the computers were called *peripheral computers* because they performed no computation but merely transferred information from one peripheral device to another. Since this operation was performed independently of the main computer, this was an "offline" operation.

There are several observations that can be made at this time. Inasmuch as the peripheral computers are required to perform only rather simple tasks, they can be quite simple, slow, and inexpensive. Furthermore, there need not always be two peripheral computers. If there is a relatively low peripheral load, one peripheral computer might handle it all—possibly switching from input processing to output processing every few hours. On the other hand, if substantial peripheral processing is required, many peripheral computers may be used.

During the early 1960s, a typical installation, such as that of MIT, might have consisted of three peripheral computers (e.g., IBM 1401s) to service one main computer (e.g., IBM 7094). At that time magnetic tapes were used instead of DASDs, although the basic concepts were still very similar to the approach described above.

The offline peripheral processing technique solved the problems presented earlier, but it also introduced several new problems in regard to (1) human intervention, (2) turnaround, and (3) scheduling. Since human operators were required to move the input DASDs from the input peripheral computer to the main computer and to perform a simpler task for output processing, there were many opportunities for human error and inefficiency. Many jobs (i.e., a batch of jobs) were recorded on the input DASD before it was moved to the main computer. The entire input DASD had to be processed and the output DASD filled before the latter was moved to the output peripheral computer. Then, finally, the individual job's output could be separated and given to its owner.

This *batch processing* approach, though efficient from the computer's point of view, made each job wait in line at each step and often increased its turnaround time. As a result of this batching processing, it was difficult to provide the desired priority scheduling. For example, if two high-priority jobs were to be run but were in separate batches, one would have to wait until the other's batch was completely processed.

5-6.2.2 DIRECT-COUPLED SYSTEMS

The major drawback to the offline peripheral processing approach was the need to physically move the input and output DASDs between the main computer and the peripheral computer. Several solutions to this problem have been developed. Figure 5-14 illustrates a configuration in which the input and output DASDs are physically connected to both the peripheral computer and the main computer, thus eliminating the need for manual handling. This configuration is called a Direct-Coupled System (DCS). Normally, a single powerful, peripheral computer, such as an IBM 7044, served as the peripheral computer to an IBM 7094 main computer.

The direct-coupled system approach eliminates most of the problems of offline peripheral processing. No human intervention is required and since jobs can be processed as soon as the peripheral computer places them on the input DASD, there is no "batch processing" turnaround time delay, nor any scheduling restrictions.

An actual direct-coupled system might use a single, shared DASD for both input and output or several shared DASDs. It is important to coordinate carefully the use of a shared DASD; mechanisms must be provided so that the main computer knows that a job has been placed on the input DASD and where it is located; similar requirements exist for output. This coordination adds substantial complexity to the system. Furthermore, since both the peripheral computer and main computer may wish to use the same DASD at the same time, there are frequent access conflicts that can reduce performance, thereby making the DASD a critical bottleneck.

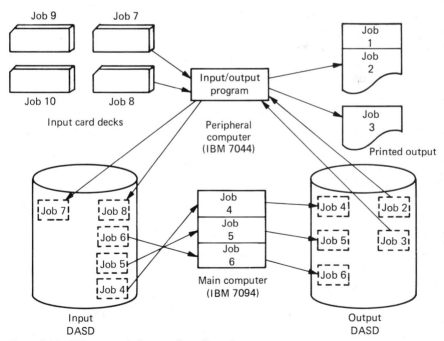

Figure 5-14 "Direct-coupled system" configuration

5-6.2.3 ATTACHED SUPPORT PROCESSOR

Another variation on this approach consists of directly connecting the peripheral and main computers together via a high-speed connection, as illustrated in Figure 5-15a. In this configuration the peripheral computer is called an *Attached Support Processor* (ASP). The support processor assumes all responsibility for controlling the input/output peripherals as well as the input and output DASD. It also performs all buffering and blocking, thereby simplifying the work required by the main computer. In this mode the attached processor has the appearance of multiple,

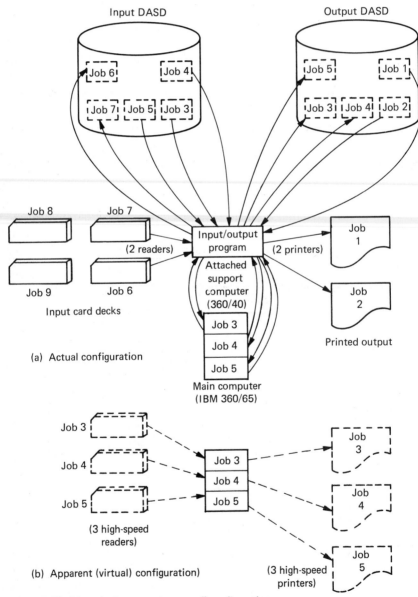

Figure 5-15 "Attached support processor" configuration

very high-speed card readers and printers (see Figure 5-15b). By analogy to the virtual memory concept presented earlier, the attached processor produces the effect of virtual devices (i.e., many more and much faster devices than really exist).

The major disadvantages of this ASP approach are that two (or more) processors are required, and since certain processors are assigned specific tasks (as a peripheral or a main processor), it is possible that at times one processor may be idle or under-utilized while another is unable to handle its load. Thus, the ASP configuration does not necessarily utilize all resources efficiently.

5-6.2.4 VIRTUAL SYSTEM

In all the solutions presented above it was assumed that one or more special computers were dedicated to the handling of input/output processing functions. Considering the powerful processing facilities available in conventional I/O channels, as well as multiprogramming capabilities, do we really need a separate computer system to handle the input/output? The answer is No. In a SPOOLing system, the main computer performs Simultaneous Peripheral Operations On Line (SPOOL), as illustrated in Figure 5-16.

In such a system, certain jobs are assigned the functions normally produced by the ASP but reside permanently on the main computer and share the use of the

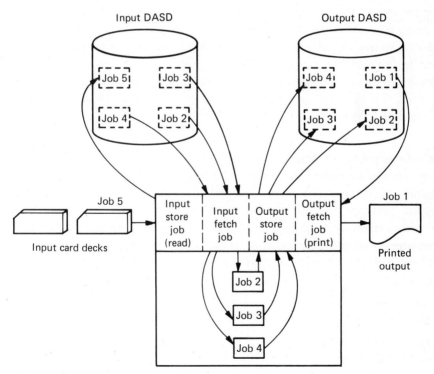

Figure 5-16 SPOOLing system

main computer with normal jobs via multiprogramming. Since these jobs are actually system jobs rather than user jobs, they are often given special names, such as "phantoms" or "daemons." In modern operating systems, many special functions are performed by such special system jobs.

Although we will examine SPOOL systems primarily from the point of view of device management and virtual devices, it should be noted that they represent an intricate mechanism that interfaces extensively with memory management, processor management, device management, and information management. Because the jobs that perform the SPOOL functions are special, permanent system jobs, memory management may handle these jobs in different ways. As a matter of fact, in some systems these jobs are incorporated into the operating system's memory area. Since there must be communication and coordination between these jobs, various facilities of processor management must be used. It is necessary to keep track of the input and output data that have been stored on the DASDs with mechanisms similar to those used by information management. Finally, efficient buffering, blocking, and I/O control must be performed to attain good performance.

The ease of implementing a SPOOL mechanism, together with the approach to be used, depends directly upon the specific facilities provided by the memory management, processor management, information management, and device management components of the operating system. In a comprehensive operating system, the role of the SPOOL programs may be a minor one, while the rest of the operating system is left to do the "hard work." On the other hand, in a more limited operating system, the SPOOL programs may have to perform many operating functions. In fact, SPOOLing often improves the system so much that it is frequently provided as part of some simple operating systems that do not support multiprogramming for user jobs or general information management. In such cases, the SPOOL programs must do a lot of work for themselves.

5-6.3 Design of a SPOOLing System

In this section we present the design of a simple SPOOLing system. The SPOOL programs are assumed to be an integral part of the operating system (rather than "normal" jobs) and perform their own specialized information management. These are typical assumptions of small to medium-scale operating systems and even of some large operating systems, such as the IBM VM/370 system (see the case studies in Chapter 9). In such systems, there are two special operating system functions (e.g., SVC supervisor calls) provided:

1 Read next input card,
   CALL READNEXT (BUFFER)
2 Print next output line,
   CALL PRINTNEXT (BUFFER)

In actuality, of course, the card is not physically read, nor the line printed at the time of these calls, since virtual devices are being used. This distinction should not be noticeable to the jobs that issue these requests.

A general input and output SPOOL system can be subdivided into four components, as illustrated in Figure 5-17. These individual components can be grouped in several ways, such as by function (input or output) or by method of gaining control (call or interrupt). The division of a program into a "call side" and an "interrupt side" is a common occurrence in handling various devices and operating system functions. The following discussion will emphasize the SPOOL function but the reader should keep the generality of the approach in mind.

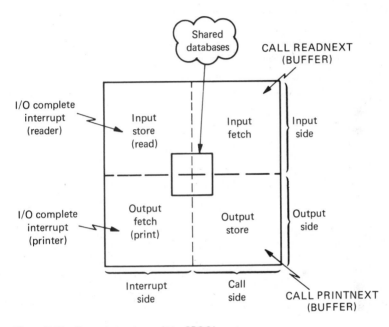

Figure 5-17   General structure of the SPOOL system

5-6.3.1 INPUT SPOOL

To simplify the design, only the input SPOOL function will be analyzed. SPOOL output is handled in a similar manner.

Two major operations must be performed by the input SPOOL facility: (1) to read physically each input card and store it on a DASD and (2) to provide access to the DASD copy of the next input card to the job during execution. This latter operation is performed at the specific request of the running job via the READNEXT call. But when is the read and store operation performed? It must be done independently of the job since, in fact, it must be completed before the job even begins. The storing of input cards physically read from the card reader is done as soon as the input is completed. Thus, the operation is initiated in response to the I/O complete indication from the card reader. This type of operation is called *interrupt-*

driven. The I/O buffering programs presented in Chapter 2 are other examples of interrupt-driven mechanisms.

The call side and interrupt side of the input SPOOL cannot function independently. The interdependencies and coordination are handled by means of certain shared databases, as suggested in Figure 5-17. The particular databases used are illustrated in Figure 5-18.

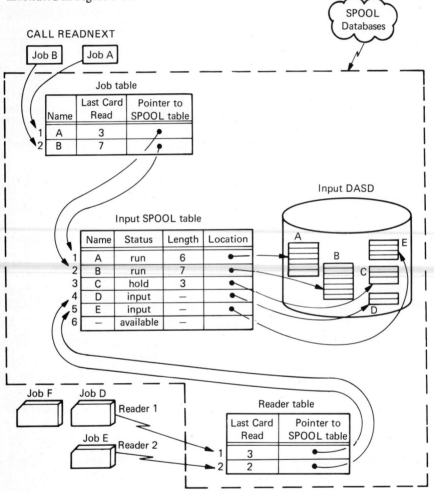

Figure 5-18 Major databases of the SPOOL system

It will be assumed that the DASD is divided into sections in such a way that each section is capable of holding an input deck of suitably large size, such as 2,000 cards. By storing each input deck on a separate cylinder, a single IBM 3330-type disk drive could be used to hold up to 400 input decks (each up to about 2,000 cards long). The reader will find more sophisticated storage techniques presented in Chapter 6.

The key database in Figure 5-18 is the Input SPOOL Table. It maintains indication of the status of each input DASD storage area (usually called SPOOL *areas*). A given SPOOL area may be unused, in which case it is *available* for use. If it is being used to hold an input deck, it may be in either *input*, *hold*, or *run* status:

input: The input deck is still being read.

hold: The input deck has been completely copied onto the DASD but the corresponding job has not been started yet.

run: The corresponding job is currently running and is reading the input data from the SPOOL area.

In addition to the above status information, the SPOOL table also stores the length of the input deck and the user-assigned job name for record and accounting purposes. Finally, the physical location of the SPOOL area is noted. In our simple implementation, the location would be the address of the cylinder containing the input deck copy.

5-6.3.2 RELATIONSHIP BETWEEN SPOOLING AND JOB SCHEDULING

At this time it is appropriate to make a minor digression. In the discussion of processor management, particularly in the case of job scheduling, it was assumed that the operating system knew which jobs were to be run and was able to choose arbitrarily which job to run next. How is the job scheduler able to do this without requiring information from the computer operator and a lot of manual shuffling of input decks?

The SPOOL facility solves most of these problems. The input SPOOL areas in "hold" status correspond to the jobs to be run. By being slightly cleverer, the input SPOOL program could read the job parameters on the job card and set corresponding fields in the input SPOOL table, such as CPU time estimate, priority, etc., in addition to job name. In this case, the SPOOL table also serves as an important database of the job scheduler and is often called the *job queue* or *job hold list*.

Furthermore, the use of virtual card readers, accomplished by the SPOOL facility, makes it possible to start arbitrary jobs and read their input data without any physical shuffling of input decks. Thus, although they are intended to serve vastly different purposes, there is a significant relationship between the job scheduler and the SPOOL facility. In practice, some systems actually merge these programs together.

5-6.3.3 INPUT SPOOL ALGORITHM

In addition to the input SPOOL table, there are two supplemental databases: (1) the *reader table* maintains information on the status of each physical card reader and the corresponding input SPOOL area being used, and (2) the *job table* maintains information on the status of all jobs currently running and the corresponding SPOOL area being used as a virtual device.

The databases are actually the most important part of the SPOOL system design. The actual routines perform rather straightforward operations that either modify or use these tables. Overall algorithms are illustrated in Figure 5-19 (a and b). When entry is made into the system either via a call or an interrupt, the corresponding job table or reader table entry, respectively, is determined. The correct SPOOL table entry and SPOOL area can then be determined. In both cases, the blocks of the SPOOL area are processed sequentially. For example, if the DASD is organized as one hundred 80-byte records per track and twenty tracks per cylinder, the SPOOL table entry designates the cylinder number, and

$$\text{track number} = \frac{\text{card number}}{20}$$

$$\text{record number} = \text{remainder}\left[\frac{\text{card number}}{20}\right]$$

Thus card 1 = (track 0, record 1) on the cylinder, and card 15 = (track 1, record 5), etc.

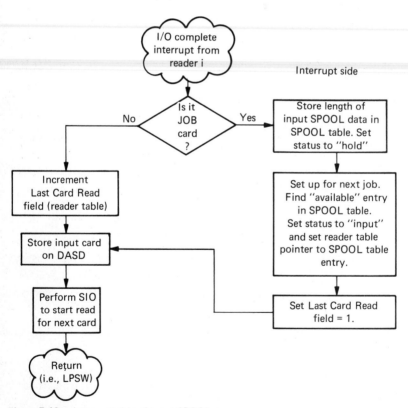

Figure 5-19a Interrupt side of input SPOOL program

Figure 5-19a illustrates the algorithm used by the interrupt side of the input SPOOL program. Whenever there is an I/O complete interrupt from a reader, the input card is stored in the next sequential record location in the appropriate SPOOL area. Before returning to the point of interrupt, I/O is initiated for the next input card. If a single 1,000-card per minute reader were used by a SPOOL system, the interrupt side would be entered approximately every 60 ms.

The interrupt side also recognizes the special job card used to start each input deck and thereby serves to separate input decks. When such a card is read, the previous input SPOOL area is known to be complete and is placed in "hold" status. An "available" SPOOL table entry and SPOOL area must be found for the new input deck. The entry is then set to "input," and information, such as job name, is transferred from the job card to the SPOOL table entry. The reader table entry is then updated to refer to the correct SPOOL table entry and the Last Card read field is reset to 1. After these tasks have been completed, normal interrupt side processing is performed as described above.

The call side operates at the specific request of the user's job as a result of READNEXT calls. The job's entry in the job table is determined and a check is made to determine if all the input has been read (i.e., Last Card Read = Length Of Input). If so, the SPOOL table entry's status is set "available" and a special error return code is returned to the job (in PL/I programs this is called an ENDFILE condition). Otherwise, the next input card is read from the DASD SPOOL area and returned to the job.

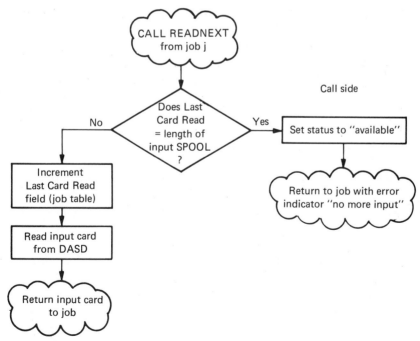

Figure 5-19b Call side of input SPOOL program

5-6.3.4 SPECIAL CASES OF INPUT SPOOL ALGORITHM

The design presented above is a usable, though not necessarily efficient, approach to a SPOOL system. There are several special cases that must be considered:

1 How does the interrupt side get started?

2 What happens if the reader is temporarily stopped because of malfunction or because there is no more input to be read at that time?

3 What happens if there are no more SPOOL table entries or SPOOL areas available to hold the next input deck (i.e., if jobs are running slowly in comparison to the input rate, there could be hundreds or even thousands of job inputs in the "hold" status)?

4 What happens if there are no SPOOL table entries in the "run" or "hold" status?

Cases 1 and 2 can be handled by the same basic technique. An initial START I/O must be performed; when the I/O complete interrupt occurs, the interrupt side will be "back in business." This initial SIO can be activated by two approaches: (1) in response to a special operator command, such as START READER 2 or (2) automatically in response to the I/O *ready interrupt,* which is generated by devices such as the IBM 2501 card reader when cards are placed in the reader's hopper and the START button is pressed.

Cases 3 and 4 require cooperation between the call side and the interrupt side. If no more SPOOL table entries are available, the interrupt side must temporarily stop reading input and merely return to the interrupted program without issuing another SIO. If the DASDs used for SPOOL areas are sufficiently large, this case should be a rare occurrence. Cooperation is required because the call side must inform the interrupt side when a SPOOL table entry becomes available. Then the interrupt side can proceed to store the job card in the available SPOOL area, set the SPOOL table entry status to "input," and issue an SIO to read additional input cards.

Case 4 is handled in a fashion similar to case 3. If there are no jobs in the "run" or "hold" status, there is no work for the processor to do. Thus, the processor is put in the WAIT state but with the interrupts enabled. The I/O complete interrupts, if input is being read, or the I/O ready interrupt, if the reader had been idle, would cause the processor to start up and transfer control to the SPOOL interrupt side. After the interrupt side had done its function, the processor would revert to the WAIT state via the LPSW done at the end of the interrupt processing.

When an input deck has finally been completely read and placed in "hold" status, the call side, or more precisely the job scheduler, must be awakened. This can be accomplished by turning off the WAIT state bit in the PSW before returning via the LPSW from the interrupt side.

Figures 5-20 (a and b) illustrates the call and interrupt side algorithms modified to handle the cases discussed above. Once again it must be emphasized that alternate implementations might be appropriate, depending upon the facilities provided in the other components of the operating system, especially in processor management. For example, in the sample operating system of Chapter 7, the coordination between the call and interrupt sides is handled by means of semaphores and the P and V operations.

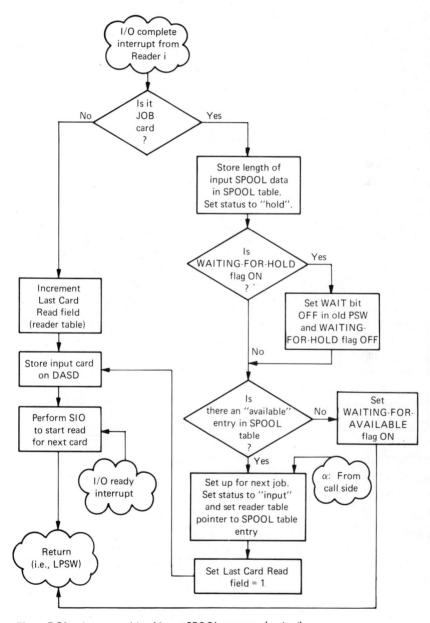

Figure 5-20a Interrupt side of input SPOOL program (revised)

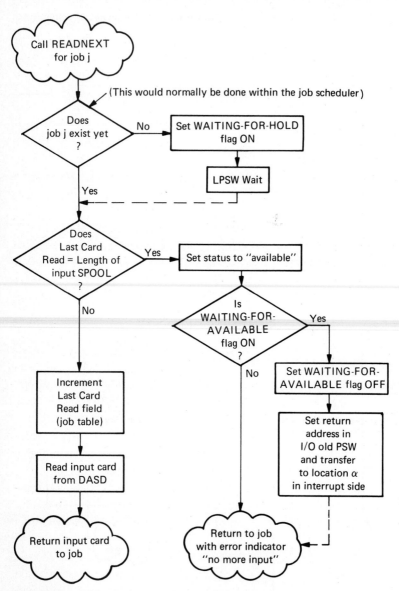

Figure 5-20b Call side of input SPOOL program (revised)

5-6.4 SPOOL System Performance Considerations

Up to this point it has been assumed that the DASD I/O performed by the SPOOL routine was unbuffered, unblocked, and nonoverlapped. We assumed that there was one 80-byte logical record stored per physical I/O record. When it was necessary to read or write a DASD record, the caller's BUFFER was used in the case of READNEXT and PRINTNEXT, or else a single area associated with each reader or printer was used by the interrupt side. Furthermore, the entire system would stop while the SPOOL program waited for its DASD I/O. We will now investigate the effectiveness of these techniques and consider alternatives.

At a speed of 1,000 cards per minute, we can read the next card in 60 ms from a card reader. How much faster is the DASD? As noted earlier, conventional large-capacity DASDs, such as the IBM 2314 and IBM 3330, take around 60 ms to read an arbitrary 80-byte record. Thus although we can use the DASDs to produce multiple virtual devices, it would seem that they are not especially faster—in fact, they may be slower.

It is important to recall that although it may take 60 ms to read an 80-byte DASD record, it only takes about 61 ms to read an 800-byte DASD record containing 10 logical 80-byte records. Since SPOOL DASD reading and writing are always sequential within a SPOOL area, if we assign an 800-byte buffer to each active SPOOL area (input, output, or run status), read and write 800-byte blocks, and deblock the buffer into 80-byte records, we attain an effective access time of 6 ms—10 times faster than the physical card reader. This means that the first READNEXT request from a SPOOL area will take 60 ms, the second through ninth requests will take less than 1 ms, i.e., the deblocking time plus other SPOOL program computation time. The tenth request will again take 60 ms, etc. Thus, on the average, 10 requests are satisfied every 60 ms. If we were to use 8000-byte DASD records, the effective access time would drop to around 1 ms—60 times faster than a physical card reader. It is not usually worthwhile to go beyond 8000-byte blocks since the normal software overhead for satisfying a SPOOL request is probably close to 1 ms anyway, and blocking does not cause this to decrease.

As noted earlier in this chapter, large physical records utilize the DASD space more effectively because of the decreased number of Inter-record Gaps. Thus, with large records, the number and/or capacity of the SPOOL areas may be substantially increased.

We can use multiprogramming to overlap this I/O time with the execution of some other job. If all the jobs were waiting for I/O at the same time, the system would then be idle for a while. By using two buffers and the technique of double buffering, it is possible to further reduce this I/O delay by reading the next block (for READNEXT) while deblocking the current block.

The use of the techniques described above could reduce the effective access time for these virtual devices to a fraction of their "real" counterparts.

Since it offers such wonderful features, why isn't the SPOOL technique used on every system? There are various reasons. For one thing, an efficient SPOOL program may be complex and consumes a reasonable amount of the operating system area. Also, a significant amount of DASD storage is needed for SPOOL areas. To get an idea of these costs, consider the amount of main memory used as SPOOL buffers. Let us assume a system with two readers, three printers, and six jobs running. Assume also that double buffering is used and the block size is 8000 bytes. How much main memory is used for buffers? With double buffering two buffers are used for each reader and printer and four buffers for each active job (two for input and two for output).

2 readers: 2 X 2 = 4 buffers
3 printers: 3 X 2 = 6 buffers
6 jobs: 6 X 4 = 24 buffers
                     34 buffers
              X 8000 bytes/buffer
             272,000 bytes

We could, of course, reduce this size significantly by using smaller blocks and single buffering (e.g., if single-buffered 800-byte blocks were used, only 13,600 bytes would be required); in any case, there would be a significant cost in terms of main memory for a SPOOL system. The figure 272,000 bytes becomes dramatic when we consider that a system with 1,000,000 bytes is considered large and there are many medium-to-small computer systems with a maximum memory capacity of less than 272,000 bytes. Thus the value of SPOOLing must be carefully weighed against its cost to determine its usefulness in any given system.

5-7 FUTURE TRENDS IN DEVICE MANAGEMENT

We expect to see many more hardware facilities made available to the software for better utilization of devices. For example, the 370 provided rotational position sensing and block multiplexing, which were not available on the earlier 360. Automatic rotational ordering is also available on some devices. We expect that even more of the software functions of device management will be implemented in hardware in the future, and that the techniques of "virtualizing" devices will become much more prevalent.

5-8 SUMMARY

This chapter has described techniques for handling the four basic functions of device management. We presented a framework for handling these functions, based upon three software modules:

1   I/O traffic controller

2   I/O scheduler

3   I/O device handler

The reader should not assume that this is the only way or the best way to handle these functions. However, we feel that this framework is conceptually the most desirable, and the one that many contemporary systems follow. The sample operating system in Chapter 7 illustrates a clean way to organize the device management routines.

QUESTIONS

5-1 We have seen that between each physical record on a tape there is an Inter-
record Gap. These gaps are needed mainly to allow a tape-drive space to
reach speed before it starts reading data, and also to give it stopping room.
A disk or drum, on the other hand, is always moving, hence it requires no
space for starting or stopping.

  1 Are IRGs on disks or drums required or in any way desirable from the
  hardware point of view?

  2 Are IRGs on disks or drums useful from the software point of view?

5-2 Assume a magnetic tape storage device with records of varying length; the
start of a record is indicated by a start-record mark and the end of a record
is indicated by an end-of-record mark.

   Assume that the tape transport moves the tape at a speed of 200 inches/
second past the recording/sensing heads. Between each I/O operation (reading or writing one record) the tape must stop. The transport mechanism
accelerates and decelerates the tape at the same rate: 40,000 inches/second^2.
The density at which information is written is 800 bits/inch and the format
of the information is eight tracks of data plus an additional parity track.

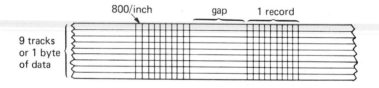

  1 What is the transfer rate of this device? That is, once the tape has come
  up to speed, at what rate (bytes/second) can information be read or
  written?

  2 What is the "local" access time (time to come up to speed) if we are reading records sequentially (seconds)?

  3 What is the length of the IRG?

  From here on, assume that the length of the interrecord gap is 3/4 inch.

  4 What percentage of the tape will have information recorded on it if we
  write 80-byte card images per record? What about 100 cards per record?

  5 Sketch a plot of percentage of tape used (ordinate) versus blocking factor
  (abscissa) where, for example, the blocking is 10 if we write 10 card
  images per record.

  6 What is the highest value of information utilization (%) of a tape if the
  maximum amount of core storage left for data areas is 24,000 bytes?
  Does this indicate that tapes are cost-ineffective?

  7 What are three problems/costs with blocking data into long records?

5-3 Assume that we have a magnetic drum storage device with a movable head. There are three positions (tracks) that the head can read/write data from/to (tracks 0,1,2). On each track there are eight records (0–7). The drum makes one revolution in 8 ms. The head can also be moved between adjunct tracks in 8 ms.

The following list of addresses for reads has been received by the routine that handles the drum.

track, record
0,2
1,2
1,3
1,5
2,4
2,3

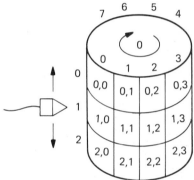

1 How much time will it take to perform the above I/O requests in the order given (first come, first served)? You may assume for this part that when you start to perform reads, the drum/head is at location 0,0.

2 What is an optimal order for servicing these requests? Describe in words the algorithms you used.

3 Explain how each of the following may be of use in a routine for optimizing I/O requests to the drum.

a An instruction to sense the current position of the drum/head.

b An instruction to move the head to a specific track that releases the channel from being tied up as soon as the instruction is executed (it doesn't have to wait for the operation to complete).

c A head move time of 2 ms. Be specific.

4 What effects would you expect the following to have on the response time of the drum system?

a More tracks are added.

b A second movable head on the opposite side of the drum is added.

5-4 The following table lists four types of storage devices. For each type: Indicate whether it is a serial, completely direct, or direct access device (column 1). Show how it compares with the other devices listed in the indicated characteristic (1 = largest capacity, lowest average access time, ..., 4 = smallest capacity, highest average access time); (see columns 2 and 3).

Provide the information requested (columns 4, 5, and 6).

Discuss which policy technique (dedicated, shared, virtual) would be most applicable and why.

Storage device	1 Serial, direct or completely direct	2 Storage capacity	3 Average access time (random accesses)	4 Method of addressing a record	5 Method of locating a record	6 Example of appropriate application for device
Magnetic tape						
Moving-head disk						
Fixed-head drum						
Extended core storage						

5-5

1 What is the function of the I/O traffic controller?

2 What is the function of the I/O device handlers?

3 What is the function of the I/O scheduler?

4 What address space does the traffic controller reside in?

5 What address space do the device handlers reside in?

5-6 One of the goals of system designers is to increase efficiency or throughput. We have discussed the effects of different job and process scheduling algorithms on system performance. Since all of a job's I/O is subject to the whims of the I/O scheduler, the I/O scheduler, too, has an impact on system performance.

1 Describe the conditions under which improvements in the performance of the I/O scheduler would have a large impact on overall system performance.

2 Describe conditions under which improvements in the performance of the I/O scheduler would have little effect on system performance.

5-7 List two problems that force some operating systems to use the technique of device dedication.

5-8

1 List three problems introduced by allowing users to share a device.

2 What makes a disk more "sharable" than a tape?

5-9 Conceptually, telecommunications devices, such as teletypes, can be handled in the same way as other input/output devices. There are a few special characteristics that do require attention. First, the output rate is fairly slow—at 10 characters per second, an 80-byte line takes 8 seconds to print. Second, the input rate is limited by the speed of the human typist (in fact, the typist may even stop for lunch in the middle of a line).

There are three major types of hardware interfaces for telecommunications devices: (1) interrupt, (2) poll, and (3) buffered. For the *interrupt type*, when a key is pressed, an interrupt is generated. The interrupt handler must then issue a read SIO to get the data byte. For the *poll type*, when a read SIO is issued, either a data byte will be returned (if a key had been pressed) or an error condition will be indicated (if a key had not been pressed since the last successful read SIO). For the *buffered type*, when a read SIO is issued, the channel automatically transfers each character as it is typed to consecutive memory locations until an end of message key is pressed—this is usually the carriage return key.

For each of these hardware interfaces, identify major problem areas and specify a design for a corresponding device handler.

5-10 There are two general strategies for handling remote terminal input/output: by character or by line. In the by-character mode, there is a separate SIO and interrupt for each character. In the by-line mode, there is one SIO and interrupt for the entire line. In general, the by-line mode is more efficient since it requires much less interrupt handling and imposes less severe timing demands (in by-character mode, an interrupt must be completely processed and another SIO issued within 100 ms of the preceding interrupt).

Assume that a line has a maximum length of 132 characters. Give any additional information that would be helpful in answering questions below and show how you would use the information.

1   Which mode seems best for handling five terminals connected to a small timesharing system? Why?

2   Which mode seems best for handling the 4,000 terminals connected to an airline reservation system? Why?

3   Is there any value to a compromise strategy (e.g., interrupt after 16 bytes entered or at end of line, whichever comes first)? Explain.

5-11

1   What is the difference between the technique of buffering and the technique of blocking?

2   Give examples of the uses of both techniques.

3   What three advantages does each technique offer?

5-12   In many systems that use SPOOLing a job cannot be started until *all* its input deck has been copied onto DASD. Also, its output will not start until the job has terminated (i.e., until *all* its output has been copied onto DASD).

For parts (1), (2), and (3) of this question we will consider the following five jobs (each 100K bytes):

JOB NUMBER	RUN TIME	NUMBER INPUT CARDS	NUMBER OUTPUT LINES
1	3 min.	100	2,000
2	2 min.	200	600
3	4 min.	1,000	4,000
4	1 min.	2,000	400
5	6 min.	700	5,000

We will assume that these jobs do not use any other I/O and that the reading of input cards and the writing of output lines are rather uniformly distributed throughout the jobs (i.e., they do *not* necessarily read all the input at the beginning of the job and write all the output at the very end).

Furthermore, we will assume that these jobs are to be run on a multiprogrammed computer system with one card reader and two printers. Since the system has over 1M bytes of memory, all five jobs can be in memory at the same time. The card reader averages 1,000 cards/minute input, and each printer averages 1,000 lines/minute output.

The run time for a job is the amount of time it would take if it were running alone (no multiprogramming) and all I/O requests took zero time. Basically, the run time tells how much CPU time is needed for the job.

The total elapsed time for a job, without multiprogramming, is equal to the *input I/O time + run time + output I/O time*. For example, if Job 1 were run all by itself (run = 3 min., cards = 100, print = 2,000), we would compute:

Input I/O time = 100/1,000 = 0.1 min.
Run time = 3 min.
Output I/O time = 2,000/1000 = 2.0 min.
Total time = 5.1 minutes

The above computation was based upon the assumptions that there was multiprogramming and that all I/O was *not* overlapped (i.e., the CPU stops whenever an I/O request is in process).

1 Assuming *no* SPOOLing and *no* I/O buffering, what is the optimum manner in which to run these jobs? What is the total run time from start to finish for all five jobs? What is the average turnaround time (i.e., time from first card of job read to last line of output printed, for each job)?

2 Assuming no SPOOLing but one *card buffering* (i.e., start an SIO for the *next* card each time a card is requested by the program), what is the optimum manner in which to run these jobs? What is the total run time? What is the average turnaround time?

3 Assuming SPOOLing (ignore time required to read/write DASD), what is the optimum manner in which to run these jobs? What is the total run time? What is the average turnaround time?

4 In (3) we assumed that a job couldn't be started until entire SPOOL completed, etc. Let us assume that a single job is submitted at 3 AM Sunday (not usually a busy time) and that there are no other jobs to be run. Assume also that this is a 5-minute run job that reads 2,000 cards and prints 4,000 lines.

   a Assuming no SPOOLing or double buffering, how long will it take to complete this job?

   b Assuming no SPOOLing, but allowing one card buffering, how long will it take to complete this job?

   c Assuming a SPOOLing system as described above, how long will it take to complete this job?

   d Assuming we modified our SPOOLing system so that we could start reading cards from the DASD even though the entire job's input has not been SPOOLed, and likewise start printout before the job has terminated, how long will it take to complete this job using our modified SPOOLing system?

5 Describe briefly how the modified SPOOLing system of (4d) above could be implemented (i.e., how does it differ from conventional SPOOLing system implementation)?

    a Is there any extra synchronization required for this modified system?

    b Are there any circumstances whereby using this modified SPOOLing technique could adversely affect system throughput? (*Hint:* consider job scheduling and unexpected job arrivals.)

5-13 We have discussed the concept of blocking logical records and its advantages. One of the major drawbacks of blocking is the amount of core required for buffering large physical records. Block sizes as high as 16K bytes are not uncommon for large machines using tapes. For a double-buffering access method this means that 32K must be set aside for buffers. Given a 360 with 8K of memory available and one tape drive and one printer, is it possible to list a tape with 120-byte logical records blocked with a blocking factor of 100 (12,000-byte physical records)? If so, how? If not, why not? Be specific.

5-14 We have discussed the use of SPOOLing routines to simulate virtual card readers and printers for several users at once in a multiprogrammed system. The basic process involves using a disk or drum as a large buffer area and writing programs to make these buffers look like readers or printers. Using very similar techniques it is possible to simulate virtual disk drives where several users could be using the same disk at once as if it were several distinct disks. Given that this setup cannot possibly be as fast as separate disk drives, are there any circumstances that might justify the overhead involved in the simulation? Be specific.

5-15

    1 What advantages are there in using a DASD (e.g., disk) as opposed to tape for input SPOOLing? Do these advantages also apply to output SPOOLing?

    2 Suppose we have a program with the following structure:

in which we loop through several thousand times. The program, being slightly intelligent, uses a double-buffering scheme for output to the printer. One line at a time gets printed.

      If such a program is run under an operating system with SPOOLing, the operating system must perform the I/O programming. What must be done to the I/O? How will this affect the execution speed of the program? Will the system throughput be increased if several such programs are run concurrently?

    3 Most minicomputers have been designed as single-user systems. Therefore, each user is allowed to do his own I/O (i.e., no privileged or problem state). Each user is in complete control of interrupts, I/O queuing, and so on.

Imagine such a system with a card reader, printer, and disk. If this system is converted into a two-user multiprogrammed computer, which device will be least affected? Why?

4 Consider the following I/O initiation sequence from the system described in (3).

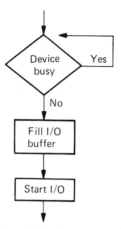

If the second user is added, how must the I/O flowchart be changed? (*Hint*: not all three devices will be affected.)

5 In this system one device will be almost impossible to share without operator intervention. Which one? Why?

5-16

1 List three benefits of SPOOLing. Give a one-sentence explanation of each.

2 Normally we use SPOOLing only for card readers, punches, and printers. List two possible reasons for using SPOOLing for tapes. What problems could be solved?

3 Considering the reasons advanced in (2), why don't we normally SPOOL tapes?

4 Is SPOOLing feasible for all types of I/O devices?

5-17 Two approaches can be taken for spooling input/output. One is to provide GET/PUT routines that directly write disk records with no printer or reader CCWs. The other is to provide an SIO routine that accepts a CCW chain for the simulated device and interprets it. Discuss the pros and cons of each approach.

5-18 Channels, as we have discussed them, require real physical addresses in their CCWs. If we want to use a paged memory without making hardware modifications to the I/O channel, a problem will arise if we attempt a read or write operation and, in the midst of its processing, the relevant page is chosen for removal. Two possibilities exist as a solution to this problem.

1 Wire down the buffer in the VM and change the CCWs to real addresses. That is, somehow keep the paging software from selecting the buffer page(s) for removal.

2 Set aside a buffer within the (nonpaged) area of the operating system and when I/O is complete (for a read) move the data into the page(s) in the virtual memory.

   a How would you implement (1) above? That is, what databases and/or routines would have to change? How would you determine which pages must be wired down?

   b If a user's buffer crossed a page boundary and his two pages were not contiguous in real core, how would you accomplish a read operation under (1)?

   c Under (2) above we are assuming that real memory is divided into a paged section and an operating system area. If a user requests I/O and there is no room left in the operating system area for his buffer, would he have to wait for space to be freed or could the operating system recover part of the paged area for use as a buffer? If so, how and what problems would it create?

   d What will determine which is a better scheme? List one advantage and disadvantage of each scheme.

   e Would I/O handling be simplified if the channel could process CCWs with virtual addresses (rather than requiring real addresses)? Why or how?

5-19 You are in charge of setting up a payroll system for a medium-sized company. You have already done most of the programming and all that remains is to decide on the physical layout of the payroll master file. You have already decided that the logical layout of the file should be sequential, ordered on the Social Security number, and that the length of each individual's record is 128 bytes. The basic hardware for your system is an IBM model 370-165 with a 3330 disk drive. Assume the following characteristics for the disk drive:

Records of information are stored on each track separated by IRGs. Each cylinder contains 19 tracks and it takes no arm motion to read records from the same cylinder. Reading records from different cylinders does require arm motion. The time required to read any record on the disk is arm motion time + rotational delay + transfer time. Further assume that the delay between reading of two adjacent records on a track is IRG size + transfer rate. The following statistics apply: rotational period = 16.7 ms; average rotational delay = 8.4 ms; adjacent cylinder arm motion time = 10 ms; random cylinder arm motion = 55 ms max., 30 ms average; transfer rate = 1.24 μs/byte; IRG size = 135 bytes; track size = 13,165 bytes, which implies that number of records per track = 13,165/(135 + d1) where d1 is record length. You may assume that the time from when an SIO is issued until the disk drive is connected is negligible.

Assume that the software you have already provides four basic functions: (1) updating payroll file to show hours worked yesterday, (2) printing payroll checks and summary reports once a week, (3) adding new employees, and (4) removing ex-employees. Since you have already written the programs, timing information is available. Ignore printer and reader times. The updating program issues I/O requests every 75 μs, starting from the front of the file and working to the back, the paycheck program issues I/O requests every 1 ms, and the employee adding and deleting programs issues I/O requests every 50 μs.

You are considering three possible physical file layout schemes. The first is purely sequential—starting at record 1, cylinder 1, track 1 and then progressing to track 2, then track 3 . . . track 19, then cylinder 2, track 1, record 1, and so on. With the second scheme each record, in addition to its 128 bytes of information, must have 6 bytes that contain the disk address of the next record, a chained structure. The records are randomly distributed throughout the disk space they require. To read the whole file you start at cylinder 1, track 1, record 1 and it tells you where to go for the next record. The third method is a refinement of the second method. The file is divided into cylinder boundaries with all the records of a cylinder lying within a range of Social Security numbers kept in an in-core cylinder index table. Within a cylinder, however, records are randomly distributed. To find a record under this scheme you look in the cylinder index table to find the cylinder and then chain from the first record of the cylinder (identified in the table) to the record you want.

Answer each of the following questions for each of the above three methods assuming 20,000 employees. Assume also that for the chained methods there is always a supply of "overflow records" for each cylinder. These records are chained from a known location and may be used to add employees.

1 How much disk space is required for the master file?
2 How long does it take to print all the paychecks?
3 How long does it take to add an employee? Two employees?
4 How long does it take to remove an employee? Two employees?
5 How long does it take to update all the records?
6 What has to happen when there are no longer any overflow records for a cylinder? How long does this take?
7 Which of the three schemes would you pick and why?

Information Management

6

6-1 INTRODUCTION

Information management is concerned with the storage and retrieval of information entrusted to the system in much the same manner as a library. The following are the basic functions of information management.

1 Keeping track of all information in the system through various tables, the major one being the file directory—sometimes called the Volume Table of Contents (VTOC). These tables contain the name, location, and accessing rights of all information within the system.

2 Deciding policy for determining where and how information is stored and who gets access to the information. Factors influencing this policy are efficient utilization of secondary storage, efficient access, flexibility to users, and protection of access rights to the information requested.

3 Allocating the information resource. Once the decision is made to let a process have access to information, the allocation modules must find the desired information, make the desired information accessible to the process, and establish the appropriate access rights.

4 Deallocating of the resource. Once the information is no longer needed, temporary table entries and other such resources may be released. If the user has updated the information, the original copy of that information may be updated for possible use by other processes.

The modules of information management are sometimes collectively referred to as the *file system*. Information management is conceptually simple. Yet information is one of the most important resources of an operating system and perhaps the one most poorly managed in contemporary systems.

In Figure 1-9 we placed the modules of information management in a single outer ring of the kernel of the operating system. However, a full implementation of this manager can be quite complicated. Thus our approach is to further delineate the modules of the information manager into levels, as shown in Figure 6-1. Such a delineation was first presented by Madnick (1969) and is a framework for implementing a file system.

Each level of the file system follows structured programming techniques. Each level depends only on levels below it and only calls downward. This hierarchical approach for the design of the file system does not require that the rest of the operating system be implemented in the hierarchical manner implied in Figure 6-1.

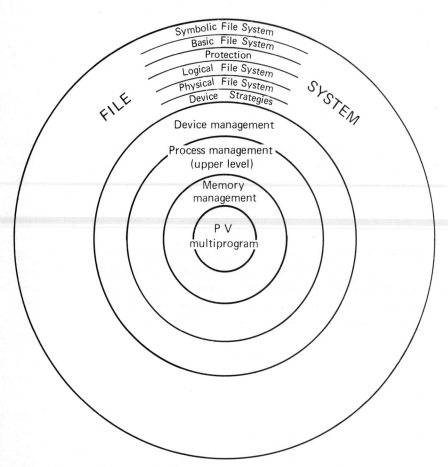

Figure 6-1   Kernel of an operating system

The file system is intended to provide convenient management of both permanent (long-term) and temporary (short-term) information. The programmer is freed from problems such as the allocation of space for his information, physical storage formats, and I/O accessing. One goal of a file system is to allow the programmer to concern himself only with the logical structure and operations performed in processing his information. File systems may also make it possible to share information among users and protect information from unauthorized access.

We will present only basic file system concepts in this chapter. It is useful to distinguish among file systems (i.e., basic information management mechanisms), data management systems, and database systems.

A *file system* is concerned only with the simple logical organization of information. It deals with collections of unstructured and uninterpreted information at the operating system level. Each separately identified collection of information is called a *file* or *data set*.

A *data management system* performs some structuring but no interpretation of the information, e.g., the system may know that each file is divided into entries of a certain size and although it allows the programmer to manipulate these entries it doesn't know what they mean (IBM's IMS-II is a data management system).

A *database system* is concerned with both the structure and interpretations of data items. An example is an airline reservations system, which allows a user to ask "How many people are there on flight 904?"

This chapter focuses mainly on file systems. Data management and database systems are discussed only briefly in Section 6-7. A *file* is a collection of related information units (*records*). For example, in an inventory control application, one line of an invoice is a data item, a complete invoice is a record, and a complete set of such records is a file.

File systems have evolved from simple mechanisms for keeping track of system programs to more complex ones that provide users and the operating system with the means for storing, retrieving, and sharing information. Thus the file system is needed by other components of the operating system as well as by user jobs.

Let us first take a simple user request for information and analyze the steps necessary to fulfill that request. From this simple example we will construct a general model of a file system. We then apply that model to design more flexible file systems.

6-2   A SIMPLE FILE SYSTEM

Let us consider the steps needed to process the following PL/I-like statement:

READ FILE (ETHEL)   RECORD (4)   INTO LOCATION (12000)

This is a request to read the fourth record of the file named ETHEL into a memory location 12000. Such a request invokes elements of the file system.

For the purpose of this example, let us assume that the file ETHEL is stored on a disk, as shown in Figure 6-2 (see Chapter 5 for details on storage devices). The file ETHEL is the shaded portion and consists of seven logical records. Each logical record is 500 bytes long. The disk consists of 16 physical blocks of 1000 bytes each. (We call the physical units of the storage device *blocks* to differentiate from the logical units of interest to the programmer which are called *records*—these are analogous to PL/I data structures.) We can store two logical records of file ETHEL into each physical block. Instead of using the physical two-component (track number, record number) address, we will assign each physical block a unique number, as indicated in Figure 6-2.

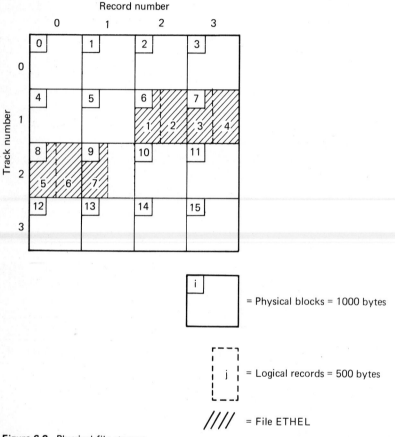

Record number

= Physical blocks = 1000 bytes

= Logical records = 500 bytes

= File ETHEL

Figure 6-2 Physical file storage

6-2.1 File Directory Database

Information on each existing file's status, for example, name and location, must be maintained in a table. As noted above, this table is often called a file directory or a Volume Table of Contents in many systems, most notably IBM's OS/360.

The name Volume Table of Contents comes from viewing the storage device medium as a "container of information" and thus a *volume*. The distinction between a storage device and a volume becomes important when removable volumes (e.g., disk pack, tape reel) are used. These volumes can be physically removed from their original storage device and placed on another storage device of the same type, sometimes even on a different computer system.

Figure 6-3 depicts a sample file directory. Each entry contains information necessary to find and access a file. The logical organization, i.e., programmer's view, is described in terms of the logical record length and the number of records in the file. (At this time we assume that all records within a file are the same length; other file organizations are presented later in Section 6-7.)

The physical location of the file on the storage device can be determined by means of the starting block number information in conjunction with the logical record length and number of records. File ETHEL, for example, consists of seven 500-byte records that require 3500 bytes of storage. Since the physical blocks are 1000 bytes long, four blocks are needed to hold file ETHEL. The first of these blocks, noted in the file directory, is 6. Thus, ETHEL occupies physical storage blocks 6, 7, 8, and 9, as previously depicted in Figure 6-2.

An important point here is that we distinguish between logical structuring and physical structuring. The file ETHEL is logically structured from the user's point of view as a sequential file, i.e., it consists of seven records numbered 1 through 7. It is also physically stored as a sequential file, i.e., its records are stored adjacent to one another in consecutive physical blocks. However, the physical structure of ETHEL need not be sequential. The blocks of ETHEL could be scattered all over secondary storage, and a mapping between the logical records and the physical blocks might then become quite complicated. Examples of other such structurings are presented later in Section 6-8.

There are six entries listed in the file directory of Figure 6-3. Three of these

ENTRY NUMBER	NAME	LOGICAL RECORD SIZE	NUMBER OF LOGICAL RECORDS	ADDRESS OF FIRST PHYSICAL BLOCK	PROTECTION AND ACCESS CONTROL
1	MARILYN	80	10	2	Access by everyone
2	Free	1000	3	3	(Free)
3	ETHEL	500	7	6	Read only
4	JOHN	100	30	12	Read for MADNICK Read/Write for DONOVAN
5	Free	1000	2	10	(Free)
6	Free	1000	1	15	(Free)

Figure 6-3 Sample file directory

(MARILYN, ETHEL, and JOHN) correspond to real user files. The other three entries are needed merely to account for presently unused storage space. Thus the file directory indicates the usage of all the physical storage blocks. (*Note:* blocks 0 and 1 are reserved for special purposes to be explained later.)

6-2.2 Steps to Be Performed

Figure 6-4 presents the steps that must be performed to satisfy a request, such as:

READ FILE (ETHEL)   RECORD (4)   INTO LOCATION (12000)

These steps utilize the sample file directory depicted in Figure 6-3. The reader should follow through the steps, one at a time, to confirm the correctness of the algorithm.

STEP NUMBER	ACTION
Step 1	The file directory is searched to find the entry for ETHEL (entry number 3).
Step 2	Information about ETHEL is retrieved and extracted from the file directory entry, namely: logical record size, address of first physical block, and protection and access control information.
Step 3	Based on the protection information, a decision is made whether to allow the requesting process to access ETHEL.
Step 4	The Logical Record Address specified (record 4 of ETHEL) is transformed into a Logical Byte Address Logical Byte Address = (record number −1) × (record size) which is (4−1) × (500) = 1500.
Step 5	The Logical Byte Address is then transformed into a Physical Byte Address. Logical Byte Address 1500 corresponds to byte 500 within the second 1000-byte physical block of ETHEL, which corresponds to physical block 7.
Step 6	Physical block 7 is read into a 1000-byte buffer area in main memory. This is accomplished by an I/O program similar to those described in Chapters 2 and 5.
Step 7	Record 4 is extracted from the buffer area and moved into the user's area at location 12000. That is, locations 500 through 999 of BUFFER are moved to locations 12000 through 12499 in main memory.

Figure 6-4 Steps involved in processing READ request

6-3 GENERAL MODEL OF A FILE SYSTEM

In this section a general model of a file system is introduced (Madnick, 1969). Figure 6-5 indicates the key components of a file system. Most of these components correspond to generalizations of specific steps of Figure 6-4.

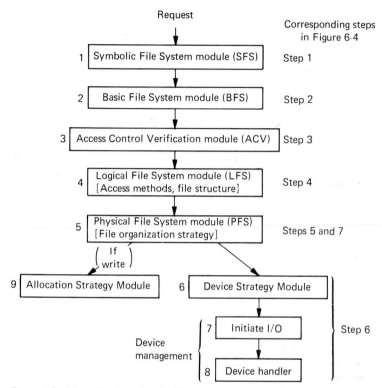

Figure 6-5 Hierarchical model of a file system

Reflecting the ideas introduced in Chapter 1, the components in this file system are organized as a structured hierarchy. Each level in the hierarchy depends only on levels below it. This concept improves the possibility of systematic debugging procedures. For example, once the lowest level is debugged, changes at higher levels have no effect. Debugging can proceed from lowest to highest levels.

Although the particular details presented in this chapter (e.g., format of file directory, file maps) may vary significantly from system to system, the basic structure is common to most contemporary file systems. For example, depending on the structure of a specific file system, certain of the modules in Figure 6-5 may be merged together, further subdivided, or even eliminated—but the underlying structure should still be the same.

6-3.1 File Directory Maintenance

Before discussing the functions of the file system components, it is important to answer certain questions about the file directory, such as: How are the file directory entries created and filled in? Where is the file directory stored? Is it necessary to search the entire directory for every request?

In a basic system such as IBM's Basic Operating System/360 (BOS/360), the programmer must keep track of available storage space and maintain the file directory by control cards similar to:

CREATE ETHEL, RECSIZE=500, NUMRECS=7, LOCATION=6
DELETE JOHN

The CREATE command adds a new entry to the file directory and the DELETE command removes an old one.

If the entire file directory is kept in main memory all the time, a significant amount of memory may be needed to store it. A more general approach is to treat the file directory as a file and place it on the storage volume. Furthermore, if the file directory is stored on the volume, the files may be easily transferred to another system by physically transferring the volume (tape reel, disk pack, etc.) containing these files as well as the corresponding file directory.

If the file directory is stored on the volume, then it may take a substantial amount of time to search it for each access to a file. Although the directory may be quite large, possibly containing thousands of entries, usually only a few files are ever used at one time. Thus if we copy the entries for files that are currently in use into main memory, the subsequent search times can be substantially reduced. Many file systems have two special requests, OPEN, to copy a specific file directory entry into main memory, and CLOSE, to indicate the entry is no longer needed in main memory. Likewise, we talk about a file being *open* or *closed* depending upon the current location of its file directory entry.

6-3.2 Symbolic File System

The first processing step is called the Symbolic File System (SFS). A typical call would be:

CALL SFS (function, file name, record number, location),
such as:
CALL SFS (READ, "ETHEL", 4, 12000)

The Symbolic File System uses the file name to locate that file's unique file directory entry. This function corresponds to step 1 in Figure 6-4.

In our simple system we had assumed a one-to-one correspondence between file names and files. In more advanced file systems, the facility must exist to have several files with the same name and be able to call the same file by different names. To implement such facilities, we divide the file directory of Figure 6-3 into two separate directories, a Symbolic File Directory (SFD) and a Basic File Directory (BFD) as shown in Figure 6-6. The symbolic file system must search the symbolic file directory to determine a unique identifier (ID) for the file requested (see Figure 6-6a). This ID is used instead of the file's name to locate entries in the Basic File Directory. The Basic File System allows operations on files using the ID such as:

CALL BFS (READ,5,4,12000)

where 5 is ETHEL's ID.

Since the SFDs are usually kept on the storage device (see ID 2 in Figure 6-6b), entries for files that are currently in use (called *active* or *opened* files) are copied into main memory. These copies can be used to eliminate repeated I/O access to the same entry on the storage device. We will call this table of active file entries the Active Name Table (ANT).

	NAME	UNIQUE IDENTIFIER (ID)
1	MARILYN	3
2	ETHEL	5
3	JOHN	6

←—16 bytes—→←— 4 bytes—→
←——— 20 bytes per entry ——→

(a) Sample Symbolic File Directory

ID	LOGICAL RECORD SIZE	NUMBER OF LOGICAL RECORDS	ADDRESS OF FIRST PHYSICAL BLOCK	PROTECTION AND ACCESS CONTROL
1	—	—	0	(Basic File Directory)
2	20	3	1	(Symbolic File Directory)
3	80	10	2	Access by everyone
4	1000	3	3	(Free)
5	500	7	6	Read only
6	100	30	12	Read for MADNICK Read/write for DONOVAN
7	1000	2	10	(Free)
8	1000	1	15	(Free)

(b) Sample Basic File Directory

Figure 6-6 Sample Symbolic and Basic File Directories

In summary the Symbolic File System is responsible for:

1 The Symbolic File Directory
2 The Active Name Table
3 Communication with the Basic File System.

6-3.3 Basic File System

The second processing step is called the Basic File System (BFS). A typical call would be:

CALL BFS (function, file ID, record number, location),

such as:

CALL BFS (READ, 5, 4, 12000)

which was shown in Section 6-3.2. The Basic File System uses the file ID to locate that file's entry in the Basic File Directory (see Figure 6-6b) and copies the entry into main memory. This function corresponds to step 2 in Figure 6-4.

By permanently assigning the Symbolic File Directory a specific ID (e.g., ID 2 in Figure 6-6b), the SFS can use the facilities of the BFS to search the directory for the desired name and ID. For example, the PL/I program segment

```
         DECLARE  1    SFD_ENTRY,
                       2 NAME   CHARACTER (16),
                       2 ID        FIXED BINARY (31);
         DO    I = 1 TO  3;
                  CALL  BFS (READ, 2, I, SFD_ENTRY);
                  IF  SFD_ENTRY.NAME = DESIRED_NAME
                  THEN GO TO FOUND;
                  END;
         FOUND:     DESIRED_ID = SFD_ENTRY.ID;
```

could be used to search the symbolic file directory.

The BFD entries for active files are saved in an Active File Table (AFT). This eliminates repeated access to the BFD for the same entry.

The AFT entry is used instead of the file ID for the next step, the Access Control Verification (ACV), which processes calls such as

CALL ACV (READ, 2, 4, 1200)

where AFT entry 2 contains the information for file ID 5 (file ETHEL).

In summary, the Basic File System is responsible for:

1   The Basic File Directory

2   The Active File Table

3   Communication with the Access Control Verification module

For the simple file system of Section 6-2, it is quite easy to combine the SFS and BFS functions. In later sections we will introduce additional functionality where this logical separation is much more significant.

6-3.4   Access Control Verification

The third processing step is called Access Control Verification (ACV). A typical call would be

CALL ACV (function, AFT entry, record number, location)

such as

CALL ACV (READ, 2, 4, 12000)

which was shown in Section 6-3.3. The Access Control Verification acts as checkpoint between the Basic File System and the Logical File System. It compares the desired function (e.g., READ, WRITE) with the allowed accesses indicated in the AFT entry. If the access is not allowed, an error condition exists and the file system request is aborted. If the access is allowed, control passes directly to the Logical File System. This function corresponds to step 3 in Figure 6-4.

6-3.5   Logical File System

The fourth processing step is called the Logical File System (LFS). A typical call would be

CALL LFS (function, AFT entry, record number, location)

such as

CALL LFS (READ, 2, 4, 12000)

which is identical, in form, to the ACV call shown in Sections 6-3.3 and 6-3.4. The Logical File System converts the request for a logical record into a request for a logical byte string. That is, a file is treated as a sequential byte string without any explicit record format by the Physical File System. In this simple case of fixed-length records, the necessary conversion can be accomplished by using the record length information from the AFT entry. That is, the

Logical Byte Address = (Record Number − 1) × Record Length

and

Logical Byte Length = Record Length

This function corresponds to step 4 in Figure 6-4.

The Logical Byte String Address and Length are used instead of the record number for the next step, the Physical File System, which processes calls such as

CALL PFS (READ, 2, 1500, 500, 12000)

Note that by permanently assigning the BFD file a specific ID (such as ID 1 in Figure 6-6b) and a specific AFT entry number (such as AFT entry 1), the Basic File System can call upon the Logical File System to read and write entries in the Basic File Directory. (It is necessary to have a special procedure for fetching BFD entry 1 into AFT entry 1 when the system is initially started or restarted.)

In summary, the Logical File System is responsible for:

1 Conversion of record request to byte string request
2 Communication with the Physical File System

Examples of more complex logical record organizations, such as variable-length records, are presented in later sections.

6-3.6 Physical File System

The fifth processing step is called the Physical File System (PFS). A typical call would be

CALL PFS (function, AFT entry, byte address, byte length, location)

such as

CALL PFS (READ, 2, 1500, 500, 12000)

which was shown in Section 6-3.5. The Physical File System uses the byte address plus the AFT entry to determine the physical block that contains the desired byte string. This block is read into an assigned buffer in main memory, using the facilities of the Device Strategy Module, and the byte string is extracted and moved to the user's buffer area. This function corresponds to steps 5 and 7 in Figure 6-4.

The mapping from Logical Byte Address to Physical Block Number, for the simple contiguous organization of Figure 6-2, can be accomplished by:

$$\text{Physical Block Number} = \frac{\text{Logical Byte Address}}{\text{physical block size}} + \text{address of first physical block}$$

For the request for the byte string starting at Logical Byte Address 1500, the Physical Block Number is:

$$\text{Physical Block Number} = \frac{1500}{1000} + 6 = 1 + 6 = 7$$

which is the block containing record 4 of file ETHEL (see Figure 6-2).

The location of the byte string within the physical block can be determined by:

$$\text{Physical Block Offset} = \text{remainder}\left[\frac{\text{Logical Block Address}}{\text{physical block size}}\right]$$

such as:

$$\text{Physical Block Offset} = \text{remainder}\left[\frac{1500}{1000}\right] = 500.$$

Thus, the byte string starts at the offset 500 within the physical block, as expected from Figure 6-2.

In order to perform these calculations, the Physical File System must know the mapping functions and physical block size used for each storage device. If these were the same for all devices, the information could be built into the PFS routines. Usually there are variations depending upon the device type (e.g., a large disk may be handled differently from a small drum). Thus, this information is usually kept on the storage volume itself and read into the Physical Organization Table (POT) when the system is first started.

If a WRITE request were being handled and the corresponding physical block had not been assigned, the Physical File System would call upon the Allocation Strategy Module (ASM) for the address of a free block of secondary storage. In the simple file system of Section 6-2, all the blocks are allocated in advance by a special CREATE facility, as discussed in Section 6-3.1.

In summary, the Physical File System is responsible for:

1 Conversion of logical byte string request into Physical Block Number and Offset
2 The Physical Organization Table
3 Communication with the Allocation Strategy Module and the Device Strategy Module

Later sections will introduce many more physical system organizations and performance considerations that have an impact on the physical file system.

6-3.7 Allocation Strategy Module

The Allocation Strategy Module (ASM) is responsible for keeping track of unused blocks on each storage device. A typical call would be:

CALL ASM (POT entry, number of blocks, first block)

such as:

CALL ASM (6, 4, FIRSTBLOCK)

where POT entry 6 corresponds to the storage device on which file ETHEL is to reside and FIRSTBLOCK is a variable in which the address of the first of the four blocks requested is returned.

The ASM may be invoked by a special setup procedure, such as the CREATE command of Section 6-3.1, or automatically by the Physical File System as indicated in Figure 6-5.

Figure 6-6b indicates how the location of groups of available blocks can be recorded in the Basic File Directory by treating them as special files. Other techniques for maintaining this information are presented in subsequent sections.

6-3.8 Device Strategy Module

The Device Strategy Module (DSM) converts the Physical Block Number to the address format needed by the device (e.g., physical block 7 = track 1, record 3, as shown in Figure 6-2). It sets up appropriate I/O commands for that device type. This function corresponds to step 6 in Figure 6-4. All previous modules have been device-independent. This one is device-dependent. Control then passes to the I/O scheduler.

6-3.9 I/O Scheduler and Device Handler

These modules correspond to the device management routines that were discussed in Chapter 5. They schedule and perform the reading of the physical block containing the requested information.

6-3.10 Calls and Returns Between File System Modules

After the physical I/O is completed, control is returned to the Device Strategy Module. The DSM checks for correct completion and returns control to the PFS, which extracts the desired information from the buffer and places it into the desired location. A "success" code is then returned back through all other modules of the file system.

Why isn't an immediate return made to the uppermost level? There are two reasons: (1) An error may be detected at any level, and that level must return the appropriate error code (for example, the Logical File System may detect the attempted access of an address beyond the file); and (2) any level may generate several calls to lower levels (for example, the Symbolic File System may call the Basic File System several times to read entries from the Symbolic File Directory).

A function of all levels of Figure 6-5 is verification, which is substantiating the validity of the request. The Symbolic File System checks to see whether or not a file exists. The Access Control Verification checks to see whether or not access is permitted. The Logical File System checks to see whether the requested logical address is within the file. The Device Strategy Module checks to see whether or not such a device exists.

6-3.11 Shortcomings of Simple File System Design

Let us summarize some of the assumptions, inefficiencies, and inadequacies of our simple file-system system:

1 *Symbolic File System*
We assumed that each file had a single unique name.

2 *Access Control Verification*
How are files shared? How can the same file have different protection rights for different uses?

3 *Logical File System*
We assumed that each file consisted of fixed-length records, and that these records were viewed as sequential. How are accesses to variable-length records handled? Are there other file structuring methods? Are there more flexible methods for the user?

4 *Physical File System*
Are there physical structurings other than sequential? Are these more efficient in space? In accesses? We assumed that for each request this module would activate an access to the disk. What if the request following READ ETHEL RECORD (4) were READ ETHEL RECORD (3)? Isn't record 3 in the system buffer area already?

5 *Allocation Strategy*
How are files stored on secondary storage? Are there fragmentation problems when files are deleted? In other words, is secondary storage being used efficiently?

6 *Device Strategy Module*
Can this module restructure or reorder requests to match more efficiently the characteristics of the device on which the information is stored?

In the sections that follow we will explore more general techniques for each of these levels, techniques that give the user more flexibility and may thus increase the system's efficiency.

6-4 SYMBOLIC FILE SYSTEM

The SFS's function is to map the user's symbolic reference to an ID. Let us develop a scheme that will offer additional features beyond those of Section 6-3.

1   Multiple Names Given to the Same File

This feature, sometimes called *aliases*, could be useful if several different programs assumed different names for the same file. The user may also find certain names to be more meaningful under different circumstances.

2   Sharing Files

This feature, sometimes called *linked* files, gives multiple users access to the same physical file, offering them more flexibility and, frequently, greater system efficiency. This is because buffers in main memory as well as secondary storage space can be shared. If, for example, several users are accessing the same file, only one master copy of that file need exist. An early version of M.I.T.'s CTSS timesharing system (see Chapter 9) provides an example of the inefficiency that can result from a system that does not allow the sharing of files. There was a very popular program called DOCTOR that simulated a psychiatrist. Over half the users on the system had a separate copy of this program. Due to the large size of this program, there was a time when over half the secondary storage consisted of copies of DOCTOR.

3   The Same Name Given to Different Files

Since many users create and use files, it is possible that two different programmers may accidently choose the same name for a file (e.g., TEST). Thus when one of them uses the control cards as follows:

```
DELETE TEST /* delete my old copy*/
CREATE TEST /* create a new copy*/
```

he may be deleting the other programmer's file TEST. Likewise, the READ and WRITE requests will use the same file for both programmers. Maintaining a manual file name registry to avoid duplicate names would be a time-consuming and awkward solution.

4   Subdividing Files into Groups

A given user (or group of users) may be responsible for a large number of files. These files may logically belong to separate projects or tasks. To help keep track of these files in an organized way, it is desirable to group related files together. Such a group is often called a *library* (or *partitioned data set* in IBM terminology).

The symbolic file name is a very convenient way for a programmer to remember and refer to this file, but we have noted several shortcomings to the simple file directory scheme presented. We therefore suggest a more flexible file-naming scheme that incorporates all the additional features we have listed above.

6-4.1   Directory Files

Notice that in Figure 6-6 we separated the file directory into two separate components: the Symbolic File Directory and the Basic File Directory. The SFD is concerned with file naming whereas the BFD is concerned with the physical file. We can generalize this mechanism in two ways: (1) have multiple symbolic directories, and (2) treat symbolic directories as files.

To eliminate or at least minimize naming conflicts, each programmer or programmer group can be assigned a separate SFD. Thus there is a need for a Master Directory that specifies the BFD entry for each programmer's private SFD.

Note that in Figure 6-6b the Master Directory has a unique ID, i.e., it is always entry 2 in the Basic File Directory. This allows the Symbolic File System to access the Master Directory via the Basic File System.

6-4.2 Sample Hierarchical File Structure

Figure 6-7 illustrates the details of a simple hierarchical file structure consisting of seven data files and four SFD files in addition to the Basic File Directory. The

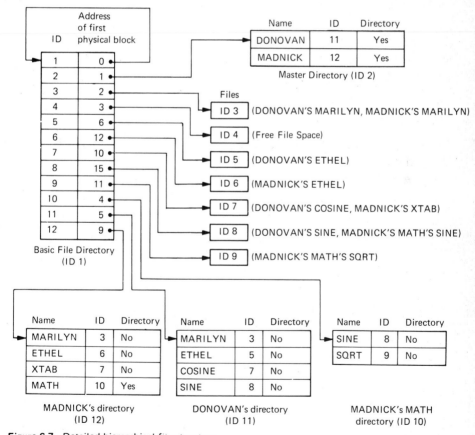

Figure 6-7 Detailed hierarchical file structure

first BFD entry is for the BFD itself; the second entry is always assigned to the Master Directory file. Remember that for all practical purposes it is just like every other file with a file directory entry, containing record length, etc.

The Master Directory file has an entry for each programmer's Symbolic File Directory. In this case, there are two programmers, DONOVAN and MADNICK. Each programmer's directory has entries for all files accessible to him. DONOVAN has four files, MARILYN, ETHEL, COSINE, and SINE, whereas MADNICK has four files, MARILYN, ETHEL, XTAB, and MATH where MATH itself is a Symbolic File Directory with entries for two files, SINE and SQRT.

Notice that the file MARILYN is really the same file (i.e., same ID) for both programmers; this is often called a *linked file*. On the other hand, DONOVAN's file ETHEL is not the same as MADNICK's file ETHEL (i.e., different IDs). There are several other flexible features illustrated in this example. (Note that DONOVAN's file COSINE and MADNICK's file XTAB are really the same file.) The reader should confirm these observations by studying Figure 6-7.

A *hierarchical file organization* such as the one described above is often diagrammed as a tree structure as shown in Figure 6-8. Several file systems (e.g., MULTICS) allow the programmer to create multilevel subsidiary directories, sometimes called private libraries, so that the structure may become several levels deep, as illustrated by the MATH directory in Figures 6-7 and 6-8.

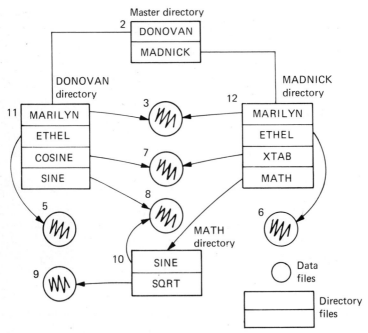

Figure 6-8 Abstract view of a hierarchical file structure

6-5 BASIC FILE SYSTEM

When the Basic File System is called, it is given the unique ID of the file requested. The BFS first searches the AFT to determine whether the file is already "opened." If not, the Basic File System searches the Basic File Directory for the entry of the requested file. It then places the information from the entry into the AFT.

If the unique ID assigned to a file is the same as the file's entry number in the Basic File Directory, there is no "searching" required to find the entry in the BFD.

Under certain circumstances, such as when a user wishes to delete a file (e.g., DELETE DONOVAN'S ETHEL), it is desirable to know if this file appears in more than one Symbolic File Directory entry. Frequently, this is accomplished by keeping a count in the BFD entry of the number of SFD entries that point to it. Whenever a link or alias is made, this count is increased. Whenever a link or alias is removed, this count is decreased. (When the file itself is deleted, the Symbolic File System must find and delete all corresponding Symbolic File Directory entries.)

6-6 ACCESS CONTROL VERIFICATION

Access control and sharing must be considered in conjunction with each other. For example, a user could protect his information by placing the entire computer system in a locked vault accessible only to him. In some of its installations the government takes an approach somewhat similar to this one by having three separate computer systems—one for top secret information, another for secret information, and yet another for confidential material. Usually, however, this extreme form of protection is not desirable.

In addition to user flexibility, there are several system advantages in allowing a controlled sharing facility:

1 It saves duplication of files. On one system, for example, there was a single shared copy of a certain 128K program that resided on disk. When the shared copy was removed, about 50 private copies appeared equal to about 6.4M bytes of disk space.

2 It allows synchronization of data operations. If two programs are updating bank balances, it is desirable that they both refer to the exact same file at all times. (Note that appropriate interlocks, as discussed in Chapter 4, are needed to coordinate the update actions.)

3 It improves the efficiency of system performance, e.g., if information is shared in memory, a possible reduction in I/O operations may occur.

In this section we will suggest three techniques for keeping track of and enforcing access control rights—access control matrix, passwords, and cryptography.

6-6.1 Access Control Matrix and Access Control Lists

Most systems have mechanisms for identifying the user that originates a job. This mechanism is needed to insure correct billing for computer usage. The identification may be by visual identification by the computer operator or special identification codes (similar to telephone credit card numbers) submitted as part of the job. We will not pursue this mechanism any further but we will assume that each user can be identified.

An access control matrix is a two-dimensional matrix. One dimension lists all users of the computer, the other dimension lists all files in the system as shown in Figure 6-9. Each entry in the matrix indicates that user's access to that file (e.g., DONOVAN can read file PAYROLL, DONOVAN can both read and write file STOCKPRICE, but MADNICK can read only file STOCKPRICE). The Access Control Verification module compares the user's access request with his allowed access to the file—if they do not match, the access is not permitted.

	Donovan	Madnick	Ziering	Bad guy	• • •
SORT	E	RWE	E	E	
PL/I	RWE	E	E	None	
Stock price	RW	R	R	R	
Payroll	R	RW	R	None	

Segments (rows) / *Users* (columns)

Figure 6-9 Access control matrix

The access control matrix of Figure 6-9 is conceptually simple but poses certain implementation problems. For example, at M.I.T. there are about 5,000 authorized users and about 30,000 online files. A two-dimensional matrix would require 5,000 X 30,000 = 150,000,000 entries. There are various techniques that are logically identical to Figure 6-9 but much more economical to implement. One approach, used in several systems, such as MULTICS, associates an Access Control List (ACL) with each file in the system. The ACL lists the authorized users of this file and their allowed accesses. Logical grouping of users, usually by project, and the special grouping ALL OTHERS greatly reduce the length of the ACL.

For example, if DONOVAN had a file, DATA, which he wished to allow only MADNICK and CARPENTER to read, the ACL would be:

FILE	ACL
DATA	DONOVAN (ALL ACCESS), MADNICK (READ), CARPENTER (READ), ALL OTHERS (NO ACCESS)

Note that this required only 4 ACL entries, not 30,000 as would be required for a complete access control matrix. Since most users allow sharing very selectively (public files use "ALL OTHERS" to allow unrestricted access to a large group of users), the Access Control Lists are usually quite short. The ACL information can be efficiently stored as part of the Basic File Directory entry and copied into the Active File Table entry when the file is in use. This makes examination of access control efficient.

6-6.2 Passwords

Access Control Lists, and similar such mechanisms, may take up large amounts of space. Moreover, their maintenance may be complicated, since they may be of varying lengths. Maintenance mechanisms must be implemented either for chaining together all entries of an ACL or reserving blocks large enough to contain the largest ACL.

An alternative method for enforcing access control is through passwords. Associated with each file in the file directory is a password. The user requesting access to that file must provide the correct password. If you wish to allow another user to access one of your files, you merely tell him the password for that file. This method has an advantage in that only a small, fixed amount of space is needed for protection information for each file. Its disadvantage is that a dishonest systems programmer may be able to get all the passwords, since the protection information is stored in the system. This disadvantage also applies to the ACL method.

Another disadvantage of passwords is that access control cannot easily be changed. How does a user selectively retrieve the passwords? If he wishes to deny access of a file to a user who has the password, how does he do it? He can change the password, but now he has to inform all the users who are to be allowed access.

6-6.3 Cryptography

Both the password and the Access Control List methods are disadvantageous in that the "access keys" are permanently stored in the system. Another method is to cryptographically encode all files. All users may access the encoded files but only an authorized user knows the way to decode the contents.

The decoding (for reading) and encoding (for writing) of the file may be done by the Access Control Verification module. The requesting user provides an argument—

the code key. The user may change that argument whenever he wishes. There are many techniques for encoding information (Skatrud, 1969). One is simply to use the key to start a random number generation. The encoder adds successive random numbers to the bytes of the file to be encoded. Decoding subtracts these numbers to obtain the original data back. An authorized user knows how to start the random number generator with the same code key for decoding as was used for encoding.

In this scheme the code key does not have to be stored in the system. The user needs to enter it only while he is encoding or decoding the file. Thus, there is no table that a dishonest systems programmer can read to find all code keys or allow himself access. Cryptography has the advantage of not having the key stored in the system, but it does incur the cost of encoding and decoding of files.

6-6.4 Summary

The access control mechanisms described in this section may be used independently or in combination. The issues of privacy, security, protection, sharing, and access control have received considerable attention by researchers. Additional information can be found in the bibliography: Comber (1969), Conway (1972), Graham (1967), Graham and Denning (1972), Hoffman (1969), Lampson (1969, 1971), Molho (1970), Needham (1972), Scherf (1973), Schroeder (1969), Skatrud (1969), and Weissman (1969).

6-7 LOGICAL FILE SYSTEM

The Logical File System is concerned with mapping the structure of the logical records onto the linear byte-string view of a file provided by the Physical File System. In particular, it must convert a request for a record into a request for a byte string.

In the sample file system of Section 6-2, the Logical File System provides facilities for direct access, based on record number, to any of the records, all of which are the same length. In conventional file systems and data management systems many additional record structures are supported. These are often called *access methods*, such as:

1 Sequentially structured fixed-length records (sequential and direct access)
2 Sequentially structured variable-length records (sequential and direct access)
3 Sequentially structured keyed records
4 Multiple-keyed records
5 Chained structured records
6 Relational or triple-structured records

6-7.1 Sequentially Structured Fixed-length Records

For this record organization, the user views his file as a sequence of fixed-length records (i.e., all records are the same length), as shown in Figure 6-10. This structure is useful for storing "card-image" and "print-image" files as well as SPOOL files.

Record number

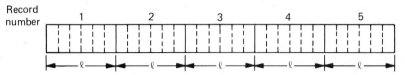

Figure 6-10 Sequential fixed-length records (all records ℓ bytes long)

6-7.1.1 SEQUENTIAL ACCESS

For sequential access, on each request the user wishes to have the "next" record— the same as reading cards from a card reader. This request would look similar to

READ FILE (ETHEL) NEXT INTO LOCATION (BUFFER)

where the explicit record number is omitted.

In order to implement this facility, the Logical File System must maintain a Current Logical Byte Address (CLBA) in the AFT entry for the file. When the file is initially opened, the CLBA is set to 0. Subsequently, after processing each request, the CLBA is updated by

$$CLBA = CLBA + RL$$

where RL is the record length.

6-7.1.2 DIRECT ACCESS

For direct access the user explicitly specifies the record desired. This request is the same as our earlier example:

READ FILE (ETHEL) RECORD (4) INTO LOCATION (BUFFER)

The CLBA can be computed by the simple formula:

$$CLBA = (RN - 1) \times RL$$

where RN is the designated record number.

6-7.2 Sequentially Structured Variable-length Records

For this record organization, the user views his file as a sequence of records of possibly differing lengths. This structure is useful for storing names, employment histories, and printer output (with trailing blanks omitted), as shown in Figure 6-11.

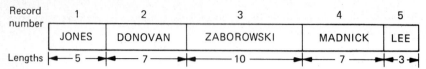

Record number

1	2	3	4	5
JONES	DONOVAN	ZABOROWSKI	MADNICK	LEE

Lengths |←— 5 —→|←— 7 —→|←——— 10 ———→|←— 7 —→|←3→|

Figure 6-11 Sample of sequentially structured variable-length records

There are various ways of storing these records. Note that it is necessary to be able to identify the boundaries of each record. For example, in Figure 6-11, how do we know that there are two separate records, JONES and DONOVAN, instead of one record, JONESDONOVAN? Figure 6-12 presents a format that can be used to handle this situation. In this approach the length of each record is stored in the file.

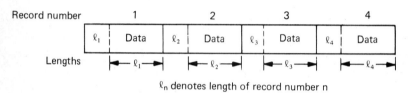

Record number

	1		2		3		4
ℓ_1	Data	ℓ_2	Data	ℓ_3	Data	ℓ_4	Data

Lengths |←— ℓ_1 —→| |←— ℓ_2 —→| |←— ℓ_3 —→| |←— ℓ_4 —→|

ℓ_n denotes length of record number n

Figure 6-12 Sequentially structured variable-length records

6-7.2.1 SEQUENTIAL ACCESS

A sequential access request might look like

READ FILE (NAMES) NEXT INTO LOCATION (BUFFER) LENGTH (N)

where the variable N is set to the length of the record that was read. The length of the BUFFER area must be equal to or larger than the largest record in the file.

Let us assume that the length field, ℓ_n, of Figure 6-12, is 2 bytes long, so that records can be up to 64K bytes long. If the CLBA is always set to the beginning of the length field for the *next* record (e.g., it is set to 0 initially), the length, N, can be extracted from the 2-byte string at location CLBA. The record itself can then be read as the N-byte string at location CLBA + 2. Since we can determine the byte address and length for both steps, the Physical File System can be used to process these requests. The CLBA is updated in preparation for the next request by

$$CLBA = CLBA + 2 + N$$

6-7.2.2 DIRECT ACCESS

A direct access request would look like

READ FILE(NAMES) RECORD(3) INTO LOCATION(BUFFER) LENGTH(N)

The logical byte address for a direct access to a sequentially structured variable-length record is found essentially by sequencing through records until you find the right record. That is, if record 3 is requested

$$CLBA = \ell_1 + 2 + \ell_2 + 2$$

where ℓ_1 and ℓ_2 are the lengths of record 1 and record 2, and can be found by accessing these records sequentially.

Direct access can be very inefficient, but there are several methods for improving the efficiency, such as the following:

1 Keep track of the number and address of the last record requested. If the present request is a record number larger than the last one accessed, then go forward. If less, then start sequencing from the beginning of the file.

2 Keep a table of record numbers and LBAs.

3 Each time a record is accessed its LBA could be kept by the user's program for possible future use (e.g., the OS/360–NOTE/POINT facility). This would make possible very fast subsequent accesses.

6-7.3 Sequentially Structured Keyed Records

A different type of access is based on content rather than record number or address. An example would be a request for the record containing Madnick's payroll information. Such single-keyed records may be depicted as in Figure 6-13 where $k_1, \ldots, k_n$ denote keys, e.g., $k_4 = $ MADNICK.

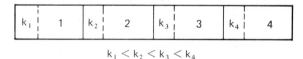

$$k_1 < k_2 < k_3 < k_4$$

Figure 6-13 Sequential single-keyed record

All records are kept in ascending order based on the keys, i.e., k_1, k_2, k_3, etc. For example, MADNICK would follow DONOVAN but precede ZIERING.

The Logical Byte Address for either sequential or direct access may be computed by searching all records for the one with the correct key. In order to avoid such a massive search, a separate *symbol table* or *index table* file may be used to indicate correspondences between keys and the LBA of the record. (See Figure 6-14.)

In practical systems the Index Table may be divided into levels. Figure 6-15 depicts the structure used by IBM's Indexed Sequential Access Method (ISAM). The master index points to the secondary index. The secondary index contains the starting locations of subsets of the data items.

Every n^{th} record in the data file is left empty for inserts. A request requires one access to the master index, one access to the secondary index, and a sequential search of the records in the subset.

	Key	Location
k_1	ADLER	
k_2	DONOVAN	
k_3	MADNICK	
k_4	ZIERING	
	• • •	• • •

Figure 6-14 Sample index table for Figure 6-13

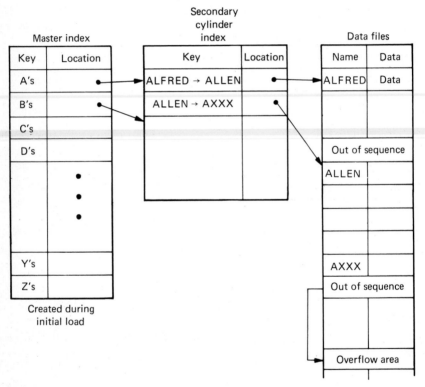

Location files

Figure 6-15 An ISAM structuring

This scheme will work well under the following conditions:

1 Most entries are initially created all at once and submitted in sorted form.

2 Insertions or deletions are a small proportion (less than 10 percent) of the file in order to minimize use of overflow areas.

3 The functions use sequential reference by key order.

There are other implementations that provide more flexibility and/or better performance (see IBM's Virtual Sequential Access Method).

6-7.4 Multiple-keyed Records (Inverted File Structure)

The following four fields in a record—(ID=1743, NAME=DONOVAN, SS#=030-34-2674, JOB=FASTEST PROFESSOR AT MIT)—all identify the same person. Sometimes users wish to organize their data so that they can be referenced by any one of several keys. This is similar to library indexing of books by title, author, and subject. The major techniques for this are:

1 Multiple indexes (note that the Index Tables may exceed the size of the data!).

2 Chaining records with the same keys together.

6-7.5 Chained Structured Records

The keyed and multiple-keyed record structures are not usually offered as part of a basic file system, but rather are built on top of one. They are data management systems, and provide facilities for complex record structures. A chained structured record organization provides a more complex data management facility.

An example can be found in Figure 6-16a, which shows the "bill of materials" (i.e., list of components) for each assembly used to produce a television set. Figure 6-16b presents the same information in a "tree" or "chained" form.

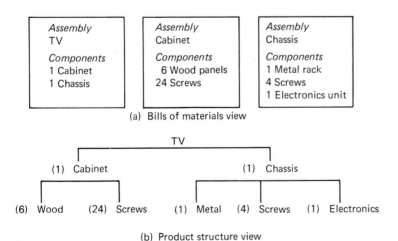

(a) Bills of materials view

(b) Product structure view

Figure 6-16 Sample chained structure records

Such a structuring allows a *top down* access, e.g., how many screws are there in a TV; or a *bottom up* access, e.g., what assemblies use screws? We will leave the discussion of the implementation of such systems to the references, such as Chapin (1969) and Senko (1973).

6-7.6 Relational or Triple-structured Records

Another database organization that may be built on top of a basic file system is a relational or triple structure (Codd, 1970). Logical records may bear a relation to other records, e.g., Frank is John's father. Figure 6-17 depicts three relations.

RECORD 1	—	RELATION	—	RECORD 2
FRANK	—	FATHER	—	JOHN
JOHN	—	BROTHER	—	PAUL
JOHN	—	FATHER	—	JAMES

Figure 6-17   A relational database

Questions that a user may ask of such a system are:

Who is JAMES' FATHER (i.e., ? — FATHER — JAMES)
Name all the FATHERS (i.e., ? — FATHER — ?)

Such systems are discussed in Codd (1970) and Senko (1973).

6-8 PHYSICAL FILE SYSTEM

The primary function of the PFS is to perform the mapping of Logical Byte Addresses into Physical Block Addresses. In the organization of Figure 6-5, the Logical File System calls the Physical File System, passing to it the logical byte address and length of the information requested. The PFS may first call the Allocation Strategy Module (if a write request) and then the Device Strategy Module, or it may call the DSM directly.

In our division of responsibility, the PFS keeps track of the mapping from Logical Byte Address to the blocks of physical storage. In previous sections the simple mapping function (Physical Block Address = first physical block of file $+ \frac{\text{Logical Byte Address}}{\text{block size}}$) was a consequence of the simple physical storage structure of the file. All blocks were stored as in Figure 6-2, i.e., contiguous on secondary storage.

In this section let us briefly discuss three additional considerations:

1 Minimizing I/O operations
2 Allowing logical record size independent of physical block size
3 Allowing noncontiguous allocation of file space

6-8.1   Minimizing I/O Operations

If all the records of file ETHEL (see Figure 6-2) were to be read sequentially, it would require seven I/O operations (each operation reading one physical block) to read the seven logical records using the algorithm presented in Figure 6-4. Since the entire file occupies only four physical blocks, we might suspect that we could reduce the number of I/O operations by eliminating redundant operations.

The number of I/O operations can be reduced by keeping track of which physical blocks are in core. Quite sophisticated algorithms can be used to determine which blocks to keep in core. For each I/O read operation a physical block is copied into a buffer in main memory. If we keep track of which physical block is presently in the buffer, we can modify step 5 of the algorithm (Figure 6-4) to test whether or not the desired block has already been read. If the block is already in the buffer, the I/O read operation (step 6) can be skipped.

In the case of file ETHEL, the request for record 1 will cause physical block 6 to be copied into the buffer. The subsequent request for record 2 will operate on the buffer without the need for any additional I/O operation. The request for record 3 will then cause physical block 7 to be copied into the buffer, and so on. In this way the entire file ETHEL can be processed sequentially with only four I/O operations instead of seven.

This technique, often called *file buffering*, has a number of variations. For example, a separate buffer may be assigned to each opened file, or a pool of buffers may be shared by all files. Furthermore, to minimize the detrimental effects of random accessing, as opposed to sequential accessing, and to allow certain I/O overlapping, it may be desirable to assign multiple buffers to a single file (whence comes the term "double buffering"). The considerations involved with effective file buffering strategies are very similar to those relating to the page replacement algorithms discussed in Section 3-6.2 and the device management buffering discussed in Section 5-3.2.

6-8.2   Allowing Logical Record Size Independent of Physical Block Size

In the simple system of Section 6-2, a physical record must hold some integral number of logical records, with no space left over. There are, unfortunately, situations in practice in which the programmer desires to process logical records of lengths that are not an even factor of block length. There are various ways to solve this problem. For example, we can effectively store fifty 13-byte logical records in the 1000-byte blocks by using 20-byte logical records, which are really 13-byte records each with 7 bytes of wasted space. This strategy, though effective, is not efficient in the use of secondary storage space.

Many storage devices allow a certain amount of flexibility in the format of the individual tracks. For example, some, such as the IBM 2314 and 3330, permit the programmer to change the track format from sixteen 1000-byte blocks (see Figure 6-1) to thirty 500-byte blocks. This format change is not usually linear since a certain amount of extra space must be used for the Inter-record Gap (IRG) of every block no matter how long it is (see Chapter 5).

In general, the strategy of changing track formats is not very convenient. A more general approach is to modify steps 5 and 7 of Figure 6-4 (as shown in Figure 6-18) and thus allow logical records to straddle physical blocks. This approach also has the benefit of allowing logical records that are larger than the maximum size physical block.

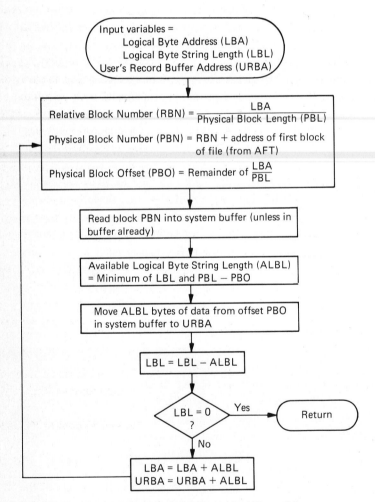

Figure 6-18 Revised version of steps 5, 6, and 7 of Figure 6-4

6-8.3 Allowing Noncontiguous Allocation of File Space

Contiguous allocation of file space, as assumed in the simple system of Section 6-2, is not always practical or possible. Various reasons are presented in Section 6-9 (Allocation Strategy Module) that follows. If the physical blocks of a file are not contiguous, a different algorithm is needed to map from logical byte address to physical block number. Two popular techniques are (1) chained blocks and (2) file maps. There are also many variations on these basic techniques.

6-8.3.1 CHAINED BLOCKS

In a chained blocks mapping, each physical block contains the address of the next "logically contiguous" block. Figure 6-19 shows file ETHEL which has been assigned blocks 6, 9, 10, and 14 (see Figure 6-2 for comparison). The Basic File Directory entries contain the address of the first physical blocks, as before, but subsequent block addresses are found by means of the address pointers (often called *chains*).

The address pointer may be stored within the physical block, thereby decreasing the data capacity of the block slightly (i.e., holds only 998 bytes per block instead of 1000 bytes), or as part of the header field (e.g., key field) of the data block which is possible on many devices such as the IBM 3330.

The chained blocks approach is efficient for sequential access to the blocks (corresponding to sequential access to the logical records) but quite inefficient for direct access for reasons similar to those discussed in Section 6-7.2.2. The chained block technique is used in the CTSS system described in Chapter 9.

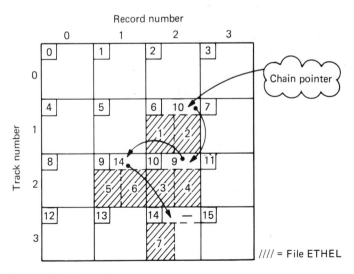

Figure 6-19 Chained blocks

6-8.3.2 FILE MAPS

Another approach to noncontiguous allocation is to use a File Map Table to map each Logical Block Address to its physical block address (similar to the file maps used for paging discussed in Section 3-6.2.1). This file map may be stored as part of the entry in the BFD or in a separate block. Figure 6-20 illustrates the latter approach. Block 6 is used to hold the file map whereas blocks 7, 9, 10, and 14 are used to hold the data records.

When the file is opened, all or part (if the file is especially large) of the file map is copied into memory as part of the Active File Table information. In this way the mapping can be done as efficiently as the contiguous allocation mapping. The mapping function becomes

$$\text{Physical Block Address} = \text{File Map}\left(\frac{\text{Logical Byte Address}}{\text{block size}}\right)$$

which is just an indexed table access.

If the file map is very large, it may require several physical blocks. In this case, it may be necessary to have file maps for the file maps. This is the case with the VM/370 system described in Chapter 9.

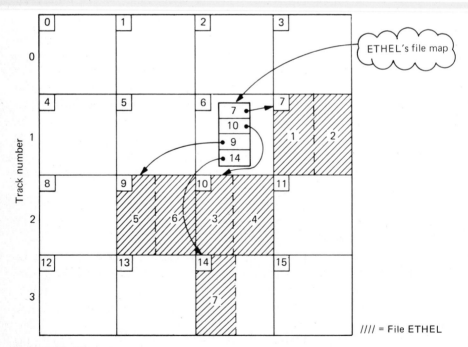

Figure 6-20 File map

6-9   ALLOCATION STRATEGY MODULE

Some systems require manual allocation of file space by using the LOCATION field of a CREATE control card as discussed in Section 6-3.1. This forces the programmer to keep track manually of space, which may be a very cumbersome task when using a typical storage device with 10,000 to 100,000 blocks or more. Also, since there are usually many programmers using the same storage device, it is necessary for a programmer to keep track of everyone else's files if he wishes to know what spaces are available. Assuming contiguous allocation, the following control cards:

CREATE ETHEL, RECSIZE = 500, NUMRECS = 7, LOCATION = 6
CREATE JOHN, RECSIZE = 100, NUMRECS = 7, LOCATION = 6

which cause files ETHEL and JOHN to overlap, would not be recognized as errors in many simple file systems. (This overlap may even be desirable under some strange circumstances, but it is usually indicative of an error in manual allocation.)

For the reasons discussed above, it is desirable for the programmer merely to specify

CREATE ETHEL, RECSIZE = 500, NUMRECS = 7
CREATE JOHN, RECSIZE = 100, NUMRECS = 30

and let the file system allocate the necessary space. In general, the programmer has no interest in the specific location anyway.

6-9.1   Automatic Allocation

There are numerous techniques by which the system can keep track of space. One simple way is to maintain "dummy" or "free" file directory entries, one for each contiguous area of blocks not assigned as shown in Figures 6-3 and 6-6b. Then, to satisfy the request for four blocks for ETHEL, the file system looks for a free file directory entry that specifies an area of four blocks or longer. Figure 6-21 illustrates this process for the control cards referred to above.

The IBM OS/360, for example, uses a similar automatic allocation technique (see Chapter 9 for more details).

6-9.2   Dynamic Allocation

There are two problems connected with the automatic allocation technique described above: (1) it leads to fragmentation of secondary storage; and (2) users often don't know in advance how big their files are going to be (e.g., the size of the output object deck file from a compiler is a function of the size and characteristic of the input source program).

As in the case of fragmentation of main memory, two techniques may be used to utilize secondary storage more efficiently: (1) relocation, e.g., some systems, such

ENTRY NO.	NAME	LOGICAL RECORD SIZE	NUMBER OF LOGICAL RECORDS	ADDRESS OF FIRST PHYSICAL BLOCK	PHYSICAL BLOCKS
1	MARILYN	80	40	2	(2, 3, 4, 5)
2	Free	1000	4	6	(6, 7, 8, 9)
3	STU	132	5	10	(10)
4	Free	1000	5	11	(11, 12, 13, 14, 15)
5					
6					

(a) Before CREATES are processed

ENTRY NO.	NAME	LOGICAL RECORD SIZE	NUMBER OF LOGICAL RECORDS	ADDRESS OF FIRST PHYSICAL BLOCK	PHYSICAL BLOCKS
1	MARILYN	80	40	2	(2, 3, 4, 5)
2	ETHEL	500	7	6	(6, 7, 8, 9)
3	STU	132	5	10	(10)
4	JOHN	100	30	11	(11, 12, 13)
5	Free	1000	2	14	(14, 15)
6					

(b) After CREATES are processed

Figure 6-21 Automatic file space allocation

as IBM's 1130 Disk Monitor System, do compact the files on the disks periodically; (2) noncontiguous file space allocation. By using noncontiguous allocation not only is fragmentation avoided but also it is easy to dynamically increase the size of a file during program execution. These are the motivations for use of file maps or chained blocks as introduced in Section 6-8.3.

6-9.2.1 FREE FILE MAPS

The allocation technique depicted by Figure 6-21 works well when there are only a few large free areas. If there are a large number of small free areas, the file directory can become very large and inefficient. One solution to this problem is to use a special file map (similar to those of Section 6-8.3.2) that contains a list of all available blocks. Whenever a block must be allocated, it is removed from this list. Whenever one or more blocks are deallocated (e.g., a file is deleted), these blocks are added to the free file map.

6-9.2.2 FREE CHAIN

Another allocation approach is to chain together all free blocks (in a manner similar to Section 6-8.3.1). In this case, there is no searching required. Whenever a block is needed, it is removed from the front of the chain (the first block in the chain). Conversely, when a block is deallocated, it is placed on the beginning of the chain.

6-9.2.3 BIT MAP

Another popular approach uses a sequence of bits, called a *bit map*, to indicate the status of each of the blocks. The status of the sixteen blocks of Figure 6-21a could be represented by the 16-bit string:

1111110000100000

where a 1 means the corresponding block is in use and a 0 means that block is free. This technique is used in the VM/370 system described in Chapter 9.

The principal advantage of the bit map scheme is that it can be kept in core, because it can be quite small. Thus the allocation can be performed at great speed.

6-10 DEVICE STRATEGY MODULE, I/O INITIATOR, DEVICE HANDLER

The basic functions of these routines are as follows:

1 Map the physical address into a device address (e.g., the physical address of file ETHEL record 4 is physical block 7, which is device address track 1, record 3).
2 Create the channel program, e.g., a program to do the following:
  a Seek to track 1
  b Search track 1 for record 3
  c Wait until disk reaches it
  d Read
3 Request the I/O, that is, call the I/O scheduler to schedule this I/O.
4 Handle the I/O interrupts and error conditions that may occur.

The algorithms for these routines have been covered previously in Chapter 5 (Device Management).

6-11 TRENDS IN INFORMATION MANAGEMENT

One may note the following similarities between the file system and the segmentation and paging concepts discussed in Chapter 3.

1 The notions of file and segment both involve the logical organization of information (i.e., files correspond to segments).
2 Both files and segments may be of arbitrary size and may grow in size dynamically.

3 Files and segments require two-dimensional addressing (i.e., file name and record number corresponds to segment name and byte number).

4 The file directory functionally corresponds to a segment map.

5 The file map functionally corresponds to a page map.

6 The memory buffers functionally correspond to memory blocks used for holding pages.

Once we recognize these similarities, we have two alternatives:

1 We can ignore the similarities and have separate mechanisms for the file system and paging/segment (e.g., OS/VS2, VM/370).

2 We can integrate the file system and the segmentation and paging mechanisms (e.g., MULTICS, TSS/360).

If a system is designed to integrate memory management and information management, hardware can be designed to help. For example, much of the reading and writing of files could be placed into hardware and only the initial access (OPEN, CLOSE) left in software. This situation is illustrated in Figure 6-22 where the segmentation and demand paging mechanisms of the MULTICS are shown on the left and the corresponding file system functions are shown on the right.

The hardware of Figure 6-22 is activated by a symbolic reference to some external segment. The hardware checks to see if that segment has been assigned a segment number (i.e., linkage bit set). If not, it produces an interrupt that activates a software module to search the file system hierarchy for the requested segment. This hardware and software module performs the function of the Symbolic File System— namely, it uniquely identifies the requested file.

Once the file has been identified, the hardware attempts to complete the access to that file. If the page table for that file is not in memory, the hardware produces an interrupt and the segment fault software is activated. Then the software finds the page tables and loads them into core. This function corresponds to opening a file and setting up the Active File Table—the task of the Basic File System.

The hardware again attempts to complete its access to the file. If the page of the file being accessed is not in core, the hardware produces an interrupt that activates the page fault mechanism. This function corresponds to transforming a logical reference into a physical address, which is the function of the Physical File System.

If space in core is needed for the requested page, the page removal algorithm is called (corresponding to the allocation module). Lastly, the I/O is performed to bring the page into core. Once the page is in core, the software and the hardware complete its access.

In the future we will probably see many more systems that merge many of the modules of memory management and information management.

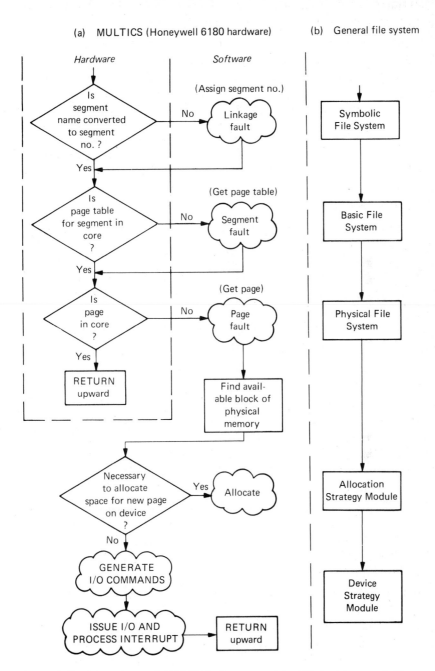

Figure 6-22 Comparisons of MULTICS file system (simplified with general file system model)

QUESTIONS

6-1

1 What purpose do the OPEN and CLOSE commands serve in a file system?
2 Could this purpose still be accomplished if explicit OPEN and CLOSE commands were to be eliminated from the file system? How?
3 What disadvantages or inefficiencies exist for your solution to (2)? (I.e., why do we normally have explicit OPEN and CLOSE commands?)

6-2 In the file system design presented in this chapter, we discussed the advantages of buffers to minimize the total number of I/O operations performed. Let us consider a situation where there are n files open (actively in use) and n buffers. (For the purposes of our example, let us assume that n = 3 and that the files are named A, B, and C.)

There are several strategies for allocating buffer usage to a file. Two possibilities are as follows:

- Assign a particular buffer to each file permanently.
- Treat the buffers as a pool and dynamically assign buffers to files as needed (similar to memory allocation on a demand paging system).

1 What advantages are there to assigning more than one buffer to a file? Give a sample sequence of requests that illustrates this strategy.
2 Describe a reasonable algorithm for dynamic assignment of buffers to files. Briefly describe your rationale. (In particular, when is a buffer assigned to a file and which buffer is selected?)

   a Describe a sequence of file system requests that operate very efficiently for the one-buffer-per-file strategy.

   b Likewise, describe a sequence that operates very inefficiently (e.g., buffer is useless, an I/O operation is required every time).

   c Describe a sequence of file system requests that operate very efficiently for the dynamic buffer assignment strategy. It would be nice if this sequence were the same as (b) above.

   d Likewise, describe a sequence that operates very inefficiently. It would be nice if this were the same as (a) above.

3 Based upon (c) and (d) above, which strategy would you choose? Why? Explain your criteria and assumptions.
4 Could the user provide any information to the file system that would be helpful to the buffer assignment problem?

6-3 If there were a single file directory for all files, would there still be a use for a per volume file directory? Why?

6-4 As was done in Figure 6-4, list the steps to satisfy the following READ requests.

1 READ FILE (ETHEL) RECORD (1) INTO LOCATION (12000).
2 READ FILE (ETHEL) RECORD (2) INTO LOCATION (12000).

6-5 State which module of the file system hierarchy handles each of the following problems, and how.
   1 Fragmentation of secondary storage
   2 Allowing the same name to be given to different files
   3 Adding a new logical structure, e.g., keyed files
   4 Adding a new physical structuring method
   5 Buffering
   6 Blocking

6-6 In the section on the Allocation Strategy Module (Section 6-9), we discussed several techniques for storage space allocation in information management (e.g., user specified allocation, automatic contiguous allocation, and dynamic allocation). The automatic allocation scheme of Section 6-9.1 is very similar to the partitioned memory technique.
   1 We noted that fragmentation on the storage device could be eliminated by recompacting the information. Typical disk and drum devices do not have relocation registers, so how can we relocate files?
   2 Why are recompacting and relocation of files often avoided?

6-7 Given the ability to have arbitrarily long file names and given also that users agree to use standardized naming conventions (e.g., incorporate name in file name), is there any difference between having a single-level, one-long-name file system and a hierarchical file directory system?

6-8 Your boss has been fortunate enough to win $7,000,000 worth of green stamps at his local grocery store and has gone out and purchased the latest in peripheral gear for the computer center, a spherical drum! It rotates in one direction and has well-defined circular tracks, although each track does not have the same storage capacity. Your job is to design a device/information management routine to handle this god-sent creation.

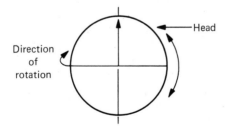

   1 Each track is numbered (0–100) and the end (0 and 100) tracks hold only half as much as the middle tracks (49, 50, 51) and track-to-track head movement is 10 ms. Where would be a good place (track) to put the volume file directory? Why?

2 Would you initiate a different pricing scheme for putting files on different parts of the drum? Why would a price differential even be considered?

3 How would you handle the allocation on this device? (*Note:* assume that it is not reasonable to use a single block size for the entire device.)

4 You now inherit $1,000,000 and decide to change the head mechanism so that only one track spirals around the sphere. (See picture below.) Does this buy you anything or does it cause trouble?

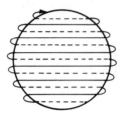

5 What color should the device be painted?

6-9

1 Given the hierarchical file system discussed, what effects would the removal of each of the following components have? What measures would be needed to compensate for its removal? (In each case assume that all other portions of the system except the one indicated are still present.)

  a file map

  b programmers' private directories

  c length entry in file directory

2 Why does the file directory contain an entry for itself?

6-10 In Section 6-7.3 we described the Index-Sequential Access Method (ISAM) which makes it possible to specify the next record to be read or written by either:

1 Next record (ordered by key)

2 Record that matches a particular key

ISAM accomplishes the former access mode by physically writing the records sequentially ordered by key when the file was created (i.e., the input data must be sorted in advance). It accomplishes the latter access mode by three I/O operations:

● Read and search master index to determine which cylinder the data are on (typically 200 or fewer entries).

● Read and search the cylinder index to determine which of the tracks the data are on (typically 20 or fewer entries).

● Read and search the track for the corresponding record that matches a key (typically 40 or fewer entries).

(*Note:* 200 × 20 × 40 = 160,000 data records; that's a lot!)

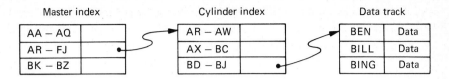

Master index			Cylinder index			Data track	
AA − AQ			AR − AW			BEN	Data
AR − FJ			AX − BC			BILL	Data
BK − BZ			BD − BJ			BING	Data

1 Propose an alternative implementation of an ISAM-type access method. You may consider various table-lookup techniques (e.g., binary search, hashing), chained records, etc. (*Note:* read the other parts of this question before answering this part.)

2 ISAM requires only 1 or 0 (if in buffer) I/O operations to get the next sequential (ordered) record (ignoring overflow, etc.). How many I/O operations does your approach require?

3 ISAM requires only three I/O operations to get a particular record accessed by key. How many I/Os do you need?

4 How might additional buffer space reduce number of I/O operations for ISAM?

5 Insertions and deletions are awkward with ISAM. They can cause the data track to become partially unsorted (a minor annoyance that can complicate sequential reading, e.g., BEN, BING, BILL, etc.). Furthermore, if too many insertions are made to a data track, the new data must be placed in an "overflow area." This can greatly reduce performance for both sequential and direct-access usage. How does your scheme handle insertions and deletions? How efficient is your scheme compared with ISAM?

6 List briefly the advantages and disadvantages of your scheme compared with ISAM. In particular, note any points that are not covered by parts 2 and 5

6-11 Interstellar Biodegradable Manufacturing Company has developed a laser holographic memory device. This device has a random access time almost as fast as main memory (e.g., 5 *micro*seconds, *not milli*seconds) and a capacity and cost comparable to disk storage.

This device has two peculiar attributes:

- All information must be stored or read as increments of 128 bytes (i.e., each addressable location holds 128 bytes). It can access and read/write 128 bytes in 10 microseconds.

- Since writing requires use of the high-intensity laser, a given record cannot be rewritten more than 100 times; otherwise, the material starts to degenerate (biodegradably). A record can be safely read an unlimited number of times.

The device is to be used to hold the file system information. We are considering changes to our existing file system.

1 Considering the speed of this device, is there any value in having multiple main memory buffers? Explain why or why not?

2 How would information management handle the restriction on the number of rewrites allowed? Explain your technique briefly but clearly.

3 What modules of the file system would have to be affected by your solution to part (2). Explain briefly.

6-12 In a file system with multilevel directories, it is often very inconvenient for a user to refer to one of his files by its fully qualified name. A file name such as SYSCATLG.SYSMASTER.SYSDIR.GROUP.USER.ALPHA should not have to be written out in its entirety; we would like the programmer to be able to call it ALPHA. What extra bookkeeping must the file system perform in order to make this possible?

6-13 In Section 6-6.1 the concept of an Access Control List (ACL) for each file was introduced. The ACL lists all the users authorized to access that file. Consider an alternate implementation whereby a User Control List (UCL) is associated with each user. The UCL lists all the files that the user is authorized to access. Does the UCL approach offer any advantages over the ACL? Which scheme would you recommend and why?

6-14 Assuming that a file of variable-length records is organized as shown in Figure 6-11, present a flowchart or PL/I program (similar in style to the one in Section 6-3.3) for a Logical File System routine that can be used for direct-access reading. State any assumptions necessary. (*Note:* this routine may call only upon the services of the Physical File System routines.)

6-15 Secondary storage space requirements can be reduced by using data compression techniques within a file. One scheme is to never allocate a storage block whose contents are all zeros. Furthermore, if a currently allocated storage block is altered (by writing a record of zeros) so that it becomes all zeros, it is deallocated.

1 Describe a situation in which this technique is likely to save substantial space.

2 Which modules of the file system must be changed to incorporate this feature? Why?

6-16 Since many files are used sequentially or partly sequentially, it is desirable to have all the blocks clustered together on the storage device (i.e., on the same or adjacent cylinders). Present an algorithm for dynamic allocation (see Section 6-9.2) that clusters the blocks.

6-17 In a hierarchical file directory environment (see Figure 6-8), it is necessary to specify a complete path to uniquely identify a file (e.g., DONOVAN's SINE might be different from MADNICK's MATH's SINE). A user program could specify the complete path name or, for simplicity, merely its local name (e.g., SINE). In order to resolve the potential ambiguity that results, search rules (default or user specified) are used to determine which directories should be searched and in which order.

1 What benefits does the local name plus search rules offer over use of complete path names?
2 What modules of the file system are affected by this strategy?
3 Present an implementation of this search rules scheme. Describe any additional control cards, tables, and/or special subroutines needed.

<table>
<tr><td>

Design of a
Sample Operating System

</td><td>

</td></tr>
</table>

7-1 INTRODUCTION

In this chapter we present a sample operating system intended to be a pedagogical aid to the understanding of the principles of operating systems and the way in which the various modules are connected.

In contrast to other operating systems, e.g., OS/360, or MULTICS, whose main purpose is not pedagogical, this system is simple and easy for students to learn. It is also comparatively small in that it occupies fewer than 2,500 cards of assembly language statements.

This operating system does not include language processors or utility programs, but instead implements a basic system nucleus that provides features such as multi-programming dynamic memory allocation, and device management to which any level supervisor and associated programs could be easily fitted. These are the features most essential to learning the fundamentals of operating systems.

The system does include a simple top-level supervisor to provide processing of the job streams. Thus the operating system is complete in that it could be used for some real-world application such as controlling a large number of real-time devices.

Finally, this system has deliberately been designed in a modular and structured manner. As a result, the relevant sections for processor management, memory management, and device management in particular can easily be identified. Although the specific implementation is for the IBM System/360, the algorithms and techniques are applicable to most contemporary computer systems. All databases are described in a PL/I-type declaration structure to facilitate ease of reading. The 360

This sample operating system is based upon the Master's thesis "Design and Implementation of an Example Operating System" by John D. DeTreville, M.I.T., June 1972. Others, notably Richard Swift and Paul Fredette, assisted in debugging it. This work was supported in part by Project MAC, an M.I.T. research program sponsored by the Advanced Research Projects Agency, Department of Defense, under Office of Naval Research Contract Number Nonr-4102(01).

assembly language code is also provided for the reader interested in studying the detailed implementation or in actually running the operating system.

7-2 OVERVIEW OF THE SYSTEM

The sample system is a multiprogramming system designed for the IBM System/360. Any types of I/O devices can be supported, but currently system support is provided only for card readers and line printers. User programs can, however, provide their own routines for nonstandard devices. No file system is provided.

Memory allocation for the user programs is in the form of dynamic partition allocation. The user must specify the amount of storage required for his job in terms of 2K-byte increments from 2K bytes upward. The system currently requires about 6K bytes for its own routines; the rest of memory is available for user programs and system tables.

The system is capable of supporting multiple job streams coming from different input devices (in this case, readers), with the output being directed to different output devices (in this case, printers). Each job stream consists of a number of jobs stacked in order, as illustrated in Figure 7-1.

A job consists of a $JOB card, followed by a single object deck, followed by optional data. The format of the $JOB card is

$JOB,core,name=devtype,name=devtype,. . .

as in

$JOB,8K,FILEA=IN,FILEB=OUT

The core field gives the amount of core required for the job; in this example it is 8K. The "name=devtype" field can be repeated any number of times, including zero. The "name" gives the name by which the user program can reference this device. The name chosen is up to the user; thus, flexible, device-independent referencing of devices is provided. The "devtype" indicates the type of device to be assigned. At present, three types of devices are available.

The type "IN" specifies the system input unit, i.e., the card reader for this job stream. The type "OUT" specifies the system output unit, i.e., the line printer. The type "EXCP" indicates a nonstandard device for which the user will supply his own handler routine. Currently, the $JOB card can contain, at most, one reference to IN, one reference to OUT, and one reference to EXCP.

The object deck, which immediately follows the $JOB card, has the same format as the standard OS/360 object deck. However, external references are not allowed (i.e., subroutine linkage facilities are not provided). Following the object deck are the card input data to the user program for cases where there is a reference to "IN" on the $JOB card.

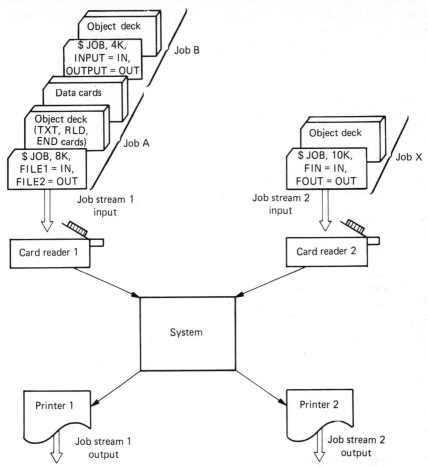

Figure 7-1   Overview of multiple job stream multiprogramming system

The user's program may use parallel processing (i.e., create multiple processes), and there are features to control this, along with flexible facilities for communication between different parallel execution paths of the program. The system automatically schedules the various jobs in the system, and their processes. The sophistication of the scheduling is, of course, limited by the brevity of the implementation. The system could easily be extended to provide more advanced features and facilities.

7-3 DESIGN OVERVIEW

The design of the sample operating system follows closely the framework presented in Figure 7-2.

We build our concept of an operating system around a process. We recognize that there are certain requirements necessary to support processes. A process in the

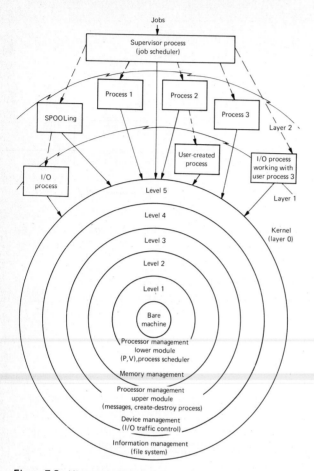

Figure 7-2 Hierarchical operating system structure

proper environment could call certain basic functions. Unfortunately, most present-day hardware does not provide these basic functions.

Thus our first design task is to build the basic functions (extended machine) for process support. These comprise the nucleus or kernel of the operating system. Examples of these basic functions are the P and V operations, basic multiprocessing support, and traffic controlling. The reader can think of these software functions as being executed in the same way as hardware instructions.

7-3.1 Extended Machine Approach

It is best to think of the kernel as being an extended machine that consists of a number of extended instructions. In this implementation, the extended instructions are accomplished by means of the Supervisor Call instruction. For example, the instruction sequence:

```
              LA    2,REQUEST      SET ARGUMENTS
              SVC   C'A'           ALLOCATE MEMORY
              .
              .
              .
REQUEST   DC    F'32'          REQUEST 32 BYTES
LOCATION  DS    A              ADDRESS SUPPLIED BY SYSTEM
ALIGN     DC    F'8'           DOUBLEWORD ALIGNMENT
```

will request 32 bytes, doubleword aligned, from memory management. A complete listing of SVC primitives and their associated calling sequences is presented in Section 7-5.2.

Certain operating system functions can be provided in the form of special system processes rather than system primitives. In this sample system there are several such processes, including the supervisor processes (job stream handlers) and the device handler processes. Each job stream has a separate supervisor handler process, and there is a separate device handler process for each device used. Furthermore, a user's process may create additional processes. Processes that belong to the same job are called a *process group*.

7-3.2 Summary of Concepts Used

Many of the features of this operating system were originally introduced elsewhere. The concept of a system implemented on various hierarchical levels was introduced by Dijkstra (1968), who also introduced the concept of the process synchronization semaphore. Madnick (1969) extended the hierarchical approach into file system design. The form of the message system for interprocess communication comes from Hansen (1970), who also elucidated the concept of a system nucleus. Much of the terminology and many of the concepts in process control were introduced by Saltzer (1966) and implemented in MULTICS, from which several ideas in this area were taken. The view of the operating system as a group of resource management modules (and the way in which these break down) comes from Donovan (1972). Additionally, several key characteristics were taken from such operating systems as OS/360, MFT (IBM, 8) and MVT (IBM, 1), and CTSS (Corbato, 1962; Crisman, 1965).

7-4 LEVELS AND LAYERS OF THE SAMPLE OPERATING SYSTEM

The hierarchical construction of the kernel is such that each successive level, from the bottom up, depends only on the existence of those levels below it, and not on those above it. This approach has the advantage of pedagogical clarity, offers debugging ease, and may be relevant to the development of new theory.

The five levels and layers (or modules) of the sample operating system are:

Levels   –   ⎡ Process Management, lower module (lowest)
                 | Memory management module
                 ⎣ Process Management, upper module

Layers   –   ⎡ Device Management
                 ⎣ Supervisor Process module   (highest)

The functions of process management have been split into a lower module and an upper module, one on either side of memory management. This is because certain parts of process management (those in the upper module) depend on memory management routines, but memory management itself depends on certain process management routines that must be in a module below memory management.

The supervisor process module and the user program operate in very nearly the same environment. This results from the extended machine approach, and gives simplicity to the operating system.

7-4.1 Process Management, Lower Module

This module of process management provides processor multiplexing, as well as basic primitive operations for interprocess synchronization. It may be viewed as the "multiprogramming support" module.

The module schedules and runs processes that are eligible to be run. A process in the system is usually eligible to be run unless it is waiting for the completion of some external event, such as the completion of an input/output operation, or for a signal from another process. Processes are scheduled by the traffic controller in a simple round-robin fashion. A process may run until it becomes temporarily ineligible to run, for reasons referred to above, or until a certain amount of time— in this system, 50 ms—called the quantum of time, passes, after which the process is stopped but remains eligible to continue running later. In either case, the traffic controller then selects another process and causes it to begin to run.

This module also provides basic primitives for the synchronization of processes. These primitives are called the P and V operations. Both operations act on a semaphore, which has an associated integer value. The P operation has two possible effects. If the value of the semaphore is greater than zero, it merely causes one to be subtracted from that value. If the value of the semaphore is zero or less, it causes one to be subtracted from its value and the process issuing the P operation must wait for a signal from another process, thus becoming temporarily ineligible. This signaling will be caused by another process executing a V operation on the same semaphore.

The V operation also follows one of two possible courses of action. If there are no processes currently waiting because of a P operation on this semaphore (i.e., if the semaphore value is nonnegative), it adds one to the value of the semaphore and continues. If there are processes waiting, the semaphore is incremented by one and a signal is sent to one of the processes to stop waiting; that process then becomes eligible for scheduling. A flowchart of these operations is presented in Figure 7-3.

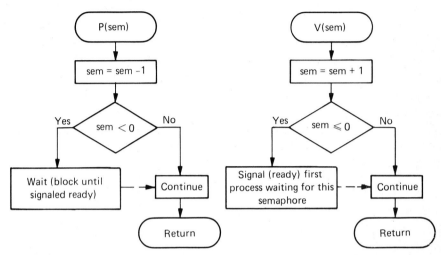

Figure 7-3 P and V operations

The P and V operations, together with semaphores, have several useful applications. For example, a semaphore with an initial value of one can be associated with some database to serve as a lock on that database. If all processes accessing that database perform a P operation on the associated semaphore before accessing the database and then perform V operations on that semaphore afterward, it is possible for only one process to access the database at any one time, thus ensuring the integrity of that database.

This module may be entered explicitly through SVCs, such as P and V, or implicitly through timer interrupt (quantum exceeded).

7-4.2 Memory Management Module

This module performs the operations necessary for dynamic allocation and freeing of memory. It is used for job partition allocation as well as for allocating space used by the operating system. It provides routines that will, on request, allocate a block of memory of a given size and a given address alignment (e.g., on a double-word boundary), or free a block of memory of a given size at a given location. To accomplish this, the module, using a best fit algorithm, keeps a list of "free" storage, taking from or adding to this list as requests are processed. Communication with this module is by means of explicit SVC calls.

The memory management module uses the process management lower module for several purposes. To guarantee that the same piece of memory is not accidentally allocated to two processes, memory management "locks" its databases via an SVC P as described in the previous section. After the memory has been allocated and the tables correctly updated, the database may be "unlocked" and made available to other processes.

7-4.3 Process Management, Upper Module

This module provides routines for the control of processes (e.g., their creation and deletion from the system), and also provides for interprocess communication with buffered messages. Communication with this module is in the form of explicit calls.

The module provides a method by which messages may be sent between processes. A process may issue an SVC call requesting that a k-character message be sent to a process of a certain name. A process can also issue a call to read the text and name of the sender. Messages may be of arbitrary length and any number of messages may be waiting to be read by a process.

As can be seen from the above, this is the level at which we introduce the concept of a process name. Names are chosen at process-creation time and are used to reference processes within this upper module. As mentioned earlier, this module also introduces the concept of a group, which is the set of processes associated with a job within the system.

This upper module depends directly on both the process management lower module and the memory management module. It uses the P and V primitives to provide synchronization between the sender and the receiver in message processing. Also, since this module runs in the process of its caller, there is an implicit dependency on the traffic controller. The memory management module is called to allocate or free space needed to store system information concerning processes, and to provide temporary buffers to store messages.

7-4.4 Device Management Module and Processes

This module provides the routines necessary to issue the appropriate input/output commands to external devices. Like the other higher layers (i.e., the supervisor process module and user program), this module runs in a separate process (in this case, one per device). Communication with this process is through messages sent to it, and the status of the result is returned via messages that it sends back.

When necessary, the device management process is provided with sufficient information to issue input/output instructions via the message facility. Its major purpose is to issue the I/O and then, after an interrupt occurs, interpret the status information available for a return message.

This module depends directly on the process management lower module in that it uses semaphores as locks against two processes simultaneously attempting to access the same device. A semaphore is used as a lock on a block of information concerning the device. Another semaphore is used to wait for an interrupt by performing a P operation on the semaphore with initial value 0.

A special portion of the device management routine handles interrupts. When an I/O interrupt occurs, the interrupt handler immediately gets control and uses the device number from the interrupt code to find the corresponding Unit Control Block. The UCB contains the semaphore used by the device management process to wait for I/O completion. The handler performs a V operation on this semaphore and then merely returns to preinterrupt status by reloading the I/O old PSW. Thus an I/O interrupt is converted into a V operation.

The device management in this sample operating system is simple. There are two reasons for this. First, all I/O devices are dedicated: there are no shared or virtual devices supported. Second, the only I/O devices supported, card readers and printers, operate via a multiplexor channel; thus, we can treat each device as if it has its own channel and avoid the need for an I/O scheduler.

7-4.5 Supervisor Module and Process

This module serves as the job scheduler. It runs as a separate process, one per job stream (thus, one per group). It can use all the features provided by the previous modules to create an interface for the processing of user jobs.

The supervisor process allocates a partition for each job in sequence the size of which is specified on the $JOB card. It creates and starts the appropriate device management processes. It then loads the user's object deck into the partition and creates and starts a process in that partition. After all this has been done, the supervisor process is not needed again until the user's job ends. It stops running and waits for a message signaling completion to come from the user program. When completion is signaled, the supervisor process cleans up by destroying any processes it might have created for this job and freeing the partition allocated, and then it goes on to the next job in the input stream.

7-4.6 The User Program and Process

The user program is loaded into the partition of memory allocated to it by the supervisor process. At first, just one process is created for the user's job, but this process can create others to run in parallel. When the job is completed, primitives are provided by which the user program can signal either successful or unsuccessful completion.

The user program runs in problem state and with nonzero protection key. Within these restrictions, the program can utilize most of the facilities of the other modules of the system. Certain nucleus routines, such as the P and V operations, are restricted and cannot be accessed by the user's program. The interprocess communication message facility (process management, upper level) can be used to accomplish the same synchronization as the P and V operation.

7-5 NUCLEUS DATABASES AND ROUTINES

In the following sections each of the levels of the operating system just described will be presented in greater detail. For complete information the reader should examine the actual program listings reproduced at the end of this chapter.

All the major databases are given for each level. The descriptions consist of a PL/I-style structure declaration followed by details on each of the fields. As you will see, the databases are the key ingredient of an operating system. If the databases are well designed, creating actual routines that manipulate them becomes a simple matter.

7-5.1 Supervisor Call (SVC) Handler

Several routines don't conveniently fit our hierarchical level structure. The most notable case is the SVC handler used to activate the extended machine instructions and transfer between levels. The SVC instruction on the 370 provides for a 1-byte operand; this byte is used to store a mnemonic for the operation to be performed (e.g., SVC C'P', SVC C'V'). When an SVC instruction is issued, a supervisor call interrupt occurs and control transfers to the SVC handler routine. The handler examines the SVC code to determine whether it corresponds to a legitimate operation and whether the caller is allowed to request the operation. (Recall that certain operations are not available to user programs.) After a copy of the registers has been saved, control is transferred to the specified routine by means of a Load PSW instruction.

7-5.2 Listing of Nucleus Routines

Figure 7-4 lists the nucleus routines. The SVC code and function are specified for each routine. In addition, the list indicates (1) the routine that processes it; (2) the save area used (I=interrupt save area, F=fault save area, M=memory save area, S=system semaphore save area); (3) whether the routine is interruptable (I=interruptable; NI=not interruptable); and (4) whether the routine is user-callable (U=user-callable; NU=not user-callable).

The save areas are assigned so that, in the course of one module's calling on another, no save area is ever overlaid. Note, as the following descriptions of routines show, that the calls that might cause the traffic controller to be entered,

SVC CODE	FUNCTION	ROUTINE	SAVE AREA	INTERRUPTABLE	USER CALLABLE
P	The P synchronization primitive	XP	S	NI	NU
V	The V synchronization primitive	XV	S	NI	NU
.	Enter traffic controller	XPER	I	NI	NU
!	Enter smc section	XEXC	I	NI	NU
,	Leave smc section	XCOM	I	NI	NU
A	Allocate a block of memory	XA	M	I	NU
E	Allocate a block of workspace memory	XE	M	I	NU
F	Free a block of memory	XF	M	I	NU
B	Link a block onto the FSB chain	XB	I	NI	NU
C	Create process	XC	F	I	U
D	Destroy process	XD	F	I	U
H	Halt job and signal supervisor	XH	F	I	U
I	Insert a PCB into the chain	XI	I	NI	NU
J	Remove a PCB from the chain	XJ	I	NI	NU
N	Find a PCB given its name	XN	I	NI	U
R	Read message	XR	F	I	U
S	Send message	XS	F	I	U
Y	Start process	XY	F	NI	U
Z	Stop process	XZ	F	I	U
?	Abnormally terminate this job	XQUE	I	NI	U

Figure 7-4 List of SVC operations

namely XP and XPER, must use the I save area when changing between processes. All save areas except the System Semaphore save area exist on a per process basis (see PCB database description).

All these routines run in key 0, allowing unrestricted memory references. Routines XP, XV, XB, XI, XJ, XN, XY, XPER, XEXC, XCOM, and XQUE operate with interrupts disabled (masked off) while the others operate with interrupts enabled. Disabling interrupts assures the routine that no processes can run while that routine is in operation.

All routines that operate with interrupts on (namely XA, XAUTO, XF, XH, XC, XD, XR, XS, and XZ) call the XEXC (enter "system must complete" mode) routine upon entry and the XCOM (leave "system must complete" mode) routine upon exit. This is to assure that a process will not be destroyed while it still has an important system lock set.

Only certain selected routines are callable directly by the user. These are XC, XD, XH, XN, XR, XS, XY, XZ, and XQUE routines; the rest are usable only by the other system routines. These primitives of process management upper module are safe for the user to call; allowing a direct call to the others could lead to a breach of security.

Arguments are passed to the nucleus routine in an area pointed to by register 2. Any returned values must be placed in this argument list (e.g., location of memory area allocated by SVC C'A').

7-6 PROCESSOR MANAGEMENT (LOWER MODULE) DATABASES

The processor management (lower module) routines and databases are used by most of the operating system's routines. The Process Control Block (PCB) and semaphores are especially important databases.

7-6.1 Process Control Block

The Process Control Block stores the information associated with a process. There is one PCB for every process in the system. The PCB is defined by:

```
DECLARE
1  PCB BASED  (PCBPTR)  ALIGNED,
    2  NAME CHARACTER  (8),
    2  NEXT_PCB_THIS_GROUP POINTER,
    2  LAST_PCB_THIS_GROUP POINTER,
    2  NEXT_PCB_ALL POINTER,
    2  LAST_PCB_ALL POINTER,
    2  STOPPED BIT  (1),
    2  BLOCKED BIT  (1),
    2  IN_SMC BIT  (8),
    2  STOP_WAITING BIT  (1),
    2  MESSAGE_SEMAPHORE_COMMON LIKE  (SEMAPHORE),
    2  MESSAGE_SEMAPHORE_RECEIVER LIKE  (SEMAPHORE),
    2  FIRST_MESSAGE POINTER,
    2  NEXT_SEMAPHORE_WAITER POINTER,
    2  STOPPER_SEMAPHORE LIKE  (SEMAPHORE),
    2  STOPPEE_SEMAPHORE LIKE  (SEMAPHORE),
    2  AUTO_STORAGE_SIZE FIXED BINARY  (31,0),
    2  AUTO_STORAGE_ADDRESS POINTER,
    2  INTERRUPT_SAVE_AREA LIKE  (SAVE_AREA),
    2  FAULT_SAVE_AREA LIKE  (SAVE_AREA),
    2  MEMORY_SAVE_AREA LIKE  (SAVE_AREA);
```

where the fields are as follows:

NAME: This field contains an eight-character string giving the name for this process. A name is supplied for a process by the process that creates it. These names are used to reference processes in calls to the process management upper module routines.

NEXT_PCB_THIS_GROUP: This is a pointer to the next PCB in the same group. The set of processes in the system is divided into a number of mutually exclusive subsets known as groups; the processes in each group are chained together in a circular list. This pointer is the forward pointer in that chain. All names within a group are unique, and naming of processes is always relative to a group.

LAST_PCB_THIS_GROUP: This is the backward pointer for the chain of PCBs in this group.

NEXT_PCB_ALL: In addition to being chained together in the group-oriented fashion mentioned above, all PCBs in the system are independently linked into a single circular list. This is for purposes of process management, lower module (the traffic controller, in particular), which is not concerned with groups. The process group is an upper-module concept within process management. This pointer is the forward pointer within this chain.

LAST_PCB_ALL: This is the backward pointer for the chain of all PCBs.

STOPPED: This bit is zero when the associated process is not stopped, and one when it is. A process is not considered runnable by the traffic controller if it is stopped. When a process is first created, it is in the stopped state, and may be started by some other process performing a "start process" primitive for it. A non-stopped process may be stopped by another process in the same group performing a "stop process" primitive for it, usually as a prelude to destroying it.

BLOCKED: This bit is zero when the associated process is not blocked, and one when it is. A process that is blocked is not considered runnable by the traffic controller. A process is normally not blocked, but can go blocked if it performs a P operation on a semaphore with a nonpositive value. It will be made nonblocked when some other process performs a V operation on the semaphore.

IN_SMC: This byte is nonzero if the process is in an smc section and zero if it is not. (The term "smc" stands for "system must complete.") If a process is in an smc section, an attempt to stop that process will be deferred until that process leaves the smc section. There are primitives to enter and leave an smc section. Since smc sections may be nested, this byte indicates the depth of nesting.

STOP_WAITING: This bit is one if a stop request is waiting for this process to leave an smc section and zero if there is no stop request waiting. It is set by the "stop process" primitive.

MESSAGE_SEMAPHORE_COMMON: This is a semaphore with an initial value of one. Whenever another process attempts to send a message to this process or if the process attempts to read a message sent to it, this semaphore is used as a lock on the message chain pointed to by FIRST_MESSAGE during the period when the message chain is being searched or modified.

MESSAGE_SEMAPHORE_RECEIVER: This semaphore is used to regulate a process receiving message. Its initial value is zero. Whenever a message is sent to this process, the sending process performs a V operation on the semaphore, thus adding one to its value. Whenever an attempt is made to read a message sent to this process, a P operation is performed on the semaphore. Thus if no messages were currently readable, the "read message" routine would wait until there were some.

FIRST_MESSAGE: This is a pointer to the first message waiting to be read by this process. If there are no messages readable by this process (i.e., if the value of the MESSAGE_SEMAPHORE_RECEIVER is zero), the value of the pointer is meaningless.

NEXT_SEMAPHORE_WAITER: All processes currently waiting on the same semaphore are chained together in a linear list. The head of this list is pointed to by a field in the semaphore, and the PCBs in the list are linked together by this field. The length of the list is taken to be the maximum of zero and the negative of the value as stored in the semaphore.

STOPPER_SEMAPHORE: This semaphore is used to wait on stopping a process in an smc section. The process attempting to do the stopping performs a P operation on the semaphore, which has an initial value of zero, whenever it notices that the process it is trying to stop has a nonzero IN_SMC byte. When the process to be stopped attempts to execute a "leave smc" section primitive and finds the STOP_WAITING bit set, it performs a V operation on the semaphore, and then a P operation on the STOPPER_SEMAPHORE. This situation is explained further in Section 7-11.10.

STOPPEE_SEMAPHORE: This semaphore, which has an initial value of zero, is used to stop a process that has had a stop postponed until it leaves an smc section. It performs a P operation on this semaphore, thus blocking itself until the stopping process can complete the stop request.

AUTO_STORAGE_SIZE: This entry contains the number of bytes of memory (if any) allocated to a process for special workspace by the SVC C'E' operation. The information is used to ensure that the storage is correctly freed when the process is destroyed. If no storage has been allocated, its value is zero.

AUTO_STORAGE_ADDRESS: This pointer is the address of the first byte of any special storage allocated by SVC C'E'. It is used to free the storage when the process is destroyed. Its initial value of zero remains unchanged if no such storage is allocated.

INTERRUPT_SAVE_AREA, FAULT_SAVE_AREA, MEMORY_SAVE_AREA: These are save areas; their formats are all the same and are described in the SAVE_AREA section below. They are used to save a copy of the registers, PSW, and other status information when an SVC routine is called. The particular save area used in each case was indicated earlier in Figure 7-4.

7-6.2 Save Areas

Whenever a system routine needs a save area for storing the status conditions at the time of entry, in order to restore them upon exit, it uses one of the three save areas in the PCB or the system save area (P or V only). The save areas look like this:

```
DECLARE
1  SAVE_AREA BASED (SAVE_AREA_POINTER),
    2  OLD_PSW LIKE (PSW),
    2  OLD_REGISTERS  (0:15)  LIKE (REGISTER),
    2  TEMPORARY  (3)  BIT  (32);
```

where the fields are used as follows:

OLD_PSW: This is the old PSW upon entry to the routine.

OLD_REGISTERS: These are the old general purpose registers upon entry to the routine.

TEMPORARY: This is a temporary storage area of three words. It is used mainly to construct argument lists (which must be held in storage) for calling other routines. If a routine ever needs more than three words of temporaries, it can use these three words to construct a call to the memory allocation routine.

7-6.3 Semaphores

Semaphores are used for basic, low-level synchronization of processes. They can be accessed either by P or V operations, or their value field can be examined directly. Their format is as follows:

```
DECLARE
1  SEMAPHORE BASED  (SEMAPHORE_POINTER),
    2  VALUE FIXED BINARY  (31,0),
    2  FIRST_WAITER POINTER;
```

where the fields are used as follows:

VALUE: This is the value of the semaphore. A P operation always subtracts one from this value, and a V operation always adds one. The initial value of the semaphore must be nonnegative.

FIRST_WAITER: For semaphores with negative values, this is the pointer to the first in a list of PCBs chained together by their NEXT_SEMAPHORE_WAITER pointers. The length of the list is the magnitude of the semaphore value. A P operation on a semaphore with nonpositive value places the PCB for that process at the end of the list, whereas a V operation on a semaphore with negative value modifies this pointer essentially to take the first PCB off the list (after which it receives a wakeup); thus we have a First-in First-out queue.

7-6.4 RUNNING

This is a pointer to the PCB of the process currently being run. It is set by the traffic controller, and is used whenever it is necessary to access the PCB for "this" (the current) process.

7-6.5 NEXTTRY

This is a pointer to the PCB of the process that the traffic controller will next try to run. The pointer is set by the traffic controller to be the same as the NEXT_PCB_ALL pointer in the PCB pointed to by RUNNING; however, it may be modified by the execution of a V operation.

7-6.6 NEXTTRY_MODIFIED

This bit is zero if NEXTTRY has not been modified since being set by the traffic controller, and one if it has.

7-6.7 SYSTEM_SEM_SAVE_AREA

This is a save area used by processor management (lower module) when switching processes. Its use is indicated in Figure 7-4.

7-6.8 Sample Databases

An example of the key processor management databases, as they might appear in actual operation, is shown in Figure 7-5. In order to simplify the diagram, only a portion of the total PCB fields are included.

Two process groups, consisting of a total of seven processes, and three semaphores are included in the example. JOB1, IN1, and OUT1 form one process group and JOB2, JOB2SUB, IN2, and OUT2 form the other. IN2 is the currently running process and OUT2 is the candidate to be run next. Processes IN1, JOB2, and JOB2SUB are "blocked" while waiting on semaphores. IN1 is waiting for a V operation on semaphore A. JOB2 and JOB2SUB are both waiting on semaphore B. When a V operation is performed on semaphore B, process JOB2SUB will be made "ready" but process JOB2 will still be "blocked" while waiting on B.

7-7 PROCESSOR MANAGEMENT (LOWER MODULE) ROUTINES

7-7.1 Traffic Controller

The traffic controller serves the purpose of creating a process-oriented environment. It runs "between processes," as it were. It gains control whenever a timer

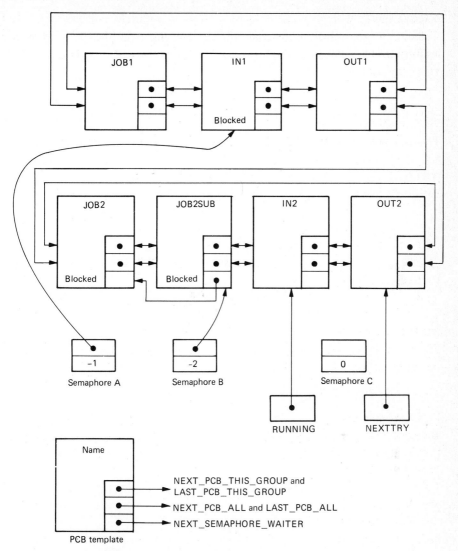

Figure 7-5 Sample processor management databases

runout trap is detected, a **P** operation is performed on a semaphore with nonpositive value, or control is specifically relinquished to it via the SVC C'.' (XPER) operation.

The traffic controller performs the basic task of processor multiplexing and shares the computer's processor among the various processes runnable at any one time. A process is said to be runnable if both the **STOPPED** and **BLOCKED** bits of the PCB are off. When a process is entered, it runs until its quantum of time is consumed (a timer runout trap is set to occur 50 ms after a process is entered), or if it must wait for synchronization with another process (a **P** operation is performed on a semaphore with nonpositive value), or when it specifically relinquishes control to the traffic controller via a special call. The overall flow to the traffic controller is illustrated in Figure 7-6.

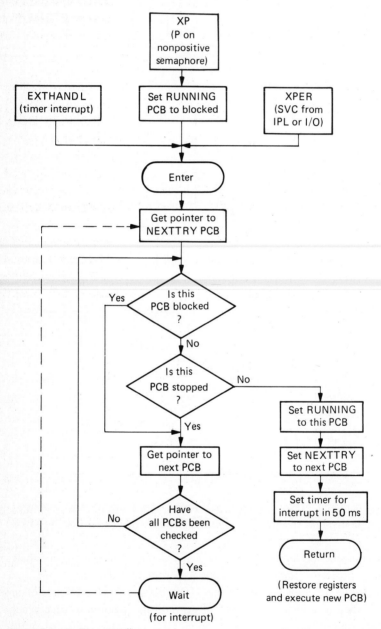

Figure 7-6   Traffic controller

All entries to the traffic controller transfer immediately to routine XPER. This routine runs in key 0 with all interrupts disabled. The old registers and PSW of the process just left are stored in the PCB's INTERRUPT_SAVE_AREA.

Beginning with the process pointed to by NEXTTRY, the traffic controller searches through all PCBs in the system and uses the NEXT_PCB_ALL chain to find the first PCB that is neither stopped nor blocked. If there is such a PCB, the traffic controller sets RUNNING to this PCB, sets NEXTTRY to point to the next PCB in the "all" chain, sets the timer to interrupt in 50 ms, and proceeds to call a standard service routine to reload the registers and PSW from the INTERRUPT_SAVE_AREA in the RUNNING PCB, thus beginning to run this new process.

If all PCBs in the "all" chain are stopped or blocked, the traffic controller loads a PSW with location set to XPER, but with the wait state on and interrupts enabled. Later, when an input/output interrupt occurs, the old PSW's wait bit is set off before it is reloaded. Thus the traffic controller waits until an input/output interrupt occurs before it has another try at scheduling. In this situation, there can be no processes runnable until such an interrupt occurs, although there should always be one runnable immediately afterwards.

7-7.2 Routine XP (P Operation)

This routine implements the P primitive. Upon entry, it is assumed that register 2 points to a semaphore. The routine subtracts one from the value, and then returns if the result is nonnegative.

If the result is negative, however, the PCB for this process is inserted at the end of the list of processes waiting on this semaphore. After the information from the SYSTEM_SEM_SAVE_AREA is transferred to the INTERRUPT_SAVE_AREA in the PCB, control transfers directly to the traffic controller.

7-7.3 Routine XV (V Operation)

This routine implements the V primitive. Upon entry, it is assumed that register 2 points to a semaphore. The routine adds one to the value of that semaphore. If the resulting value is greater than zero, it returns.

If the value is zero or less, this means there are processes waiting on the semaphore. The first process is removed from the list, and its BLOCKED bit is set to zero, thus allowing the process to be scheduled once again.

To allow the newly awakened process to be scheduled within a short time the XV routine typically sets the NEXTTRY pointer to point to this PCB, and then sets the NEXTTRY_MODIFIED bit on. This is not done, however, when the bit is already on. Thus, if one process wakes up a large number of others in the course of its execution, the first to be awakened is the first to be run after the current one. The XV routine then returns.

7-7.4 Routine XPER (Enter Traffic Controller)

This is a direct entry to the traffic controller. It is used only by the IPL routine to start the system going, or by the input/output interrupt handler if it must schedule a special process quickly for real-time response.

7-7.5 Routine XEXC (Enter SMC)

This routine serves to notify that an SMC section is about to be entered. The routine increments the IN_SMC byte in its PCB by one and returns.

7-7.6 Routine XCOM (Leave SMC)

This routine serves to notify that an SMC section is being left. It decrements the IN_SMC byte by one. If the value is still positive, the routine returns. If the value is zero, the STOP_WAITING bit in the PCB is checked. If it is off, XCOM returns.

If the STOP_WAITING bit is on, however, then it is reset to zero, a V operation is performed on the STOPPER_SEMAPHORE, and a P operation is performed on the STOPPEE_SEMAPHORE.

7-8 MEMORY MANAGEMENT DATABASES

7-8.1 Free Storage Block (FSB)

All FSBs are chained together in order of increasing size. No two FSBs are ever adjacent in memory; rather, any two adjacent blocks would be collapsed together into a single larger block.

Whenever an allocation is requested, a block is unlinked from the free storage list. When a block is freed, it is linked back onto the list, after collapsing any adjacent blocks.

The format of a Free Storage Block is:

```
DECLARE
1  FREE_STORAGE_BLOCK BASED  (FSB_POINTER),
    2  NEXT POINTER,
    2  SIZE FIXED BINARY  (31,0),
    2  UNUSED  (FREE_STORAGE_BLOCK.SIZE – 8)  CHAR  (1);
```

where the fields used are as follows:

NEXT: This is a pointer to the next FSB in the ascending-size-order chain of FSBs. For the last FSB on the chain, this field contains all zeros (null).

SIZE: This field contains the size of the FSB. The size is stored in bytes, but all FSBs contain an integral number of doublewords since all requests to the memory management module specify that the allocated area is to be on at least a doubleword boundary. Recall that only the system routines may call upon memory management.

UNUSED: This field fills out the remainder of the block to bring the actual size up to the amount specified in the size field.

7-8.2   Free Storage Block Pointer (FSBPTR)

This pointer (FSBPTR) points to the first Free Storage Block in the ascending-order-of-size chain. If there are no blocks in the chain, this pointer contains all zeros (null).

7-8.3   Free Storage Block Semaphore (FSBSEM)

This semaphore, with an initial value of one, controls access to the free storage list by serving as a lock. Any memory management routine, upon entering a section where it examines or modifies the free storage list, does a P operation on this semaphore, thus ensuring the integrity of this database, and after it stops using this database it does a V operation.

7-8.4   Memory Semaphore (MEMORY)

This semaphore, with an initial value of zero, controls waiting for memory. If a process attempts to allocate memory but is unable to do so, it performs a P operation on this semaphore, thus blocking itself. When it is reawakened by another process releasing some memory, it reattempts the allocation, possibly blocking itself again, until the request can be satisfied.

A sequence of V operations is performed on this semaphore whenever a block of memory is freed. The number of V operations performed is equal to the number of processes waiting on the semaphore at that time.

7-8.5   Sample Databases

An example of the key memory management databases is shown in Figure 7-7. Total main storage, in this example, is 20K bytes. The operating system, system tables, and user programs occupy 13K bytes. The remaining 7K bytes of free space are divided into three portions of 1K, 2K, and 4K bytes. These portions are chained together via FSBPTR and the next pointers of each FSB.

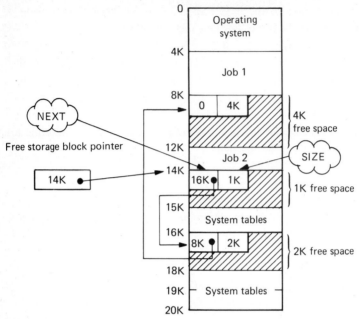

Figure 7-7   Sample memory management databases

Note, for example, that if the system requested 3K bytes from memory management, the 4K free area would be divided into two pieces, one of 3K, which would be returned to the caller, and one of 1K, which would remain as a free area. The free list chain would also have to be reorganized to reflect the fact that the new 1K free area was smaller than the existing 2K free area (recall that the chain is kept in ascending order of free area sizes).

7-9   MEMORY MANAGEMENT ROUTINES

7-9.1   Routine XA (Allocate a Block of Memory)

This routine serves to allocate a block of memory. On entry, it assumes that register 2 points to an argument list, which contains the size of the block desired, expressed in bytes, a fullword space into which the routine returns the address of the allocated area, and a power of two, indicating what type of boundary the allocation requires. For example, an argument of eight would indicate that doubleword alignment was desired.

The routine first does a P operation on the FSBSEM semaphore. It then goes through the free storage list until it finds a block large enough to contain the requested area. It calculates which parts of that block must be relinked onto the free storage list, i.e., those that exist on either side of the allocated area. In order to minimize breakage, the allocated area with the specified alignment is selected as close to the beginning of the block as possible. The routine performs this relinking by using the B primitive. The address of the allocated area is inserted into its place in the argument list, and after the routine performs a V operation on the FSBSEM semaphore, it returns.

If, however, there is no way to satisfy the request (i.e., the routine reaches the end of the free storage list without finding a suitable block), the routine does a V operation on the FSBSEM semaphore to unlock the free storage database, and then it does a P operation on the MEMORY semaphore. This has the effect of waiting until someone frees some memory. The routine, after waiting, returns to the beginning and reattempts the allocation.

A second entry point is available in this routine: the SVC C'E' will cause memory management to allocate workspace storage for this process. Since this call stores the size and beginning address fields in the PCB, only one such call per process is permitted. When a process that has allocated storage in this manner is destroyed, the storage is automatically returned to the free storage list. Otherwise, this entry point acts exactly like the XA routine described above.

7-9.2   Routine XB (Link a Block onto the FSB Chain)

This routine performs the function of linking a block of storage onto the free storage list on the assumption that compacting of the new area with existing FSBs is not necessary. Thus XB can be called directly from routine XA. On entry, it assumes that register 2 points to an argument list containing the size of the area to be placed on the FSB chain, measured in bytes, and the address of the area. Since this routine is called only by those routines (XA and XF) that have already done a P operation on the FSBSEM semaphore, it need not worry about database interference from other processes.

After the routine searches through the free storage list to find the point at which the new block should be inserted, it performs the relinking and formats the new block to look like a FSB. It then returns.

7-9.3   Routine XF (Free a Block of Memory)

This routine frees areas of storage, and compacts the new areas with current FSBs if necessary. On entry, it assumes that register 2 points to an argument list containing the size of the area to be freed, measured in bytes, and the address of the area.

The routine first does a P operation on the FSBSEM semaphore to lock the free storage list. It then searches through the free storage list to see if there are any FSBs defining a region of memory contiguous with the one being freed. It there are, these are removed from the free storage list, and the address and size of the block being freed are recomputed. When the end of the list is reached, the routine does a B operation, calling routine XB, to link the block onto the free storage list.

After examining the value of the MEMORY semaphore to determine the number of processes waiting for memory to be freed, the routine performs that number of V operations on the MEMORY semaphore. It then returns.

7-10   PROCESSOR MANAGEMENT (UPPER MODULE) DATABASES

The processor management upper module shares several databases with its lower module companion. In particular, the Process Control Block contains fields for both lower and upper module use (e.g., semaphore chain field is used by lower module only; process name field by upper module only). In addition, the upper module must also handle message-related databases.

7-10.1   Messages

Messages are used for interprocess communication as implemented by the process management upper module. Their structure is:

DECLARE
1 MESSAGE BASED (MESSAGE_POINTER),
   2 SENDER POINTER,
   2 NEXT POINTER,
   2 SIZE FIXED BINARY (31,0),
   2 TEXT CHARACTER (MESSAGE.SIZE);

where the fields are as follows:

SENDER: This is a pointer to the PCB of the process that sent the message.

NEXT: All messages currently waiting to be read by a process are chained together by their NEXT fields. The first message is pointed to by the FIRST_MESSAGE FIELD of the PCB.

SIZE: This is the number of characters in the text of the message.

TEXT: This character field is a copy of the text of the message, as supplied by the sender.

7-10.2   Sample Databases

Figure 7-8 illustrates the relationship between messages and the PCBs. In this example, three messages were sent to process A, two from B and one from C. When A issues an SVC Receive Message, he will be given the message HELLO sent by B. At this time, the MESSAGE_SEMAPHORE_RECEIVER will decrease from 3 to 2. The next Receive Message for A gets GOOD-DAY and a third Receive Message gets LET'S GO. If process A requests another message, but no more have arrived, then when A performs the P operation on the MESSAGE_SEMAPHORE_RECEIVER, the latter will decrease to −1 and block the process until another message is sent to it. Process B, in this example, is already in this situation. B sent a message ARE YOU READY? to C and is waiting for an answer.

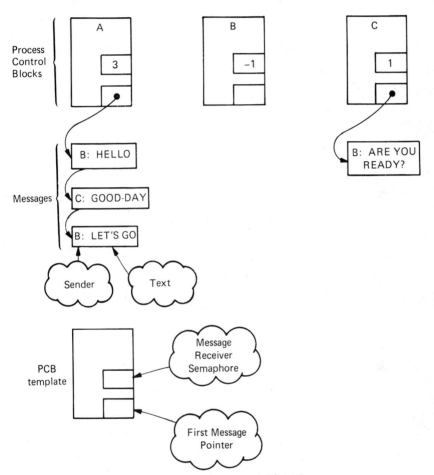

Figure 7-8 Sample processor management (upper module) databases

7-11 PROCESSOR MANAGEMENT (UPPER MODULE) ROUTINES

7-11.1 Routine XC (Create a Process)
This routine performs the "create process" function. On entry, register 2 is assumed to point to an argument list consisting solely of a name for the process to be created.

The routine first checks that the name is not already used in this group. If it is, an error routine is entered by calling routine XQUE. If not, routine XA is called to allocate an area for the new PCB. The new PCB has the name stored into it, the STOPPED bit turned on, the BLOCKED bit turned off, the semaphores set to their initial values, and the IN_SMC byte set to zero. It then calls the XI routine to link this PCB into the two PCB chains. The routine then returns.

7-11.2   Routine XD (Destroy a Process)

This routine performs the "destroy process" function. On entry, it assumes that register 2 points to an argument list consisting solely of a name for the process to be destroyed. The process to be destroyed must have been previously stopped by the "stop process" function (routine XZ).

The routine uses the XN routine to determine the address of the PCB for the process to be destroyed. If the XN routine cannot find the named process in this group, the error routine is entered (routine XQUE). The process to be destroyed must be in the stopped state. Routine XJ is called to unlink the PCB from the two process chains, thus keeping other processes from sending it messages. Then all messages waiting to be read by this process are freed. Next the PCB entries dealing with special workspace storage are checked, and any such storage is freed. Finally, the storage for the PCB is freed (all freeing here is done by the XF routine), and the XD routine returns.

7-11.3   Routine XH (Halt Job and Signal Supervisor)

This routine performs the "halt this job" function. It takes no argument list.

The sole processing performed by this routine is sending a message (via routine XS) to the supervisor process "*IBSUP" stating that the job should be halted and that normal conditions prevail. The routine then loops continually, reading and discarding messages waiting to be processed, and eventually blocking itself permanently when all messages have been released.

7-11.4   Routine XI (Insert PCB into Chains)

This routine performs the function of chaining a PCB into the two PCB chains. On entry, it assumes that register 2 points to a PCB.

The PCB is chained onto the all-PCB chain and the this-group chain immediately following the PCB for the running process. The routine then returns.

7-11.5   Routine XJ (Remove PCB from Chains)

This routine performs the function of removing a PCB from the two PCB chains. On entry, it assumes that register 2 contains a pointer to the PCB.

The PCB is removed from the two chains by modifying the links. This routine does not free the storage; that is left up to the caller. It then returns.

7-11.6   Routine XN (Find PCB by Name)

This routine serves the function of finding a PCB for a process if it is given the name of that process. On entry, register 2 points to an argument list consisting of a name and an area into which it returns a pointer to the PCB.

The routine searches along the NEXT_PCB_THIS_GROUP chain starting with the PCB for the running process, until it finds a PCB containing the desired name; it then stores the pointer in the argument list and returns. If it cannot find a PCB with the desired name, it stores a zero pointer in the argument list and returns.

7-11.7   Routine XR (Read a Message)

This routine performs the "read message" function. On entry, register 2 points to an argument list containing an area for the name of the sender, and a number giving the size of the area supplied to receive the text, followed by the area to receive the message text.

The routine first performs a P operation on its MESSAGE_SEMAPHORE_RECEIVER, which causes the process to wait if no messages have yet arrived. The routine then does a P operation on the MESSAGE_SEMAPHORE_COMMON to lock the message chain. Both these semaphores are, of course, the ones in the current process PCB. The first message is then taken off the message list and the chain is unlocked. The text is moved into the receiving area, and truncated or padded with blanks as necessary. Then the size field in the argument list is modified so that it contains the number of significant characters transmitted. The name of the sending process is copied from its PCB and placed into the argument list. Finally, the storage for the message in the message list is freed and the routine returns.

7-11.8   Routine XS (Send a Message)

This routine performs the "send a message" function. On entry, register 2 points to an argument list containing the name of the destination process and a count for the number of characters in the text, followed by the text itself.

The routine first finds the PCB for the process by the given name; if there is no such PCB, it enters an error routine by calling routine XQUE. If it finds the PCB, the routine does a P operation on the MESSAGE_SEMAPHORE_COMMON in that PCB to lock the message chain (after allocating a region of memory large enough to hold the message block). Then that message block is chained onto the end of the message list, the length of the message list being determined by the value of that PCB's MESSAGE_SEMAPHORE_RECEIVER. The message block is filled with a pointer to the sender's PCB, a null NEXT pointer, the count of the text, and the text itself. The routine then does a V operation on the MESSAGE_ SEMAPHORE_COMMON and a V operation on the MESSAGE_SEMAPHORE_ RECEIVER, and returns.

7-11.9   Routine XY (Start Process)

This routine serves to start a process that is in the "stopped" state. On entry, register 2 contains a pointer to an argument list consisting of the name of the process to be started and an address in memory at which the process should start running. The registers that should be loaded for that process in the beginning are those that existed when the SVC call occurred. This is the method of passing arguments to newly created processes.

The routine first gets a pointer to the PCB of the process of the given name. If there is no such PCB, an error routine is entered by calling routine XQUE. The routine then stores in that PCB's INTERRUPT_SAVE_AREA the registers specified and a PSW with the address specified. The remainder of the PSW is identical to the old PSW that existed when this routine was called. The STOPPED bit in the PCB is then turned off, and the routine returns.

7-11.10   Routine XZ (Stop Process)

This routine performs the "stop process" operation. On entry, register 2 points to an argument list consisting solely of the name of the process to be stopped.

The routine first gets a pointer to the PCB of the process of the given name. If there is no such PCB, an error routine is entered by calling routine XQUE. If that PCB's IN_SMC byte is zero, the routine simply turns the STOPPED bit on and returns.

However, if the IN_SMC byte is nonzero, which indicates that the process is still in a "system must complete" section, then the STOP_WAITING bit is set on, and a P operation is performed on the STOPPER_SEMAPHORE. By the time the process next begins to run, the process to be stopped has left the smc section, and the stop can be performed normally.

There is one exception to the above: a nonsystem process cannot stop a system process. (A system process is identified by a name beginning with an asterisk (*).)

7-11.1 Routine XQUE (Abnormal Termination)

This routine serves to terminate a job abnormally. It operates in the same way as the XH routine, but generates a message indicating that an error has occurred.

7-12 DEVICE MANAGEMENT DATABASES

Most device management modules operate as separate processes concurrently with the user's processes. In addition, some databases are used by the I/O interrupt handler as well as by the device management processes.

7-12.1 Unit Control Block

A UCB is stored in a permanently allocated area for every unit (card reader, printer, etc.) attached to the system. Its format is:

```
DECLARE
1 UNIT_CONTROL_BLOCK BASED (UCB_POINTER),
    2 ADDRESS FIXED BINARY (31,0),
    2 USER_SEMAPHORE LIKE (SEMAPHORE),
    2 WAIT_SEMAPHORE LIKE (SEMAPHORE),
    2 STATUS BIT (64),
    2 FAST_PROCESSING_REQUIRED BIT (1);
```

where the fields are as follows:

ADDRESS: This is the physical unit and channel address to be used in the Start I/O instruction (e.g., X'000E' for one of the printers).

USER_SEMAPHORE: This semaphore, with an initial value of one, locks the Unit Control Block to prevent more than one process at a time from trying to issue requests to a unit.

WAIT_SEMAPHORE: This semaphore, with an initial value of zero, is used by device handling routines to wait for an interrupt. By performing a P operation on it, this process becomes blocked (i.e., the semaphore becomes negative). When an interrupt occurs, the interrupt routine performs a V operation on the WAIT_SEMAPHORE in the appropriate UCB.

STATUS: This field records the status of the device, as stored by interrupt routines. It usually contains a copy of the most recent Channel Status Word stored for this device.

FAST_PROCESSING_REQUIRED: This bit is zero if fast processing is not required and one if it is. If fast processing is required, the interrupt routine transfers to the traffic controller after performing the V operation on the WAIT_SEMAPHORE. As shown in the sections on the traffic controller and the V operation, this causes the process waiting for the interrupt to start running immediately.

7-12.2 CAW Semaphore (CAWSEM)

This semaphore, with an initial value of one, serves as a lock on the Channel Address Word. Any routine performing a Start I/O instruction, which requires access to the CAW, does a P operation on this semaphore before storing into it, and a V after the Start I/O instruction.

7-13 DEVICE MANAGEMENT ROUTINES AND PROCESSES

Device management is divided into device handling processes and a special I/O interrupt handler. The device handling routines themselves reside in special processes, one per device. They are originally created by the top-level supervisor, and communication with them is by means of the message primitives provided by the upper module of process control.

The fielding and handling of input/output interrupts are performed by a special routine that is invoked whenever an I/O interrupt occurs. It runs for a very short time, just long enough to store status information and perform a V operation on the WAIT_SEMAPHORE in the appropriate UCB. It then returns to the processing of the interrupted process.

7-13.1 Reader Handler Routine and Process

This routine controls card readers; it is shared by all reader processes. On entry, it has the UCB address in register 3 and the protection key to be used in register 4. The routine then goes into a loop wherein it reads messages. If the messages are not of the form "READxxxx," where xxxx represents a 4-byte binary storage address, the message is rejected and another message is read.

However, if the message is of the correct form, the routine performs a P operation on the USER_SEMAPHORE in the UCB so as to keep other processes from using the device for the interim. The routine then constructs a Channel Control Block, which contains an appropriate Channel Command Word. The operation specified in the CCW is a "read" request, with the address as specified in the message received. If the message is from a user process, the key of the address specified is checked to be sure it matches the key supplied to the routine by the system. The count is 80 characters, and all flags controlling chaining, special interrupts, etc., are set to zero. A CAW is then constructed with the address of the CCW and a zero key. Next, a P operation is done on the CAWSEM semaphore, the CAW is set, the Start I/O instruction for the appropriate reader is issued, and a V operation is done on the CAWSEM semaphore. Then a P operation is done on the WAIT_SEMAPHORE in the UCB, and the process waits until an interrupt occurs.

After the interrupt handler has awakened the process, the status as stored by the interrupt routine is then examined. If the status indicates successful or unsuccessful completion of the request, the process examines the card, as described in the next paragraph. If, however, the operation has not completed, the process goes back to continue waiting.

The process now examines the process name of its invoker. If the name starts with an asterisk, it is assumed to be part of the supervisor process module (see the section on the supervisor process module for naming conventions) and a message reading either OK or NO depending on the success of the request, is returned. However, if the name of the invoking process does not start with an asterisk, it is assumed that it is a user process, and the situation is more complicated.

First, if the card just read in was a $JOB card, this indicates the end of the data for this program. Thus, a NO message is sent back to the caller after the card is saved in a special area and the user's copy is blanked out. Then the process enters a loop wherein it answers all user requests with a NO until it gets a system request. At this point it stores the card in the specified area and returns the message OK.

7-13.2 Printer Handler Routine and Process

This routine handles output for printers; it is shared by all printer handler processes. Its operation is directly analogous to that of the reader handler. Messages are of the form PRINxxxx, where xxxx represents the address to be printed from. (No data checking is based on process name.)

7-13.3 General Device Handler Routine (EXCP) and Process

This routine handles the interface for devices wherein the user wishes to provide his own input/output commands. The method of initialization and operation is similar to the reader and printer handlers described above, but the messages sent to the routine are of the form EXCPxxxxcccc, where xxxx represents the unit and channel address and cccc represents the address of the first Channel Command Word to be used. The EXCP routine uses xxxx to find the UCB for that device, and then starts the I/O.

When an interrupt occurs for an EXCP device, the EXCP interface returns a message of the form sssssss where sssssss is the status returned by the device and the channel.

By including the FAST_PROCESSING_REQUIRED bit in the UCB, it is possible to attain very fast processing of EXCP interrupts.

The routine again waits for a message from the user. If the message reads AGAIN, the routine waits for another I/O interrupt and returns the status to the user, thus enabling him to check for both channel and device end. If the message says OK, the routine releases the UCB and gets ready to read another EXCP-type message.

7-13.4 Input/Output Interrupt Handling Routine

The I/O interrupt routine performs handling of the input/output interrupts occurring after an input/output request. Essentially, the routine operates in whatever process was running when the interrupt occurred. The routine performs a small number of operations and then returns to resume the interrupted process.

First, it finds the UCB for the device causing the interrupt. It inserts the CSW status information into the status field of the UCB by means of the OR operation and then performs a V operation on the WAIT_SEMAPHORE in that UCB. Normally the routine returns at this point by reloading the old registers and the old PSW. The old PSW is always modified to turn off the wait bit if it is on. (For the significance of this, see the traffic controller section.)

If, however, the FAST_PROCESSING_REQUIRED bit in the UCB is on, the routine uses the XPER routine to transfer directly into the traffic controller in order to run a new process. Since the NEXTTRY field has usually been modified to point to the PCB for the device handler process, the routine does indeed provide fast processing.

7-14 SUPERVISOR ROUTINE AND PROCESS

The supervisor processes serve to schedule jobs and prepare them for execution. There is one supervisor process per job stream. Our example contains one job stream per card reader. Since each supervisor process exists in a separate process group, there is no communication between processes: they are invisible to each other. Each supervisor process is named *IBSUP and each *IBSUP has two auxiliary processes, *IN and *OUT, that handle the job stream's input and output devices, respectively.

7-14.1 Job Stream Processing Routine

After reading a $JOB card (the first card of each job) the supervisor process first sends the card to the printer. It then determines the amount of memory required and allocates that amount on a 2K boundary because of the protection hardware. All of the storage protection keys in that area are set to the key assigned to the user program. The routine then creates a process called USERPROG, which will become the process whereby the user program first begins to run.

The supervisor process then scans the device assignment fields, which are of the form name=devtype. (Note that "name" cannot begin with an asterisk.) For each field, it creates a process called "name," and starts the process in an interface routine for that devtype. For devtype either IN or OUT, the routine used is one that reads messages from the user process, sends them unchanged to process *IN or *OUT, as appropriate, waits for a reply from that process, and then sends the reply to the original calling process. For devtype EXCP, the interface routine is the one described in Section 7-13.3.

The supervisor then reads the user's object deck into his partition. Relocation is performed as necessary. When this is completed, the process USERPROG's PCB is modified to run in user mode under the specified key. The user process can then start to run.

After starting the USERPROG process, the supervisor process waits for a message to be returned. This message can be a "success" or a "failure." In either case, the content of the message is printed on the printer and the supervisor process destroys all the processes created for or by the user job, frees the partition of memory allocated, and goes to the next job.

If there are no more jobs to be run, the supervisor process will become blocked because it will try to read input messages that it will never get.

The overall flow of the job stream processor routine is shown in Figure 7-9. While the details are not especially important, the reader should note that the routine relies on many of the facilities of the extended machine (e.g., SVC's such as A, C, D, F, N, P, R, S, V, Y, and Z). It has been observed that most of the operating system routines will have been used by the job stream processor even before the first user's process is started.

7-14.2 Supervisor Initiation

The supervisor process, as we have seen, creates and controls all the processes of the system. But where do the supervisor processes come from? How are the various SVC routines initialized? Operating system initialization can be complex; in some systems it may take many minutes of execution. In this sample operating system, initialization is performed by the Initial Program Load Routine (IPLRTN). The operating system code, including IPLRTN, is first loaded via an Initial Program Load mechanism as described in Chapter 2. Once loaded, control transfers to IPLRTN.

IPLRTN runs free of most of the rest of the system. There is no point in IPLRTN until the very end at which time the traffic controller can be logically entered. There are pointers set to ensure that, if the traffic controller does get entered during this period before initialization is complete, the system will stop cold. Such a transfer could, for example, be caused by too little memory.

The initialization routine first sets up a PCB for itself in a permanently allocated area. Then it sets pointers RUNNING and NEXTTRY, as well as all the chains within the PCB, to point to that PCB. Next, all available memory (i.e., memory not used by the system) is placed on the free storage list, and all the protection keys are set to zero.

Much of the nucleus is now operational and can be used. Other PCBs are created, one for each supervisor process and each in a group by itself (thus the "create process" primitive cannot be directly used here). Each process created is named *IBSUP. IPLRTN calls "start process" for each of these processes, and starts them in the job stream processor routine. Register 3 then points to an argument list containing a pointer to the UCB for the reader and a pointer to the UCB for the printer (all UCBs are stored in a permanently assigned part of memory), and register

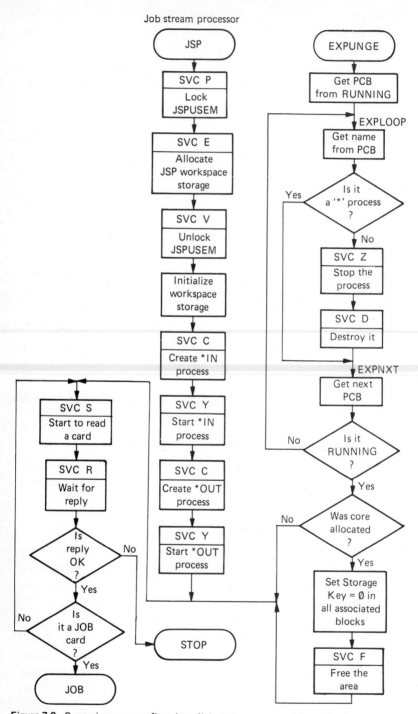

Figure 7-9 Supervisor process flowchart (job stream processor) (part 1)

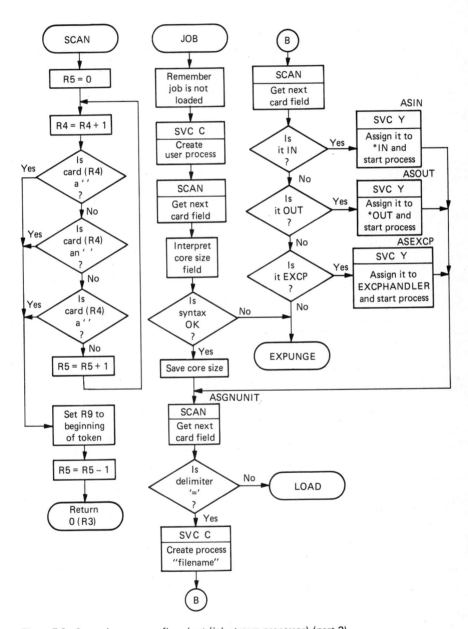

Figure 7-9 Supervisor process flowchart (job stream processor) (part 2)

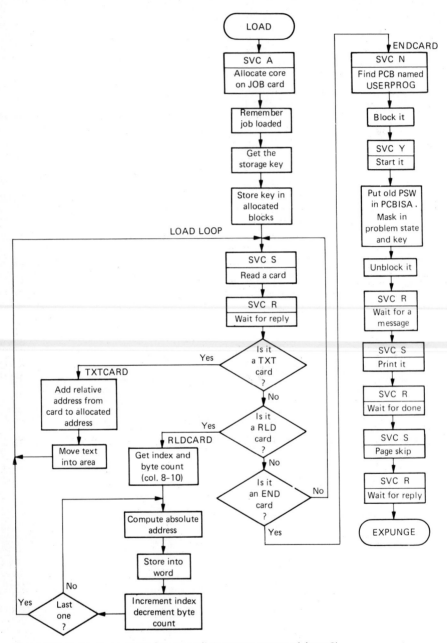

Figure 7-9 Supervisor process flowchart (job stream processor) (part 3)

4 contains the protection key to be used for the user programs of this job stream. After starting all these supervisor processes, the initialization routine modifies its

PCB to read "stopped," and only then transfers (via routine **XPER**) to the traffic controller to begin running the supervisor processes. The flowchart for the initialization routine is shown in Figure 7-10.

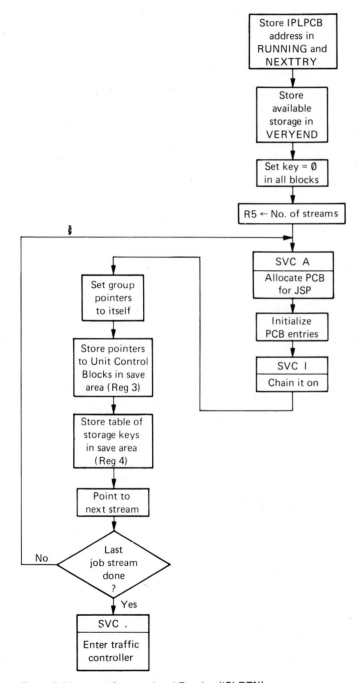

Figure 7-10 Initial Program Load Routine (IPLRTN)

Upon entry, the supervisor process first creates and starts processes called *IN and *OUT, passing them pointers to their UCBs in register 3 and to their protection keys in register 4, as explained earlier. Processing of the job streams then begins.

7-15 USER PROGRAMS AND PROCESSES

User programs run in a process or processes of their own. They start out, as mentioned above, in one process called USERPROG. However, more processes may be created later; the system facilitates the creation of subsidiary processes. User processes cannot have names starting with an asterisk, nor can they destroy a process with a name beginning with an asterisk. Thus supervisor processes are protected against user processes.

7-15.1 User Termination

Two routines, XH and XQUE, signal success and failure, respectively. XH is usually called by the user program, whereas XQUE is usually called by a system routine invoked by the user upon detection of an error condition. Both routines send a message to the supervisor process and then block themselves.

7-15.2 User Execution

While they are running, user processes may use many of the operating system primitives, for example, "send message" and "receive message." Input and output can be performed by receiving or sending messages to the system input and output processes, respectively.

A very simple user program is illustrated in Figure 7-11. This program merely prints the message USER PROGRAM ENTRY SUCCESSFUL and then terminates. The $JOB control card to be used is also shown at the top of the figure. The name PRINTER used in MSGONE must match the PRINTER=OUT on the $JOB card.

7-16 PARTIAL TRACE OF SVC FLOW

The sequence and location of SVC instruction execution, starting from IPLRTN, are shown in Figure 7-12. This trace was obtained by using a special 360 simulator called SIM360 developed at M.I.T. (Donovan, 1974). For the sake of brevity, only a short portion of the trace is included. The reader can use this trace together with the listings in Section 7-17 to follow the flow of control through the system.

$JOB,2K,READER=IN,PRINTER=OUT

LOC	OBJECT CODE	ADDR1	ADDR2	STMT		SOURCE STATEMENT		
00000				1	USER	CSECT		
00000				2		BALR	15,0	ESTABLISH ADDRESSABILITY.
00002				3		USING	*,15	
				4	*			
00002	4120 F00E		00010	5		LA	2,MSGONE	SEND MESSAGE TO PRINTER.
00006	0AE2			6		SVC	C'S'	...
				7	*			
00008	4120 F0A6		000A8	8		LA	2,MSGTWO	WAIT FOR REPLY INDICATING
0000C	0AD9			9		SVC	C'R'	THAT PRINTING IS COMPLETED.
				10	*			
0000E	0AC8			11		SVC	C'H'	HALT JOB.
				12	*			
00010	D7D9C9D5E3C5D940			13	MSGONE	DC	CL8'PRINTER'	... NAME OF PROCESS
00018	00000008			14		DC	F'8'	... LENGTH OF MESSAGE
0001C	D7D9C9D500000024			15		DC	C'PRIN',A(PRINT1)	... TEXT OF MESSAGE
00024	E4E2C5D940D7D9D6			16	PRINT1	DC	CL132 'USER PROGRAM ENTRY SUCCESSFUL.' TEXT PRINTED.	
				17	*			
000A8				18	MSGTWO	DS	CL8	... NAME OF PROCESS RETURNED HERE.
000B0	00000004			19		DC	F'4'	... LENGTH OF RETURN AREA.
000B4				20		DS	CL4	... STATUS RETURNED FROM 'PRINTER'.
				21		END		

Figure 7-11 Sample user job

```
MASSACHUSETTS INSTITUTE OF TECHNOLOGY          SYSTEM / 360 SIMULATOR
PROGRAM TRACE LISTING.   0 CONDITIONS ENABLED.

LOC   TRACE TYPE            COUNT   TIME
----  ----------------      -----   ----------


0FA4 SVC INTERRUPT A          78        85  PSW: 00 0 0 00C1  '01'B '00'B 0 000FA4

0610 SVC INTERRUPT !         104       173  PSW: FF 0 0 005A  '01'B '00'B 0 000610

061C SVC INTERRUPT P         139       293  PSW: FF 0 0 00D7  '01'B '00'B 0 00061C

069C SVC INTERRUPT B         201       432  PSW: FF 0 0 00C2  '01'B '10'B 0 00069C

06A2 SVC INTERRUPT V         239       554  PSW: FF 0 0 00E5  '01'B '10'B 0 0006A2

06B2 SVC INTERRUPT ,         272       674  PSW: FF 0 0 006B  '01'B '10'B 0 0006B2

0FB0 SVC INTERRUPT I         314       855  PSW: 00 0 0 00C9  '01'B '00'B 0 000FB0

0FA4 SVC INTERRUPT A         365       990  PSW: 00 0 0 00C1  '01'B '10'B 0 000FA4

0610 SVC INTERRUPT !         391     1,078  PSW: FF 0 0 005A  '01'B '00'B 0 000610

051C SVC INTERRUPT P         426     1,198  PSW: FF 0 0 00D7  '01'B '00'B 0 00061C

069C SVC INTERRUPT B         488     1,337  PSW: FF 0 0 00C2  '01'B '10'B 0 00069C

06A2 SVC INTERRUPT V         526     1,459  PSW: FF 0 0 00E5  '01'B '10'B 0 0006A2

06B2 SVC INTERRUPT ,         559     1,579  PSW: FF 0 0 006B  '01'B '10'B 0 0006B2

0FB0 SVC INTERRUPT I         601     1,760  PSW: 00 0 0 00C9  '01'B '10'B 0 000FB0

0FE4 SVC INTERRUPT .         651     1,895  PSW: 00 0 0 004B  '01'B '10'B 0 000FE4

11BC SVC INTERRUPT P         699     2,004  PSW: FF 0 0 00D7  '01'B '00'B 0 0011BC

11C2 SVC INTERRUPT E         732     2,123  PSW: FF 0 0 00C5  '01'B '00'B 0 0011C2
```

Figure 7-12   Partial trace of SVC flow (part 1)

```
MASSACHUSETTS INSTITUTE OF TECHNOLOGY          SYSTEM / 360 SIMULATOR
PROGRAM TRACE LISTING.   1 CONDITIONS ENABLED.

LOC  TRACE TYPE           COUNT   TIME
----  -----------------   -----   ----------

0610 SVC INTERRUPT !       758    2,210  PSW: FF 0 0 005A  '01'B '00'B 0 000610

061C SVC INTERRUPT P       793    2,330  PSW: FF 0 0 00D7  '01'B '00'B 0 00061C

069C SVC INTERRUPT B       855    2,469  PSW: FF 0 0 00C2  '01'B '10'B 0 00069C

06A2 SVC INTERRUPT V       893    2,591  PSW: FF 0 0 00E5  '01'B '10'B 0 0006A2

06B2 SVC INTERRUPT ,       928    2,712  PSW: FF 0 0 006B  '01'B '00'B 0 0006B2

11CC SVC INTERRUPT V       970    2,864  PSW: FF 0 0 00E5  '01'B '00'B 0 0011CC

122E SVC INTERRUPT C      1020    3,034  PSW: FF 0 0 00C3  '01'B '00'B 0 00122E

078E SVC INTERRUPT N      1044    3,124  PSW: FF 0 0 00D5  '01'B '00'B 0 00078E

079A SVC INTERRUPT !      1079    3,246  PSW: FF 0 0 005A  '01'B '00'B 0 00079A

07A8 SVC INTERRUPT A      1113    3,372  PSW: FF 0 0 00C1  '01'B '00'B 0 0007A8

0610 SVC INTERRUPT !      1139    3,460  PSW: FF 0 0 005A  '01'B '00'B 0 000610

061C SVC INTERRUPT P      1174    3,580  PSW: FF 0 0 00D7  '01'B '00'B 0 00061C

069C SVC INTERRUPT B      1236    3,719  PSW: FF 0 0 00C2  '01'B '10'B 0 00069C

06A2 SVC INTERRUPT V      1274    3,840  PSW: FF 0 0 00E5  '01'B '10'B 0 0006A2

06B2 SVC INTERRUPT ,      1307    3,960  PSW: FF 0 0 006B  '01'B '10'B 0 0006B2

07BE SVC INTERRUPT I      1349    4,135  PSW: FF 0 0 00C9  '01'B '00'B 0 0007BE

07C0 SVC INTERRUPT ,      1387    4,257  PSW: FF 0 0 006B  '01'B '00'B 0 0007C0

1230 SVC INTERRUPT Y      1427    4,407  PSW: FF 0 0 00E8  '01'B '00'B 0 001230
```

Figure 7-12 Partial trace of SVC flow (part 2)

```
MASSACHUSETTS INSTITUTE OF TECHNOLOGY              SYSTEM / 360 SIMULATOR
PROGRAM TRACE LISTING.    1 CONDITIONS ENABLED.

LOC   TRACE TYPE              COUNT    TIME
----  ----------------       -----    ----------


0A18 SVC INTERRUPT   N  1451    4,497   PSW: 00 0 0 00D5   '01'B '00'B 0 000A18

123A SVC INTERRUPT   C  1495    4,681   PSW: FF 0 0 00C3   '01'B '00'B 0 00123A

078E SVC INTERRUPT   N  1519    4,770   PSW: FF 0 0 00D5   '01'B '00'B 0 00078E

079A SVC INTERRUPT   !  1559    4,897   PSW: FF 0 0 005A   '01'B '00'B 0 00079A

07A8 SVC INTERRUPT   A  1593    5,023   PSW: FF 0 0 00C1   '01'B '00'B 0 0007A8

0610 SVC INTERRUPT   !  1619    5,111   PSW: FF 0 0 005A   '01'B '00'B 0 000610

061C SVC INTERRUPT   P  1654    5,231   PSW: FF 0 0 00D7   '01'B '00'B 0 00061C

069C SVC INTERRUPT   B  1716    5,369   PSW: FF 0 0 00C2   '01'B '10'B 0 00069C

06A2 SVC INTERRUPT   V  1754    5,491   PSW: FF 0 0 00E5   '01'B '10'B 0 0006A2

06B2 SVC INTERRUPT   ,  1787    5,611   PSW: FF 0 0 006B   '01'B '10'B 0 0006B2

07BE SVC INTERRUPT   I  1829    5,786   PSW: FF 0 0 00C9   '01'B '00'B 0 0007BE

07C0 SVC INTERRUPT   ,  1867    5,907   PSW: FF 0 0 006B   '01'B '00'B 0 0007C0

123C SVC INTERRUPT   Y  1907    6,058   PSW: FF 0 0 00E8   '01'B '00'B 0 00123C

0A18 SVC INTERRUPT   N  1931    6,147   PSW: 00 0 0 00D5   '01'B '00'B 0 000A18


NORMAL SIMULATOR TERMINATION FOR PROGRAM PROGRAM
          SIMULATED REAL TIME:      6,330.562
          SIMULATED CPU TIME:       6,330.562
```

Figure 7-12 Partial trace of SVC flow (part 3)

7-17 SAMPLE OPERATING SYSTEM PROGRAM LISTINGS

The following pages contain the actual program listings of the sample operating system. This 370 assembly language code is provided for the reader interested in studying the detailed implementation, or in actually running the sample operating system.

Although the program has been tested, its primary purpose is to illustrate general structure. We do not, therefore, guarantee its correctness. In the questions at the end of this chapter, the reader is asked to propose changes or corrections to this operating system design.

```
                                       2331+**********************************************
                                       2332+**                                          *
                                       2333+**                                          *
                                       2334+**        *  *  *  *  *                     *
                                       2335+**        *  *  *  *  *                     *
                                       2336+**              SAMPLE OPERATING SYSTEM     *
                                       2337+**                   VERSION 2.00           *
                                       2338+**              DEVELOPED AT MIT, 1973      *
                                       2339+**                                          *
                                       2340+**                                          *
                                       2341+**********************************************

000000                                 2343+       PRINT ON,NODATA,GEN
008000                                 2344+PROGRAM CSECT

008000                                 2346+CORESIZE EQU   32768 BYTES OF CORE IN OBJECT MACHINE

000000                                 2348+       USING *,0 COMMUNICATIONS AREA

000000 000000000000F6E                 2350+IPLPSW  DC    B'00000000',B'00000000',X'0000',X'00',AL3(IPLRTN)
000008                                 2351+IPLCCW1 DC    D .            IPL CCW #1
000010                                 2352+IPLCCW2 DC    D .            IPL CCW #2
000018                                 2353+EXTOLD  DS    D .            EXTERNAL OLD PSW
000020                                 2354+SVCOLD  DS    D .            SVC OLD PSW
000028                                 2355+PGMOLD  DS    D .            PROGRAM INTERRUPT OLD PSW
000030                                 2356+MCHKOLD DS    D .            MACHINE CHECK OLD PSW
000038                                 2357+IOOLD   DS    D .            I/O INTERRUPT OLD PSW
000040                                 2358+CSW     DS    D .            CHANNEL STATUS WORD
000048                                 2359+CAW     DS    F .            CHANNEL ADDRESS WORD
00004C                                 2360+UNUSED0 DS    F .
000050 FFFFFFFF                        2361+TIMER   DC    F'-1' .        TIMER
000054 00000000                        2362+UNUSED1 DC    F'0'
000058 000000000000027A                2363+EXTNEW  DC    B'00000000',B'00000000',X'0000',X'00',AL3(EXTHANDL)
000060 00000000000002B2                2364+SVCNEW  DC    B'00000000',B'00000000',X'0000',X'00',AL3(SVCHANDL)
000068 00000000000002B0                2365+PGMNEW  DC    B'00000000',B'00000000',X'0000',X'00',AL3(PGMHANDL)
000070 00200000000000EF4               2366+MCHKNEW DC    B'00000000',B'00000010',X'0000',X'00',AL3(0)
000078 00000000000001648              2367+IONEW   DC    B'00000000',B'00000000',X'0000',X'00',AL3(IOHANDL)
000080 000180                          2368+       ORG   *+X'100' SPACE OVER STAND ALONE DUMP AREA
000180 00001648                        2369+FSBPTR  DC    A(VERYEND)     FSB POINTER
000184 00000001000000000               2370+FSBSEM  DC    F'1,0' .       FSB SEMAPHORE
00018C 00000000000000000               2371+MEMORY  DC    F'0,0' .       MEMORY SEMAPHORE
000194 00000001000000000               2372+CAWSEM  DC    F'1,0' .       CAW SEMAPHORE

00019C                                 2374+TRAPSAVE DS   16F .          STORAGE FOR EXTERNAL INTERRUPTS
0001DC                                 2375+IOHSAVE DS    16F .          STORAGE FOR I/O INTERRUPTS

00021C                                 2377+SYSSEMSA DS   CL84 .         SYSTEM SEMAPHORE SAVE AREA

000270                                 2379+RUNNING DS    A .            RUNNING
000274                                 2380+NEXTRY  DS    A .            NEXTRY
000278                                 2381+NEXTRYM DS    C,0H .         NEXTRY MODIFIED
```

SAMPLE OPERATING SYSTEM   VERSION 2.00

LOC   OBJECT CODE   ADDR1 ADDR2   STMT   SOURCE STATEMENT

                                        2383+***
                                        2384+**   **
                                        2385+**   EXTERNAL, PROGRAM, AND SVC INTERRUPT HANDLERS **
                                        2386+**   **
                                        2387+***

00027A   0019C   2389+EXTHANDL EQU *   EXTERNAL INTERRUPT HANDLER
00027A 900F 019C   2390+   STM   0,15,TRAPSAVE .   SAVE REGISTERS
00027E 0510   2391+   BALR 1,0 .   ESTABLISH ADDRESSING
000280   0001B   2392+   USING *,1
000280 9580 001B   2393+   CLI   EXTOLD+3,X'80' .   SEE IF TIMER TRAP
000284 4770 1028   002A8   2394+   BNE   EXTHRET .   IF NOT, IGNORE
000288 58F0 0270   00270   2395+   L   15,RUNNING .   SET UP REGISTERS FOR TRAFFIC
00028C   00019   2396+   USING PCB,15 .   CONTROLLER (XPER)
00028C 95FF F019   00019   2397+   CLI   PCBBLOKT,X'FF' .   IF BLOCKED, NO PROCESS IS
000290 4780 1028   002A8   2398+   BE   EXTHRET .   RUNNABLE, SO RETURN
000294 41E0 F04C   0004C   2399+   LA   14,PCBISA .   GET SAVE AREA
000000   0000E   2400+   USING SA,14
000298 D207 E003 0018 00000 00018   2401+   MVC   SAPSW,EXTOLD .   AND STORE OLD STUFF INTO IT
00029E D23F E008 019C 00008 0019C   2402+   MVC   SAREGS,TRAPSAVE
0002A4 47F0 12EA   0056A   2403+   B   XPER .   THEN GO TO TRAFFIC SCHEDULER
0002A8   0019C   2404+EXTHRET EQU *
0002A8 980F 019C   2405+   LM   0,15,TRAPSAVE .   TO IGNORE AN INTERRUPT, RELOAD
0002AC 8200 0018   00018   2406+   LPSW EXTOLD .   AND TRANSFER BACK

0002B0   0019C   2408+PGMHANDL EQU *   PROGRAM INTERRUPT HANDLER
0002B0 0A6F   2409+   SVC   C'?' .   IN ANY CASE, AN ERROR

```
LOC     OBJECT CODE      ADDR1 ADDR2   STMT    SOURCE STATEMENT

                                       2411*   ****************************************************
                                       2412*   *                                                  *
                                       2413*   *              SVC INTERRUPT HANDLER               *
                                       2414*   *                                                  *
                                       2415*   *  FOR ALL ROUTINES ENTERED BY SVC INTERRUPT, THE  *
                                       2416*   *  FOLLOWING REGISTERS CONTAIN THIS INFORMATION:   *
                                       2417*   *                                                  *
                                       2418*   *  REGISTER  1 - BASE REGISTER FOR ROUTINE         *
                                       2419*   *  REGISTER  2 - POINTER TO ARGUMENT LIST (IF ANY) *
                                       2420*   *  REGISTER 14 - POINTER TO SAVEAREA USED FOR THIS SVC *
                                       2421*   *  REGISTER 15 - POINTER TO PCB PRESENTLY RUNNING  *
                                       2422*   *                                                  *
                                       2423*   ****************************************************
0002B2                          019C   2425*   SVCHANDL EQU  *                  SVC HANDLER
0002B2  900F 019C              0019C   2426*            STM  0,15,TRAPSAVE .     SAVE REGISTERS
0002B6  0590                          2427*            BALR 9,0 .               ESTABLISH ADDRESSING
0002B8                                 2428*            USING *,9
0002B8  98AE 905C              00314   2429*            LM   10,14,SVCCONST     INITIALIZE REGISTERS
0002BC  43A0 0023              00023   2430*            IC   10,SVCOLD+3 .       GET SVC CODE
0002C0  43AA 9070              00328   2431*            IC   10,SVCHTABL(10) .   TRANSLATE INTO TABLE OFFSET
0002C4  41AA 9170        00002 00428   2432*            LA   10,SVCRTN(10) .     REG 10 -> THE CORRECT PSW
0002C8  9500 A002              00302   2433*            CLI  2(10),X'00' .       IS THIS CALL PROTECTED?
0002CC  4780 904A              00270   2434*            BE   SVCHPROT .          THEN SEE IF WE CAN CALL IT
0002D0  58F0 0270                      2435*   SVCOK    L    15,RUNNING .        GET PCB POINTER
000000                                 2436*            USING PCB,15
0002D4  9500 A003              00302   2437*            CLI  3(10),X'00' .       IS IT A SYSTEM SAVEAREA?
0002D8  4780 9026              00003   2438*            BE   SYSSEM .            DON'T USE REG 14 AS PCB PTR
0002DC  18EF                          2439*            LR   14,15 .             ELSE, SET UP PCB POINTER
0002DE  43BA 0003              00003   2440*   SYSSEM   IC   11,3(10) .          GET POINTER TO SAVE AREA OFFSET
0002E2  5AEB 9210              004C8   2441*            A    14,SVCSAVE(11) .    REG 14 -> SAVE AREA
0002E6  95AB 0023              00023   2442*            CLI  SVCOLD+3,C'.' .     ARE WE CALLING XPER?
0002EA  4780 9042              002FA   2443*            BE   SVCXPER .           IF SO, DON'T SAVE RETURN STATUS
0002EE  D207 E000 0020   00000 00020   2444*            MVC  SA,14
0002F4  D23F E008 019C   00008 0019C   2445*            MVC  SAPSW,SVCOLD .      SAVE PSW
                                       2446*            MVC  SAREGS,TRAPSAVE .   SAVE REGISTERS
0002FA  581A 0004              00004   2447*   SVCXPER  L    1,4(10) .           MAKE ADDRESSING EASY WITHIN
0002FE  8200 A000              00000   2448*   SVCHPROT LPSW 0(10) .             ROUTINE, AND GO THERE
000306  58C0 0020              00020   2449*            L    12,SVCOLD .         GET PROTECTION KEY
000308  14CD                          2450*            NR   12,13 .             IS IT A USER?
00030C  4780 9018              002D0   2451*            BZ   SVCOK
000310  41A0 91F8              004B0   2452*            LA   10,SVCRTN+136 .     IF NO, THAT'S FINE
        47F0 9018              002D0   2453*            B    SVCOK .             ELSE SET UP CALL TO XQUE
                                       2454*            DROP 9
000314  0000000000000000...            2455*   SVCCONST DC   3F'0',X'00F00000',F'0'

000328  8484848484848484               2457*   SVCHTABL DC   256X'84' .         TABLE OF PSW OFFSETS
0003FF                                 2458*            ORG  SVCHTABL+C'P'
0003FF  00                            2459*            DC   AL1(0)
00040D                                 2460*            ORG  SVCHTABL+C'V'
00040D  08                            2461*            DC   AL1(8)
000382                                 2462*            ORG  SVCHTABL+C'!'
000382  10                            2463*            DC   AL1(16)
000393                                 2464*            ORG  SVCHTABL+C','
000393  18                            2465*            DC   AL1(24)
```

```
LOC     OBJECT CODE       ADDR1 ADDR2  STMT    SOURCE STATEMENT

000394  0003EA                          2466+        ORG   SVCHTABL+C'B'
0003EA  2003E9                          2467+        DC    AL1(32)
0003EB  40                              2468+        ORG   SVCHTABL+C'A'
0003E9  0003EE                          2469+        DC    AL1(40)
0003EE  30                              2470+        ORG   SVCHTABL+C'F'
0003EE  3D                              2471+        DC    AL1(48)
0003EF  0003F1                          2472+        ORG   SVCHTABL+C'I'
0003F1  38                              2473+        DC    AL1(56)
0003F2  0003F9                          2474+        ORG   SVCHTABL+C'J'
0003F9  40                              2475+        DC    AL1(64)
0003FA  000373                          2476+        ORG   SVCHTABL+C'.'
000373  48                              2477+        DC    AL1(72)
000374  000401                          2478+        ORG   SVCHTABL+C'R'
000401  50                              2479+        DC    AL1(80)
000402  00040A                          2480+        ORG   SVCHTABL+C'S'
00040A  58                              2481+        DC    AL1(88)
00040B  0003EB                          2482+        ORG   SVCHTABL+C'C'
0003EB  60                              2483+        DC    AL1(96)
0003EC  0003FD                          2484+        ORG   SVCHTABL+C'N'
0003FD  68                              2485+        DC    AL1(104)
0003FE  000410                          2486+        ORG   SVCHTABL+C'Y'
000410  70                              2487+        DC    AL1(112)
000411  78                              2488+        ORG   SVCHTABL+C'Z'
000412  0003EC                          2489+        DC    AL1(120)
0003EC  80                              2490+        ORG   SVCHTABL+C'D'
0003ED  000397                          2491+        DC    AL1(128)
000397  88                              2492+        ORG   SVCHTABL+C'?'
000398  0003F0                          2493+        DC    AL1(136)
0003F0  90                              2494+        ORG   SVCHTABL+C'H'
0003F1  0003ED                          2495+        DC    AL1(144)
0003ED  98                              2496+        ORG   SVCHTABL+C'E'
0003EE  000428                          2497+        DC    AL1(152)
                                        2498+        ORG   SVCHTABL+256

000428                                  2500+SVCRTN  DS    0D
                                        2501+*   .                   THE PSWS                    * * * * * * *
                                        2502+*   IN THE FOLLOWING PSWS, THE THIRD BYTE INDICATES
                                        2503+*   WHETHER THE SVC IS RESTRICTED:
                                        2504+*        X'00' -> OPERATING SYSTEM ONLY
                                        2505+*        X'FF' -> AVAILABLE TO USER ALSO
                                        2506+*
                                        2507+*   THE FOURTH BYTE INDICATES WHICH SAVE AREA TO USE;
                                        2508+*   SVCSAVE BELOW SHOWS THE CODE VALUES.

000428  00000000000004EE                2508+        DC    B'00000000',B'00000000',X'0000',AL3(XP)
000430  0000000000000534                2509+        DC    B'00000000',B'00000000',X'0004',AL3(XV)
000438  00000000400005C0                2510+        DC    B'00000000',B'00000000',X'0004',AL3(XEIC)
000440  00000000400005D2                2511+        DC    B'00000000',B'00000000',X'0004',AL3(XEXC)
000448  00000000400007D4                2512+        DC    B'00000000',B'00000000',X'0004',AL3(XCOM)
000450  FF0000C00000600                 2513+        DC    B'11111111',B'00000000',X'000C',AL3(XB)
000458  FF0000C000006B6                 2514+        DC    B'11111111',B'00000000',X'000C',AL3(XA)
000460  00000000400087A                 2515+        DC    B'00000000',B'00000000',X'000C',AL3(XF)
000468  000000004000008A6               2516+        DC    B'00000000',B'00000000',X'0004',AL3(XI)
000470  00000000400056A                 2517+        DC    B'00000000',B'00000000',X'0004',AL3(XJ)
000478  FF00FF08000008EC                2518+        DC    B'11111111',B'00000000',X'FF08',AL3(XPER)
000480  FF00FF0800000978                2519+        DC    B'11111111',B'00000000',X'FF08',AL3(XR)
000488  FF00FF0800000780                2520+        DC    B'11111111',B'00000000',X'FF08',AL3(XS)
```

```
SAMPLE OPERATING SYSTEM    VERSION 2.00

LOC    OBJECT CODE    ADDR1 ADDR2  STMT    SOURCE STATEMENT

000490 0000FF0400000BCA              2521+       DC   B'00000000',B'00000000',X'FF04',X'00',AL3(XN)
000498 0000FF0800000A0A              2522+       DC   B'00000000',B'00000000',X'FF08',X'00',AL3(XY)
0004A0 FF00FF0800000A42              2523+       DC   B'11111111',B'00000000',X'FF08',X'00',AL3(XZ)
0004A8 FF00FF080000007C6             2524+       DC   B'11111111',B'11111111',X'FF08',X'00',AL3(XD)
0004B0 0000FF0400000A8E              2525+       DC   B'00000000',B'00000000',X'FF04',X'00',AL3(XQUE)
0004B8 FF00FF0800000842              2526+       DC   B'11111111',B'00000000',X'FF08',X'00',AL3(XH)
0004C0 FF00000C00000608              2527+       DC   B'11111111',B'00000000',X'000C',X'00',AL3(XAUTO)

                                     2529+SVCSAVE DS   0F .             THE SAVE AREA OFFSETS
0004C8 0000021C                      2530+       DC   A(SYSSEMSA) .     CODE 00 -> SYSSEMSA
0004C8 0000004C                      2531+       DC   A(PCBISA-PCB) .   CODE 04 -> INTERRUPT SAVE AREA
0004D0 000000A0                      2532+       DC   A(PCBFSA-PCB) .   CODE 08 -> FAULT SAVE AREA
0004D4 000000F4                      2533+       DC   A(PCBMSA-PCB) .   CODE 0C -> MEMORY SAVE AREA

                                     2535+*********************************************************************
                                     2536+**                                                                 **
                                     2537+**  RETURN SEQUENCE FOR REQUEST DRIVEN ROUTINES AND TRAFFIC CONTROLLER  **
                                     2538+**                                                                 **
                                     2539+*********************************************************************

0004D8                               2541+       DS   0D
0004D8 00000000000004E0              2542+RETURN  DC   B'00000000',B'00000000',X'0000',X'00',AL3(RETURNR)

0004E0                               2544+RETURNR EQU  * .               RETURN ROUTINE FOR SVC'S & XPER
0004E0 D207 0420 E000   00020 00000  2545+       MVC  SVCOLD,SAPSW .     SAVE PSW IN A SAFE PLACE
0004E6 980F E008        00008        2546+       LM   0,15,SAREGS .      RELOAD REGISTERS
0004EA 8200 0420        00020        2547+       LPSW SVCOLD .           AND RETURN
```

```
      SAMPLE OPERATING SYSTEM          VERSION 2.00

LOC     OBJECT CODE     ADDR1  ADDR2   STMT   SOURCE STATEMENT

                                       2549*  ***************************************
                                       2550*  *                                     *
                                       2551*  *        REQUEST DRIVEN ROUTINES      *
                                       2552*  *                                     *
                                       2553*  ***************************************

                                       2555*  ***************************************
                                       2556*  *                                     *
                                       2557*  *                                     *
                                       2558*  *              XP ROUTINE             *
                                       2559*  *                                     *
                                       2560*  *  FUNCTION: TO IMPLEMENT "P" PRIMITIVE FOR SEMAPHORES
                                       2561*  *  DATABASES: UPON ENTRY, REGISTER 2 CONTAINS ADDRESS SM
                                       2562*  *             SM      DS 0D   SEMAPHORE DEFINITION
                                       2563*  *             SMVAL   DS F    VALUE
                                       2564*  *             SMPTR   DS A    POINTER TO FIRST WAITER
                                       2565*  *  ROUTINES USED: XPER
                                       2566*  *  PROCEDURE: SUBTRACT ONE FROM SMVAL; IF NON-NEGATIVE, RETURN.
                                       2567*  *             IF NEGATIVE, PLACE RUNNING PROCESS AT END OF LIST
                                       2568*  *             OF PROCESSES WAITING ON SM. BLOCK CALLING PROCESS;
                                       2569*  *             ENTER TRAFFIC CONTROLLER.
                                       2570*  *  ERROR CHECKS: NONE
                                       2571*  *  INTERRUPTS: OFF
                                       2572*  *  USER ACCESS: NO
                                       2573*  ***************************************

0004EE                                 2575+XP      EQU   *              THE XP ROUTINE
0004EE                                 2576+        USING *,1
000000                                 2577+        USING SM,2           ARGUMENT IS A SEMAPHORE
0004EE  5830 2000            00000     2578+        L     3,SMVAL        GET THE VALUE
0004F2  0630                           2579+        BCTR  3,0            SUBTRACT ONE
0004F4  5030 2000            00000     2580+        ST    3,SMVAL        AND STORE IT BACK
0004F8  1233                           2581+        LTR   3,3            SET CONDITION CODE
0004FA  4740 1014            00502     2582+        BM    XPWAIT         IF IT'S NEGATIVE, MUST WAIT
0004FE  8200 04D8     004D8            2583+        LPSW  RETURN         ELSE RETURN NOW
000502  4140 2004            00004     2584+XPWAIT  LA    4,SMPTR        START GOING DOWN
000506  5850 2004            00004     2585+        L     5,SMPTR        CHAIN OF POINTERS
                                       2586+        DROP  15
000000                                 2587+        USING PCB,5
00050A  1255                           2588+XPLOOP  LTR   5,5            IF REACHED END
00050C  4780 102E            0051C     2589+        BZ    XPTHEN         ADD OUR PCB ON. ELSE,
000510  4140 5030            00030     2590+        LA    4,PCBNSW       INCREMENT POINTERS
000514  5850 5030            00030     2591+        L     5,PCBNSW
000518  47F0 107C            0050A     2592+        B     XPLOOP         AND TRY AGAIN
                                       2593+        DROP  5
000000                                 2594+        USING PCB,15
00051C  D203 4000 0270  00000 00270    2595+XPTHEN  MVC   0(4,4),RUNNING WE'RE AT THE END
000522  5050 F030            00030     2596+        ST    5,PCBNSW       STORE NULL POINTER
000526  92FF F019            00019     2597+        MVI   PCBBLOKT,X'FF' AND WE'RE BLOCKED
00052A  D253 F04C 021C  0004C 0021C    2598+        MVC   PCBISA,SYSSEMSA SWITCH SAVE AREAS
000530  47F0 107C            0056A     2599+        B     XPER           SO RUN SOMEONE ELSE
                                       2600+        DROP  2
```

```
SAMPLE OPERATING SYSTEM          VERSION 2.00

LOC     OBJECT CODE   ADDR1 ADDR2    STMT    SOURCE STATEMENT

                                     2602 ** *  *  *  *  *  *  *  *  *  *  *  *  *  *  *  *  *  *
                                     2603 **
                                     2604 **
                                     2605 **                          XV ROUTINE
                                     2606 **
                                     2607 **  FUNCTION:  TO IMPLEMENT "V" PRIMITIVE FOR SEMAPHORES
                                     2608 **  DATABASES: UPON ENTRY, REGISTER 2 CONTAINS ADDRESS SM
                                     2609 **             SM      DS 0D   SEMAPHORE DEFINITION
                                     2610 **             SMVAL   DS F    VALUE
                                     2611 **             SMPTR   DS A    POINTER TO FIRST WAITER
                                     2612 **  ROUTINES USED: NONE
                                     2613 **  PROCEDURE: ADD ONE TO SMVAL. IF > ZERO, RETURN. IF ZERO OR
                                     2614 **             LESS, REMOVE FIRST PROCESS FROM WAITER CHAIN;
                                     2615 **             UNBLOCK IT; IF NEXTTRYM NOT SET, SET IT AND SET
                                     2616 **             NEXTTRY TO THAT PROCESS; RETURN; IF NEXTTRYM SET,
                                     2617 **             RETURN.
                                     2618 **  ERROR CHECKS: NONE
                                     2619 **  INTERRUPTS: OFF
                                     2620 **  USER ACCESS: NO
                                     2621 ** *  *  *  *  *  *  *  *  *  *  *  *  *  *  *  *  *  *

000534                               2623+XV       EQU   *                    THE XV ROUTINE
000534                               2624+         USING *,1
000000                               2625+         USING SM,2
000534  5830 2000         00000      2626+         L     3,SMVAL              ARGUMENT IS A SEMAPHORE
000538  5A30 18F4         00B28      2627+         A     3,=F'1'              GET THE VALUE
00053C  5030 2000         00000      2628+         ST    3,SMVAL              ADD ONE
000540  47D0 1014         00548      2629+         BNP   XVWAKEUP             AND STORE IT BACK
000544  8200 04D8   004D8            2630+         LPSW  RETURN               IF <=0, SOMEONE'S WAITING
000548  5840 2004         0004       2631+XVWAKEUP L     4,SMPTR              ELSE RETURN
                                     2632+         DROP  15                   GET THE FIRST OF THE GUYS
000000                               2633+         USING PCB,4
00054C  D203 2004 4030   00004 00030 2634+         MVC   SMPTR,PCBNSW         REMEMBER THE REST
000552  9200 4019         00019      2635+         MVI   PCBBLOKT,X'00'       WE'RE NO LONGER BLOCKING HIM
000556  95FF 0278         00278      2636+         CLI   NEXTTRYM,X'FF'       IS NEXT TRY MODIFIED?
00055A  4780 1032         00566      2637+         BE    XVRET                IF SO, WELL OK
00055E  5040 0274         00274      2638+         ST    4,NEXTTRY            ELSE MODIFY NEXTTRY
000562  92FF 0278         00278      2639+         MVI   NEXTTRYM,X'FF'       AND SAY SO
000566  8200 04D8         004D8      2640+XVRET    LPSW  RETURN               GET BACK
                                     2641+         DROP  2,4
```

```
LOC      OBJECT CODE      ADDR1  ADDR2   STMT    SOURCE STATEMENT

                                         2643+   *****************************************
                                         2644+   *                                       *
                                         2645+   *                                       *
                                         2646+   *                                       *
                                         2647+   *        XPER ROUTINE (TRAFFIC CONTROLLER)   *
                                         2648+   *                                       *
                                         2649+   *   FUNCTION: TO IMPLEMENT MULTIPROGRAMING   *
                                         2650+   *   DATABASES: NONE                      *
                                         2651+   *   ROUTINES USED: NONE                  *
                                         2652+   *   PROCEDURE: STARTING WITH NEXTTRY, SEARCH FOR PROCESS ON ALL  *
                                         2653+   *     PCB CHAIN NOT BLOCKED OR STOPPED; IF FOUND, USE AS  *
                                         2654+   *     NEW RUNNING, FOR 50 MS OF TIME AND RETURN. ELSE,   *
                                         2655+   *     ENTER WAIT STATE WITH INTERRUPTS ON, AND TRY TO    *
                                         2656+   *     SCHEDULE AGAIN AFTER INTERRUPT; RETURN.            *
                                         2657+   *   ERROR CHECKS: NONE                   *
                                         2658+   *   INTERRUPTS: OFF                      *
                                         2659+   *   USER ACCESS: NO                      *
                                         2660+   *****************************************
00056A                          00078    2661+XPER     EQU  *                 ROUTINE XPER: TRAFFIC SCHEDULER
00056A 8000 0078                         2662+         SSM  IONEW             MASK OFF INTERRUPTS
00056E 0510                              2663+         BALR 1,0
                                         2664+         USING *,1
000570 58A0 0274                00274    2665+         L    10,NEXTTRY        START LOOKING AT NEXTTRY
000574 188A                              2666+         LR   11,10             REMEMBER WHICH THAT WAS
                                         2667+         USING PCB,10
000576 95FF A019                00019    2668+GWLOOP   CLI  PCBBLOKT,X'FF'    IF IT'S BLOCKED,
00057A 4780 1016                00586    2669+         BE   GWINC             IGNORE
00057E 95FF A018                00018    2670+         CLI  PCBSTOPT,X'FF'    ELSE, IF IT'S NOT STOPPED,
000582 4770 1030                05A0     2671+         BNE  GWRUN             WE CAN RUN IT
000586 4770 A010                00010    2672+GWINC    L    10,PCBNPALL       ELSE, GO TO THE NEXT
00058A 19AB                              2673+         CR   10,11             IF WE'VE SEEN ALL, QUIT
00058C 4770 1006                00576    2674+         BNE  GWLOOP            ELSE TRY AGAIN
000590 8200 1028                00598    2675+         LPSW IDLE              SIT AND WAIT
000598 0D                                2676+IDLE     DS   0D
000598 FE020000000056A                   2677+         DC   B'11111110',B'00000010',X'00000',X'000',AL3(XPER)
0005A0 D203 0274 A010    00274  00010    2679+GWRUN    MVC  NEXTTRY,PCBNPALL  GET A NEW NEXTTRY
0005A6 9200 0278                00278    2680+         MVI  NEXTTRYM,X'00'    NOT MODIFIED
0005AA 50A0 0270                00270    2681+         ST   10,RUNNING        GET A NEW RUNNING
0005AE 41E0 A04C                0004C    2682+         LA   14,PCBISA
0005B2 D203 0050 104C    00050  0104C    2683+         MVC  TIMER,QUANTUM     INTERRUPT AFTER 50 MS
0005B8 8200 04D8                004D8    2684+         LPSW RETURN            AND GO TO RETURNR
0005BC 00000F00                          2685+QUANTUM  DC   X'00000F00'       QUANTUM OF TIME
                                         2686+         DROP 10
000000                                   2687+         USING PCB,15
```

```
SAMPLE OPERATING SYSTEM          VERSION 2.00

LOC   OBJECT CODE  ADDR1 ADDR2   STMT  SOURCE STATEMENT

                                 2689** ****************************************************
                                 2690**                    XEXC ROUTINE
                                 2691** ****************************************************
                                 2692**
                                 2693**       FUNCTION: TO ENTER SMC SECTION
                                 2694**       DATABASES: NONE
                                 2695**       ROUTINES USED: NONE
                                 2696**       PROCEDURE: INCREMENT SMC BYTE IN PCB BY ONE; RETURN.
                                 2697**       ERROR CHECKS: NONE
                                 2698**       INTERRUPTS: OFF
                                 2699**       USER ACCESS: NO
                                 2700**
                                 2701** ****************************************************
                                 2703+*XEXC  EQU   *           ROUTINE XEXC: ENTER SMC SECTION
005C0                            2704+      USING *,1
005C0                            2705+      SR    8,8
005C0 1B88                       2706+      IC    8,PCBINSMC  ADD ONE TO IN SMC BYTE
005C2 4380 F01A         0001A    2707+      LA    8,1(8) .
005C6 4188 0001                  2708+      STC   8,PCBINSMC
005CA 4280 F01A         0001A    2709+      LPSW  RETURN .     AND LEAVE
005CE 8200 04D8         004D8
                                 2711** ****************************************************
                                 2712**                    XCOM ROUTINE
                                 2713** ****************************************************
                                 2714**
                                 2715**       FUNCTION: TO LEAVE SMC SECTION
                                 2716**       DATABASES: NONE
                                 2717**       ROUTINES USED: XP, XV
                                 2718**       PROCEDURE: DECREMENT SMC BYTE IN PCB BY ONE; IF NOT ZERO,
                                 2719**                  RETURN. ELSE, CHECK FOR STOP WAITING; IF STOP
                                 2720**                  WAITING, ALLOW STOP AND BLOCK SELF; RETURN. IF NO
                                 2721**                  STOP WAITING, RETURN.
                                 2722**       ERROR CHECKS: NONE
                                 2723**       INTERRUPTS: OFF
                                 2724**       USER ACCESS: NO
                                 2725**
                                 2726** ****************************************************
                                 2728+*XCOM  EQU   *           ROUTINE XCOM: LEAVE SMC
005D2                            2729+      USING *,1
005D2                            2730+      SR    8,8
005D2 1B88                       2731+      IC    8,PCBINSMC
005D4 4380 F01A         0001A    2732+      BCTR  8,0 .        SUBTRACT ONE FROM IN SMC BYTE
005D8 0680                       2733+      STC   8,PCBINSMC
005DA 4280 F01A         0001A    2734+      LTR   8,8 .
005DE 1288                       2735+      BNZ   XCOMRET      IS IT ZERO?
005E0 4770 102A         005FC    2736+      CLI   PCBSW,X'00'  NO, THEN GET BACK. OTHERWISE,
005E4 9500 F01B         0001B    2737+      BE    XCOMRET      IS STOP WAITING?
005E8 4780 102A         005FC    2738+      MVI   PCBSW,X'00' . IF NOT, RETURN
005EC 9200 F01B         0001B    2739+      LA    2,PCBSRS     STOPS NOT WAITING AFTER THIS
005F0 4120 F034         00034    2740+      SVC   C'V'         WE'LL "V" THE STOPPER,
005F4 0AE5                       2741+      LA    2,PCBSES .
005F6 4120 F03C         0003C    2742+      SVC   C'P'         AND "P" THE STOPPEE.
005FA 0AD7                       2743+*XCOMRET LPSW RETURN .    AND HERE (IF EVER) WE RETURN
005FC 8200 04D8         004D8
```

```
LOC     OBJECT CODE   ADDR1 ADDR2   STMT   SOURCE STATEMENT

                                    2745+  ******************************************
                                    2746+  *                                        *
                                    2747+  *                                        *
                                    2748+  *              XA ROUTINE                *
                                    2749+  *             XAUTO ROUTINE              *
                                    2750+  *   FUNCTION: TO ALLOCATE MEMORY          *
                                    2751+  *   DATABASES: UPON ENTRY, REGISTER 2 CONTAINS ADDRESS XAX:
                                    2752+  *      XAX      DS 0D
                                    2753+  *      XAXSIZE  DS F    SIZE OF BLOCK TO BE ALLOCATED
                                    2754+  *      XAXADDR  DS F    ADDRESS OF FIRST BYTE OF BLOCK
                                    2755+  *      XAXALGN  DS F    ALIGNMENT OF BLOCK
                                    2756+  *   ROUTINES USED: XEXC, XCOM, XP, XV,
                                    2757+  *   PROCEDURE: LOCK FSB SEMAPHORE. SEARCH FREE STORAGE FOR LARGE
                                    2758+  *      ENOUGH MEMORY BLOCK; ALIGN BOUNDARY; USE XB TO
                                    2759+  *      CHAIN ANY LEFTOVER BLOCKS TO FREE STORAGE LIST;
                                    2760+  *      PLACE ADDRESS OF ALLOCATED BLOCK IN XAXADDR; UNLOCK
                                    2761+  *      FSB SEMAPHORE; RETURN. IF CAN'T SATISFY REQUEST
                                    2762+  *      UNLOCK FSB SEMAPHORE. APPLY XP ROUTINE TO MEMORY
                                    2763+  *      SEMAPHORE; BLOCKING PROCESS RUNNING UNTIL MEMORY
                                    2764+  *      FREED; THEN UNBLOCK; TRY TO SATISFY REQUEST AGAIN.
                                    2765+  *   ERROR CHECKS: NONE
                                    2766+  *   INTERRUPTS: ON
                                    2767+  *   USER ACCESS: NO
                                    2768+  *                                        *
                                    2769+  ******************************************

000600                              2771+ *XA      EQU   *               THE XA ROUTINE, TO ALLOCATE
000600                              2772+          USING *,1             SET REGISTER ZERO TO ONE TO
000600  4100 0001        00001      2773+          LA    0,1               INDICATE C'A' CALL
000604  47F0 100E        0060E      2774+ *        B     XACOM           AUTO STORAGE ENTRY POINT
000608                              2775+ *XAUTO   EQU   *
000608                              2777+          USING *,0             REG0=0 INDICATES C'F' CALL
000608  1B00                        2778+          SR    0,0             RESET BASE REGISTER PROPERLY
00060A  5810 1824        00E2C      2779+          L     1,=A(XAX)
00060E  085A                        2780+ *XACOM   USING XAX,1           ENTER SMC
000610  1872                        2781+          LR    7,2             ARGUMENT LIST
000000                              2782+          USING XAX,7
000612  5860 7000        7000       2783+          LA    0,XAXSIZE       GET THE SIZE REQUESTED
000616  4120 0184        0184       2784+ *XATOP   LA    2,FSBSEM        LOCK THE FSB SEMAPHORE
00061A  0AD7                        2785+          SVC   C'P'
00061C  4150 0180        0180       2786+          LA    5,FSBPTR        START LOOKING DOWN
000620  5840 0180        0180       2787+          L     4,FSBPTR        THE FREE STORAGE LIST
000624  5880 7008        0008       2788+          L     8,XAXALGN       WE WOULD HAVE TO START AT WITH
000628  0680                        2789+          BCTR  8,0             THIS CONSTANT TO FIND ALIGNMENT
000000                              2790+          USING FSB,4
00062A  1244                        2791+          LTR   4,4             IF AT THE END,
00062C  4780 1056        00656      2792+ *XALOOP  BZ    XAWAIT          WAIT UNTIL A "FREE" OP
000630  1BD4                        2793+          LR    13,0            FIND THE LOCATION
000632  0600                        2794+          BCTR  13,0            IN THIS BLOCK WITH THIS
000634  16D8                        2795+          OR    13,8            ALIGNMENT
000636  41DD 0001        00001      2796+          LA    13,1(13)        THAT'S IT
00063A  189D                        2797+          LR    9,4             AND NOW GET IN REG 9
00063C  1B94                        2798+          SR    9,4             WHAT IS WASTED AT THE FRONT
00063E  5830 4004        00004      2799+          L     3,FSBSIZE       GET SIZE MINUS WASTE AT
```

```
LOC    OBJECT CODE  ADDR1 ADDR2  STMT  SOURCE STATEMENT
000642 1B39                      2800+        SR    3,9 .              FRONT, LEAVING EFFECTIVE SIZE
000644 1963                      2801+        CR    6,3 .              IS IT ENOUGH?
000646 47D0 1062          00662  2802+        BNP   XAFOUND            EUREKA!
00064A 4150 4000   00000         2803+        LA    5,FSBNEXT .        OH WELL, GET THE NEXT FREE
00064E 5840 4000   00000         2804+        L     4,FSBNEXT .        STORAGE BLOCK ON THE CHAIN
000652 47F0 102A          0062A  2805+        B     XALOOP .           BETTER LUCK NEXT TIME
000656 0AE5                      2806+XAWAIT  SVC   C'V' .             NEED TO WAIT
000658 4120 018C          0018C  2807+        LA    2,MEMORY .         SO WE LET OTHER PEOPLE GET IN
00065C 0AD7                      2808+        SVC   C'P' .             SO THEY'LL WAKE US UP
00065E 47F0 1016          00616  2809+        B     XATOP .            AND THEN WE'LL TRY AGAIN
000662 50D0 7004          00004  2810+XAFOUND ST    13,XAXADDR         WE'VE NOW GOT THE ADDRESS
000666 D203 5000 4000 00000 00000 2811+       MVC   0(4,5),FSBNEXT .   UNLINK THE BLOCK OUT
00066C 58C0 4004          00004  2812+        L     12,FSBSIZE .       GET THE WHOLE BLOCK SIZE
000670 4120 0048          00048  2813+        LA    2,SATEMP .         START MAKING UP ARG LISTS
000000                           2814+        USING XBX,2 .            FOR THE XB RTN
000674 18AD                      2815+        LR    10,13 .            THE STARTING LOCATION
000676 1BA4                      2816+        SR    10,4 .             MINUS THE START OF THE BLOCK
000678 4780 1086          00686  2817+        BZ    XANF .             IF NONE WASTED AT FRONT, SKIP
00067C 5040 2004          00004  2818+        ST    4,XBXADDR .        ELSE FREE, STARTING THERE
000680 50A0 2000          00000  2819+        ST    10,XBXSIZE .       UP TO THE BEGINNING OF THE
000684 0AC2                      2820+        SVC   C'B' .             ALLOCATION; INSERT IT IN CHAIN
000686 18BD                      2821+XANF    LR    11,13 .            THE STARTING ADDR PLUS THE SIZE
000688 1AB6                      2822+        AR    11,6 .             GIVES THE FIRST UNUSED ADDR
00068A 1BCA                      2823+        SR    12,10 .            MINUS THE WASTE AT FRONT,
00068C 1BC6                      2824+        SR    12,6 .             MINUS THE PART ALLOCATED. IF
00068E 4780 109C          0069C  2825+        BZ    XARETURN .         NONE LEFT OVER, GOOD
000692 50B0 2004          00004  2826+        ST    11,XBXADDR .       ELSE STORE ADDRESS AND
000696 50C0 2000          00000  2827+        ST    12,XBXSIZE .       SIZE, AND LINK ONTO
00069A 0AC2                      2828+        SVC   C'B' .             FREE STORAGE LIST
                                 2829+        DROP
00069C 4120 0184          00184  2830+XARETURN LA   2,FSBSEM .         WE ARE DONE, SO NOW SOMEONE
0006A0 0AE5                      2831+        SVC   C'V' .             ELSE CAN COME IN
0006A2 1200                      2832+        LTR   0,0 .              IS THIS FOR AUTOMATIC STORAGE?
0006A4 4770 10B0          006B0  2833+        BNZ   XABACK .           IF NOT, RETURN NOW
0006A8 5060 F044          00044  2834+        ST    6,PCBASIZE .       OTHERWISE, STORE SIZE AND
0006AC 50D0 F048          00048  2835+        ST    13,PCBAADDR .      ADDRESS OF AUTOMATIC STORAGE
0006B0 0A6B                      2836+XABACK  SVC   C'.' .             LEAVE SMC SECTION
0006B2 8200 04D8          004D8  2837+        LPSW  RETURN .           GET BACK JOJO
                                 2838+        DROP  4,7
```

```
LOC     OBJECT CODE  ADDR1 ADDR2   STMT    SOURCE STATEMENT

                                   2840**  **********************************************
                                   2841**  *
                                   2842**  *
                                   2843**  *
                                   2844**  *               XF ROUTINE
                                   2845**  *
                                   2846**  *    FUNCTION: TO FREE MEMORY
                                   2847**  *    DATABASES: UPON ENTRY, REGISTER 2 CONTAINS ADDRESS XFX:
                                   2848**  *               XFX     DS 0D
                                   2849**  *               XFXSIZE DS F    SIZE OF BLOCK TO BE FREED
                                   2850**  *               XFXADDR DS A    ADDRESS OF FIRST BYTE OF BLOCK
                                   2851**  *    ROUTINES USED: XEXC, XFP, XB, XV, XCOM
                                   2852**  *    PROCEDURE: LOCK FSB SEMAPHORE; SEARCH FREE STORAGE LIST TO
                                   2853**  *               FIND IF ANY FREE BLOCK CONTIGUOUSLY FOLLOWS OR
                                   2854**  *               PRECEDES BLOCK TO BE FREED; IF THERE IS ANY,
                                   2855**  *               COMPACT THEM INTO SINGLE BLOCK OF COMBINED SIZE;
                                   2856**  *               USE XB TO CHAIN COMPACTED BLOCK ONTO FREE STORAGE
                                   2857**  *               LIST; WAKEUP ALL PROCESSES WAITING ON MEMORY
                                   2858**  *               SEMAPHORE; UNLOCK FSB SEMAPHORE; RETURN.
                                   2859**  *    ERROR CHECKS: NONE
                                   2860**  *    INTERRUPTS: ON
                                   2861**  *    USER ACCESS: NO

0006B6                             2863+XF       EQU   *,1          THE XF ROUTINE, TO FREE STORAGE
0006B6                             2864+         USING *,1
0006B6  015A                       2865+         SVC   C'!'         ENTER SMC SECTION
0006B8  1872                       2866+         LR    7,2
000000                             2867+         USING XFX,7        THE ARGUMENT LIST
0006BA  5830 7000       00000      2868+         L     3,XFXSIZE    GET THE SIZE
0006BE  5840 7004       00004      2869+         L     4,XFXADDR    AND THE ADDRESS
0006C2  1853                       2870+         LR    5,3          GET ADDRESS OF THE END OF THE
0006C4  1A54                       2871+         AR    5,4          BLOCK TO BE FREED
0006C6  4120 0184       00184      2872+         LA    2,FSBSEM     LOCK FSBSEM
0006CA  0AD7                       2873+         SVC   C'P'
0006CC  4180 0180       00180      2874+         LA    8,FSBPTR     START LOOKING DOWN THE FREE
0006D0  5860 0180       00180      2875+         L     6,FSBPTR     STORAGE LIST, FOR COMPACTION
000000                             2876+         USING FSB,6
0006D4  1266                       2877+XFLOOP   LTR   6,6          ARE WE THROUGH?
0006D6  4780 105E       00714      2878+         BZ    XFLINK .     IF SO, JUST ADD IT ON
0006DA  5890 6000       00000      2879+         L     9,FSBNEXT    IF NOT, GET THE NEXT PTR
0006DE  1965                       2880+         CR    6,5 .        IS THIS BLOCK RIGHT AFTER OURS?
0006E0  4770 103A       00714      2881+         BNE   XFTHEN .     IF NOT, OK, BUT IF IT IS,
0006E4  5098 6004       00004      2882+         ST    9,0(8) .     WE CAN COMPACT. SO UNCHAIN IT
0006E8  5830 6004       00004      2883+         A     3,FSBSIZE    AND REMEMBER THE NEW SIZE
0006EC  47F0 1050       00706      2884+         B     XFBACKUP .   AND ON TO THE NEXT
0006F0  18A6                       2885+XFTHEN   LR   10,6          MAYBE IT'S RIGHT BEFORE OURS
0006F2  5AA0 6004       00004      2886+         A    10,FSBSIZE    GET ENDING ADDRESS OF FREE BLOCK
0006F6  19A4                       2887+         CR   10,4 .        IS IT RIGHT BEFORE OURS?
0006F8  4770 1052       00708      2888+         BNE   XFINC .      OH FUDGE! NO!
0006FC  5098 0000       00004      2889+         ST    9,0(8) .     I SO, UNCHAIN IT
000700  1846                       2890+         LR    4,6          GET NEW BEGINNING LOCATION
000702  5830 6004       00004      2891+         A     3,FSBSIZE    AND NEW SIZE OF FREE BLOCK
000706  1868                       2892+XFBACKUP LR    6,8          BACK UP ONE FSB
000708  4180 6000       00000      2893+XFINC    LA    8,FSBNEXT    ON TO THE NEXT FSB
00070C  5860 6000       00000      2894+         L     6,FSBNEXT
```

435

```
LOC     OBJECT CODE   ADDR1  ADDR2   STMT   SOURCE STATEMENT

000710  47F0 101E            006D4   2895+        B     XPLOOP .          TRY, TRY AGAIN
000714  4120 E048            00048   2896+XPLINK  LA    2,SATEMP .        START TO CALL XB
000000                               2897+        USING XBX,2
000718  5030 2000            00000   2898+        ST    3,XBXSIZE .       STORE SIZE
00071C  5040 2004            00004   2899+        ST    4,XBXADDR .       AND ADDRESS
000720  0AC2                         2900+        SVC   C'B' .            LINK IT ONTO THE FSB CHAIN
000000                               2901+        USING SM,2
000722  4120 018C            0018C   2902+        LA    2,MEMORY .        GET VALUE OF MEMORY SEMAPHORE
000726  41B0 0001            00001   2903+        LA    11,1(0,0) .       SUBTRACT FROM ONE; IT'S A HANDLE
00072A  5BB0 2000            00000   2904+        S     11,SMVAL .        ON THE # OF PEOPLE WAITING
                                     2905+        DROP  2
00072E  46B0 1088            0073E   2906+XPVLOOP BCT   11,XPVDO .        LOOP IF ANYONE ELSE IS WAITING
000732  4120 0184            00184   2907+        LA    2,FSBSEM .        WE'RE THROUGH SO
000736  0AE5                         2908+        SVC   C'V' .            UNLOCK FSBSEM
000738  0A6B                         2909+        SVC   C'k' .            LEAVE SMC
00073A  8200 04D8            004D8   2910+        LPSW  RETURN .          RETURN
00073E  0AE5                         2911+XPVDO   SVC   C'V' .            WAKE SOMEONE UP
000740  47F0 1078            0072E   2912+        B     XPVLOOP .         TRY AGAIN FOR ANOTHER
                                     2913+        DROP  6,7
```

```
LOC     OBJECT CODE   ADDR1 ADDR2   STMT   SOURCE STATEMENT

                                    2915* ****************************************************
                                    2916* *
                                    2917* *
                                    2918* *
                                    2919* *                        XB ROUTINE
                                    2920* * FUNCTION:  TO CHAIN A STORAGE BLOCK ONTO FREE STORAGE LIST
                                    2921* * DATABASES: UPON ENTRY, REGISTER 2 CONTAINS ADDRESS XBX:
                                    2922* *            XBX      DS  0D
                                    2923* *            XBXSIZE  DS  F     SIZE OF BLOCK
                                    2924* *            XBXADDR  DS  A     ADDRESS OF FIRST BYTE OF BLOCK
                                    2925* * ROUTINES USED: NONE
                                    2926* * PROCEDURE: SEARCH FREE STORAGE LIST TO FIND WHERE TO INSERT
                                    2927* *            FREE BLOCK IN ORDER OF INCREASING SIZE; FORMAT
                                    2928* *            BLOCK LIKE A FSB; INSERT; RETURN.
                                    2929* * ERROR CHECKS: NONE
                                    2930* * INTERRUPTS: OFF
                                    2931* * USER ACCESS: NO
                                    2932* * COMMENTS: SINCE XB ROUTINE ONLY CALLED BY XA AND XF, PSB
                                    2933* *           SEMAPHORE IS ALREADY LOCKED.
                                    2934* ****************************************************

000744                             2936 +XB        EQU   *,1
000744                             2937 +          USING *,1
000000                             2938 +          USING XBX,2
000744  5830 2000    00000         2939 +          L     3,XBXSIZE .     ARGUMENT LIST
000748  5840 2004    00004         2940 +          L     4,XBXADDR .     GET THE SIZE
00074C  4180 0180    00180         2941 +          LA    8,FSBPTR .      AND THE ADDRESS
000750  5860 0180    00180         2942 +          L     6,FSBPTR .      START LOOKING DOWN THE CHAIN
000754  1266                       2943 +          LTR   6,6 .           IF ZERO POINTER, WE ARE AT
000756  4780 102C    00770         2944 +          BZ    XBINSERT .      END OF CHAIN ALREADY
000000                             2945 +          USING FSB,6
00075A  5930 6004    00004         2946 +XBLOOP    C     3,FSBSIZE .     IF THE SIZE OF OURS IS LESS,
00075E  47D0 102C    00770         2947 +          BNP   XBINSERT .        TIME TO INSERT
000762  4180 6000    00000         2948 +          LA    8,FSBNEXT .     ELSE GO ON TO THE NEXT
000766  5860 6000    00000         2949 +          L     6,FSBNEXT .
00076A  1266                       2950 +          LTR   6,6 .           IF NOT ALREADY THROUGH
00076C  4770 1016    0075A         2951 +          BNZ   XBLOOP .        BRANCH BACK
000770  5048 0000    00000         2952 +XBINSERT  ST    4,0(8) .        NOW, LINK OURS ON
                                   2953 +          DROP  6
000000                             2954 +          USING PSB,4
000774  5060 4000    00000         2955 +          ST    6,FSBNEXT .     MAKE OURS POINT TO THE NEXT
000778  5030 4004    00004         2956 +          ST    3,FSBSIZE .     WITH THE RIGHT SIZE
00077C  8200 04D8    004D8         2957 +          LPSW  RETURN .        AND RETURN
                                   2958 +          DROP  2,4
```

437

```
LOC    OBJECT CODE      ADDR1 ADDR2   STMT   SOURCE STATEMENT

                                      2960+  ****************************************************
                                      2961+  *                                                  *
                                      2962+  *                                                  *
                                      2963+  *                                                  *
                                      2964+  *                  XC ROUTINE                      *
                                      2965+  *                                                  *
                                      2966+  *                                                  *
                                      2967+  *                                                  *
                                      2968+  *  FUNCTION:  TO CREATE A PROCESS
                                      2969+  *  DATABASES: UPON ENTRY, REGISTER 2 CONTAINS ADDRESS XCX:
                                      2970+  *                 XCX     DS 0D
                                      2971+  *                 XCXNAME DS CL8  NAME OF PROCESS TO BE CREATED
                                      2972+  *  ROUTINES USED: XEXC, XCOM, XN, XA, XI, XQUE
                                      2973+  *  PROCEDURE:  USE XA TO ALLOCATE NEW PCB; PLACE XCXNAME IN PCB;
                                      2974+  *              INITIALIZE SEMAPHORES; STOP; BLOCK; OUT OF SMC;
                                      2975+  *              CALL XI TO LINK PCB INTO PCB CHAINS; RETURN SMC;
                                      2976+  *  ERROR CHECKS: IF NAME ALREADY USED IN THIS GROUP, XQUE ENTERED.
                                              *  INTERRUPTS: ON
                                              *  USER ACCESS: YES
                                              ****************************************************

000780                                2978+XC      EQU  *              THE XC ROUTINE: CREATE A PROCESS
000780                                2979+        USING *,1
000780 1872                           2980+        LR   7,2
000000             00048              2981+        USING XCX,7
000782 4120 E048         00048        2982+        LA   2,SATEMP .       ARGUMENT LIST
000000                                2983+        USING XN,2 .          A XN-LIKE ARGUMENT LIST
000786 D207 2000 7000  00000 00048    2984+        MVC  XNXNAME,XCXNAME . GET THE NAME
00078C 0AD5                           2985+        SVC  C'N' .           AND CALL TO FIND THE PCB
00078E D503 2008 16B0  00008 00E30    2986+        CLC  XNXADDR,=A(0) .  SEE IF THERE
000794 4770 1044         007C4        2987+        BNE  XCERR .          IF ALREADY EXISTS, BAD
000798 0A5A                           2988+        SVC  C'!' .           ENTER SMC SECTION
                                      2989+        DROP 2
000000                                2990+        USING XAX,2 .         READY TO CALL XA
00079A D203 2000 16B4  00000 00E34    2991+        MVC  XAXSIZE,=A(LENPCB) . WE KNOW THE SIZE
0007A0 D203 2008 16B8  00008 00E38    2992+        MVC  XAXALGN,=P'8' .  AND THE ALIGNMENT
0007A6 0AC1                           2993+        SVC  C'A' .           SO CALL
0007A8 5820 2004         00004        2994+        L    2,XAXADDR .      FIND THE ADDRESS
                                      2995+        DROP 2,15
000000                                2996+        USING PCB,2 .         FILL IN THE PCB
0007AC D207 2000 7000  00000 00000    2997+        MVC  PCBNAME,XCXNAME . GIVE IT A NAME
0007B2 92FF 2018         00018        2998+        MVI  PCBSTOPT,X'FF' . IT'S STOPPED
0007B6 D232 2019 19F9  00019 01179    2999+        MVC  PCBBLOKT(PCBISA-PCBBLOKT),TEMPLATE+1  INITIALIZE PCB
0007BC 0AC9                           3000+        SVC  C'I' .           THREAD IT ON
0007BE 0A6B                           3001+        SVC  C',' .           LEAVE SMC SECTION
0007C0 8200 04D8         004D8        3002+        LPSW RETURN .         AND RETURN
0007C4 0A6F                           3003+XCERR   SVC  C'?' .           IF ALREADY EXISTS, ERROR
                                      3004+        DROP 2,7
```

438

```
SAMPLE OPERATING SYSTEM        VERSION 2.00

LOC    OBJECT CODE    ADDR1 ADDR2    STMT    SOURCE STATEMENT

                                     3006**  **********************************************************
                                     3007**  *                                                        *
                                     3008**  *                                                        *
                                     3009**  *                                                        *
                                     3010**  *                       XD ROUTINE                       *
                                     3011**  *                                                        *
                                     3012**  *  FUNCTION: TO DESTROY A PROCESS                         *
                                     3013**  *  DATABASES: UPON ENTRY, REGISTER 2 CONTAINS ADDRESS XDX: *
                                     3014**  *                 XDX      DS 0D                          *
                                     3015**  *                 XDXNAME  DS CL8  NAME OF PROCESS TO BE DESTROYED *
                                     3016**  *  ROUTINES USED: XEXC, XJ, XS, XN, XF, XCOM, XQUE        *
                                     3017**  *  PROCEDURE: USE XN TO FIND PCB FOR PROCESS TO BE DESTROYED; *
                                     3018**  *                 USE XJ TO UNLOCK PCB FROM PROCESS CHAINS; IF ANY *
                                     3019**  *                 MESSAGES FOR THIS PROCESS, FREE STORAGE FOR THEM; *
                                     3020**  *                 IF THERE IS ANY AUTOMATIC STORAGE, FREE IT; *
                                     3021**  *                 FREE STORAGE FOR PCB; RETURN.          *
                                     3022**  *  ERROR CHECKS: IF NAME DOESN'T EXIST OR PROCESS NOT STOPPED, *
                                     3023**  *                 XQUE ENTERED.                           *
                                     3024**  *  INTERRUPTS: ON                                        *
                                     3025**  *  USER ACCESS: YES                                      *
                                     3026**  *                                                        *
                                             **********************************************************

0007C6                               3027+XD     EQU   *
0007C6                               3028+       USING *,1
0007C6  1872                         3029+       LR    7,2
000000                               3030+       USING XDX,7
0007C8  4120 E048            00048   3031+       LA    2,SATEMP .            ARG LIST
000000                               3032+       USING XNX,2                READY TO CALL OUT
0007CC  D207 2000 00000  7000 00000  3033+       MVC   XNXNAME,XDXNAME .    WILL CALL XN
0007D2  0AD5                         3034+       SVC   C'N' .               GET NAME
0007D4  5820 2008            00008   3035+       L     2,XNXADDR .          AND CALL
                                     3036+       DROP  2                    GET ADDRESS
0007D8  1222                         3037+       LTR   2,2 .                IF ADDRESS IS NULL,
0007DA  4780 107A            00840   3038+       BZ    XDERR .              IT'S AN ERROR
000000                               3039+       USING PCB,2
0007DE  95FF 2018            00018   3040+       CLI   PCBSTOPT,X'FF' .      IF NOT STOPPED,
0007E2  4770 107A            00840   3041+       BNE   XDERR .              IT'S AN ERROR.
0007E6  0A5A                         3042+       SVC   C'!' .               ENTER SMC SECTION
                                     3043+       DROP  2
000000                               3044+       USING PCB,15
0007E8  0AD1                         3045+       SVC   C'J' .               ELSE UNTHREAD THE ENTRY
0007EA  1882                         3046+       LR    8,2 .                REMEMBER THE PCB PTR
0007EC  4120 E048            00048   3047+       LA    2,SATEMP .           READY TO CALL OUT AGAIN
000000                               3048+       USING PCB,8
                                     3049+       DROP  15
0007F0  5890 802C            0002C   3050+       L     9,PCBPM .            GET FIRST MESSAGE
0007F4  1299                         3051+XDLOOP  LTR   9,9 .               ANY MORE MESSAGES?
0007F6  4780 1054            0081A   3052+       BZ    XDCHECK .            IF NOT, FINISH UP
000000                               3053+       USING MSG,9
0007FA  58A0 9004            00004   3054+       L     10,MSGNEXT .         ELSE REMEMBER NEXT
0007FE  58B0 9008            00008   3055+       L     11,MSGSIZE .         GET THE SIZE
000802  41BB 000F            0000F   3056+       LA    11,15(11) .          AND MAKE IT SOME NUMBER
000806  5480 1676                    3057+       N     11,=F'-8' .          OF DOUBLEWORDS
000000                               3058+       USING XPX,2
00080A  5090 2004            00004   3059+       ST    9,XPXADDR .          FREE THE LOCATION
00080E  5080 2000            00000   3060+       ST    11,XPXSIZE .         THE NUMBER OF WORDS
```

```
             SAMPLE OPERATING SYSTEM        VERSION 2.00

LOC    OBJECT CODE       ADDR1 ADDR2  STMT   SOURCE STATEMENT

000812 0AC6                           3061+          SVC   C'F' .                DO IT
000814 189A                           3062+          LR    9,10 .                ON TO THE NEXT
000816 47F0 102E            007F4     3063+          B     XDLOOP .              GET NEXT MESSAGE
00081A D503 8048 166A  00048 00E30    3064+XDCHECK   CLC   PCBAADDR(4),=A(0) .   HAS AUTOMATIC STORAGE BEN
000820 4780 1068            00E30     3065+          BE    XDTHEN .              ALLOCATED? IF NOT, GO FINISH UP
000824 4120 8044            00044     3066+          LA    2,PCBASIZE .          SET UP ARGUMENT LIST
000828 0AC6                           3067+          SVC   C'F' .                FREE IT
00082C 4120 E048            00048     3068+          LA    2,SATEMP .            RESET REGISTER 2
000832 5080 2004            00004     3069+XDTHEN    ST    8,XPFXADDR            READY TO FREE THE PCB
000838 D203 2000 166E  00000 00E34    3070+          MVC   XPFXSIZE,=A(LENPCB) . THE SIZE
00083C 0AC6                           3071+          SVC   C'F' .                FREE IT
       0A6B                           3072+          SVC   C'?' .                LEAVE SMC
       0A6F                           3073+          LPSW  RETURN .              AND RETURN
000840 8200 04D8            004D8     3074+XDERR     SVC   C'?',9,8              IF PROCESS DOES NOT EXIST
                                      3075+          DROP  2,7,9,8
000000                                3076+          USING PCB,15


*************************************************************
                                      3078+*                                                    *
                                      3079+*                                                    *
                                      3080+*                  XH ROUTINE                        *
                                      3081+*                                                    *
                                      3082+*  FUNCTION:  TO HALT A JOB                          *
                                      3083+*  DATABASES:  NONE                                  *
                                      3084+*  ROUTINES USED:  XS, XR                            *
                                      3085+*  PROCEDURE:  SEND MESSAGE TO SUPERVISOR PROCESS FOR THIS JOB
                                      3086+*                INDICATING NORMAL TERMINATION. TRIES TO READ
                                      3087+*                MESSAGES FOREVER LOOPING; BLOCKS ITSELF, THEREBY
                                      3088+*                NEVER RETURNING.                    *
                                      3089+*  ERROR CHECKS:  NONE                               *
                                      3090+*  INTERRUPTS:  ON                                   *
                                      3091+*  USER ACCESS:  YES                                 *
                                      3092+*  COMMENTS:  USER NORMALLY USES THIS ROUTINE TO END A JOB. *
                                      3093+*                                                    *
*************************************************************

000842                                3096+XH        EQU   *                     THE XH ROUTINE: HALT A JOB
                                      3097+          USING *,1
000842 4120 1012            00854     3098+          LA    2,XHMSG1              SEND A MESSAGE TO *IBSUP
000846 0AE2                           3099+          SVC   C'S'                  SEND IT
000848 4120 102A            0086C     3100+XHLOOP    LA    2,XHMSG2              READY TO HEAR A REPLY
00084C 0AD9                           3101+          SVC   C'R'                  WHICH NEVER COMES
00084E 47F0 1006            00848     3102+          B     XHLOOP                BUT IF IT DOES WERE READY
000854                                3103+          DS    0F                    SAY TO *IBSUP
000854 5CC9C2E2E4D74040               3104+XHMSG1    DC    CL8'*IBSUP' .         TWELVE CHARACTERS
00085C 0000000C                       3105+          DC    F'12' .               SAVING WERE OK
000860 D7D9D6C7D9C1D440               3106+          DC    CL12'PROGRAM HALT' .  WHO SENDS US A MESSAGE
00086C                                3107+XHMSG2    DS    CL8 .                 ONE CHARACTER
000874 00000001                       3108+          DC    C'1' .                WHICH GOES HERE
000878                                3109+          DS    CL1,0H .
```

440

```
LOC    OBJECT CODE  ADDR1 ADDR2  STMT   SOURCE STATEMENT

                                 3111*  ***************************************************
                                 3112*  *                                               *
                                 3113*  *                    XI ROUTINE                  *
                                 3114*  *                                               *
                                 3115*  *   FUNCTION: TO CHAIN A PCB ONTO PROCESS CHAINS *
                                 3116*  *   DATABASES: UPON ENTRY, REGISTER 2 CONTAINS ADDRESS OF A PCB *
                                 3117*  *   ROUTINES USED: NONE                          *
                                 3118*  *   PROCEDURE: POINTER USED TO CHAIN PCB INTO ALL PCB CHAIN AND *
                                 3119*  *              THIS GROUP CHAIN RIGHT AFTER RUNNING PCB; RETURN. *
                                 3120*  *   ERROR CHECKS: NONE                           *
                                 3121*  *   INTERRUPTS: OFF                              *
                                 3122*  *   USER ACCESS: NO                              *
                                 3123*  *                                               *
                                 3124*  ***************************************************
00087A                           3126*XI    EQU   *,;              THE XI ROUTINE: THREAD IN A PCB
00087A                           3127*       USING *,;
00087A 58A0 F010         00010   3128*       L     10,PCBNPALL .   GET THE NEXT 'ALL' PCB
00087E 5020 F010         00010   3129*       ST    2,PCBNPALL .    STORE THIS PCB RIGHT AFTER MINE
000000                           3130*       DROP  15
000000                           3131*       USING PCB,10
000882 5020 A014         00014   3132*       ST    2,PCBLPALL .    THE NEXT ONE DOWN POINTS BACK
000000                           3133*       DROP  10
000000                           3134*       USING PCB,2
000886 50F0 2014         00014   3135*       ST    15,PCBLPALL .   THIS PCB POINTS BACK
00088A 50A0 2010         00010   3136*       ST    10,PCBNPALL .   AND FORWARD
000000                           3137*       DROP  2
000000                           3138*       USING PCB,15
00088E 58A0 F008         00008   3139*       L     10,PCBNPTG .    GET NEXT "THIS GROUP" PCB
000892 5020 F008         00008   3140*       ST    2,PCBNPTG .     RUNNING PCB POINTS TO NEW MEMBER
000000                           3141*       DROP  15              OF PROCESS GROUP
000000                           3142*       USING PCB,10
000896 5020 A00C         0000C   3143*       ST    2,PCBLPTG .     NEXT PCB DOWN POINTS BACK
000000                           3144*       DROP  10
000000                           3145*       USING PCB,2
00089A 50F0 200C         0000C   3146*       ST    15,PCBLPTG .    AND WE POINT BACKWARD
00089E 50A0 2008         00008   3147*       ST    10,PCBNPTG .    AND FORWARD
000000                           3148*       DROP  2
0008A2 8200 04D8         004D8   3149*       LPSW  RETURN .        RETURN
000000                           3150*       USING PCB,15
```

```
SAMPLE OPERATING SYSTEM          VERSION 2.00

LOC    OBJECT CODE    ADDR1 ADDR2    STMT    SOURCE STATEMENT

                                     3152+**********************************************************
                                     3153+*                                                        *
                                     3154+*                                                        *
                                     3155+*                        XJ ROUTINE                      *
                                     3156+*                                                        *
                                     3157+*        FUNCTION: TO UNCHAIN A PCB FROM PROCESS CHAINS   *
                                     3158+*        DATABASES: UPON ENTRY, REGISTER 2 CONTAINS ADDRESS OF A PCB *
                                     3159+*        ROUTINES USED: NONE                              *
                                     3160+*        PROCEDURE: POINTERS TO PCB IN ALL PCB CHAIN AND THIS GROUP *
                                     3161+*                   CHAIN MODIFIED WITHOUT FREEING STORAGE; RETURN. *
                                     3162+*        ERROR CHECKS: NONE                               *
                                     3163+*        INTERRUPTS: OFF                                  *
                                     3164+*        USER ACCESS: NO                                  *
                                     3165+**********************************************************

0008A6                               3167+XJ      EQU   *,1               THE XJ ROUTINE: UNTHREAD A PCB
0008A6                               3168+        USING *,1
                                     3169+        DROP  15
000000                               3170+        USING PCB,2
0008A6 5880 2014       00014         3171+        L     11,PCBLPALL .     GET PRECEDING PCB
0008AA 58A0 2010       00010         3172+        L     10,PCBNPALL .     AND FOLLOWING ONE IN "ALL"
                                     3173+        DROP  2                 CHAIN
000000                               3174+        USING PCB,11
0008AE 50A0 B010       00010         3175+        ST    10,PCBNPALL .     LAST POINTS TO NEXT
                                     3176+        DROP  11
000000                               3177+        USING PCB,10
0008B2 5080 A014       00014         3178+        ST    11,PCBLPALL .     NEXT POINTS TO LAST
                                     3179+        DROP  10
000000                               3180+        USING PCB,2
0008B6 5880 200C       0000C         3181+        L     11,PCBLPTG .      REDO FOR THIS GROUP PCB CHAIN
0008BA 58A0 2008       00008         3182+        L     10,PCBNPTG
                                     3183+        DROP  2
000000                               3184+        USING PCB,11
0008BE 50A0 B008       00008         3185+        ST    10,PCBNPTG .      LAST POINTS TO NEXT
                                     3186+        DROP  11
000000                               3187+        USING PCB,10
0008C2 5080 A00C       0000C         3188+        ST    11,PCBLPTG .      NEXT POINTS TO LAST
                                     3189+        DROP  10
0008C6 8200 04D8       004D8         3190+        LPSW  RETURN .          AND RETURN
000000                               3191+        USING PCB,15
```

```
SAMPLE OPERATING SYSTEM        VERSION 2.00

LOC    OBJECT CODE   ADDR1 ADDR2      STMT   SOURCE STATEMENT

                                      3193+**********************************************************
                                      3194+*                                                        *
                                      3195+*                                                        *
                                      3196+*                        XN ROUTINE                      *
                                      3197+*    FUNCTION: TO FIND THE PCB FOR A PROCESS GIVEN ITS NAME ONLY *
                                      3198+*    DATABASES: UPON ENTRY, REGISTER 2 CONTAINS ADDRESS XNX: *
                                      3199+*                 XNX      DS 0D                           *
                                      3200+*                 XNXNAME  DS CL8   NAME OF PROCESS        *
                                      3201+*                 XNXADDR  DS A     ADDRESS OF PCB         *
                                      3202+*    ROUTINES USED: NONE                                  *
                                      3203+*    PROCEDURE: SEARCH THIS GROUP PCB CHAIN FOR NAME; IF FOUND, *
                                      3204+*                 STORE POINTER IN XNXADDR. IF NOT FOUND, STORE *
                                      3205+*                 ZERO IN XNXADDR. RETURN.                *
                                      3206+*    ERROR CHECKS: NONE                                   *
                                      3207+*    INTERRUPTS: OFF                                       *
                                      3208+*    USER ACCESS: YES                                      *
                                      3209+*                                                        *
                                      3210+**********************************************************

0008CA                                3212+XN         EQU   *                    THE XN ROUTINE: FIND A NAMED PCB
0008CA                                3213+           USING *,1
000000                                3214+           USING XNX,2                THE ARG LIST
0008CA 18AF                           3215+           LR    10,15 .              FIRST PCB TO LOOK AT IS OURS
                                      3216+           DROP  15
000000                                3217+           USING PCB,10
0008CC 58A0 A008        00008         3218+XNLOOP     L     10,PCBNPTG           LOOK AT NEXT PCB
0008D0 D507 A000 2000 00000 00000     3219+           CLC   PCBNAME,XNXNAME .    HAS IT THE RIGHT NAME?
0008D6 4780 101A        008E4         3220+           BE    XNFOUND .            IF YES, OH JOY.
0008DA 19AF                           3221+           CR    10,15 .              IF NOT, ARE WE THROUGH?
0008DC 4770 1002        008CC         3222+           BNE   XNLOOP .             IF NOT, TRY NEXT PCB
0008E0 41A0 0000        00000         3223+           LA    10,0 .               ELSE, IT'S NOT HERE
0008E4 50A0 2008        00008         3224+XNFOUND    ST    10,XNXADDR .         FOUND IT, SAY WHERE.
0008E8 8200 04D8        004D8         3225+           LPSW  RETURN .             AND RETURN
                                      3226+           DROP  2,10
000000                                3227+           USING PCB,15
```

```
LOC     OBJECT CODE   ADDR1 ADDR2   STMT   SOURCE STATEMENT

                                    3229** *****************************************
                                    3230** *
                                    3231** *                    XR ROUTINE
                                    3232** *
                                    3233** *
                                    3234** *   FUNCTION: TO READ A MESSAGE
                                    3235** *   DATABASES: UPON ENTRY, REGISTER 2 CONTAINS ADDRESS XRX:
                                    3236** *       XRX        DS  0D
                                    3237** *       XRXNAME    DS  CL8   NAME OF SENDER PROCESS
                                    3238** *       XRXSIZE    DS  F     SIZE OF MESSAGE TEXT
                                    3239** *       XRXTEXT    DS  C     TEXT OF MESSAGE
                                    3240** *   ROUTINES USED: XP, XEXC, XN, XCOM, XP
                                    3241** *   PROCEDURE: USE XP ON MESSAGE SEMAPHORE RECEIVER TO SEE IF ANY
                                    3242** *       MESSAGES WAITING; IF NONE, PROCESS BLOCKED UNTIL
                                    3243** *       THERE IS ONE; LOCK MESSAGE CHAIN; REMOVE A MESSAGE
                                    3244** *       FROM CHAIN AND UNLOCK IT; MOVE TEXT OF MESSAGE,
                                    3245** *       PADDING WITH BLANKS OR TRUNCATING AS NECESSARY;
                                    3246** *       INDICATE CORRECT MESSAGE LENGTH AND NAME OF
                                    3247** *       MESSAGE SENDER; FREE STORAGE USED TO HOLD MESSAGE,
                                    3248** *       AND RETURN.
                                    3249** *   ERROR CHECKS: NONE
                                    3250** *   INTERRUPTS: ON
                                    3251** *   USER ACCESS: YES
                                    3252** *****************************************

0008BC                              3254+XR      EQU   *             THE XR ROUTINE: READ A MESSAGE
0008BC   1872                       3255+        USING *,1
000000                              3256+        LR    7,2
0008EE   4120 F024         00024    3257+        USING XRX,7
0008F2   0AD7                       3258+        LA    2,PCBMSR      ARG LIST
0008F4   0A5A                       3259+        SVC   C'P'          SEE IF MESSAGES WAITING
0008F6   4120 F01C         0001C    3260+        SVC   C'!'          ENTER SMC SECTION
0008FA   0AD7                       3261+        LA    2,PCBMSC      THEN LOCK THE MESSAGE CHAIN
0008FC   5850 F02C         0002C    3262+        SVC   C'P'
000000                              3263+        L     5,PCBPM       GET THE FIRST MESSAGE
000900   D203 F02C 5004 0002C 00004 3264+        USING MSG,5
000906   0A85                       3265+        MVC   PCBPM,MSGNEXT   REMEMBER THE NEXT
000908   5860 7008         00008    3266+        SVC   C'V'          UNLOCK THE MESSAGE CHAIN
00090C   5860 1554         0E240    3267+        L     6,XRXSIZE     GET THE BUFFER CAPACITY
000910   9240 700C         0091C    3268+        S     6,=F'2'       MINUS 1, MINUS 1
000914   4740 1030                  3269+        MVI   XRXTEXT,C' '  MOVE IN A BLANK
000918   4460 1080                  3270+        BM    KRNOB
00091C   4166 0001                  3271+        EX    6,XRFILL      THEN FILL THE REST WITH BLANKS
000920   5960 5008         00008    3272+XRNOB   LA    6,1(6)        THEN GET PROPER BUFFER COUNT
000924   4740 1042                  3273+        C     6,MSGSIZE     COMPARE WITH MESSAGE LENGTH
000928   5860 5008                  3274+        BL    XRTHEN        IF LESS, HANDLE ACCORDINGLY
00092C   0660                       3275+        L     6,MSGSIZE     ELSE COUNT FOR MVC IS MESSAGE
00092E   1266                       3276+        BCTR  6,0           SIZE MINUS ONE
000930   4740 104C                  3277+XRTHEN  LTR   6,6           ANY CHARACTERS TO MOVE?
000934   4460 1086                  3278+        BM    XRAFT         IF NOT, DON'T
000938   4166 0001                  3279+        EX    6,XRMOVE      ELSE MOVE THEM
00093C   5870 7008                  3280+XRAFT   LA    6,1(6)        THEN GET MESSAGE LENGTH
000940   58A0 5000                  3281+        ST    6,XRXSIZE     STORE IT
                                    3282+        L     10,MSGSENDR   GET SENDER'S PCB
                                    3283+        DROP  15
```

```
        SAMPLE OPERATING SYSTEM         VERSION 2.00

LOC     OBJECT CODE   ADDR1 ADDR2   STMT    SOURCE STATEMENT

000000                              3284+         USING  PCB,10
000094  D207 7000 A000 00000        3285+         MVC    XRXNAME,PCBNAME .     AND STORE SENDER'S NAME
00009A  5860 5008                   3286+         L      6,MSGSIZE .          GET SIZE OF MESSAGE TEXT,
00009E  4166 000C                   3287+         LA     6,LENMSG(6) .         ADD SIZE OF MESSAGE BLOCK
0000A2  4166 0007                   3288+         LA     6,7(6) .             AND TRUNCATE
0000A6  5460 1550                   3289+         N      6,=F'-8' .            UP
0000AA  1825                        3290+         LR     2,5 .                AND SET UP POINTER TO XPX
000000                              3291+         USING  XPX,2
00009C  5050 2004                   3292+         ST     5,XPXADDR .          STORE ADDRESS
0000A0  5060 2000                   3293+         ST     6,XPXSIZE .          STORE SIZE
0000A4  0AC6                        3294+         SVC    C'F' .               AND FREE THE MESSAGE BLOCK
0000A6  0A6B                        3295+         SVC    C'.' .               LEAVE SMC
0000A8  8200 04D8                   3296+         LPSW   RETURN .             AND RETURN
0000AC  D200 700D 700C 0000  0000   3297+XRFILL   MVC    XRXTEXT+1,XRXTEXT .  FILL WITH BLANKS
0000B2  D200 700C 500C 0000  0000   3298+XRMOVE   MVC    XRXTEXT,MSGTEXT .    MOVE TEXT
                                    3299+         DROP   2,5,7,10
000000                              3300+         USING  PCB,15

                                    3302+**********************************************************
                                    3303+**                                                      **
                                    3304+**                                                      **
                                    3305+**                     XS ROUTINE                       **
                                    3306+**                                                      **
                                    3307+** FUNCTION:  TO SEND A MESSAGE.                         **
                                    3308+** DATABASES: UPON ENTRY, REGISTER 2 CONTAINS ADDRESS XSX: **
                                    3309+**                 XSX,     DS  0D                       **
                                    3310+**                 XSXNAME  DS  CL8  NAME OF TARGET PROCESS **
                                    3311+**                 XSXSIZE  DS  F    SIZE OF TEXT         **
                                    3312+**                 XSXTEXT  DS  C    TEXT OF MESSAGE      **
                                    3313+** ROUTINES USED: XP, XV, XEXC, XCOM, XA, XN, XQUE        **
                                    3314+** PROCEDURE:  USE XN TO GET POINTER TO PCB OF TARGET PROCESS; **
                                    3315+**            USE XP, XV TO GET POINTER TO PCB OF TARGET PROCESS; **
                                    3316+**            USE LENGTH OF MESSAGE AND XA TO ALLOCATE BLOCK FOR **
                                    3317+**            MESSAGE; LOCK MESSAGE CHAIN OF TARGET PROCESS; **
                                    3318+**            PUT MESSAGE BLOCK AT END OF CHAIN: STORE SENDER **
                                    3319+**            NAME, SIZE AND TEXT OF MESSAGE; UNLOCK CHAIN; **
                                    3320+**            INDICATE MESSAGE CHAIN IS ONE LONGER; RETURN. **
                                    3321+** ERROR CHECKS: IF NO PROCESS BY GIVEN NAME, ENTER XQUE. **
                                    3322+** INTERRUPTS: ON                                        **
                                    3323+** USER ACCESS: YES                                      **
                                    3324+**                                                      **
                                    3302+**********************************************************
                                    3303+**                                                      **
                                    3304+**                                                      **
                                    3305+**                     XS ROUTINE                       **
                                    3306+**                                                      **
                                    3307+** FUNCTION:  TO SEND A MESSAGE.                         **
                                    3308+** DATABASES: UPON ENTRY, REGISTER 2 CONTAINS ADDRESS XSX: **
                                    3309+**                 XSX,     DS  0D                       **
                                    3310+**                 XSXNAME  DS  CL8  NAME OF TARGET PROCESS **
                                    3311+**                 XSXSIZE  DS  F    SIZE OF TEXT         **
                                    3312+**                 XSXTEXT  DS  C    TEXT OF MESSAGE      **

000978                    XS        3325+XS       EQU    *.
000978                              3326+         USING  *,1
000978  1872                        3327+         LR     7,2 .                THE XS ROUTINE: SEND MESSAGES
000000                              3328+         USING  XSX,7 .
00097A  4120 E048       00048       3329+         LA     2,SATEMP .           ARG LIST
000000                              3330+         USING  XNX,2 .              READY TO CALL OUT
00097E  D207 2000 7000 00000 00000  3331+         MVC    XNXNAME,XSXNAME .    ABOUT TO CALL XN
000984  0AD5                        3332+         SVC    C'N' .               SEE NAME OF TARGET PROCESS
000986  5840 2008       00008       3333+         L      4,XNXADDR .          SEE WHERE IT IS
00098A  1244                        3334+         LTR    4,4 .                IS THERE INDEED ONE?
00098C  4780 108A       00A02       3335+         BZ     XSERR .              IF NOT ,ERROR
000000                              3336+         USING  PCB,4
```

```
LOC    OBJECT CODE     ADDR1 ADDR2   STMT          SOURCE STATEMENT

000000                               3337+      DROP  2,15                  READY TO CALL YA
000990 0A5A                          3338+      USING XIX,2                 ENTERING SMC SECTION
000992 5830 7008        00008        3339+      SVC   C*1,2 .               GET THE STATED SIZE
000996 4133 000C        0000C        3340+      L     3,XSXSIZE .           PLUS THE AMOUNT OF OVERHEAD
00099A 4133 0007        00007        3341+      LA    3,LBMSG(3) .          AND TRUNCATE
00099E 5430 14C4        0E3C         3342+      LA    3,7(3) .              UP
0009A2 5030 2000        00000        3343+      N     3,=F'-8'
0009A6 D203 2008 14C0 00008 0E38     3344+      ST    3,XAXSIZE .           THAT'S THE SIZE OF THE REGION TO
0009AC 0AC1                          3345+      MVC   XAXALGN,=F'8' .       ALLOCATE ON A DOUBLEWORD BOUND
0009AE 5850 2004        00004        3346+      SVC   C*A'                  SO ALLOCATE ALREADY
0009AE                               3347+      L     5,XAXADDR .           GET THE ADDRESS
                                     3348+      DROP  2
0009B2 4120 401C        0001C        3349+      LA    2,PCBMSC              GET THE MESSAGE CHAIN SEMAPHORE
0009B6 0AD7                          3350+      SVC   C*P*                  AND LOCK IT
0009B8 4180 402C        0002C        3351+      LA    8,PCBPM               THEN START DOWN THE MESSAGE
0009BC 5890 402C        0002C        3352+      L     9,PCBPM               CHAIN
000000                               3353+      USING MSG,9
0009C0 1299                          3354+XSLOOP LTR   9,9                  ARE WE THROUGH?
0009C2 4780 105A        009D2        3355+      BZ    XSADD .               IF SO ADD IT ON.
0009C6 4180 9004        00004        3356+      LA    8,MSGNEXT             IF NOT, ON TO THE NEXT
0009CA 5890 9004        00004        3357+      L     9,MSGNEXT .
0009CE 47F0 1048        009C0        3358+      B     XSLOOP                AND TRY AGAIN
0009D2 5058 0000                     3359+XSADD  ST    5,0(8) .             CHAIN OURS ON THE END
                                     3360+      DROP
000000                               3361+      USING MSG,5
0009D6 D203 5204 14B8 00004 0E30     3362+      MVC   MSGNEXT,=A(0) .       SET NEXT POINTER NULL
0009DC 50F0 5000        00000        3363+      ST    15,MSGSENDR .         STORE THE SENDER
0009E0 5860 7008        00008        3364+      LT    6,XSXSIZE .           GET THE TEXT LENGTH
0009E4 5060 5008        00008        3365+      L     6,MSGSIZE .           AND STORE IT
0009E8 0660                          3366+      BCTR  6,0 .                 ONE LESS
0009EA 1266                          3367+      LTR   6,6 .                 TEST LENGTH
0009EC 4740 107C        009F4        3368+      BM    XSAFT .               IF ZERO, NOTHING TO MOVE
0009F0 4460 108C        00A04        3369+      EX    C*V,XSMOVE .          ELSE, MOVE IT
0009F4 4120 4024        00024        3370+XSAPT  LA    2,PCBMSR .           UNLOCK THE MESSAGE CHAIN
0009F8 0AE5                          3371+      SVC   C*V* .                THEN SAY THERE'S
0009FA 0AE5                          3372+      SVC   C*V' .                ONE MORE MESSAGE
0009FC 0A6B                          3373+      LPSW  =X .                  LEAVE SMC SECTION
0009FE 8200 04D8        004D8        3374+      SVC   C*? .                 AND RETURN
000A02 016F                          3375+XSERR  MVC   MSGTEXT,XSXTEXT .
000A04 D200 530C 700C 0000C 0000C    3376+XSMOVE DROP  PCB,15               THE MOVE FOR THE TEXT
                                     3377+
000000                               3378+
```

```
LOC     OBJECT CODE     ADDR1 ADDR2     STMT    SOURCE STATEMENT

                                        3380***********************************************************
                                        3381**                                                        *
                                        3382**                    XY ROUTINE                          *
                                        3383**                                                        *
                                        3384**      FUNCTION: TO START A PROCESS                       *
                                        3385**      DATABASES: UPON ENTRY, REGISTER 2 CONTAINS ADDRESS XYX: *
                                        3386**                  XYX      DS  0D                         *
                                        3387**                  XYYNAME  DS  CL8   NAME OF PROCESS TO BE STARTED *
                                        3388**                  XYYADDR  DS  A     STARTING ADDRESS OF PROCESS *
                                        3389**      ROUTINES USED: XN, XEXC, XCOM, XQUE               *
                                        3390**      PROCEDURE: USE XN TO GET POINTER TO PCB OF PROCESS TO BE *
                                        3391**                  STARTED; STORE IN PCB INTERRUPT SAVE AREA REGISTERS *
                                        3392**                  AND PSW WITH STARTING ADDRESS AS SENT FROM STARTING *
                                        3393**                  PROCESS; STOPPED BIT TURNED OFF; RETURN. *
                                        3394**      ERROR CHECKS: IF NO PROCESS BY GIVEN NAME, XQUE ENTERED. *
                                        3395**      INTERRUPTS: OFF                                    *
                                        3396**      USER ACCESS: YES                                   *
                                        3397**                                                        *
                                        3398***********************************************************

000A0A                                  3400+XY     EQU   *,1                     THE XY ROUTINE: START A PROCESS
000A0A                                  3401+       USING *,1
000A0A  1872                            3402+       LR    7,2
000A0A                                  3403+       USING XY,7 .                   THE ARG LIST
000A0C  4120 E048          00048        3404+       LA    2,SATEMP .              READY TO CALL OUT
000000                                  3405+       USING XN,2
000A10  D207 2000 7000  00000 00000     3406+       MVC   XNYNAME,XYYNAME .       GIVE XN A NAME
000A16  0AD5                            3407+       SVC   C'N' .                   CALL XN
000A18  58A0 2008            00008      3408+       L     10,XNXADDR .            WHERE IS THE PCB?
000A1C  12AA                            3409+       LTR   10,10 .                 OR IS THERE ONE?
000A1E  4780 1036            00A40      3410+       BZ    XYERR .                 IF NOT, OH HISS BOO
                                        3411+       DROP  2,14,15
                                        3412+       USING PCB,10
000A22  41D0 A04C            0004C      3413+       LA    13,PCBISA .             GET INTO THAT PCB'S ISA
000000                                  3414+       USING SA,13
000A26  D207 D000 E000  00000 00000     3415+       MVC   SAPSW,(SAPSW-SA)(14) .  GIVE IT THE CALLER'S PSW
000A2C  D202 D005 E008  00005 00008     3416+       MVC   SAPSW+5(3),XYXADDR+1 .  BUT AT THE REQUESTED ADDRESS
000A32  D23F D008 E008  00008           3417+       MVC   SAREGS,(SAREGS-SA)(14)  .GIVE IT HIS REGISTERS
000A38  9200 A018            00018      3418+       MVI   PCBSTOPT,X'00' .        IT'S NO LONGER STOPPED
000A3C  8200 04D8            004D8      3419+       LPSW  RETURN .                AND RETURN
000A40  0A6F                            3420+XYERR  SVC   C'2' .                  WE DONE BAD
000000                                  3421+       DROP  7,10,13
000000                                  3422+       USING SA,14
                                        3423+       USING PCB,15
```

```
SAMPLE OPERATING SYSTEM        VERSION 2.00

LOC    OBJECT CODE  ADDR1 ADDR2   STMT   SOURCE STATEMENT

                                  3425+**********************************************
                                  3426+**
                                  3427+**
                                  3428+**
                                  3429+**
                                  3430+**                   XZ ROUTINE
                                  3431+**
                                  3432+**
                                  3433+**   FUNCTION: TO STOP A PROCESS
                                  3434+**   DATABASES: UPON ENTRY, REGISTER 2 CONTAINS ADDRESS XZX:
                                  3435+**              XZX     DS  0D
                                  3436+**              XZXNAME DS  CL8  NAME OF PROCESS TO BE STOPPED
                                  3437+**   ROUTINES USED: XN EXC, XCOM, XQUE, XP
                                  3438+**   PROCEDURE: CHECK THAT USER PROC'S CAN'T STOP SYSTEM
                                  3439+**              PROCESS. USE XN TO GET PCB POINTER. IF IN SMC, SET
                                  3440+**              STOPPING BIT AND BLOCK SELF UNTIL STOP
                                  3441+**              PERFORMED; ELSE SET STOPPED BIT AND RETURN.
                                  3442+**   ERROR CHECKS: IF NO PROCESS BY GIVEN NAME OR USER TRIES TO
                                  3443+**                STOP A SYSTEM PROCESS, XQUE ENTERED.
                                  3444+**   INTERRUPTS: ON
                                  3445+**   USER ACCESS: YES
                                  3446+**
                                  3447+**
                                  3448+**********************************************

000A42                            3445+*XZ    EQU   *                THE XZ ROUTINE: STOP A PROCESS
000A42 1872                       3446+       USING *,1
000000                            3447+       LR    7,2
000A44 955C F000   00000          3448+       USING XZ,7              ARG LIST
000A48 4780 1012                  3449+       CLI   PCBNAME,C'**'     IS STOPPER A * PROCESS?
000A4C 955C 7000   00000          3450+       BE    XZFINE            THAT'S OK
000A50 4780 104A         00A8C    3451+       CLI   XZXNAME,C'**'     IF NOT, IS STOPPEE A * ?
000A54 4120 E048         00A8C    3452+       BE    XZERR             CAN'T DO THAT
000A58 D207 2000 7000 00000       3453+XZFINE LA    2,SATERP          READY TO CALL OUT
000A5E 0AD5                       3454+       USING XNXNAME,XZXNAME   WILL CALL XN
000A60 58A0 2008         00008    3455+       MVC   XNXNAME,XZXNAME   GIVE IT THE NAME
000A64 12AA                       3456+       SVC   C'N'              AND DO THE CALL
000A66 4780 104A         00A8C    3457+       L     10,XNXADDR        GET THE PCB'S ADDRESS
000A6A 0A5A                       3458+       LTR   10,10             SEE IF NULL
                                  3459+       BZ    XZERR             IF SO, ERROR.
                                  3460+       SVC   C'!'              ENTER SMC
                                  3461+       DROP  2,15
000000                            3462+       USING PCB,10
000A6C 9500 A01A   0001A          3463+XZSTOP CLI   PCBINSMC,X'00'    SEE IF IN SMC
000A70 4770 103C         00A7E    3464+       BNE   XZINSMC,C'**'     IF SO, BAD
000A74 92FF A018   00018          3465+       MVI   PCBSTOPT,X'FF'    ELSE JUST STOP IT
000A78 0A6B                       3466+       SVC   C'.'              LEAVE SMC
000A7A 8200 04D8   004D8          3467+       LPSW  RETURN            AND RETURN
000A7E 92FF A01B   0001B          3468+XZINSMC MVI  PCBSW,X'FF'       IF IN SMC, SAY STOP WAITING
000A82 4120 A034         00034    3469+       LA    2,PCBSRS          AND STOP OURSELVES AGAINST
000A86 0AD7                       3470+       SVC   C'P'              A SEMAPHORE
000A88 47F0 102A         00A6A    3471+       BV    XZSTOP            THEN WE CAN REALLY STOP IT
000A8C 0A6F             00A6C     3472+XZERR  SVC   C'?'              AN ERROR
                                  3473+       DROP  10,7
000000                            3474+       USING PCB,15
```

SAMPLE OPERATING SYSTEM   VERSION 2.00

LOC   OBJECT CODE   ADDR1 ADDR2   STMT   SOURCE STATEMENT

```
                                   3476+ *******************************************************
                                   3477+ *                                                     *
                                   3478+ *                                                     *
                                   3479+ *                   XQUE ROUTINE                      *
                                   3480+ *                                                     *
                                   3481+ *    FUNCTION: TO SIGNAL ERROR CONDITION              *
                                   3482+ *   DATABASES: NONE                                   *
                                   3483+ * ROUTINES USED: XR, XS                               *
                                   3484+ *   PROCEDURE: SEND MESSAGE TO SUPERVISOR PROCESS FOR THIS JOB *
                                   3485+ *             INDICATING ABNORMAL TERMINATION; TRY TO READ *
                                   3486+ *             MESSAGES, FOREVER LOOPING; BLOCK ITSELF, THEREBY *
                                   3487+ *             NEVER RETURNING.                        *
                                   3488+ * ERROR CHECKS: NONE                                  *
                                   3489+ *  INTERRUPTS: OFF                                    *
                                   3490+ * USER ACCESS: YES                                    *
                                   3491+ *******************************************************
000A8E                             3493+XQUE     EQU   *                       THE XQUE ROUTINE: ERROR!
000A8E                             3494+         USING *,1
000A8E  4120 1012      00AA0       3495+         LA    2,XQUEM1 .              SEND AN ERROR MESSAGE TO *IBSUP
000A92  0AE2                       3496+         SVC   C'S'
000A94  4120 102A      00AB8       3497+XQUELOOP LA    2,XQUEM2 .              WAIT FOR REPLY
000A98  0AD9                       3498+         SVC   C'R'
000A9A  47F0 1006      00A94       3499+         B     XQUELOOP .              BUT IGNORE IT
000AA0                             3500+         DS    0F
000AA0  5CC9C2E4D074040            3501+XQUEM1   DC    CL8'*IBSUP'
000AA8  0000000C                   3502+         DC    F'12'
000AAC  D7D9D6C7D9C1D440           3503+         DC    CL12'PROGRAM FLOP'
000AB8                             3504+XQUEM2   DS    CL8
000AB8  F'1'                       3505+         DC    F'1'
000AC0  00000001                   3506+         DS    CL1,0H
000AC4                             3507+         DROP  14,15
```

449

```
       SAMPLE OPERATING SYSTEM                VERSION 2.00
  LOC   OBJECT CODE   ADDR1 ADDR2   STMT  SOURCE STATEMENT

                                    3509  ****************************************************
                                    3510  ****                                            ****
                                    3511  ****            INPUT/OUTPUT ROUTINES           ****
                                    3512  ****                                            ****
                                    3513  ****************************************************

                                    3515  *
                                    3516  *
                                    3517  *    SYSTEM SUPPLIED DEVICE HANDLER FOR READERS
                                    3518  *
                                    3519  *    ****************************************************

000AC6                              3521  RDRHANDL EQU   *  .            THE READER HANDLER
                                    3522           USING UCB,3 .         STARTED WITH REG3 -> UCB
000AC6 0510                         3523           BALR  1,0
                                    3524           USING *,1
000AC8 4120 1140   00C08           3525           LA    2,RDRHSEM .      ESTABLISH ADDRESSING
000ACC 0AD7                         3526           SVC   C'P' .          LOCK OURSELVES UNTIL WE SET UP
000ACE 4120 1150   00C18           3527           LA    2,RDRHAAS .      AN AUTOMATIC STORAGE AREA
                                    3528           USING TAX,2           READY TO ALLOCATE
000AD2 0AC5                         3529           SVC   C'E' .          ALLOCATE
000AD4 58C0 2004   00004           3530           L     12,XAXADDR .     GET A PTR
                                    3531           DROP  2 .
000AD8 4120 1140   00C08           3532           LA    2,RDRHSEM .
000ADC 0AE5                         3533           SVC   C'V' .          AND UNLOCK OURSELVES
000ADE 8840 0010   00010           3534           SRL   4,16 .           SHIFT KEY
000AE2 1BAA                         3535           SR    10,10 .         CLEAR REG 10
                                    3536           USING RDRHAS,12       AUTOMATIC AREA
000AE4 9200 C07A   0007A           3537           MVI   JOBBIT,X'00' .   INITIALIZE
000AE8 4160 C000   00000           3538           LA    2,RDRHCCB .      GET PTR TO CCB
000AEC 4120 C008   00008           3539  RDRHLOOP LA    2,RDRHMSG .      TRY TO READ A MESSAGE
                                    3540           USING XRX,2
000AF0 D203 2008 1370  00008 00E38 3541           MVC   XRXSIZE,=F'8' .  WE CAN TAKE 8 CHARS
000AF6 0AD9                         3542           SVC   C'R' .          READ IT
000AF8 D503 137C 200C  00E44 0000C 3543           CLC   =C'READ',XRXTEXT .  IF 1ST WORD IS READ, OK
000AFE 4770 1024   00AEC           3544           BNE   RDRHLOOP .       ELSE IGNORE
000B02 5802 2010   00010           3545           L     5,XRXTEXT+4 .    GET 2ND WORD OF THE TEXT
                                    3546           DROP  2
000B06 4120 3004   00004           3547           LA    2,UCBUS .        LOCK THE UCB AND ITS UNIT
000B0A 0AD7                         3548           SVC   C'P' .
000B0C 4120 C008   00008           3549           LA    2,RDRHMSG .      RESET ADDRESSING POINTER
                                    3550           USING XRX,2
000B10 95FF C07A   0007A           3551           CLI   JOBBIT,X'FF' .   HAVE WE JUST READ $JOB CARD?
000B14 4770 1066   00B2E           3552           BNE   RDRHMORE .       IF NO, GO CHECK PROTECTION. ELSE
000B18 955C 2000   00000           3553           CLI   XRXNAME,C'*' .   IS JSP CALLING US?
000B1C 4770 10D8   00BA0           3554           BNE   RDRHNO .         IF NOT, TELL HIM NO.
000B20 D24F 5000 C01C  00000 0001C 3555           MVC   0(80,5),RDRHTEMP .  IF IT IS, GIVE JSP THE $JOB CARD
000B26 9200 C07A   0007A           3556           MVI   JOBBIT,X'00' .   SAY WE DON'T HAVE $JOB WAITING
000B2A 47F0 10F4   00BBC           3557           B     RDRHSOK .        AND SEND MESSAGE BACK
                                    3558           DROP  2
000B2E 955C C008   00008           3559  RDRHMORE CLI   RDRHMSG,C'*' .   IS SYSTEM CALLING?
000B32 4780 108C   00B54           3560           BE    RDRHPOK .        THEN PROTECTION OK. ELSE
000B36 18B5                         3561           LR    11,5 .          GET ADDRESS THAT'S TO HOLD CARD,'
000B38 54B0 114C   00C14           3562           N     11,PROTCON1 .    GET THE 2K BOUNDARY
000B3C 09AB                         3563           ISK   10,11 .         FIND STORAGE KEY
```

SAMPLE OPERATING SYSTEM   VERSION 2.00

```
LOC     OBJECT CODE        ADDR1  ADDR2  STMT            SOURCE STATEMENT

000B3E  19A4                             3564+          CR   10,4 .                DOES IT MATCH OURS?
000B40  4770 10D8                 00BA0  3565+          BNE  RDRHNO .              IF NOT, TELL HIM NO
000B44  41B5 004F                 0004F  3566+          LA   11,79(5) .            CHECK LAST BYTE ADDR OF CARD
000B48  54B0 114C                 00C14  3567+          N    11,PROTCON1 .         GET THE 2K BOUNDARY
000B4C  09AB                             3568+          ISK  10,11 .               FIND STORAGE KEY
000B4E  19A4                             3569+          CR   10,4 .                DOES IT MATCH OURS?
000B50  4770 10D8                 00BA0  3570+          BNE  RDRHNO .              IF NOT, TELL HIM NO
000B54  5450 1148                 00C10  3571+RDRHPOK   ST   5,CCBCON1 .           MAKE ADDRESS INTO
000B58  5050 C000          00000         3572+          ST   5,RDRHCCB .           A CCW (OR CCB)
000B5C  9602 C000          00000         3573+          OI   RDRHCCB,X'02' .
000B60  D203 C004 1380     00004  00BA0  3574+          MVC  RDRHCCB+4,=F'80' .    WE'LL READ EIGHTY CHARACTERS
000B66  D203 3014 1368     00014  00B30  3575+          MVC  UCBCSW(4),=A(0) .     CLEAR THE LAST CSW THERE
000B6C  D203 3018 1368     00018  00B30  3576+          MVC  UCBCSW+4(4),=A(0) .
000B72  4120 0194                 00194  3577+          LA   2,CAWSEM .
000B76  0AD7                             3578+          SVC  C'P' .                LOCK THE CAW
000B78  5060 0048                 00048  3579+          ST   6,CAW .               THAT'S THE CAW
000B7C  5870 3000          00000         3580+          L    7,UCBADDR .           GET THE UNIT ADDRESS
000B80  9C00 7000          00000         3581+          SIO  0(7) .                START THE I/O
000B84  4770 1134                 00BFC  3582+          BNZ  RDSTATUS .            BRANCH IF SIO UNSUCCESSFUL
000B88  0AE5                             3583+          SVC  C'V' .                THEN UNLOCK THE CAW
000B8A  4120 300C                 0000C  3584+RDRHWAIT  LA   2,UCBWS .             NOW WAIT FOR AN INTERRUPT
000B8E  0AD7                             3585+          SVC  C'P' .                CHECK THE STATUS
000B90  9105 3018                 00018  3586+          TM   UCBCSW+4,X'05' .
000B94  4780 10C2                 00B8A  3587+          BZ   RDRHWAIT .            IF NOT FINISHED, WAIT
000B98  9101 3018                 00018  3588+          TM   UCBCSW+4,X'01' .      CHECK FOR EXCEPTION
000B9C  4780 10E2                 00BAA  3589+          BZ   RDRHOK .              IF NOT, ALL IS GROOVY
000BA0  D201 C078 139C     00078  00BC2  3590+RDRHNO    MVC  RDRHM+12(2),=C'NO' .  ELSE MESSAGE BACK IS NO
000BA6  47F0 10FA                 00BC2  3591+          B    RDRHSEND .            GET READY TO SEND
000BAA  955C C008                 00008  3592+RDRHOK    CLI  0(5),C'*' .           IS THE SYSTEM CALLING?
000BAE  4780 10F4                 00B68  3593+          BE   RDRHSOK .             THAT'S FINE, OTHERWISE,
000BB2  D504 13A0 1116     003A0  00116  3594+          CLC  =C'$JOB',0(5) .       WAS IT A $JOB CARD?
000BB8  4780 1116                 00BDE  3595+          BE   ENDADATA .            OOPS! WE HIT END OF DATA STREAM
000BBC  D201 C078 139E     00078  00BE4  3596+RDRHSOK   MVC  RDRHM+12(2),=C'OK' .  GROOVINESS MESSAGE
000BC2  D203 C074 1378     00074  00BE0  3597+RDRHSEND  MVC  RDRHM+8(4),=F'2' .    SAY THERE ARE 2 CHARACTERS
000BC8  D207 C06C C008     0006C  00008  3598+          MVC  RDRHM+0(8),RDRHMSG+0 . SEND BACK TO SAME GUY
000BCE  4120 300C                 0000C  3599+          LA   2,UCBUS .             NOW UNLOCK UCB AND UNIT
000BD2  0AE5                             3600+          SVC  C'V' .
000BD4  4120 C06C                 0006C  3601+          LA   2,RDRHM .             SET UP MESSAGE
000BDA  0AE2                             3602+          SVC  C'S' .                AND SEND IT
000BDE  D201 C078 1024     00078  00AEC  3604+ENDADATA  MVC  RDRHM+12(2),=C'NO' .  TELL USER NO MORE CARDS
000BE4  D24F C01C 5000     0001C  00000  3605+          MVC  RDRHTEMP(80),0(5) .   SAVE THE $JOB CARD
000BEA  9240 5000                 00000  3606+          MVI  0(5),C' ' .           BLANK OUT THE USER'S COPY
000BEE  D24E 5001 5000     00001  00000  3607+          MVC  1(79,5),0(5) .
000BF4  92FF C07A                 0007A  3608+          MVI  JOBBIT,X'FF' .        INDICATE WE HAVE A NEW $JOB CARD
000BFA  47F0 10FA                 00BC2  3609+          B    RDRHSEND .            AND SEND MESSAGE BACK
000BFE  4120 300C                 0000C  3610+RDSTATUS  LA   2,UCBWS .             UNLOCK THE CAW
000C02  0AD7                             3611+          SVC  C'P' .                AND WAIT FOR AN INTERRUPT
000C04  47F0 108C                 00B54  3613+          B    RDRHPOK .             AND TRY TO RESTART THE I/O
                                         3614+          DROP 3,12

000C08  00000001 00000000                3616+RDRHSEM   DC   F'1,0'
000C10  00FFFFFF                         3617+CCBCON1   DC   X'00FFFFFF'           MASK
000C14  00FFF800                         3618+PROTCON1  DC   X'00FFF800'
```

```
  LOC  OBJECT CODE  ADDR1 ADDR2   STMT   SOURCE STATEMENT

000C18 00000000                   3619*RDRHAAS  DC    A(LENRDRHA)  ALLOCATE ARGLIST FOR STORAGE
000C1C 00000000                   3620*         DC    F'0'
000C20 00000008                   3621*         DC    F'8'

                                  3623** ********************************************
                                  3624** *                                        *
                                  3625** *  SYSTEM SUPPLIED DEVICE HANDLER FOR PRINTERS  *
                                  3626** *                                        *
                                  3627** ********************************************

000C24                            3629*PRTHANDL  EQU   *                THE PRINTER HANDLER
000000                            3630*          USING UCB,3            ENTERED WITH REG3 -> THE UCB
000C24 0510                       3631*          BALR  1,0
000C26                            3632*          USING *,1              ESTABLISH ADDRESSING
000C26 4120 110A          00D30   3633*          LA    2,PRTHSEM        LOCK UNTIL ALLOCATE STORAGE
000C2A 0AD7                       3634*          SVC   C'P' .
000C2C 4120 1112          00038   3635*          LA    2,PRTHAAS .      READY TO ALLOCATE
000000                            3636*          USING XAX,2
000C30 0AC5                       3637*          SVC   C'E' .
000C32 58C0 2004          00004   3638*          L     12,XAXADDR .     GET THE ADDRESS
000000                            3639*          DROP  2
000C36 4120 110A          00D30   3640*          LA    2,PRTHSEM .      UNLOCK TO ROUTINE
000C3A 0AE5                       3641*          SVC   C'V' .           SHIFT KEY
000C3C 8840 0010          00010   3642*          SRL   4,16 .           CLEAR REG 10
000C40 1BAA                       3643*          SR    10,10 .          ADDRESSING IN THE AUTO AREA
000000                            3644*          USING PRTHAAS,12
000C42 4160 C000          00000   3645*          LA    6,PRTHCCB .      MAKE A CAW
000C46 4120 C008          00008   3646*PRTHLOOP  LA    2,PRTHMSG .      READY TO READ A MESSAGE
000000                            3647*          USING XRX,2
000C4A D203 2008 1212 00008 0E38 3648*          MVC   XRXSIZE,=F'8' .  WE CAN TAKE 8 CHARACTERS
000C50 0AD9                       3649*          SVC   C'R' .           READ IT
000C52 5850 2010          00010   3650*          L     5,XRXTEXT+4 .    LOAD THE ADDRESS
000C56 D503 1226 200C 00E4C 0000C 3651*          CLC   =C'PRIN',XRXTEXT . IS IT A PRIN REQUEST?
000C5C 4780 1048          00C6E   3652*          BE    PRTHPRIN
000C60 D503 122A 200C 00E50 0000C 3653*          CLC   =C'STC1',XRXTEXT . OR A SKIP REQUEST?
000C66 4780 108A          00CB0   3654*          BE    PRTHSTC1 .
000C6A 47F0 1020          00C46   3655*          B     PRTHLOOP .       IF NEITHER, IGNORE
000000                            3656*          DROP  2
000C6E 4120 3004          00004   3657*PRTHPRIN  LA    2,UCBUS          LOCK THE UCB AND UNIT
000C72 0AD7                       3658*          SVC   C'P' .           IS SYSTEM CALLING?
000C74 95SC C008    00008 00008   3659*          CLI   PRTHMSG,C'*' .   IS SYSTEM CALLING?
000C78 4780 1074          00C9A   3660*          BE    PRTHPOK .        THEN PROTECTION OK.  ELSE
000C7C 18B5                       3661*          LR    11,5 .           GET ADDRESS THAT'S TO HOLD MSG,
000C7E 54B0 0C14          00C14   3662*          N     11,PROTCON1 .    FIND THE 2K BOUNDARY
000C82 09AB                       3663*          CR    10,4 .           DOES IT MATCH OURS?
000C84 19AA                       3664*          CR    10,1 .
000C86 4770 10D0          00CF6   3665*          BNE   PRTHNO .         IF NOT, TELL HIM
000C8A 41B5 00B3          00083   3666*          LA    11,131(5) .      CHECK LAST BYTE ADDRESS OF LINE
000C8E 54B0 0C14          00C14   3667*          N     11,PROTCON1 .    GET THE 2K BOUNDARY
000C92 09AB                       3668*          CR    10,4 .           DOES IT MATCH OURS?
000C94 19AA                       3669*          CR    10,1 .
000C96 4770 10D0          00CF6   3670*          BNE   PRTHNO .         IF NOT, TELL HIM NO
000C9A 5450 0C10          00C10   3671*PRTHPOK   N     5,CCBCON1 .      MAKE A WRITE REQUEST
```

```
LOC      OBJECT CODE       ADDR1 ADDR2   STMT          SOURCE STATEMENT

000C9E   5050 C000               00000   3672+          ST    5,PRTHCCB               FOR THE CCB
000CA2   9609 C000               00004   3673+          OI    PRTHCCB,X'09'           PRINT COMMAND CODE
000CA6   D203 C004 122E    00004 00E54   3674+          MVC   PRTHCCB+4,=P'132'       WE'LL PRINT 132 CHARACTERS
000CAC   47F0 1096               0CBC    3675+          B     PRTHCOMM                BRANCH TO COMMON SECTION
000CB0   D207 C000 11FA    00000 00E20   3676+PRTHSTC1  MVC   PRTHCCB(8),=X'8900000020000001' SKIP TO TOP OF PAGE
000CB6   4120 3004               00004   3677+          LA    2,UCBUS                 LOCK THE UCB AND UNIT
000CBA   0AD7                    0194    3678+          SVC   C'P'
000CBC   4120 0194               00194   3679+PRTHCOMM  LA    2,CAWSEM                LOCK THE CAW
000CC0   0AD7                            3680+          SVC   C'P'
000CC2   5060 0048               00048   3681+          ST    6,CAW                   STORE OUR CAW
000CC6   D203 3014 120A    00014 00E30   3682+          MVC   UCBCSW(4),=A(0)         CLEAR THE LAST CSW THERE
000CCC   D203 3018 120A    00018 00E30   3683+          MVC   UCBCSW+4(4),=A(0)
000CD2   5870 3000               00000   3684+          L     7,UCBADDR               GET THE ADDRESS
000CD6   9C00 7000               00000   3685+          SIO   0(7)                    START THE I/O
000CDA   4770 10FC               0D22    3686+          BNZ   PTSTATUS                BRANCH IF SIO UNSUCCESSFUL
000CDE   0AE5                            3687+          SVC   C'V'                    AND UNLOCK THE CAW
000CE0   4120 300C               0000C   3688+PRTHWAIT  LA    2,UCBWS                 START TO WAIT
000CE4   0AD7                            3689+          SVC   C'P'
000CE6   9105 3018               00018   3690+          TM    UCBCSW+4,X'05'          IS THE UNIT READY?
000CEA   4780 10BA               0CE0    3691+          BZ    PRTHWAIT                IF NOT, ITS STILL ON. WAIT
000CEE   9101 3018               00018   3692+          TM    UCBCSW+4,X'01'          WAS THERE AN EXCEPTION?
000CF2   4780 10DA               0D00    3693+          BZ    PRTHOK                  IF NOT, GOOD
000CF6   D201 C028 123E    00028 00E64   3694+PRTHNO    MVC   PRTHM+12(2),=C'NO'      THERE WAS, SO SAY SO
000CFC   47F0 10E0               0D06    3695+          B     PRTHSEND
000D00   D201 C028 1240    00028 00E66   3696+PRTHOK    MVC   PRTHM+12(2),=C'OK'      NO ERRORS
000D06   D203 C024 121A    00024 00E40   3697+PRTHSEND  MVC   PRTHM+8(4),=F'2'        SENDING 2 CHARACTERS
000D0C   D207 C01C C008    0001C 00C08   3698+          MVC   PRTHM+0(8),PRTHMSG+0    SEND TO OUR SENDER
000D12   4120 3004               00004   3699+          LA    2,UCBUS
000D16   0AE5                            3700+          SVC   C'V'                    UNLOCK THE UCB
000D18   4120 C01C               0001C   3701+          LA    2,PRTHM
000D1C   0AE2                            3702+          SVC   C'S'                    SEND IT
000D1E   47F0 1020               0C46    3703+          B     PRTHLOOP                AND READ ANOTHER MESSAGE
000D22   4120 0194               00194   3704+PTSTATUS  LA    2,CAWSEM                UNLOCK THE CAW
000D26   0AE5                            3705+          SVC   C'V'
000D28   4120 300C               0000C   3706+          LA    2,UCBWS                 AND WAIT FOR AN INTERRUPT
000D2C   0AD7                            3707+          SVC   C'P'
000D2E   47F0 1096               0CBC    3708+          B     PRTHCOMM                AND TRY TO RESTART THE I/O

000D30   0000 0001 0000 0000             3710+PRTHSEM   DC    F'1,0'   LOCK
000D38   00000030                        3711+PRTHAAS   DC    A(LENPRTHA)  XA ARG LIST FOR AUTO STORAGE
000D3C   00000000                        3712+          DC    F'0'
000D40   00000008                        3713+          DC    F'8'
```

```
        SAMPLE OPERATING SYSTEM I          VERSION 2.00

LOC    OBJECT CODE  ADDR1 ADDR2   STMT  SOURCE STATEMENT

                                  3715+ *******************************************
                                  3716+ ***
                                  3717+ ***  SYSTEM ROUTINE FOR USER SUPPLIED DEVICE HANDLER  ***
                                  3718+ ***
                                  3719+ *******************************************

000044                            3721+EXCPHNDL EQU  *                 EXCP DEVICE HANDLER
000044                            3722+     USING UCB,3                 WILL HAVE REG 3 -> UCB
000044 0510                       3723+     BALR 1,0
000046                            3724+     USING *,1                   ESTABLISH ADDRESSING
000046 4120 10C6      00E0C       3725+     LA   2,EXCPHSEM .           LOCK OURSELVES UNTIL WE HAVE
00004A 0AD7                       3726+     SVC  C'P'.                  SET UP AUTOMATIC STORAGE
00004C 4120 10CE      00E14       3727+     LA   2,EXCPHAAS .           READY TO ALLOCATE
000050                            3728+     USING XAX,2
000050 0AC5                       3729+     SVC  C'E'.                  ALLOCATE
000052 58C0 2004      00004       3730+     L    12,XAXADDR .           GET POINTER TO AUTO STORAGE
                                  3731+     DROP 2
000056 4120 10C6      00E0C       3732+     LA   2,EXCPHSEM .           AND UNLOCK OURSELVES
00005A 0AE5                       3733+     SVC  C'V'.
00005C 184B                       3734+     LR   4,11
00005C 8940 0008      00008       3735+     SLL  4,8 .                  SHIFT KEY FOR CAW
000062                            3736+     USING EXCPHAS,12            FOR ADDRESSING AUTO AREA
000062 4120 C000      00000       3737+EXCPLOOP LA  2,EXCPHMSG .        TRY TO READ A MESSAGE
000000                            3738+     USING XRX,2
000066 D203 2008 1112 00008       3739+     MVC  XRXSIZE,=P'12' .       WE'LL TAKE 12 CHARACTERS
00006C 0AD9                       3740+     SVC  C'R'.
00006E D503 1116 200C 00E5C       3741+     CLC  =C'EXCP',XRXTEXT .     IS IT AN EXCP MESSAGE?
000074 4770 101C      0000C       3742+     BNE  EXCPLOOP .             IF NOT, IGNORE IT
000078 5850 2010      00010       3743+     L    5,XRXTEXT+4 .          REG 5 CONTAINS CHAN AND DEV
00007C 5860 2014      00014       3744+     L    6,XRXTEXT+8 .          REG 6 CONTAINS ADDR OF CCWS
                                  3745+     DROP 2
000080 4170 112E      00074       3746+     LA   7,UCBTABLE .           GET PTR TO UCB TABLE
000084 5957 0000      00000       3747+EXCPCOMP C  5,0(7) .             COMPARE UNIT ADDRESS
000088 4780 09DA      09DA        3748+     BE   EXCPFIND .             THAT'S THE UCB WE WANT
00008C 4177 0020      00020       3749+     LA   7,UCBLENG(7) .         GET PTR TO NEXT UCB
000090 5970 111A      0E60        3750+     C    7,=A(UCBTBEND) .       ARE WE THROUGH WITH TABLE?
000094 4770 103E      0E84        3751+     BNE  EXCPCOMP .             IF NOT, LOOK SOME MORE
000098 0A6F                       3752+     SVC  C'?'.                  ELSE ERROR
00009A 1837                       3753+EXCPFIND LR 3,7 .                SET REG 3 TO UCB PTR
00009C 4120 3004      00004       3754+     LA   2,UCBUS                LOCK THE UCB
0000A0 0AD7                       3755+     SVC  C'P'.                  OR IN USER'S KEY
0000A2 1664                       3756+     OR   6,4 .                  CLEAR THE LAST CSW THERE
0000A4 D203 3014 0E30 00014 0E30  3757+     MVC  UCBCSW(4),=A(0)
0000AA D203 3018 0E30 00018 0E30  3758+     MVC  UCBCSW+4(4),=A(0)
0000B0 4120 0194      00194       3759+     LA   2,CANSEM .             LOCK CAW
0000B4 0AD7                       3760+     SVC  C'P'.
0000B6 5060 0048      00048       3761+     ST   6,CAW .                STORE OUR CAW
0000BA 9C00 0000      00000       3762+     SIO  0(5) .                 START THE I/O
0000BE 0AE5                       3763+     SVC  C'V'.                  UNLOCK CAW
0000C0 4120 300C      0000C       3764+EXCPWAIT LA 2,UCBWS .            NOW WAIT FOR AN INTERRUPT
0000C4 0AD7                       3765+     SVC  C'P'.
0000C6 D207 C024 3014 00024 00014 3766+     MVC  EXCPHM+12(8),UCBCSW .  GIVE USER HIS CSW
0000CC D203 C020 1112 00020 1112  3767+     MVC  EXCPHM+8(4),=P'12'
0000D2 D207 C018 0000 00018 00000 3768+     MVC  EXCPHM(8),EXCPHMSG
0000D8 4120 C018      00018       3769+     LA   2,EXCPHM
```

LOC	OBJECT CODE	ADDR1	ADDR2	STMT	SOURCE STATEMENT	
000DDC	0AE2			3770+	SVC	C'S'	AND SEND THE MESSAGE
000DDE	4120 C000		00000	3771+	LA	2,EXCPHMSG .	AND WAIT FOR A REPLY
000000				3772+	USING	XRX,2	
000DE2	D203 2008 10F2	00008	00E38	3773+	MVC	XRXSIZE(4),=F'18' .	
000DE8	0AD9			3774+	SVC	C'R' .	FROM THE USER
000DEA	D501 1120 200C	00E66	0000C	3775+	CLC	C'OK',XRXTEXT .	AM I DONE?
000DF0	4780 10BA		0E00	3776+	BE	EXCPDONE	DOES HE WANT ANOTHER CSW?
000DF4	D504 1127 200C	00E6D	000C0	3777+	CLC	C'AGAIN',XRXTEXT .	
000DFA	4780 107A			3778+	BE	EXCPWAIT .	WRONG MESSAGE
000DFE	0A6F			3779+	SVC	C'?' .	
				3780+	DROP		
000E00	4120 3004		00004	3781+	EXCPDONE LA	2,JCBUS .	UNLOCK UNIT
000E04	0AE5			3782+	SVC	C'V'	AND GET ANOTHER MESSAGE
000E06	47F0 101C		00D62	3783+	B	EXCPLOOP	
				3784+	DROP	3,12	
000E0A	0000			3785+	EXCPHSEM DC	F'1,0'	
000E0C	0000000100000000			3786+	EXCPHAAS DC	A(LENEXCPA) .	ALLOCATION OF AUTO STORAGE
000E14	00000030			3787+	DC	F'0'	
000E18	00000000			3788+	DC	F'8'	
000E1C	00000008						
000E20				3789+	LTORG		
000E20	89000000020000001			3790+		=X'89000000020000001'	
000E28	00000001			3791		=F'1'	
000E2C	00000600			3792		=A(XA)	
000E30	00000148			3793		=A(O)	
000E34	00000008			3794		=A(LENPCB)	
000E38	FFFFFFF8			3795		=F'-8'	
000E3C	FFFFFFF8			3796		=F'8'	
000E40	00000002			3797		=F'2'	
000E44	D9C5C1C4			3798		=C'READ'	
000E48	00000050			3799		=F'80'	
000E4C	D7D9C9D5			3800		=C'PRIN'	
000E50	E2E3C3F1			3801		=C'STC1'	
000E54	00000084			3802		=F'132'	
000E58	0000000C			3803		=F'12'	
000E5C	C5E7C3D7			3804		=C'EXCP'	
000E60	00C0EF4			3805		=A(UCBTBEND)	
000E64	D5D6			3806		=C'NO'	
000E66	D6D2			3807		=C'OK'	
000E68	5BD1D6C26B			3808		=C'$JOB,'	
000E6D	C1C7C1C9D5			3809		=C'AGAIN'	
				3810			

```
SAMPLE OPERATING SYSTEM    VERSION 2.00

LOC    OBJECT CODE   ADDR1 ADDR2  STMT   SOURCE STATEMENT

                                  3812 *********************************************
                                  3813 **                                         **
                                  3814 **            UNIT CONTROL BLOCKS           **
                                  3815 **                                         **
                                  3816 *********************************************

000E74                            3818 +UCBTABLE DS  0F .       TABLE OF UNIT CONTROL BLOCKS
                                  3819 *                        UCB FOR READER 1
000E74 00000012                   3820 +UCBRDR1  DC  X'00000012' . DEVICE ADDRESS,
000E78 0000000100000000           3821          DC  F'1,0' .      USER SEMAPHORE,
000E80 0000000000000000           3822          DC  F'0,0' .      WAIT SEMAPHORE,
000E88 0000000000000000           3823          DC  F'0,0' .
000E90 00                         3824          DC  X'00' .       CHANNEL STATUS WORD
000E94                            3825          DS  0F
                                  3826 *                        UCB FOR PRINTER 1
000E94 00000010                   3827 +UCBPRT1  DC  X'00000010' . DEVICE ADDRESS,
000E98 0000000100000000           3828          DC  F'1,0' .      USER SEMAPHORE,
000EA0 0000000000000000           3829          DC  F'0,0' .      WAIT SEMAPHORE,
000EA8 0000000000000000           3830          DC  F'0,0' .
000EB0 00                         3831          DC  X'00' .       CHANNEL STATUS WORD
000EB4                            3832          DS  0F
                                  3833 *                        UCB FOR READER 2
000EB4 0000000C                   3834 +UCBRDR2  DC  X'0000000C' . DEVICE ADDRESS,
000EB8 0000000100000000           3835          DC  F'1,0' .      USER SEMAPHORE,
000EC0 0000000000000000           3836          DC  F'0,0' .      WAIT SEMAPHORE,
000EC8 0000000000000000           3837          DC  F'0,0' .
000ED0 00                         3838          DC  X'00' .       CHANNEL STATUS WORD
000ED4                            3839          DS  0F
                                  3840 *                        UCB FOR PRINTER 2
000ED4 0000000E                   3841 +UCBPRT2  DC  X'0000000E' . DEVICE ADDRESS,
000ED8 0000000100000000           3842          DC  F'1,0' .      USER SEMAPHORE,
000EE0 0000000000000000           3843          DC  F'0,0' .      WAIT SEMAPHORE,
000EE8 0000000000000000           3844          DC  F'0,0' .
000EF0 00                         3845          DC  X'00' .       CHANNEL STATUS WORD
000EF4                            3846          DS  0F
000EF4                            3847 +UCBTBEND EQU *
```

```
LOC    OBJECT CODE   ADDR1  ADDR2  STMT   SOURCE STATEMENT

                                   3849+ ****************************************
                                   3850+ **
                                   3851+ **
                                   3852+ **            I/O INTERRUPT HANDLER
                                   3853+ ****************************************

000EF4                             3855+IOHANDL  EQU  *  .                  THE I/O INTERRUPT HANDLER
000EF4 900F 01DC            01DC   3856+         STM  0,15,IOHSAVE          SAVE REGISTERS
000EF8 0510                        3857+         BALR 1,0
                                   3858+         USING *,1                  ESTABLISH ADDRESSING
000EFA 94FD 0039     00039         3859+         NI   IOOLD+1,X'FD' .       TURN OFF WAIT BIT
000EFE 5860 16FE            015F8  3860+         L    6,=A(UCBTABLE) .      GET POINTER TO UCB TABLE
000F02 D501 6002 003A 00002        3861+IOCOMP   CLC  2(2,6),IOOLD+2 .      COMPARE DEVICE AND CHANNEL
000F08 4780 1022            00F1C  3862+         BE   IODVFND .             IF EQUAL, REG 6 INDICATES PTR
000F0C 4166 0020            00020  3863+         LA   6,UCBLENG(6) .        INCREMENT TO NEXT ENTRY
000F10 5960 1702            015FC  3864+         C    6,=A(UCBTBEND) .      ARE WE AT END OF TABLE?
000F14 4770 1008            00F02  3865+         BNE  IOCOMP .              IF NOT DONE, TRY NEXT UCB
000F18 47F0 106C            00F66  3866+         B    IOBACK .              ELSE, IGNORE IT
000000                             3867+         USING UCB,6 .              IT'S A UCB PTR
000F1C D203 6014 0040 00014 00040  3868+IODVFND  MVC  UCBCSW(4),CSW .       MOVE IN THE NEW CSW
000F22 5870 0044            00044  3869+         L    7,CSW+4 .             GET STATUS BYTE
000F26 5670 6018            00018  3870+         O    7,UCBCSW+4 .          OR IN NEW STATUS INFORMATION
000F2A 5070 6018            00018  3871+         ST   7,UCBCSW+4 .          AND STORE IT BACK
000F2E D201 601A 0001A 00046       3872+         MVC  UCBCSW+6(2),CSW+6 .   MOVE IN BYTE COUNT
000F34 4120 600C            0000C  3873+         LA   2,UCBWS .
000F38 9500 601C     0001C         3874+         CLI  UCBPPR,X'00' .        IS FAST PROCESSING
000F3C 4780 106A            00F64  3875+         BE   IONOPPR .             REQUIRED? IF NOT, RETURN
000F40 58F0 0270            00270  3876+         L    15,RUNNING .          IF SO, STOP GUY NOW RUNNING
000000                             3877+         USING PCB,15
000F44 95FF F019     00019         3878+         CLI  PCBLOKT,X'FF' .       IS ANYONE REALLY RUNNING?
000F48 4780 1062            00F5C  3879+         BE   IOWAIT .              IF NOT, START UP SLEEPER
000F4C 41D0 F04C            0004C  3880+         LA   13,PCBISA .           IF SO, STOP RUNNING PROCESS
000000                             3881+         USING SA,13
000F50 D207 D000 00000 00038       3882+         MVC  SAPSW,IOOLD .         SAVE PROCESS WHICH WAS
000F56 D23F D008 00008 001DC       3883+         MVC  SAREGS,IOHSAVE .      INTERRUPTED
                                   3884+         DROP 13,15
000F5C 9200 027B     0027B         3885+IOWAIT   MVI  NEXTRYM,X'00' .       MAKE NEXTRY NOT MODIFIED
000F60 0AE5                        3886+         SVC  C'V' .                SO CAN FAST PROCCESS SLEEPER
000F62 0A4B                        3887+         SVC  C'.' .                GO PROCESS IT RIGHT AWAY
000F64 0AE5                        3888+IONOPPR  SVC  C'V' .                AND WAKE UP THE SLEEPER
000F66 980F 01DC            001DC  3889+IOBACK   LM   0,15,IOHSAVE .        RELOAD OUR REGISTERS
000F6A 8200 0038            00038  3890+         LPSW IOOLD .               AND STEALTHILY RETURN
                                   3891+         DROP 1,6
```

```
LOC     OBJECT CODE    ADDR1 ADDR2   STMT   SOURCE STATEMENT

                                     3893+  *****************************************************************
                                     3894+  *                                                               *
                                     3895+  *                    IPL ENTERED ROUTINE                        *
                                     3896+  *                                                               *
                                     3897+  *  FUNCTION:  TO INITIALIZE SYSTEM PARAMETERS, SET STORAGE KEYS,*
                                     3898+  *             AND CREATE MULTIPLE JOB STREAMS.                  *
                                     3899+  *                                                               *
                                     3900+  *****************************************************************

000F6E                               3902+IPLRTN  EQU   *                 THE IPL-ENTERED ROUTINE
000F6E 0510                          3903+        BALR  1,0               ESTABLISH ADDRESSING
000F70                               3904+        USING *,1 .
000F70 41F0 1098        01008        3905+        LA    15,IPLPCB .       I'M RUNNING
000F74 50F0 0270        00270        3906+        ST    15,RUNNING'       INITIALIZE 'RUNNING'
000F78 50F0 0274        00274        3907+        ST    15,NEXTTRY'       INITIALIZE 'NEXTTRY'
000F7C D207 1608 15D0  01578 01540   3908+        MVC   VERYEND,=A(0,CORESIZE-(VERYEND-PROGRAM))  FREE CORE
000F82 4130 0008        00008        3909+        LA    3,8 .             SET ZERO KEY AND FETCH PROTECT
000F86 5820 11BC        0112C        3910+        L     2,CORESIZ         START PAST THE LAST BLOCK
000F8A 5820 1690        01600        3911+IPLCL   S     2,=F'2048'        GO TO THE PREVIOUS BLOCK
000F8E 4740 1028        00F98        3912+        BM    IPLTH'            IF NEGATIVE, WE'RE THROUGH HERE
000F92 0832                          3913+        SSK   3,2 .             ELSE SET THE STORAGE KEY TO
000F94 47F0 101A        00F8A        3914+        B     IPLCL .           ZERO AND WORK BACKWARDS
000F98 1B44                          3915+IPLTH   SR    4,4 .             INDEX IN TABLES FOR INPUT STREAM
000F9A 5850 1074        00FE4        3916+        L     5,STREAMS .       HOW MANY STREAMS?
000F9E 4120 11E0        01150        3917+IPLLOOP LA    2,IPLAPCBS .      READY TO ALLOCATE A PCB
000000                               3918+        USING IAX,2
000FA2 0AC1                          3919+        SVC   C'A'              ALLOCATE
000FA4 5820 2004        00004        3920+        L     2,XAXADDR         GET THE ADDRESS
000FA8 D253 2000 11F0  00000 01160   3921+        MVC   0(TYPLEN,2),TYPPCB .   MAKE IT LOOK LIKE A PCB
000FAE 0AC9                          3922+        SVC   C'I' .            CHAIN IT ON
000000                               3923+        USING PCB,2
000FB0 5020 2008        00008        3924+        ST    2,PCBNPTG .       BUT PUT IT IN A GROUP BY ITSELF
000FB4 5020 200C        0000C        3925+        ST    2,PCBLPTG .
000000                               3926+        DROP  2
000000                               3927+        USING PCB,15
000FB8 50F0 F00C        0000C        3928+        ST    15,PCBLPTG .      LIKEWISE FOR THE IPL PCB
000FBC 50F0 F008        00008        3929+        ST    15,PCBNPTG .
000000                               3930+        DROP  15
000000                               3931+        USING PCB,2
000FC0 4180 204C        0004C        3932+        LA    8,PCBISA .        GET THE NEW PCB'S ISA
000000                               3933+        USING SA,8
000FC4 4190 8008        00008        3934+        LA    9,SAREGS .        ABOUT TO FIX INIT REGS
000000                               3935+        USING REGS,9
000FC8 41A0 1078        00FE8        3936+        LA    10,UCBTAB
000FCC 1AA4                          3937+        AR    10,4
000FCE D203 900C A000  0000C 00000   3938+        MVC   REG3,0(10)        REG3 -> (RDRUCB,PTRUCB)
000FD4 D203 9010 A008  00010 00008   3939+        MVC   REG4,KEYTAB-UCBTAB(10) .  REG4 = KEY
000000                               3940+        DROP  9
000FDA 4144 0004        00004        3941+        LA    4,4(4) .          GO TO NEXT JOB STREAM
000FDE 4650 102E        00F9E        3942+        BCT   5,IPLLOOP .       DO FOR EACH STREAM
000FE2 0A4B                          3943+        SVC   C'.' .            THEN ENTER TRAFFIC CONTROLLER

000FE4 00000002                      3945+STREAMS DC    F'2' .            NUMBER OF STREAMS
```

```
LOC     OBJECT CODE       ADDR1 ADDR2  STMT  SOURCE STATEMENT

000FE8                                 3947*UCBTAB   EQU  *  .                    TABLE OF PTRS TO UCB BLOCKS
000FE8  00000FF8                       3948*         DC   A(UCBLP1)
000FEC  00001000                       3949*         DC   A(UCBLP2)

000FF0                                 3951*KEYTAB   EQU  *  .                    TABLE OF PROTECTION KEYS
000FF0  00100000                       3952*         DC   X'00100000'
000FF4  00200000                       3953*         DC   X'00200000'

000FF8  00000E7400000E94               3955*UCBLP1   DC   A(UCBRDR1,UCBPRT1)
001000  00000EB400000ED4               3956*UCBLP2   DC   A(UCBRDR2,UCBPRT2)

001008                                 3958*         DS   0D
001008  4040404040404040               3959*IPLPCB   DC   CL8' '  .              IPL ROUTINE PCB
001010  0000100800001008               3960*         DC   4A(IPLPCB)
001020  FF000000                       3961*         DC   X'FF000000'  .         INITIALIZED FLAGS
001024  0000000100000000               3962*         DC   P'1,0'
        0000000000000000               3963*         DC   5P'0,0'
001054  0002000000000000               3964*         DC   X'0002000000000000'
00105C                                 3965*         DS   CL76
0010A8                                 3966*         DS   CL84
0010FC                                 3967*         DS   CL84

001150  00000148                       3969*IPLAPCBS DC   A(LENPCB)  .           ALLOC LIST PPR PCB'S
001154  00000000                       3970*         DC   A(0)
001158  00000008                       3971*         DC   P'8'
00115C  00008000                       3972*CORESIZ  DC   A(CORESIZE)  .         BYTES OF CORE IN OBJECT MACHINE

001160                                 3974*         DS   0D
001160  5CC9C2E2E4D74040               3975*TYPPCB   DC   CL8'*IBSUP'  .         A TEMPLATE *IBSUP PCB
001168  0000000000000000               3976*         DC   4A(0)
001178  00000000                       3977*TEMPLATE DC   X'00000000'  .
00117C  0000000100000000               3978*         DC   P'1,0'
001184  0000000000000000               3979*         DC   5P'0,0'
0011AC  FF00000000000011B4             3980*         DC   X'FF00000000',AL3(JSP) INITIALIZED FLAGS
000054                                 3981*TYPLEN   EQU  *-TYPPCB
```

459

```
LOC     OBJECT CODE   ADDR1 ADDR2   STMT  SOURCE STATEMENT

                                    3983 ****************************************
                                    3984 ***
                                    3985 ***               JOB STREAM PROCESSOR
                                    3986 ***
                                    3987 ****************************************

0011B4                              3989+JSP   EQU   *                     THE JOB STREAM PROCESSOR
0011B4 0510                         3990+      BALR  1,0 .                  (PROCESS *IBSUP)
0011B6                              3991+      USING *,1 .                  ESTABLISH ADDRESSING
0011B6 4120 13AA          01560     3992       LA    2,JSPSUSEM .          LOCK OURSELVES UNTIL
0011BA 0AD7                         3993       SVC   C'P' .                WE CAN ALLOCATE STORAGE
0011BC 4120 13B2          01568     3994       LA    2,JSPAAS .            READY TO ALLOCATE
                                    3995+      USING XAX,2
0011C0 0AC5                         3996       SVC   C'E' .                ALLOCATE
0011C2 58C0 2004          00004     3997       L     12,XAXADDR .          PTR TO AUTO AREA
                                    3998+      DROP  2
000000                              3999+      USING JSPAS,12 .            USE FOR ADDRESSING
0011C6 4120 13AA          01560     4000       LA    2,JSPSDSEM .          UNLOCK OURSELVES
0011CA 0AE5                         4001       SVC   C'V' .
0011CC D207 C164 1422  00164 0016C  4002       MVC   TREAD+0(8),=CL8'*IN' . INITIALIZE VALUES IN AUTOMATIC
0011D2 D203 C16C 144E  0016C 01604  4003       MVC   TREAD+8(4),=F'8' .                 STORAGE
0011D8 D203 C170 1452  00170 01608  4004       MVC   TREAD+12(4),=C'READ'
0011DE 4120 C084          00084     4005       LA    2,CARD
0011E2 5020 C174          00174     4006       ST    2,CARD
0011E6 D207 C190 142A  00190 01508  4007       MVC   USERL+0(8),=CL8'USERPROG'
0011EC D20B C178 1352  00178 01508  4008       MVC   WRITE(12),SKIP
0011F2 D203 C184 1456  00184 0160C  4009       MVC   WRITE+12(4),=C'PRIN'
0011F8 4150 C000          00000     4010       LA    5,LINE
0011FC 5050 C188          00188     4011       ST    5,WRITE+16
001200 D203 C188 144A  00188 01600  4012       MVC   CORE+8(4),=F'2048'
001206 D207 C1B8 142A  001B8 01508  4013       MVC   TALK+0(8),=CL8'USERPROG'
00120C D203 C1C0 145A  001C0 01610  4014       MVC   TALK+8(4),=F'12'
001212 D203 C1D8 145E  001D8 01614  4015       MVC   ANYBACK+8(4),=F'1'
001218 D203 C1B4 1462  001B4 01618  4016       MVC   BLDTEMP,=A(0)
00121E 5040 C18C          0018C     4017       ST    4,KEY                 STORE KEY
001224 1853                         4018+      LR    5,3 .                 GET PTR TO UCB PTR BLOCK
001228 5835 0000          00000     4019       L     3,0(5) .              GET READER POINTER
001228 4120 1362          01518     4020       LA    2,INSEQ .             READY TO CREATE & START *IN
00122C 0AC3                         4021       SVC   C'C' .                START
00122E 0AE8                         4022       SVC   C'Y' .
001234 4120 136E          01524     4023       L     3,4(5) .              GET PTR TO PRINTER UCB
001238 0AC3                         4024       LA    2,OUTSEQ .            READY TO CREATE & START *OUT
00123A 0AE8                         4025       SVC   C'C' .                START
                                    4026       SVC   C'Y' .

00123C 4120 C164          00164     4028+LOOP   LA    2,TREAD .            READY TO READ A CARD
001240 0AE2                         4029+      SVC   C'S' .                START TO READ
001242 D203 C0DC 1466  000DC 0161C  4030+      MVC   RREPLY1=F'132' .      132 CHARS FOR REPLY
001248 4120 C0D4          000D4     4031+      LA    2,RREPLY
00124C 0AD9                         4032       SVC   C'R' .                LISTEN FOR REPLY
00124E D501 C0E0 1476  000E0 01626  4033       CLC   REPLY(2),=C'OK' .     IS REPLY 'OK'?
001254 4770 10B0          01266     4034       BNE   STOP .                IF NOT, STOP
001258 D504 1478 0084  01478 00084  4035       CLC   =C'$JOB,',CARD .      HAVE WE A JOB CARD?
00125E 4780 10B6          0126C     4036       BE    JOB .                 GOOD!
001262 47F0 1086          0123C     4037       B     LOOP .                ELSE LOOP
```

```
LOC     OBJECT CODE       ADDR1  ADDR2   STMT          SOURCE STATEMENT

001266  4120 134A                01500   4038*STOP     LA   2,JSPNEVER .         WAIT FOR A "V" OPERATION
00126A  0AD7                              4039*         SVC  C1P* .               THAT NEVER COMES
00126C  9200 C1DD                001DD    4041*JOB      MVI  LOADED,X'00' .       REMEMBER NOT LOADED
001270  D283 C000 1432    00000  015B8    4042*         MVC  LINE,=CL8' ' .       CLEAR A LINE, PUT IN
001276  D27B C008 C007    00008  00007    4043*         MVC  LINE+8(124),LINE+7 . ALL BLANKS
00127C  D24F C000 C084    00000  00084    4044*         MVC  LINE(80),CARD .      TO PRINTER
001282  4120 C178                00178    4045*         LA   2,WRITE .            GET READY TO SEND $JOB CARD
001286  0AE2                              4046*         SVC  C'S' .               SEND IT
001288  4120 C0D4                000D4    4047*         LA   2,RREPLY             AND WAIT FOR REPLY
00128C  0AD9                              4048*         SVC  C'R' .
00128E  4120 C190                00190    4049*         LA   2,USERL .            CREATE USERPROG
001292  0AC3                              4050*         SVC  C'C' .
001294  4140 C088                00088    4051*         LA   4,CARD+4             START TO SCAN CARD
001298  4530 131A                01400    4052*         BAL  3,SCAN .             GET NEXT TOKEN
00129C  4180 0800                00800    4053*         LA   8,2048 .             FIRST GUESS AT CORE SIZE
0012A0  5870 13A6                015BC    4054*         L    7,CORETABS .         GET CORE TABLE SIZE
0012A4  4160 110A                013A6    4055*         LA   6,CORETAB .          INDEX INTO CORE TABLE
0012A8  4780 1110                01110    4056*CORELOOP EX   5,CORECOMP           IS THIS THE CORE SPEC?
0012AC  4780 11C0                012C0    4057*         BE   COREOK               IF SO, BINGO!
0012B0  4188 0800                00800    4058*         LA   8,2048(8)            ELSE UP OUR GUESS
0012B4  4166 0004                00004    4059*         LA   6,4 (6)              AND OUR INDEX
0012B8  4670 10F2                010F2    4060*         BCT  7,CORELOOP           AND TRY AGAIN
0012BC  47F0 12CA                012CA    4061*         B    EXPUNGE .            ELSE THROW HIM AWAY
0012C0  D500 9000 6000    00000  00000    4062*CORECOMP CLC  0(0,9),0(6)          EX'D TO TEST AGAINST CORE TABLE
0012C6  5080 C1A8                001A8    4063*COREOK   ST   8,CORE .             REMEMBER CORE REQUIREMENT
0012CA  4530 131A                01400    4064*ASGNUNIT BAL  3,SCAN .             GET NEXT TOKEN
0012CE  957E 4000                00000    4065*         CLI  0(4),C'='            IS IT AN '='?
0012D2  4770 119C                0119C    4066*         BNE  LOAD .               IF NOT, LOAD IN THE OBJECT DECK
0012D6  955C 9000                00000    4067*         CLI  0(9),C'*'            HAS USER NAMED IT STARTING
0012DA  4120 C19C                0019C    4068*         BE   EXPUNGE .            WITH * ? IF SO, THROW HIM OUT
0012DE  D207 C19C 15B8    0019C  015B8    4069*         LA   2,SEQ .              ELSE CREATE A PROCESS
0012E4  4450 115C                0115C    4070*         MVC  SEQ,=CL8' '          BLANK OUT THE NAME
0012E8  0AC3                              4071*         EX   5,UNAMMOV .          THEN MOVE THE RELEVANT
0012EA  4120 C19C                0019C    4072*         SVC  C'C' .               CHARACTERS AND CREATE
0012EE  4530 131A                01400    4073*         LA   2,SEQ .              WE'LL START IT IN A MOMENT
0012F2  4450 1162                01162    4074*         BAL  3,SCAN .             SCAN AGAIN
0012F6  4780 1174                01174    4075*         EX   5,CMPIN .            IS IT 'IN'?
0012FA  4450 1168                01168    4076*         BE   ASIN .               IF SO, ASSIGN IT AS IN
0012FE  4780 1184                01184    4077*         EX   5,CMPOUT .           IF IT'S 'OUT',
001302  4450 116E                0116E    4078*         BE   ASOUT .              ASSIGN IT AS OUT
001306  4780 118C                0118C    4079*         EX   5,CMPEXCP .          IS IT 'EXCP'?
00130A  47F0 12CA                012CA    4080*         BE   ASEXCP .             IF SO, ASSIGN IT AS EXCP
00130E  4120 C19C                0019C    4081*         B    EXPUNGE .            ERROR: GO ON TO NEXT JOB
001312  D500 9000 019C    9000   0019C    4082*UNAMMOV  MVC  SEQ(0),0(9)          MOVE THE UNIT'S PROCESS NAME
001318  D500 9000 1633    00000  01633    4083*CMPIN    CLC  0(0,9),=C'IN' .      DOES IT SAY 'IN'?
00131E  D500 9000 1620    00000  01620    4084*CMPOUT   CLC  0(0,9),=C'OUT' .     DOES IT SAY 'OUT'?
001324  D500 9000 1636    00000  01636    4085*CMPEXCP  CLC  0(0,9),=C'EXCP' .    DOES IT SAY 'EXCP'?
00132A  4180 1422                015D8    4087*ASIN     LA   11,=C18'*IN* .        POINT TO NAME OF READER HANDLER
001330  D203 C1A4 146E    001A4  01624    4088*SETDIM   MVC  UNITRTN,=A(DIM)       USE A DIM AS THE INTERFACE
001336  0AE8                              4089*         SVC  C'Y' .
001338  47F0 12CA                012CA    4090*         B    ASGNUNIT .
00133C  4180 143A                0143A    4091*ASOUT    LA   11,=C18'*OUT* .       POINT TO NAME OF PRINTER HANDLER
001340  47F0 1178                01178    4092*         B    SETDIM .
```

```
                    SAMPLE OPERATING SYSTEM          VERSION 2.00

  LOC   OBJECT CODE       ADDR1 ADDR2  STMT  SOURCE STATEMENT

001342 D203 C1A4 1472 001A4 01628 4093+ASEXCP  MVC  UNITRTN,=A(EXCPHNDL) .   USE FOR USER SUPPLIED
001348 58B0 C18C             0018C 4094+        L    11,KEY
00134C 0AE8                        4095+        SVC  C'Y' .                    I/O ROUTINE
00134E 47F0 1114             012CA 4096+        B    ASGNUNIT

001352 4120 C1A8             001A8 4098+LOAD    LA   2,CORE .                  READY TO ALLOCATE THE REGION
001356 0AC1                        4099+        SVC  C'A' .                    AND ALLOCATE IT
001358 92FF C1DD       001DD       4100+        MVI  LOADED,X'FF' .            REMEMBER THAT WE'RE LOADED
00135C 5890 C1AC             001AC 4101+        L    9,CORE+4 .                GET THE FIRST ADDRESS
001360 5840 C18C             0018C 4102+        L    4,KEY .                   GET THE KEY
001364 8840 0010             0010  4103+        SRL  4,16
001368 1839                        4104+        LR   3,9 .
00136A 1A38                        4105+        AR   3,8                       GET THE BLOCK FOLLOWING OURS
00136C 5B30 144A             0144A 4106+LOADSK  S    3,=F'2048' .              GET THE PREVIOUS BLOCK
001370 1939                        4107+        CR   3,9 .                     HAVE WE PASSED THE START?
001372 4740 11C6             0137C 4108+        BL   LOADLOOP .                IF SO, START LOADING
001376 0843                        4109+        SSK  4,3 .                     ELSE SET THIS BLOCK TO THE KEY,
001378 47F0 11B6             0136C 4110+        B    LOADSK                    AND BRANCH BACK
00137C 4120 C164             00164 4111+LOADLOOP LA  2,TREAD .                 READ IN OBJECT DECK.
001380 0AE2                        4112+        SVC  C'S' .                    GET A CARD A*READING.
001382 D502 CODC       000DC       4113+        MVC  RREPLY1,=F'132'          WAIT FOR ANSWER
001388 4120 C0D4             000D4 4114+        SVC  C'R' .
00138A 0AD9                        4115+        LA   2,RREPLY
00138E D502 C085 1485 00085 0163B 4116+TXTCARD CLC  CARD+1(3),=C'TXT' .       IS IT A TXT CARD?
001394 4780 11FA             11FA  4117+        BE   TXTCARD
001398 D502 C085 1488 00085 0163E 4118+        CLC  CARD+1(3),=C'RLD' .       IS IT A RLD CARD?
00139E 4780 1214             013CA 4119+        BE   RLDCARD
0013A2 D502 C085 148B 00085 01641 4120+        CLC  CARD+1(3),=C'END' .       IS IT AN END CARD?
0013A8 4780 1272             0137C 4121+        BE   ENDCARD
0013AC 47F0 11C6             0137C 4122+        B    LOADLOOP                  IF NONE, IGNORE.

0013B0 58A0 C088             00088 4124+TXTCARD L    10,CARD+4                 GET THE RELATIVE ADDRESS
0013B4 1AA9                        4125+        AR   10,9                      PLUS THE ABSOLUTE ADDRESS
0013B6 48B0 C08E             0008E 4126+        LH   11,CARD+10                GET THE COUNT
0013BA 06B0                        4127+        BCTR 11,0                      DECREMENTED.
0013BC 44B0 120E             013CA 4128+        EX   11,TXTMOV                 AND MOVE THE TEXT.
0013C0 47F0 11C6             0137C 4129+        B    LOADLOOP                  AND READ ANOTHER CARD! OH WOW!
0013C4 D200 A000 C094 00000 00094 4130+TXTMOV  MVC  0(0,10),CARD+16

0013CA 48B0 C08E             0008E 4132+RLDCARD LH   11,CARD+10                GET THE BYTE COUNT
0013CE 41D0 C098             00098 4133+        LA   13,CARD+20                AND AN INDEX INTO THE CARD
0013D2 58AD 0000             00000 4134+RLDLOOP L    10,0(13)                  GET THE LOCATION TO BE RLD'D
0013D6 1AA9                        4135+        AR   10,9                      GET THE ABSOLUTE ADDRESS
0013D8 9103 D003       00003       4136+        TM   3(13),X'03'              IS IT A FULLWORD?
0013DC 4770 1254             0140A 4137+        BNZ  NOTALGND                  IF NO, HANDLE AS THREE BYTES
0013E0 587A 0000             00000 4138+        L    7,0(10)                   GET THAT WORD (HAD BETTER BE
0013E4 1A79                        4139+        AR   7,9                       ONE) ADD THE RELOCATION
0013E6 507A 0000             00000 4140+        ST   7,0(10)                   ADDRESS, AND STORE IT BACK
0013EA 9101 D00D       0000D       4141+RLDCONT TM   13(13),X'01'             CHECK FOR LONG OR SHORT FIELD
0013EE 4770 1244             013FA 4142+        BNZ  SHORT                     AND BRANCH ACORDINGLY
0013F2 47F0 1248             013FE 4143+        B    RLDFINI
0013F6 41D0 0008             00008 4144+        LA   13,8                      SKIP EIGHT BYTES
0013FA 41D0 0004             00004 4145+SHORT   LA   13,4                      SKIP FOUR BYTES
0013FE 1AD4                        4146+RLDFINI AR   13,4                      INCREMENT THE CARD INDEX
001400 1BB4                        4147+        SR   11,4                      DECREMENT THE BYTE COUNT
```

```
LOC     OBJECT CODE   ADDR1 ADDR2  STMT   SOURCE STATEMENT

001402  4720 121C           013D2  4148*        BP   RLDLOOP .            AND TRY AGAIN
001406  47F0 11C6           0137C  4149*        B    LOADLOOP .           OR READ ANOTHER CARD
00140A  D202 C1B5  A000 001B5 00000  4150*NOTALGND MVC  RLDTEMP+1(3),0(10) . PUT ADDRESS HERE
001410  5870 C1B4           001B4  4151*        L    7,RLDTEMP .          RELOCATE IT
001414  1A79                       4152*        AR   7,9
001416  5070 C1B4           001B4  4153*        ST   7,RLDTEMP .          AND PUT IT BACK TO
00141A  D202 A000  C1B5 00060 001B5  4154*        MVC  0(3,10),RLDTEMP+1 . WHERE IT BELONGS
001420  9400 C1B4           001B4  4155*        NI   RLDTEMP,X'00' .      CLEAR OUT TEMPORARY
001424  47F0 123A           013EA  4156*        B    RLDCONT .            AND LOOP BACK

001428  4120 C190           00190  4158*ENDCARD  LA   2,USERL .           FIND THE PCB FOR USERPROG
00142C  0AD5                       4159*        SVC  C'N' .               GET THE ADDRESS,
00142E  4120 C198           00198  4160*        L    4,USERL+8 .
000000                             4161*        USING PCB,4
001432  92FF 4019           00019  4162*        MVI  PCBBLOKT,X'FF' .     TEMPORARILY BLOCK IT
001436  5090 C198           00198  4163*        ST   9,USERL+8 .          STORE THE BEGINNING ADDRESS
00143A  0AE8                       4164*        SVC  C'Y' .               THEN START IT
00143C  5850 C18C           0018C  4165*        L    5,KEY .              GET THE KEY,
001440  5650 404C           0004C  4166*        O    5,PCBISA+0 .         THEN OR THIS INTO THE
001444  5050 404C           0004C  4167*        ST   5,PCBISA+0 .         FIRST WORD OF THE PCB
001448  9601 404D           0004D  4168*        OI   PCBISA+1,X'01' .     OR IN A 'PROGRAM STATE' BIT
00144C  9200 4019           00019  4169*        MVI  PCBBLOKT,X'00' .     AND THEN UNBLOCK IT
                                   4170*        DROP 4
001450  4120 C1B8           001B8  4171*        LA   2,TALK .             LISTEN TO WHAT IT SAYS
001454  0AD9                       4172*        SVC  C'R' .

001456  D207 C000 1432 00008 015E8  4174*        MVC  LINE(8),=CL8' ' .    JOB FINISHED, CLEAR A LINE
00145C  D27B C008 C007 00008 00007  4175*        MVC  LINE+8(124),LINE+7  MOVE THE MESSAGE ONTO THE LINE
001462  D20B C000 C000 00008 00000  4176*        MVC  LINE+12(12),TALK+12  AND SAY TO WRITE IT
001468  4120 C178           00178  4177*        LA   2,WRITE .
00146C  0AE2                       4178*        SVC  C'S' .
00146E  4120 C1D0           001D0  4179*        LA   2,ANYBACK .
001472  0AD9                       4180*        SVC  C'R' .               WAIT FOR THE ANSWER
001474  4120 1352           01508  4181*        LA   2,SKIP .
001478  0AE2                       4182*        SVC  C'S' .               SKIP TO THE TOP OF THE NEXT PAGE
00147A  4120 C1D0           001D0  4183*        LA   2,ANYBACK .
00147E  0AD9                       4184*        SVC  C'R' .

001480  5850 0270           00270  4186*EXPUNGE  L    5,RUNNING .          EXPUNGE A JOB: LOOK AT ALL PCBS
001484  4120 C19C           0019C  4187*        LA   2,SEQ .
000000                             4188*        USING PCB,5
001488  D207 C19C 0019C 00008 00000  4189*EXPLOOP  MVC  SEQ(8),PCBNAME .    GET THE PROCESS NAME
00148E  5840 C19C           0019C  4190*        LA   4,PCBNPTG .           GET THE NEXT PTR
001492  955C C19C           0019C  4191*        CLI  SEQ+0,C'*' .          IS IT A '*' PROCESS?
001496  4780 12E8           0149E  4192*        BE   EXPNXT .              IF SO, SKIP OVER
00149A  0AE9                       4193*        SVC  C'Z' .                ELSE STOP IT
00149C  0AC4                       4194*        SVC  C'D' .                AND DESTROY IT
00149E  1854                       4195*EXPNXT   LR   5,4 .                GO TO THE NEXT PCB
0014A0  5950 0270           00270  4196*        C    5,RUNNING .           ARE WE THROUGH?
0014A4  4770 12D2           01488  4197*        BNE  EXPLOOP .             IF NOT, LOOP AGAIN
0014A8  9500 C1DD           001DD  4198*        CLI  LOADED,X'00' .        WAS CORE ALLOCATED?
0014AC  4780 1086           0123C  4199*        BE   LOOP .                IF NOT, GO READ NEXT $JOB CARD
0014B0  1844                       4200*        SR   4,4 .                 ELSE GET A ZERO KEY
0014B2  1839                       4201*        LR   3,9 .                 AND A POINTER TO THE NEXT
0014B4  1138                       4202*        AR   3,8 .                 BLOCK AFTER OURS.
```

463

```
LOC    OBJECT CODE       ADDR1 ADDR2  STMT SOURCE STATEMENT

0014B6 5B30 144A               01600  4203*LOADCL   S     3,=F'2048'      GO TO THE PREVIOUS BLOCK
0014BA 1939                           4204*         CR    3,9             ARE WE THROUGH?
0014BC 4740 1310               014C6  4205*         BL    LOADD           IF SO, GO FREE CORE
0014C0 0843                           4206*         SSK   4,3             ELSE CLEAR STORAGE KEY
0014C2 47F0 1300               014B6  4207*         B     LOADCL          AND LOOP BACK
0014C6 4120 C1A8               001A8  4208*LOADD    LA    2,CORE          FREE THE STORAGE
0014CA 0AC6                            4209*         SVC   C'F'
0014CC 47F0 1086               0123C  4210*         B     LOOP            READ ANOTHER $JOB CARD

0014D0 1B55                            4212*SCAN     SR    5,5             START TOKEN COUNT AT ZERO
0014D2 4144 4000               00001  4213*SCANLOOP LA    4,1(4)          GO TO NEXT CHARACTER
0014D6 956B 4000         00000        4214*         CLI   0(4),C','       DO WE HAVE A DELIMITER? OF SO,
0014DA 4780 1340               014F6  4215*         BE    TOKSTART
0014DE 957E 4000         00000        4216*         CLI   0(4),C'='       DITTO
0014E2 4780 1340               014F6  4217*         BE    TOKSTART
0014E6 9540 4000         00000        4218*         CLI   0(4),C' '       DITTO
0014EA 4780 1340               014F6  4219*         BE    TOKSTART
0014EE 4155 0001               00001  4220*         LA    5,1(5)          AND UP COUNT
0014F2 47F0 131C               014D2  4221*         B     SCANLOOP        AND LOOP
0014F6 1894                            4222*TOKSTART LR    9,4             SET REG9 TO START
0014F8 1895                            4223*         SR    9,5             OF THIS TOKEN
0014FA 0650                            4224*         BCTR  9,0             LESS ONE FOR EXECUTE INSTRUCTION
0014FC 07F3                            4225*         BR    3

0014FE 0000
001500 0000000000000000              4227*JSPNEVER DC    F'0,0'    .      A GOOD WAY TO DIE: P(JSPNEVER)
001508 5CD6E4E340404040              4228*SKIP     DC    CL8'*OUT' .      MESSAGE BLOCK FOR NEW PAGE
001510 00000008                      4229*         DC    F'8'
001514 E2E3C3F1                      4230*         DC    CL4'STC1'
001518 5CC9D54040404040              4231*INSEQ    DC    CL8'*IN'  .      SEQ TO CREATE & START *IN
001520 00000AC6                      4232*         DC    A(RDHANDL)
001524 5CD6E4E340404040              4233*OUTSEQ   DC    CL8'*OUT' .      SEQ TO CREATE & START *OUT
00152C 00000C24                      4234*         DC    A(PRTHANDL)
001530                               4235*CORETAB  EQU   *                TABLE OF CORE SIZES
001530 F2D24040                      4236*         DC    CL4'2K'
001534 F4D24040                      4237*         DC    CL4'4K'
001538 F6D24040                      4238*         DC    CL4'6K'
00153C F8D24040                      4239*         DC    CL4'8K'
001540 F1F0D240                      4240*         DC    CL4'10K'
001544 F1F2D240                      4241*         DC    CL4'12K'
001548 F1F4D240                      4242*         DC    CL4'14K'
00154C F1F6D240                      4243*         DC    CL4'16K'
001550 F1F8D240                      4244*         DC    CL4'18K'
001554 F2F0D240                      4245*         DC    CL4'20K'
001558 F2F2D240                      4246*         DC    CL4'22K'
00155C 0000000B                      4247*CORETABS DC    A((*-CORETAB)/4) . CORE TABLE SIZE
001560 0000000100000000              4248*JSPSUSEM DC    F'1,0'    .      SEMAPHORE TO LOCK ROUTINE
001568 000001E0                      4249*JSPRAS   DC    A(LENJSPAS) .    ALLOCATE LIST FOR AUTO STORAGE
00156C                               4250*         DS    A
001570 00000008                      4251*         DC    F'8'
```

LOC   OBJECT CODE   ADDR1 ADDR2   STMT   SOURCE STATEMENT

```
                                          4253+***********************************************************
                                          4254+*                                                         *
                                          4255+*                  DEVICE INTERFACE MODULE                *
                                          4256+*                                                         *
                                          4257+***********************************************************
                                          4258+*        FUNCTION: TO INTERFACE BETWEEN USERPROG AND DEVICE HANDLER
                                          4259+*       DATABASES: NONE
                                          4260+*   ROUTINES USED: XA, XP, XV, XR, XS
                                          4261+*       PROCEDURE: ALLOCATE AUTOMATIC STORAGE; START TO READ MESSAGE
                                          4262+*                  FROM USER: SEND MESSAGE TO DEVICE HANDLER;
                                          4263+*                  CONTINUE LOOPING, SENDING MESSAGES FROM USER TO
                                          4264+*                  DEVICE HANDLER AND BACK.
                                          4265+*     ERROR CHECKS: NONE
                                          4266+*      INTERRUPTS: ON
                                          4267+*     USER ACCESS: YES
                                          4268+***********************************************************
001574                                    4270+DIM      EQU   *                   THE DEVICE INTERFACE MODULE
001574  0510                              4271+         BALR  1,0
001576                                    4272+         USING *,1                  ESTABLISH ADDRESSING
001576  4120 1042              015B8      4273+         LA    2,DIMSEM             LOCK UNTIL GET STORAGE
001574  0AD7                              4274+         SVC   C'P'
001574C 4120 104A              015C0      4275+         LA    2,DIMAAS             READY TO ALLOCATE STORAGE
000000                                    4276+         USING XAX,2
001580  0AC5                              4277+         SVC   C'A'                 DO IT
001582  58C0 2004              00004      4277+         L     12,XAXADDR           GET THE ADDRESS
                                          4278+         USING *,12
001586  4120 1042              015B8      4279+         DROP  2
001582                                    4280+         LA    2,DIMSEM             UNLOCK OURSELVES
001586  4120 1042              015B8      4281+         SVC   C'V'
001588  0AE5                              4282+         USING DIMAS,12             USE 12 FOR AUTO STORAGE
000000                                    4283+         MVC   DIMLMS,C(11)         MOVE NAME OF RECEIVER
00158C  D207 C090 B000 00090  00098       4284+         LA    8,132               REG 8 = SIZE OF MESSAGE
001592  4180 0084              00084      4285+DIMLOOP  ST    8,DIMMSG+8           GET READ1 TO READ A MESSAGE
001596  5080 C008              00008      4286+         LA    2,DIMMSG
00159A  4120 C000              00000      4287+         SVC   C'R'                 READ
00159E  0AD9                              4288+         MVC   DIMTEMP,DIMMSG       SAVE SENDER NAME
00159E  D207 C098 C000 00098  00000       4289+         MVC   DIMMSG,DIMLMS        SEND IT BACK TO THE LAST GUY
0015A6  D207 C000 C090 00000  00090       4290+         SVC   C'S'                 SEND IT
0015AC  0AE2                              4291+         MVC   DIMLMS,DIMTEMP       AND REMEMBER WHO TO SEND TO NEXT
0015AE  D207 C090 C098 00090  00098       4292+         B     DIMLOOP             RELOOP
0015B4  47F0 1020              01596      4293+DIMSEM   DC    P'1,0'               SEMAPHORE FOR ENTRY
0015B8  0000000100000000                  4294+DIMAAS   DC    A(DIMLEN)            ALLOCATE SEQ FOR AUTO STORAGE
0015C0  000000A0                          4295+         DC    A(0)
0015C4  00000000                          4296+         DC    F'8'
0015C8  00000008                          4297+         DROP  12
```

```
LOC     OBJECT CODE          ADDR1 ADDR2  STMT    SOURCE STATEMENT

                                           4299+           LTORG
0015D0  0000000000006988                   4299+   =A(0,CORESIZE-(VERYEND-PROGRAM))
0015D8  5C9D5404040040                     4300    =CL8'*IN*'
0015E0  E42C5D9D79D6C7                     4301    =CL8'USERPROG'
0015E8  4040404040404040                   4302    =CL8' '
0015F0  5C6D6E2304040040                   4303    =CL8'*OUT*'
0015F8  00000E74                           4304    =A(UCBTABLE)
0015FC  00000EF4                           4305    =A(UCBTBEND)
001600  00000800                           4306    =F'2048'
001604  00000008                           4307    =F'8'
001608  D9C5C1C4                           4308    =C'READ'
00160C  D7D9C9D5                           4309    =C'PRIN'
001610  0000000C                           4310    =F'12'
001614  00000001                           4311    =F'1'
001618  00000000                           4312    =A(0)
00161C  D6E4E340                           4313    =C'OUT'
001620  00000084                           4314    =F'132'
001624  00001574                           4315    =A(DTM)
001628  00000D44                           4316    =A(EXCPHNDL)
00162C  D6D2                               4317    =C'OK'
00162E  5BD1D6C26B                         4318    =C'$JOB,'
001633  C9D540                             4319    =C'IN '
001636  C5E7C3D740                         4320    =C'EXCP '
00163B  E3E7E3                             4321    =C'TXT'
00163E  D9D3C4                             4322    =C'RLD'
001641  C5D5C4                             4323    =C'END'
001648                                     4325+VERYEND  DS    D .    BEGINNING OF FREE STORAGE
```

466

```
LOC      OBJECT CODE  ADDR1 ADDR2   STMT   SOURCE STATEMENT

                                    4327   ******************************************  ****
                                    4328   **
                                    4329   **          DATABASE DEFINITIONS
                                    4330   **
                                    4331   ******************************************

000000                              4333  +PCB        DSECT            PROCESS CONTROL BLOCK DEFINITION
000000                              4334  +PCBNAME     DS    CL8 .      NAME
000008                              4335  +PCBNPTG     DS    F .        NEXT POINTER THIS GROUP
00000C                              4336  +PCBLPTG     DS    F .        LAST POINTER THIS GROUP
000010                              4337  +PCBNPALL    DS    F .        NEXT POINTER ALL
000014                              4338  +PCBLPALL    DS    F .        LAST POINTER ALL
000018                              4339  +PCBSTOPT    DS    C .        STOPPED
000019                              4340  +PCBBLOKT    DS    C .        BLOCKED
00001A                              4341  +PCBINSMC    DS    C .        IN SMC
00001B                              4342  +PCBSW       DS    C .        STOP WAITING
00001C                              4343  +PCBMSC      DS    CL8        MESSAGE SEMAPHORE COMMON
000024                              4344  +PCBMSR      DS    CL8        MESSAGE SEMAPHORE RECEIVER
00002C                              4345  +PCBFM       DS    F .        FIRST MESSAGE
000030                              4346  +PCBNSW      DS    CL8 .      NEXT SEMAPHORE WAITER
000034                              4347  +PCBSBS      DS    CL8 .      STOPPER SEMAPHORE
00003C                              4348  +PCBSES      DS    CL8 .      STOPPEE SEMAPHORE
000044                              4349  +PCBRASIZE   DS    A .        AUTOMATIC STORAGE SIZE
000048                              4350  +PCBRAADDR   DS    A .        AUTOMATIC STORAGE ADDRESS
00004C                              4351  +PCBISA      DS    CL84 .     INTERRUPT SAVE AREA
0000A0                              4352  +PCBFSA      DS    CL84 .     FAULT SAVE AREA
0000F4                              4353  +PCBMSA      DS    CL84 .     MEMORY SAVE AREA
000148                              4354  +           DS    0D .       (ALIGN)
000148                              4355  +LENPCB      EQU   *-PCB      (LENGTH)

000000                              4357  +SA          DSECT            SAVE AREA DEFINITION
000000                              4358  +SAPSW       DS    D .        PROGRAM STATUS WORD
000008                              4359  +SAREGS      DS    CL64 .     REGISTERS
000048                              4360  +SATEMP      DS    CL12 .     TEMPORARIES

000000                              4362  +REGS        DSECT            REGISTERS DEFINITION
000000                              4363  +REG0        DS    F .        REGISTER 0
000004                              4364  +REG1        DS    F .        REGISTER 1
000008                              4365  +REG2        DS    F .        REGISTER 2
00000C                              4366  +REG3        DS    F .        REGISTER 3
000010                              4367  +REG4        DS    F .        REGISTER 4
000014                              4368  +REG5        DS    F .        REGISTER 5
000018                              4369  +REG6        DS    F .        REGISTER 6
00001C                              4370  +REG7        DS    F .        REGISTER 7
000020                              4371  +REG8        DS    F .        REGISTER 8
000024                              4372  +REG9        DS    F .        REGISTER 9
000028                              4373  +REG10       DS    F .        REGISTER 10
00002C                              4374  +REG11       DS    F .        REGISTER 11
000030                              4375  +REG12       DS    F .        REGISTER 12
000034                              4376  +REG13       DS    F .        REGISTER 13
000038                              4377  +REG14       DS    F .        REGISTER 14
00003C                              4378  +REG15       DS    F .        REGISTER 15
```

LOC	OBJECT CODE	ADDR1 ADDR2	STMT	SOURCE STATEMENT	
000000			4380+FSB	DSECT	FREE STORAGE BLOCK DEFINITIONS
000000			4381+FSBNEXT	DS A	NEXT
000004			4382+FSBSIZE	DS F	SIZE
000000			4384+SM	DSECT	SEMAPHORE DEFINITION
000000			4385+SMVAL	DS F	VALUE
000004			4386+SMPTR	DS F	PTR
000000			4388+MSG	DSECT	MESSAGE DEFINITION
000000			4389+MSGSENDR	DS A	POINTER TO SENDER'S PCB
000004			4390+MSGNEXT	DS A	NEXT
000008			4391+MSGSIZE	DS F	SIZE
00000C			4392+MSGTEXT	DS 0C	TEXT
00000C			4393+LENMSG	EQU *-MSG	(LENGTH)
000000			4395+XAX	DSECT	XA ARGUMENT LIST
000000			4396+XAXSIZE	DS F	SIZE
000004			4397+XAXADDR	DS A	ADDRESS
000008			4398+XAXALGN	DS F	ALIGNMENT
000000			4400+XPX	DSECT	XP ARGUMENT LIST
000000			4401+XPXSIZE	DS F	SIZE
000004			4402+XPXADDR	DS A	ADDRESS
000000			4404+XBX	DSECT	XB ARGUMENT LIST
000000			4405+XBXSIZE	DS F	SIZE
000004			4406+XBXADDR	DS A	ADDRESS
000000			4408+XCX	DSECT	YC ARGUMENT LIST
000000			4409+XCXNAME	DS CL8	NAME
000000			4411+XDX	DSECT	XD ARGUMENT LIST
000000			4412+XDXNAME	DS CL8	NAME
000000			4414+XNX	DSECT	XN ARGUMENT LIST
000000			4415+XNXNAME	DS CL8	NAME
000008			4416+XNXADDR	DS A	ADDRESS
000000			4418+XRX	DSECT	XR ARGUMENT LIST
000000			4419+XRXNAME	DS CL8	NAME
000008			4420+XRXSIZE	DS F	SIZE
00000C			4421+XRXTEXT	DS 0C	TEXT
000000			4423+XSX	DSECT	XS ARGUMENT LIST
000000			4424+XSXNAME	DS CL8	NAME
000008			4425+XSXSIZE	DS F	SIZE
00000C			4426+XSXTEXT	DS 0C	TEXT
000000			4428+XYX	DSECT	XY ARGUMENT LIST
000000			4429+XYXNAME	DS CL8	NAME
000008			4430+XYXADDR	DS A	ADDR
000000			4432+XZX	DSECT	XZ ARGUMENT LIST
000000			4433+XZXNAME	DS CL8	NAME

468

```
LOC   OBJECT CODE   ADDR1 ADDR2   STMT   SOURCE STATEMENT

000000                            4435+RDRHAS    DSECT           .         READER HANDLER AUTOMATIC STORAGE
000000                            4436+RDRHCCB   DS    2F        .         CCB
000008                            4437+RDRHMSG   DS    CL8       .         MESSAGE BLOCK FOR REQUESTS
000010                            4438+          DS    F'8'      .
000014                            4439+          DS    CL8       .
00001C                            4440+RDRHTEMP  DS    CL80      .         AREA FOR $JOB IN DATA STREAM
00006C                            4441+RDRHM     DS    CL8       .         MESSAGE BLOCK FOR REPLY
000074                            4442+          DS    F'2'      .
000078                            4443+          DS    CL2       .
00007A                            4444+JOBBIT    DS    1C        .
000080                            4445+          DS    0D        .
000080                            4446+LENRDRHA  EQU   *-RDRHAS  .         (LENGTH)

000000                            4448+PRTHAS    DSECT           .         PRINTER HANDLER AUTO STORAGE
000000                            4449+PRTHCCB   DS    2F        .         CCB
000008                            4450+PRTHMSG   DS    CL8       .         MESSAGE BLOCK FOR REQUESTS
000010                            4451+          DS    F'2'      .
000014                            4452+          DS    CL8       .
00001C                            4453+PRTHM     DS    CL8       .         MESSAGE BLOCK FOR REPLYS
000024                            4454+          DS    F'2'      .
000028                            4455+          DS    CL2       .
000030                            4456+          DS    0D        .
000030                            4457+LENPRTHA  EQU   *-PRTHAS  .         (LENGTH)

000000                            4459+EXCPHAS   DSECT           .         EXCP HANDLER AUTOMATIC STORAGE
000000                            4460+EXCPHMSG  DS    CL8       .         MESSAGE BLOCK FOR REQUESTS
000008                            4461+          DS    F'12'     .
00000C                            4462+          DS    CL12      .
000018                            4463+EXCPHM    DS    CL8       .         MESSAGE BLOCK FOR REPLY
000024                            4464+          DS    F'12'     .
000030                            4465+          DS    CL12      .
000030                            4466+          DS    0D        .
000030                            4467+LENEXCPA  EQU   *-EXCPHAS .

000000                            4469+UCB       DSECT           .         UNIT CONTROL BLOCK DEFINITION
000000                            4470+UCBADDR   DS    F         .         ADDRESS
000004                            4471+UCBUS     DS    PL8       .         USER SEMAPHORE
00000C                            4472+UCBWS     DS    PL8       .         WAITER SEMAPHORE
000014                            4473+UCBCSW    DS    PL8       .         CHANNEL STATUS WORD
00001C                            4474+UCBPPR    DS    CL1       .         PAST PROCCESSING REQUIRED
000020                            4475+          DS    0F        .
000020                            4476+UCBLENG   EQU   *-UCB     .

000000                            4478+JSPAS     DSECT           .         JSP AUTOMATIC STORAGE
000000                            4479+LINE      DS    CL132     .         PRINTED LINE
000084                            4480+          DS    0F        .
000084                            4481+CARD      DS    CL80      .         CARD READ
000084                            4482+          DS    0F        .
0000DC                            4483+RREPLY    DS    P         .
0000DC                            4484+RREPLY1   DS    P         .         MESSAGE BLOCK FOR REPLIES
000164                            4485+REPLY     DS    CL132     .
000164                            4486+TREAD     DS    0F        .
000164                            4487+          DS    CL8'*IN'  .
00016C                            4488+          DS    F'8'      .
000170                            4489+          DS    CL4'READ' .         MESSAGE BLOCK FOR READING
```

SAMPLE OPERATING SYSTEM   VERSION 2.00

LOC	OBJECT CODE	ADDR1	ADDR2	STMT	SOURCE STATEMENT	
000174				4490+ACARD	DS	A(0)
000178				4491+WRITE	DS	CL8'*OUT' . MESSAGE BLOCK TO PRINT A LINE
000180				4492+	DS	P'8'
000184				4493+	DS	CL4'PRIN'
000188				4494+	DS	A(LINE)
00018C				4495+KEY	DS	P'1'
000190				4496+USERBL	DS	P LIST FOR MANIPULATING USERPROG
000198				4497+	DS	CL8'USERPROG' .
00019C				4498+SEQ	DS	CL8' ' . COMMON ARG LIST FOR I/O PROCESS
0001A4				4499+UNITRTN	DS	A
0001A8				4500+CORE	DS	P . MEMORY ALLOCATE AND FREE
0001AC				4501+	DS	A SEQUENCE
0001B0				4502+	DS	P'2048'
0001B4				4503+RLDTEMP	DS	P MESSAGE BLOCK FOR MESSAGE FROM
0001B8				4504+TALK	DS	CL8'USERPROG' . USERPROG
0001C0				4505+	DS	P'12' . MESSAGE BLOCK FOR IGNORING MESS
0001C4				4506+	DS	CL12
0001D0				4507+ANYBACK	DS	CL8 . IF CORE ALLOCATED
0001D8				4508+	DS	P'1'
0001DC				4509+	DS	CL1
0001DD				4510+LOADED	DS	C .
0001E0				4511+	DS	0D
0001E0				4512+LENJSPAS	EQU	*-JSPAS . (LENGTH)
000000				4514+DIMAS	DSECT	. DEVICE INTERFACE MODULE STORAGE
000000				4515+DIMMSG	DS	CL8 . MESSAGE BLOCK
000008				4516+	DS	P'132'
00000C				4517+	DS	CL132
000090				4518+DIMLMS	DS	CL8 . LAST MESSAGE SENDER
000098				4519+DIMTEMP	DS	CL8 . TEMPORARY
0000A0				4520+	DS	0D
0000A0				4521+DIMLEN	EQU	*-DIMAS . (LENGTH)
				4522	END	

SYMBOL	LEN	VALUE	DEFN	REFERENCES
ACARD	4	000174	4490	4006
ANYBACK	8	0001D0	4507	4015 4179 4183
ASEXCP	6	001342	4093	4080
ASGNUNIT	4	0012CA	4064	4090 4096
ASIN	4	00132A	4087	4076
ASOUT	4	001333	4091	4078
CARD	80	000084	4481	4005 4035 4044 4051 4116 4118 4120 4124 4126 4130 4132 4133
CAW	4	000008	2359	3579 3681 3761
CAWSEM	4	000194	2372	3577 3679 3759
CCBCON1	4	000C10	3617	3571 3671
CMPEXCP	6	001324	4085	4079
CMPIN	6	00131B	4083	4075
CMPOUT	6	00131E	4084	4077
CORE	4	0001A8	4500	4012 4063 4098 4101 4208
CORECOMP	6	0001C0	4062	4056
CORELOOP	4	0012A8	4056	4060
COREOK	4	0001A6	4063	4057
CORESIZ	4	00115C	3972	3910
CORESIZE	1	08000D	2346	3908 3972 4300
CORETAB	6	001530	4235	4055 4247
CORETABS	4	00155C	4247	4054
CSW	8	000040	2358	3868 3869 3872
DIM	1	001574	4270	4088 4316
DIMAAS	4	0015C0	4294	4275
DIMAS	1	0015C0	4294	4282 4521
DIMLEN	1	000000	4521	4294
DIMLMS	8	000090	4518	4283 4289 4291
DIMLOOP	4	001596	4285	4292
DIMSG	8	000000	4515	4285 4286 4288 4289
DIMSEM	8	0015B8	4519	4273 4280
DIMTEMP	8	000098	4519	4288 4291
ENDADATA	6	000BDE	3604	3595
ENDCARD	4	001428	4158	4121
EXCPCOMP	4	000D84	3747	3751
EXCPDONE	4	000E00	3781	3776
EXCPFIND	2	000D9A	3753	3748
EXCPHAAS	4	000E14	3786	3727
EXCPHAS	8	000000	4459	3736 4467
EXCPHM	8	000018	4463	3766 3767 3768 3769
EXCPHMSG	8	000000	4460	3737 3768 3771
EXCPHNDL	1	000D44	3721	4093 4317
EXCPHSEM	4	000E0C	3785	3725 3732
EXCPLOOP	4	000D62	3737	3742 3783
EXCPWAIT	4	000DC0	3764	3778
EXPLOOP	6	001488	4189	4197
EXPNXT	2	00149E	4195	4192
EXPUNGE	4	001480	4186	4061 4068 4081
EXTHANDL	1	00027A	2389	2363
EXTHRET	4	0002A8	2405	2394 2398
EXTNEW	1	000058	2363	2393 2401 2406
EXTOLD	8	000018	2353	2390 2876 2945 2954
FSB	1	000000	4380	2790 2803 2804 2811
FSBNEXT	4	000180	2369	2786 2787 2874 2879 2893 2894 2948 2949 2955
FSBPTR	4	000180	2369	2786 2787 2874 2875 2893 2894 2942
FSBSEM	4	000184	2370	2784 2830 2872 2907 2941

SYMBOL	LEN	VALUE	DEFN	REFERENCES
PSBSIZE	4	000004	4382	2799 2812
GWINC	4	000586	2672	2669
GWLOOP	6	0005A0	2668	2674
GWRUN	6	0005A0	2679	2671
IDLE	1	000598	2677	2675
INSEQ	8	001518	4231	4020
IOBACK	4	000F66	3889	3866
IOCOMP	6	000F02	3868	3865
IODEVFND	6	000F1C	3868	3862
IOHANDL	1	000EF4	3855	2367 3883 3889
IOHSAVE	6	0001DC	2375	3856
IONEW	1	000078	2367	2662
IONOFPR	2	000F64	3888	2875
IOOLD	8	000038	2357	3859 3861 3882 3890
IOWAIT	4	000F5C	3885	3879
IPLAPCBS	4	001150	3969	3917
IPLCCW1	8	000008	2351	
IPLCCW2	8	000010	2352	
IPLCL	4	000F8A	3911	3914
IPLLOOP	4	000F9E	3917	3942
IPLPCB	8	001008	3959	3905 3960
IPLPSW	1	000000	2350	2350
IPLRTN	1	000F6E	3902	3912
IPLTH	2	000F98	3915	3915
JOB	1	00126C	4041	4036
JOBBIT	1	00007A	4444	3537 3551 3556 3608
JSP	1	0011B4	3989	3980
JSPAAS	4	001568	4249	3994
JSPAS	1	000000	4478	3999
JSPNEVER	4	001500	4227	4038
JSPSUSEM	4	001560	4248	3992 4000
KEY	4	00018C	4495	4017 4094 4102 4165
KEYTAB	1	000FF0	3951	3939
LENEXCPA	1	0001E0	4467	3786
LENJSPAS	1	0001E0	4512	4249
LENMSG	1	00000C	4393	3287 3341 3795 3969
LENPCB	1	000148	4355	2991 3070
LENPRTHA	1	000030	4457	3711
LENRDRHA	1	000080	4446	3619
LINE	132	000000	4479	4010 4042 4043 4044 4174 4175 4175 4175 4176
LOAD	1	001352	4098	4066
LOADCL	4	0014B6	4203	4207
LOADD	1	0014C6	4208	4205
LOADED	1	0001DD	4510	4041 4100 4198 4129 4149
LOADLOOP	4	00137C	4111	4108 4122
LOADSK	4	00136C	4106	4110
LOOP	4	00123C	4028	4037 4199 4210
MCHKNEW	1	000070	2366	
MCHKOLD	8	00018C	2356	
MEMORI	4	000030	2371	2807 2902
MSG	4	000000	4388	3053 3264 3353 3361 4393
MSGNEXT	4	000004	4390	3054 3265 3356 3357 3362
MSGSENDR	4	000008	4389	3282 3363
MSGSIZE	4	000008	4391	3055 3273 3275 3286
MSGTEXT	1	00000C	4392	3298 3376 3365

SYMBOL	LEN	VALUE	DEFN	REFERENCES
NEXTTRY	4	000274	2380	2638 2665 2679
NEXTTRYM	1	000278	2381	2636 2639 2680
NOTALGND	6	00140A	4150	4117
OUTSEQ	8	015524	4233	4024
PCB	1	000000	4333	2531 2532 2533 2587 2594 2633 2667 2687 2996 3039 3044 3048 3076 3131 3138 3142 3145 3150 3170 3174 3177 3180 3184 3187 3191 3217 3227 3284 3336 3378 3412 3423 3462 3474 3877 3923 3927 3931 4161 4188 4355
PCBAADDR	4	000048	4350	2835 3064 3066 3066
PCBASIZE	4	000044	4349	2834 3066
PCBBLOKT	1	000019	4340	2397 2597
PCBFM	4	00002C	4345	2532 2597 2635 2668 2731 2733 2999 3351 3878 4162 4169
PCBFSA	84	0000A0	4352	2531 2597 2682 2999 3178 3880 4166 4167 4168
PCBINSMC	1	00001A	4341	2399 3135 3171
PCBISA	84	00004C	4351	2598 2682 2999 3181 3188 3413 3880 3932
PCBLPALL	4	000014	4338	3132 3135 3171 3175 3929 4190
PCBLPTG	4	00000C	4336	3143 3146 3188 3925 3928
PCBMSA	84	0000F4	4353	2533 3181 3185
PCBMSC	8	00001C	4343	3261 3349 3371
PCBMSR	8	000024	4344	3258 3371
PCBNAME	8	000010	4334	2997 3219 3285 3449 4189
PCBNPALL	8	000010	4337	2672 2679 3128 3129 3136 3147 3182 3185
PCBNPTG	4	000008	4335	2590 2591 2596 3139 3140 2634
PCBNSW	4	000030	4346	2741
PCBSES	8	00003C	4348	2739 3469
PCBSRS	8	000034	4347	2670 2738 2998
PCBSTOPT	1	000018	4339	2736 3040 3418 3465
PCBSW	1	00001B	4342	2365 3468
PGMHANDL	1	0002B0	2408	2365
PGMNEW	1	000068	2365	2344
PGMOLD	8	000028	2355	2344
PROGRAM	1	000000	2344	3908 4300
PROTCON1	1	000C14	3618	3562 3567 3662 3667
PRTHAAS	1	000D38	3711	3635
PRTHANDL	1	000C24	3629	3634
PRTHAS	1	000000	4448	4234 4457
PRTHCCB	4	000000	4449	3645 3672 3673 3674 3676
PRTHCOMM	4	000CBC	3679	3675 3679 3703 3707
PRTHLOOP	4	000C46	3646	3655 3694 3696
PRTHM	8	00001C	4453	3694 3697 3698 3701
PRTHMSG	8	000008	4450	3646 3659 3670
PRTHOK	6	000CF6	3594	3660 3665
PRTHPOK	4	000D00	3671	3652
PRTHPRIN	4	000C9A	3557	3633 3640
PRTHSEM	4	000C6E	3710	3633
PRTHSEND	6	000D30	3697	3652
PRTHSTC1	6	000D06	3676	3654
PRTHWAIT	4	000CB0	3688	3691
PTSTATUS	2	000CE0	3704	3686
QUANTUM	4	000D22	2685	3683
RDRHAAS	1	0005BC	3521	3527
RDRHANDL	1	000C18	3619	4232
RDRHAS	4	000AC6	3536	3556 3573 3574
RDRHCCB	4	000000	4435	3538 3572 3573
RDRHLOOP	4	000AEC	3539	3544 3603 4446

SYMBOL	LEN	VALUE	DEFN	REFERENCES															
RDREM	8	00006C	4441	3590	3596	3597	3598	3601	3604										
RDREMORE	4	00082E	3559	3552	3559	3559	3598												
RDREMSG	8	000008	4437	3554	3549	3592	3598												
RDREHNO	6	0008A0	3590	3554	3565	3570													
RDREHOK	4	0008AA	3592	3589															
RDREHPOK	4	000C08	3571	3560	3613														
RDREHSEM	6	0008C2	3616	3571	3532														
RDREHSEND	80	00001C	3597	3525	3609														
RDREHSOK	2	0008B8	3596	3591	3593														
RDREHTEMP	2	0008FC	4440	3555	3605														
RDREHWAIT	1	000000	3584	3555															
RDSTATUS			3610	3587															
REGS			4362	3582															
REG0	4	000000	4363	3935															
REG1	4	000004	4364																
REG10	4	000028	4373																
REG11	4	00002C	4374																
REG12	4	000030	4375																
REG13	4	000034	4376																
REG14	4	000038	4377																
REG15	4	00003C	4378																
REG2	4	000008	4365	3938															
REG3	4	00000C	4366	3939															
REG4	4	000010	4367																
REG5	4	000014	4368																
REG6	4	000018	4369																
REG7	4	00001C	4370																
REG8	4	000020	4371																
REG9	4	000024	4372																
REPLY	132	0000E0	4485																
RETURN	1	0009D8	2542	2583	2630	2640	2684	2709	2743	2837	2910	2957	3002	3073	3149	3190	3225	3296
				3374	3419	3467													
RETURNR	1	0004E0	2584																
RLDCARD	4	0013CA	4132	2542															
RLDCONT	4	0013EA	4141	4119	4156														
RLDFINI	2	0013FE	4146	4184															
RLDLOOP	4	0013D2	4134	4148															
RLDTEMP	4	0001B4	4503	4016	4150	4151	4153	4154	4155										
RREPLY	8	0000D4	4483	4031	4047														
RREPLY1	8	0000DC	4484	4030	4113	4114													
RUNNING	1	000270	2379	2395	2435	2595	2681	2876	3906										
SA	1	000270	4357	2400	2444	2414	2415	3415	3422	3417									
SAPSW	8	000000	4358	2401	2445	2545	2415	3415	3416										
SAREGS	64	000008	4359	2402	2446	2546	3417	3417	3883	3882	3934								
SATEMP	12	000048	4360	2813	2896	2982	3031	3047	3068	3329	3404	3453							
SCAN	2	0014D0	4212	4052	4064	4074													
SCANLOOP	2	0014D2	4213	4221															
SEQ	8	00019C	4498	4069	4070	4073	4082	4187	4189	4191									
SETDIM	6	00132E	4088	4092															
SHORT	8	0013FA	4145	4142															
SKIP	1	001508	4228	4008	4181														
SM	1	000000	4384	2577	2625	2901	2904												
SMPTR	4	000004	4386	2584	2585	2631	2634												
SMVAL	4	000000	4385	2578	2580	2626	2628												
STOP	4	001266	4038	4034															

SYMBOL	LEN	VALUE	DEFN	REFERENCES							
STREAMS	4	000FE4	3945	3916							
SVCCONST	4	000314	2455	2429							
SVCHANDL	1	0002B2	2425	2364							
SVCHPROT	4	000302	2449	2434							
SVCHTABL	1	000328	2457	2431	2486	2458 2488	2460 2490	2462 2492	2464 2494	2466 2496	2468 2498
SVCNEW	1	000060	2364								
SVCOK	8	0002D0	2435	2451	2453	2445	2449	2545	2547		
SVCOLD	8	000020	2354	2430	2442						
SVCRTN	8	0004C8	2500	2432	2452						
SVCSAVE	4	0004C8	2529	2441							
SVCXPER	4	0002FA	2447	2443							
SYSSEM	4	0002DE	2440	2438							
SYSSEMSA	84	00021C	2377	2530	2598						
TALK	8	0001B8	4504	4013	4014	4171	4176				
TEMPLATE	4	001178	3977	2999							
TIMER	4	000050	2361	2683							
TOKSTART	2	0014F6	2222	4215	4217	4219	4226	2446			
TRAPSAVE	4	00019C	2374	2390	2402	2405	4028	4111			
TREAD	4	000164	4486	4002	4003	4004					
TXTCARD	4	0013B0	4124	4117							
TXTMOV	6	0013C4	4130	4128							
TYPLEN	1	00005A	3981	3921	3981						
TYPPCB	8	001160	3975	3522	3630	3722	3867	4476			
UCB	1	000000	4469	3580	3684	3586	3588	3682	3683	3690	3692 3757 3758 3766 3868 3870 3871 3872
UCBADDR	4	000014	4470	3575	3576						
UCBCSW	4	00001C	4474	3874	3863						
UCBFPR	1	000020	4476	3749							
UCBLENG	4	000FF8	3955	3948							
UCBLP1	4	001000	3956	3949							
UCBLP2	4	000E94	3827	3955							
UCBPRT1	4	000ED4	3841	3956							
UCBPRT2	4	000E7A	3820	3956							
UCBRDR1	4	000EB4	3834	3936	3939						
UCBRDR2	1	000FE8	3947	3746	3860	3864	4305	4306			
UCBTAB	1	000E7A	3818	3750	3806	3657	3677	3699	3754	3781	
UCBTABLE	8	000004	3847	3587	3599	3611	3705	3764	3873		
UCBTBEND	8	00000C	4471	3584							
UCBUS	6	001312	4472	4071							
UNAMMOV	4	0001A4	4082	4088	4093						
UNITRTN	4	00004C	4499								
UNUSED0	8	000054	2360	4007	4049	4158	4160	4163			
UNUSED1	8	000190	2362	4369	3908	3908	4300				
USERL	1	001648	4496	4008	4009	4011	4045	4177			
VERYEND	1	000178	4325	2513	2778	2779	3793				
WRITE	2	000600	4491	2833							
XA	2	0006B0	2771	2774							
XABACK	4	00060E	2836	2802							
XACOM	2	000662	2780	2805							
XAPOUND	2	00062A	2810	2817							
XALOOP	2	000686	2791	2625							
XANF	4	00069C	2821	2809							
XARETURN	4	000616	2830								
XATOP			2784								

CROSS-REFERENCE

SYMBOL	LEN	VALUE	DEFN	REFERENCES
XAUTO	1	000608	2775	2527
XAWAIT	2	000656	2806	2792
XAX	1	000000	4395	2782 2990 3338 3528 3636 3728 3918 3995 4276
XAXADDR	4	000000	4397	2810 2994 3347 3530 3638 3730 3920 3997 4278
XAXALGN	4	000008	4398	2788 2992 3345
XAXSIZE	4	000000	4396	2783 2991 3344
XB	1	000744	2936	2512
XBINSERT	4	000770	2952	2944 2947
XBLOOP	4	00075A	2946	2951
XBX	1	000000	4404	2814 2897 2938 2940
XBXADDR	4	000004	4406	2818 2826 2899
XBXSIZE	4	000000	4405	2819 2827 2898 2939
XC	1	000780	2978	2520
XCERR	2	0007C4	3003	2987
XCOM	4	0005D2	2728	2511 2735
XCOMRET	4	0005FC	2743	2735
XCX	1	000000	4408	2981 2984 2997
XCXNAME	8	0007C6	4409	2984 2997
XD	1	00081A	3027	2524
XDCHECK	6	000840	3074	3052
XDERR	2	0007F4	3051	3038
XDLOOP	2	00082E	3069	3063 3041
XDTHEN	1	000000	4411	3065
XDI	8	000000	4412	3030
XDXNAME	1	0005C0	2863	3033
XEXC	1	0006B6	2892	2510
XF	2	000706	2893	2514
XFBACKUP	2	000714	2896	2884
XFINC	2	0006D4	2877	2888
XFLINK	2	0006F0	2885	2878
XFLOOP	2	00073F	2911	2895
XFTHEN	1	00072E	2906	2861
XFVDD	2	000000	4402	2906 3058 3291 3292
XFVDLOOP	1	000000	4401	2912 3059 3069 3293
XFX	1	000000	3096	2367 3060 3070
XFXADDR	4	000848	3100	2869
XFXSIZE	4	00085A	3104	2868
XH	1	00086C	3107	2526
XHLOOP	8	00087A	3126	3102
XHMSG1	8	0008A6	3167	3098
XHMSG2	1	0008CA	3212	3100
XI	1	0008CC	3224	2515
XJ	1	0008E4	3218	2516
XN	1	0008CC	3220	2521
XNFOUND	4	000000	3222	
XNLOOP	4	000008	4414	
XNX	1	000000	4416	2983 3032 3214 3330 3405 3454
XNXADDR	4	0004EE	4415	2986 3035 3224 3333 3408 3457
XNXNAME	8	00056A	2575	2984 3033 3219 3331 3406 3455
XPER	1	00050A	2661	2508 2517 2599 2677
XPLOOP	2	00051C	2588	2403
XPTHEN	6	000502	2595	2592
XPWAIT	6	000A8E	2584	2589
XQUE	1	000A8E	3493	2582 2525

SYMBOL	LEN	VALUE	DEFN	REFERENCES
XQUELOOP	4	000A94	3497	3499
XQUEM1	8	000AA0	3501	3495
XQUEM2	8	000AB8	3504	3497
XR	1	0008EC	3254	2518
XRAPT	4	000938	3280	3278
XRFILL	6	00096C	3297	3271
XRMOVE	6	000972	3298	3279
XRNOB	4	00091C	3272	3270
XRTHEN	2	00092E	3277	3274
XRX	1	000000	3257	3540 3550 3647 3650 3651 3653 3738 3741 3743 3744 3772 3775 3777
XRXNAME	8	000000	4418	3553
XRXSIZE	4	000008	4419	3267 3285 3541 3648 3739 3773
XRXTEXT	1	00000C	4420	3269 3281 3298 3543 3545
XS	1	0009D8	3325	2519
XSADD	4	0009D2	3359	3355
XSAPT	2	0009F4	3370	3368
XSERR	2	000A02	3375	3335
XSLOOP	2	0009C0	3354	3358
XSMOVE	6	000A04	3376	3369
XSX	1	000000	4423	3328
XSXNAME	8	000000	4424	3331
XSXSIZE	4	000008	4425	3340 3364
XSXTEXT	1	00000C	4426	2509
XV	1	000534	2623	2637
XVRET	4	000566	2640	2629
XVWAKEUP	1	000548	2631	2522
XY	1	000A0A	3400	3410
XYERR	2	000A40	3420	3403
XYX	1	000008	4428	3416
XYXADDR	4	000000	4429	3406
XYXNAME	8	000000	4430	
XZ	1	000A42	3445	2523
XZERR	2	000A8C	3472	3452 3459
XZFINE	4	000A54	3453	3450
XZINSMC	4	000A7E	3468	3464
XZSTOP	4	000A6C	3463	3471
XZX	1	000000	4432	3448
XZXNAME	8	000000	4433	3451 3455

NO STATEMENTS FLAGGED IN THIS ASSEMBLY

2332 SYSIN SOURCE RECORDS
4984 SYSPRINT OUTPUT RECORDS

QUESTIONS

We have divided all questions into four categories:

1 General
2 Fixing minor operational flaws
3 Major modifications to existing modules
4 Major additions to existing system

GENERAL

7-1 How many processes would exist in the sample operating system if two user jobs were running, each using a card reader and a printer?

7-2 What is the difference between disabling (masking) interrupts and using the "enter system_must_complete (smc)" primitive?

7-3 If all processes are CPU-bound, is the process scheduler algorithm "fair" to all user jobs? (Consider the case where one of the user processes creates ten subordinate processes to perform computations for it.) How could process scheduling be changed to be "fairer"?

7-4 The workspace storage facility (SVC C'E') is presently restricted to operating system processes. Could user processes be allowed to use this facility? What would be affected?

7-5 Explain how Send Message and Receive Message can be used by a user process to accomplish the same functions as P and V.

7-6 Why does our sample operating system have two distinct levels of process management?

7-7

1 In the sample operating system, the Allocate and Free (memory management) SVCs are not user-callable (i.e., they are restricted to operating system routines only). Why is this restriction made? (*Hint:* Consider deadly embrace possibilities.)

2 Can the above problem be resolved? That is, can memory management be made user-callable without introducing the problems alluded to in (1)? What restrictions, requirements, or constraints would have to be imposed?

3 Memory management is used internally to generate PCBs, message control blocks, etc. Can these internal usages result in a deadly embrace? Give a simple example.

4 Propose a solution to the example you have given for (3).

FIXING MINOR OPERATIONAL FLAWS AND MINOR IMPROVEMENTS

7-8 Stopped Processes: Currently, after the "stop process" primitive (routine XZ) has been used, the stopped process cannot be restarted by the "start process" primitive (routine XY). This is because the stopped process may be in the middle of the "leave smc section" primitive (routine XCOM) while waiting on a semaphore that no other process will ever access. Devise a test for such a condition in the "start process" routine.

7-9 User Semaphores: Currently, the semaphore operations P and V are not callable by user processes. This is because certain system information (e.g., a pointer to the PCB of the first process waiting on the semaphore) is stored in the semaphore itself. Therefore, if the semaphore were stored in the user's partition, this pointer's integrity could not be guaranteed. Thus, the system currently allows only system routines to call the P and V routines, and these calling routines pass only system semaphores (stored outside of any user's partition and accessible only by system routines) as arguments. The reader should propose a facility that programs could use for semaphore-type syn-chronization. Basically, it would have to have an entry point for creating semaphores in a system area at the user's request, and for passing back a name for the created semaphore to be used in future pseudo-P and pseudo-V requests. The principal benefit to be derived from this exercise, in addition to gaining familiarity with P and V, is an increased awareness of the problems of memory allocation. Full records would have to be kept of the name associated with each semaphore, and also of the semaphores allocated by the user's processes, so that these records could be freed at the end of the job. This bookkeeping would serve to get the reader into the details very quickly.

7-10 Automatic Storage: Presently, the workspace storage facility (SVC C'E') allows only one work area to be allocated per process. Design an extension to this facility to allow multiple uses of SVC C'E' in a process.

7-11 Messages: A pointer to the sender's PCB is stored in each message chain for the receiver's PCB. What error could occur if a sender's process were destroyed before the receiver had read the message? How could this prob-lem be avoided?

7-12 Accounting Information: The system as now implemented performs no accounting. Modify the system to expect another field on the $JOB card, of the form USER=username, where username is the name of the user to whom this work is to be charged. At the end of the job, an accounting tailsheet is printed containing the username, the resources used, and the total cost. As an adjunct to this problem, the reader should develop a pricing scheme. Note that it will be necessary to collect the resource usage statistics (e.g., processor time) used by the job.

MAJOR MODIFICATIONS TO EXISTING MODULES

This category includes changes to the system that are merely modifications to its present structure, but which nevertheless have major impact on the system and are important pedagogically.

7-13 Deadlock Recovery: Currently, if the processes running in the system request more memory than memory management is able to provide, and no process exists to free memory, a deadlock will be reached. This can seriously degrade system performance, if it does not stop the system completely. By means of a test the operating system should be able to see that all processes in the system are currently blocked and that none of them is runnable or ever will be runnable (because there are no input/output operations currently being performed). This test, which could be performed by the traffic controller, would cause a selected job to be thrown off the system. Here, the detection of a deadlock situation is easy, but the modifications to the system would cause problems. Currently, the method used to throw a job off the system includes sending a message that requires memory to be allocated. The amount of memory required is just a few words, but it would most probably be impossible to supply if such a situation arose. A more important problem pedagogically is that we would have the traffic controller, the most basic part of the system, very far removed from the problem. This is a serious problem from the viewpoint of modularity, and its resolution is not obvious.

7-14 Deadlock Avoidance: Another problem related to memory allocation deadlocks is the detection of partial deadlocks. A situation may arise where five job streams were in the system, four of which were involved in a deadlock while the fifth had a long compute-bound program running, one that had no current use for programs using the memory allocation. After completing its compute-bound section, this job may free enough memory to allow the others to run, but it would be more likely to get caught in the same deadlock. An important but intellectually difficult assignment would be to extend the traffic controller to detect the possibility of this type of deadlock and deal with it as in the previous problem.

7-15 Device Assignment: Currently, each job can request one reader and one printer, when the device to be assigned is determined before the request is made. This is certainly not the most efficient method, especially in cases where there are more printers than readers, but it is a simple one and does eliminate the problem of device deadlocks. A real improvement in system performance could be gained if a reader used by a job were to be released whenever there were no more cards to be read for that job, thus allowing a supervisor process created at that time to begin processing the next job.

MAJOR ADDITIONS TO THE EXISTING SYSTEM

This category is concerned with the addition of major new features to the system. These can, of course, take any form. A few representative ones are considered below.

7-16 Secondary Storage Support: Add routines to the system to handle secondary storage devices, such as disks. The modifications would come in the job stream processor and in the device management routines.

7-17 File System Design: Once disk management is available, it is possible to add a file system. Specific ways of doing this can vary, but it should be noted that, from the user's viewpoint, the fields on the $JOB card can easily provide for this design.

7-18 Spooling and Job Scheduling: With disk management and a simple file system, we could perform input and output spooling. And, with spooling, the addition of various job scheduling algorithms would become feasible.

Interdependencies: Performance Evaluation

The purpose of this chapter is threefold:

1 To give the reader a general "feel" for some of the possible tradeoffs between resources.
2 To introduce and give a starting point to the literature on the modeling and analysis of interdependencies.
3 To demonstrate the value of analyzing possible tradeoffs *before* a system is built or configured. To fulfill this last purpose, we present an analysis of two specific situations.

Since the scope and number of interdependencies are endless, we cannot discuss them all. However, we can suggest to the reader an approach which may help him answer some of the basic questions that may confront him. For example, if you, the reader, had a computer system and your boss gave you a fixed amount of money to improve system performance, would you buy more core? A faster CPU? More disks? More channels? After reading this chapter, we hope you will have some general ideas, or know how to utilize the literature for help, or be able to perform a mathematical analysis in order to answer your questions.

Let us illustrate the influence of one resource manager on another. If one were to use a memory management scheme that offers high utilization of memory, such as paging, and the best multiprogramming processor management schemes offering high utilization of processors and low wait time, one would expect to have the best possible system. Not necessarily. The two schemes might interact in such a way as to produce *thrashing*, a phenomenon in which the processor is spending most of its time in overhead functions instead of executing user process. We will discuss for each resource manager in turn what is involved in a tradeoff, and then deal with some of the tradeoffs over which the user has control. We will then present an analysis of two aspects of the independencies of processor and

and memory management: a swapping versus a paging system. We will also give an analysis of thrashing.

The reader can refer to the annotated bibliography for more detail on interdependencies. (See Interdependencies, Modeling.) Our formal analysis of thrashing uses a modeling technique called *Markov modeling* (Feller, 1969; Drake, 1967). The literature contains examples of further applications of this useful analysis technique.

In the bibliography we have listed some 20 references that discuss the modeling of some aspects of system behavior as well as 6 articles on performance evaluation and measurement. There are over 19 articles that analyze different aspects of paging performance. All these references may be used to extend the material in this chapter.

8-1 MEMORY MANAGEMENT

In Chapter 3 we discussed a series of memory management techniques, each of which progressively provided better utilization of memory (e.g., contiguous allocation, partitioned, relocatable partitioned). However, each improvement in memory utilization required more CPU time.

Before choosing a memory management technique, one should analyze the tradeoff of memory versus CPU time. For example, let us assume that each partition in the relocatable partition scheme depicted in Figure 8-1 is 500,000 bytes. Therefore, at a "move" speed of 4,000,000 bytes per second, 125 milliseconds

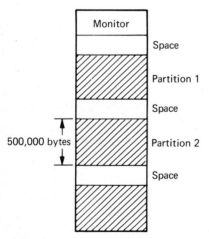

Figure 8-1 A relocatable partitioned scheme

would be required to move one partition. If the majority of jobs on the system were student jobs, it might take longer to move a job than to run it. A typical student job might run for only 100 milliseconds (execution of 100,000 instructions).

8-2 PROCESSOR MANAGEMENT

In Chapter 4 we discussed processor management and demonstrated that multiprogramming increased processor utilization, but at a cost of memory and I/O device loading.

In Section 3-2.2, we calculated the percent of I/O wait time of the CPU as a function of both the degree of multiprogramming and the percent of I/O wait for each job in a monoprogrammed environment.

Figure 8-2 gives a typical curve for the amount of CPU time ($T_{I/O}$) waiting for I/O as a function of the number of jobs multiprogrammed in the system. We have assumed that all jobs are equal, and, when run alone, that each job results in the same fixed amount of I/O wait time. Data for a particular group of jobs showing percent of I/O waits can be found in Table 3-1.

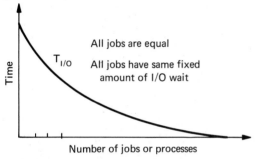

Figure 8-2 A typical curve for I/O wait time as more equal jobs are added to system

The implication of Figure 8-2 is that when $T_{I/O}$ goes to zero (more multiprogramming), the CPU is fully utilized. That is, the CPU is continuously doing useful work for the users. However, there may be a point at which additional multiprogramming results in so much overhead that less CPU time is spent on user processes.

This overhead results from two factors:

1 The I/O queuing requires CPU time. This is usually a constant amount, e.g., 1 ms, but for large numbers of jobs the overhead time grows.

2 There are only a finite number of channels, control units, and I/O devices. Eventually contention develops (e.g., eight requests are made to the same disk drive, the first of which is satisfied in 100 ms, the last not for 800 ms). Thus for large numbers of processes the CPU may become increasingly more idle as processes wait for busy devices.

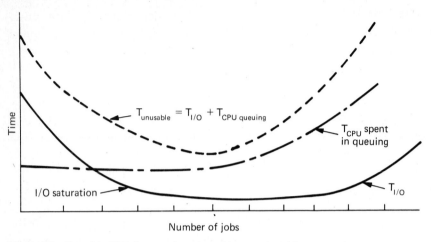

Figure 8-3 Unusable CPU time as a function of increased multiprogramming

Figure 8-3 shows the total CPU time that is not usable (time spent waiting for I/O or in the overhead of maintaining queues). Note that after a certain degree of multiprogramming system performance may decrease. (This example is *not* taken from a paging system; paging may further degrade performance when too much multiprogramming is allowed.) For any given system, there is a point at which increased multiprogramming has a negative effect both on memory and I/O device loadings.

8-3 DEVICE MANAGEMENT

In Chapter 5 we discussed several techniques for improving the management of devices (e.g., queue reordering, buffering, blocking, SPOOLing). How effective are these techniques in improving system performance? For many systems, such elaborate techniques may introduce more overhead than they can possibly save in efficiency (Teorey, 1972). An example would be a system in which two jobs were multiprogrammed, each with a 25 percent I/O wait. How much time is the CPU idle? Table 3-1 indicates that the CPU is idle 4 percent of the time. In such a system, how much savings can the cleverest device management techniques provide us? Since multiprogramming reduces the I/O wait time to 4 percent, we can only hope to further reduce this wait to zero! Thus any device management technique that consumes over 4 percent of the CPU time in overhead is costing more in overhead than it can possible save in efficiency.

The reader should not infer, however, that this argument applies to all systems inasmuch as many jobs have much more than 25 percent I/O wait time.

In this section let us examine the tradeoffs involved in the use of the following techniques:

Queue reordering

Blocking/buffering

Data packing techniques

8-3.1 Queue Reordering

Let us take some numbers to illustrate when queuing may not be appropriate. Consider the range of CPUs and their typical instruction speeds (Figure 8-4). Now consider several disks and their corresponding access speeds (Figure 8-5). Note that the access speed is the time between a START I/O to a device and the I/O complete from that device. During this time the CPU may have to wait. Take, for example, the access speed of the 2314, which is 75 ms; this is the maximum time (worst case) that the CPU may be idle. In practice, in a multiprogrammed environment, the CPU would not wait that long because it would most probably execute another process.

COMPUTER	TIME FOR 1 INSTRUCTION (MICROSECONDS)	TIME FOR 1000 INSTRUCTIONS (MILLISECONDS)
360/30	30	30
360/40	10	10
360/50	3	3
360/65	1	1
370/158	0.4	0.4
370/168	0.2	0.2

Figure 8-4 Instruction speeds for computers

	Disk	Access speed (milliseconds)
Moving arm	IBM 2311	125
	IBM 2314	75
	IBM 3330	35
Drumlike	IBM 2301	10
	IBM 2305	5

Figure 8-5 Disk speeds

A typical queuing routine may execute 1,000 instructions. Thus on the 360/30, it would take *longer* to queue than to randomly access the 2301 or 2305, and it would be close on the 2314. On the 360/65, even for the 2305 it is worthwhile to queue if there is a substantial I/O load. *Note:* if the I/O load is moderate and we are multiprogramming, the I/O might be *all* overlapped—thus the queuing time would be all CPU overhead.

8-3.2 Blocking/Buffering

Blocking and buffering are device management techniques for reducing the number of I/Os and making better use of I/O device capacity.

However, the costs incurred are more memory for the buffers, and more CPU time to deblock. On many systems, the memory could be better used for additional multiprogramming than for extra buffers, and then perhaps I/O device capacity would not be a concern. For example, at 4K per buffer, two double-buffered files (input and output) equal 16K. This might equal or exceed the size of a typical "small" job (360/30s go up to only 64K).

8-3.3 Data Packing Techniques

In the following example, each of the three record-packing techniques offers a tradeoff in CPU time, I/O accesses, or memory. Our example has the typical characteristics of a card SPOOLing situation where: (1) output spool lines are only ≈ 80 to 132 bytes; and (2) of the 80 bytes average, about 50 percent are blanks, often in sequences.

Technique 1

Always write 132-byte records (assume disk block = 1320 bytes) = 10 records per block.

Technique 2

Truncate trailing blanks and write variable length records (average 16 records per block), thus reducing I/O time.

Technique 3

Encode all sequences of multiple blanks (e.g., 2 bytes| FF | n | means n blanks belong here for n > 2), possibly up to 20 records per block, thus reducing I/O time but increasing CPU time.

The reader should attempt to answer the following questions:

1 Can technique 2 ever require more I/Os than 1?

2 How about 3 versus 2?

3 What about block size and number of buffers?

    a (10 users running) × (2 input + 2 output) = 40 buffers

b (40 buffers) × (4000 bytes per buffer) = 160,000 bytes for buffers [if only 1 buffer per spool ≈ ½ space (80K), are added buffers worth 80K?]

In a system designed by one of the authors, technique 2 was chosen because the system was CPU-limited.

8-4 INFORMATION MANAGEMENT

In Chapter 6 we discussed techniques for the management of information. The secondary storage allocation techniques focused mostly on flexibility for the user (e.g., dynamic allocation enabled the user files to grow). However, the possibility of saving secondary storage space itself should be considered. The following are four techniques for saving secondary storage space, each of which costs CPU time.

1 Blocking—grouping of logical records.
2 Multifile blocking—grouping of files together. This eliminates wasted space due to "file breakage." (File lengths are seldom even multiples of physical block length.)
3 Encoding—for example, replacing strings of zeros by a code and a number indicating the number of zeros.
4 Semantic compacting—for example, the statement:

LET ALPHA = BETA + GAMMA

may be stored

471839

where each digit denotes a keyword or symbol.

8-5 TRADEOFFS OVER WHICH THE USER HAS CONTROL

The following three techniques may be used to increase the speed of algorithms at the cost of more memory.

1 Using hash tables (Donovan, 1972; Morris, 1968)—a user may use hash-coding techniques to manage tables that must be searched, thereby assuring fast access. However, to assure this fast access, the hash tables must be sparsely filled (e.g., half-filled). Thus it may take twice as much space to store information using hashed tables as it does to store it in tables suited for binary search techniques.
2 Tabulating functions—a user may use tables instead of computing functions (e.g., store all needed sine values rather than computing them each time).
3 Reducing or eliminating I/O—a user may keep his information in core. This is a direct tradeoff of core space for I/Os.

8-6 INFLUENCES

In order to take advantage of techniques for saving CPU time or space the user must be aware of some of the operating system's algorithms or else he may get "out of synchronization" and actually degrade system performance. Naturally, he must also be aware of the cost of each resource before he makes any tradeoffs.

The user should also take into account his own temperament; if for example, he is impatient, he will demand fast turnaround, no matter what the cost.

8-6.1 Influence of a Multiprogrammed System on the User

It is important for a user to know whether his system is multiprogrammed or not. For example, if the system is not multiprogrammed, it is common to have jobs of 100K and core of 256K; in such systems space is not usually a problem. Therefore, a user may freely use more space to save CPU time. Figure 8-6 depicts the performance curve of a user's algorithm as it uses greater space (e.g., more buffers). As space becomes more plentiful, the user can turn to hashing or similar table-processing techniques, thus reducing his execution time.

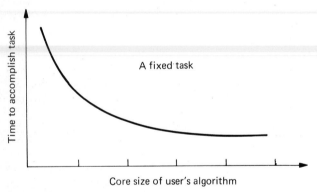

Figure 8-6 Possible user program performance

On a multiprogrammed system, however, if one user increases his core usage, the system cannot multiprogram as many users, which could reduce system performance. Figure 8-7 depicts a typical curve for system performance (throughput) for a fixed core size in a multiprogrammed environment. Point 1 of Figure 8-7 represents a situation in which each job in the system has a small amount of core. If each job were given more core, system performance could be improved, e.g., by reducing I/O (point 2).

However, as users use more and more core, other users are excluded, thus reducing multiprogramming (point 3) and degrading system performance. The best size core is at point 2, but this would vary with the types of jobs in the system.

Some measurements of costs have been taken on the user tradeoff of I/O access

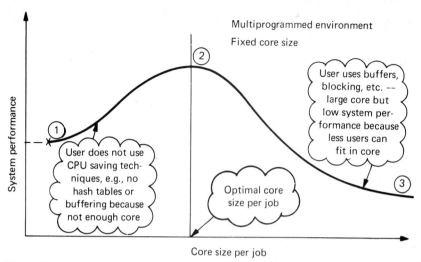

Figure 8-7 System performance in a multiprogramming environment as users use more and more core

versus CPU time. On a fully loaded CP-67 it was found that 12 ms of CPU time equaled one I/O device access (Bard, 1971). That is, if a user could (by buffering, blocking, etc.) spend less than 12 ms of CPU time and save one I/O, he would come out ahead.

One tradeoff over which a user has less control showed that 11 ms of user CPU time equals the cost involved in 1.4 page I/Os. Thus if a user could perform more CPU calculations and thereby reduce his paging requirements, he would reduce costs. Since paging is (or should be) invisible to the user, this equality is not readily usable.

8-6.2 Psychological Tradeoffs

Recently, the authors were involved in providing a financial reporting package for a small company. Since the reports were to be printed in alphabetical order but not stored alphabetically in the database, there were two possible algorithms:

1 For each item, search the database and print the line.
2 Perform a sort on the database and print the entire sorted database.

The second was the more efficient for the database size, but one of the authors could not stand the suspense of having the computer spend a considerable amount of time in internal sorting before receiving answers. He thus reprogrammed the algorithm in the inefficient fashion of the first algorithm.

8-7 SWAPPING VERSUS PAGING

In this section we analyze a tradeoff between memory management and processor management. We consider two memory management techniques:

1 Swap System (e.g., TSO, CTSS, PDP-10)—a swap system uses a memory management technique in which an address space is placed in core before the assignment of a processor. If another process is to be activated, the first address space is swapped out onto secondary storage, and the new user is swapped in. (See Section 3-9.1.)

2 Demand Paging System (e.g., TSS/360, VM 370, 370 OS, CP-67 MULTICS)—see Section 3-6.

We wish to measure two parameters:

1 Responsiveness of a system—time in which a system is capable of responding to a user

2 Throughput—average amount of time taken per job

For each of these memory management schemes we will vary the time quantum (length of time a process has a processor), a function directly related to the responsiveness of the system.

8-7.1 Sample Program and System

Figure 8-8 gives the characteristics of a sample machine. We assume the characteristics of a sample program to be:

size = 100K words (100 pages)

run time = 1 second (10^6 instructions)

Our objective is to make an analysis of total run time for the sample program on the system of Figure 8-8, using a swapping and a paged memory management technique. That is, our objective is to replace the "?" of Figure 8-9.

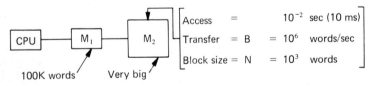

$$\begin{bmatrix} \text{Access} & = & 10^{-2} \text{ sec (10 ms)} \\ \text{Transfer} & = B & = 10^6 \text{ words/sec} \\ \text{Block size} = N & = 10^3 \text{ words} \end{bmatrix}$$

100K words   Very big

Figure 8-8 Sample machine for page vs. swap analysis

8-7.2 Case 1: Time Quantum = ∞

For case 1 we let the time quantum = ∞ (i.e., a job runs until it is complete). A consequence of this large time quantum is that the system is not responsive to any process other than the one running. Thus there could be long periods when the system would not respond to most users.

CASE NUMBER	SYSTEM RESPONSIVENESS	TIME QUANTUM	MEMORY MANAGEMENT SCHEME	TOTAL RUN TIME
1	Slow	Time quantum = ∞	Swapped	?
			Paged	?
2	Medium	Time quantum = 500 ms	Swapped	?
			Paged	?
3	Fast	Time quantum = 50 ms	Swapped	?
			Paged	?

Figure 8-9 Comparison of page vs. swapped analysis

8-7.2.1 SWAP SYSTEM

Figure 8-10 depicts memory usage in a swapping system as a function of time for tq = ∞ (very large). The sample program must first be found (accessed) and loaded before it can be executed.

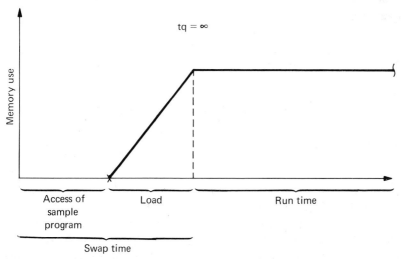

Figure 8-10 Memory usage for sample program for Case 1 swapping

The total run time of the sample program for tq = ∞ and a swapping system may be calculated by using Figure 8-10. That is,

Total run = swap time + run

Total run time = access + load + run

Total run time = $10^{-2} + \dfrac{10^5}{10^6} + 1.0$

Total run time = $\underbrace{10^{-2}}_{\substack{10\text{ ms} \\ \text{access}}} + \underbrace{10^{-1}}_{\substack{100\text{ ms} \\ \text{load}}} + \underbrace{1}_{1\text{ sec}} = \boxed{1.11\text{ sec}}$

8-7.2.2 DEMAND PAGING SYSTEM

Again wè assume that once the job is started, it runs until completion (tq = ∞). Figure 8-11 depicts memory usage as a function of time for the sample program using a demand-paged system.

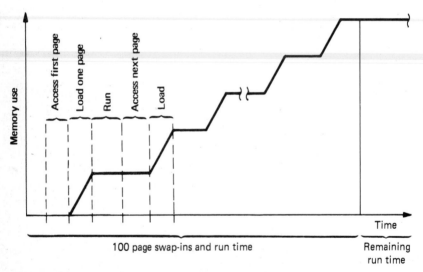

Figure 8-11 Memory usage for Case 1 using demand paging

In Figure 8-11 we have assumed, for simplicity, that the program makes a new page reference every 5 ms (e.g., in 500 ms every page will have been accessed at least once) and we use demand paging. The system accesses the first page of the sample program, then loads it. The program runs for 5 ms before an access and load of another page takes place. The process continues until all pages are accessed.

Then the sample program runs until it reaches completion. We have assumed no computing while reading.

Total run time can be computed as follows:

Total run time = (number of pages) × (page swap-in) + run

Total run time = 100 × (access + page-load) + run

$$= 10^2 \ (10^{-2} + \frac{10^3}{10^6}) + 1.0$$
$$= 10^2 \ (10^{-2} + 10^{-3}) + 1.0$$
$$= 10^2 \ (1.1 \times 10^{-2}) + 1.0$$
$$= 1.1 + 1.0 = \boxed{2.1 \ \text{sec}}$$

8-7.3 Case 2: Time Quantum = 500 ms

We repeat our analysis using a time quantum of 500 ms. That is, the system allows the CPU to spend only 500 ms on a job before it starts to unload that job. If the job is not finished after 500 ms, it is unloaded and then reloaded at some later time and run for another 500 ms. This process is repeated until the job is complete.

8-7.3.1 SWAP SYSTEM

Figure 8-12 depicts memory utilization for the sample program in a swap system with tq = 500 ms. Thus the execution of the sample program for tq = 500 ms and a swapping system requires two swap-in fetches and one swap-out unfetch; we assume that all take the same amount of time.

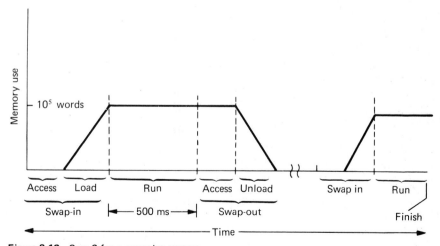

Figure 8-12 Case 2 for a swapping system

Total run time = 3 × (swaps) + run

$$= 3 \times (10^{-2} + 10^{-1}) + 1$$

$$= 3 \times (.11) + 1$$

$$= .33 + 1 = \boxed{1.33 \text{ sec}}$$

8-7.3.2 DEMAND PAGING SYSTEM

We will load pages as before, but when timeslice is ended, we push out all pages at once in the same way as with the swap system. This swapping out allows the memory to be used by other users. It is a technique used in many systems, and it is called *load on demand and postpage*.

Figure 8-13 depicts the dynamics of this case.

Total run time is computed as follows:

Total run time = 2 × 100 page fetches + 1 swap-out + run

$$= 2\,[100\,(10^{-2} + 10^{-3})] + [10^{-2} + 10^{-1}] + 1$$

$$= 2\,[100\,(.011)] + (.11) + 1$$

$$= 2.2 + .11 + 1 = \boxed{3.31 \text{ sec}}$$

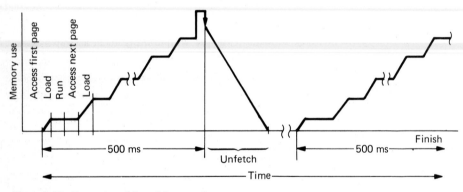

Figure 8-13 Dynamics of Case 2 for paged system

8-7.4 Case 3: Time quantum = 50 ms

What if we reduce the time quantum to 50 ms? This should provide a far more responsive system.

8-7.4.1 SWAP SYSTEM

Now 20 fetches + 19 unfetches are required.

Total run time = 39 × (access + load) + run

$$= 39 \times (10^{-2} + 10^{-1}) + 1$$

$$= 39 \times (.11) + 1$$

$$= 4.29 + 1.0 = \boxed{5.29 \text{ sec}}$$

8-7.4.2 DEMAND PAGING SYSTEM

In 50 ms interval only 10 pages are touched and thus loaded/unloaded each time.

Total run time = 20 × (10 page fetches) + 19 unfetches + run

$$= 20 \times 10 \times (10^{-2} + 10^{-3}) + 19 \times (10^{-2} + 10^{-2}) + 1$$

access   load   unfetch

$$= 20 \times 10 \times .011 + 19 \times (.02) + 1$$
$$= 2.2 + .38 + 1 = \boxed{3.58 \text{ sec}}$$

8-7.5 Conclusion

Figure 8-14 gives a summary of the results. Note that in timeshared systems the run times tend to be quite small, much less than 500 ms, due to I/O requests even if the time quantum allowed is quite large.

CASE NUMBER	RESPONSIVENESS	TIME QUANTUM	MEMORY MANAGEMENT SCHEME	TOTAL RUN TIME
1	Slow	Time quantum = ∞	Swapped	1.11
			Paged	2.1
2	Medium	Time quantum = 500 ms	Swapped	1.33
			Paged	3.31
3	Fast	Time quantum = 50 ms	Swapped	5.29
			Paged	3.58

Figure 8-14 Results of paged vs. swapped analysis

Depending upon the choice of tq, which is related to the responsiveness of the system, the decision between swap or demand paging may differ. tq = ∞ roughly corresponds to batch operating systems, whereas tq = 500 ms and tq = 50 ms correspond to highly interactive timesharing systems.

Thus if a highly responsive system with high throughput is desired, a paging system is the better choice. This simple analysis indicates that for this job mix a swapping system is best for a batch system.

8-8 THRASHING

In the last section we saw the advantages of paging. We have also discussed the advantages of multiprogramming. If we combine these two techniques, would we have too much of a good thing? Paging is a memory management function, while multiprogramming is a processor management function. Are the two interdependent? Yes, because combining them may lead to a drastic degradation of system performance. This degradation is loosely called thrashing (Schwartz, 1972; Denning, 1968; Randel, 1968). Among the definitions of thrashing that have been used are the following:

1 Thrashing is the point at which a system drives its disks, at their natural residency frequency, into doing so much I/O that the disk looks like a MAYTAG washing machine in its drying cycle.
2 Thrashing is the region in which the system is doing a lot of work but with no results.
3 Thrashing is the point at which the total CPU time devoted to a job in multiprogramming is equal to the total CPU time that would be devoted to that job in a monoprogrammed environment, that is, the point at which multiprogramming loses to monoprogramming.

Our approach to thrashing is to discuss specific problems connected with it; we do so by means of examples [see Denning (1968) for another approach to thrashing analysis].

This section presents a formal analysis of total CPU time (run time, I/O wait, paging time, etc.) spent on a job versus the number of jobs multiprogrammed in a demand-paged system. We will show that for a given type of job there exists a degree of multiprogramming above which the total time spent on a job is equal to the total time that would have been spent on it in a monoprogrammed system. That point is called the *thrashing point*, the region where multiprogramming is self-defeating.

We will indicate where that region is in a multiprogramming system running a number of identical jobs, a sample of which we describe below.

8-8.1   Description of the Sample Job

8-8.1.1   MACHINE CHARACTERISTICS

We assume that the hardware resembles the 360/370 and that it has the following characteristics:

The memory size $= 256K$ bytes.

The CPU speed $= 2 \times 10^{-6}$ seconds per instruction.

The drum has 40 ms rotation, 20 ms average access, and transfer time is small compared with access.

There are other I/O devices, e.g., disks or printers.

There is a demand paging system using a "single bit" LRU removal algorithm similar to MULTICS (Corbato, 1969) or CP-67 (Bard, 1973).

There are 4K-byte pages (note that drum access is 20 ms; therefore, it takes 20 ms to retrieve a single page).

8-8.1.2 PROGRAM CHARACTERISTICS

This section discusses the characteristics of the sample program (actually a 360 assembler) and ways in which to measure them. It is a function of the operation system to exploit these characteristics in order to improve throughput and efficiency. Note we assumed that this program is the only program on the system, i.e., every job is running a copy of this program.

There are two classes of program characteristics: explicit characteristics, which are simple to measure, and implicit characteristics, which are more difficult to measure (Coffman, 1968; Brawn, 1968; Hatfield, 1972).

Explicit Characteristics

Program size = 160,000 bytes.

Runs for 1,000,000 instructions = 2 sec CPU.

It issues 60 I/O requests; each I/O takes 50 ms; thus if a program ran by itself (no multiprogramming), wait time for I/O $(T_{I/O})$ = 3 seconds.

Thus, percent of I/O wait = $\dfrac{T_{I/O}}{\text{total time}}$ = $\dfrac{3}{5}$ = 60 percent.

Implicit Characteristics

In Section 3-6.3 we presented various ways to characterize a program's behavior in a demand-paged environment (Figure 3-36 illustrates a program's address reference pattern). One useful aggregate measure of a program's paging characteristics is its parachor curve (see Section 3-6.3.2), which gives the total number of page exceptions for various memory sizes. Figure 8-15 presents the parachor curve for our sample program under investigation.

8-8.2 Analysis of Total CPU Time Spent Running the Sample Program

The objective of this section is to calculate the total CPU time (T_{TOTAL}) devoted to the job, i.e., the time the CPU spends executing the job and waiting for I/O for the job, plus the time spent waiting for page I/O. We wish to calculate this time as a function of the system's degree of multiprogramming. That is, we calculate T_{TOTAL} for one job in the system, the T_{TOTAL} when there are two jobs, and

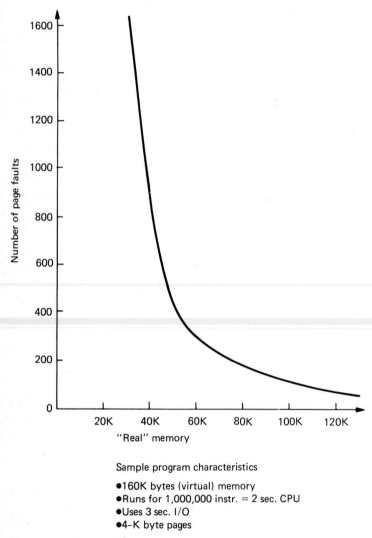

Sample program characteristics

- 160K bytes (virtual) memory
- Runs for 1,000,000 instr. = 2 sec. CPU
- Uses 3 sec. I/O
- 4-K byte pages

Figure 8-15 Experimentally observed paging behavior of the sample program

so on. We assume memory will be divided equally among jobs (e.g., if there are four jobs in the system, each job gets 64K bytes). Thus, as more jobs enter the system, page faults will go up since less memory is available to the program (Figure 8-15).

8-8.2.1 ACCOUNTING PHILOSOPHY

Let us define the concepts of T_{TOTAL}, T_{CPU}, $T_{I/O}$, and T_{PAGE} as follows:

T_{CPU} = CPU time for execution

$T_{I/O}$ = nonoverlapped I/O time

T_{PAGE} = nonoverlapped page I/O time

In defining the above terms, we have used an accounting concept that assumes all CPU time must be charged to some user. In other words, there is no overhead account—if you use the CPU, you pay for it.

If your job issues an I/O request and no other job can be executed at that time, then you pay for the idle CPU time—$T_{I/O}$. If your job causes a page fault and there is no other job that the CPU can execute while the page is being retrieved, you pay for the CPU idle time—T_{PAGE}.

You may say that this is unfair, since it was just your misfortune that the CPU had nothing else to do when you issued your I/O, while another user may be luckier and find the CPU able to execute another job. However, it all evens out in the long run.

We want T_{TOTAL} as a function of the number of jobs in the system. Let us make the computations of T_{CPU}, $T_{I/O}$, and T_{PAGE} as a function of the number of jobs multiprogrammed on the system. Each job is identical to our sample job. Figure 8-16 gives the values of T_{CPU}, $T_{I/O}$, and T_{PAGE}. These values are computed as follows.

	I/O			PAGE				CPU	TOTAL	UTIL-IZA-TION
Number of jobs	% Non-overlapped I/O wait	$T_{I/O}$	Memory per job	Number page faults per job	% Page wait per job	% Non-overlapped page wait	T_{PAGE}	T_{CPU}	T_{TOTAL}	%
1	60.0	3.00	256	33	24.8	24.8	.660	2.000	5.660	35.34
2	31.0	.898	128	33	24.8	04.0	.084	2.000	2.982	67.07
3	13.4	.310	85	185	64.9	18.9	.466	2.000	2.776	72.05
4	04.8	.100	64	290	74.4	20.6	.518	2.000	2.618	76.39
5	01.4	.028	51	415	80.6	19.9	.496	2.000	2.524	79.24
6	00.4	.008	43	600	85.7	24.1	.636	2.000	2.644	75.64
7	00.1	.002	37	1200	92.3	36.2	1.134	2.000	3.136	63.78
8	00.01	.0002	32	1600	94.1	60.9	3.116	2.000	5.116	39.09
1	2	3	4	5	6	7	8	9	10	11

Figure 8-16 $T_{I/O}$, T_{PAGE}, T_{CPU} tabulated results (in seconds)

8-8.2.2 T_{CPU}

T_{CPU} is the time the CPU spent executing instructions for the job. This time remains constant, regardless of how many jobs are on a system:

$T_{CPU} = (10^6 \text{ instructions}) \times (2 \times 10^{-6} \text{ instructions per sec}) = 2 \text{ sec}$

8-8.2.3 $T_{I/O}$

A job runs for a short period of time before it issues an I/O request. The $T_{I/O}$ (I/O wait) for a single job is 3 seconds. This was one of the characteristics of the sample program.

If two jobs are running, then the I/O wait time will go down, since the CPU can execute the second job while the first job is waiting for I/O. Using the analysis of Section 3-2.2 and Table 3-1, we can make all the entries in the $T_{I/O}$ column.

If w is the percentage (probability) of nonoverlapped I/O, then:

$T_{I/O} = w \times (\text{run time})$

$T_{I/O} = w \times (T_{CPU} + T_{I/O})$

therefore $T_{I/O} = \dfrac{w}{1 - w} \times T_{CPU}$

Column 3 ($T_{I/O}$) can thus be computed from column 2 and T_{CPU}.

8-8.2.4 T_{PAGE}

To calculate T_{PAGE}, we need to know how long the CPU is idle while waiting for a page. The intermediate steps in the calculation of T_{PAGE} are shown in Figure 8-16, columns 4, 5, 6, 7, and 8.

First, we assume that each job gets a portion of memory equal to the size of primary memory divided by the number of jobs. This gives the column "memory per job." Based on memory per job the "number of page faults per job" column is then taken from Figure 8-15. The "percentage wait per job" column is computed, assuming that the job is running alone. The formula is:

$$\frac{(\text{number of page faults}) \times (\text{time to process a page fault})}{(\text{number of page faults}) \times (\text{time to process a page fault}) + T_{CPU}}$$

This column was calculated by assuming a page fault time of 20 milliseconds and $T_{CPU} = 2$ seconds. Now using the same Markov model as for nonoverlapped I/O wait time, given page wait for a single job, we can compute "percent nonoverlapped page wait" using Table 3-1. If we call this percent wait w', we can use the following relation to calculate T_{PAGE}.

$T_{PAGE} = \dfrac{w'}{1 - w'} \times T_{CPU}$ (same derivation as for $T_{I/O}$)

Thus $T_{TOTAL} = T_{CPU} + T_{I/O} + T_{PAGE}$.

8-8.2.5 T_TOTAL

Figure 8-17 summarizes the results, and Figure 8-18 plots this summary.

NUMBER OF JOBS	T_{CPU}	$T_{I/O}$	T_{PAGE}	T_{TOTAL}	CPU UTILIZATION PERCENTAGE
1	2.000	3.000	.660	5.660	35.34
2	2.000	.898	.084	2.982	67.07
3	2.000	.310	.466	2.776	72.05
4	2.000	.100	.518	2.618	76.39
5	2.000	.028	.496	2.524	79.24
6	2.000	.008	.636	2.644	75.64
7	2.000	.002	1.134	3.136	63.78
8	2.000	.0002	3.116	5.116	39.09

Figure 8-17 Overall performance: treating I/O and paging independently

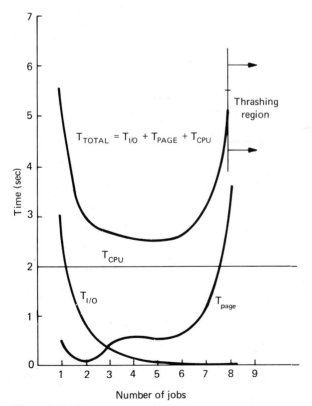

Figure 8-18 Sample program analysis: nonoverlapped processing time

8-8.3 Conclusions

8-8.3.1 OPTIMAL NUMBER OF JOBS

From Figure 8-18 it is clear that the optimal number of jobs is in the range of 3 to 6. Running more than eight jobs requires more CPU time for each job in a multiprogrammed environment than would be needed to run each in a monoprogrammed environment. Note that if we tried to multiprogram 15 users, for example, there would be about 16K (four pages) for each. T_{TOTAL} would be very poor (over 160 seconds per job)—a 32-fold, 3,200 percent stretchout! This is an extreme case of thrashing, since only about 5 to 10 percent of CPU time is devoted to T_{CPU}.

One task of the system designer is to decide on the number of jobs he will allow in a multiprogrammed environment. In actuality, since the job characteristics are usually varied, he decides on a range. Typically, this range, for most systems, is from four to eight jobs. The MULTICS and VM/370 systems, described in Chapter 9, incorporate techniques to limit the degree of multiprogramming in order to avoid thrashing. The reader is referred to these descriptions for additional information.

8-8.3.2 ASSUMPTIONS

In our analysis of thrashing, we made several assumptions for the sake of simplification. More complicated analyses have been done (Buzen, 1973; Sekino, 1972), but the results are essentially the same as those shown in Figure 8-17. However, let us further analyze three of our assumptions.

1 $T_{I/O}$ and T_{PAGE} *Are Independent.* In our analysis we assumed that $T_{I/O}$ and T_{PAGE} were independent. But, in fact, they are not, since when a job is waiting for I/O, it cannot produce any page faults and vice versa. A queuing model (Schwartz, 1973) was made of the sample system that recognized these dependencies. The results, as shown in Figures 8-19 and 8-20, are contrasted with our earlier results. Although the particular values differ from those of our simpler analysis, the overall shape of the curves are quite similar as is the thrashing region point.

Number of jobs	CPU utilization percentage
1	36.4%
2	62.8
3	70.3
4	65.2
5	66.3
6	63.5
7	47.1
8	43.4

Figure 8-19 Overall performance: combined I/O wait and page wait model

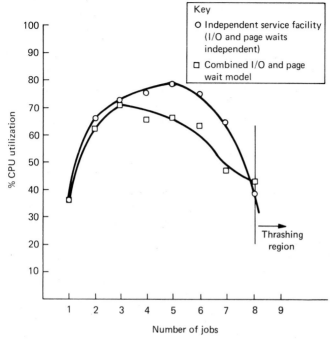

Figure 8-20 Sample program analysis: CPU utilization percentage

2 *Each Job Should Receive an Equal Amount of Memory.* Let us use the page fault relationship experimentally observed and reported in Figure 8-19 to show that dividing memory equally among the jobs was in fact a good policy. That is, our memory division did not aggravate the thrashing depicted in Figure 8-18.

Let us assume that there are four jobs for our memory allocation scheme, which would give each user 64K bytes. Thus, using Figure 8-15, the total page faults of the system would be

4 × 293 = 1,172 page faults

Now let us transfer 8K from one user to another (e.g., two users have 64K partitions, one user has 56K, and the fourth has 72K).

Total page faults = 2 × 293 + 359 + 237 = 586 + 359 + 237 = 1,182

This is an increase of 10 in the number of page faults. Thus, given the convexity of the parachor curve and the simple round-robin scheduling, it is reasonable to assign each job an equal amount of memory. This may not necessarily be the best strategy under a biased scheduling algorithm.

3 *Constant I/O and Paging Times.* We assumed in our analysis that I/O and page request service times were constant. In actual systems there is only a finite number of separate channels and devices, therefore, system performance would

be even worse than that of Figure 8-18 due to queuing delays caused by over-loading of the channels' and I/O devices' capacity.

8-8.3.3 FACTORS AFFECTING THRASHING

Our analysis has covered only *one* case. Other factors to be considered in analyzing a specific system are:

Program pattern (page fault curve, I/O amount, CPU amount)

Type of hardware (memory size, speed of drum, etc.)

Type of operating system (memory and processor management algorithms)

8-9 CONCLUSIONS

Taking the "best" memory processor, device, or information management schemes and combining them all into one system will not necessarily produce the "best" system.

We have touched on a few of the tradeoffs that a system designer and/or user may wish to use to make a system better suited to his needs. We have presented analytical techniques for measuring these tradeoffs and providing the information necessary to make system decisions. Many more analysis examples and techniques can be found in the articles included in the bibliography.

QUESTIONS

8-1 Section 8-1 gave an analysis of memory management assuming that each partition was 500,000 bytes. How would the results of the analysis differ if the partition size were 100,000 bytes?

8-2 Scheduling is one of the basic operations involved in resource management; basically, we have a limited number of resources that must be shared among multiple processes over time. The success of any system can be measured by how well an algorithm for scheduling resources performs its task. For any two of the four main resources (memory, processor, device, or information):

1 Present a general method of measuring how well an algorithm for scheduling these resources works, explaining why this method is a good one.

2 Discuss some interdependencies that can develop in a scheduling algorithm for two resources.

3 Identify similarities in the scheduling algorithms for the two chosen resources that emerge from your answer to (1). In other words, what similarities exist in scheduling resources in general? What differences exist?

8-3

1 Give an example of a collection of jobs and characteristics for which relocation partition is superior to fixed partitions. State your assumed memory and CPU speeds.

2 Using the same collection of jobs, give a CPU and memory speed in which fixed partitions would be superior to relocation.

8-4 The purpose of this problem is to do some computations that would exemplify the phenomenon depicted in Figure 8-3, that is, too much multiprogramming may be bad. Assume the following:

1 You have a multiprogrammed, nonpaged system.

2 The system has 16 disk drives.

3 Jobs do sequential I/O, i.e., a program will tend to access the same or adjacent cylinders.

4 Each job will have two disk files associated with it.

5 The I/O access time to files on the same or adjacent cylinders is 20 ms. The I/O access time to all other files is 50 ms.

6 The average job makes 20 I/O operations. If it were in a monoprogrammed environment, the average job would have a 40 percent I/O wait. However, in our multiprogrammed system, after a point, as the number of jobs increased, the effective I/O wait per job would go up because of two factors:

a The job would have to wait for a drive that another job was using, e.g., if only two jobs were on the system, the four accessible files would not be likely to be on the same disks; however, if 64 jobs were on the system, some of the 128 files would be on the same disk.

b In a monoprogrammed environment most of the disk accesses would reference cylinders sequentially. However, in our example, as the number of jobs increased, the probability that a disk arm would not be positioned correctly would go up.

Therefore, each job's effective I/O speed is slowed down after a degree of multiprogramming.

1 Compute the CPU per job.

2 Compute the probability of an access to disk A due to another job between two successive accesses to a file on disk A. With this give an expression of the expected I/O access time, when multiprogrammed, as a function of N, the number of jobs.

3 Compute the expected number of I/O requests to disk A between two successive I/O operations to a file on disk A.

4 What is the average CPU time per job between two I/O operations?

5 Statistically, will a disk ever have backlogged requests on this system?

6 What is the expected I/O wait per job as a function of the number of jobs, and what is the expected I/O percentage as a function of the number of jobs?

7 Compute the above values for up to 20 jobs.

8-5 If a system is multiprogrammed and there are four jobs in core, each of which has an average I/O wait time of 20 percent, what is the maximum amount by which the total unusable CPU time can be reduced if clever device management techniques are used? Explain your answer.

8-6 Your local IBM computer salesman has come to your office to sell you some new "improved" equipment (only slightly more expensive). You are to evaluate the expected effect of the proposed system changes upon CPU utilization.

The following alternatives are available:

1 Since most of your program I/O is for printed output (which is SPOOLed), the printer can be changed from 1,000 lines/minute to 10,000 lines/minute and the SPOOL disk from 200 ms average access time to 20 ms average access time.

2 The paging drum can change from 20 ms average access time to faster than 2 ms access time.

3 The memory size can be changed from 256K bytes to 2 million bytes.

4 The CPU and memory can change to the faster System/380 that executes 5 million instructions per second instead of the current 0.5 million instructions per second.

5 All of the above.

For each system change described, you should do the following:

1 Indicate which T's are affected (i.e., T_{CPU}, $T_{I/O}$, T_{PAGE}, as shown in Figure 8-18). In what way are they affected? Why?

2 State how the change affects the optimal number of jobs that should be run (Figure 8-20). That is, does the maximum point of curve move left or right? Why?

3 Using Figure 8-20 as a base, sketch the new CPU utilization curve and mark it 1, 2, 3, 4, or 5 to correspond with the system modification.

4 Briefly discuss how much you would pay for each of these proposed changes.

8-7 Repeat the analysis of paging versus swapping we made in Section 8-7, with the addition of a more realistic paging model. That is, until a certain amount of pages are in core, there will be many page faults. Beyond this point the page fault frequency goes down. Use Figure 8-15 to characterize the program's paging behavior.

Case Studies

9-1 INTRODUCTION

The purpose of this chapter is fourfold:

1 To illustrate important algorithms used in real operating systems
2 To demonstrate the applicability of our framework in describing real systems
3 To provide the user with a starting point for studying the particular systems described
4 To describe the following systems:

   a IBM's 370 VS1, VS2; 360 MVT, MFT, BOS, which we have chosen because of their widespread use

   b Compatible Time-Sharing System (CTSS), which has historic significance as an early timesharing system and exemplifies some excellent techniques.

   c MULTICS, which is a timesharing system with advanced features and concepts

   d VM 370 and CP-67/CMS, which are examples of the virtual machine concept

   The systems selected exemplify good batch, timesharing, and real-time systems. Our contention is that all operating systems perform the same functions, that is, the mechanics are the same, only the policies differ. For example:

   A batch system's scheduling policy may be to maximize average throughput.

   A timesharing system's scheduling policy is to provide good response. Response time must be directly proportional to user expectations: the user wants the machine to perform certain tasks quickly, namely, those he thinks are easy. Thus, a timesharing system may give preference to the interactive user and simple tasks.

   A real-time system's scheduling policy must make the system capable of handling large amounts of data; it must be able to analyze or handle data faster than they come in and it must also respond to time events.

All these systems have resource managers, but the policies of the managers are different. A good exercise, based on the sample operating system in Chapter 7, is to have readers perform the following tasks: given the sample operating system (1) make a good batch system, (2) make a good timesharing system, and (3) make a good real-time system.

It is not the purpose of this chapter to describe each system in detail; instead we present important features of each so that the reader can seek out the appropriate documentation. Nor can we attempt to describe all systems or even the major ones. Our hope is that the reader will use our conceptual approach to analyze other systems for himself.

It is important to realize that real operating systems are seldom static in design. They continually undergo changes and alterations, thus making an up-to-date, comprehensive description difficult, if not impossible, to undertake. For this reason the following case studies should be viewed merely as examples of the kinds of resource management techniques and algorithms that are likely to be found in real systems. These examples should serve not only to broaden the reader's experiences and insight but also to provide a perspective for the study of other systems and a conceptual starting point for a deeper study of the systems outlined.

Since some aspects of these systems have been discussed in earlier chapters, some of the descriptions are quite short.

9-2 IBM SYSTEM/360 AND SYSTEM/370 OPERATING SYSTEMS

9-2.1 Philosophy

The IBM operating systems for the System/360 and System/370 are part of a family that has been evolving since 1964. Figure 9-1 lists the major operating systems, while Figure 9-2 divides them into two somewhat compatible groups. In addition, most of these systems have many options. We will primarily focus our attention on the group 2 systems, the descendents of OS/360.

One of the most distinctive features of these operating systems is their memory management routines. Primary Control Program (PCP) was an early operating system intended for small 360s. Therefore, it used a simple, single contiguous partition memory management scheme. (IBM no longer supports PCP.) Multiprogram with Fixed Tasks (MFT) was intended for medium-sized 360s; its nucleus requires approximately 64K bytes. It uses a fixed partitioned memory management scheme. MFT is a good system if you can match partition size with your job mix ahead of time. Multiprogramming with Variable Tasks (MVT) (IBM, 16) is intended for the larger 360s and is a variable partitioned system whose nucleus requires

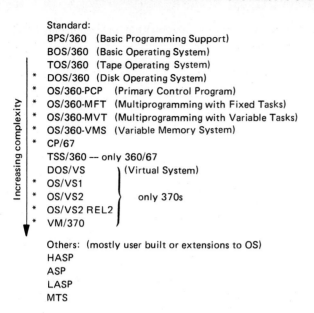

Standard:
BPS/360 (Basic Programming Support)
BOS/360 (Basic Operating System)
TOS/360 (Tape Operating System)
* DOS/360 (Disk Operating System)
* OS/360-PCP (Primary Control Program)
* OS/360-MFT (Multiprogramming with Fixed Tasks)
* OS/360-MVT (Multiprogramming with Variable Tasks)
* OS/360-VMS (Variable Memory System)
* CP/67
TSS/360 -- only 360/67
DOS/VS   (Virtual System)
* OS/VS1
* OS/VS2   only 370s
* OS/VS2 REL2
* VM/370

Increasing complexity

Others: (mostly user built or extensions to OS)
HASP
ASP
LASP
MTS

* = Systems we will talk about

Figure 9-1 360/370 operating systems

Group 1	Group 2
BOS	OS/360–PCP
TOS	OS/360–MFT
DOS	OS/360–MFT–II (now OS/360–MFT)
DOS – II (now DOS)	OS/360–MVT
DOS/VS	OS/VS1
	OS/VS2
For small 360/370s, e.g., 360/25, 360/30, 360/40 370/125, 370/135	For medium to large 360/370s, e.g., 360/50, 360/65, 360/75, 360/85 370/145, 370/158, 370/168
Simpler	More complex

Note: The systems within group 1 are relatively compatible, as are the systems within group 2. However, the two groups are not especially compatible (a source of trouble to IBM and its customers).

Figure 9-2 Two main groups of 360/370 operating systems

128K bytes or more. It is a good system for job mixes with unpredictable memory needs.

OS/360 Variable Memory System (VMS) was intended to free the user from having to specify his job size in advance, but it was never actually released. VMS was a predecessor to MVT and provided dynamic allocation (nonrelocatable) software segmentation. The above memory management techniques have been discussed earlier in Section 3-3.

OS/VS1 and OS/VS2 (IBM, 14; IBM, 15) are based on MFT and MVT, respectively, but they utilize the paging hardware of the 370s to provide users with much larger virtual memories. CP-67 and VM/370, which are virtual machine monitors, will be discussed in Section 9-5.

The 370 hardware (IBM, 5) provided the potential for more flexible operating systems and made it possible for the operating system to better utilize its resources. Specifically, the 370 has Dynamic Address Translation (DAT) (IBM, 17), which consists of paging and the simple form of segmentation discussed in Sections 3-5.1 and 3-6.1. The segmentation is limited to 256 segments and, as a result, is not as generally usable as the Honeywell 6180 with 256K segments. VS1 does not use the segmentation hardware, and VS2 uses it only marginally.

To assist device management, the 370 also has a block multiplexor channel with rotational position sensing, as discussed in Section 5-5.3.1.

9-2.2 Memory Management

9-2.2.1 PARTITIONED MEMORY MANAGEMENT

MFT uses a memory management scheme of static partitions, while MVT uses a variable partitioned scheme, as discussed in Chapter 3. With both MVT and MFT, the user must specify the maximum memory needs in advance. VMS, the system never released, did not require this—it would dynamically allocate more space as a job needed it. For example, Figure 9-3 depicts a situation where Job 1 and Job 2

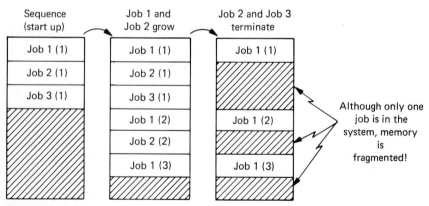

Figure 9-3 VMS memory allocation

requested more space and VMS dynamically assigned it to them; this resulted, however, in serious fragmentation problems.

9-2.2.2 DEMAND-PAGED MEMORY MANAGEMENT

OS/VS1 (Virtual Storage 1) is based on OS/360-MFT, while OS/VS2 (Virtual Storage 2) is based on OS/360 MVT. Both initially used the same partition scheme as MFT and MVT, but in virtual store rather than real store. (See Figure 9-4.)

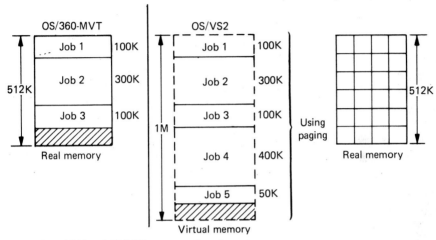

Figure 9-4 MVT and OS/VS2 memory allocation schemes

Keeping MFT- and MVT-type systems under virtual storage has the following advantages:

1 It requires only simple changes to MFT and MVT. (This is the principal advantage.)
2 It provides larger memory.
   a Fragmentation cost is minimized (fragmentation of virtual storage is cheap).
   b Scheduling is eased.
   c Economical "slop" is allowed (e.g., requesting large partitions but using only a portion of them).
3 It reflects 360/370 architecture.
4 It makes more OS options possible (e.g., SPOOLing)—this is less costly since pageable partitions can be used.

It has the following disadvantages:

1 It doesn't really use segmentation. (On VS2, partitions are multiples of 64K segments; thus, they can use segment fault hardware to control protection rather than the storage protection keys, which had caused a limit of 15 partitions.)

2 The total address space for all jobs is less than or equal to 16M.

3 There is no more sharing than on MVT (although larger memory makes MVT-type sharing more feasible).

There are other considerations also. For example, the virtual store of VS1 and VS2 is intended to be used in limited amounts, such as from 1.5 to 2 times real memory size. (The 16M limit also helps to bound this.) Thus paging (i.e., page swaps) is minimal (around 5 to 10 pages per second) compared with timesharing systems where virtual memory equals 10 to 100 times real memory size and paging is as high as 50 to 100 pages per second.

The initial VS2 implementation was substantially modified in its second release so as to support a separate virtual memory of up to 16M bytes for each job's partition. Figure 9-5 is a conceptual view of the virtual memory of VS2 release 1 and release 2.

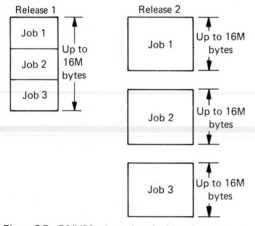

Figure 9-5 OS/VS2 release 1 and release 2 virtual memories

The page replacement scheme of VS1 and VS2 is a *modified LRU*. A single-bit "reference bit" is used to note whether a page has been used. However, by periodically "strobing" these bits and maintaining lists as in Figure 9-6, VS develops sets of successively Less Recently Used. The more sets there are and the more often the strobing is done, the more accurately the working set can be maintained. With low page rates for VS1 and VS2, we don't need too many lists or too much strobing.

9-2.3 Processor Management

9-2.3.1 JOB SCHEDULERS

Most of the 360/370 operating systems have similar job schedulers. Basically they are all priority schedulers with a great degree of flexibility. Take, for example, MFT. Four actions are important:

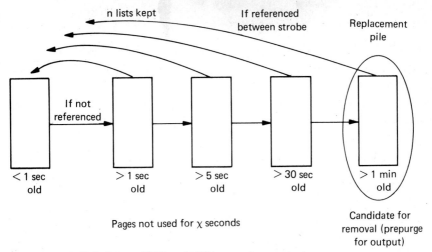

Figure 9-6   Simplified view of VS1 and VS2 page replacement scheme

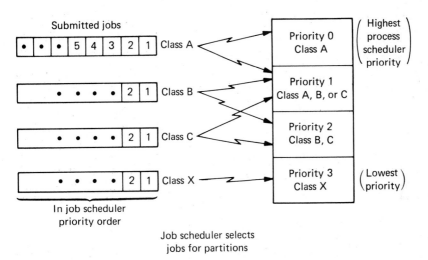

Figure 9-7   Sample class assignment for an MFT system

1   The operator sets the class of job that each partition can service. Each partition has a specific process scheduler priority, as illustrated in Figure 9-7.

2   All jobs are classified into A, B, C . . . X, Y, Z jobs. The requirements for membership in each class is established by all users or it is dictated by the operator. A typical convention may be as follows:

Class A—I/O-bound jobs

Class B—balanced

Class C—CPU-bound jobs

Class X—express

3 Each user specifies on a job card the class of his job and its priority within that class.

4 The operator presumably sets the charging policy to discourage lying about the class of a job. For example, class A jobs receive a 10 percent reduction in costs of I/O but pay a 15 percent surcharge on CPU. Conversely, class C jobs receive a reduction in CPU charge rate. Thus, if a user misrepresents a class C job as class A, it is costly for him.

Basically, the job scheduler or SPOOLer orders all submitted jobs first by class, then by priority within that class. A partition may service more than one job class. In this case the classes are ordered as primary, secondary, etc. When a partition becomes free in MFT, the scheduler chooses the highest priority job in the highest priority class serviced by that partition.

Note that the configuration of Figure 9-7 (with the convention of class A being I/O-bound, class B balanced, and class C CPU-bound) favors I/O-bound jobs for both job scheduling and process scheduling. A user with a class C job may be tempted to lie and call his job a class A, since it is then more likely to run. But if the charging policy described above were in effect, he would be charged more. The operator can, of course, configure the system to favor any type of job.

In MVT, how does the operator set the priorities and classes associated with each partition inasmuch as the number of partitions varies from one to fifteen? MVT provides a program called an *initiator* for each potential partition. The operator gives each initiator information on the class and priority of jobs that it will "fight" for, i.e., find memory and create a partition.

For MVT and VS2 there are options available at system generation that can further tailor the job scheduler to fit the needs of particular job mixes. An example is roll-out. If a job with a high priority enters the system, a low-priority job running in a partition of the same class may be rolled out.

9-2.3.2 PROCESS SCHEDULERS

Process scheduling is based on priorities. The scheduler will always assign the processor to the job running in the highest priority partition. Several options are available to tailor the process scheduler to the needs of a particular installation, including:

1 Automatic Priority Grouping (APG), whereby the system dynamically assigns priorities to jobs to balance system utilization by favoring jobs doing a lot of I/O.

2 Timeslicing, whereby a group of jobs shares the processor on a round-robin timesliced basis. This prevents the situation whereby one high-priority job may dominate a processor and, as a result, other high-priority jobs may not be executed for a long time.

9-2.4   Device Management

Most 360/370 operating systems allow the user the option of specifying various device management functions that may improve the performance of his job. Several of them are listed below:

1   Channel Separation/Affinity (SEP/AFF). The user may specify that a particular data set (file) be allocated on a device serviced by the same or different channels. For example, if the user knew two data sets would be accessed at the same time, he would request that they be assigned to different channels.

2   I/O Unit or Volume. The user can specify the type of device or a particular device (e.g., tape 17) that a data set is to be stored on.

3   Allocation. Data sets can grow dynamically. The user is allowed up to 16 non-continuous parts. He specifies the size of the first part as primary; the remaining 15 parts are linked as needed, but the size of each is the size specified as secondary.

4   Synchronous Error. The user can specify I/O error handlers.

5   Buffer Pool. The user specifies where buffers come from. The following three specifications may be used:

(BUILD): static—the buffer is within the user program.

(GETPOOL): explicit—the system is asked for a buffer.

(AUTOMATIC): the system assigns buffers as needed.

6   Buffer Assignment. The user can specify double buffering or dynamic.

7   Chained Scheduling. The user can specify rotational position sensing. (The system performs I/O-seek reordering.)

8   Split Seek. The user requests the system to preseek before I/O. (This is not necessary on a 370 block multiplexor channel since a seek does not tie up the channel.)

In addition to these device management functions, the user can specify the following, which relate strongly to information management.

1   Record Format (RECFM), either fixed (F), variable (V), or undefined (U)

2   Record Length (LRECL)

3   Block Size (BLKSIZE)

4   Symbolic Data Set Name (DDNAME)

5   Data Set Organization (DSORG), either Physical Sequential (PS), Index Sequential (IS), Partitioned (PO), or Direct Access (DA)

9-2.5 Information Management

9-2.5.1 SPACE ALLOCATION

Let us start by asking how a user allocates a file. He may either specify the file in a device-independent way, e.g.,

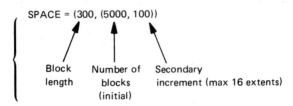

SPACE = (300, (5000, 100))

Block length — Number of blocks (initial) — Secondary increment (max 16 extents)

or in cylinders, which are device-dependent, as

SPACE = (CYL, (3,1)), UNIT = 3330

9-2.5.2 VOLUME TABLE OF CONTENTS (VTOC)

How does the system keep track of files? Associated with each volume is a Volume Table of Contents (VTOC) in which each entry consists of a 44-byte key and 96 bytes of data. There are six types of entries:

1 Information about a data set and its first three extents (pointer to type 3 entry if additional extents)
2 Additional information for index sequential data set (pointed to by type 1 entry)
3 Information on up to 13 additional extents
4 VTOC entry (no extents)
5 Free area (information about 26 available extents)
6 Shared cylinder allocation information

The type 6 entry allows the storage of parts of two data sets to be split on the same cylinder. For example, an input file and an output file may be accessed in such a way that if part of the input file were on the same cylinder as part of the output file, efficient I/O could be achieved.

9-2.5.3 CATALOG

Once a file is created, how does the system keep track of which volume it is on? Residing on a special volume (SYSRES) is a special file, the *catalog*. The name and volume location of a file may be stored in the catalog.

9-2.5.4 PARTITIONED DATA SETS

OS allows libraries of small files, that is, partitioned data sets. Figure 9-8 depicts a sample OS library. The library consists of one data set the top portion of which

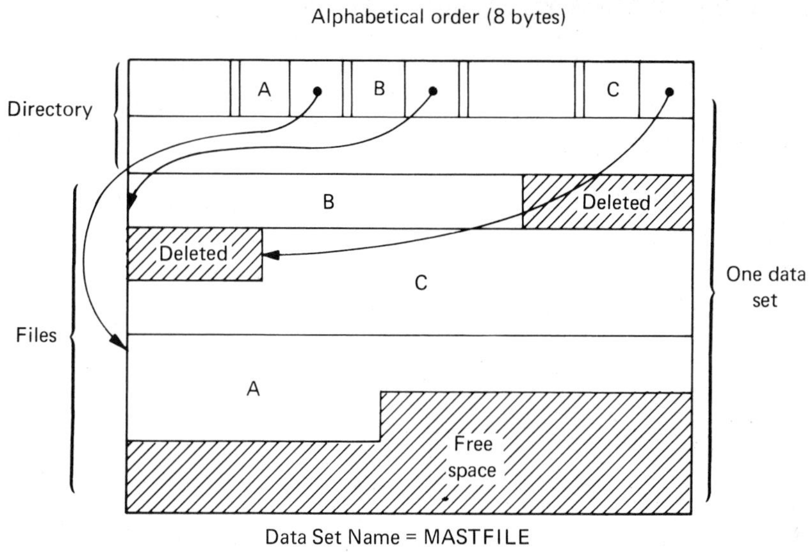

Alphabetical order (8 bytes)

Data Set Name = MASTFILE

Figure 9-8 A library data set

is a directory. A member of the data set (i.e., a file) may be referenced as MASTFILE(A).

OS provides facilities for deletion of entries in a library, but does not keep track of holes or try to use them. It is a common experience in OS to run out of space in libraries. For example, each time B is deleted and a new B added, the size of the data set increases. If the user wants to delete holes, he must copy all files and delete the old library. DOS and the IBM 1130 Disk Monitor provide a facility where holes are deleted automatically by relocating all files in a partitioned data set under some specified conditions (e.g., 50 percent holes).

9-2.5.5 ACCESS METHOD
OS supports two types of access methods to files:

1 Queued Access: the user invokes this type of access by GET/PUT macros. These are used for sequential access. With the queued-access method the system automatically blocks and deblocks, buffers, and does I/O overlap.

2 Basic Access: The user invokes this type of access by the READ/WRITE macros. These are used for either sequential or direct access. For direct access the user may give any of the following:

a Relative record number (for fixed length records only)

b Relative track and key

c Relative track and record number

d Actual address

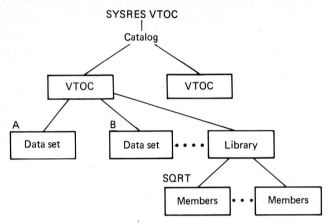

Figure 9-9a Limited hierarchy of OS 360/370

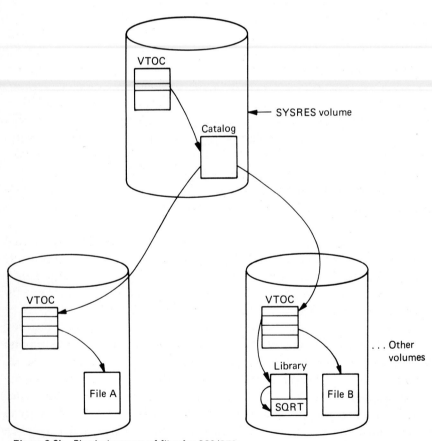

Figure 9-9b Physical storage of files for 360/370

With the basic access method the system processes physical blocks, not records. Blocking and deblocking are the user's responsibility, as is synchronization. This means that the user must check for I/O complete. (He may use the CHECK macro.)

9-2.5.6 DIRECTORY HIERARCHY

In summary, the OS 360/370 file system operates on a limited hierarchical structure. Members of this hierarchy are the VTOC of the SYSRES volume, the catalog, the libraries, members of libraries, and data sets. Figure 9-9a shows the logical structure of this file system, and Figure 9-9b depicts the physical storage of these files.

9-3 THE COMPATIBLE TIME-SHARING SYSTEM (CTSS)

9-3.1 Philosophy and History

The Compatible Time-Sharing System (CTSS) was first demonstrated in rudimentary form in 1961 (Corbato, 1962), came into general use at M.I.T. in 1963 (Crisman, 1965), and was terminated in 1973. We discuss CTSS because it was one of the first timesharing systems, it is simple, and it has historic significance. (Many subsequent systems have been based on the CTSS design.) It incorporated important resource management techniques, some of which are yet to be duplicated, and it is a system that can easily be implemented on other computers.

CTSS is built on a modified IBM 7094. Normal use supports 30 users in a time-shared mode and a batch job stream under the Fortran Monitor System (FMS). It is a compatible system in that programs running under the normal FMS batch processing system also run under CTSS. Each user in a timeshared mode may create and store files. He may cause the execution of these files or of system files (such as compilers, assemblers, editors). For inputting files, users have a wide selection of editors ranging from line editors, context editors, and general macro-editors.

CTSS was used to develop much of the software for the MULTICS system and played an important role in the early development of the CP/CMS system. It demonstrated the value of a software factory approach (tools for developing software) in decreasing the development cost and time for software and increasing the quality of documentation and efficiency of code. We strongly urge the use of systems like CTSS for the development of software.

Figure 9-10 presents a sample CTSS terminal session. The user and CTSS converse by using a terminal similar to a teletype or electric typewriter. In this interaction user input is typed in lower case, CTSS output in upper case. In this sample session a program is entered into the CTSS file system, then modified, compiled, and tested several times. The program, written in the MAD language, is intended merely to read two numbers from the user's console and then compute and output the square root of the sum and the product.

```
   login ml416 madnick
   W 1315.1
PASSWORD
   PARTY LINE BUSY, STANDBY LINE HAS BEEN ASSIGNED
   M1416 2286 LOGGED IN    1/10/66   1315.6 from 20000K
   CTSS BEING USED IS       DMN2C5

LAST LOGOUT WAS 1/6/66 1756.0
R 6.783+750


edl simple mad
W 1316.4
 FILE SIMPLE   MAD NOT FOUND.
INPUT
normal mode is integer
floating point a
        print comment$numbers,pleeuhz''''''''ase$
        read data
        a=sqrt(b+c)
        d=bc
end of?           end of program

EDIT
t
1 mode
NORMAL MODE IS INTEGER
r       normal mode is integer
n
r       floating point a,d
1 a
        PRINT COMMENT$NUMBERS,PLEASE$
1 a=
        A=SQRT(B+C)

c /t/t./
        A=SQRT.(B+C)
1 d=
        D=BC
i
INPUT
        print results a,d
        execute exit.


EDIT
file
R 5.833+4.250


print simple mad
W 1321.3

SIMPLE     MAD    01/10  1321.4

        NORMAL MODE IS INTEGER
        FLOATING POINT A,D
        PRINT COMMENT$NUMBERS,PLEASE$
        READ DATA
        A=SQRT.(B+C)
```

user typing

CTSS typing

Creating and modifying MAD program named SIMPLE.

Figure 9-10 CTSS sample session (part 1)

```
        D=BC
        PRINT RESULTS A,D
        EXECUTE EXIT.
        END OF PROGRAM
R .616+416
```

```
mad simple
Wl321.9
  THE FOLLOWING NAMES HAVE OCCURRED ONLY ONCE IN THIS PROGRAM.
  COMPILATION WILL CONTINUE.
        BC
        B
        C
LENGTH 00072.   TV SIZE 00006.   ENTRY 00016
R 2.766+.533
```
Complete
SIMPLE.

```
edl simple mad
W 1322.8
Edit
1 bc
        D=BC
c /b/b*/
        D=B*C
file
R 3.516+1.450
```
making correction
to program.

```
mad simple
W 1323.7
LENGTH 00071.   TV SIZE 00006.   ENTRY 000015
R 2.216+.750
```
Compile
SIMPLE again.

```
loadgo simple
W 1324.1
EXECUTION.
NUMBERS,PLEASE
b=7,c=2*
```
Load
and
execute
SIMPLE
program.

```
        A = 2.707999E 26,            D = 14.000000
   EXIT CALLED. PM MAY BE TAKEN.
R 6.166.1.050
```

```
edl simple mad
W 1325.5
EDIT
1 mode
        NORMAL MODE IS INTEGER
d
1 read
        READ DATA
1       whenever (b+c).1.0.,transfer to tag
1 exit
        EXECUTE EXIT.
```

Figure 9-10 CTSS sample session (part 2)

```
c //tag 2/
TAG2    EXECUTE EXIT.
i
INPUT
tag     print comment$negative argument$
        transfer to tag2

EDIT
file
R 2.950+3.150

mad simple
W 1523.1
LENGTH 00107.   TV SIZE 00006.   ENTRY 00020
R 2.966+.900

loadgo simple
W 1523.7
EXECUTION.
NUMBERS,PLEASE
b=7.,c=2.*

        A =   3.000000, D = 14.000000
  EXIT CALLED. PM MAY BE TAKEN.
R 6.566+1.083

loadgo simple
W 1524.7
EXECUTION.
NUMBERS,PLEASE
b=-7.,c=,2.*
NEGATIVE ARGUMENT
  EXIT CALLED.   PM MAY BE TAKEN.
R 6.216+.816

delete simple *
W 1526.1
R 1.716+366


logut
W 1528.2
 LOGUT NOT FOUND.
READY.


logout
W 1528.4
 M1416  2286 LOGGED OUT  1/10/66    1536.3 FROM 20000K
 TOTAL TIME USED=    00.7 MIN.
```

Figure 9-10 CTSS sample session (part 3)

9-3.2 Hardware

As noted in section 9-3.1, CTSS is built around a modified IBM 7094. The hardware characteristics of a 7094 are:

Memory size = 32K words

Word size = 36 bits

Typical instruction format =

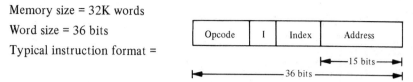

The major modifications are a second 32K core memory (as shown in Figure 9-11) and a relocation and bounds register. Since all instructions have a 15-bit address—not enough to address the combined 64K words—an addressing bit register was added to direct any access to A or B core. A core is used for the operating system and B core is primarily used for user programs. Two 7-bit registers were added as relocation and bounds registers. (Specifications of bounds and relocation are in 256-word blocks.) The bounds register could be used to prevent a user's program from accessing outside its address space.

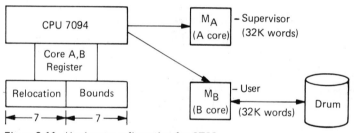

Figure 9-11 Hardware configuration for CTSS

A drum is used to swap the user's programs in and out. The entire 32K B core can be swapped in or out in about 250 ms.

For our discussion of CTSS, a user = a process = a job.

9-3.3 Memory Management

The basic memory management algorithm that CTSS uses is called an *onion-skin* swapping algorithm. CTSS performs no multiprogramming. A user is assigned as much memory as he needs starting at location 0 of B core. His initial needs are determined by the size of his program. Additional memory may be requested during execution for tables and data areas. At any time, each user has a specific memory bound, which is the maximum memory address that he is using. When a different user is to be run, the currently running user's programs and data must be swapped out. To minimize swapping overhead, only enough memory is swapped out to load the next user.

Figure 9-12 depicts the memory usage of four users over a period of time. Note that when user 3 was swapped in he did not require all of user 2 to be swapped out; therefore, when user 2 was subsequently swapped in much of his address space was already in memory. Note that at time 5, in order to swap in user 4, user 1 had to be swapped out along with residual portions of users 3 and 2.

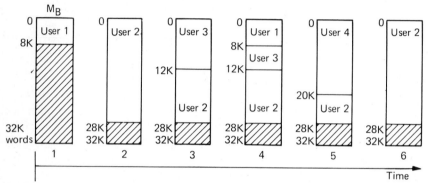

Figure 9-12 Onion-skin algorithm

Because all jobs began at location 0 of B core, the relocation register was never actually used in CTSS. It could have been used either to multiprogram or to overlap swap-in and execute times, but these facilities were not provided. Why do we need the bounds register? Because with the onion-skin algorithm there may be part of another user's job in core and this must be protected.

9-3.4 Processor Management

A user is assigned the processor until one of the following occurs:

His timeslice is up.

He makes an error.

He completes.

He does console I/O.

Note that a user cannot be swapped out until all of his current I/O is complete (except console I/O). Every 200 ms CTSS regains control of the processor to determine if console I/O was completed or if another user should run. The model of Figure 9-13 depicts the various process states. The states are as follows:

Submit—corresponds to a user dialing his data set phone.

Log in—user has dialed in, but no resources have been assigned to him.

Working—corresponds to a ready state in that a process is capable of being run; all it needs is to be swapped in and assigned a processor.

There are several categories of wait states in CTSS. The states differ depending on the event being awaited. These categories are:

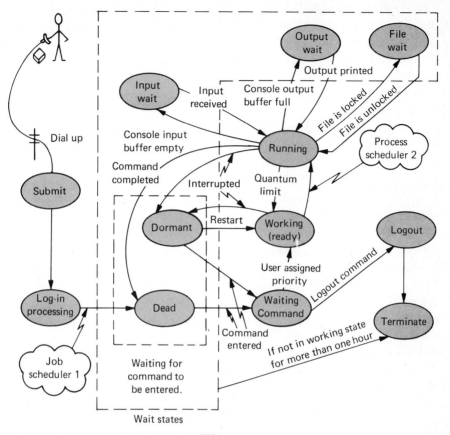

Figure 9-13 State diagram of a process in CTSS

In-wait—jobs that try to read from the console input buffer when the buffer is empty.

Out-wait—jobs that have filled up their console output buffer region. These go into a wait state until the output has been printed.

File-wait—jobs waiting to read a shared file that is locked.

Waiting command—jobs that have just entered a command and are waiting to be assigned a priority level in the working state.

Dormant—jobs that have been interrupted in the midst of a command; the job can continue from point of interrupt or accept a new command.

Dead—jobs that have terminated their previous command and are waiting for the next command.

Note that there is no disk- or tape-I/O-blocked state. Jobs do not go blocked when doing disk I/O, that is, they keep their assigned CPU while performing disk or tape I/O. Recall that there is only one complete job in memory at a time, thus, conventional multiprogramming to overlap I/O is not possible.

9-3.4.1 JOB SCHEDULER

Cloud 1 of Figure 9-13 represents the job scheduler; on CTSS this scheduling is fairly simple. There is a specific maximum number of users (e.g., 30) allowed on the system at one time. Thus, the first 30 users who log in are accepted. If the system already has 30 users, no others are allowed in. If any additional users try to dial in, the system hangs up the phone. No information is kept on users who try to log in but fail.

This simple job scheduler does limit the system load effectively but it also encourages various forms of antisocial behavior. For example, consider 10 students working on a project. Each of them agrees to come to work very early (e.g., 7 AM) twice a month, each on a different day of the month. When the "early bird" arrives he logs in 10 terminals that are kept logged in all day long for the benefit of this group.

The job scheduler was extended to cope with some of these problems. All users are assigned to groups (i.e., most users are members of research groups at M.I.T.). Each group is assigned a specific number of *primary lines*. Let us assume that the group of students above are assigned two primary lines. The first two users from this group to log in are assigned these primary lines. If the system is fully loaded, no additional users from this group are allowed. On the other hand, if the system is not fully loaded, additional users from this group are allowed on the system; they are assigned *secondary lines* (also called *standby lines*).

If a user from another group with a primary line available wishes to log in, the system picks a standby line user and automatically logs him out.

The algorithm for choosing the user to be logged out changes periodically to prevent users (who do not want to be logged out) from subverting it. One version logs out the user who had consumed the most CPU time at that point. The justification is that the user has had his chance. (Wise freshmen watch their time usage carefully and when they have used more than most other users, they sometimes log in again, thus setting their usage to zero.)

In addition to limiting the load to a maximum of 30 users, the job scheduler gives a user who dials the system 2 minutes to log in. If he does not properly identify himself by that time, he is disconnected.

One of the most exciting, and frustrating, aspects of scheduling algorithms is the unpredictability of the effect. An example based on CTSS may illustrate this point. How was the 30-user limit determined? It assumed that each user imposed a certain load on the system. Since a user's behavior is not constant, the limit was frequently either too conservative or too permissive. A special job scheduler was allegedly developed that monitored the overall system load and, if the load increased beyond a specific limit, it automatically terminated a user in order to decrease the load.

Let us trace the behavior of this load-balancing scheme on the assumption that load currently exceeds the critical point. A logout procedure is started in order to terminate a user (e.g., close files, update accounting information). The logout procedure takes several seconds to complete. While this logout is underway, the load-balancing algorithm checks again and finds that the load has actually increased! (This is caused by the intensive load of the logout procedure.) Thus another user is selected to be terminated. This further increases the load and additional users must be terminated. Eventually the load-balancing algorithm is satisfied—after all, the users have been terminated! It is not known if this algorithm was ever actually used, but it does indicate the potential dangers of "clever" scheduling algorithms.

9-3.4.2 PROCESS SCHEDULER

Cloud 2 of Figure 9-13 represents the process scheduler. Several algorithms have been tried, most of which are quite sophisticated (Scherr, 1965). The objective of the CTSS algorithm is to give good response to the interactive user at the expense of the noninteractive user who is doing extensive computation.

The algorithm accomplishes its goals by establishing eight ready queues (0 through 7). The interactive users tend toward the low-number queues and the compute-bound users toward the high-numbered queues. The process scheduler runs all jobs in low-number queues (favoring the interactive job) first. But jobs in higher-numbered queues are given a large time quantum when they are run, thus reducing the swap-time overhead for large compute-bound jobs. Jobs in each queue are assigned a time quantum to run; this is a function of the queue number. The basic quantum Q equals 500 ms.

Run quantum $= Q \times 2^n$

where n denotes level number.

Initially, all user jobs start in either level 2 or level 3.

> If the job is fewer than 4K words, it starts in level 2 (run quantum = 2 seconds).
>
> If the job is greater than 4K words, it starts in level 3 (run quantum = 4 seconds).

If a job is not finished by the end of its current quantum, it moves to the next higher level (4, 5, 6, 7).

Preemption is also allowed if the current job has run longer than the preempting job's quantum. For example, if level 7 is running, a level-3 job that becomes ready does not get swapped in unless level 7 has run at least as long as the level-3 time quantum. This policy tends to avoid the possibility that a job will be swapped in and immediately preempted. The job swap time is quite substantial on CTSS because of the relatively slow speed of the swapping drum.

There are several other rules that govern the handling of the job queue. When the user's job receives input from the teletype, it is classified as interactive and automatically assigned to level 2. Furthermore, if a job in ready state is not run within 1 minute, the job moves to the next lower queue. For example, consider a job that drifts down to queue number 7; as long as jobs are in queues 0, 1, 2, 3, 4, 5, or 6, it will never be run. The 1-minute limit assures that if that job were not run within 1 minute, it would move up to level 6. Thus, this limit guarantees that every job will run at least once every 8 minutes, even if only for 500 ms (if it has to reach queue 0 to be run).

In order to reduce the overhead of examining unused terminals (e.g., the user stepped out for lunch), a job in a nonworking state for more than 1 hour is automatically terminated and logged out of the system.

In addition to the jobs originating from the online users (these are called *foreground jobs*), there are several other jobs in the system. One job runs the Fortran Monitor System that operates as a batch-processing operating system (this is called the *background job*). This background job is usually assigned a lower priority level than the foreground jobs since it never receives teletype input—it is treated as a noninteractive job.

There are several other system jobs, called daemons or helpful spirits. These daemons continually examine the file system and make copies onto tape of files that have been modified or created recently. This provides for a reasonably current backup copy in case of a serious system failure.

9-3.5 Device Management

Since there is no multiprogramming, device management is rather straightforward. Only three types of I/O are performed.

1 Console: Each job is assigned an output and input buffer area for console I/O. All console I/O is handled by the supervisor in A core; input from the console is placed in the job's buffer area in A core whether or not that job is in B core. Appropriate changes are made in the user's state when input has been received. A running job's console output is directed to its output buffer area in A core and, as soon as possible, the supervisor performs the I/O. If the buffer area is filled, then the job goes into out-wait state.

2 Disk I/O: Disk or drum I/O takes place under two circumstances—a user reading a file, or memory management swapping a user in or out. The user reading a file is performed on demand and that user is considered to be running during this I/O. Memory management does the swapping.

3 Tape I/O: The user initiates tape I/O in the same way as for disk I/O, i.e., he must be running. Printer I/O, card reader I/O, etc., are performed only by background FMS users; they are all directed to a tape, which is then carried to an offline computer (1401) for actual processing.

9-3.6 Information Management

The file system of CTSS was and still is one of the more advanced systems. It has features that other systems do not have even today. For example, in most abnormal logout conditions (e.g., system shutdown time), the system saves a snapshot of each job so that the user can restart it. Information management has the following features:

1 The user may write and maintain programs and data on disk.

2 System programs are stored on secondary storage and maintained in a similar manner to user programs and data.

3 All files are symbolically referenced.

4 There may be multiple files accessible at one time.

5 Access to files may be restricted (e.g., read only).

6 A standard physical record format is used throughout the system regardless of logical record format (one record/track format).

7 A backup system automatically copies files onto tape.

8 Sharing of files between users is allowed.

9 A modular design is used to simplify implementation and maintenance.

The file structure is organized on a two-level hierarchical basis, as depicted in Figure 9-14. A master file directory lists all user directories, the system directory, and library files. Each user directory has an entry for each file. All the physical records for a file are chained together as shown in Figure 9-14. This makes

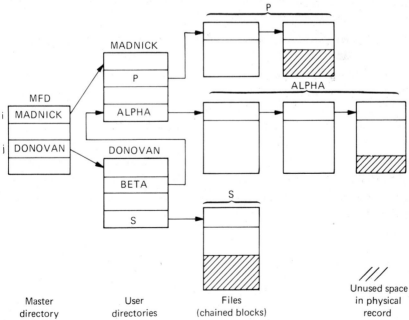

Figure 9-14 Hierarchical file system of CTSS

sequential file processing (which was most common) efficient but random access quite inefficient.

A special permit-and-link file lists the access rights of all files in the system and the users who have established links to other uses' files.

A user, Madnick, can allow another user, Donovan, to access his files by means of a PERMIT command, such as PERMIT DONOVAN ALPHA READ ONLY, which means I Will Allow Donovan to Read My File Named ALPHA. If a user wishes to take advantage of this permission, he must use a LINK command, such as LINK MADNICK ALPHA BETA, which says I Wish to Access Madnick's File ALPHA under the Name BETA in My Directory.

Each file's directory entry contains information on "time last changed" and "time last copied." A system job, the backup daemon mentioned earlier, continually runs through all the directories looking for files where time last changed is greater than time last copied. When it finds such a file, it is copied onto magnetic tape and the time last copied updated. If a file is ever destroyed, either accidentally by a user or because of system error, a copy can be obtained from these backup tapes.

9-4 MULTIPLEXED INFORMATION AND COMPUTING SYSTEM (MULTICS)

9-4.1 Philosophy and History

The Multiplexed Information and Computing System (MULTICS) was a cooperative effort involving Project MAC[1] of M.I.T., Bell Telephone Laboratories, and the computer department of the General Electric Company.[2] The MULTICS development was begun in 1964 at Project MAC; it has been in general use at M.I.T. since 1969. The MULTICS Project was introduced in a series of six papers presented at the 1965 Fall Joint Computer Conference (including Corbato, 1965). The principal goal was to develop a working prototype of a *computer utility*. The computer utility is a generalization of the timesharing concept whereby a central facility is capable of dispensing efficient and effective computer resources to remote users in a manner analogous to the electric and telephone utilities. Special attention was given to security and privacy issues. Since we have taken examples from the MULTICS system throughout this book we need touch only briefly on certain interesting details here.

---

[1] Project MAC (MAC stands for Man and Computer, Multiple Access Computer, or Machine Aided Cognition—take your choice) is a major research group at M.I.T. exploring the use of computers in many areas. Project MAC was also responsible for much of the development of CTSS at M.I.T.

[2] This group is now part of Honeywell Information Systems Incorporated. The original MULTICS hardware, known as the GE 645, is now called the HIS 645.

In addition to designing and developing the system, a major goal of the project was the clarification of the concepts underlying good design and implementation techniques. We strongly urge that in the development of all systems careful consideration be given to the three design techniques employed in implementing MULTICS (Corbato, 1969):

1 Design before you implement.
2 Use a timesharing system for implementation (in the case of MULTICS, CTSS was used; MULTICS is now being used by Honeywell Information Systems for the implementation of future systems).
3 Use a high-level language (e.g., PL/I) for all machine-independent functions.

MULTICS at its inception was a very ambitious effort. Its design incorporated many unique concepts along with other concepts that previously had been used only in limited ways. It is difficult to identify the most outstanding aspect since there are so many. One of the most notable accomplishments is the exploitation of paging and segmentation to merge much of the memory management and information management functions (see Sections 3-7, 3-8, and 6-11). The references, especially Organick (1972) and Corbato (1972), highlight many more details.

9-4.2 Hardware

The original MULTICS system used the GE 645 (now HIS 645) hardware, which was a specially modified version of the GE 635 system. In order to take advantage of advances in computer hardware manufacturing as well as the experience gained from using MULTICS, the HIS 645 was replaced by the newer HIS 6180 system in 1973. Most of the hardware features relevant to our discussion are applicable to both the HIS 645 and 6180.

The hardware of an HIS 6180 consists of one or more CPUs, as depicted in Figure 9-15. Memory is organized as 36-bit words with appropriate paging and segmentation hardware to provide a virtual memory (Bensoussan, 1969) as described earlier in Section 3-8. Several other systems pioneered similar demand paging (Fotheringham, 1961) and segmentation (Burroughs, 1961). This approach is also used in the hardware of other recent systems (Comfort, 1965; Motobayashi, 1969). The exact details of the hardware can be found in the Honeywell manuals or even more clearly in Organick (1972). Here we mention only the pertinent features.

Memory is addressed by an ordered pair (name, offset) where "name" denotes a segment and "offset" denotes word number in that segment. The hardware and software transform this two-dimensional address into a specific core address. The hardware supports up to 2^{18} segments per process; each segment may be up to 2^{18} words long. However, MULTICS restricts the segment size to 2^{16} words. The hardware allows a segment to be divided into pages of either 64 words or 1,024 words.

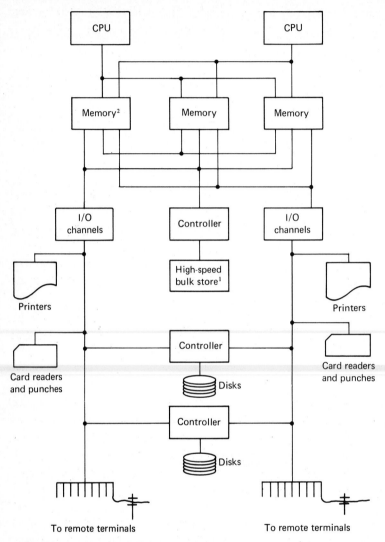

1 The high-speed bulk store was a "Firehose" Drum on the HIS 645 and large-capacity core memory on the HIS 6180.

2 Three memory modules of 128K words each.

Figure 9-15 Example of MULTICS hardware configuration

The MULTICS software presently uses 1,024-word pages for most segments. The use of multiple page sizes in an early version was abandoned due to excessive complexity in physical memory management.

The hardware performs all addressing using a Segment Map Table, called the *descriptor segment* (pointed to by the *descriptor base register*), and page tables. This form of addressing is performed as described in Section 3-8. There are two primary formats for instructions. Type 0 is for referencing data or instructions within the same segment, while type 1 may be used to reference data or instruction in any segment (Figure 9-16).

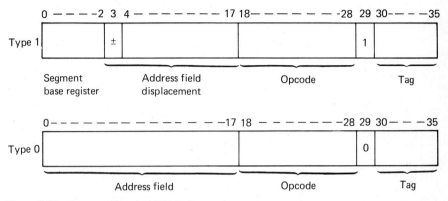

Figure 9-16 Formats of typical H6180 instructions

There are eight base registers, any one of which can be selected by the segment base register field. Multilevel indirect addressing, as described in Section 3-7.2.4, is available and may be used for both intra- and intersegment references. Organick (1972) describes other modes and types of address formation.

9-4.3 Memory Management

The memory management modules support a paged-segmented environment. All memory references are mapped through Page Map Tables and Segment Map Tables (Corbato, 1969; Daley, 1968) as discussed in Chapters 3 and 6. Segments can go up to 64K words and each process can have up to 256K segments. The segmentation supports dynamic linking and sharing.

9-4.3.1 MULTICS MEMORY HIERARCHY

On most contemporary timesharing systems demand-paged memory management and information management are handled separately. Usually a high-performance device, such as a "paging drum" (Denning, 1967), is used to hold pages of the user's address space that are not in main memory whereas larger capacity, though slower, devices such as moving-arm disks are used to hold the user's files. MULTICS handles all files as segments and performs all "file I/Os" by means of the demand paging mechanisms. Thus, there is no explicit separation.

Although this unified view of segments and files is quite elegant in concept, its implementation poses several problems. If moving-arm disks are used solely, the paging rates necessary for good performance cannot be attained (e.g., rates of 50- to 100-page swaps per second are common in a heavily loaded timesharing system).

On the other hand, exclusive use of high-performance drums would be prohibitively expensive (e.g., online storage of 400,000,000 bytes or more is common for a large timesharing system—this would require over 50 expensive drums to handle). To cope with this dilemma, MULTICS uses a storage hierarchy (Madnick, 1973) that employs both high-cost–high-performance devices and low-cost–low-performance devices as shown in Figure 9-17. For brevity, we will refer to the main memory, drum storage, and disk storage, as L1, L2, and L3 memories, respectively.

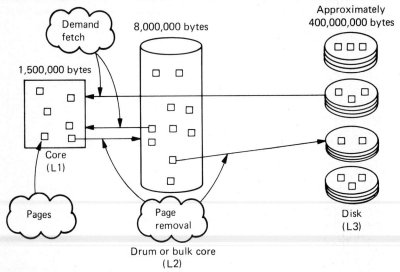

Figure 9-17   Memory hierarchy of MULTICS

The presence of both L2 and L3 memories necessitates a means to determine where a file should be placed. Ideally, we desire that most I/O be directed to the L2 memory rather than L3. This is difficult to accomplish in view of the small capacity of L2. Initially, MULTICS made this decision based upon simple rules, such as:

1   All temporary segments and stack segments are placed on the drum.
2   Carefully (and manually) selected system segments, especially certain nonresident portions of the operating system, are placed on the drum.
3   All other segments are placed on the disks.

These rules were sufficient to direct 90 percent of all page I/Os to the drum even though it held only about 1 percent of the files (Madnick, 1973).

Although impressive, this performance is not good enough. If we assumed that the average access time to the drum and disk are 10 ms and 100 ms, respectively, the effective access time—as defined in Section 3-10.3.4—would be 0.90×10 ms $+ 0.10 \times 100$ ms $= 19$ ms. If the percentage of drum I/Os could be increased to 95 percent, the effective access time drops to 14.5 ms—a decrease of about 25 percent. This improvement is possible by considering certain shortcomings of the rules described above: (1) Frequently used or long-running user procedure segments are always swapped between L1 and L3, and (2) L2 space may be wasted holding segments that are not actually being used (e.g., the temporary segments of a user who is out to lunch but didn't log out). Thus, we would like to move the user procedure segments onto L2 and move "useless" segments from L2 to L3.

MULTICS maintains a dynamic memory hierarchy using a set of rules such as:

1 If a page fault occurs, the necessary page is moved into L1 from L2—if there is a copy on L2—otherwise from L3.

2 If L1 is full and a page must be removed, it is moved to L2.
   a If there is a copy of the page on L2, it is overwritten. (If the page has not been changed, the writing is not necessary.)
   b If a copy does not exist on L2, space for a copy is found.

3 If L2 is full in step 2b, a page must be moved from L2 to L3 to make room for the new page from L1. (If the page has not been changed—always true for pure procedure segments—there is no need to physically move it since a copy already exists on L3.)

Note that it is possible for identical copies of the same pure procedure to exist on L1, L2, and L3.

Variations on the Least Recently Used (LRU) algorithm are used to select pages for removal from L1 and L2. One additional measure of the effectiveness of the dynamic memory is the duration of the page on the L2 storage. It has been reported that, on the average, a page remains on L2 for over 45 minutes before being moved back to L3.

9-4.3.2 PAGE REMOVAL ALGORITHM

The page removal algorithm attempts to approximate LRU by using a 1-bit "used bit" as discussed in Section 3-6.2.7. Further, for each process, memory management maintains a page trace that is a list of the last 200 page faults taken. When a process becomes ineligible (see Section 9-4.4), this list is examined to determine which pages to postpurge (i.e., remove all at once) now and which to prepage (i.e., bring in all at once) when the process becomes eligible again later. (Those worthy of prepaging are remembered and paged in if they are not already in core at reload time.) The decision to postpurge or prepage involves the following six criteria, which are applied to each page in the page trace.

1 Is the page still in core?
2 Has it been used (referenced bit *on* in the page-table word)?
3 Has it been modified?
4 Is this page part of a nonshared segment?
5 Did the page come from the paging drum?
6 Has the page been used during the current eligible period?

The actions that may be taken on the basis of the answers are:

1 Postpurge the page now.

2 Prepage the page later, if necessary.

3 Consider the page to be part of the working set.

4 Make the page the next to be considered for removal when space is needed.

These actions may be taken in any combination. The actual decisions are made by means of a table that indicates the actions to be taken for each of the 2^6 criteria possibilities.

The count of all pages determined to be part of the working set represents the current estimate of the working set size; this count is recorded in the Active Process Table (APT) entry for that process.

When computations make rather abrupt changes (e.g., start new phase), their working sets (and sizes) can also be expected to change abruptly. Accordingly, we want the working-set estimator to be responsive to such changes. More specifically, a system routine, hcs_$reset_working_set, is provided for this purpose. The system is a heavy user of this routine. Upon each return to command level, the Listener (i.e., command processor) calls hcs_$reset_working_set, which goes through the page-trace table resetting every used bit to zero in the page-table words of the corresponding pages that are still in core. The Listener then puts the process into a blocked state to await another interaction. In so doing, the computation (quite conveniently) touches pages of all the key segments that should remain part of the working set and be preloaded when the process becomes eligible once again; for instance, the stacks, combined linkage segment, the typewriter I/O mechanism and its databases, the interprocess communication facility and its databases (including the Listener itself, naturally).

User programs may call hcs_$reset_working_set at any time; this may occur at a point where there is a known abrupt change in the nature of the computation, as, for instance, between two passes of a compiler, or after the execution of a section of a computation that has touched numerous pages that will not be referenced again. Proper use of hcs_$reset_working_set causes the unwanted pages to be purged sooner and so frees core for more immediate use during the processing of subsequent page faults. The practice also lowers the core commitment for this process and may generally work for the mutual benefit of all processes in the system (i.e., result in more throughput from more effective utilization of core).

9-4.3.3 RINGS OF PROTECTION

In addition to the segmentation protection attributes described in Section 3-7, MULTICS employs the concept of *rings of protection*. For a comprehensive explanation of this concept and its implementation, the reader is directed to Graham (1968) and Organick (1972).

The rings of protection are based on the concepts of: (1) "need to know" and (2) "firewalls" to minimize damage due to errors. An example may help to illustrate the usage. Consider a "grading program" used in a computer subject. This program is used to test the correctness of subroutines written by students. In a typical two-state (supervisor-state or user-state) operating system, where do we put this grading program? If it is placed in user state along with the student's subroutines, how can it be protected from damage by the student (accidental or malicious)? One of our students had written his subroutine to put a 100 at the correct location in the GRADES segment used by the grading program. When this was accidentally discovered, the student replied: "It was harder to fool the grader than doing the required assignment, but this was much more fun."

We could incorporate the grader into the protected operating system, but besides being operationally difficult, this makes the operating system vulnerable to any errors in the grading program.

MULTICS solves this problem by generalizing from a two-state system to a hierarchical n-state system. Segments in state i have access to segments in states $> i$ but no access (except by procedure call) to segments in states $< i$. This concept of protection rings provides a nice mechanism for enforcing the hierarchical operating system view discussed in Chapter 1 and used in the sample operating system of Chapter 7.

The hardware of the HIS 6180 supports eight protection rings. Rings 0 to 3 are reserved for the operating system, rings 4 to 7 are available to the user. Figure 9-18 illustrates how these rings can be used to handle the grading problem situation. The operating system itself is divided into rings to minimize the impact of an error in a noncritical subroutine.

9-4.3.4 MAIN MEMORY USAGE

Even in a demand-paged environment, certain portions of the operating system must be permanently assigned areas of main memory either for efficiency or logical prerequisites (e.g., the page fault interrupt handler must be in main memory). Figure 9-19 depicts the approximate memory usage of the MULTICS system operating on the HIS 645 at Project MAC.

The wired-down supervisor consists of all nonpageable parts of the supervisor. A major system table is the Active Segment Table (AST). This table contains an entry for every active segment in the system, i.e., every segment that has its page table in core. The other major table is the Active Process Table (APT), i.e., the hold and ready list.

A process in the hold state requires about 128 words for its APT and AST entries. When a process moves into the ready, running, or blocked state, its main memory table requirements rise to about 3,200 words—largely for the descriptor segments (segment maps).

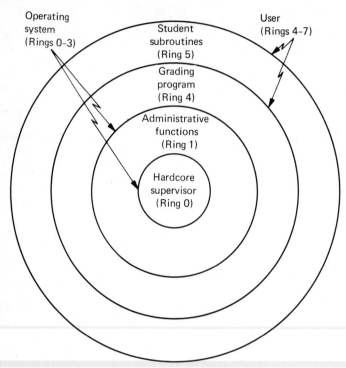

Figure 9-18 Usage of protection rings in MULTICS

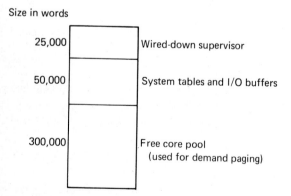

Figure 9-19 MULTICS memory requirements

It is important to note that on the MULTICS system the functions of memory management, the file system, and the hardware all overlap. For example, the file system maintains the AST and is therefore able to reduce (because of sharing pure procedures) the core requirements of a process that needs a sharable segment already in core.

9-4.4 Processor Management

Processor management is composed of modules that handle the transition of process states as shown in Figure 9-20.

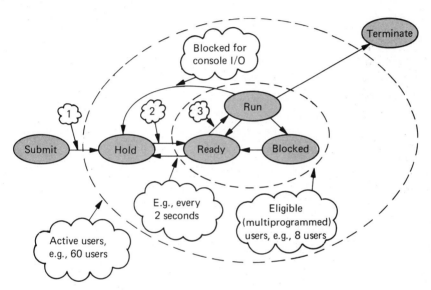

Figure 9-20 MULTICS-process state diagram

Processor management is subject to two restraints: The first constraint is the need to ensure good response time; this limits the number of users allowed entry into the hold state. The exact number of users at any given time depends on the load and configuration of the system at that time.

The second constraint is to prevent thrashing; this limits the number of users multiprogrammed at any one time. If, for example, 60 users were allowed to multiprogram and the available user core was 300,000 words (Figure 9-19), each user would get approximately 5,000 words or only five pages (1K-word pages). The number of page faults would then be very large. If, on the other hand, only eight users were multiprogrammed, each user would get over 30 pages, and there would be little chance of excessive page faults.

Thus the processor manager timeshares "in the large" for good response time and multiprograms "in the small" for effective utilization of resources. At any time, certain processes are selected to be *eligible* (i.e., multiprogrammed) for a given length of time, such as 2 seconds, after which they will be placed back into hold state. A user that goes blocked for console I/O also gets placed back in the hold state. A process remains eligible while blocked for page I/O.

The number of users allowed to be eligible at one time depends on both system configuration and user characteristics; however, it is usually between two and ten.

In reference to Figure 9-20, key questions in scheduling are:

1 How does the system select the users to be let into the system (cloud 1)?

2 How does the system decide which of the processes in the hold state is to be made eligible and for how long (cloud 2)?

3 How does the system decide which process in the ready state is run and for how long (cloud 3)?

Different algorithms have been tried for all three questions. A possible criterion for answering question 1 is guaranteeing fast response time; a criterion for answering question 2 is guaranteeing good utilization. One algorithm used for question 3 simply picked one process arbitrarily and gave it all the resources using the other processes to absorb the I/O wait. This forces one user to complete very fast.

9-4.4.1 LOAD CONTROL

The algorithm for cloud 1 is as follows. All users are given weights:

Ordinary user:	1 unit
Batch job:	1 1/2 units
Restricted user:	1/2 unit

The operator sets the maximum number of units allowed on the system. The weighting is intended to represent the resources used, e.g., the batch user is not interactive and never pauses for console input, thereby using more computer resources than the timesharing user. The M.I.T. HIS 6180 normally allows 100 units for two CPUs and three memories (each 128K words) and 50 units for one CPU and two memories.

All MULTICS users are grouped into *load control groups*. Each load control group is allocated a certain number of units. If a group's units are exceeded, no more users in that group are normally allowed on. If a user is on, and at some later time the total number of units for his group is exceeded, he is then automatically logged out after a grace period. The group leader can set the length of time of the grace period.

Users within a control group are divided into two basic classes: privileged and nonprivileged. A privileged user may preempt a nonprivileged one. This scheme is similar to the one used in CTSS (Section 9-3.4.1).

9-4.4.2 JOB SCHEDULER

Cloud 2 corresponds to a job scheduler. This scheduler must select the processes to be made eligible and then place them in the ready state.

The hold list may be viewed as a set of n queues, one per priority level. Each user process is initially assigned a range of priority levels (ℓ_1, ℓ_2), starting at level ℓ_1. The range (ℓ_1, ℓ_2) offers some clue as to the type of timesharing service the process will be given. At any given time a process has a current priority level ℓ such that $1 < \ell_1 < \ell < \ell_2 < n$.

Interactive processes would range from 1 to some value k_1 while absentee processes (i.e., batch) would range from some value k_2 to n, with k_2 perhaps having a higher priority level than k_1 as suggested by the straddling brackets:

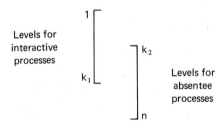

In keeping with the policy of giving fast response to short interactions, priority level 1 is awarded to processes that are expected to make brief use of a processor. For instance, a process that has initiated a console read call and has given up the processor while waiting for the user to type the next input line wants the opportunity to resume (with a short spurt of execution) when the input has been entered. Such a process will be assigned the priority level of 1.

Lower priority levels are reserved for longer-running interactive processes and for *absentee processes*. (Absentee processes are similar to background jobs in CTSS.) The priority range for absentee processes is expected to be (k_2, n), where $1 < k_2$. Note that if $k_2 < k_1$, there would be some straddling of the interactive user's priority range, which is $(1, k_1)$. In any case, service for short absentee jobs will be better than for longer absentee jobs.

The highest priority ineligible process is made eligible (i.e., it moves from hold state to ready state) when its working set can fit into memory (i.e., the sum of the working set estimates of all eligible processes should be less than the size of pageable memory). The amount of available memory increases whenever an eligible process becomes ineligible. As a result of this working-set size constraint, the number of processes being multiprogrammed varies over time.

When a process is made eligible, it must be "loaded." Loading includes setting up certain descriptor segments (mentioned in Section 9-4.3.4) and prepaging all pages designated at the time the process was last unloaded (described in Section 9-4.3.2).

A noneligible process may preempt an eligible process in order to give good response to interactive users issuing commands of short duration. If the preempted process came from priority level k, it is rescheduled by being placed on top of the level k queue with a time allotment equal to whatever time is still unused from its last scheduling algorithm.

The net effects are that a preempted process becomes eligible whenever the preempting process loses eligibility. Thus, suppose A, at priority level 3, preempts B at level 4. Process B is rescheduled at the top of level 4. If shortly afterward A incurs a timer runout, it will lose its eligibility and be rescheduled at the bottom of the queue at level 4. B will be picked to run next, if no other process was added to the list ahead of B while A was running.

9-4.4.3 PROCESS SCHEDULING

The algorithm for cloud 3 corresponds to the process scheduler. In the MULTICS system processes in the ready list are assigned priorities. The process scheduler always gives the processor to the ready process with the highest priority.

Associated with each hold queue is a time quantum q_0. Processes that use up their entire CPU quantum are returned to the hold state and placed in the next lower queue with a time quantum of $2 \times q_0$. Information on the position in the queues and timeslice time is kept in the APT.

When a running process enters a wait state for the occurrence of a system event, the CPU will be given to the ready and eligible process that has the highest priority. When the awaited event occurs, the waiting process is readied and if it has a higher priority than the currently running process, the running process yields the processor. The system always runs the highest priority ready process.

Since a process specifically retains its eligibility when it enters the wait state due to page I/O, it is entirely possible for all the eligible processes to be in the wait state simultaneously. In this event, since there is no eligible processes to run, the processor is given to an idle process that can be regarded as always ready and always having the lowest priority.

9-4.5 Device Management

The MULTICS I/O system provides a generalized device-independent interface, similar to that of IBM's Operating Systems, for all I/O devices that can be processed sequentially (this is called *stream I/O* in both MULTICS and PL/I terminology). Stream I/O can be used for remote terminals, card readers and punches, magnetic tapes, paper tapes, etc. Even a segment can be treated as a source or sink for sequential stream I/O.

To carry out a read or write for a stream, the device manager must look up the device associated with the I/O stream and convert the request into the appropriate CCWs [Data Control Words (DCWs) in HIS terminology]. This conversion is performed by a specialized module for each device called a Device Interface Module (DIM).

The I/O system is conceptually pictured in Figure 9-21.

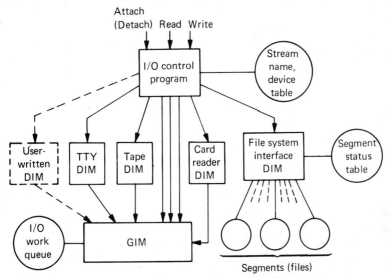

Figure 9-21   Complete simplified view of the MULTICS I/O system organization

On the HIS 645 MULTICS system I/O is performed with the aid of the Generalized I/O Controller (GIOC). The GIOC is the device scheduler, normally a software function. It manages and multiplexes the I/O channels.

The DIM converts a device-independent request into a device-dependent one. To do so, it must compile a program for the GIOC. The compiled program reflects the idiosyncracies of the particular device to which the stream is attached. The program may include line controls in the case of remote terminals, select instructions in the case of tapes, and so forth. In addition, the DIM may have to convert the internal character code used by the system into an appropriate character code for the device. Typewriter terminals, for example, come in many different varieties, and virtually every variety has a different character code.

The DIM, after compiling a program for the GIOC, calls a module that serves as an interface for the GIOC. It is the DIM's responsibility to interact with the GIOC Interface Module (GIM) until this I/O request has been completed. This may require several calls to the GIM depending on the format of the channel programs that the GIOC can provide to the channels for execution.

The GIM program is responsible for the overall management of the GIOC. The GIM answers interrupts (i.e., it is the interrupt handler for the GIOC), recognizing completion of tasks and transmitting to the DIM appropriate status information.

In Figure 9-21 the entry point Attach must be employed in order to establish the appropriate stream-name-to-device association in the attach table. The entry point Detach is used to nullify a previous Attach stream-name-to-device pairing.

The DIMs and the GIOC also perform:

Rotational position sensing

Drum queuing

Overlapping of I/O as much as is possible

SPOOLing

9-4.6 Information Management

Two concepts are important in MULTICS information management: (1) treating a file as a segment (Daley, 1968) and (2) a complete hierarchical file structure. Treating a file as a segment allows many of the functions of the file system to be performed by the segmentation hardware (see Chapters 3 and 6). The hierarchical structure allows great user flexibility, elaborate sharing and protection rights, and access to files (see Chapter 6).

For certain applications, namely, large data management systems, the files may become larger than 256K words, the maximum size of a segment. These large files cannot be completely handled by the segmentation hardware. In such a case, multisegment files must be used. If the I/O system (device management) interface is used, there is no difference to the user between single segment and multiple segment files.

Since the overall structure of a hierarchical file structure has already been discussed we will only focus on two areas of the MULTICS file system: Segment Control and Directory Control.

The Segment Control Module (SCM) performs the mapping from symbolic name to segment number. If a new segment is created, SCM determines where to place it in the file hierarchy. The SCM also performs the protection function in that, after a segment is identified, it is made known to the executing process with appropriate access rights.

The SCM maintains the Known Segment Table (KST) containing all segments that are part of a process and the Active Segment Table (AST) containing all segments currently used by active processes.

The Directory Control Module (DCM) is involved in making modifications to the directory structure. All inquiries about the status or location of segments ultimately invoke the DCM because only this module is permitted to read and alter the contents of the directory segments.

The MULTICS file system incorporates the previously discussed concepts of rings, links, hierarchical structure, and dynamic linking.

9-5 VIRTUAL MACHINE/370 (VM/370)

9-5.1 Philosophy and History

Virtual Machine/370 (VM/370) is an example of a Virtual Machine Monitor (VMM) system. A VMM is a special form of operating system that multiplexes only the physical resources among the users—no other functional enhancements are provided. In particular, the extended machine (see Section 1-5.1) provided by a VMM is identical to the bare machine on which the VMM runs! In this way, VM/370, for example, makes one System/370 appear to be many separate System/370s, as illustrated in Figure 9-22. VM/370 accomplishes this feat by controlling the multiplexing of the physical hardware resources in a manner analogous to the way that the telephone company multiplexes communications enabling separate and, hopefully, isolated conversations over the same wires.

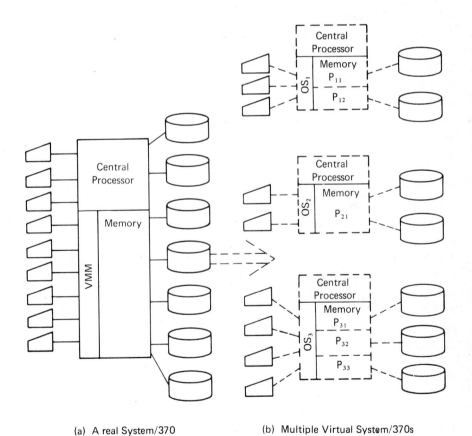

(a) A real System/370

(b) Multiple Virtual System/370s

Figure 9-22 Real and virtual machines

The VMM concept, once understood, is quite simple and logical. Unfortunately, it is sufficiently different from most conventional operating systems that many people have difficulty in understanding the concept. The papers by Buzen (1973), Goldberg (1973), Madnick (1969), and Parmelee (1972) should be studied for additional insight.

At first the idea of replicating the bare machine interface may seem foolish since you end up back where you started. The key difference is that VM/370 produces the effect of multiple bare machines. In this way each user appears to have his own 370 computer. Thus, each user can select the operating system (e.g., OS/360, DOS, etc.) of his choice to run on his "private" computer. This fact is depicted by the operating systems OS_1, OS_2, and OS_3 in Figure 9-22. A more graphical picture of the relationship between virtual machine interfaces and operating system interfaces, used by Buzen (1973), is shown in Figure 9-23.

How does VM/370 produce this feat? How do the users of VM/370 communicate with it? Programs running under VM/370, usually operating systems, physically execute in problem state but can behave as if they were in supervisor state. When they issue a privileged instruction, such as START I/O or SET STORAGE KEY, an interrupt occurs and control transfers to VM/370. The interrupt is handled in such a way that the program thinks that the privileged instruction was actually executed. Thus, these privileged instruction interrupts are the subtle interfaces between users and VM/370.

9-5.1.1 HISTORY

Work on the Control Program–40/Cambridge Monitor System (CP–40/CMS) commenced at the IBM Cambridge Scientific Center (CSC) in 1964 (Parmelee, 1972). This project used an IBM System/360 Model 40 modified to include hardware to support simple demand paging. There were two parts to the software: (1) Control Program–40, the virtual machine monitor and (2) Cambridge Monitor System, a simple easy-to-use one-user operating system. The CP–40/CMS project was a research effort having the following objectives: (1) study of various timesharing techniques and methods; (2) evaluation of hardware requirements for timesharing; (3) implementation of a timesharing system for in-house use; and (4) development of a method for observing the dynamic interaction between operating systems and their hardware environment. The CP–40/CMS system was in general use at IBM CSC by early 1967 and supported up to 15 users.

Two developments had considerable impact on the evolution from CP–40/CMS to VM/370. First, the proliferation of IBM System/360 operating systems noted in Section 9-2 introduced major operational headaches in computer installations that had to run more than one operating system—due to compatibility or special features. Second, IBM's Time-Sharing System/360 (TSS/360), designed to operate

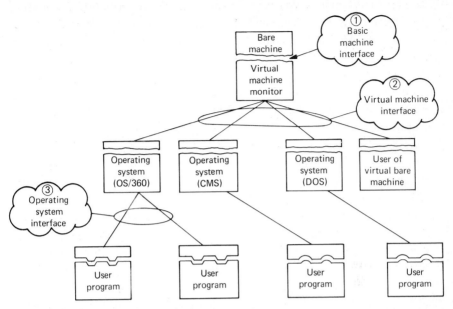

Figure 9-23 Virtual machine organization

on the special System/360 Model 67 hardware (a special model that had Dynamic Address Translation hardware to support demand paging), was falling behind schedule. As a result, in 1966 an effort was started to develop a version of CP-40/CMS to operate on the Model 67 hardware. In 1967 the CP-67/CMS system was made available to installations that had the special Model 67 hardware. The rapidity with which CP-67/CMS was developed is at least partially explained by the clean separation between the CP-67 and CMS components.

The VM/370 system, announced in 1972, is a descendant of the CP-40/CMS and CP-67/CMS systems. It can operate on any IBM System/370 equipped with Dynamic Address Translation, as described in Sections 3-6, 3-7, and 3-8.

9-5.1.2 USES AND RATIONALE
The virtual machine has many uses and advantages (Buzen, 1973):

1 Concurrent running of dissimilar operating systems by different users. For example, one user may be checking out a new release of an OS while others are using a tried and proven version.
2 Elimination of certain conversion problems. The user can run his DOS programs under DOS and his MVT programs under MVT and run both operating systems on the same hardware.

3 Software development. Programs can be developed and debugged for machine configurations that are different from those of the host (i.e., VM/370 can produce virtual 370s that are different from the real 370, such as larger main memory).

4 Test of network facilities. Processor-to-processor communication can be simulated between several virtual machines under one VM monitor.

5 Evaluation of program behavior. Virtual machine monitors must intercept certain instructions for interpretive execution rather than allowing them to execute directly on the bare machine. These intercepted instructions include I/O requests and most other supervisory calls. Hence, if it is desired to measure the frequency of I/O operations or the amount of supervisory overhead in a system, it is possible to modify the virtual machine monitor so as to collect these statistics and then run the system under that modified monitor. In this way no changes have to be made to the system itself. A large body of experimental data has been collected by using virtual machine monitors in this fashion (Hatfield, 1971; Morrison, 1973).

6 Reliability. Virtual machine monitors typically do not require a large amount of code or a high degree of logical complexity. This makes it feasible to carry out comprehensive checkout procedures and thus ensure high overall reliability as well as the integrity of any special privacy and security features that may be present.

7 Security and privacy. The high degree of isolation between independent virtual machines aids in ensuring privacy and security (Madnick, 1973). Basically, privacy between users is ensured because an operating system has no way of determining whether it is running on a virtual machine or a bare machine and, therefore, no way of spying on or altering any other coexisting virtual machine.

9-5.1.3 RELATIONSHIP BETWEEN CP AND CMS

VM/370 consists of two major components: (1) Control Program (CP), the virtual machine monitor, which performs the functions of processor, memory, and I/O device multiplexing to produce the virtual machines; and (2) Conversational Monitor System (CMS), a simple operating system that performs the functions of command processing, information management, and limited device management (i.e., all the functions needed by a user at a console of a timesharing system; see the CTSS example in Section 9-3). Since CMS uses single contiguous memory allocation and provides no multiprogramming, it has extremely simple memory and processor management.

CP and CMS are typically used together although an individual may choose to use any other System/360 or System/370 operating system, such as OS/360, DOS,

DOS/APL, OS/VS-1 or OS/VS-2, instead of CMS. CP and CMS represent a clean division in the VM/370 design. By dividing the system into two roughly equal pieces, the design and implementation are substantially simplified. Furthermore, since both CP and CMS are built on a bare machine interface, they can be implemented and debugged in parallel rather than serially.

In both CP-40/CMS and CP-67/CMS, the CMS component was first debugged on a real machine before being used on a virtual machine. In fact, major portions of CMS were operational before the CP component was completed. It is likely that many operating systems in the future will exploit the virtual machine approach.

9-5.1.4 SIMULATION OF THE SYSTEM/360 AND SYSTEM/370

CP, in conjunction with the System/370 hardware facilities, simulates the processor, memory, I/O devices, operator's console, and system control panel. For each virtual machine CP maintains a set of tables containing the description and status of the virtual machine's components. Where appropriate, these tables correlate the hardware components of the host 370 with components of the virtual system. Thus, for example, a keyboard device such as an IBM 2741 communications terminal is used to simulate the system control panel and operator's console of each virtual machine.

System Control Panel

CP associates with each virtual machine a keyboard device (either remote or locally attached) and maps onto this device the major portion of the functions available on the system control panel. Thus the RESET button on the System/370 panel becomes the typed character sequence RESET, which causes CP to initiate a detailed step-by-step simulation that resets the appropriate status data in the tables describing the virtual System/370. In the same fashion, CP simulates other features of the system control panel.

CPU

In the System/370 the distinction between problem and supervisor state enables CP to execute most of a virtual machine's instructions directly. When the CPU is in problem state, any attempt to execute an instruction that changes or interrogates the state of the system, i.e., a privileged instruction, causes a program interruption. Thus, by executing virtual machine instructions only while in the problem state, CP is ensured of regaining control whenever a privileged instruction is encountered. When such an event occurs, VM simulates the appropriate functional effect of the privileged instruction as follows: From a table describing the virtual CPU, its status is determined—specifically, whether it is in problem or supervisor state. If the virtual machine thought it was in problem state, CP would have to simulate a program interruption to the virtual machine. This entails storing the virtual machine's CPU status in the virtual machine program old Program Status Word (PSW) location, fetching the virtual machine's program new PSW, and updating appropriately the data in CP's table for the virtual CPU. If the virtual machine thought it was in supervisor state, CP would have to decode the instruction and perform a simulation of that instruction. For example, for a virtual machine's SSK instruction, CP must determine the key value and block address and then, if the corresponding page is in main storage, set its key to the value specified. If the page is not in main storage, CP must store the key value in the appropriate swap table entry. In either case, CP must appropriately update the tables (and hardware) to reflect the change in the virtual machine's status before it can resume running the virtual machine.

I/O System

All I/O is simulated. When a virtual machine attempts to execute an I/O instruction, control is transferred to CP via an interrupt. There are three major situations: (1) If such an I/O device physically exists and has been assigned to that virtual machine, the I/O is directly executed. (2) If a similar I/O device exists, the I/O commands are appropriately modified and then executed—such as simulating many small disks by using separate areas of a single large disk. (3) Certain devices may be extensively simulated, such as virtual card readers and printers, using techniques similar to SPOOLing (see Section 5-6).

Memory

Demand paging is used to provide each virtual machine with its own virtual memory.

9-5.2 Hardware

The CP component of VM/370 uses the standard IBM System/370 hardware with the Dynamic Address Translation feature. Nonprivileged instructions executed by programs on a user's virtual machine can be directly processed by the hardware (with occasional page fault interrupts). Privileged instructions result in program interrupts that require special processing by the CP software. Certain memory addresses (e.g., timer, PSWs, CAW, CSW) as well as I/O device addresses are not directly translated by the hardware but are handled by CP. Certain models of the System/370 provide a special "microcode assist," whereby some of the special interrupt processing is performed directly by the hardware. (See Appendix B for a discussion of microprogramming.)

Due to the multiplexing of the processor, as well as the fact that the virtual machines are run partly by direct hardware execution and partly by CP software simulation, rigid timing dependencies cannot be guaranteed. Most other aspects of real System/370s can be reproduced for the virtual System/370s.

It is interesting to note that many contemporary computer systems do not lend themselves to "virtualization" (Goldberg, 1973). This situation can occur if the "sensitive" instructions (i.e., the instructions that affect or examine the virtual machine's state) are not also privileged instructions. For example, on one computer, when running in problem state, all privileged instructions are ignored (i.e., they are treated as "no-operation" and do not cause an interrupt). On another computer the instruction to transfer from supervisor state to problem state (this is done by LPSW on the System/370) is not a privileged instruction; thus, a virtual machine monitor would not be able to determine which state the virtual machine thinks it is in. There is considerable research interest in formally defining computer designs for correct and efficient operation of virtual machines.

9-5.3 Memory Management

CP uses demand paging with postpaging for memory management. The overall paging scheme is based on an LRU approximation similar to the description in Section 3-6.2.7. Tables are used by CP to describe the characteristics of each virtual machine, including its memory size. CP can provide each virtual machine with a virtual memory of up to 16M bytes; normally each virtual machine's memory is limited to 320K bytes.

CP supports both virtual machines with the basic System/360 addressing (i.e., no Dynamic Address Translation) and the System/370 addressing with Dynamic Address Translation. As an example, in basic addressing mode on a translation exception interruption, CP must determine whether the address is in the address span of the virtual machine's storage. If it is outside the span, it must present an addressing exception interruption to the virtual machine. Alternatively, it must make a memory block available (a function of the page replacement algorithm), find in the swap table the location on auxiliary store of the image of the needed page, bring it into main storage, and set its storage keys to the values specified by the swap table. When these actions are complete, CP can resume running the virtual machine.

Additional software mechanisms are needed to produce a virtual System/370 with Dynamic Address Translation. These mechanisms must direct a page fault to its rightful owner, either CP or the virtual machine. A page fault may result from two causes:

1 The virtual machine explicitly removed the page from its address space (i.e., the page fault would have occurred even if run on a real machine).

2 The page was removed due to CP's memory management (i.e., this page fault would not have occurred on a real machine).

To implement a virtual machine with paging on a real machine with paging, additional tables are needed to keep track of not only the status of pages as the virtual machine "sees" them but also their real status. In other words, we must simulate the function of the paging hardware.

To support a virtual system/370 with address translation (which we will call a V370R) CP utilizes the host 370's DAT hardware to simulate the translation hardware of the V370R. The segment and page tables of the operating system in the V370R, such as OS/VS1, indicating how its virtual addresses are to be translated into "real" addresses must be combined with CP's tables indicating how the V370R's "real" addresses are to be mapped onto the main storage of the host System/370. In CP, the combined tables are called *shadow segment tables* and *shadow page tables* (see Figure 9-24).

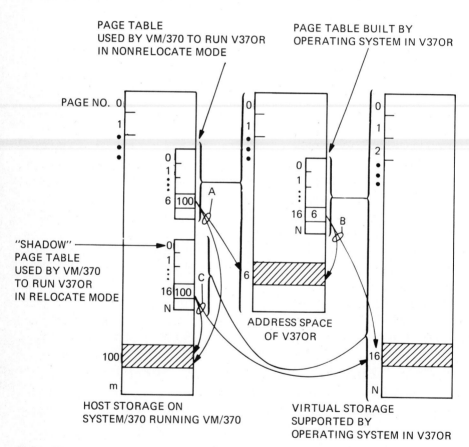

Figure 9-24 Use of shadow tables to support a virtual System/370 with Dynamic Address Translation

We will present a short example to illustrate the use of these shadow tables. CP's map may indicate that page 6 of the virtual machine's storage is at page 100 of the host System/370's storage (see Figure 9-24, point A). If the virtual machine is a V370R in relocate mode, it has a map relating virtual addresses to real addresses that may indicate, for example, that page 16 is in block 6 (Figure 9-24, point B).

To effect the functional simulation of the V370R's map of virtual addresses to its "real" storage, CP must build a shadow table that maps virtual page 16 to real page 100 (Figure 9-24, point C). When running a V370R in nonrelocate mode, CP uses its normal page tables, and when the V370R enters relocate mode, CP uses the shadow tables. It is in this fashion that CP maintains a functional simulation of sufficient fidelity to allow OS/VS1, OS/VS2, as well as VM/370 itself to be run in a V370R.

A more detailed description of the memory management mechanisms can be found in Parmelee (1972) and the VM/370 manuals.

9-5.4 Processor Management

The goals of CP's processor management are similar to those of MULTICS (Section 9-4) in that they (1) limit the number of jobs being multiprogrammed at any one time to prevent thrashing and (2) give preference to interactive jobs. The process state diagram for CP is presented in Figure 9-25.

The jobs being multiprogrammed (called eligible jobs in MULTICS terminology) are divided into two lists or queues, called Q1 and Q2. The remaining jobs are kept in hold states for Q1 or Q2. I/O-intensive and interactive jobs tend to migrate to Q1 whereas CPU-intensive jobs tend toward Q2. To prevent thrashing and ensure good system utilization, limits are placed on the number of jobs allowed in Q1 and Q2. Typical Q1 and Q2 limits are shown in Figure 9-26.

A new job initially entering the system or immediately after receiving input from the user at the terminal is placed in the hold state for Q1. When a vacancy occurs in Q1 Ready, the oldest job in Q1 Hold is selected. (Jobs move from Q2 Hold to Q2 Ready in a similar manner.) The jobs in Q1 Ready are selected to be run in round-robin order. Jobs in Q2 Ready are run only when there are no jobs in Q1 Ready. Thus, a strong preference is given to interactive or I/O-intensive jobs.

If a job must wait for console I/O, it is removed from Q1 and Q2. When the input is received it reenters Q1 Hold and repeats the sequence described above.

A job from Q1 or Q2 is placed in Q2 Hold if:

1 It is in Q1, and if
    a It has run more than its time quantum (e.g., 50 ms) without requesting any I/O, or

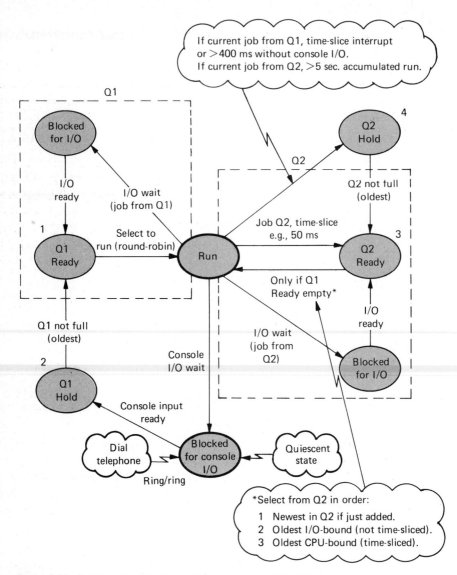

Figure 9-25 Process state diagram for CP component of CP-67/CMS

MAIN MEMORY SIZE (BYTES)	256K	512K	768K	1024K
Q1 limit	3	6	9	12
Q2 limit	1	3	6	9

Figure 9-26 CP-67 Job/process scheduler-typical queue sizes

b It has accumulated 400 ms of CPU time without requesting any console I/O.

2 It is in Q2 and has accumulated 2 seconds of CPU time without requesting any console I/O.

The operator of the computer can set a limit on the total number of users allowed to dial into the system.

9-5.5 Device Management

CP uses all three device management strategies. It uses:

SPOOLed—for I/O to reader, printer, punch

Dedicated—for I/O to tape (CP may, of course, dedicate anything else, e.g., disk, printer)

Shared—for I/O to disk (minidisk), communications controller (lines)

CP must take the following steps for the dedicated or shared strategies:

1 Copy CCWs into system area.

2 Translate addresses of CCWs to reflect physical addresses (bring data pages into main memory if necessary).

3 Translate channel commands that indicate data areas crossing page boundaries into multiple data-chained commands. This is necessary because, in general, contiguous virtual pages are not contiguous in real storage.

4 Schedule I/O.

5 Simulate the I/O interrupt to the virtual machine when the I/O is complete.

6 Release data pages.

SPOOLing is interrupt-driven as described in Chapter 5. Terminals are semi-SPOOLed, with only one I/O CCW chain (copied into special CP buffers).

The device manager keeps track of all devices by maintaining tables with descriptions of the I/O structure of each virtual machine. These tables indicate not only the existence of each I/O element but also the status of the element (e.g., busy or free) and the real hardware component to which it corresponds. Thus when a virtual machine issues an SIO instruction, CP must first determine that the I/O address is valid in the virtual machine's I/O structure and that the elements composing the virtual I/O path (channel, control unit, device) are free. CP must then mark the virtual path busy and build an equivalent I/O task for the real hardware.

Taking an example from the simplest level, a virtual machine's SIO to an IBM 3330 Direct Access Storage Device at I/O address 190 could result in CP's issuing an SIO to a real 3330 at I/O address 332. The real path may, of course, be busy (as when an I/O request for another virtual machine is utilizing the required channel), and, if so, this new I/O request must be deferred until the real path becomes free. When it is free, CP can issue an SIO instruction and proceed with the instructions following the virtual machine's SIO. When the I/O request is completed, CP must reflect this fact in the tables describing the virtual machine's I/O structure; in particular, it must indicate that the previously busy virtual path has become free and that an interruption is pending. Then, when the virtual CPU becomes enabled for the interruption, CP must simulate the effects of the interruption, including the updating of the virtual machine's Channel Status Word.

The I/O handling procedure just described is followed in cases where direct counterparts exist for the elements of the virtual machine's I/O structure. Where no direct counterparts are available, CP must effect detailed simulation of the data flow through the virtual machine I/O structure. For example, virtual 2311 Direct Access Storage Devices (an older storage device) could be simulated using the 3330 storage devices if we wished to run an operating system requiring use of 2311 devices in a virtual machine.

9-5.6 Information Management

The CP component of VM/370 does not provide any information management facilities since none is provided on the bare System/370 hardware. Information management is usually obtained by means of selecting an operating system to run on the virtual machine produced by VM/370. The Conversational Monitor System (CMS) is such an operating system, and it is provided as a component of VM/370. CMS itself could, conceptually, be run on a bare System/370 as a single-user operating system, but it has been specially designed to perform well in a virtual machine environment.

CMS requires a System/370 configuration (virtual or real) with two or more secondary storage devices. In a virtual machine environment, these storage devices may be actual 2314 or 3330 units (dedicated assignment) or, more typically, mini-disks that are portions (i.e., one or more cylinders) of a real device simulated by CP to appear as real devices with smaller than normal capacity (e.g., a 10-cylinder 2314 rather than the standard 200-cylinder 2314).

CMS maintains a separate file directory for each storage device in a manner similar to OS/360's Volume Table of Contents (VTOC). One of the storage devices, called the System Disk, is used to hold the nonresident portions of CMS as well as various system programs, such as assemblers, compilers, or utility programs. The other storage devices are used to hold the user's permanent files, as shown in Figure 9-27.

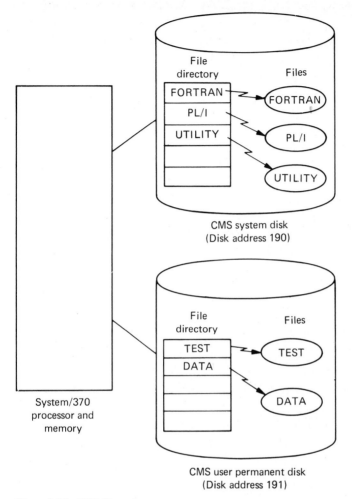

Figure 9-27   CMS file system

CP allows two or more virtual storage devices to be mapped onto the same real storage device. Thus, for example, there is usually only one real CMS System Disk in the system, and all CMS virtual machines share the same disk. CP can prevent users from modifying the contents of the System Disk (i.e., it is read-only, writing is not permitted).

CMS files are identified by three designators: a file name, a file type, and a file mode. The file type indicates the usage of the file, for example, FORTRAN for a FORTRAN source file, TEXT for an object (machine language) file, LISTING for the output of a compiler or assembler. The file mode designates a specific disk (e.g., the System Disk is "S," the Permanent Disk is "A"). Thus, TEST FORTRAN A is a FORTRAN source program, named TEST, located on the user's permanent disk, named A. For many CMS commands the file type and/or file mode may be omitted since default actions are defined.

Figure 9-28 indicates the storage device structure used by the CMS file system (somewhat simplified). The entire device is formated into 800-byte blocks. Certain blocks are used to hold the file directory and space allocation directory. (A Master Directory Block, not shown in Figure 9-28, is used to indicate the locations of directories.) During normal operation these directories are copied into memory. All the remaining blocks are used as: (1) file map blocks, (2) file data blocks, or (3) unused blocks.

The Space Allocation Directory is a *bit map* used to keep track of the unused blocks. If there are n blocks on the device, this directory is n bits long. Thus, a device with 4,000 blocks (4,000 $\times$ 800 = 3,200,000 bytes of storage) needs a Space Allocation Directory of 4,000 bits (500 bytes). If the ith bit is a zero, then block number i is unused.

The file directory contains an entry for each file on that storage device. Each entry specifies the name, current length, and other status information. In addition, each entry specifies the storage block number of that file's primary file map. The primary file map consists of two tables of block numbers, one specifying up to 60 data blocks, the other up to 40 secondary file map blocks.

A few examples will help to illustrate the usage of these file maps. A source file consisting of 250 80-byte records requires 20,000 bytes of storage (25 800-byte file data blocks). The addresses of these 25 data blocks are stored in the primary file map; no secondary file maps are needed. An output listing file consisting of 5,000 132-byte records requires 660,000 bytes of storage (825 800-byte file data blocks). The addresses of the first 60 data blocks are stored in the primary file map. Two additional secondary file maps are needed (each holds 400 block numbers) to store the addresses of the remaining 765 data blocks. The CMS file map structure allows for more efficient direct access to records within a file in comparison to the CTSS file system (described in Section 9-3.6).

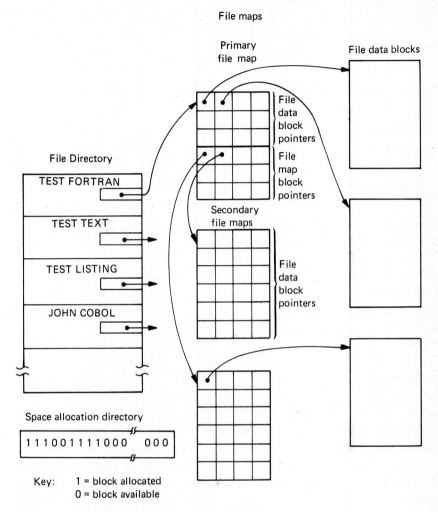

Figure 9-28 Storage device structure used by CMS file system

QUESTIONS[3]

9-1 The HIS 645 allows a segment to consist entirely of either 64-word or 1024-word pages by means of a bit in the corresponding segment table entry.

1 Explain how 64-word pages may be useful to decrease page breakage, especially for small segments.

2 What problems are introduced if the system uses both 64-word and 1024-word pages?

3 Present approaches to cope with the problems of (2).

9-2 In CTSS all I/O is performed directly with no I/O overlap or multiprogramming. Present a technique for incorporating multiprogramming and overlapping of swapping and execution. Comment upon the likely performance impact of these changes.

9-3 MULTICS performs most I/O (other than paging) by use of system buffer areas. Data are moved to or from the user's buffer area for reading or writing, respectively. VM/370, on the other hand, "locks" the pages containing the user's buffer area into main memory and performs the I/O directly to or from the user's area.

1 Present and evaluate the advantages and disadvantages of each approach.

2 Recommend an approach and justify it.

9-4 In VM/370 Q1 jobs have a strict priority preference over Q2 jobs.

1 Is it possible that a Q2 job will never be run?

2 Suggest a modification to VM/370's processor management to provide at least guaranteed minimum service to Q2 jobs.

9-5 It is possible to combine many aspects of information management and memory management on systems that use paging and segmentation. Figures A, B, and C below illustrate three possible ways of structuring these parts of the system. Briefly state a reason for choosing each approach.

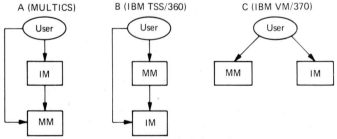

MM = memory management, IM = information management

---

[3]The instructor may wish to supplement this chapter by use of more detailed reference manuals on OS, CTSS, MULTICS, VM/370, or some other operating system. If so, the students may be assigned to investigate and write more detailed descriptions of resource managers of these systems.

9-6   The IBM 360 MVT system is primarily interrupt-driven. That is, when one user causes an interrupt (I/O or SVC), another process is begun. However, IBM has also included the option of timeslicing groups of tasks.

1   Discuss the merits and drawbacks of each method.

2   How might a priority structure be implemented for each of these methods (a structure in which higher priority jobs will be executed first)? (*Hint:* There are never more than eight jobs in core at one time.)

   IBM also provides for the temporary dynamic expansion of a job beyond its originally specified region size by means of ROLL-OUT/ROLL-IN. When a job needs more core storage, this feature attempts to obtain unassigned storage. If it fails, it rolls out a blocked job and temporarily assigns its storage to the requesting job. When the requesting job releases the storage, the other job is rolled back in.

3   Discuss the value of this feature. Consider time, priorities, etc. What problems might be caused by the use of this feature?

9-7   In this chapter we discussed CTSS's process scheduling algorithm (see Section 9-3.4.2). Call the basic time quantum Q (500 ms in CTSS) and the maximum static time X (1 minute in CTSS) i.e., if a job doesn't get run for X minutes, it moves up to the next higher priority level.

   For the following jobs, assume Q = 100 ms and X = 1 second.

JOB COMMAND	RUN TIME	SIZE
Editor	400 ms	3K
Compiler	5 sec	20K
APL	500 ms	10K
Tape dump	1 sec	2K

1   Assuming that all the commands are entered at the same time in the order listed, plot for each job its quantum level versus time.

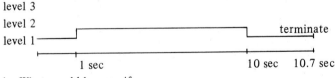

b   What would happen if

   i) $Q \to \infty$

   ii) $Q \to 0$

   iii) $X \to \infty$

   iv) $X \to 0$

c   What would be the criteria for an optimum value of X, Q?

9-8 The diagram below illustrates the logical organization of the IBM CP-67 time-sharing system:

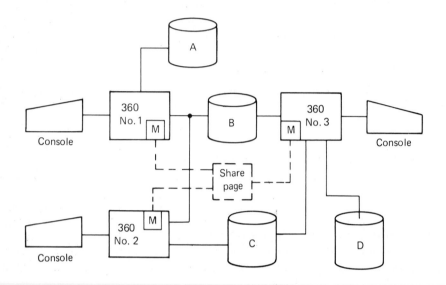

Each user appears to have his own 360 with its own private (nonshared) memory. The disks themselves may be connected to more than one user's 360. For example, disk B is connected to all three users' 360s, but disk C is connected only to users 2 and 3. Thus some form of sharing is possible via the shared disk drives.

1 Assuming that there is no other physically shared memory except via disk drives, would there by any problems in developing a file-sharing facility (e.g., two or more users reading or writing files on a shared disk)? (*Note:* There is a separate copy of the file system on each user's 360.)

This question probes some of the problems associated with adding a hierarchical data file structure and dynamically controlled sharing. One change in CP-67 is provided.

A shared block of memory is available that is common to all users' 360s. This shared block, 4096 bytes long, is illustrated by dotted lines in the diagram above. (For example, locations 4096–8192 are common to all the machines.)

Every time reading or writing into a file occurs, a lock is produced in the shared block for each user. A read lock is differentiated from a write lock. Several users may read from the same file, but only one may write into it at any one time. Subsequent attempts to access that file by other users loop until that write lock is released. Typically, the wait time is short. In addition, there is a lock associated with the overall shared page, which is set with the special 360 test-and-set instruction.

2   What information must be included in a lock?

3   Why would you need to differentiate between a read lock and a write lock? In particular, why do we need a read lock?

4   Why is there a lock on the shared page? Describe what might happen if that lock were not utilized.

5   Since locks are maintained by each independent 360 machine, many problems can arise. Define some of these problems. (*Hint:* Each user has a STOP button that allows him to stop his process and leave his machine temporarily.) Also, only one shared 4096-byte block exists. What problems would this cause?

6   Suggest solutions to (5) and/or propose a better design for achieving dynamic sharing. Try to determine, for example, what you would do when a user is waiting to access the shared page or some particular file.

9-9   The Humble Timesharing Co. (HTS) is a small struggling timesharing service bureau handling about 50 simultaneous remote users (jobs). HTS uses the standard Bonanza I Real-Time Multiprogramming Timesharing Universal Operating System (with paging and segmentation). After hiring Frank Fasttalker as head salesman, HTS now has 100 simultaneous users and is having trouble maintaining adequate throughput. Harry Moredough, HTS's computer agent, has suggested four changes to improve throughput:

a   Buy more main memory.

b   Purchase the new and faster Model 2 CPU.

c   Replace the old Elephant Model A drums with the new and faster Pachyderm B drums.

d   Switch to the Bonanza II operating system with improved information management features.

For each of these suggestions describe circumstances (job mix, environment, e.g., CPU-bound) where (1) the change will have significant results and (2) the change will result in very little improvement.

9-10   You are now reasonably familiar with the structure of OS/360 as well as MULTICS and VM/370. As you may recall, the standard 360 does not provide any relocation, paging, or segmentation hardware; thus OS/360 uses a partitioned allocation scheme.

You are the chief systems programmer for a computer leasing company. Your company finds that it has a warehouse full of 360s (including some 360/67s) because of the development of IBM's new 370. It has been suggested that all the 360s be upgraded to include the paging segmentation features of the 360/67, since it is such a neat machine.

Since most of your potential customers currently use OS/360—and wish to continue to use it (it's habit-forming)—you have been asked to make incremental changes to OS/360 to take advantage of this neat hardware. Remember, since you have to do all the coding and debugging yourself, the changes should be minimal (you are, of course, allowed to work 24 hours a day).

1 Under what user circumstances would this new hardware and operating system be of no advantage to performance?

2 Under what user circumstances would this new hardware and operating system be of advantage to performance?

3 How would you handle memory management? In particular, what changes would you make to current OS/360 memory management?

4 What problems does the use of paging have for device management? How would you solve these problems in order to get very good I/O performance?

5 What problems does current OS/360 have when it removes a low-priority job from memory (roll-out) to make room for a high-priority job? Does the paging/segmentation hardware help decrease this problem? How?

9-11 For students who successfully completed question 1-15, this question is the next step.

1 Define and describe an operating system superior to OS, CTSS, MULTICS, and VM/370.

2 Produce complete flowcharts.

3 Implement this operating system in either 360 machine language or PL/I.

10-1 CROSS REFERENCES TO ANNOTATED BIBLIOGRAPHY[1]

BASIC PRINCIPLES
Altucher et al., 1966
Donovan, 1972
Kapur, 1970
Knuth, 1968
Martin, 1971
Morris, 1968
Pankhurst, 1968
Presser and White, 1972
Price, 1971

DEBUGGING AIDS
Josephs, 1969
Kulsrud, 1969
Van Horn, 1967

EXECUTIVES (Monitors, Supervisors)
Gaines, 1971
Huxtable, Warwick, 1967
Reiter, 1967
Rosin, 1969

FILE SYSTEMS (Information Management)
Bensoussan, 1969
Chapin, 1969
Katzan, 1971
Madnick, 1969

HARDWARE
Ahearn, Dishon, and Snively, 1972
Amdahl and Amdahl, 1967
Cashman, 1972
Femling, 1971

HIGHER-LEVEL LANGUAGES
Boehm, 1973
Corbato, 1969
Donovan, 1972

HISTORICAL
Rosen, 1969
Rosin, 1969

JOB CONTROL LANGUAGE
Brown, 1970
Cadow, 1970

LANGUAGE PROCESSORS
Donovan, 1972
Freiburghouse, 1969
Mclure, 1972

MEMORY MANAGEMENT (Design Philosophies)
Abate and Dabner, 1969
Belady and Knehner, 1969
Coffman, 1969
Considine and Weis, 1969

---

[1] For the reader's convenience we have grouped the references under a number of main subject areas. The annotated bibliography follows this list.

Denning, 1968
Denning, 1967
Dennis, 1965
Femling, 1971
Fields, 1971
Fotheringham, 1961
Funchel and Heller, 1967
Johnson, 1973
Katzan, 1971
Liptay, 1968
Madnick, 1973
Mattson et al., 1970
Meade, 1970
Randell and Kuehner, 1967
Reiter, 1967
Risko, 1968
Ross, 1967
Teorey, 1972
Teorey and Pinkerton, 1971
Vareha, Rutledge, and Gold, 1969
Wilkes, 1965

MICROPROGRAMMING
Hussen, 1970
Rosin, 1969
Wilkes, 1969

MODELING
Abate and Dubner, 1969
Arden and Bottner, 1969
Belady, 1966
Buzen, 1971
Buzen, 1973
Coffman, 1969
Coffman and Ryan, 1971
Denning, 1969
Denning, 1967
Denning and Schwartz, 1972
Drake, 1967
Estrin, Muntz, and Uzgalis, 1972
Feller, 1968
Fuchi, Tanaka, Manago, and Yuba, 1969
Goldberg, 1973
Katz, 1966
Kay, 1972
Kleinrock, 1970
MacDougal, 1970
Madnick, 1968
McKinney, 1969
Nielson, 1967
Oppenheimer and Weizer, 1967
Schwartz, 1973
Sekino, 1972
Teorey, 1972
Teorey and Pinkerton, 1971
Winograd, Morganstein, and Herman, 1971

MULTICS
Bensoussan, Clingen, and Daley, 1969
Corbató, 1969
Corbató and Vyssotosky, 1965
Corbató, Clingen, and Saltzer, 1972
Daley and Dennis, 1968
Feieritag and Organick, 1971
Freiburghouse, 1969
Organick, 1972
Saltzer and Gintell, 1969
Schroeder, 1971
Sekino, 1972

MULTIPROGRAMMING
Arden and Bottner, 1969
Browne, Lan, and Baskett, 1972
Buzen, 1971
Hellerman and Smith, 1970
Lehman and Rosenfeld, 1968
MacDougal, 1970
Schwartz, 1973

OPERATING SYSTEMS AND THEIR
PRINCIPLES
Betourne, Boulenger, Ferrie, Kaiser,
    Krakowiak, and Mossiere, 1970
Conti, Gibson, and Pittowsky, 1968
Crisman, 1965
Denning, 1971
Dennis and Van Horn, 1966
Dijkstra, 1968
Donovan, 1972
Enwin and Jensen, 1970
Gaines, 1971
Hansen, 1970
Ho-Nien, Peck, and Pollard, 1969
Jones, 1969
Katzan, 1970
Liskov, 1972
McFarland, 1970
Needham and Hartley, 1969
Saltzer, 1966
Sevick et al., 1972
Watson, 1970

PAGING AND PAGING SYSTEMS
Bard, 1973
Belady, Nelson, and Shedler, 1969
Brawn and Gustavson, 1968
Coffman and Varian, 1968
Corbató, 1969
Denning, 1969
Denning, 1968
Denning and Schwartz, 1972
Gustavson, 1968

Hatfield, 1972
Madnick, 1973
Oppenheimer and Weizer, 1967
Randell and Kuehner, 1968
Schroeder, 1971
Schwartz, 1973
Seligman, 1968
Spirn and Denning, 1972
Vareha, Rutledge, and Gold, 1969
Winograd, Morganstein, and Herman, 1971

PERFORMANCE EVALUATION AND
MEASUREMENT
Abate and Dubner, 1969
Arden and Bottner, 1969
Calingaert, 1967
Cantrell, 1968
Hatfield, 1972
Karush, 1969
Lehman and Rosenfeld, 1968
Lucas, 1971
Saltzer and Gintell, 1969
Schroeder, 1971
Wulf, 1969

PROCESSES AND PROCESS
COMMUNICATION
Bernstein, Deflefsen, and Kerr, 1969
Dijkstra, 1968
Dijkstra, 1968
Gaines, 1971
Habermann, 1972
Horning and Randell, 1973
Spier and Organick, 1969
Varney, 1971

PROTECTION
Comber, 1969
Conway, Maxwell, and Morgan, 1972
Graham, 1967
Graham and Denning, 1972
Hoffman, 1969
Lampson, 1971
Lampson, 1969
Madnick and Donovan, 1973
Molho, 1970
Needham, 1972
Scherf, 1973
Schroeder and Saltzer, 1972
Skatrud, 1969
Weissman, 1969

PROVING THEOREMS
Dijkstra, 1965
Fontao, 1971

Habermann, 1971
Kahn, 1971

SCHEDULING
Abell, Rosen, and Wagner, 1970
Baskett, 1971
Browne, Lan, and Basket, 1972
Buzen, 1971
Coffman and Kleinrock, 1968
Hansen, 1971
Kleinrock, 1970
Lampson, 1968
Oppenheimer and Weizer, 1967
Rodriguez-Rosell, 1971
Teorey, 1972
Teorey and Pinkerton, 1971
Varney, 1971

STRUCTURED PROGRAMMING AND
RELIABLE SOFTWARE
Dahl, Dijkstra, and Hoare, 1972
Liskov, 1972
Mealy et al., 1968

SYSTEM DEADLOCK
Bensoussan, 1969
Coffman, Elphick, and Shoshani, 1971
Dijkstra, 1968
Easton, 1971
Fontao, 1971
Habermann, 1969
Havender, 1968
Holt, 1972
Murphey, 1968
Saltzer, 1966

SYSTEMS PROGRAMMING
Donovan, 1972
Neumann, 1969
Presser and White, 1972

TIMESHARING
Considine and Weis, 1969
Corbató, 1962
Earl and Bugly, 1969
Foster, 1971
Hargraves, 1969
Karush, 1969
Kleinrock, 1970
Lichtenberger, 1965
Linde, Weissman, and Fox, 1969
Madnick, 1966
McKinney, 1969
Motobayashi, 1969
Reiter, 1967
Scherr, 1965
Schwartz, 1964

Watson, 1970
Weissman, 1969
Wilkes, 1968
Winogrand, Morganstein, and Herman,
1971

VIRTUAL MEMORY
Belady, 1966
Bensoussan, Clingen, and Daley, 1969

Coffman and Ryan, 1971
Daley and Dennis, 1968
Denning, 1970
Hatfield, 1971
Madnick, 1972
Morrison, 1973
Parmelee et al, 1972
Sayer, 1969
Winograd, Morganstein, and Herman,
1971

10-2 ANNOTATED BIBLIOGRAPHY[1]

Abate, J. and H. Dubner: "Optimizing the Performance of a Drum-Like Storage," *IEEE TC*, vol. C-18, no. 11, pp. 992–996, Nov. 1969.

The paper covers the analysis of an auxiliary storage system that manages information with head-per-track access and is hardware-queued to service requests with minimal rotational latency. An abstracted view of the memory subsystem permits determination of the waiting time for a transaction in the queues. Expected performance is presented by graphical depictions of the results of the study.

Abell, V. A., S. Rosen, and R. E. Wagner: "Scheduling in a General Purpose Operating System," *Proceedings, AFIPS, 1970, FJCC*, vol. 37, pp. 89–96.

The MACE operating system on a CDC 6000 series computer is discussed in terms of job scheduling and job management techniques. Scheduling interdependencies are brought out.

Ahearn, G. R., Y. Dishon, and R. N. Snively: "Design Innovations of the IBM 3830 and 2835 Storage Control Units," *IBM Journal of Research and Development*, vol. 16, no. 1, pp. 11–18, Jan. 1972.

This article illustrates the use of microprocessors to produce sophisticated and flexible mass storage control units.

Altucher et al. (The Computer Usage Company): *Programming the IBM System/360*, John Wiley & Sons, Inc., New York, 1966.

Basic System/360 assembler language is presented. Starts off on the ground floor.

---

[1] Abbreviations are as follows:

AFIPS	American Federation of Information Processing Societies
CACM	Communications of the Association of Computing Machinery
FJCC	Fall Joint Computer Conference
IEEE TC	Institute of Electrical and Electronic Engineers, Transactions on Computers
IFIP	International Federation of Information Processing
JACM	Journal of the Association of Computing Machinery
SJCC	Spring Joint Computer Conference

Amdahl, G. M. and L. D. Amdahl: "Fourth-Generation Hardware," *Datamation*, pp. 25–26, Jan. 1967.

Arden, B. W. and Bottner: "Measurement and Performance of a Multiprogramming System," *Second ACM Symposium on Operating Systems Principles*, Princeton University, pp. 130–146, Oct. 1969.
A pragmatic approach to performance evaluation is suggested. Detailed measurements on the Michigan Time Sharing (MTS) system precede an analysis of the data (the measurement techniques are discussed). The measurements were designed to extract data relevant to performance analyses that fit formal yet realistic system models. Specifics of the models include a central serverlike model used to determine ideal system response time. It is concluded that a good load measure for efficiency is the ratio of ideal to actual response time.

Bard, Y.: "Performance Criteria and Measurement of a Time-Sharing System," *IBM Systems Journal*, vol. 10, pp. 193–216, 1971.
A study of tradeoffs between CPU, I/O, and paging.

Bard, Y.: "A Characterization of Program Paging in a Time Sharing Environment," *Cambridge Scientific Center*, G320-2083, Feb. 1973.
A review of analyzing program behavior (program paging in a fixed-core partition) with a static parachor curve results in the conclusion that the curve is not accurate enough because a program's resident set size and paging frequency are time/load-dependent quantities.

Baskett, F.: "The Dependence of Computer System Queues upon Processing Time Distribution and Central Processor Scheduling," *Third ACM Symposium on Operating Systems Principles*, Stanford University, pp. 109–113, Oct. 1971.
The method of stages is employed to investigate an upper and lower bound to round-robin scheduling. A model called a processor-sharing central server is used. Nonexponential service distributions are included. The use of actual data is verifying the model indicates usefulness of the results.

Belady, L. A.: "A Study of Replacement Algorithms for a Virtual Storage Computer," *IBM Systems Journal*, vol. 5, no. 5, pp. 78–101, 1966.
Motivation for virtual storage computers is provided as an introduction to the study of one of their more dynamic variants: block replacement mechanisms. The development of probabilistic models to study typical algorithms ranges the gamut from random, which requires no special information, to so-called optimal (MIN), which manages replacement with perfect future knowledge of reference patterns. Replacement statistics were gathered by a program monitor and used as input to a replacement algorithm, which was then employed to attain predictive results. The algorithms are studied and compared in detail.

Belady, L. A. and C. J. Knehner: "Dynamic Space Sharing in Computer Systems," *CACM*, vol. 12, no. 5, pp. 282–288, May 1969.
Various demand paging algorithms are presented.

Belady, L. A., R. A. Nelson, and G. S. Shedler: "An Anomaly in Space-Time Characteristics of Certain Programs Running in a Paging Environment," *CACM*, vol. 12, no. 6, pp. 349–353, June 1969.
The interesting problem of an increasing number of program page faults as the

number of pages available to the program increases is uncovered through an example of an FIFO page-replacement strategy.

Bensoussan, A.: "Overview of the Locking Strategy in the File System," *Multics Systems Programmers Manual*, Section BG. 19.00, pp. 1-10, Nov. 1969.

Discussed is an approach to implementing parallel processing in ring 0 that results in synchronizing of processes each time a ring 0 datum, the value of which is subject to modification, is shared. It is found necessary to associate a lock with each data set type involved (i.e., a directory, a branch in a directory, etc.) The algorithm selected to handle the synchronization and sharing includes an interesting backup operation termed *decompute*.

Bensoussan, A., C. T. Clingen, and R. C. Daley: "The Multics Virtual Memory," *Second ACM Symposium on Operating Systems Principles*, Princeton University, pp. 30-42, Oct. 1969.

Sharing information is automated by operations in a segmented environment where "each potentially sharable (segment) carries its own independent attribute of size and access privilege." Considerations with respect to design and implementation of such an environment in MULTICS are discussed, and the need for virtual memory mechanisms to back up the segmented address space is motivated. Discussion of software and hardware interaction in this context is included.

Bernstein, A. J., G. D. Deflefsen, and R. H. Kerr: "Process Control and Communication," *Second ACM Symposium on Operating Systems Principles*, Princeton University, pp. 60-66, 1969.

The "exec" is an operating system designed for a GE 600 computer. The multipurpose monitor has an interesting process structure that is described in this paper. The process environment consists of up to four parts called *logical segments*, which are relocated and protected by *Base Address Registers*. The communications structure implemented is revealed and examples of its use are provided.

Betourne, C., J. Boulenger, J. Ferrie, C. Kaiser, S. Krakowiak, and J. Mossiere: "Process Management and Resource Sharing in the Multiaccess System ESOPE," *CACM*, vol. 13, no. 12, pp. 727-733, Dec. 1970.

The design principles of a hierarchically organized, process-based computer operating system are presented. Implementation details are forgone in the attempt to explain underlying relationships among process management, virtual memory activities, file system organization, and user management. The paper is detailed enough to give more than a mere flavor of the issues.

Boehm, Barry W., "Software and Its Impact: A Quantitative Assessment," *Datamation*, pp. 48-59, May 1973.

This paper summarizes some of the results of a study conducted for the Air Force Systems Command. The study investigated the costs of software development and factors that affect these costs.

Brawn, B. S. and F. G. Gustavson: "Program Behavior in a Paging Environment," *Proceedings, AFIPS, 1968, FJCC*, vol. 33, pt. II, pp. 1019-1032.

Programming style affects program performance in demand-paged virtual storage computers, and this paper gives empirical test results, for both mono- and multiprogrammed job execution, on real core constraints, page replacement algorithms, and program style/program locality. It is observed that style may be more important than physical system and design decisions, i.e., choice of page replacement algorithm.

Brown, G. D.: *System/360: Job Control Language*, John Wiley & Sons, Inc., New York, 1970.
This book gives a brief overview of IBM System/360 JCL and system-related concepts.

Browne, J. C., J. Lan, and F. Baskett: "The Interaction of Multiprogramming Job Scheduling and CPU Scheduling," *Proceedings, AFIPS, 1972, FJCC*, vol. 41, pt. 1, pp. 13–22.
A system simulation of a CDC 6600 system is employed to assess the dependency of overall system performance on the effects of both job scheduling and CPU scheduling algorithms. This simulation study touches on some interesting inter-dependencies.

The Burroughs Corporation: *The Descriptor—A Definition of the B5000 Information Processing System*, The Burroughs Corporation, Detroit, 1961. This early paper introduces the concept of a "descriptor" and a form of segmented address space.

Buzen, J. P.: "Computational Algorithms for Closed Queuing Networks with Exponential Servers," *CACM*, vol. 16, no. 9, Sept. 1973.
This paper provides a brief description of the Central Server Model along with a set of algorithms useful in analyzing many queueing network models.

Buzen, J. P.: "Queuing Network Models of Multiprogramming," doctoral dissertation, Harvard University, 1971.
Buzen reviews in detail the past research in the area of scheduling philosophies and includes a comprehensive bibliography. He presents a conceptual model of multiprogramming called the Central Server Model and proceeds to develop a rationale for performance evolution based on his model. He derives new computational algorithms that make solution of the analytical model fast and efficient. A great starting point for those interested in research in this area.

Buzen, J. P. and U. O. Gagliardi: "The Evolution of Virtual Machine Architecture," *National Computer Conference*, pp. 291–299, 1973.
The historical development and motivation of virtual machine architecture is presented. Some unresolved issues are presented.

Cadow, H. W.: *OS/360: Job Control Language*, Prentice-Hall, Inc., Englewood Cliffs, N.J., 1970.
A complete overview of system-related concepts is presented here.

Calingaert, P.: "System Performance Evaluation: Survey and Appraisal," *CACM*, vol. 10, no. 1, pp. 12–18, Jan. 1967.
Measures of performance, such as throughput, turnaround, and availability are defined. The use of instruction mixes and kernels is presented. The roles of analysis, simulation, and synthesis are discussed.

Cantrell, H. N. and A. L. Ellison: "Multiprogramming System Performance Measurement and Analysis, *Proceedings, AFIPS, 1968, SJCC*, vol. 32, pp. 213-221. A good analysis is given here.

Chapin, N.: "Common File Organization Techniques Compared," *Proceedings, AFIPS, 1969, FJCC*, vol. 35, pp. 413-422.
Some of the basic definitions are presented, i.e., file organization versus file structure and data management. Sequential, indexed sequential, and random file organization are compared in concept. Detailed yet concise information is provided. An interesting time-flow-graph approach is used to differentiate among the various file access methods.

Codd, E. F.: "A Relational Model of Data for Large Shared Data Banks," *CACM*, vol. 13, no. 6, pp. 377-387, June 1970.
Future users of large data banks must be protected from having to know how the data are organized in the machine (the internal representation). Activities of users at terminals and most application programs should remain unaffected when the internal representation of data is changed and even when some aspects of the external representation are changed. Changes in data representation will often be needed as a result of changes in query, update, and report traffic and natural growth in the types of stored information.
   Inadequacies of tree-structured files are discussed. A model based on n-ary relations, a normal form for database relations, and the concept of a universal data sublanguage are introduced. In Section 2, certain operations on relations (other than logical inference) are discussed and applied to the problems of redundancy and consistency in the user's model.

Coffman, E. G., Jr.: "Analysis of a Drum Input/Output Queue under Scheduled Operation in a Paged Computer System," *JACM*, vol. 16, no. 1, pp. 73-90, Jan. 1969.
Scheduling page I/O operations is the key to the design of efficient virtual memory environments of this kind. In this paper, a model for a rotating magnetic drum is studied in detail in the context of these systems. The analysis results in a determination of drum utilization as well as other vital and often referenced statistics (e.g., Sekino's thesis uses the parameters for utilization determined here to model secondary memory operations). An example of well-developed mathematical modeling.

Coffman, E. G., Jr., M. J. Elphick, and A. Shoshani: "System Deadlocks," *ACM Computing Surveys*, vol. 3, no. 2, pp. 67-78, June 1971.
A short example opens the discussion of deadlock and leads to a definition that specifies necessary conditions for embrace. State graphs are then shown to be effective means for detecting the said conditions. Detection and recovery techniques are then evaluated in terms of the cost of their approach. Included in the paper is a presentation of deadlock avoidance using information on resource requirements (which is done when full information must be provided as well as when full requirements are not known).
   This paper surveys the most salient features of current techniques and makes makes thèm both understandable and readable.

Coffman, E. G., Jr. and L. C. Varian: "Further Experimental Data on the Behavior of Programs in a Paging Environment," *CACM*, vol. 11, no. 7, pp. 471–474, July 1968.

The dynamic behavior of programs operating under a demand paging, memory management algorithm is studied in order to gather empirical data on program paging characteristics. The data are gathered from the interpretative execution of sample programs. Relevant statistics (i.e., number of instructions between page faults) are presented. These statistics are useful for studying alternative page replacement algorithms and the effect of memory size on program paging.

Coffman, E. G., Jr. and T. A. Ryan: "A Study of Storage Partitioning Using Mathematical Model of Locality," *Third ACM Symposium on Operating Systems Principles*, Stanford University, pp. 122–129, Oct. 1971.

The concern here for virtual memory management is centered around two basic strategies: fixed partitioning and dynamic partitioning. Proposed for studying these schemes is a probabilistic model of locality, which is a stationary Gaussian process based on the concept of working set. Advantages of the dynamic scheme, such as producing economies when working-set size varies dynamically, are clearly demonstrated.

Coffman, E. G., Jr. and L. Kleinrock: "Computer Scheduling Methods and Their Counter Measures," *Proceedings, AFIPS, 1968, SJCC*, vol. 32, pp. 11–21.

The paper presents the methods of priority scheduling available and discusses their strengths and weaknesses on the basis of performance criteria such as response time and resource availability. Also, those approaches to undermining a service discipline so as to achieve high-priority usage are mentioned in the interest of designing a workable queuing mechanism. The paper serves as an excellent reference work on scheduling measures. It is very readable since relationships are made qualitatively, while the mathematical basis for the conclusions is left to the bibliography.

Comber, E. V.: "Management of Confidential Information," *Proceedings, AFIPS, 1969, FJCC*, vol. 35, pp. 135–143.

This qualitative approach to analyzing the underlying "philosophical and ethical questions that are inherent in the concept of 'privacy' " is valuable not only because it reflects the basic properties a well-protected system should have but also because it serves as a good referral for someone interested in a basic, stepwise description of privacy. It can be read on various levels, since the experienced systems analyst can read further into the suggested criteria and system services suggested.

Comfort, W. T.: "A Computing System Design for User Services," *Proceedings, AFIPS, 1965, FJCC*, vol. 27, pt. 1, pp. 619–628

Considine, J. P. and A. H. Weis: "Establishment and Maintenance of a Storage Hierarchy for an On-Line Data Base under TSS/360," *Proceedings, AFIPS, 1969, FJCC*, vol. 35, pp. 433–440.

Management of an online accessible database, restricted by limited storage, was facilitated by establishment of a dynamic storage volume hierarchy. Described are the commands implemented for governing just such a system for TSS/360. The commands give a flavor of the operational requirements of online database systems.

Conti, C. J., D. H. Gibson, and S. H. Pittowsky: "Structural Aspects of the System/ 360 Model 85: I. General Organization," *IBM Systems Journal*, vol. 7, no. 1, pp. 2-14, 1968.
A description of an early baffer (cache) memory system is given.

Conway, R. W. Maxwell, and H. Morgan: "Selective Security Capabilities in ASAP— A File Management System," *Proceedings, AFIPS, 1972, SJCC*, vol. 40, pp. 1181-1186.
This is a short paper on the development of a file management system that explains those precautions taken to prevent users from retrieving information they are not allowed to. Although implementation issues concerning protection in more general purpose systems are not treated, a flavor for protection issues is afforded.

Corbató, F. J.: "A Paging Experiment with the MULTICS System," in Feshbach and Ingard (eds.), *In Honor of Philip M. Morse*, M.I.T. Press, Cambridge, Mass., 1969, pp. 217-228.
A detailed description of the MULTICS paging algorithm lends insight into how one goes about implementing such a system feature. The MULTICS algorithm has a parametric nature that appears as FIFO at one extreme and LRU at the other. Experiments demonstrate its performance characteristics.

Corbató, F. J.: "PL/1 as a Tool for System Programming," *Datamation*, pp. 68, 73-76, May 1969.
This paper presents a candid evaluation of the nature of implementing and using PL/1 for programming a major computer system development effort. Discussed in the context of MULTICS, both advantages and disadvantages of the language are related. The overall conclusion is that since PL/1 has many desirable features not found in other higher level languages, it was able to provide the necessary environment for the involved development work.

Corbató, F. J., C. T. Clingen, and J. H. Saltzer: "Multics—The First Seven Years," *Proceedings, AFIPS, 1972, SJCC*, vol. 40, pp. 571-584.
A view of the design goals, background development, and general nature of MULTICS is provided in a very readable exposé. The technical issues underlying the success of MULTICS are relegated to the references and concentration is on presenting a thorough picture of an information-processing utility. The insight gained from MULTICS as a learning experience is of particular interest to the system designer.

Corbató, F. J. et al.: "An Experimental Time-Sharing System," *Proceedings, AFIPS, 1962, SJCC*, vol. 21, pp. 335-344.
A discussion of the timesharing system CTSS is given here.

Corbató, J. F. and V. A. Vyssotosky: "Introduction and Overview of the MULTICS System," *Proceedings, AFIPS, 1965, FJCC*, vol. 27, pp. 185-196.
This basic overview presents the original MULTICS design goals and the complement of hardware upon which the system operates.

Crisman, P. A.: *The Compatible Time-Sharing System; A Programmer's Guide*, 2d ed., M.I.T. Press, Cambridge, Mass., 1965.

Dahl, O. J., E. W. Dijkstra, and C. A. Hoare: *Structured Programming*, Academic Press, London and New York, 1972.
Overall, concern is with analyzing the conceptual tools available for the design of programs and the prevention of programming oversights and errors. Chapter 1 consists of Dijkstra's notes on Structured Programming, which give a description of the top-down programming method. Chapter 2 contains Hoare's notes on Data Structuring. This is an application of Dijkstra's principles to the design of data structures including their implementation and use. Chapter 3 contains Dahl and Hoare's Hierarchical Program Structures, which provide a synthesis of the first two chapters and expounds the close theoretical and practical connections between design of data and design of programs using Simula 1967 constructs.

Daley, R. C. and J. B. Dennis: "Virtual Memory, Processes, Sharing in MULTICS," *CACM*, vol. 11, no. 5, p. 306, May 1968.
The concepts of process and address space as used by MULTICS are described, details of the MULTICS addressing mechanism follow, and dynamic linking is explained. A good discussion of those features of a system that permit users to cooperate in their programming efforts.

Denning, P. J.: "Effects of Scheduling on File Memory Operations," *Proceedings, AFIPS, 1967, SJCC*, vol. 30, pp. 9-18.
The object of this paper is to present an overview of file system organization as a backdrop for a discussion to maximize file I/O throughput (i.e., the average number of requests serviced per unit time). Both disk and drum models are incorporated into a system model and various policies for their operation are investigated, i.e., drum (FCFS, SATF) and disk (SSTF, SATF, FLFS).

Denning, P. J.: "Equipment Configuration in Balanced Computer Systems," *IEEE TC*, vol. C-18, no. 11, pp. 1008-1114, Nov. 1969.
The equipment configuration in a balanced computer is defined as the proper relative capacities of processor and memory resources that create demands that match available equipment. The solution results, gathered by reasoning from basic probabilistic arguments, are presented in the form of theorems that relate to a selected balance policy. Application to a demand paging system is presented.

Denning, P. J.: "The Working Set Model for Program Behavior," *CACM*, vol. 11, no. 5, pp. 323-333, May 1968.
A dynamic management technique for paged memories is the goal achieved through use of "the working set model" of handling program behavior. The working set is defined as "the collection of [the program's] most recently used pages." Probabilistic arguments lead to analytical expressions for relevant barometers such as paging traffic. In addition, the model is used to formulate a resource allocation policy based on system demand.

Denning, P. J.: "Third Generation Computer Systems," *ACM Computing Surveys*, vol. 3, no. 4, pp. 175-216, Dec. 1971.

This is a review of the basic concepts of operating systems features found in computer systems from the mid-sixties to the present. Common system properties are cited and programming objectives are discussed in context. Also, issues basic to the areas of memory management, process management, resource allocation, and protection are opened for discussion. The fully annotated bibliography covers many current and useful papers and books in the field.

Denning, P. J.: "Thrashing: Its Causes and Prevention," *Proceedings, AFIPS, 1968, FJCC*, vol. 33, pp. 915-922.
The interdependency between memory management and processor utilization is uncovered in a discussion of thrashing behavior. Of particular interest is the effect of page fetch time T on the effective busy time of the processor. At the end, Denning briefly speculates on reducing T by using a three-level memory system and possibly using small page sizes (since access delay is assumed to be minimal for second-level store).

Denning, P. J.: "Virtual Memory," *ACM Computing Surveys*, vol. 2, no. 3, pp. 153-190, Sept. 1970.
Reviewed are the basic concepts associated with the development of virtual memory management strategies. A contrast between segmentation and paging lends insight into implementation issues. The outgrowth of this discussion of "mechanisms" is a discussion of policies, i.e., where, when, and how you access and store information. This, in turn, provides motivation for a look at program behavior. Related issues of locality of reference, working set, and thrashing arise and are placed in perspective. The article combines present knowledge on virtual systems and provides a stepping stone for future research. An extensive bibliography is provided.

Denning, P. J. and S. C. Schwartz: "Properties of the Working-Set Model," *CACM*, vol. 15, no. 3, pp. 191-198, March 1972.
A mathematical model is presented with emphasis on the time-varying nature of the working-set characteristics. Algorithms for estimating the relationship between working-set size and missing page rate are developed in a manner that permits both time average and stochastic arguments to complement each other nicely. The analysis includes the relationships existing among average working-set size, missing page rate, and the interference-interval distribution.

Dennis, J. B.: "Segmentation and the Design of Multiprogramming Computer Systems," *JACM*, vol. 12, no. 4, pp. 589-602, Oct. 1965.
The concept of segmented name and address space is described, as well as an approach to their implementation. This latter issue involves discussion of hardware and software support. Comparisons with other addressing structures are made.

Dennis, J. B. and E. C. Van Horn: "Programming Semantics for Multiprogrammed Computations," *CACM*, vol. 9, no. 3, pp. 143-155, March 1966.
One of the original references on development of systems to support segmentation, sharing, parallel execution of programs, and multiprogramming. The concept of capabilities is developed and use is made of hierarchical directories in providing protection and sharing.

Dijkstra, E. W.: "Cooperating Sequential Processes," *Programming Languages*, Academic Press, 1968, pp. 43-111.

Semaphores are conceptual/physical mechanisms for coordinating process activity and thus for facilitating resource management. The approach to their use is motivated by example and explained in depth. Constrained allocation to avoid deadly embrace is discussed in context.

Dijkstra, E. W.: "Solution of a Problem in Concurrent Programming Control," *CACM*, vol. 8, no. 9, pp. 569-570, Sept. 1965.

The problem posed to the reader is to determine a control mechanism that permits only one of N computers to be in its critical section at any one moment. The computers are engaged in cyclical processes and can communicate via a common store. The proprietary critical sections are execution periods that cannot be interrupted. Both a solution and a proof are provided. This short paper is a classic example of both conscientious and valuable research.

Dijkstra, E. W.: "The Structure of the T. H. E. Multiprogramming System," *CACM*, vol. 11, no. 5, pp. 341-346, May 1968.

An overview of the design and development of a distributed operating system is presented with a personal touch. The system by nature implements multiprogramming among a group of the cooperating processes that are incorporated in a hierarchical software system. The different levels of the hierarchy handle specific tasks in the interest of facilitating logical design, efficient operation, and system verification. The basic nature of process synchronization is advanced by a description of semaphore operation. The paper proposes that these design techniques can be successful in large system efforts.

Donovan, J. J.: *Systems Programming*, McGraw-Hill Computer Science Series, McGraw-Hill Book Co., New York, 1972. This book covers the background material necessary for systems programming. It contains chapters on machine architecture, assembly language, assemblers, macroprocessors, loaders, higher-level languages, formal systems, compilers, and operating systems. Examples are based on the IBM 360-370 and questions accompany each topic area.

Donovan, J. J. and S. E. Madnick: *Software Projects: Pedagogical Aids for Software Education and Research,* McGraw-Hill Book Co., New York, 1976.

This book discusses an environment, specific tools, and a philosophy for teaching software that have been used for the past six years at M.I.T. and other universities, as well as in industry, for computer software courses. Specifically, the book provides documentation, including teacher's manual, student write-ups, and maintenance manuals, on the following:

1   Problems and environments
    a   A simulator for the 360 on a machine language level
    b   Assembly language problems and grading programs
    c   I/O - interrupt exercises
    d   Problems for job schedulers, paging, and device handlers, and environment simulators for testing solutions to these problems

e   Large design and implementation problems—e.g., writing major components of operating systems or compilers, and environments for running these implementations
2   Mechanisms for reducing the computer costs of running student runs
   a   A monitor to run under OS/360 that greatly reduces costs
   b   A fast PL/I (F) compiler

Drake, A. W.: *Fundamentals of Applied Probability Theory*, McGraw-Hill Book Co., New York, 1967, Chap. 5.
Fundamentals of probability are presented in a readable manner. A good chapter on Markov models.

Earl, D. B. and F. L. Bugly: "Basic Time Sharing: A System of Computing Principles," *Second ACM Symposium on Operating Systems Principles*, Princeton University, pp. 75-79, 1969.
A vocabulary for talking about timeshared operating systems is described. Included in the definition language are basic system structures that can be used to express the design concepts of contemporary computers.

Easton, W. B.: "Process Synchronization without Long-Term Interlocks," *Third ACM Symposium on Operating Systems Principles*, Stanford University, pp. 95-100, Oct. 1971.
A check mechanism is proposed that precludes the need for critical sections. Shared objects are assigned a version number, which is used by executing processes to determine if modification has taken place. Scheduling no longer necessitates locking and unlocking of common information. Included in the paper are examples, and a philosophy for a system architecture that revolves around this concept.

Erwin, J. D. and D. E. Jensen: "Interrupt Processing with Queued Content-Addressable Memories," *Proceedings, AFIPS, 1970, FJCC*, vol. 37, pp. 621-627.
An interrupt-handling mechanism is described that minimizes software time spent by the operating system in organizing responses to the appropriate request. A queued content-addressable memory is employed to facilitate interrupt processor operations.

Estrin, G., R. R. Muntz, and R. C. Uzgalis: "Modeling, Measurement, and Computer Power," *Proceedings, AFIPS, 1972, SJCC*, vol. 40, pp. 725-738.
This survey article selects criteria for assessment of a computer utilities power. This forms the backdrop for a discussion of models of such systems, of intelligent measurement methods, and of the results obtained by applying such techniques at the user interface. The pervasive implication is the need for heavier dependence on modeling both in design and implementation of computer systems.

Fano, R. M.: "On the Social Role of Computer Communication," *IEEE*, vol. 60, no. 11, pp. 1249-1253, Nov. 1972.
This is an interesting overview and worth reading.

Feller, W.: *An Introduction to Probability Theory and Its Applications*, vol. 1, 3d ed., John Wiley & Sons, Inc., New York, 1968.

One of the most complete references on basic probability theory. It can be read on many levels, and it goes deep into the basics in both theory and example. It contains detailed discussions on continuous-time Markov models.

Feieritag, R. J. and E. I. Organick: "The Multics Input/Output System," *Third ACM Symposium on Operating Systems Principles*, Stanford University, pp. 17-23, Oct. 18-20, 1971.

A description of a device interface module that converts generalized I/O requests into specific instructions for the appropriate devices is presented. This MULTICS subsystem permits system programmers to be less concerned about IOCS operations. Applications within the MULTICS environment are provided.

Fields, S.: "Silicon Disk Memories Beat Drums," *Electronics*, pp. 85-86, May 24, 1971.

This article gives examples of new low-latency (e.g., 100 microseconds) direct access storage devices.

Fine, G. H. and P. V. McIsaac: "Simulation of a Time-Sharing System," *Management Science*, vol. 12, no. 6, pp. B180-B194, Feb. 1966.

Fontao, R. O.: "A Concurrent Algorithm for Avoiding Deadlocks," *Third ACM Symposium on Operating Systems Principles*, Stanford University, pp. 72-79, Oct. 18-20, 1971.

"Simultaneous" execution of an algorithm for embrace avoidance is found to provide an efficient mechanism for determining page requests prior to allocation. The algorithm requires knowledge of the maximum number of resource requirements by class for each process and uses the information for dynamic operation. The mathematics of the actual algorithm (concurrency-after-request) and a proof of its correctness are provided. The complexity is found to be of the second order in N, similar to the Habermann algorithm.

Foster, C. C.: "An Unclever Time-Sharing System," *ACM Computing Surveys*, vol. 3, no. 1, pp. 23-48, March 1971.

This University of Massachusetts system may not be clever in its straightforward approach to implementing timesharing with *U*nlimited *M*achine *A*ccess from *S*cattered *S*ites (the UMASS-2 facility); however, this does not prevent its presentation from being both instructive and informative. Approaches to the structural design and implementation of the system on a CDC 3600 are detailed as well as background reasoning for selected design directions. The value of the paper is in its machine-independent approach to discussing the related concepts.

Fotheringham, J.: "Dynamic Storage Allocation in the Atlas Computer Including an Automatic Use of a Backing Store," *CACM*, vol. 4, no. 10, pp. 435-436, Oct. 1961.

An early paper that briefly describes the Atlas system. Though short, it presents the basic ideas rather clearly. The Atlas system pioneered work in demand paging.

Freiburghouse, R. A.: "The Multics PL/1 Compiler," *Proceedings, AFIPS, 1969, FJCC*, vol. 35, pp. 187–199.

The design objectives of the MULTICS compiler are outlined as well as an overview of its basic operation. Explained in more detail are its five phases: syntactic translation, declaration processing, semantic translation, optimization, and code generation. Examples are used to explain the major operating modules in these functions. This article is suggested for the reader familiar with the underlying concepts since it goes one step beyond and uncovers interesting complications and interdependencies.

Fuchi, K., H. Tanaka, Y. Manago, and T. Yuba: "A Program Simulator by Partial Interpretation," *Second ACM Symposium on Operating Systems Principles*, Princeton, N.J., pp. 97–104, 1969.

Debugging supervisor programs remains a major task in any system development effort. A technique called "partial interpretation" described in this paper suggests running the exec programs as user programs and simulating those privileged instructions in its execution locus. Other instructions would be executed as usual. The result is speedy, hardware-feature-independent checkout. The simulation configuration is described. This approach is similar to the virtual machine system (e.g., CP-67 and VM/370).

Funchel, K. and S. Heller: "Consideration in the Design of a Multiple Computer System with Extended Core Storage," *First ACM Symposium on Operating Systems Principles*, Gatlinburg, Tenn., Oct. 1967.

Application of large quantities of addressable but not executable fast, random access memory to improve system performance is discussed. The results of the study are based on a configuration of dual CDC 6600s' sharing of extended core storage at Brookhaven National Laboratories.

Gaines, R. S.: "An Operating System Based on the Concept of a Supervisory Computer," *Third ACM Symposium on Operating Systems Principles*, Stanford University, pp. 17–23, Oct. 18–20, 1971.

An interesting approach to designing a monitor function module is presented. The concept of a "software implemented supervisory computer" is developed through discussion and example. The main idea is to keep a small, stable supervisor that can be combined with other processes through primitives to perform complicated tasks. Discussed also is the interprocess communication facility, which performs a key role in the unit.

Goldberg, R. P.: "Architecture of Virtual Machines," *Proceedings, AFIPS, National Computer Conference*, vol. 42, pp. 309–318, 1973.

This paper develops a model that represents the mapping and addressing of resources by a process executing on a virtual machine. By deriving properties of the model, the author clarifies and contrasts existing virtual machine systems. The most important result of the model is that its proper interpretation implies the Hardware Virtualizer as the direct natural implementation of the virtual machine model. Some of the characteristics of the Hardware Virtualizer are developed and the operation is then illustrated through the use of a concrete example.

Graham, R. M.: "Protection in an Information Processing Utility," *First ACM Symposium on Operating Systems Principles*, Gatlinburg, Tenn., Oct. 1967. (Also *CACM*, vol. 11, no. 5, p. 365, May 1968.)

Motivated by an interesting discussion of system environment and the resulting need for privacy, the properties of an adequate protection mechanism are outlined. The solution to the protection problem chosen is based on a model of a segmented computer system proposed by Dennis. Extension of the model with a ring number permits implementation of layered protection, since each segment attains access privileges based on its ring assignment. In addition to discussion of this hardware mechanism, software support necessary is also outlined. A more detailed discussion of the mechanism and the actual implementation aspects with respect to MULTICS can be found in the paper by Schroeder and Saltzer.

Graham, G. S. and P. J. Denning: "Protection—Principles and Practice," *Proceedings, AFIPS, 1972, SJCC*, vol. 40, pp. 417–430.

Protection requirements are placed in perspective and an abstract model that yields a discussion of the implications for permitting cooperation between mutually suspicious subsystems is presented. The majority of the work is based on Lampson's model, with extensions studied in several important areas. The basic approach taken is to present a theoretical basis for protection and then to discuss some of the associated implementation issued. Analysis is kept within the realm of the current level of knowledge. A useful bibliography for anyone interested in more details is provided.

Gustavson, F. G.: "Program Behavior in a Paging Environment," *Proceedings, AFIPS, 1968, FJCC*, vol. 33, pt. 11, pp. 1019-1032.

Investigation of the virtual memory concept proceeds with a summary of a study conducted on the M44/44X timeshared, paged experimental IBM system. Although the paper deals particularly with the complement of hardware available, information on measurement techniques, program behavior under paging, memory management (automatic versus programmer controlled), and data correlation will be valuable to others studying similar systems.

Habermann, A. N.: "Prevention of System Deadlocks," *CACM*, vol. 12, no. 7, pp. 373-377, July 1969.

A less restrictive allocation algorithm that grants requests on the basis of the current resource pool and the possibility of introducing a deadlock is presented. The means for completely specifying the system's realizable, safe, and unsafe states is based on the vector, matrix description of the system. The algorithms are shown to impose both necessary and sufficient conditions to prevent deadlock. The issue of ordering responses to request or reacting to an unsafe request are mentioned, in conclusion, as system-dependent decisions.

Habermann, A. N.: "Synchronization of Communicating Processes," *Third ACM Symposium on Operating Systems Principles*, Stanford University, pp. 80-85, Oct. 1971. (Also *CACM*, vol. 15, no. 3, pp. 171-176, March 1972.)

The concept of "critical section" is incorporated into a design philosophy for a process communication system. The design prevents more than one process from executing sensitive deposit and request procedures concurrently, while at the same time permitting simultaneous read capability on messages. Theorematic development and proof of corrections form the structure of the presentation.

Hansen, P. B.: "Short Term Scheduling in Multiprogramming Systems," *Third ACM Symposium on Operating Systems Principles*, Stanford University, pp. 101-105, Oct. 1971.

The design principle of "treating all system processes in a uniform manner at the most elementary level of scheduling" surfaces here. It is an evolution of the work of Dijkstra, Lampson, and Saltzer. The approach presented is a more viable alternative than previous work of the authors on the RC4000 system where I/O and computational processes were distinct from a scheduling point of view. Description of short- and medium-term scheduling (hardware management and user management) are provided with Pascal, a language similar to Algol 60. Heavy reliance is placed on the concept of critical sections.

Hansen, P. B.: "The Nucleus of a Multiprogramming System," *CACM*, vol. 13, no. 4, pp. 238-241, April 1970.

The basic characteristics of a hierarchical operating system based on the concept of process execution are presented. The discussion is based on the RC4000 system and includes the related issues of system nucleus, internal/external processes, process communication, and process hierarchy. A key observation is that flexible systems of this sort make possible multipurpose, replaceable operating systems.

Hargraves, R. F. Jr. and A. G. Stephenson: "Design Considerations for an Educational Time-Sharing System, *Proceedings, AFIPS, 1969, SJCC*, vol. 34, pp. 657-664.

A discussion of the Dartmouth timesharing system is given.

Hatfield, D. J.: "Experiments on Page Size, Program Access Patterns, and Virtual Memory Performance," *IBM Journal of Research and Development*, vol. 16, no. 1, pp. 58-66, Jan. 1972.

Results based on various experiments with page size and access patterns are presented. Empirical evidence that demonstrates the "page size" anomaly is provided. This behavior is characterized by drastically increased (sometimes more than double) paging I/Os when a decrease in page size by one-half occurs. The results were based on instruction traces of real IBM System/360 programs. (See Madnick (1973) for a later work which places limits on paging I/Os due to this phenomenon.)

Hatfield, D. J. and J. Gerald: "Program Restructuring for Virtual Memory," *IBM Systems Journal*, vol. 10, no. 3, pp. 168-192, 1971.

This paper presents techniques to improve performance in a demand-paged environment by ordering subroutines. This ordering provides clustering of subroutines that are to be frequently used together so that they are on the same page.

Havender, J. W.: "Avoiding Deadlocks in Multitasking Systems," *IBM Systems Journal*, vol. 7, no. 2, pp. 74-84, 1968.

The issue of allocation of resources in a multitasking environment is addressed in an effort to demonstrate techniques that could be employed to avoid system deadlocks. These techniques are enumerated. The job initiator is taken as an example in its task of allocating data sets, devices, and memory. A technique of a numbering scheme that orders requests for disk storage, memory, and then devices is found to be satisfactory for avoiding deadlocks in job setup and execution.

Hellerman, H. and H. J. Smith, Jr.: "Throughput Analysis of Some Idealized Input, Output, and Compute Overlap Configurations," *ACM Computing Surveys*, vol. 2, no. 2, pp. 111–118, June 1970.
This tutorial approach to multiprogramming operation develops a flavor for system operations by deriving performance equations for idealized cases of input, output, and compute intervals. The performance evaluation parameter used is system throughput (the reciprocal of job time spent in the system to complete). One can gain a good understanding of the concept of multiprogramming by trying to work through a few of the cases studied.

Ho-Nien, Liu, W. S. Peck, and P. T. Pollard: "Resource Management Subsystem for a Large Corporate Information System," *Proceedings, AFIPS, 1969, FJCC*, vol. 35, pp. 441–461.
The variety of uses to which general purpose computer systems have been put yields a multitude of reports on the required computer power needs for different applications. This paper describes a subsystem for efficiently incorporating the complex data needs of a corporate information system into the resource environment of the computer to ensure maximum use of equipment. Both batch and online uses are described since the overview covers the approach to orderly system design that was employed.

Hoffman, L. J.: "Computer and Privacy: A Survey," *ACM Computing Surveys*, vol. 1, no. 2, pp. 83–103, June 1969.
Motivation for discussion of the subject is based on the broadening horizon of computer applications, i.e., "public data bank grids"; the problem of controlling access to sensitive information and its delicate moral implications are first addressed. Then a review of the technical methods currently available for controlling information are presented. The schemes as well as their weaknesses are cited. Some of the successful approaches in the selected areas of privacy include the use of randomly selected passwords, pseudo-random encoded messages, and dialup and callback systems, among many others. Areas for future research are also outlined.

Holt, R. C.: "Some Deadlock Properties of Computer Systems," *ACM Computing Surveys*, vol. 4, no. 3, pp. 179–196, Sept. 1972.
The intention of the paper is to present a methodology for the logical study of the nature of computer system deadlocks. The goal is the building of more reliable computer systems. Included in the presentation are the related concepts of process, deadlock, reusable resources, and consumable resources. Meaningful examples are employed to bring across the issues. The formal modeling of systems is introduced through the use of graph theoretic arguments. General

resource systems are studied and the necessary and sufficient conditions for deadlocks to occur are specified. A good bibliography serves as further introduction to current research in this area.

Horning, J. J. and B. Randell: "Process Structuring," *ACM Computing Surveys,* vol. 5, no. 1, pp. 5–30, March 1973.

The term *process* had meant many things to many people. Herein lies a classification of processes and thus a perspective definition. Combinations and abstractions of processes are defined as a means to master the complexity of systems design and documentation. Hierarchical organization is found to be a subset of this more general analysis. This paper gives complete descriptions of a process and its environment.

Husson, S. S.: *Microprogramming: Principles and Practice,* Prentice-Hall, Englewood Cliffs, N.J., 1970.

A comprehensive introduction to the concepts and usage of microprogramming. Detailed case studies of several microprogrammed computers, such as IBM System/360 Model 50, Honeywell 4200, and RCA Spectra 45, are presented.

Huxtable, D. H. R., and M. T. Warwick: "Dynamic Supervisors—Their Design and Construction," *First ACM Symposium on Operating Systems Principles,* Gatlinburg, Tenn., Oct., 1967.

Here is a detailed description of the executive system of a computer facility. The technology of implementation of such a module is an integral part of the presentation. It reads almost like a user's manual for the design of systems supervisors. The practical nature of this paper rests on the use of its contents in designing and implementing an actual Disk Operating System Supervisor.

IBM, 1: *IBM System/360 MVT, Control Program Logic Summary,* Form Y28-6658-0.

IBM, 2: *IBM System/360: Principles of Operation,* Form GA22-6821.

IBM, 3: *IBM System/360: System Summary,* Form A22-6810.

IBM, 4: *IBM System/370: Principles of Operation,* Form GA22-7000.

IBM, 5: *IBM System/370: System Summary,* Form GA22-7001-1.

IBM, 6: *IBM System/360: Assembler Language Programming,* Form GC28-6514.

IBM, 7: *IBM System/370: OS/VS and DOS/VS Assembler Language,* Form GC33-4010.

IBM, 8: *IBM System/360: Operating System, Planning for Multiprogramming with a Fixed Number of Tasks,* Version II (MFT II), Form C27-6939-0.

IBM, 9: *A Guide to IBM System/370, Model 155,* Form GC20-1729, pp. 11–18.

IBM, 10: *A Guide to IBM System/370, Model 165,* Form GC20-1730, pp. 14–24.

IBM, 11: *IBM System/370 Model 155: Functional Characteristics,* Form GA22-6942.

IBM, 12: *IBM System/370 Model 165: Functional Characteristics,* Form GA22-6935, pp. 14–16.

IBM, 13: *Introduction to OS/VS2 Release 2,* Form GC28-0661.

IBM, 14: *IBM Virtual Machine Facility/370 Introduction,* Form GC20-1800.

IBM, 15: *Planning Guide OS/VS2*, Form GC28-0600.

IBM, 16: *IBM System/360 Operating System: MVT Guide*, Form GC28-6720.

IBM, 17: *Introduction to Virtual Storage in System/370*, Form GR20-4260.

IBM, 18: *IBM System/360 and System/370 Bibliography*, Form GA22-6822.

IBM Cambridge Scientific Center: *CP/CMS Program Logic Manual*, IBM, Cambridge, Mass., 1969.
Description of the IBM CP/CMS implemented on a 360/67. This is a good implementation of virtual machines.

Johnson, David S.: "Near-Optimal Bin Packing Algorithms," *MIT Project MAC Report TR-109*, Cambridge, Mass., June 1973.
This report analyzes various dynamic partitioned allocation algorithms including First Fit and Best Fit. Other algorithms are also studied. Results of an empirical study of average case behavior are provided.

Jones, P. D.: "Operating System Structures," *IFIP Congress Proceedings*, North-Holland Publishing Co,, Amsterdam, 1969, pp. 525-530.
Effort here concentrates on comparing a small chunk of representative operating systems on such basic design characteristics as hardware, major features, and tradeoffs. The systems looked at are CDC 6600/Chippewa, OS/360, and the Atlas Supervisor.

Josephs, W. H.: "An On-Line Machine Language Debugger for OS/360," *Proceedings, AFIPS, 196, FJCC*, vol. 35, pp. 179-186.
This practical system is called DYDE and is invoked through the appropriate JCL upon batch entry. For example, debugging facilities are made available through an IBM 2260 display and are initiated when DYDE receives control. An environment for debugging can be established through break points and then actual data can be displayed from the program. A good overview of a debugging system, including some of the more interesting implementation details, is provided.

Kahn, G.: "An Approach to Systems Correctness," *Third ACM Symposium on Operating Systems Principles*, Stanford University, pp. 86-94, Oct. 1971.
A graph theoretic approach to the description and theorem-proving aspects of small-scale operating systems is presented. The graphical technique explained provides for token flow, merging of communications lines, queues, nodes, and input/output. Sample proofs that relate to small systems are used to demonstrate the value of the methodology.

Kapur, G. K.: *IBM 360 Assembler Language Programming*, John Wiley & Sons, Inc., New York, 1970.
A well-written book that starts on the ground floor and steps its way up to some sophisticated concepts and programming techniques. Examples are drawn from Disk Operating System.

Karush, A. D.: "Two Approaches for Measuring the Performance of Time Sharing Systems," *Second ACM Symposium on Operating Systems Principles*, Princeton University, pp. 150-166, 1969.
Two state-of-the-art performance measures for timesharing systems (stimulus/

response and software hook) are described and applied to the ADEPT time-sharing system (an SDC product).

Katz, J. H.: "Simulation of a Multiprocessor Computer System," *Proceedings, AFIPS, 1966, SJCC*, vol. 28, pp. 127–139.
A revealing model of IBM's direct-coupled system.

Katzan, H., Jr.: "Operating Systems Architecture," *Proceedings, AFIPS, 1970, SJCC*, vol. 36, pp. 109–118.
A good summary of operating systems architecture is given here.

Katzan, H., Jr.: "Storage Hierarchy Systems," *Proceedings, AFIPS, 1971, SJCC*, vol. 38, pp. 325–336.
Provides a good summary of various memory management and file system techniques.

Kay, I. M.: "An Over-the-Shoulder Look at Discrete Simulation Languages," *Proceedings, AFIPS, 1972, SJCC*, vol. 40, pp. 791–798.
A consultant's view of the folklore of simulation systems is presented in this brief exposé. Classified by family type, the languages covered are also categorized by original developer. The broad range of applications of these languages is outlined for the reader interested in learning about the breadth of simulation accomplishments.

Kleinrock, L.: "A Continuum of Time-Sharing Scheduling Algorithms," *Proceedings, AFIPS, 1970, SJCC*, vol. 36, pp. 453–458.
A class of scheduling algorithms based on a two-parameter system for specifying customer priority are generalized and treated with an operable model. The parameters selected are based on customer service time, and their relative values yield results on a broad range of scheduling algorithms, i.e., FCFS to RR. The analysis techniques facilitate a study of the selfish-RR algorithm that lies between the earlier two on the continuum.

Knuth, D.: *The Art of Computer Programming: Fundamental Algorithms*, vol. 1, Addison-Wesley, Reading, Mass., 1968.
Covered are fundamental programming techniques and information structures. The book is valuable for anyone interested in systems programming. It includes detailed coverage of list, tree, and multilinked structures. Various dynamic partitioned memory management algorithms are presented and compared.

Kulsrud, H. E.: "Helper: An Interactive Extensible Debugging System," *Second ACM Symposium on Operating Systems Principles*, Princeton University, pp. 105–111, 1969.
Advances in the art of debugging, especially in interactive graphics-oriented systems, are presented. The structure of Helper provides the backdrop and substance of the discussion. Operation of this compiler, simulator, debugging software, and controller package is explained through actual computer runs.

Lampson, B. W.: "A Scheduling Philosophy for Multiprocessing Systems," *CACM*, vol. 11, no. 5, pp. 347–360, May 1968.
The issues basic to processor management are presented. First, processes are characterized in order to understand the concept of processor multiplexing.

Then, the features of a system needed to implement multiplexing are discussed in depth. These include priority schemes, ready-list management, time scheduling, hardware, and locks. Some of the key ideas presented originated with the Saltzer thesis.

Lampson, B. W.: "Dynamic Protection Structures," *Proceedings, AFIPS, 1969, FJCC*, vol 35, pp. 27–38.

In a computer utility, how can the structures that provide protection be protected themselves? This issue is the one to which Lampson directs his attention. In other words, how are the processes that execute user programs identified, passed around, created, destroyed, used, and shared? The structure of the methodology is formed from concepts such as capabilities, domains, and access keys.

Lampson, B. W.: "Protection," *Proceedings of the Fifth Princeton Conference on Information Sciences and Systems*, pp. 437–443, 1971.

An introduction reflects on properties of existing systems concerning protection and access control. Then, a "message system" is described as a model for implementing the general features of a protection scheme. The concept of domain is introduced as a discrete information sphere that desires interaccess communication. Finally, to beef up the model capabilities, an "object system" is developed to provide external domain control. Implementation techniques are included in the analysis. This brief exposé lays groundwork for a practical model of dynamic protection.

Lehman, Meir M. and Jack L. Rosenfeld, "Performance of a Simulated Multiprogramming System," *Proceedings, AFIPS, 1968, FJCC*, vol. 32, pp. 1431–1442.

This paper reports on the results of experiments performed by A. L. Scherr ("Analysis of Main Storage Fragmentation," *Proceedings of IBM Symposium on Storage Hierarchy Systems*, TR.00.1556, pp. 159–174, Dec. 30, 1966). Scherr had shown that a 65 percent wait factor was typical for many 360/65 installations. Lehman and Rosenfeld conducted additional experiments on the effect of multiprogramming on system I/O wait time.

Lichtenberger, W. W. and M. W. Pirtle: "A Facility for Experimentation in Man-Machine Interaction," *Proceedings, AFIPS, 1965, FJCC*, vol. 27, pp. 185–196.
The XDS-940 timesharing system is discussed.

Linde, R. R., C. Weissman, and C. Fox: "The ADEPT-50 Time Sharing System," *Proceedings, AFIPS, 1969, FJCC*, vol. 35, pp. 39–50.

The architecture and construction of a timesharing executive is discussed in depth. The system product is a result of an advanced development prototype, general purpose, timeshared, data management system implemented by SDC for government use on an IBM System/360. The design features a modular approach and results in a distributed executive. A good overall picture of executive design is provided.

Liptay, J. S.: "Structural Aspects of the System/360 Model 85: II. The Cache," *IBM Systems Journal*, vol. 7, no. 1, pp. 15–21, 1968.

Carrying the slave memory concept of Wilkes into a system product, IBM managed to offset the slow cycle time of main memory with a small high-speed buffer. The result is improved CPU utilization. The study that resulted in the Model 85 architecture is presented in detail, validating the contentions expressed by Wilkes.

Liskov, B. H.: "A Design Methodology for Reliable Software Systems," *Proceedings, AFIPS, 1972, FJCC*, vol. 41, pt. 1, pp. 191–200.

This presentation is structured in two working modules. Criteria that a system design should meet are first discussed. These include clear levels of delegated responsibility, i.e., hierarchical functionality and structured programming. Guidelines for implementing the system are then provided to aid the designer in achieving his goal. These guidelines center around achieving efficient system modularity. Such papers as this are a first step toward the "refinement, extensions, and clarification" of the methodology of top-down design and structured programming.

Liskov, B. H.: "The Design of the Venus Operating System," *CACM*, vol. 15, no. 3, pp. 144–156, March 1972.

The value of flexibility in a microprogram software-implemented operating system is exposed in a description that provides insight into guiding design principles. A primary objective of the effort was to evaluate the effect of architecture (variable firmware support base) on the development of system software (you can exploit the system and define its functions simply). The actual system is characteristic of a fourth-generation machine, including sophisticated resource management such as a hierarchical process-oriented environment, segmented virtual memory, and multiprogramming of 16 concurrent processes. This paper is highly recommended as an example of state-of-the-art pragmatic research.

Lucas, H. J., Jr.: "Performance Evaluation and Monitoring," *ACM Computing Surveys*, vol. 3, no. 3, pp. 79–92, Sept. 1971.

This often referenced categorization of efforts in the area of computer performance evaluation and monitoring performs a much needed function. In an area where a new methodology is advancing, Lucas attempts to classify the goals and techniques applied. For example, he cites three general purposes of system evaluation: selector evaluation, performance projection, and performance monitoring. Then he tabulates the various techniques on their suitability in achieving the said goals. The techniques are also explained in brief. The approach taken to unify such a broad body of knowledge is appropriate.

MacDougal, M. H.: "Computer System Simulation: An Introduction," *ACM Computing Surveys*, vol. 2, no. 3, pp. 191–209, Sept. 1970.

The underlying aspects of constructing a simulation model are uncovered by approaching the study of a disk-based multiprogramming system with a higher level (as opposed to simulation) language. Maintenance of variable-length event lists, queues for shared resources, and statistics gathering are all explained. This paper is a great place to begin if you are interested in system simulation principles. In addition, a fully annotated bibliography provides references for more in-depth research.

Madnick, S. E.: "Multi-Processor Software Lockout," *Proceedings of the ACM National Conference*, 1968.
This is a study of processor idle time in a multiprocessor system in which modification of a shared database is an activity exclusive to one processor at any instant. Analysis by a continuous-time Markov model results in predictions on the level of processor lockout as a function of the number of system processors.

Madnick, S. E.: "Storage Hierarchy Systems," *MIT Project MAC Report TR-105*, Cambridge, Mass., 1973. Multilevel storage hierarchies are discussed and analyzed in this report. A major contribution here is the formalization of the page size anomaly and the development of an algorithm—tuple-coupling—to limit the bad effects of decreasing page size.

Madnick, S. E., "Time-Sharing Systems: Virtual Machine Concept vs. Conventional Approach," *Modern Data*, vol. 2, no. 3, pp. 34-36, March 1966.
An early paper highlighting the characteristics and benefits of a virtual machine approach to timesharing.

Madnick, S. E. and J. W. Alsop: "A Modular Approach to File System Design," *Proceedings, AFIPS, 1969 SJCC*, vol. 34, pp. 1-14.
An approach to designing file systems based on "hierarchical modularity" is presented. The outcome is a general model of a file system, and it is observed that file systems studied by the authors fit into this model, although some abstraction may be required.

Madnick, S. E., and J. J. Donovan, "Application and Analysis of the Virtual Machine Approach to Information System Security and Isolation," *Proceedings of the ACM Workshop on Virtual Computer Systems*, March 1973.
The separation of operating system and virtual machine monitor interfaces is shown to provide better security and isolation than conventional operating systems.

Martin, W. A.: "Sorting," *ACM Computing Surveys*, vol. 3, no. 4, pp. 147-174, Dec. 1971.
This article surveys the field of sorting and presents the best algorithms known for given applications. The ideas are selected from a reference list of over 100 books and articles. A suggested first stop for anyone who wants to find out about this art.

Mattson, R. et al.: "Evaluation Techniques for Storage Hierarchies," *IBM Systems Journal*, vol. 9, no. 2, pp. 78-117, 1970.
Stack processing is found to be a useful tool for analyzing the performance of page replacement algorithms in a demand paging environment. Examined from a theoretical point of view are FIFO, LRU, LFU, OPT, and random replacement algorithms with the intent of uncovering their basic properties.

McFarland, C.: "A Language Oriented Computer Design," *Proceedings, AFIPS, 1970, FJCC*, vol. 37, pp. 629-640.
Proposed is the idea of designing the hardware, executive, and computer languages to maximize the compatibility of their interactions in a functional

system. Such an experimental effort is conceptualized for the reader. One interesting overall design goal is that of having hardware-implemented software functions. Insight is thus provided into an interdependency often overlooked in system planning.

McKinney, J. M.: "A Survey of Analytical Time-Sharing Models," *ACM Computing Surveys*, vol. 1, no. 2, pp. 105-116, vol. 1, no. 2.

The concept of computer timesharing is introduced as groundwork for the discussion of research and related results on analytical models of such systems. Part of the background also includes a discussion of service disciplines relevant to timesharing applications such a RR, FB, and external priority. The condensation of research and results serves as a common reference point for the analyst interested in timesharing modeling. An annotated bibliography is included.

Mclure, R. M.: "An Appraisal of Compiler Technology," *Proceedings, AFIPS, 1972, SJCC*, vol. 40, pp. 1-10.

An overview of production-line compilers that attempts to unify some of the current design issues is presented. It briefly touches on current techniques in syntactic analysis, internal representation, tables and their management, as well as implementation issues. Code generation and optimization are also briefly mentioned. Meant for the initiated reader, hints on new or adequate techniques for specific situations are made. D. Gries' book, *Compiler Construction for Digital Computers*, is cited in the references as "the best single book available which has a good bibliography for further study."

Meade, R. M.: "On Memory System Design," *Proceedings, AFIPS, 1970, FJCC*, vol. 37, pp. 33-44.

The theoretical and statistical basis for the design of memory hierarchy systems is explained with an eye toward cost-effective operation. Block size, buffer capacity, interlevel control algorithms, transfer ratios, and performance measures are treated in the discussion, which gives a respectful overview of the major issues and tradeoffs encountered in memory design.

Mealy, C. H. et al.: "Program Transferability Study," Rome Air Development Center, Griffiss AFB, Technical Report No. RADC-TR-68-341 (available from the U.S. Clearinghouse for Federal Scientific and Technical Information), Nov. 1968.

This report presents an extensive study on the subject of transferability. A wide range of languages, programs, and environments are considered and three attack levels are proposed: (1) administrative control of documentation, programs, etc.; (2) extensions to the existing operating system/language system base to enhance transferability; and (3) the long-term development of an "Advanced Transferability Environment." The advantages and the shortcomings of each approach are discussed and recommendations are made.

Molho, L.: "Hardware Aspects of Secure Computing," *Proceedings, AFIPS, 1970, SJCC*, vol. 36, pp. 135-143.

The issues of logic failure and subversion as well as their countermeasures are presented conceptually with specific examples drawn from the hardware aspects of an IBM 360/50 system. Based on the discussion, general ideas on hardware design that relate to secure computing are pointed out, such as fail-secure operation, failure detection, and data checking. Insight is provided into the difficult task of ensuring system integrity.

Morris, R.: "Scatter Storage Techniques," *CACM*, vol. 12, no. 1, pp. 38-44, May 1968.
Hash coding is discussed in some detail. This is a good reference for providing a review of the methodology as well as specific details for implementation, i.e., resolving conflicting entries.

Morrison, J. E.: "User Program Performance in Virtual Storage Systems," *IBM Systems Journal*, vol. 12, no. 3, pp. 216-237, 1973.
This paper presents the factors of user programs that affect demand paging performance. Programming techniques for improving performance are suggested.

Motobayashi, S., T. Masuda, and N. Takahashi: "The HITAC 5020 Time Sharing System'" *Proceedings of the 24th National Conference of the ACM*, ACM Publication P-69, pp. 419-429, 1969.
Description of the HITAC 5020 system, which incorporates and extends many of the concepts introduced in the MULTICS system.

Murphey, J. E.: "Resource Allocation with Interlock Detection in a Multi-task System," *Proceedings, AFIPS, 1968, FJCC*, vol. 33, pt. II, pp. 1169-1176.
A queue management technique that detects embrace-causing resource requests is described. Implementation is performed with either a wait matrix or a precedence matrix. The former permits simple yes/no detection and requires release and repeated request of all resources held upon embrace. The latter provides a mechanism for determining a minimal set of resources to release upon deadlock. The paper demonstrates the technique through example and also suggests areas for future research.

Needham, R. M.: "Protection Systems and Protection Implementations," *Proceedings, AFIPS, 1972, FJCC*, vol. 41, pt. 1, pp. 571-578.
A scheme for protection of main memory computer information is proposed that bases its operation on manipulation of indirection tables. The decision to select this mechanism follows from an analysis of disadvantages of lock-key methods. The requirements of such a table-driven protection scheme are outlined and the problem of invalid arguments is treated in context.

Needham, R. M. and D. F. Hartley: "Theory and Practice in Operating System Design," *Second ACM Symposium on Operating Systems Principles*, Princeton University, pp. 8-12, Oct. 1969.
Touched upon are SPOOLing design, deadly embrace, and multiprogramming efficiency in a discussion that intends to mediate between a theoretical and commonsense design base. Areas where more of the particular approach to design might be fruitful are suggested.

Neumann, P. G.: "The Role of Motherhood in the Pop Art of System Programming," *Second ACM Symposium on Operating Systems Principles*, Princeton University, pp. 13-18, 1969.
Yardsticks for measuring software systems are proposed in the hope that they will be obeyed in practice rather than just paid lip service (what do you think

that has to do with motherhood?). Those desirable system features such as debugging, documentation, flexibility, modularity, portability, are defined and those to be shunned most are exposed. The approach to presentation is light and the reading easy.

Nielsen, N. R.: "Computer Simulation of Computer System Performance," *Proceedings, ACM National Conference, 1967*, pp. 581-590.
Reports on simulations of early versions of the IBM TSS/360 system showing clearly the idle time resulting from a poorly balanced system.

Oppenheimer, G. and N. Weizer: "Resource Management for a Medium Scale Time Sharing Operating System," *First ACM Symposium on Operating Systems Principles*, Gatlinburg, Tenn., Oct. 1967.
Described are the essential characteristics of task scheduling on an RCA Spectra 70/46 computer in an effort to afford a basic structure for balancing system performance and resource utilization. On the basis of simulation studies using a GPSS-like language, an evaluation of alternative scheduling and paging algorithms is performed.

Organick, E. I.: *The Multics System: An Examination of Its Structure*, The M.I.T. Press, Cambridge, Mass., 1972.
This book is the first and presently the only generally available comprehensive description of the MULTICS system. A complete MULTICS bibliography is also included.

Pankhurst, R. J.: "Program Overlay Techniques," *CACM*, vol. 11, no. 2, pp. 119-125, Feb. 1968.
Automatic, semiautomatic, and manual overlay mechanisms are described as key virtual memory management techniques. An example is drawn from the semiautomatic overlay processor and CDC 6600.

Parmelee, R. P., T. I. Peterson, C. C. Sullivan, and D. S. Hatfield: "Virtual Storage and Virtual Machine Concepts," *IBM Systems Journal*, vol. 11, no. 2, pp. 99-130, 1972.
This provides a good description of CP-67/CMS and an annotated bibliography of all aspects of virtual machines.

Presser, L. and J. R. White: "Linkers and Loaders," *ACM Computing Surveys*, vol. 4, no. 3, pp. 149-169, Sept. 1972.
This tutorial approach to linking and loading stages of language translation introduces the central concepts of these "man/computer communication processes." The main focus is on the modular view of linkage editing combined with simple relocatable loading as performed on the IBM System/360. The task of linking together independently translated modules is treated in depth with examples. Secondary functions such as overlay processing, program modification, and library access are also mentioned.

Price, C. E.: "Table Look Up Techniques," *ACM Computing Surveys*, vol. 3, no. 2, June 1971
A treatment of the basic methodology of static table searching that includes basic information on sequential, merge, binary, estimated entry, and direct

lookup is provided. Hash addressing also receives attention. This paper fills out the body of knowledge on table management presented by Martin and is a review of Chapter 4 in Donovan's book.

Randell, B. and C. J. Kuehner: "Demand Paging in Perspective," *Proceedings, AFIPS, 1968, FJCC*, vol. 33, pt. II, pp. 1011–1018.

Demand paging is defined and then effort is concentrated on surveying techniques used to improve demand paging system performance. Hardware methods are discarded as brute force while software methods are discussed in greater depth. These techniques include tuning the program load and adjusting operating system strategies, i.e., scheduling and resource allocation. The summary and conclusion provide valuable insight into paging system operations.

Randell, B. and C. J. Kuehner: "Dynamic Storage Allocation Systems," *First ACM Symposium on Operating Systems Principles*, Gatlinburg, Tenn., Oct. 1967. Dynamic storage allocation systems are characterized according to their functional capabilities and the underlying techniques employed in their implementation. Four basic characteristics are used to assess current automatic storage techniques on contemporary systems such as B5500, MULTICS, 360/67 among others. The authors develop a framework for studying various hardware facilities used for memory allocation.

Reiter, Allen, "A Resource Allocation Scheme for Multi-User On-Line Operation of a Small Computer," *Proceedings, AFIPS, 1967, SJCC*, vol. 30, pp. 1–8, 1967. This paper describes an operating system designed for small computers (e.g., the IBM 360/30). It employs an interesting memory management scheme based upon use of software techniques to support a form of dynamic segment swapping.

Risko, F. D.: "New Horizons for Magnetic Bulk Storage Devices," *Proceedings, AFIPS, 1968, FJCC*, vol. 33, pt. II, pp. 1361–1368.

An interesting overview of memory devices is provided, including useful criteria for evaluation of bulk storage. The hardware state of the art is uncovered and future trends toward laser memories are discussed. This article provides an interesting comparison with our reality today.

Rodriguez-Rosell, Juan: "Experimental Data on How Program Behavior Affects the Choice of Scheduler Parameters," *Third ACM Symposium on Operating Systems Principles*, Stanford University, pp. 156–163, Oct. 1971.

This is a report on the working-set characteristics of programs (empirical measurements of working-set size) and their relationship to choice of processor-scheduling parameters (quantum size). Experiments on system programs run under a fully interpretative simulator yielded a variety of results, which are presented in graphical form.

Rosen, S.: "Electronic Computers: A Historical Survey," *ACM Computing Surveys*, vol. 1, no. 1, pp. 7–36, March 1969.

This interesting, detailed, yet brief history of computer systems and their manufacturers may rightly fit into the "all you ever wanted to know about" category. The main concentration of information is confined to developments within the

United States. The three well-known generations of computers are placed in perspective and an extensive bibliography documents the research.

Rosin, R. F.: "Contemporary Concepts of Microprogramming and Emulation," *ACM Computing Surveys*, vol. 1, no. 4, pp. 197–212, 1969.
The approach in the paper is to demonstrate the control functions of a hypothetical machine by applying and contrasting the current techniques in microprogramming in a natural tutorial manner. Some of the currently available systems that make use of microprogramming are presented. In addition, areas for future research are outlined.

Rosin, R. F.: "Supervisory and Monitor Systems," *ACM Computing Surveys*, vol. 1, no. 1, pp. 37–54, March 1969.
A chronological report of the developments in the executive operating system functions of computer utilities is presented in detail. Although depth is sacrificed for completeness, this article can be profitably read by an initiate to the field. The perspective afforded is a must for the veteran computer body.

Ross, D. T., "The AED Free Storage Package," *CACM*, vol. 10, no. 8, pp. 481–492, Aug. 1967.
This paper describes the dynamic storage allocation facilities provided in the Free Storage Package of the AED-1 Compiler System. This package allows the user to separate the available free space into *zones* and employ different allocation algorithms for each zone.

Saltzer, J. H.: "Traffic Control in a Multiplexed Computer System," *MIT Project MAC Report TR-30*, Cambridge, Mass., 1966.
Cambridge, Mass., 1966.
Assuming familiarity with issues such as reliability, accessibility, and sharing, this thesis goes on to discuss the nature of an operating system and a key module, the traffic controller, for managing functions within a computer utility. The approach is tutorial in nature and exposes many advanced concepts that are now forming integral parts of present-day computing systems, i.e., interprocess communication facilities and multiple-processor multiplexing. A well-laid management scheme is thus proposed, and it is noted that such concepts form the backbone of the MULTICS system.

Saltzer, J. H. and J. W. Gintell: "The Instrumentation of MULTICS," *Second ACM Symposium on Operating Systems Principles*, Princeton University, pp. 167–174, 1969.
This article serves as a working survey of measurement tools used for the maintenance and study of a computer utility. Included in the repertoire are special hardware clocks and data channels, general purpose programmed probing and recording tools, and specialized measurement facilities. Mention is made of the particular hardware/software instrumentation used in a demand paging environment.

Sayer, D.: "Is Automatic 'Folding' of Programs Efficient Enough to Displace Manual?" *CACM*, vol. 12, no. 12, pp. 656–660, Dec. 1969.
Program rearrangement for virtual memory systems is discussed in this paper. The performance of automatically arranged (folded) programs is shown to have

potential for use in computing systems, and the advantages of such techniques are demonstrated. The dynamic mechanism is contrasted with compilers of 10 years ago and the author predicts that acceptance of the associated methodology will come with time in a similar fashion.

Scherf, J.: "Data Security: A Comprehensive and Annotated Bibliography," master's thesis, M.I.T. Sloan School of Management, Cambridge, Mass., 1973.

Scherr, A. L.: "An Analysis of Time-Shared Computer Systems," *MIT Project MAC Report TR-18*, Cambridge, Mass., 1965.
An extensive analysis of some of the algorithms and performance of CTSS is presented.

Schroeder, M. D.: "Performance of the GE-645 Associative Memory While MULTICS Is in Operation," *ACM Workshop on System Performance Evaluation*, pp. 227–245, April 1971.
Discussion of segmentation and paging on MULTICS precedes a discussion and evaluation of the associative memory used by the processor to perform address translations for memory references.

Schroeder, M. D. and J. H. Saltzer: "A Hardware Architecture for Implementing Protection Rings," *CACM*, vol. 15, no. 3, March 1972.
Hardware mechanisms called rings are suggested (Graham) as a feasible technique for controlling access in a timeshared, multiprogrammed, multiprocessor, segmented virtual memory computer system, i.e., MULTICS. The scenario for the discussion is based on the complement of equipment available on the modified version of the original Honeywell 645 computer. Yet, discussion is sufficiently general to be of value to anyone interested in protection for segmented systems. Included in the paper are underlying principles of operation useful for handling domain changing with calls and returns. The hardware mechanisms are presented.

Schwartz, D. S.: "Multiprogramming in a Page on Demand Computer System: Performance Models and Evaluation," master's thesis, Department of Electrical Engineering, M.I.T., Cambridge, Mass., 1973.
This paper contains a literature review on current computer modeling efforts in the areas of both analytical and simulation models. Presented is an analysis of multiprogramming role time and average CPU utilization with three different modeling techniques. The results are placed in perspective and the modeling techniques are compared and contrasted.

Schwartz, J., E. G. Coffman, and L. Weissman: "A General Purpose Time-Sharing System," *Proceedings, AFIPS, 1964, SJCC*, vol. 25, pp. 397–411.
A discussion of the System Development Corporation timesharing system is given here.

Sekino, A.: "Performance Evaluation of Multiprogrammed Time-Shared Computer Systems," *M.I.T. Project MAC Report TR-103*, Cambridge, Mass., 1972.
This report presents a complete analytical analysis of an existing multi-purpose computer system. With an eye toward validating his model on MULTICS, Sekino developed a general model for a timeshared, multiprogrammed, multiprocessor, demand-paged, virtual storage computer.

Senko, M. E., E. B. Altman, M. M. Astrahan, and P. L. Fehder: "Data Structures and Accessing in Data-base Systems," *IBM Systems Journal*, vol. 1, pp. 30-93, 1973.

Presented in three parts is a descriptive analysis of database information systems. Part I reviews the evolution of database systems to reveal the direction of their growth and applications. Part II discusses the structuring of information and introduces a new fundamental approach to this structuring. Part III presents a framework, the Data Independent Accessing Model (DIAM), for describing information and its stored representations.

Sevick, K. C., et al.: "Project SUE as a Learning Experience," *Proceedings, AFIPS, 1972, FJCC*, vol. 41, pt. 1, pp. 331–338.
This research project has many design aspects that integrate and advance the current work in hierarchical operating systems development. Presented to the reader as a status report, it is possible to gain insight into what the substance of such a system is and how it is organized. The bibliography includes references to some of the other technical reports produced for this ongoing project.

Skatrud, R. O.: "A Consideration of the Application of Cryptographic Techniques to Data Processing," *Proceedings, AFIPS, 1969, FJCC*, vol. 35, pp. 111-119.
The approach taken here is to describe two digital cryptographic techniques that have potential applications in data processing systems. The background reviews cryptographic techniques used since the days of the Romans. The two methods concentrated on are digital substitution and digital route transposition, and they are explained with reasonable clarity.

Spier, M. J. and E. I. Organick: "The MULTICS Interprocess Communication Facility," *Second ACM Symposium on Operating Systems Principles*, Princeton University, pp. 33–91, Oct. 1969.
Explained is the environment within which an IPC (Interprocess Communication) facility would operate as part of MULTICS. The fundamentals of the process communication facility are described in a machine-independent fashion. Specialization to MULTICS follows and applications for systems designers are surveyed.

Spirn, J. R. and P. J. Denning: "Experiments with Program Locality," *Proceedings, AFIPS, 1972, FJCC*, vol. 41, pt. 1, pp. 611–621.
The concept of program locality is explicitly defined and references to previous work in the area are provided. Then definitions on locality of reference are classified into intrinsic and extrinsic locality models and effort is concentrated on estimating the ability of extrinsic measurements, i.e., working set, to measure true intrinsic localities. Models for intrinsic locality are reviewed and criteria for the actual experimentation are determined in order to try to give realistic comparisons of expected performance. Sample programs are used to generate data for comparison, and the working-set model is found to be a good estimator of program locality.

Teorey, T. J.: "Properties of Disk Scheduling Policies in Multiprogrammed Computer Systems," *Proceedings, AFIPS, 1972, FJCC*, vol. 41, pt. 1, pp. 1–12. Mention is made of key research previously done in the area of disk-scheduling analysis with adequate references provided. The article then delves into many mathematical manipulations as part of a derivation of analytical expressions for performance of these commonly studied scheduling algorithms (often, in the past, simulation had to be employed in their analysis). It is hoped by the author that the results will provide information to aid in deciding whether to undertake scheduling or not, and, if so, which policy is best for the given application. The policies covered are discussed in terms of operating systems and hardware.

Teorey, T. J. and T. B. Pinkerton: "A Comparative Analysis of Disk Scheduling Policies," *Third ACM Symposium on Operating Systems Principles*, Stanford University, pp. 114–121, Oct. 1971. Based on the performance criteria of expected seek time and expected waiting time, policies such as FCFS, SSTF, SCAN, and N-Step Scan are compared for movable head disks. Both analytical and simulational results are obtained. Optimal policies for a given environment are chosen. This is a very complete discussion of current analysis technology in this area.

Van Horn, E. C.: "Design for Asynchronously Reproducible Multiprocessing," *M.I.T. Project MAC Report TR-34*, Cambridge, Mass., 1966. Presented are software mechanisms for implementing a lock.

Van Horn, E. C.: "Three Criteria for Designing Computing Systems to Facilitate Debugging," *First ACM Symposium on Operating Systems Principles*, Gatlinburg, Tenn., 1967. Three key criteria deemed important to the user interface in terms of program testing are outlined. These are input recordability, input specifiability, and asynchronous reproducibility of output. The scope of the criteria is outlined and their implications for computer design to aid in debugging are discussed.

Vareha, A. L., R. M. Rutledge, and M. M. Gold: "Strategies for Structuring Two Level Memories in a Paging Environment," *Second ACM Symposium on Operating Systems Principles*, Princeton University, pp. 54–59, 1969. Discussed are the principles for the effective utilization of a two-level, directly executable memory, the algorithms considered, and the experience gained in their use. The paper is based on a 360/67 timesharing system. It was found that introduction of a slower, second-level bulk memory led to reduced paging and improved performance.

Varney, R. C.: "Process Selection in a Hierarchical Operating System," *Third ACM Symposium on Operating Systems Principles*, Stanford University, pp. 106–108, Oct. 1971. A new model is presented for processor sharing in a process-scheduling environment. Flexible models of operation are possible, such as multiprogramming, real time, and timesharing. Description and use of a processor selector tree are presented for use in adaptive scheduling.

Watson, R. W.: *Timesharing System Design Concepts*, McGraw-Hill Computer Science Series, McGraw-Hill Book Co., New York, 1970.
A good book in exposing timesharing design concepts. The author discusses two systems, MULTICS and SDS 940.

Weissman, C.: "Security Controls in the ADEPT-50 Time-Sharing System," *Proceedings, AFIPS, 1969, FJCC*, vol. 35, pp. 119-134.
Described are the security controls of the Adept-50 timesharing system (see Linde) that "handle sensitive information in classified government and military facilities." Four security objects are identified: user, terminal, job, and file. Each object is assigned a security profile that describes its security properties, and then a set theoretic model of access rights is employed to specify timesharing security control among the cited resources. The paper is quite detailed in its coverage, thus implicitly generating a secure feeling about the approach.

Wilkes, M. V.: "Slave Memories and Dynamic Storage Allocation," *IEEE TC* vol. EC-14 no. 2, pp. 270-271, April 1965.
This short note discusses techniques for increasing effective memory speed of typical core storage hierarchy systems. Introduced is the idea of slave memories, both small and large, as auxiliary storage systems, with access times much faster than its main core counterpart. Application areas are mentioned and techniques are outlined that minimize hardware complexity.

Wilkes, M. V.: "The Growth of Interest in Microprogramming: A Literature Survey," *Computing Surveys*, vol. 1, no. 3, pp. 139-145, Sept. 1969.
The origin of the term *microprogramming* is explained and defined (by the renowned father of the art) for those who may intend to apply it otherwise. The author then unfolds an international picture of the increasing awareness of this design tool through a brief review of relevant papers (55 articles document the research). This approach generates an implicit belief in the power, flexibility, and future of this firmware commodity for use in the computer field.

Wilkes, M. V.: *Time Sharing Computer Systems*, American Elsevier Publishing Co., New York, 1968.
This book is recommended for those interested in timesharing systems.

Winograd, J., S. J. Morganstein, and R. Herman: "Simulation Studies of a Virtual Memory, Time-Shared, Demand Paging Operating System," *Third ACM Symposium on Operating Systems Principles*, Stanford University, pp. 149-155, Oct. 1971.
A detailed system simulator called Sim/61 is described. It provides a detailed model of a virtual memory, timeshared, demand-paged system environment. The model is used for load and configuration studies as well as algorithm evaluation for task scheduling. The various simulation experiments are briefly outlined. This article provides an excellent example of the success achieved with Simscript as a computer analysis tool.

Wulf, W. A.: "Performance Monitors for Multiprogramming Systems," *Second ACM Symposium on Operating Systems Principles*, Princeton University, pp. 175-181, 1969.

Self-monitoring, self-adjusting systems have been a goal of computer system engineers since the mid-sixties and yet this issue has remained largely academic. Proposed here is a scheme for improving the throughput of multiprogramming systems based on measures of both system and process activity. The main concentration is on improving resource utilization through mix-monitoring. Simplified forms of this macro/micro dynamic analysis have been implemented by the author on a B5500.

Appendix A

IBM
System/370
Reference
Summary *

Second Edition (September 1972)

This edition supersedes GX20-1850-0. It includes information related to dynamic address translation, program event recording, and new timing facilities.

The card is intended primarily for use by S/370 assembly language programmers. It contains basic machine information summarized from the *System/370 Principles of Operation* (GA22-7000), frequently used information from *OS/VS and DOS/VS Assembler Language* (GC33-4010), command codes for various I/O devices, and a multi-code translation table.

The names of machine instructions new with System/370 are shown in italics. Some instructions and other CPU functions are model-dependent or optional; for those available on a particular model, the user is referred to the functional characteristics manual for that model.

IBM Corporation, Technical Publications Department,
1133 Westchester Avenue, White Plains, N. Y. 10604

*Reprinted by permission of International Business Machines Corporation.

MACHINE INSTRUCTIONS

②

NAME	MNEMONIC	OP CODE	FORMAT	OPERANDS
Add (c)	AR	1A	RR	R1,R2
Add (c)	A	5A	RX	R1,D2(X2,B2)
Add Decimal (c)	AP	FA	SS	D1(L1,B1),D2(L2,B2)
Add Halfword (c)	AH	4A	RX	R1,D2(X2,B2)
Add Logical (c)	ALR	1E	RR	R1,R2
Add Logical (c)	AL	5E	RX	R1,D2(X2,B2)
AND (c)	NR	14	RR	R1,R2
AND (c)	N	54	RX	R1,D2(X2,B2)
AND (c)	NI	94	SI	D1(B1),I2
AND (c)	NC	D4	SS	D1(L,B1),D2(B2)
Branch and Link	BALR	05	RR	R1,R2
Branch and Link	BAL	45	RX	R1,D2(X2,B2)
Branch on Condition	BCR	07	RR	M1,R2
Branch on Condition	BC	47	RX	M1,D2(X2,B2)
Branch on Count	BCTR	06	RR	R1,R2
Branch on Count	BCT	46	RX	R1,D2(X2,B2)
Branch on Index High	BXH	86	RS	R1,R3,D2(B2)
Branch on Index Low or Equal	BXLE	87	RS	R1,R3,D2(B2)
Compare (c)	CR	19	RR	R1,R2
Compare (c)	C	59	RX	R1,D2(X2,B2)
Compare Decimal (c)	CP	F9	SS	D1(L1,B1),D2(L2,B2)
Compare Halfword (c)	CH	49	RX	R1,D2(X2,B2)
Compare Logical (c)	CLR	15	RR	R1,R2
Compare Logical (c)	CL	55	RX	R1,D2(X2,B2)
Compare Logical (c)	CLC	D5	SS	D1,(L,B1),D2(B2)
Compare Logical (c)	CLI	95	SI	D1(B1),I2
Compare Logical Characters under Mask (c)	CLM	BD	RS	R1,M3,D2(B2)
Compare Logical Long (c)	CLCL	0F	RR	R1,R2
Convert to Binary	CVB	4F	RX	R1,D2(X2,B2)
Convert to Decimal	CVD	4E	RX	R1,D2(X2,B2)
Diagnose (p)		83		
Divide	DR	1D	RR	R1,R2
Divide	D	5D	RX	R1,D2(X2,B2)
Divide Decimal	DP	FD	SS	D1(L1,B1),D2(L2,B2)
Edit (c)	ED	DE	SS	D1(L,B1),D2(B2)
Edit and Mark (c)	EDMK	DF	SS	D1(L,B1),D2(B2)
Exclusive OR (c)	XR	17	RR	R1,R2
Exclusive OR (c)	X	57	RX	R1,D2(X2,B2)
Exclusive OR (c)	XI	97	SI	D1(B1),I2
Exclusive OR (c)	XC	D7	SS	D1(L,B1),D2(B2)
Execute	EX	44	RX	R1,D2(X2,B2)
Halt I/O (c,p)	HIO	9E00	S	D2(B2)
Halt Device (c,p)	HDV	9E01	S	D2(B2)
Insert Character	IC	43	RX	R1,D2(X2,B2)
Insert Characters under Mask (c)	ICM	BF	RS	R1,M3,D2(B2)
Insert Storage Key (p)	ISK	09	RR	R1,R2
Load	LR	18	RR	R1,R2
Load	L	58	RX	R1,D2(X2,B2)
Load Address	LA	41	RX	R1,D2(X2,B2)
Load and Test (c)	LTR	12	RR	R1,R2
Load Complement (c)	LCR	13	RR	R1,R2
Load Control (p)	LCTL	B7	RS	R1,R3,D2(B2)
Load Halfword	LH	48	RX	R1,D2(X2,B2)
Load Multiple	LM	98	RS	R1,R3,D2(B2)
Load Negative (c)	LNR	11	RR	R1,R2
Load Positive (c)	LPR	10	RR	R1,R2
Load PSW (n,p)	LPSW	82	S	D2(B2)
Load Real Address (c,p)	LRA	B1	RX	R1,D2(X2,B2)
Monitor Call	MC	AF	SI	D1(B1),I2
Move	MVI	92	SI	D1(B1),I2
Move	MVC	D2	SS	D1(L,B1),D2(B2)
Move Long (c)	MVCL	0E	RR	R1,R2
Move Numerics	MVN	D1	SS	D1(L,B1),D2(B2)
Move with Offset	MVO	F1	SS	D1(L1,B1),D2(L2,B2)
Move Zones	MVZ	D3	SS	D1(L,B1),D2(B2)
Multiply	MR	1C	RR	R1,R2
Multiply	M	5C	RX	R1,D2(X2,B2)
Multiply Decimal	MP	FC	SS	D1(L1,B1),D2(L2,B2)
Multiply Halfword	MH	4C	RX	R1,D2(X2,B2)
OR (c)	OR	16	RR	R1,R2
OR (c)	O	56	RX	R1,D2(X2,B2)
OR (c)	OI	96	SI	D1(B1),I2
OR (c)	OC	D6	SS	D1(L,B1),D2(B2)
Pack	PACK	F2	SS	D1(L1,B1),D2(L2,B2)

MACHINE INSTRUCTIONS (Contd)

NAME	MNEMONIC	OP CODE	FOR-MAT	OPERANDS
Purge TLB (p)	PTLB	B20D	S	
Read Direct (a,p)	RDD	85	SI	D1(B1),I2
Reset Reference Bit (c,p)	RRB	B213	S	D2(B2)
Set Clock (c,p)	SCK	B204	S	D2(B2)
Set Clock Comparator (p)	SCKC	B206	S	D2(B2)
Set CPU Timer (p)	SPT	B208	S	D2(B2)
Set Program Mask (n)	SPM	04	RR	R1
Set Storage Key (p)	SSK	08	RR	R1,R2
Set System Mask (p)	SSM	80	S	D2(B2)
Shift and Round Decimal (c)	SRP	F0	SS	D1(L1,B1),D2(B2),I3
Shift Left Double (c)	SLDA	8F	RS	R1,D2(B2)
Shift Left Double Logical	SLDL	8D	RS	R1,D2(B2)
Shift Left Single (c)	SLA	8B	RS	R1,D2(B2)
Shift Left Single Logical	SLL	89	RS	R1,D2(B2)
Shift Right Double (c)	SRDA	8E	RS	R1,D2(B2)
Shift Right Double Logical	SRDL	8C	RS	R1,D2(B2)
Shift Right Single (c)	SRA	8A	RS	R1,D2(B2)
Shift Right Single Logical	SRL	88	RS	R1,D2(B2)
Start I/O (c,p)	SIO	9C00	S	D2(B2)
Start I/O Fast Release (c,p)	SIOF	9C01	S	D2(B2)
Store	ST	50	RX	R1,D2(X2,B2)
Store Channel ID (c,p)	STIDC	B203	S	D2(B2)
Store Character	STC	42	RX	R1,D2(X2,B2)
Store Characters under Mask	STCM	BE	RS	R1,M3,D2(B2)
Store Clock (c)	STCK	B205	S	D2(B2)
Store Clock Comparator (p)	STCKC	B207	S	D2(B2)
Store Control (p)	STCTL	B6	RS	R1,R3,D2(B2)
Store CPU ID (p)	STIDP	B202	S	D2(B2)
Store CPU Timer (p)	STPT	B209	S	D2(B2)
Store Halfword	STH	40	RX	R1,D2(X2,B2)
Store Multiple	STM	90	RS	R1,R3,D2(B2)
Store Then AND System Mask (p)	STNSM	AC	SI	D1(B1),I2
Store Then OR System Mask (p)	STOSM	AD	SI	D1(B1),I2
Subtract (c)	SR	1B	RR	R1,R2
Subtract (c)	S	5B	RX	R1,D2(X2,B2)
Subtract Decimal (c)	SP	FB	SS	D1(L1,B1),D2(L2,B2)
Subtract Halfword (c)	SH	4B	RX	R1,D2(X2,B2)
Subtract Logical (c)	SLR	1F	RR	R1,R2
Subtract Logical (c)	SL	5F	RX	R1,D2(X2,B2)
Supervisor Call	SVC	0A	RR	I
Test and Set (c)	TS	93	S	D2(B2)
Test Channel (c,p)	TCH	9F	S	D2(B2)
Test I/O (c,p)	TIO	9D	S	D2(B2)
Test under Mask (c)	TM	91	SI	D1(B1),I2
Translate	TR	DC	SS	D1(L,B1),D2(B2)
Translate and Test (c)	TRT	DD	SS	D1(L,B1),D2(B2)
Unpack	UNPK	F3	SS	D1(L1,B1),D2(L2,B2)
Write Direct (a,p)	WRD	84	SI	D1(B1),I2
Zero and Add Decimal (c)	ZAP	F8	SS	D1(L1,B1),D2(L2,B2)

Floating-Point Instructions

NAME	MNEMONIC	OP CODE	FOR-MAT	OPERANDS
Add Normalized, Extended (c,x)	AXR	36	RR	R1,R2
Add Normalized, Long (c)	ADR	2A	RR	R1,R2
Add Normalized, Long (c)	AD	6A	RX	R1,D2(X2,B2)
Add Normalized, Short (c)	AER	3A	RR	R1,R2
Add Normalized, Short (c)	AE	7A	RX	R1,D2(X2,B2)
Add Unnormalized, Long (c)	AWR	2E	RR	R1,R2
Add Unnormalized, Long (c)	AW	6E	RX	R1,D2(X2,B2)
Add Unnormalized, Short (c)	AUR	3E	RR	R1,R2
Add Unnormalized, Short (c)	AU	7E	RX	R1,D2(X2,B2)
Compare, Long (c)	CDR	29	RR	R1,R2
Compare, Long (c)	CD	69	RX	R1,D2(X2,B2)
Compare, Short (c)	CER	39	RR	R1,R2
Compare, Short (c)	CE	79	RX	R1,D2(X2,B2)
Divide, Long	DDR	2D	RR	R1,R2
Divide, Long	DD	6D	RX	R1,D2(X2,B2)
Divide, Short	DER	3D	RR	R1,R2

a. Direct control feature.
c. Condition code is set.
n. New condition code is loaded.

p. Privileged instruction.
x. Extended precision floating-point feature.

Floating-Point Instructions (Contd)

④

NAME	MNEMONIC	OP CODE	FOR-MAT	OPERANDS
Divide, Short	DE	7D	RX	R1,D2(X2,B2)
Halve, Long	HDR	24	RR	R1,R2
Halve, Short	HER	34	RR	R1,R2
Load and Test, Long (c)	LTDR	22	RR	R1,R2
Load and Test, Short (c)	LTER	32	RR	R1,R2
Load Complement, Long (c)	LCDR	23	RR	R1,R2
Load Complement, Short (c)	LCER	33	RR	R1,R2
Load, Long	LDR	28	RR	R1,R2
Load, Long	LD	68	RX	R1,D2(X2,B2)
Load Negative, Long (c)	LNDR	21	RR	R1,R2
Load Negative, Short (c)	LNER	31	RR	R1,R2
Load Positive, Long (c)	LPDR	20	RR	R1,R2
Load Positive, Short (c)	LPER	30	RR	R1,R2
Load Rounded, Extended to Long (x)	LRDR	25	RR	R1,R2
Load Rounded, Long to Short (x)	LRER	35	RR	R1,R2
Load, Short	LER	38	RR	R1,R2
Load, Short	LE	78	RX	R1,D2(X2,B2)
Multiply, Extended (x)	MXR	26	RR	R1,R2
Multiply, Long	MDR	2C	RR	R1,R2
Multiply, Long	MD	6C	RX	R1,D2(X2,B2)
Multiply, Long/Extended (x)	MXDR	27	RR	R1,R2
Multiply, Long/Extended (x)	MXD	67	RX	R1,D2(X2,B2)
Multiply, Short	MER	3C	RR	R1,R2
Multiply, Short	ME	7C	RX	R1,D2(X2,B2)
Store, Long	STD	60	RX	R1,D2(X2,B2)
Store, Short	STE	70	RX	R1,D2(X2,B2)
Subtract Normalized, Extended (c,x)	SXR	37	RR	R1,R2
Subtract Normalized, Long (c)	SDR	2B	RR	R1,R2
Subtract Normalized, Long (c)	SD	6B	RX	R1,D2(X2,B2)
Subtract Normalized, Short (c)	SER	3B	RR	R1,R2
Subtract Normalized, Short (c)	SE	7B	RX	R1,D2(X2,B2)
Subtract Unnormalized, Long (c)	SWR	2F	RR	R1,R2
Subtract Unnormalized, Long (c)	SW	6F	RX	R1,D2(X2,B2)
Subtract Unnormalized, Short (c)	SUR	3F	RR	R1,R2
Subtract Unnormalized, Short (c)	SU	7F	RX	R1,D2(X2,B2)

EXTENDED MNEMONIC INSTRUCTIONS†

Use	Extended Code* (RX or RR)	Meaning	Machine Instr.* (RX or RR)
General	B or BR	Unconditional Branch	BC or BCR 15,
	NOP or NOPR	No operation	BC or BCR 0,
After	BH or BHR	Branch on A High	BC or BCR 2,
Compare	BL or BLR	Branch on A Low	BC or BCR 4,
Instructions	BE or BER	Branch on A Equal B	BC or BCR 8,
(A:B)	BNH or BNHR	Branch on A Not High	BC or BCR 13,
	BNL or BNLR	Branch on A Not Low	BC or BCR 11,
	BNE or BNER	Branch on A Not Equal B	BC or BCR 7,
After	BO or BOR	Branch on Overflow	BC or BCR 1,
Arithmetic	BP or BPR	Branch on Plus	BC or BCR 2,
Instructions	BM or BMR	Branch on Minus	BC or BCR 4,
	BNP or BNPR	Branch on Not Plus	BC or BCR 13,
	BNM or BNMR	Branch on Not Minus	BC or BCR 11,
	BNZ or BNZR	Branch on Not Zero	BC or BCR 7,
	BZ or BZR	Branch on Zero	BC or BCR 8,
After Test	BO or BOR	Branch if Ones	BC or BCR 1,
under Mask	BM or BMR	Branch if Mixed	BC or BCR 4,
Instruction	BZ or BZR	Branch if Zeros	BC or BCR 8,
	BNO or BNOR	Branch if Not Ones	BC or BCR 14,

*Second operand not shown; in all cases it is D2(X2,B2) for RX format or R2 for RR format.

CNOP ALIGNMENT†

Double Word							
Word				Word			
Half Word		Half Word		Half Word		Half Word	
Byte	Byte	Byte	Byte	Byte	Byte	Byte	Byte
0,4 0,8		2,4 2,8		0,4 4,8		2,4 6,8	

†For OS/VS and DOS/VS; source: GC33-4010.

ASSEMBLER INSTRUCTIONS†

Function	Mnemonic	Meaning
Data definition	DC	Define constant
	DS	Define storage
	CCW	Define channel command word
Program	START	Start assembly
sectioning	CSECT	Identify control section
and linking	DSECT	Identify dummy section
	DXD*	Define external dummy section
	CXD*	Cumulative length of external dummy section
	COM	Identify blank common control section
	ENTRY	Identify entry-point symbol
	EXTRN	Identify external symbol
	WXTRN	Identify weak external symbol
Base register	USING	Use base address register
assignment	DROP	Drop base address register
Control of listings	TITLE	Identify assembly output
	EJECT	Start new page
	SPACE	Space listing
	PRINT	Print optional data
Program Control	ICTL	Input format control
	ISEQ	Input sequence checking
	PUNCH	Punch a card
	REPRO	Reproduce following card
	ORG	Set location counter
	EQU	Equate symbol
	OPSYN*	Equate operation code
	PUSH*	Save current PRINT or USING status
	POP*	Restore PRINT or USING status
	LTORG	Begin literal pool
	CNOP	Conditional no operation
	COPY	Copy predefined source coding
	END	End assembly
Macro definition	MACRO	Macro definition header
	MNOTE	Request for error message
	MEXIT	Macro definition exit
	MEND	Macro definition trailer
Conditional	ACTR	Conditional assembly loop counter
assembly	AGO	Unconditional branch
	AIF	Conditional branch
	ANOP	Assembly no operation
	GBLA	Define global SETA symbol
	GBLB	Define global SETB symbol
	GBLC	Define global SETC symbol
	LCLA	Define local SETA symbol
	LCLB	Define local SETB symbol
	LCLC	Define local SETC symbol
	SETA	Set arithmetic variable symbol
	SETB	Set binary variable symbol
	SETC	Set character variable symbol

SUMMARY OF CONSTANTS†

TYPE	IMPLIED LENGTH, BYTES	ALIGNMENT	FORMAT	TRUNCA-TION/ PADDING
C	–	byte	characters	right
X	–	byte	hexadecimal digits	left
B	–	byte	binary digits	left
F	4	word	fixed-point binary	left
H	2	halfword	fixed-point binary	left
E	4	word	short floating-point	right
D	8	doubleword	long floating-point	right
L	16	doubleword	extended floating-point	right
P	–	byte	packed decimal	left
Z	–	byte	zoned decimal	left
A	4	word	value of address	left
Y	2	halfword	value of address	left
S	2	halfword	address in base-displacement form	–
V	4	word	externally defined address value	left
Q*	4	word	symbol naming a DXD or DSECT	left

†For OS/VS and DOS/VS; source: GC33-4010.
*OS/VS only.

CONDITION CODES ⑥

Condition Code Setting	0	1	2	3
Mask Bit Position	8	4	2	1

Floating-Point Instructions

Add Normalized S/L/E	zero	<zero	>zero	—
Add Unnormalized S/L	zero	<zero	>zero	—
Compare S/L (A:B)	equal	A low	A high	—
Load and Test S/L	zero	<zero	>zero	—
Load Complement S/L	zero	<zero	>zero	—
Load Negative S/L	zero	<zero	—	—
Load Positive S/L	zero	—	>zero	—
Subtract Normalized S/L/E	zero	<zero	>zero	—
Subtract Unnormalized S/L	zero	<zero	>zero	—

Fixed-Point and Decimal Instructions

Add H/F/Dec.	zero	<zero	>zero	overflow
Add Logical	zero, no carry	not zero, no carry	zero, carry	not zero, carry
Compare H/F/Dec. (A:B)	equal	A low	A high	
Load and Test	zero	<zero	>zero	
Load Complement	zero	<zero	>zero	overflow
Load Negative	zero	<zero	—	—
Load Positive	zero	—	>zero	overflow
Shift and Round Decimal	zero	<zero	>zero	overflow
Shift Left Single/Double	zero	<zero	>zero	overflow
Shift Right Single/Double	zero	<zero	>zero	—
Subtract H/F/Dec.	zero	<zero	>zero	overflow
Subtract Logical	—	not zero, no carry	zero, carry	not zero, carry
Zero and Add	zero	<zero	>zero	overflow

Logical Instructions

AND	zero	not zero	—	—
Compare Logical (A:B)	equal	A low	A high	—
Edit, Edit and Mark	zero	<zero	>zero	—
Exclusive OR	zero	not zero	—	—
Insert Characters under Mask	all zero	1st bit one	1st bit zero	—
Move Long	count equal	count low	count high	overlap
OR	zero	not zero	—	—
Test and Set	zero	one	—	—
Test under Mask	zero	mixed	—	ones
Translate and Test	zero	incomplete	complete	—

Input/Output Instructions

Halt Device	interruption pending	CSW stored	channel working	not oper
Halt I/O	interruption pending	CSW stored	burst op stopped	not oper
Start I/O, SIOF	started	CSW stored	busy	not oper
Store Channel ID	ID stored	CSW stored	busy	not oper
Test Channel	available	interruption pending	burst mode	not oper
Test I/O	available	CSW stored	busy	not oper

Miscellaneous Instructions

Load Real Address	translation available	ST entry invalid	PT entry invalid	length violation
Reset Reference Bit	zero,zero	zero,one	one,zero	one,one
Set clock	set	secure	—	not oper
Store clock	set	not set	error	not oper

EDIT AND EDMK PATTERN CHARACTERS (in hex)

20–digit selector	40–blank	5C--asterisk
21–start of significance	4B--period	6B--comma
22–field separator	5B--dollar sign	C3D9--CR

CHANNEL COMMANDS ⑦

Standard Command Code Assignments (CCW bits 0-7) for I/O Operations

xxxx 0000	Invalid		†††† ††01	Write
†††† 0100	Sense		†††† ††10	Read
xxxx 1000	Transfer in Channel		†††† ††11	Control
†††† 1100	Read Backward		0000 0011	Control No Operation

x—Bit ignored.   †Modifier bit for specific type of I/O device

3210, 3215 CONSOLES   Source: GA24-3557

Write, No Carrier Return	01	Sense	04
Write, Auto Carrier Return	09	Audible Alarm	0B
Read Inquiry	0A		

3505 CARD READER/3525 CARD PUNCH   Source: GA21-9124

Command	Binary	Hex	Bit Meanings	
Sense	0000 0100	04	SS	Stacker
Feed, Select Stacker	SS10 F011		00	1
Read Only*	11D0 F010		01	2
Diagnostic Read	1101 0010	D2	10	2
Read, Feed, Select Stacker*	SSD0 F010		F	Format Mode
Write RCE Format*	0001 0001	11	0	Unformatted
			1	Formatted
3505 only				
Write OMR Format†	0011 0001	31	D	Data Mode
			0	1—EBCDIC
3525 only			1	2—Card image
Write, Feed, Select Stacker	SSD0 0001			
Print Line*	LLLL L101		L	Line Position
				5-bit binary value

*Special feature on 3525.

3211 PRINTER/3811 CONTROL UNIT   Source: GA24-3543

	After Write	Immed		
Space 1 Line	09	0B	Write without spacing	01
Space 2 Lines	11	13	Sense	04
Space 3 Lines	19	1B	Load UCSB	FB
Skip to Channel 0	—	83	Fold	43
Skip to Channel 1	89	8B	Unfold	23
Skip to Channel 2	91	93	Load FCB	63
Skip to Channel 3	99	9B	Block Data Check	73
Skip to Channel 4	A1	A3	Allow Data Check	7B
Skip to Channel 5	A9	AB	Read PLB	02
Skip to Channel 6	B1	B3	Read UCSB	0A
Skip to Channel 7	B9	BB	Read FCB	12
Skip to Channel 8	C1	C3	Check Read	06
Skip to Channel 9	C9	CB	Diagnostic Write	05
Skip to Channel 10	D1	D3	Raise Cover	6B
Skip to Channel 11	D9	DB	Diagnostic Gate	07
Skip to Channel 12	E1	E3		

3803/3420 MAGNETIC TAPE   Source: GA32-0020

Write	01	Data Security Erase				97
Read Forward	02	Diagnostic Write Mode Set				0B
Read Backward	0C	Set Mode 1 (7-track)†				
Sense	04	Density	Parity	DC	Trans	Cmd
Sense Reserve*	F4		odd	on	off	53
Sense Release*	D4			off	off	73
Request Track-in-Error	1B	556			on	7B
Loop Write-to-Read	8B		even	off	off	63
Set Diagnose	4B				on	6B
Rewind	07		odd	on	off	93
Rewind Unload	0F			off	off	B3
Erase Gap	17	800			on	BB
Write Tape Mark	1F		even	off	off	A3
Backspace Block	27				on	AB
Backspace File	2F	Set Mode 2 (9-track)				
Forward Space Block	37	1600 bpi				C3
Forward Space File	3F	800 bpi†				CB

*Two-channel switch required.   †Special feature for NRZI operation.

CHANNEL COMMANDS (Contd)   ⑧
DIRECT ACCESS DEVICES

Source: GA26-1592 for 3830/3330
GA26-1589 for 2835/2305
GA26-3599, GA26-1606 for 2314, 2319

Command		MT Off	MT On*	Count
Control	Orient (c)	2B		Nonzero
	Recalibrate	13		Nonzero
	Seek	07		6
	Seek Cylinder	0B		6
	Seek Head	1B		6
	Space Count	0F		3 (a); nonzero (d)
	Set File Mask	1F		1
	Set Sector (a)	23		1
	Restore (a)	17		Nonzero
	Vary Sensing (c)	27		1
	Diagnostic Load (a)	53		1
	Diagnostic Write (a)	73		512
Search	Home Address Equal	39	B9	4
	Identifier Equal	31	B1	5
	Identifier High	51	D1	5
	Identifier Equal or High	71	F1	5
	Key Equal	29	A9	KL
	Key High	49	C9	KL
	Key Equal or High	69	E9	KL
	Key and Data Equal (d)	2D	AD	⎫
	Key and Data High (d)	4D	CD	Number
	Key and Data Eq. or Hi (d)	6D	ED	of bytes
Continue	Search Equal (d)	25	A5	(including
Scan	Search High (d)	45	C5	mask bytes)
	Search High or Equal (d)	65	E5	in search
	Set Status Modifier (d)	35	B5	argument
	Set Status Modifier (d)	75	F5	
	No Status Modifier (d)	55	D5	⎭
Read	Home Address	1A	9A	5
	Count	12	92	8
	Record 0	16	96	⎫ Number
	Data	06	86	of bytes
	Key and Data	0E	8E	to be
	Count, Key and Data	1E	9E	transferred
	IPL	02		⎭
	Sector (a)	22		1
Sense	Sense I/O	04		24 (a); 6 (d)
	Read, Reset Buffered Log (b)	A4		24
	Read Buffered Log (c)	24		128
	Device Release (e)	94		24 (a); 6 (d)
	Device Reserve (e)	B4		24 (a); 6 (d)
	Read Diagnostic Status 1 (a)	44		16 or 512
Write	Home Address	19		5
	Record 0	15		8+KL+DL of R0
	Erase	11		8+KL+DL
	Count, Key and Data	1D		8+KL+DL
	Special Count, Key and Data	01		8+KL+DL
	Data	05		DL
	Key and Data	0D		KL+DL

*   Code same as MT Off except as listed.   d.   2314,2319 only.
a.   3830/3330 and 2835/2305 only.   e.   Channel attachment and 2-channel
b.   3830/3330 only.   switch feature required; standard
c.   2835/2305 only.   on 2314 with 2844.

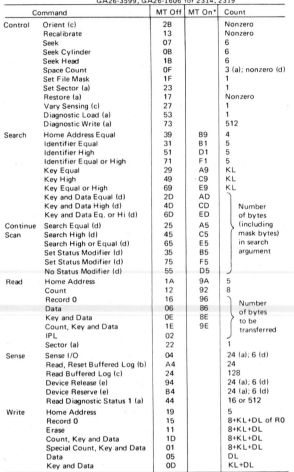

International Business Machines Corporation
Data Processing Division
1133 Westchester Avenue, White Plains, New York 10604
(U.S.A. only)

IBM World Trade Corporation
821 United Nations Plaza, New York, New York 10017
(International)

Printed in U.S.A.   GX20-1850-1

CODE TRANSLATION TABLE ⑨

Dec.	Hex	Instruction (RR)	Graphics and Controls BCDIC	EBCDIC(1)	ASCII	7-Track Tape BCDIC(2)	Card Code	Binary
0	00			NUL	NUL		12-0-1-8-9	0000 0000
1	01			SOH	SOH		12-1-9	0000 0001
2	02			STX	STX		12-2-9	0000 0010
3	03			ETX	ETX		12-3-9	0000 0011
4	04	SPM		PF	EOT		12-4-9	0000 0100
5	05	BALR		HT	ENQ		12-5-9	0000 0101
6	06	BCTR		LC	ACK		12-6-9	0000 0110
7	07	BCR		DEL	BEL		12-7-9	0000 0111
8	08	SSK			BS		12-8-9	0000 1000
9	09	ISK			HT		12-1-8-9	0000 1001
10	0A	SVC		SMM	LF		12-2-8-9	0000 1010
11	0B			VT	VT		12-3-8-9	0000 1011
12	0C			FF	FF		12-4-8-9	0000 1100
13	0D			CR	CR		12-5-8-9	0000 1101
14	0E	MVCL		SO	SO		12-6-8-9	0000 1110
15	0F	CLCL		SI	SI		12-7-8-9	0000 1111
16	10	LPR		DLE	DLE		12-11-1-8-9	0001 0000
17	11	LNR		DC1	DC1		11-1-9	0001 0001
18	12	LTR		DC2	DC2		11-2-9	0001 0010
19	13	LCR		TM	DC3		11-3-9	0001 0011
20	14	NR		RES	DC4		11-4-9	0001 0100
21	15	CLR		NL	NAK		11-5-9	0001 0101
22	16	OR		BS	SYN		11-6-9	0001 0110
23	17	XR		IL	ETB		11-7-9	0001 0111
24	18	LR		CAN	CAN		11-8-9	0001 1000
25	19	CR		EM	EM		11-1-8-9	0001 1001
26	1A	AR		CC	SUB		11-2-8-9	0001 1010
27	1B	SR		CU1	ESC		11-3-8-9	0001 1011
28	1C	MR		IFS	FS		11-4-8-9	0001 1100
29	1D	DR		IGS	GS		11-5-8-9	0001 1101
30	1E	ALR		IRS	RS		11-6-8-9	0001 1110
31	1F	SLR		IUS	US		11-7-8-9	0001 1111
32	20	LPDR		DS	SP		11-0-1-8-9	0010 0000
33	21	LNDR		SOS	!		0-1-9	0010 0001
34	22	LTDR		FS	"		0-2-9	0010 0010
35	23	LCDR			#		0-3-9	0010 0011
36	24	HDR		BYP	$		0-4-9	0010 0100
37	25	LRDR		LF	%		0-5-9	0010 0101
38	26	MXR		ETB	&		0-6-9	0010 0110
39	27	MXDR		ESC	'		0-7-9	0010 0111
40	28	LDR			(		0-8-9	0010 1000
41	29	CDR			)		0-1-8-9	0010 1001
42	2A	ADR		SM	*		0-2-8-9	0010 1010
43	2B	SDR		CU2	+		0-3-8-9	0010 1011
44	2C	MDR			,		0-4-8-9	0010 1100
45	2D	DDR		ENQ	-		0-5-8-9	0010 1101
46	2E	AWR		ACK	.		0-6-8-9	0010 1110
47	2F	SWR		BEL	/		0-7-8-9	0010 1111
48	30	LPER			0		12-11-0-1-8-9	0011 0000
49	31	LNER			1		1-9	0011 0001
50	32	LTER		SYN	2		2-9	0011 0010
51	33	LCER			3		3-9	0011 0011
52	34	HER		PN	4		4-9	0011 0100
53	35	LRER		RS	5		5-9	0011 0101
54	36	AXR		UC	6		6-9	0011 0110
55	37	SXR		EOT	7		7-9	0011 0111
56	38	LER			8		8-9	0011 1000
57	39	CER			9		1-8-9	0011 1001
58	3A	AER			:		2-8-9	0011 1010
59	3B	SER		CU3	;		3-8-9	0011 1011
60	3C	MER		DC4	<		4-8-9	0011 1100
61	3D	DER		NAK	=		5-8-9	0011 1101
62	3E	AUR		>	>		6-8-9	0011 1110
63	3F	SUR		SUB	?		7-8-9	0011 1111

1. Two columns of EBCDIC graphics are shown. The first gives standard bit pattern assignments. The second shows the T-11 and TN text printing chains (120 graphics).
2. Add C (check bit) for odd or even parity as needed, except as noted.
3. For even parity use CA.

CODE TRANSLATION TABLE (Contd)   ⑩

Dec.	Hex	Instruction (RX)	Graphics and Controls BCDIC	EBCDIC(1)	ASCII	7-Track Tape BCDIC(2)	Card Code	Binary
64	40	STH	Sp	Sp	@	(3)	no punches	0100 0000
65	41	LA			A		12-0-1-9	0100 0001
66	42	STC			B		12-0-2-9	0100 0010
67	43	IC			C		12-0-3-9	0100 0011
68	44	EX			D		12-0-4-9	0100 0100
69	45	BAL			E		12-0-5-9	0100 0101
70	46	BCT			F		12-0-6-9	0100 0110
71	47	BC			G		12-0-7-9	0100 0111
72	48	LH			H		12-0-8-9	0100 1000
73	49	CH			I		12-1-8	0100 1001
74	4A	AH	¢	¢	J		12-2-8	0100 1010
75	4B	SH	.	.	.	B A 8 21	12-3-8	0100 1011
76	4C	MH	⌑)	<	<	B A 84	12-4-8	0100 1100
77	4D		[	(	(	B A 84 1	12-5-8	0100 1101
78	4E	CVD	<	+	+	B A 842	12-6-8	0100 1110
79	4F	CVB	‡	|	|	B A 8421	12-7-8	0100 1111
80	50	ST	& +	&	&	B A	12	0101 0000
81	51				Q		12-11-1-9	0101 0001
82	52				R		12-11-2-9	0101 0010
83	53				S		12-11-3-9	0101 0011
84	54	N			T		12-11-4-9	0101 0100
85	55	CL·			U		12-11-5-9	0101 0101
86	56	O			V		12-11-6-9	0101 0110
87	57	X			W		12-11-7-9	0101 0111
88	58	L			X		12-11-8-9	0101 1000
89	59	C			Y		11-1-8	0101 1001
90	5A	A			Z		11-2-8	0101 1010
91	5B	S	$	$	$	B 8 21	11-3-8	0101 1011
92	5C	M	*	*	*	B 84	11-4-8	0101 1100
93	5D	D	]	)	)	]	B 84 1	11-5-8	0101 1101
94	5E	AL	;	;	;	¬ ^	B 842	11-6-8	0101 1110
95	5F	SL	Δ	¬	¬	_	B 8421	11-7-8	0101 1111
96	60	STD	-	-	-	`	B	11	0110 0000
97	61		/	/	/	a	A 1	0-1	0110 0001
98	62				b		11-0-2-9	0110 0010
99	63				c		11-0-3-9	0110 0011
100	64				d		11-0-4-9	0110 0100
101	65				e		11-0-5-9	0110 0101
102	66				f		11-0-6-9	0110 0110
103	67	MXD			g		11-0-7-9	0110 0111
104	68	LD			h		11-0-8-9	0110 1000
105	69	CD			i		0-1-8	0110 1001
106	6A	AD	|	|	j		12-11	0110 1010
107	6B	SD	,	,	,	k	A 8 21	0-3-8	0110 1011
108	6C	MD	% (	%	%	l	A 84	0-4-8	0110 1100
109	6D	DD	γ	_	_	m	A 84 1	0-5-8	0110 1101
110	6E	AW	\	>	>	n	A 842	0-6-8	0110 1110
111	6F	SW	⧻	?	?	o	A 8421	0-7-8	0110 1111
112	70	STE			p		12-11-0	0111 0000
113	71				q		12-11-0-1-9	0111 0001
114	72				r		12-11-0-2-9	0111 0010
115	73				s		12-11-0-3-9	0111 0011
116	74				t		12-11-0-4-9	0111 0100
117	75				u		12-11-0-5-9	0111 0101
118	76				v		12-11-0-6-9	0111 0110
119	77				w		12-11-0-7-9	0111 0111
120	78	LE			x		12-11-0-8-9	0111 1000
121	79	CE	`		y		1-8	0111 1001
122	7A	AE	ᵬ	:	:	z	A	2-8	0111 1010
123	7B	SE	# =	#	#	{	8 21	3-8	0111 1011
124	7C	ME	@ '	@	@	¦	84	4-8	0111 1100
125	7D	DE	:	'	'	}	84 1	5-8	0111 1101
126	7E	AU	>	=	=	~	842	6-8	0111 1110
127	7F	SU	√	"	"	DEL	8421	7-8	0111 1111

CODE TRANSLATION TABLE (Contd) ⑪

Dec.	Hex	Instruction and Format	BCDIC	EBCDIC(1)	ASCII	7-Track Tape BCDIC(2)	Card Code	Binary
128	80	SSM -S					12-0-1-8	1000 0000
129	81		a	a			12-0-1	1000 0001
130	82	LPSW -S	b	b			12-0-2	1000 0010
131	83	Diagnose	c	c			12-0-3	1000 0011
132	84	WRD ⎫	d	d			12-0-4	1000 0100
133	85	RDD ⎬ SI	e	e			12-0-5	1000 0101
134	86	BXH ⎭	f	f			12-0-6	1000 0110
135	87	BXLE	g	g			12-0-7	1000 0111
136	88	SRL	h	h			12-0-8	1000 1000
137	89	SLL	i	i			12-0-9	1000 1001
138	8A	SRA					12-0-2-8	1000 1010
139	8B	SLA ⎱RS		{			12-0-3-8	1000 1011
140	8C	SRDL		≤			12-0-4-8	1000 1100
141	8D	SLDL		(			12-0-5-8	1000 1101
142	8E	SRDA		+			12-0-6-8	1000 1110
143	8F	SLDA		‡			12-0-7-8	1000 1111
144	90	STM ⎫					12-11-1-8	1001 0000
145	91	TM ⎬ SI	j	j			12-11-1	1001 0001
146	92	MVI ⎭	k	k			12-11-2	1001 0010
147	93	TS -S	l	l			12-11-3	1001 0011
148	94	NI ⎫	m	m			12-11-4	1001 0100
149	95	CLI ⎬ SI	n	n			12-11-5	1001 0101
150	96	OI ⎭	o	o			12-11-6	1001 0110
151	97	XI	p	p			12-11-7	1001 0111
152	98	LM -RS	q	q			12-11-8	1001 1000
153	99		r	r			12-11-9	1001 1001
154	9A						12-11-2-8	1001 1010
155	9B			}			12-11-3-8	1001 1011
156	9C	SIO,SIOF ⎫		⌑			12-11-4-8	1001 1100
157	9D	TIO ⎬ S		)			12-11-5-8	1001 1101
158	9E	HIO,HDV ⎭		±			12-11-6-8	1001 1110
159	9F	TCH		■			12-11-7-8	1001 1111
160	A0			-			11-0-1-8	1010 0000
161	A1		~	°			11-0-1	1010 0001
162	A2		s	s			11-0-2	1010 0010
163	A3		t	t			11-0-3	1010 0011
164	A4		u	u			11-0-4	1010 0100
165	A5		v	v			11-0-5	1010 0101
166	A6		w	w			11-0-6	1010 0110
167	A7		x	x			11-0-7	1010 0111
168	A8		y	y			11-0-8	1010 1000
169	A9		z	z			11-0-9	1010 1001
170	AA						11-0-2-8	1010 1010
171	AB			└			11-0-3-8	1010 1011
172	AC	STNSM ⎱ SI		┌			11-0-4-8	1010 1100
173	AD	STOSM ⎰		[			11-0-5-8	1010 1101
174	AE			≥			11-0-6-8	1010 1110
175	AF	MC -SI		●			11-0-7-8	1010 1111
176	B0			0			12-11-0-1-8	1011 0000
177	B1	LRA -RX		1			12-11-0-1	1011 0001
178	B2	See below		2			12-11-0-2	1011 0010
179	B3			3			12-11-0-3	1011 0011
180	B4			4			12-11-0-4	1011 0100
181	B5			5			12-11-0-5	1011 0101
182	B6	STCTL ⎱ RS		6			12-11-0-6	1011 0110
183	B7	LCTL ⎰		7			12-11-0-7	1011 0111
184	B8			8			12-11-0-8	1011 1000
185	B9			9			12-11-0-9	1011 1001
186	BA						12-11-0-2-8	1011 1010
187	BB			⌐			12-11-0-3-8	1011 1011
188	BC			¬			12-11-0-4-8	1011 1100
189	BD	CLM ⎫		]			12-11-0-5-8	1011 1101
190	BE	STCM ⎬ RS		≠			12-11-0-6-8	1011 1110
191	BF	ICM ⎭		—			12-11-0-7-8	1011 1111

Op code (S format)

B202 - STIDP	B207 - STCKC
B203 - STIDC	B208 - SPT
B204 - SCK	B209 - STPT
B205 - STCK	B20D - PTLB
B206 - SCKC	B213 - RRB

CODE TRANSLATION TABLE (Contd)   ⑫

Dec.	Hex	Instruction (SS)	BCDIC	EBCDIC(1)	ASCII	7-Track Tape BCDIC(2)	Card Code	Binary
192	C0		?	{		B A 8 2	12-0	1100 0000
193	C1		A	A	A	B A 1	12-1	1100 0001
194	C2		B	B	B	B A 2	12-2	1100 0010
195	C3		C	C	C	B A 2 1	12-3	1100 0011
196	C4		D	D	D	B A 4	12-4	1100 0100
197	C5		E	E	E	B A 4 1	12-5	1100 0101
198	C6		F	F	F	B A 4 2	12-6	1100 0110
199	C7		G	G	G	B A 4 2 1	12-7	1100 0111
200	C8		H	H	H	B A 8	12-8	1100 1000
201	C9		I	I	I	B A 8 1	12-9	1100 1001
202	CA						12-0-2-8-9	1100 1010
203	CB						12-0-3-8-9	1100 1011
204	CC			⌠			12-0-4-8-9	1100 1100
205	CD						12-0-5-8-9	1100 1101
206	CE			ɤ			12-0-6-8-9	1100 1110
207	CF						12-0-7-8-9	1100 1111
208	D0		!	}		B 8 2	11-0	1101 0000
209	D1	MVN	J	J	J	B 1	11-1	1101 0001
210	D2	MVC	K	K	K	B 2	11-2	1101 0010
211	D3	MVZ	L	L	L	B 2 1	11-3	1101 0011
212	D4	NC	M	M	M	B 4	11-4	1101 0100
213	D5	CLC	N	N	N	B 4 1	11-5	1101 0101
214	D6	OC	O	O	O	B 4 2	11-6	1101 0110
215	D7	XC	P	P	P	B 4 2 1	11-7	1101 0111
216	D8		Q	Q	Q	B 8	11-8	1101 1000
217	D9		R	R	R	B 8 1	11-9	1101 1001
218	DA						12-11-2-8-9	1101 1010
219	DB						12-11-3-8-9	1101 1011
220	DC	TR					12-11-4-8-9	1101 1100
221	DD	TRT					12-11-5-8-9	1101 1101
222	DE	ED					12-11-6-8-9	1101 1110
223	DF	EDMK					12-11-7-8-9	1101 1111
224	E0		ǂ	\		A 8 2	0-2-8	1110 0000
225	E1						11-0-1-9	1110 0001
226	E2		S	S	S	A 2	0-2	1110 0010
227	E3		T	T	T	A 2 1	0-3	1110 0011
228	E4		U	U	U	A 4	0-4	1110 0100
229	E5		V	V	V	A 4 1	0-5	1110 0101
230	E6		W	W	W	A 4 2	0-6	1110 0110
231	E7		X	X	X	A 4 2 1	0-7	1110 0111
232	E8		Y	Y	Y	A 8	0-8	1110 1000
233	E9		Z	Z	Z	A 8 . 1	0-9	1110 1001
234	EA						11-0-2-8-9	1110 1010
235	EB						11-0-3-8-9	1110 1011
236	EC			⊣			11-0-4-8-9	1110 1100
237	ED						11-0-5-8-9	1110 1101
238	EE						11-0-6-8-9	1110 1110
239	EF						11-0-7-8-9	1110 1111
240	F0	SRP	0	0	0	8 2	0	1111 0000
241	F1	MVO	1	1	1	1	1	1111 0001
242	F2	PACK	2	2	2	2	2	1111 0010
243	F3	UNPK	3	3	3	2 1	3	1111 0011
244	F4		4	4.	4	4	4	1111 0100
245	F5		5	5	5	4 1	5	1111 0101
246	F6		6	6	6	4 2	6	1111 0110
247	F7		7	7	7	4 2 1	7	1111 0111
248	F8	ZAP	8	8	8	8	8	1111 1000
249	F9	CP	9	9	9	8 1	9	1111 1001
250	FA	AP		ǀ			12-11-0-2-8-9	1111 1010
251	FB	SP					12-11-0-3-8-9	1111 1011
252	FC	MP					12-11-0-4-8-9	1111 1100
253	FD	DP					12-11-0-5-8-9	1111 1101
254	FE						12-11-0-6-8-9	1111 1110
255	FF						12-11-0-7-8-9	1111 1111

MACHINE INSTRUCTION FORMATS

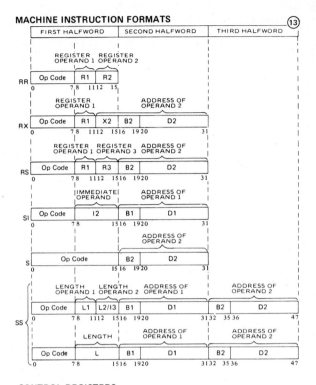

CONTROL REGISTERS

CR	Bits	Name of field	Associated with	Init.
0	0	Block-multiplex'g control	Block-multiplex'g mode	0
	1	SSM suppression control	SSM instruction	0
	8-9	Page size control	⎫	0
	10	Unassigned (zero stored)	⎬ Dynamic addr. transl.	0
	11-12	Segment size control	⎭	0
	20	Clock comparator mask	Clock comparator	0
	21	CPU timer mask	CPU timer	0
	24	Interval timer mask	Interval timer	1
	25	Interrupt key mask	Interrupt key	1
	26	External signal mask	External signals	1
1	0-7	Segment table length	⎱ Dynamic addr. transl.	0
	8-25	Segment table address	⎰	0
2	0-31	Channel masks	Channels	1
8	16-31	Monitor masks	Monitoring	0
9	0	Successful branching mask	⎫	0
	1	Instruction fetching mask	⎪	0
	2	Storage alteration mask	⎬ Program-event record'g	0
	3	Gen'l Reg. alteration mask	⎪	0
	16-31	GR identification masks	⎭	0
10	8-31	PER starting address	Program-event record'g	0
11	8-31	PER ending address	Program-event record'g	0
14	0	Check-stop control	⎱ Machine-check handling	1
	1	Synch. MCEL control	⎰	1
	2	I/O extended logout ctrl.	I/O extended logout	0
	4	Recovery report mask	⎫	0
	5	Degradation report mask	⎪	0
	6	Ext. damage report mask	⎬ Machine-check handling	1
	7	Warning mask	⎪	0
	8	Asynch. MCEL control	⎪	0
	9	Asynch. fixed log ctrl.	⎭	0
15	8-28	MCEL address	Machine-check handling	512

PROGRAM STATUS WORD (BC Mode)

(14)

Channel masks	E	Protect'n key	CMWP	Interruption code
0	6 7 8	11 12	15 16	23 24 31

ILC	CC	Program mask	Instruction address
32 34	36	39 40	47 48 55 56 63

0–5 Channel 0 to 5 masks	32–33 (ILC) Instruction length code
6 Mask for channel 6 and up	34–35 (CC) Condition code
7 (E) External mask	36 Fixed-point overflow mask
12 (C=0) Basic control mode	37 Decimal overflow mask
13 (M) Machine-check mask	38 Exponent underflow mask
14 (W=1) Wait state	39 Significance mask
15 (P=1) Problem state	

PROGRAM STATUS WORD (EC Mode)

0R00 0TIE	Protect'n key	CMWP	00	CC	Program mask	0000 0000
0	7 8	11 12	15 16	18	20 23 24	31

0000 0000	Instruction address
32 39 40	47 48 55 56 63

1 (R) Program event recording mask	15 (P=1) Problem state
5 (T=1) Translation mode	18–19 (CC) Condition code
6 (I) Input/output mask	20 Fixed-point overflow mask
7 (E) External mask	21 Decimal overflow mask
12 (C=1) Extended control mode	22 Exponent underflow mask
13 (M) Machine-check mask	23 Significance mask
14 (W=1) Wait state	

CHANNEL COMMAND WORD

Command code	Data address
0	7 8 15 16 23 24 31

Flags	00	/////////	Byte count
32	37 38 40	47 48	55 56 63

CD—bit 32 (80) causes use of address portion of next CCW.
CC—bit 33 (40) causes use of command code and data address of next CCW.
SLI—bit 34 (20) causes suppression of possible incorrect length indication.
Skip—bit 35 (10) suppresses transfer of information to main storage.
PCI—bit 36 (08) causes a channel Program Controlled Interruption.
IDA—bit 37 (04) causes bits 8–31 of CCW to specify location of first IDAW.

CHANNEL STATUS WORD (hex 40)

Key	0	L	CC	CCW address
0	3 4	5	6 7 8	15 16 23 24 31

Unit status	Channel status	Byte count
32 39 40	47 48	55 56 63

5 Logout pending	40 (80) Program-controlled interruption
6–7 Deferred condition code	41 (40) Incorrect length
32 (80) Attention	42 (20) Program check
33 (40) Status modifier	43 (10) Protection check
34 (20) Control unit end	44 (08) Channel data check
35 (10) Busy	45 (04) Channel control check
36 (08) Channel end	46 (02) Interface control check
37 (04) Device end	47 (01) Chaining check
38 (02) Unit check	48–63 Residual byte count for the
39 (01) Unit exception	last CCW used

PROGRAM INTERRUPTION CODES

0001	Operation exception	000C	Exponent overflow excp
0002	Privileged operation excp	000D	Exponent underflow excp
0003	Execute exception	000E	Significance exception
0004	Protection exception	000F	Floating-point divide excp
0005	Addressing exception	0010	Segment translation excp
0006	Specification exception	0011	Page translation exception
0007	Data exception	0012	Translation specification excp
0008	Fixed-point overflow excp	0013	Special operation exception
0009	Fixed-point divide excp	0040	Monitor event
000A	Decimal overflow exception	0080	Program event (code may be
000B	Decimal divide exception		combined with another code)

FIXED STORAGE LOCATIONS (15)

Area, dec.	Hex addr	EC only	Function
0- 7	0		Initial program loading PSW, restart new PSW
8- 15	8		Initial program loading CCW1, restart old PSW
16- 23	10		Initial program loading CCW2
24- 31	18		External old PSW
32- 39	20		Supervisor Call old PSW
40- 47	28		Program old PSW
48- 55	30		Machine-check old PSW
56- 63	38		Input/output old PSW
64- 71	40		Channel status word (see diagram)
72- 75	48		Channel address word [0-3 key, 4-7 zeros, 8-31 CCW address]
76- 79	4C		Unused
80- 83	50		Interval timer
84- 87	54		Unused
88- 95	58		External new PSW
96-103	60		Supervisor Call new PSW
104-111	68		Program new PSW
112-119	70		Machine-check new PSW
120-127	78		Input/output new PSW
132-135	84	X	External interruption [0-15 zeros, 16-31 code]
136-139	88	X	SVC interruption [0-12 zeros, 13-14 ILC, 15:0, 16-31 code]
140-143	8C	X	Program interrupt. [0-12 zeros, 13-14 ILC, 15:0, 16-31 code]
144-147	90	X	Translation exception address [0-7 zeros, 8-31 address]
148-149	94		Monitor class [0-7 zeros, 8-15 class number]
150-151	96	X	PER interruption code [0-7 code, 8-15 zeros]
152-155	98	X	PER address [0-7 zeros, 8-31 address]
156-159	9C		Monitor code [0-7 zeros, 8-31 monitor code]
168-171	A8		Channel ID [0-3 type, 4-15 model, 16-31 max. IOEL length]
172-175	AC		I/O extended logout address [0-7 unused, 8-31 address]
176-179	B0		Limited channel logout (see diagram)
185-187	B9	X	I/O address [0-7 zeros, 8-23 address]
216-223	D8		Machine-check CPU timer save area
224-231	E0		Machine-check clock comparator save area
232-239	E8		Machine-check interruption code (see diagram)
248-251	F8		Failing processor storage address [0-7 zeros, 8-31 address]
252-255	FC		Region code*
256-351	100		Fixed logout area*
352-383	160		Machine-check floating-point register save area
384-447	180		Machine-check general register save area
448-511	1C0		Machine-check control register save area
512†	200		Machine-check extended logout area (size varies)

*May vary among models; see functional characteristics manual for specific model.
†Location may be changed by programming (bits 8-28 of CR 15 specify address).

LIMITED CHANNEL LOGOUT (hex B0)

0	SCU id	Detect	Source	000	Field validity flags	TT	00	A	Seq.
0	1 3	4 7	8 12	13 15	16 23	24 26	28	29 31	

4 CPU	12 Control unit	24-25 Type of termination
5 Channel	16 Interface address	00 Interface disconnect
6 Storage ctrl. unit	17-18 Reserved (00)	01 Stop, stack or normal
7 Storage unit	19 Sequence code	10 Selective reset
8 CPU	20 Unit status	11 System reset
9 Channel	21 Cmd. addr. and key	28(A) I/O error alert
10 Main storage control	22 Channel address	29-31 Sequence code
11 Main storage	23 Device address	

MACHINE-CHECK INTERRUPTION CODE (hex E8)

MC conditions	000	00	Time	Stg. error	0	Validity
0 8	9	13	14 16	18	19 20	31

0000	0000	0000	00	Val.	MCEL length
32 39	40		45	46 48	55 56 63

0 System damage	15 Delayed	25 Region code
1 Instr. proc'g damage	16 Uncorrected	27 Floating-pt registers
2 System recovery	17 Corrected	28 General registers
3 Timer damage	18 Key uncorrected	29 Control registers
4 Timing facil. damage	20 PSW bits 12-15	30 CPU ext'd logout
5 External damage	21 PSW masks and key	31 Storage logical
7 Degradation	22 Prog. mask and CC	46 CPU timer
8 Warning	23 Instruction address	47 Clock comparator
14 Backed-up	24 Failing stg. address	

DYNAMIC ADDRESS TRANSLATION ⑯

VIRTUAL (LOGICAL) ADDRESS FORMAT

Segment Size	Page Size		Segment Index	Page Index	Byte Index
64K	4K	Bits	8 - 15	16 - 19	20 - 31
64K	2K	0 - 7	8 - 15	16 - 20	21 - 31
1M	4K	are	8 - 11	12 - 19	20 - 31
1M	2K	ignored	8 - 11	12 - 20	21 - 31

SEGMENT TABLE ENTRY

PT length	0000*	Page table address	00*	I
0 3	4 7	8	28 29	31

*Normally zeros; ignored on some models.   31 (I) Segment-invalid bit.

PAGE TABLE ENTRY (4K)

Page address	I	00	
0	11 12 13		15

12 (I) Page-invalid bit.

PAGE TABLE ENTRY (2K)

Page address	I	0	
0	12 13 14		15

13 (I) Page-invalid bit.

HEXADECIMAL AND DECIMAL CONVERSION

From hex: locate each hex digit in its corresponding column position and note the decimal equivalents. Add these to obtain the decimal value.

From decimal: (1) locate the largest decimal value in the table that will fit into the decimal number to be converted, and (2) note its hex equivalent and hex column position. (3) Find the decimal remainder. Repeat the process on this and subsequent remainders.

Note: Decimal, hexadecimal, (and binary) equivalents of all numbers from 0 to 255 are listed on panels 9 - 12.

HEXADECIMAL COLUMNS

6		5		4		3		2		1	
HEX	= DEC	HEX	= DEC	HEX	= DEC	HEX	= DEC	HEX	= DEC	HEX	= DEC
0	0	0	0	0	0	0	0	0	0	0	0
1	1,048,576	1	65,536	1	4,096	1	256	1	16	1	1
2	2,097,152	2	131,072	2	8,192	2	512	2	32	2	2
3	3,145,728	3	196,608	3	12,288	3	768	3	48	3	3
4	4,194,304	4	262,144	4	16,384	4	1,024	4	64	4	4
5	5,242,880	5	327,680	5	20,480	5	1,280	5	80	5	5
6	6,291,456	6	393,216	6	24,576	6	1,536	6	96	6	6
7	7,340,032	7	458,752	7	28,672	7	1,792	7	112	7	7
8	8,388,608	8	524,288	8	32,768	8	2,048	8	128	8	8
9	9,437,184	9	589,824	9	36,864	9	2,304	9	144	9	9
A	10,485,760	A	655,360	A	40,960	A	2,560	A	160	A	10
B	11,534,336	B	720,896	B	45,056	B	2,816	B	176	B	11
C	12,582,912	C	786,432	C	49,152	C	3,072	C	192	C	12
D	13,631,488	D	851,968	D	53,248	D	3,328	D	208	D	13
E	14,680,064	E	917,504	E	57,344	E	3,584	E	224	E	14
F	15,728,640	F	983,040	F	61,440	F	3,840	F	240	F	15
0 1 2 3		4 5 6 7		0 1 2 3		4 5 6 7		0 1 2 3		4 5 6 7	
BYTE				BYTE				BYTE			

POWERS OF 2

2^n	n
256	8
512	9
1 024	10
2 048	11
4 096	12
8 192	13
16 384	14
32 768	15
65 536	16
131 072	17
262 144	18
524 288	19
1 048 576	20
2 097 152	21
4 194 304	22
8 388 608	23
16 777 216	24

$2^0 = 16^0$
$2^4 = 16^1$
$2^8 = 16^2$
$2^{12} = 16^3$
$2^{16} = 16^4$
$2^{20} = 16^5$
$2^{24} = 16^6$
$2^{28} = 16^7$
$2^{32} = 16^8$
$2^{36} = 16^9$
$2^{40} = 16^{10}$
$2^{44} = 16^{11}$
$2^{48} = 16^{12}$
$2^{52} = 16^{13}$
$2^{56} = 16^{14}$
$2^{60} = 16^{15}$

POWERS OF 16

16^n	n
1	0
16	1
256	2
4 096	3
65 536	4
1 048 576	5
16 777 216	6
268 435 456	7
4 294 967 296	8
68 719 476 736	9
1 099 511 627 776	10
17 592 186 044 416	11
281 474 976 710 656	12
4 503 599 627 370 496	13
72 057 594 037 927 936	14
1 152 921 504 606 846 976	15

Appendix B

Introduction to Microprogramming[1]

The technique of microprogramming was first introduced in 1951 (Wilkes, 1969) as a means for designing the control unit of an otherwise conventional digital computer. By the mid-1960s both the technology and understanding of microprogramming had advanced to such an extent that it had become an important concept in most contemporary computers. A good discussion of microprogramming can be found in Husson (1970), Rosin (1969), and Wilkes (1969).

STRUCTURE OF DIGITAL COMPUTERS

Most contemporary digital computers can be logically partitioned into five distinct functional units: Input Unit (IU), Storage Unit (SU), Arithmetic and Logical Unit (ALU), Output Unit (OU), and Control Unit (CU).

The functions of the control unit are: (1) to fetch a machine instruction, (2) to decode it, (3) to gate appropriate data paths to perform the correct operation, and (4) to prepare for the processing of the next machine instruction. Such a scheme can be described as a collection of active elements (e.g., ALU, SU), passive elements (e.g., registers), and data paths connecting the active and passive elements as shown in Figure 1.

TRADITIONAL CONTROL UNITS

Traditionally, the control unit has been implemented as a combinatorial and sequential logic network. It accepts as inputs the Current Instruction Register, status bits, and clock pulses and outputs the various latch and data bus gate settings as well as control pulses to the active elements. For a moderate to large computer system with an extensive set of machine operations, the control unit usually becomes extremely complex and confusing.

MICROPROGRAMMED CONTROL UNITS

Professor M. V. Wilkes of the Cambridge University Mathematical Laboratory first used the term *microprogramming* in 1951. His object was to provide a systematic alternative to the usual ad hoc procedure for designing the control unit of a digital computer. In the process of executing a machine instruction, a sequence of transfers of information from one register in the processor to another takes place, some directly and some through an active element. Because of the analogy between the execution of individual steps in a machine instruction to the execution of the individual instructions in a program, Professor Wilkes introduced the concept of microprogramming. Most of the combinatorial and sequential logic of the traditional hardware control unit is replaced by a simple control unit in conjunction with a microprogram storage unit.

---

[1] This appendix is based upon the article "What Is Microprogramming?" by Stuart Madnick that appeared in the *Proceedings of the 1971 IEEE Computer Conference*.

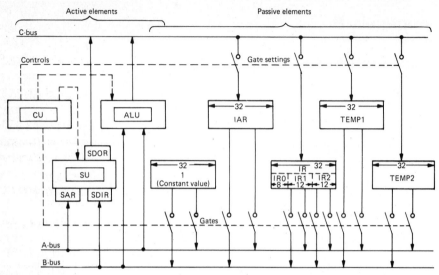

Key:

CU = Control Unit
SU = Storage Unit
ALU = Arithmetic and Logical Unit
IAR = Instruction Address Register

IR   = Instruction Register
SDIR = Storage Data In Register (32 bits)
SDOR = Storage Data Out Register (32 bits)
SAR = Storage Address Register (12 bits)

Figure 1 Structure of a simple computer

SIMPLE MICROPROGRAMMED CONTROL UNIT

A microprogrammed control unit for the simple computer shown in Figure 1 might have a microinstruction format as follows:

SU op	ALU op	A– bus	B– bus	C– bus	D

for example, a microinstruction, such as:

ALU=ADD,A=IAR,B=1,C=IAR

will connect the IAR and 1 registers to the inputs of the ALU, cause an addition to be performed, and transfer the resulting ALU output back to the IAR register. Thus, the operation IAR ← IAR+1 is performed (i.e., the IAR register is incremented by 1). A microinstruction such as:

SU=WRITE,A=IR2,B=TEMP1,C=TEMP2

causes the data currently at the Storage Data Out Register (SDOR) of the SU (i.e., result of last READ or WRITE operation) to be transferred to register TEMP2. At the same time, the data from register TEMP1 is transferred to the Storage Data In Register (SDIR) and the 12-bit IR2 field of register IR is transferred to the Storage Address Register (SAR). Then the SU will start to write the data from the SDIR into the storage location specified by the SAR.

Usually, the SU functions more slowly than the ALU and requires several cycles for completion. We will assume that an ALU operation requires one cycle and the SU requires two cycles for completion.

SAMPLE MICROPROGRAM

Let us assume that we are designing a computer with a two-address machine instruction format as follows:

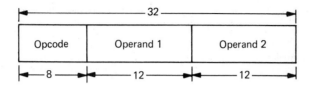

For example, the instruction

ADD X,Y

causes

$X \leftarrow X + Y$.

Let us assume that the IR register contains a copy of such a 32-bit ADD instruction and the IAR register contains the memory address of the instruction. The portion of the microprogram to accomplish the ADD machine instruction might be:

MICROINSTRUCTION   COMMENTS

1 SU=READ,A=IR1

> Start fetch of operand1. (The 12-bit IR1 field of the IR register specifies the memory address of the first operand.)

2 Idle

> Wait a cycle for the READ to complete.

3 SU=READ,A=IR2,C=TEMP1

> READ (from step 1) complete, save operand1 in TEMP1, start fetch of operand 2.

4 ALU=ADD,A=IAR,B=1,C=IAR

> Increment IAR (while SU busy doing READ). IAR now contains address of the next instruction.

5 SU=READ,A=IAR,C=TEMP2

> READ complete, save operand2 in TEMP2, start to fetch next instruction. (Note: we have started fetch for next instruction even though current instruction has not been completed.)

6 ALU=ADD,A=TEMP1,B=TEMP2,C=TEMP1

> Add operand1 and operand2.

7 SU=WRITE,A=IR1,B=TEMP1,C=IR

> Save new instruction in IR, start to store result of addition as operand1.

8 Branch to correct microroutine for next machine instruction based on operation code in IR. (The IR and IAR registers are all set for processing new instruction.)

In the last step (step 8), the IRO field (first 8 bits) of register IR are used to determine the address of the next microinstruction. For example, if the control store contains 2048 microinstructions, the 8-bit field could be expanded to an 11-bit address by appending three zeros as the low-order bits.

Notice that it is possible to have the ALU and SU operating in parallel. Many contemporary microprogrammed computers attain very high speeds by initiating several parallel operations.

This usually requires very long and elaborate microinstructions: microinstructions of over 100 bits are quite common for large-scale computers.

Although the simple microprocessor described above executed each microinstruction sequentially, it is usually necessary to provide various forms of microprogram branching (e.g., unconditional, conditional, and multi-path).

BENEFITS OF MICROPROGRAMMING

Besides providing a simpler and more orderly technique for designing a computer's control unit, microprogramming offers many additional benefits, such as:

1 *Flexibility*—it is much easier to make last-minute changes to the control unit by merely changing the microprogram.
2 *Emulation*—by changing the microprogram, the interpretation of machine instructions will also be changed. For example, it is possible to execute programs written for the earlier IBM 1401 on the newer IBM System/360 Model 30 by providing a special 1401 microprogram.
3 *More powerful machine instructions*—using the microprogram facility, it is possible and practical to implement very powerful machine instructions, such as floating point decimal arithmetic. Even the direct execution of high-level language statements is possible.
4 *Maintenance, education, and diagnosis*—the simplicity of the microprogram mechanism makes maintenance and diagnosis of errors much easier, as well as simplifying the education of maintenance personnel.

GENERAL IMPLICATIONS OF MICROPROGRAMMING

The growth and evolution of microprogramming appears to have substantial implications for the design and operation of computer systems. Already microprogramming has provided a bridge between the previously clear-cut areas of hardware and software; it has even been given an appropriate name, *firmware* (other names, such as *underware*, although colorful, seem to have been abandoned).

Eventually many of the present operating-system software functions will be transferred into firmware. Liskov (1972) describes such an experimental system. The *microcode assist* for VM/370, mentioned in Section 9-5.2 indicates this trend even on contemporary computers. As a result, the boundary line between operating-system software and firmware will become more subtle—hardware designers will have to understand more about operating systems and operating-system designers will have to understand more about hardware.

Index

(Numbers in boldface indicate pages containing the main discussion.)

Notes

Notes